SCIENCE, REASON, AND REALITY

ISSUES IN THE PHILOSOPHY OF SCIENCE

SCIENCE, REASON, AND REALITY

ISSUES IN THE PHILOSOPHY OF SCIENCE

DANIEL ROTHBART

GEORGE MASON UNIVERSITY

HARCOURT BRACE COLLEGE PUBLISHERS

Fort Worth   Philadelphia   San Diego   New York   Orlando   Austin   San Antonio
Toronto   Montreal   London   Sydney   Tokyo

Publisher	Christopher P. Klein
Acquisitions Editor	David Tatom
Product Manager	Steve Drummond
Developmental Editor	Diane Drexler
Project Editor	John Haakenson
Production Manager	Diane Gray
Art Director	Brian Salisbury

ISBN: 0-15-503529-0

Library of Congress Catalog Card Number: 97-72809

Address for Editorial Correspondence: Harcourt Brace College Publishers, 301 Commerce Street, Suite 3700, Fort Worth, TX 76102
Address for Orders: Harcourt Brace & Company, 6277 Sea Harbor Drive, Orlando, FL 32887-6777. 1-800-782-4479 (in Florida).

Website address:
http://www.hbcollege.com

Harcourt Brace College Publishers may provide complimentary instructional aids and supplements of supplement packages to those adopters qualified under our adoption policy. Please contact your sales representative for more information. If as an adopter or potential user you receive supplements you do not need, please return them to your sales representative or send them to:

Attn: Returns Department
Troy Warehouse
465 South Lincoln Drive
Troy, MO 63379

Printed in the United States of America

7 8 9 0 1 2 3 4 5 6   067   9 8 7 6 5 4 3 2 1

PREFACE

This anthology was motivated from the belief that students with no previous training in philosophy can actively engage in a serious discussion of the philosophical basis of science. Once students realize that all scientific knowledge rests on various philosophical assumptions, certain questions can be raised. What exactly are the conditions for acquiring scientific knowledge? How can we be reasonably confident that the scientists' pronouncements of success, failure, or indeed, any pronouncements at all are, in fact, warranted? What are the "objective" indications of scientific progress?

The articles of this anthology were selected and organized with certain goals in mind. First, an anthology in philosophy of science should focus on some of the central philosophical topics of the day, as discussed in the current body of philosophical literature. Of course, this goal must be balanced against limitations of length. To fulfill this goal, the present anthology is divided into the following five topics: the character of experimental evidence and its role in the appraisal of theories (Topic I), rival conceptions of a scientific explanation (Topic II), the Kuhnian conception of paradigm-driven science (Topic III), the relativist critiques of science (Topic IV), and the realist/antirealist debates concerning the possibility of a theory to refer to real-world processes (Topic V). In contrast to some anthologies on the market, the realism/antirealism controversy is prominent in the present work, reflecting the centrality of this issue in the current discussion in philosophy of science. Furthermore, the relativist critiques of science comprise a unique topic of the anthology, including selections from Bruno Latour, as well as Barry Barnes and David Bloor. Such critiques are particularly stimulating to students.

Second, the sequence of articles in each topic reflects a diversity of philosophical opinion. The present anthology avoids the problem of presenting an artificially narrow range of philosophical opinion. The selection of articles shows students how each position is subject to constructive criticism, and how some criticism motivates alternative positions.

Third, an anthology should highlight the work of the most prominent and influential scholars in the field. The present collection contains classic articles by Carnap, Hanson, Hempel, Hume, Lakatos, Popper and Kuhn (the selection from Kuhn's work includes three chapters from his *The Structure of Scientific Revolution* and one chapter from *The Essential Tension*). The anthology includes as well work by the participants currently engaged in the philosophical debate. I suspect that some of these articles may become classics for a later generation. At the end of each topic is a fairly extensive bibliography designed to assist those students wishing to pursue particular issues further.

Fourth, an anthology should be accessible to undergraduate students with no previous training in philosophy. The present anthology avoids the excessively technical terminology and highly rigorous arguments common to advanced discussions. Some selections are reprints of chapters from the author's own introductory text, such as work by Carnap, Hanson, Hempel, and Harré. Most of the other selections are equally comprehensible. A few articles may necessitate preparation by the instructor. But as a pedagogical aid, all selections are summarized briefly in the topic introductions.

The present anthology is intended as a primary text for an introductory course in philosophy of science. The instructor may supplement this work with extensive scientific writings from the natural sciences. From my experience, some writings from the modern period of science can be quite accessible to students. In another course this text could also function as a primary text for the theory of knowledge, or a course on the philosophical dimensions of science and religion.

Many people kindly offered extensive advice throughout the development of this project. My colleague Emmett Holman was particularly generous with his time and valuable suggestions. Considerable credit goes to the following reviewers for their detailed and constructive comments: Peter Achinstein, Johns Hopkins University; Michael Bishop, Iowa State University; Herbert Burhenn, The University of Tennessee at Chattanooga; Robert L. Causey, The University of Texas at Austin; Brian B. Clayton, Gonzaga University; Wayne Davis, Georgetown University; Malcolm R. Forster, University of Wisconsin-Madison; Richard Hassing, The Catholic University; John L. King, University of North Carolina at Greensboro; Hugh Lacey, Swarthmore College; Joseph LeFevre, Xavier University of Louisiana; Robert N. McCauley, Emory University; Alfred Nordmann, University of South Carolina; Bonnie Paller, California State University-Northridge; Thomas W. Platt, West Chester University; and Paul C. L. Tang, California State University-Long Beach. Many thanks go to the developmental editor, Diane Drexler, for her support and keen editorial judgment.

CONTENTS

THEORY AND OBSERVATION

INTRODUCTION

Imagine holding a diamond ring in one hand and a lead pencil in another. Contrary to expectation, scientists tell us that both the diamond and the "lead" from a pencil are composed of the same material—carbon atoms. The primary difference is the arrangement of these atoms.

We know that the apparent "disappearance" of a rabbit during a magic act is a form of trickery. But, according to astrophysicists, if any relatively small object, such as a rabbit, comes very close to a certain region of space, known as a black hole, the object eventually disappears from our universe without a trace. No one really knows what happens to it.

Why should we believe that the scientists are correct in these cases which seem to violate common sense? Exactly how is scientific understanding of nature ever possible, given the many prejudices, biases, and limitations that afflict human beings? Can scientists demonstrate that their ideas sometimes reveal the truths of nature? Absolutely not, according to some critics of science. The scientists' declarations that they have discovered truths about the world border on self-serving nonsense, closer to fraud than to fact. On this view the preference for astronomy over astrology, for example, merely reflects the propaganda victories of oppressive social institutions.

The debate concerning the possibility of genuine scientific knowledge of nature is the primary issue in the philosophy of science. What can scientists do to show that their beliefs are right? Of course, a major activity designed to demonstrate the truth of a certain belief is the performance of scientific experiments. Experiments give scientists "reliable" evidence upon which beliefs (or dis-beliefs) are founded. Scientists typically use the experimental data to justify (demonstrate, confirm, or corroborate) their beliefs about events that they have not yet observed, such as events in the future.

This goal of an experiment raises three important philosophical questions: First, *exactly how do scientists use evidence from an experiment about observed events to acquire information about unobserved events?* Scientists frequently declare that data from past experiments can be used to predict the future. But are they right? At stake here is nothing less than the capacity of scientists to justify their beliefs about the world. This important question is addressed in articles by David Hume, Rudolf Carnap, and Karl Popper.

Second, *what exactly is the character of observation reports arising from an experiment?* The whole purpose of an experiment is to provide a reliable test for determining whether or not a certain belief is correct. If the test is performed properly, the experimental data should be correct, or so one would hope. But why should anyone, especially nonscientists, believe that such data are correct? This issue is addressed in the article by Norwood Russell Hanson.

Third, scientists typically convey their beliefs about the universe through scientific theories. *What exactly is the character of a scientific theory?* This is addressed in articles by Hilary Putnam and Frederick Suppe.

S U M M A R Y   O F   R E A D I N G S

Let us begin with the first major question of Topic I: Exactly how can scientists use evidence from an experiment about observed events to acquire information about unobserved events? As David Hume argued in the eighteenth century (selection #1), there are no rational grounds for using evidence from observed phenomena to draw out information about events which have not been observed. No principle of logic or doctrine of reasoning of any kind allows us to infer knowledge of unobserved events from observed events. Hume recognizes that we strongly expect the pattern of events to remain the same, based on our experience that events of one type are constantly conjoined with events of another type. For example, I have acquired an expectation from past experience that the floor in my classroom will hold the weight of my body. This expectation grows with the frequency of such experience, leading to a belief in a cause-and-effect relationship between such events. Nevertheless, we are never warranted rationally in believing that the pattern of past events will be sustained in the future. The very possibility of rational science is at stake. If Hume is correct, we can never distinguish objective facts from psychological habit, or, according to some commentators, never distinguish sanity from insanity. How can Hume's skepticism be addressed in ways that save rational science?

Rudolf Carnap attempts to overcome Hume's challenge by appeal to the method of scientific experimentation (selection #2). For Carnap the scientific method is identical to the method of evaluating scientific ideas through the use of experimental tests. When certain beliefs are subjected to tests, two results are possible: The experimental evidence either violates or it supports the beliefs. When a violation occurs, the actual evidence contradicts what one would expect from these beliefs. In such a case scientists can reasonably claim that the ideas are inaccurate. This of course assumes that the experiment was properly designed and performed. For Carnap, when beliefs pass a sufficient number and variety of tests, the beliefs are confirmed. This confirmation never establishes the absolute certainty, because *we can never compile enough evidence to show that a scientific belief is correct for all the events it describes.* The most we can say is that the belief is very likely to be true on the basis of extensive evidence. Such evidence increases our confidence that the belief correctly describes future events, though we never achieve complete certainty.

For Karl Popper, however, Carnap's entire experimental methodology collapses (selection #3). If we follow Carnap's proposal to use experiments to predict future events, we are again confronted with the Humean obstacle. Carnap's method of experimentation cannot yield knowledge of the events we have not observed. In a very controversial proposal Popper flatly rejects all procedures which try to use evidence on behalf of a statement's truth, or even its probability. Popper's rejection is rather stunning: *Any attempt to use evidence positively to demonstrate the truth or probability of a universal statement about nature is doomed from the outset.* No matter how many tests such a statement passes, our level of confidence that the statement is true is always nil, from a rational standpoint. We can easily show that a general statement is false by discovering one (repeatable) event which violates the statement, but the chances that the statement is true never improve with further testing. The Popperian conception of rational science stresses the following: A theory can be easily dismissed, but it can never be confirmed, not even partially.

So, in rational science a theory should be subjected to severe experimental scrutiny in order to expose its weakest point. To this end, Popper advocates the following methodological principles:

(1) The best indication of a theory's success, prior to any experience, is not the number of possible events a theory can explain, but is rather the number of situations that are prohibited by the theory.

(2) Every genuinely scientific theory, as opposed to a theory of pseudoscience, must show how one type of event is prohibited.

(3) A legitimate experimental test must subject the theory to the severest possible scrutiny to exploit its "weakest point" in an effort to efficiently falsify the theory.

(4) No matter how many tests a theory passes, it is at best tentatively accepted and awaits future scrutiny.

Carnap's positive method and Popper's falsification method represent rival conceptions of rational science. As Imre Lakatos argues (selection #4), any viable methodology serves two vital functions. First, a methodology provides rules for the acceptance and rejection of theories, or what he calls research programs. Second, a methodology provides normative guidelines for the interpretation of the history of science. Rather than a collection of neutral facts, the historical study of science is driven by its own "rules for discovery" toward a rational reconstruction of the major episodes of scientific progress. For example, a positive methodology will direct the historian to the factual evidence associated with a scientific discovery, while a falsifying methodology centers on historical cases of bold conjectures and severe challenges through rigorous tests.

The second major question of Topic I is as follows: What exactly is the character of observation reports arising from an experiment? According to both Carnap and Popper, our ability to test a theory rests on discovering the "facts" of nature, and expressing "facts" through the use of observation reports. But can we ever remove all theoretical influences from such reports? According to Norwood Russell Hanson, such reports are inescapably dependent on theoretical beliefs (selection #5). For example, when looking through an X-ray tube, would a physicist see the same thing as a baby? Of course not, says Hanson. Seeing requires not only visual perception but also theoretical understanding. The infant simply cannot organize the visual landscape in the same way that a trained physicist can. For Hanson, there is more to seeing than meets the eyeball.

Obviously, the primary purpose of an experiment is to determine whether to accept a theory. But what exactly is a scientific theory? This is the third important question of Topic I. One attempt to answer this question is given by the "Received View" conception of a theory. According to this conception, a theory is an organized description of an infinite number of possible events. For example, Newton's theory of motion presumably gives information about any physical body moving in space or on earth. But there is no way to provide descriptions of all such bodies in motion, because the list would be literally endless. A more efficient method would require the use of laws of nature. A law of nature is a statement which conveys information about an infinite number of events, only some of which can be observed. For example, Newton's theory includes the first law of motion: Every physical body continues in a state of rest, or a state of uniform motion, unless compelled to change its state by an external force. We can easily apply this law to the following simple situation: A stationary billiard ball on a polished tile floor remains at rest unless it is subjected to some external force, such as bombardment by another ball. All the laws of Newton's theory should be organized into a logical system. Consequently, from some laws we can logically infer other laws, and from these still other laws can be inferred, and so on. In this way all of the laws in Newton's theory are organized very well.

The "Received View" conception of a theory assumes a definite distinction between a theoretical statement and an observational statement. Many laws of nature are theoretical statements, because they include "theoretical terms." For example, Newton's first law of motion (above) includes the theoretical term *force*. But when we apply a law to a specific situation that we observe, we must come up with observation statements. Newton's first law presumably describes in observational terms how the billiard ball will move under specific circumstances. Such descriptions provide an interpretation of the law in a specific context of application.

However, Hilary Putnam rejects the "Received View" conception (selection #6). He argues that the "Received View" rests on a bogus distinction between theoretical statements and observation statements. The primary culprit is the notion of an observation term. If "observation term" is defined as a term that always refers to observable things, then these terms simply do not arise in the scientific literature. Putnam concludes that the distinction between observational term and theoretical term cannot be drawn in a way that salvages the "Received View."

What is a viable alternative to the "Received View"? According to Frederick Suppe, the "Received View" fails to capture an important function of scientific theories (selection #7). A theory does not tell us what actually occurred or what will occur in the world, but how phenomena *would behave* under certain idealized conditions. A theory of gravitation, for example, tells us how a material object would fall, assuming no wind resistance, atmospheric interference, and so on. Of course, such conditions cannot be realized outside of an experimental test. Again, a theory should inform us what would happen under ideal circumstances. Suppe argues that such information is best provided by abstract "pictures" of phenomena in idealized settings. Consequently, such "pictures" comprise the central content of every scientific theory.

DAVID HUME
SCEPTICAL DOUBTS CONCERNING THE OPERATIONS OF THE UNDERSTANDING

PART I

20 All the objects of human reason or enquiry may naturally be divided into two kinds, to wit, *Relations of Ideas,* and *Matters of Fact.* Of the first kind are the sciences of Geometry, Algebra, and Arithmetic; and in short, every affirmation which is either intuitively or demonstratively certain. *That the square of the hypothenuse is equal to the square of the two sides,* is a proposition which expresses a relation between these figures. *That three times five is equal to the half of thirty,* expresses a relation between these numbers. Propositions of this kind are discoverable by the mere operation of thought, without dependence on what is anywhere existent in the universe. Though there never were a circle or triangle in nature, the truths demonstrated by Euclid would for ever retain their certainty and evidence.

21 Matters of fact, which are the second objects of human reason, are not ascertained in the same manner; nor is our evidence of their truth, however great, of a like nature with the foregoing. The contrary of every matter of fact is still possible; because it can never imply a contradiction, and is conceived by the mind with the same facility and distinctness, as if ever so comformable to reality. *That the sun will not rise to-morrow* is no less intelligible a proposition, and implies no more contradiction, than the affirmation, *that it will rise.* We should in vain, therefore, attempt to demonstrate its falsehood. Were it demonstratively false, it would imply a contradiction, and could never be distinctly conceived by the mind.

It may, therefore, be a subject worthy of curiosity, to enquire what is the nature of that evidence which assures us of any real existence and matter of fact, beyond the present testimony of our senses, or the records of our memory. This part of philosophy, it is observable, has been little cultivated, either by the ancients or moderns; and therefore our doubts and errors, in the prosecution of so important an enquiry, may be the more excusable; while we march through such difficult paths without any guide or direction. They may even prove useful, by exciting curiosity, and destroying that implicit faith and security, which is the bane of all reasoning and free enquiry. The discovery of defects in the common philosophy, if any such there be, will not, I presume, be a discouragement, but rather an incitement, as is usual, to attempt something more full and satisfactory than has yet been proposed to the public.

22 All reasonings concerning matter of fact seem to be founded on the relation of *Cause and Effect.* By means of that relation alone we can go beyond the evidence of our memory and senses. If you were to ask a man, why he believes any matter of fact, which is absent; for instance, that his friend is in the country, or in France; he would give you a reason; and this reason would be some other fact; as a letter received from him, or the knowledge of his former resolutions and promises. A man finding a watch or any other machine in a desert island, would conclude that there had once been men in that island. All our reasonings concerning fact are of the same nature. And here it is constantly supposed that there is a connexion between the present fact and that which is inferred from it. Were there nothing to bind them together, the inference would be entirely precarious. The hearing of an articulate voice and rational discourse in the dark assures us of the presence of some person: Why? because these are the effects of the human make and fabric, and closely connected with it. If we anatomize all the other reasonings of this nature, we shall find that they are founded on the relation of cause and effect, and that this relation is either near or remote, direct or collateral. Heat and light are collateral effects of fire, and the one effect may justly be inferred from the other.

23   If we would satisfy ourselves, therefore, concerning the nature of that evidence, which assures us of matters of fact, we must enquire how we arrive at the knowledge of cause and effect.

I shall venture to affirm, as a general proposition, which admits of no exception, that the knowledge of this relation is not, in any instance, attained by reasonings *a priori;* but arises entirely from experience, when we find that any particular objects are constantly conjoined with each other. Let an object be presented to a man of ever so strong natural reason and abilities; if that object be entirely new to him, he will not be able, by the most accurate examination of its sensible qualities, to discover any of its causes or effects. Adam, though his rational faculties be supposed, at the very first, entirely perfect, could not have inferred from the fluidity and transparency of water that it would suffocate him, or from the light and warmth of fire that it would consume him. No object ever discovers, by the qualities which appear to the senses, either the causes which produced it, or the effects which will arise from it; nor can our reason, unassisted by experience, ever draw any inference concerning real existence and matter of fact.

24   This proposition, *that causes and effects are discoverable, not by reason but by experience,* will readily be admitted with regard to such objects, as we remember to have once been altogether unknown to us; since we must be conscious of the utter inability, which we then lay under, of foretelling what would arise from them. Present two smooth pieces of marble to a man who has no tincture of natural philosophy; he will never discover that they will adhere together in such a manner as to require great force to separate them in a direct line, while they make so small a resistance to a lateral pressure. Such events, as bear little analogy to the common course of nature, are also readily confessed to be known only by experience; nor does any man imagine that the explosion of gunpowder, or the attraction of a loadstone, could ever be discovered by arguments *a priori.* In like manner, when an effect is supposed to depend upon an intricate machinery or secret structure of parts, we make no difficulty in attributing all our knowledge of it to experience. Who will assert that he can give the ultimate reason, why milk or bread is proper nourishment for a man, not for a lion or a tiger?

But the same truth may not appear, at first sight, to have the same evidence with regard to events, which have become familiar to us from our first appearance in the world, which bear a close analogy to the whole course of nature, and which are supposed to depend on the simple qualities of objects, without any secret structure of parts. We are apt to imagine that we could discover these effects by the mere operation of our reason, without experience. We fancy, that were we brought on a sudden into this world, we could at first have inferred that one Billiard-ball would communicate motion to another upon impulse; and that we needed not to have waited for the event, in order to pronounce with certainty concerning it. Such is the influence of custom, that, where it is strongest, it not only covers our natural ignorance, but even conceals itself, and seems not to take place, merely because it is found in the highest degree.

25   But to convince us that all the laws of nature, and all the operations of bodies without exception, are known only by experience, the following reflections may, perhaps, suffice. Were any object presented to us, and were we required to pronounce concerning the effect, which will result from it, without consulting past observation; after what manner, I beseech you, must the mind proceed in this operation? It must invent or imagine some event, which it ascribes to the object as its effect; and it is plain that this invention must be entirely arbitrary. The mind can never possibly find the effect in the supposed cause, by the most accurate scrutiny and examination. For the effect is totally different from the cause, and consequently can never be discovered in it. Motion in the second Billiard-ball is a quite distinct event from motion in the first; nor is there anything in the one to suggest the smallest hint of the other. A stone or piece of metal raised into the air, and left without any support, immediately falls: but to consider the matter *a priori,* is there anything we discover in this situation which can beget the idea of a downward, rather than an upward, or any other motion, in the stone or metal?

And as the first imagination or invention of a particular effect, in all natural operations, is arbitrary, where we consult not experience; so must we also esteem the supposed tie or connexion between the cause and effect, which binds them together, and renders it impossible that any other effect could result from the operation of that cause. When I see, for instance, a Billiard-ball moving in a straight line towards another; even suppose motion in the second ball should by accident be suggested to me, as the result of their contact or impulse; may I not conceive, that a hundred different events might as well follow from that cause? May not both these balls remain at absolute rest? May not the first ball return in a straight line, or leap off from the second in any line or direction? All these suppositions are consistent and conceivable. Why then should we give the preference to one, which is no more consistent or conceivable than the rest? All our reasonings *a priori* will never be able to show us any foundation for this preference.

In a word, then, every effect is a distinct event from its cause. It could not, therefore, be discovered in the cause, and the first invention or conception of it, *a priori,* must be entirely arbitrary. And even after it is suggested, the conjunction of it with the cause must appear equally arbitrary; since there are always many other effects, which, to reason, must seem fully as consistent and natural. In vain, therefore, should we pretend to determine any single event, or infer any cause or effect, without the assistance of observation and experience.

26   Hence we may discover the reason why no philosopher, who is rational and modest, has ever pretended to assign the ultimate cause of any natural operation, or to show distinctly the action of that power, which produces any single effect in the universe. It is confessed, that the utmost effort of human reason is to reduce the principles, productive of natural phenomena, to a greater simplicity, and to resolve the many particular effects into a few general causes, by means of reasonings from analogy, experience, and observation. But as to the causes of these general causes, we should in vain attempt their discovery; nor shall we ever be able to satisfy ourselves, by any particular explication of them. These ultimate springs and principles are totally shut up from human curiosity and enquiry. Elasticity, gravity, cohesion of parts, communication of motion by impulse; these are probably the ultimate causes and principles which we shall ever discover in nature; and we may esteem ourselves sufficiently happy, if, by accurate enquiry and reasoning, we can trace up the particular phenomena to, or near to, these general principles. The most perfect philosophy of the natural kind only staves off our ignorance a little longer: as perhaps the most perfect philosophy of the moral or metaphysical kind serves only to discover larger portions of it. Thus the observation of human blindness and weakness is the result of all philosophy, and meets us at every turn, in spite of our endeavours to elude or avoid it.

27   Nor is geometry, when taken into the assistance of natural philosophy, ever able to remedy this defect, or lead us into the knowledge of ultimate causes, by all that accuracy of reasoning for which it is so justly celebrated. Every part of mixed mathematics proceeds upon the supposition that certain laws are established by nature in her operations; and abstract reasonings are employed, either to assist experience in the discovery of these laws, or to determine their influence in particular instances, where it depends upon any precise degree of distance and quantity. Thus, it is a law of motion, discovered by experience, that the moment or force of any body in motion is in the compound ratio or proportion of its solid contents and its velocity; and consequently, that a small force may remove the greatest obstacle or raise the greatest weight, if, by any contrivance or machinery, we can increase the velocity of that force, so as to make it an overmatch for its antagonist. Geometry assists us in the application of this law, by giving us the just dimensions of all the parts and figures which can enter into any species of machine; but still the discovery of the law itself is owing merely to experience, and all the abstract reasonings in the world could never lead us one step towards the knowledge of it. When we reason *a priori,* and consider merely any object or cause, as it appears to the mind, independent of all observation, it never could suggest to us the notion of any distinct object, such as its effect; much less, show us the inseparable and inviolable connexion between them. A man must be very sagacious who could discover by reasoning that crystal is the effect of heat, and ice of cold, without being previously acquainted with the operation of these qualities.

PART II

28   But we have not yet attained any tolerable satisfaction with regard to the question first proposed. Each solution still gives rise to a new question as difficult as the foregoing, and leads us on to farther enquiries. When it is asked, *What is the nature of all our reasonings, concerning matter of fact?* the proper answer seems to be, that they are founded on the relation of cause and effect. When again it is asked, *What is the foundation of all our reasonings and conclusions concerning that relation?* it may be replied in one word, Experience. But if we still carry on our sifting humour, and ask, *What is the foundation of all conclusions from experience?* this implies a new question, which may be of more difficult solution and explication. Philosophers, that give themselves airs of superior wisdom and sufficiency, have a hard task when they encounter persons of inquisitive dispositions, who push them from every corner to which they retreat, and who are sure at last to bring them to some dangerous dilemma. The best expedient to prevent this confusion, is to be modest in our pretensions; and even to discover the difficulty ourselves before it is objected to us. By this means, we may make a kind of merit of our very ignorance.

I shall content myself, in this section, with an easy task, and shall pretend only to give a negative answer to the question here proposed. I say then, that, even after we have experience of the operations of cause and effect, our conclusions from that experience are *not* founded on reasoning, or any process of the understanding. This answer we must endeavour both to explain and to defend.

29   It must certainly be allowed, that nature has kept us at a great distance from all her secrets, and has afforded us only the knowledge of a few superficial qualities of objects; while she conceals from us those powers and principles on which the influence of these objects entirely depends. Our senses inform us of the colour, weight, and consistence of bread; but neither sense nor reason can ever inform us of those qualities which fit it for the nourishment and support of a human body. Sight or feeling conveys an idea of the actual motion of bodies; but as to that wonderful force or power, which would carry on a moving body for ever in a continued change of place, and which bodies never lose but by communicating it to others; of this we cannot form the most distant conception. But notwithstanding this ignorance of natural powers[1] and principles, we always presume, when we see like sensible qualities, that they have like secret powers, and expect that effects, similar to those which we have experienced, will follow from them. If a body of like colour and consistence with that bread, which we have formerly eat, be presented to us, we make no scruple of repeating the experiment, and foresee, with certainty, like nourishment and support. Now this is a process of the mind or thought, of which I would willingly know the foundation. It is allowed on all hands that there is no known connexion between the sensible qualities and the secret powers; and consequently, that the mind is not led to form such a conclusion concerning their constant and regular conjunction, by anything which it knows of their nature. As to past *Experience*, it can be allowed to give *direct* and *certain* information of those precise objects only, and that precise period of time, which fell under its cognizance: but why this experience should be extended to future times, and to other objects, which for aught we know, may be only in appearance similar; this is the main question on which I would insist. The bread, which I formerly eat, nourished me; that is, a body of such sensible qualities was, at that time, endued with such secret powers: but does it follow, that other bread must also nourish me at another time, and that like sensible qualities must always be attended with like secret powers? The consequence seems nowise necessary. At least, it must be acknowledged that there is here a consequence drawn by the mind; that there is a certain step taken; a process of thought, and an inference, which wants to be explained. These two propositions are far from being the same, *I have found that such an object has always been attended with such an effect,* and *I foresee, that other objects, which are, in appearance, similar, will be attended with similar effects.* I shall allow, if you please, that the one proposition may justly be inferred from the other: I know, in fact, that it always is inferred. But if you insist that the inference is made by a chain of reasoning, I desire you to produce that reasoning. The connexion between these propositions is not intuitive. There is required a medium, which may enable the mind to draw such an inference, if indeed it be drawn by reasoning and argument. What that medium is, I must confess, passes my comprehension; and it is incumbent on those to produce it, who assert that it really exists, and is the origin of all our conclusions concerning matter of fact.

30   This negative argument must certainly, in process of time, become altogether convincing, if many penetrating and able philosophers shall turn their enquiries this way and no one be ever able to discover any connecting proposition or intermediate step, which supports the understanding in this conclusion. But as the question is yet new, every reader may not trust so far to his own penetration, as to conclude, because an argument escapes his enquiry, that therefore it does not really exist. For this reason it may be requisite to venture upon a more difficult task; and enumerating all the branches of human knowledge, endeavour to show that none of them can afford such an argument.

All reasonings may be divided into two kinds, namely, demonstrative reasoning, or that concerning relations of ideas, and moral reasoning, or that concerning matter of fact and existence. That there are no demonstrative arguments in the case seems evident; since it implies no contradiction that the course of nature may change, and that an object, seemingly like those which we have experienced, may be attended with different or contrary effects. May I not clearly and distinctly conceive that a body, falling from the clouds, and which, in all other respects, resembles snow, has yet the taste of salt or feeling of fire? Is there any more intelligible proposition than to affirm, that all the trees will flourish in December and January, and decay in May and June? Now whatever is intelligible, and can be distinctly conceived, implies no contradiction, and can never be proved false by any demonstrative argument or abstract reasoning *a priori.*

If we be, therefore, engaged by arguments to put trust in past experience, and make it the standard of our future judgement, these arguments must be probable only, or such as regard matter of fact and real existence, according to the division above mentioned. But that there is no argument of this kind, must appear, if our explication of that species of reasoning be admitted as solid and satisfactory. We have said that all arguments concerning existence are founded on the relation of cause and effect; that our knowledge of that relation is derived entirely from experience; and that all our experimental conclusions proceed upon the supposition that the future will be comfortable to the past. To endeavour, therefore, the proof of this last supposition by probable arguments, or arguments regarding existence, must be evidently going in a circle, and taking that for granted, which is the very point in question.

31   In reality, all arguments from experience are founded on the similarity which we discover among natural objects, and by which we are induced to expect effects similar to those which we have found to follow from such objects. And though none but a fool or madman will ever pretend to dispute the authority of experience, or to reject that great guide of human life, it may surely be allowed a philosopher to have so much curiosity at least as to examine the principle of human nature, which gives this mighty authority to experience, and makes us draw advantage from that similarity which nature has placed among different objects. From causes which appear *similar* we expect similar effects. This is the sum of all our experimental conclusions. Now it seems evident that, if this conclusion were formed by reason, it would be as perfect at first, and upon one instance, as after ever so long a course of experience. But the case is far otherwise. Nothing so like as eggs; yet no one, on account of this appearing similarity, expects the same taste and relish in all of them. It is only after a long course of uniform experiments in any kind, that we attain a firm reliance and security with regard to a particular event. Now where is that process of reasoning which, from one instance, draws a conclusion, so different from that which it infers from a hundred instances that are nowise different from that single one? This question I propose as much for the sake of information, as with an intention of raising difficulties. I cannot find, I cannot imagine any such reasoning. But I keep my mind still open to instruction, if any one will vouchsafe to bestow it on me.

32   Should it be said that, from a number of uniform experiments, we *infer* a connexion between the sensible qualities and the secret powers; this, I must confess, seems the same difficulty, couched in different terms. The question still recurs, on what process of argument this *inference* is founded? Where is the medium, the interposing ideas, which join propositions so very wide of each other? It is confessed that the colour, consistence, and other sensible qualities of bread appear not, of themselves, to have any connexion with the secret powers of nourishment and support. For otherwise we could infer these secret powers from the first appearance of these sensible qualities, without the aid of experience; contrary to the sentiment of all philosophers, and contrary to plain matter of fact. Here, then, is our natural state of ignorance with regard to the powers and influence of all objects. How is this remedied by experience? It only shows us a number of uniform effects, resulting from certain objects, and teaches us that those particular objects, at that particular time, were endowed with such powers and forces. When a new object, endowed with similar sensible qualities, is produced, we expect similar powers and forces, and look for a like effect. From a body of like colour and consistence with bread we expect like nourishment and support. But this surely is a step or progress of the mind, which wants to be explained. When a man says, *I have found, in all past instances, such sensible qualities conjoined with such secret powers:* And when he says, *Similar sensible qualities will always be conjoined with similar secret powers,* he is not guilty of a tautology, nor are these propositions in any respect the same. You say that the one proposition is an inference from the other. But you must confess that the inference is not intuitive; neither is it demonstrative: Of what nature is it, then? To say it is experimental, is begging the question. For all inferences from experience suppose, as their foundation, that the future will resemble the past, and that similar powers will be conjoined with similar sensible qualities. If there be any suspicion that the course of nature may change, and that the past may be no rule for the future, all experience becomes useless, and can give rise to no inference or conclusion. It is impossible, therefore, that any arguments from experience can prove this resemblance of the past to the future; since all these arguments are founded on the supposition of that resemblance. Let the course of things be allowed hitherto ever so regular; that alone, without

some new argument or inference, proves not that, for the future, it will continue so. In vain do you pretend to have learned the nature of bodies from your past experience. Their secret nature, and consequently all their effects and influence, may change, without any change in their sensible qualities. This happens sometimes, and with regard to some objects: Why may it not happen always, and with regard to all objects? What logic, what process of argument secures you against this supposition? My practice, you say, refutes my doubts. But you mistake the purport of my question. As an agent, I am quite satisfied in the point; but as a philosopher, who has some share of curiosity, I will not say scepticism, I want to learn the foundation of this inference. No reading, no enquiry has yet been able to remove my difficulty, or give me satisfaction in a matter of such importance. Can I do better than propose the difficulty to the public, even though, perhaps, I have small hopes of obtaining a solution? We shall at least, by this means, be sensible of our ignorance, if we do not augment our knowledge.

33   I must confess that a man is guilty of unpardonable arrogance who concludes, because an argument has escaped his own investigation, that therefore it does not really exist. I must also confess that, though all the learned, for several ages, should have employed themselves in fruitless search upon any subject, it may still, perhaps, be rash to conclude positively that the subject must, therefore, pass all human comprehension. Even though we examine all the sources of our knowledge, and conclude them unfit for such a subject, there may still remain a suspicion, that the enumeration is not complete, or the examination not accurate. But with regard to the present subject, there are some considerations which seem to remove all this accusation of arrogance or suspicion of mistake.

It is certain that the most ignorant and stupid peasants—nay infants, nay even brute beasts—improve by experience, and learn the qualities of natural objects, by observing the effects which result from them. When a child has felt the sensation of pain from touching the flame of a candle, he will be careful not to put his hand near any candle; but will expect a similar effect from a cause which is similar in its sensible qualities and appearance. If you assert, therefore, that the understanding of the child is led into this conclusion by any process of argument or ratiocination, I may justly require you to produce that argument; nor have you any pretence to refuse so equitable a demand. You cannot say that the argument is abstruse, and may possibly escape your enquiry; since you confess that it is obvious to the capacity of a mere infant. If you hesitate, therefore, a moment, or if, after reflection, you produce any intricate or profound argument, you, in a manner, give up the question, and confess that it is not reasoning which engages us to suppose the past resembling the future, and to expect similar effects from causes which are, to appearance, similar. This is the proposition which I intended to enforce in the present section. If I be right, I pretend not to have made any mighty discovery. And if I be wrong, I must acknowledge myself to be indeed a very backward scholar; since I cannot now discover an argument which, it seems, was perfectly familiar to me long before I was out of my cradle.

NOTE

[1] The word, Power, is here used in a loose and popular sense. The more accurate explication of it would give additional evidence to this argument.

RUDOLF CARNAP

SELECTIONS FROM *PHILOSOPHICAL FOUNDATIONS OF PHYSICS: AN INTRODUCTION TO THE PHILOSOPHY OF SCIENCE*

THE VALUE OF LAWS: EXPLANATION AND PREDICTION

The observations we make in everyday life as well as the more systematic observations of science reveal certain repetitions or regularities in the world. Day always follows night; the seasons repeat themselves in the same order; fire always feels hot; objects fall when we drop them; and so on. The laws of science are nothing more than statements expressing these regularities as precisely as possible.

If a certain regularity is observed at all times and all places, without exception, then the regularity is expressed in the form of a "universal law." An example from daily life is, "All ice is cold." This statement asserts that any piece of ice—at any place in the universe, at any time, past, present, or future—is (was, or will be) cold. Not all laws of science are universal. Instead of asserting that a regularity occurs in *all* cases, some laws assert that it occurs in only a certain percentage of cases. If the percentage is specified or if in some other way a quantitative statement is made about the relation of one event to another, then the statement is called a "statistical law." For example: "Ripe apples are usually red," or "Approximately half the children born each year are boys." Both types of law—universal and statistical—are needed in science. The universal laws are logically simpler, and for this reason we shall consider them first. In the early part of this discussion "laws" will usually mean universal laws.

Universal laws are expressed in the logical form of what is called in formal logic a "universal conditional statement." (In this book, we shall occasionally make use of symbolic logic, but only in a very elementary way.) For example, let us consider a law of the simplest possible type. It asserts that, whatever x may be, if x is P, then x is also Q. This is written symbolically as follows:

$$(x)(Px \supset Qx).$$

The expression "(x)" on the left is called a "universal quantifier." It tells us that the statement refers to *all* cases of x, rather than to just a certain percentage of cases. "Px" says that x is P, and "Qx" says that x is Q. The symbol "$\supset$" is a connective. It links the term on its left to the term on its right. In English, it corresponds roughly to the assertion, "If . . . then . . ."

If "x" stands for any material body, then the law states that, for any material body x, if x has the property P, it also has the property Q. For instance, in physics we might say: "For every body x, if that body is heated, that body will expand." This is the law of thermal expansion in its simplest, nonquantitative form. In physics, of course, one tries to obtain quantitative laws and to qualify them so as to exclude exceptions; but, if we forget about such refinements, then this universal conditional statement is the basic logical form of all universal laws. Sometimes we may say that, not only does Qx hold whenever Px holds, but the reverse is also true; whenever Qx holds, Px holds also. Logicians call this a biconditional statement—a statement that is conditional in both directions. But of course this does not contradict the fact that in all universal laws we deal with universal conditionals, because a biconditional may be regarded as the conjunction of two conditionals.

Not all statements made by scientists have this logical form. A scientist may say: "Yesterday in Brazil, Professor Smith discovered a new species of butterfly." This is not the statement of a law. It speaks about a specified single time and place; it states that something happened at that time and place. Because statements such as this are about single facts, they are called "singular" statements. Of course, all our knowledge has its origin in singular statements—the particular observations of particular individuals. One of the big, perplexing questions in the philosophy of science is how we are able to go from such singular statements to the assertion of universal laws.

When statements by scientists are made in the ordinary word language, rather than in the more precise language of symbolic logic, we must be extremely careful not to confuse singular with universal statements. If a zoologist writes in a textbook, "The elephant is an excellent swimmer," he does not mean that a certain elephant, which he observed a year ago in a zoo, is an excellent swimmer. When he says "the elephant," he is using "the" in the Aristotelian sense; it refers to the entire class of elephants. All European languages have inherited from the Greek (and perhaps also from other languages) this manner of speaking in a singular way when actually a class or type is meant. The Greeks said, "Man is a rational animal." They meant, of course, all men, not a particular man. In a similar way, we say "the elephant" when we mean all elephants or "tuberculosis is characterized by the following symptoms . . ." when we mean, not a singular case of tuberculosis, but all instances.

It is unfortunate that our language has this ambiguity, because it is a source of much misunderstanding. Scientists often refer to universal statements—or rather to what is expressed by such statements—as "facts." They forget that the word "fact" was originally applied (and we shall apply it exclusively in this sense) to singular, particular occurrences. If a scientist is asked about the law of thermal expansion, he may say: "Oh, thermal expansion. That is one of the familiar, basic facts of physics." In a similar way, he may speak of the fact that heat is generated by an electric current, the fact that magnetism is produced by electricity, and so on. These are sometimes considered familiar "facts" of physics. To avoid misunderstandings, we prefer not to call such statements "facts." Facts are particular events. "This morning in the laboratory, I sent an electric current through a wire coil with an iron body inside it, and I found that the iron body became magnetic." That is a fact unless, of course, I deceived myself in some way. However, if I was sober, if it was not too foggy in the room, and if no one has tinkered secretly with the apparatus to play a joke on me, then I may state as a factual observation that this morning that sequence of events occurred.

When we use the word "fact," we will mean it in the singular sense in order to distinguish it clearly from universal statements. Such universal statements will be called "laws" even when they are as elementary as the law of thermal expansion or, still more elementary, the statement, "All ravens are black." I do not know whether this statement is true, but, assuming its truth, we will call such a statement a law of zoology. Zoologists may speak informally of such "facts" as "the raven is black" or "the octopus has eight arms," but, in our more precise terminology, statements of this sort will be called "laws."

Later we shall distinguish between two kinds of law—empirical and theoretical. Laws of the simple kind that I have just mentioned are sometimes called "empirical generalizations" or "empirical laws." They are simple because they speak of properties, like the color black or the magnetic properties of a piece of iron, that can be directly observed. The law of thermal expansion, for example, is a generalization based on many direct observations of bodies that expand when heated. In contrast, theoretical, nonobservable concepts, such as elementary particles and electromagnetic fields, must be dealt with by theoretical laws. We will discuss all this later. I mention it here because otherwise you might think that the examples I have given do not cover the kind of laws you have perhaps learned in theoretical physics.

To summarize, science begins with direct observations of single facts. Nothing else is observable. Certainly a regularity is not directly observable. It is only when many observations are compared with one another that regularities are discovered. These regularities are expressed by statements called "laws."

. . .

INDUCTION AND STATISTICAL PROBABILITY

[Earlier] we assumed that laws of science were available. We saw how such laws are used, in both science and everyday life, as explanations of known facts and as a means for predicting unknown facts. Let us now ask how we arrive at such laws. On what basis are we justified in believing that a law holds? We know, of course, that all laws are based on the observation of certain regularities. They constitute indirect knowledge, as opposed to direct knowledge of facts. What justifies us in going from the direct observation of facts to a law that expresses certain regularities of nature? This is what in traditional terminology is called "the problem of induction."

Induction is often contrasted with deduction by saying that deduction goes from the general to the specific or singular, whereas induction goes the other way, from the singular to the general. This is a misleading oversimplification. In deduction, there are kinds of inferences other than those from the general to the specific; in induction there are also many kinds of inference. The traditional distinction is also misleading because it suggests that deduction and induction are simply two branches of a single kind of logic. John Stuart Mill's famous work, *A System of Logic,* contains a lengthy description of what he called "inductive logic" and states various canons of inductive procedure. Today we are more reluctant to use the term "inductive inference." If it is used at all, we must realize that it refers to a kind of inference that differs fundamentally from deduction.

In deductive logic, inference leads from a set of premisses to a conclusion just as certain as the premisses. If you have reason to believe the premisses, you have equally valid reason to believe the conclusion that follows logically from the premisses. If the premisses are true, the conclusion cannot be false. With respect to induction, the situation is entirely different. The truth of an inductive conclusion is never certain. I do not mean only that the conclusion cannot be certain because it rests on premisses that cannot be known with certainty. Even if the premisses are assumed to be true and the inference is a valid inductive inference, the conclusion may be false. The most we can say is that, with respect to given premises, the conclusion has a certain degree of probability. Inductive logic tells us how to calculate the value of this probability.

We know that singular statements of fact, obtained by observation, are never absolutely certain because we may make errors in our observations; but, in respect to laws, there is still greater uncertainty. A law about the world states that, in any particular case, at any place and any time, if one thing is true, another thing is true. Clearly, this speaks about an infinity of possible instances. The actual instances may not be infinite, but there is an infinity of possible instances. A physiological law says that, if you stick a dagger into the heart of any human being, he will die. Since no exception to this law has ever been observed, it is accepted as universal. It is true, of course, that the number of instances so far observed of daggers being thrust into human hearts is finite. It is possible that some day humanity may cease to exist; in that case, the number of human beings, both past and future, is finite. But we do not know that humanity will cease to exist. Therefore, we must say that there is an infinity of possible instances, all of which are covered by the law. And, if there is an infinity of instances, no number of finite observations, however large, can make the "universal" law certain.

Of course, we may go on and make more and more observations, making them in as careful and scientific a manner as we can, until eventually we may say: "This law has been tested so many times that we can have complete confidence in its truth. It is a well-established, well-founded law." If we think about it, however, we see that even the best-founded laws of physics must rest on only a finite number of observations. It is always possible that tomorrow a counterinstance may be found. At no time is it possible to arrive at *complete* verification of a law. In fact, we should not speak of "verification" at all—if by the word we mean a definitive establishment of truth—but only of confirmation.

Interestingly enough, although there is no way in which a law can be verified (in the strict sense), there is a simple way it can be falsified. One need find only a single counterinstance. The knowledge of a counterinstance may, in itself, be uncertain. You may have made an error of observation or have been deceived in some way. But, if we assume that the counterinstance is a fact, then the negation of the law follows immediately. If a law says that every object that is P is also Q and we find an object that is P and not Q, the law is refuted. A million positive instances are insufficient to verify the law; one counterinstance is sufficient to falsify it. The situation is strongly asymmetric. It is easy to refute a law; it is exceedingly difficult to find strong confirmation.

How do we find confirmation of a law? If we have observed a great many positive instances and no negative instance, we say that the confirmation is strong. How strong it is and whether the strength can be expressed numerically is still a controversial question in the philosophy of science. We will return to this in a moment. Here we are concerned only with making clear that our first task in seeking confirmation of a law is to test instances to determine whether they are positive or negative. This is done by using our logical schema to make predictions. A law states that $(x) (Px \supset Qx)$; hence, for a given object a, $Pa \supset Qa$. We try to find as many objects as we can (here symbolized by "a") that have the property P. We then observe whether they also fulfill the condition Q. If we find a negative instance, the matter is settled. Otherwise, each positive instance is additional evidence adding to the strength of our confirmation.

There are, of course, various methodological rules for efficient testing. For example, instances should be diversified as much as possible. If you are testing the law of thermal expansion, you should not limit your tests to solid substances. If you are testing the law that all metals are good conductors of electricity, you should not confine your tests to specimens of copper. You should test as many metals as possible under various conditions—hot, cold, and so on. We will not go into the many methodological rules for testing; we will only point out that in all cases the law is tested by making predictions and then seeing whether those predictions hold. In some cases, we find in nature the objects that we wish to test. In other cases, we have to produce them. In testing the law of thermal expansion, for example, we do not look for objects that are hot; we take certain objects and heat them. Producing conditions for testing has the great advantage that we can more easily follow the methodological rule of diversification; but whether we create the situations to be tested or find them ready-made in nature, the underlying schema is the same.

A moment ago I raised the question of whether the degree of confirmation of a law (or a singular statement that we are predicting by means of the law) can be expressed in quantitative form. Instead of saying that one law is "well-founded" and that another law "rests on flimsy evidence," we might say that the first law has a .8 degree of confirmation, whereas the degree of confirmation for the second law is only .2. This question has long been debated. My own view is that such a procedure is legitimate and that what I have called "degree of confirmation" is identical with logical probability.

Such a statement does not mean much until we know what is meant by "logical probability." Why do I add the adjective "logical"? It is not customary practice; most books on probability do not make a distinction between various kinds of probability, one of which is called "logical." It is my belief, however, that there are two fundamentally different kinds of probability, and I distinguish between them by calling one "statistical probability," and the other "logical probability." It is unfortunate that the same word, "probability," has been used in two such widely differing senses. Failing to make the distinction is a source of enormous confusion in books on the philosophy of science as well as in the discourse of scientists themselves.

Instead of "logical probability," I sometimes use the term "inductive probability," because in my conception this is the kind of probability that is meant whenever we make an inductive inference. By "inductive inference" I mean, not only inference from facts to laws, but also any inference that is "nondemonstrative"; that is, an inference such that the conclusion does not follow with logical necessity when the truth of the premises is granted. Such inferences must be expressed in degrees of what I call "logical probability" or "inductive probability." . . .

INDUCTION AND LOGICAL PROBABILITY

. . .

In my conception, logical probability is a logical relation somewhat similar to logical implication; indeed, I think probability may be regarded as a partial implication. If the evidence is so strong that the hypothesis follows logically from it—is logically implied by it—we have one extreme case in which the probability is 1. (Probability 1 also occurs in other cases, but this is one special case where it occurs.) Similarly, if the negation of a hypothesis is logically implied by the evidence, the logical probability of the hypothesis is 0. In between, there is a continuum of cases about which deductive logic tells us nothing beyond the negative assertion that neither the hypothesis nor its negation can be deduced from the evidence. On this continuum inductive logic must take over. But inductive logic is like deductive logic in being concerned solely the statements involved, not with the facts of nature. By a logical analysis of a stated hypothesis h and stated evidence e, we conclude that h is not logically implied but is, so to speak, partially implied by e to the degree of so-and-so much.

At this point, we are justified, in my view, in assigning numerical value to the probability. If possible, we should like to construct a system of inductive logic of such a kind that for any pair of sentences, one asserting evidence e and the other stating a hypothesis h, we can assign a number giving the logical probability of h with respect to e. (We do not consider the trivial case in which the sentence e is contradictory; in such instances, no probability value can be assigned to h.) I have succeeded in developing possible definitions of such probabilities for very simple languages containing only one-place predicates, and work is now in progress for extending the theory to more comprehensive languages. Of course, if the whole of inductive logic, which I am trying to construct on this basis, is to be of any real value to science, it should finally be applicable to a quantitative language such as we have in physics, in which there are not only one- or two-place predicates, but also numerical magnitudes such as mass, temperature, and so on. I believe that this is possible and that the basic principles involved are the same as the principles that have guided the work so far in the construction of an inductive logic for the simple language of one-place predicates.

When I say I think it is possible to apply an inductive logic to the language of science, I do not mean that it is possible to formulate a set of rules, fixed once and for all, that will lead automatically, in any field, from facts to theories. It seems doubtful, for example, that rules can be formulated to enable a scientist to survey a hundred thousand sentences giving various observational reports and then find, by a mechanical application of those rules, a general theory (system of laws) that would explain the observed phenomena. This is usually not possible, because theories, especially the more abstract ones dealing with such nonobservables as particles and fields, use a conceptual framework that goes far beyond the framework used for the description of observation material. One cannot simply follow a mechanical procedure based on fixed rules to devise a new system of theoretical concepts, and with its help a theory. Creative ingenuity is required. This point is sometimes expressed by saying that there cannot be an inductive machine—a computer into which we can put all the relevant observational sentences and get, as an output, a neat system of laws that will explain the observed phenomena.

I agree that there cannot be an inductive machine if the purpose of the machine is to invent new theories. I believe, however, that there can be an inductive machine with a much more modest aim. Given certain observations e and a hypothesis h (in the form, say, of a prediction or even of a set of laws), then I believe it is in many cases possible to determine, by mechanical procedures, the logical probability, or degree of confirmation, of h on the basis of e. For this concept of probability, I also use the term "inductive probability," because I am convinced that this is the basic concept involved in all inductive reasoning and that the chief task of inductive reasoning is the evaluation of this probability.

When we survey the present situation in probability theory, we find a controversy between advocates of the frequency theory and those who, like Keynes, Jeffreys, and myself, speak in terms of a logical probability. There is, however, one important difference between my position and that of Keynes and Jeffreys. They reject the frequency concept of probability. I do not. I think the frequency concept, also called statistical probability, is a good scientific concept, whether introduced by an explicit definition, as in the systems of Mises and Reichenbach, or introduced by an axiom system and rules of practical application (without explicit definition), as in contemporary mathematical statistics. In both cases, I regard this concept as important for science. In my opinion, the logical concept of probability is a second concept, of an entirely different nature, though equally important.

Statements giving values of statistical probability are not purely logical; they are factual statements in the language of science. When a medical man says that the probability is "very good" (or perhaps he uses a numerical value and says .7) that a patient will react positively to a certain injection, he is making a statement in medical science. When a physicist says that the probability of a certain radioactive phenomenon is so-and-so much, he is making a statement in physics. Statistical probability is a scientific, empirical concept. Statements about statistical probability are "synthetic" statements, statements that cannot be decided by logic but which rest on empirical investigations. On this point I agree fully with Mises, Reichenbach, and the statisticians. When we say, "With this particular die the statistical probability of throwing an ace is .157," we are stating a scientific hypothesis that can be tested only by a series of observations. It is an empirical statement because only an empirical investigation can confirm it.

As science develops, probability statements of this sort seem to become increasingly important, not only in the social sciences, but in modern physics as well. Statistical probability is involved not only in areas where it is necessary because of ignorance (as in the social sciences or when a physicist is calculating the path of a molecule in a liquid), but also as an essential factor in the basic principles of quantum theory. It is of the utmost importance for science to have a theory of statistical probability. Such theories have been developed by statisticians and, in a different way, by Mises and Reichenbach.

On the other hand, we also need the concept of logical probability. It is especially useful in metascientific statements, that is, statements about science. We say to a scientist: "You tell me that I can rely on this law in making a certain prediction. How well established is the law? How trustworthy is the prediction?" The scientist today may or may not be willing to answer a metascientific question of this kind in quantitative terms. But I believe that, once inductive logic is sufficiently developed, he could reply: "This hypothesis is confirmed to degree .8 on the basis of the available evidence." A scientist who answers in this way is making a statement about a logical relation between the evidence and the hypothesis in question. The sort of probability he has in mind is logical probability, which I also call "degree of confirmation." His statement that the value of this probability is .8 is, in this context, not a synthetic (empirical) statement, but an analytic one. It is analytic because no empirical investigation is demanded. It expresses a logical relation between a sentence that states the evidence and a sentence that states the hypothesis.

Note that, in making an analytic statement of probability, it is always necessary to specify the evidence explicitly. The scientist must not say: "The hypothesis has a probability of .8." He must add, "with respect to such and such evidence." If this is not added, his statement might be taken as a statement of statistical probability. If he intends it to be a statement of logical probability, it is an elliptical statement in which an important component has been left out. In quantum theory, for instance, it is often difficult to know whether a physicist means statistical probability or logical probability. Physicists usually do not draw this distinction. They talk as though there were only one concept of probability with which they work. "We mean that kind of probability that fulfills the ordinary axioms of probability theory," they may say. But the ordinary axioms of probability theory are fulfilled by both concepts, so this remark does not clear up the question of exactly what type of probability they mean.

A similar ambiguity is found in the statements of Laplace and others who developed the classical conception of probability. They were not aware, as we are today, of the difference between logical probability and frequency probability. For that reason it is not always possible to determine which concept they meant. I am convinced, however, that most of the time—not always, of course—they meant the logical concept. Mises and other frequentists were not correct, in my opinion, in certain criticisms they made of the classical school. Mises believed that there was no other scientific concept of probability but the frequency concept, so he assumed that, if the classical writers meant anything at all by "probability," they must have meant statistical probability. Of course, they were not able to say clearly and explicitly that they meant relative frequency in the long run, but this, according to Mises, is what they implicitly meant. I do not agree. I believe that, when the classical writers made certain statements about a priori probability, they were speaking of logical probability, which is analytic and therefore *can* be known a priori. I do not regard these statements as violations of the principle of empiricism, as Mises and Reichenbach do.

Let me add a word of caution. After I had expressed this view in my book on probability, a number of colleagues—some of them my friends—pointed to certain quotations from classical authors and said that logical probability could not have been what those authors had in mind. With this I agree. In some of their statements the classical writers could not have meant logical probability; presumably, they meant frequency probability. Nevertheless, I am convinced that their basic concept was logical probability. I think this is even implied by the title of the first systematic book in the field, Jacob Bernoulli's *Ars conjectandi,* the art of conjecture. Mises' theory of probability is not an art of conjecture. It is a mathematically formulated axiomatic theory of mass phenomena. There is nothing conjectural about it. What Bernoulli meant was quite different. We have seen certain events, he said, such as the way a die has fallen, and we want to make a conjecture about how it will fall if we throw it again. We want to know how to make rational bets. Probability, for the classical writers, was the degree of certainty or confidence that our beliefs can have about future events. This is logical probability, not probability in the statistical sense.[1]

I will not go into greater detail here about my view of probability, because many technicalities are involved. But I will discuss the one inference in which the two concepts of probability may come together. This occurs when either the hypothesis or one of the premises for the inductive inference contains a concept of statistical probability. We can see this easily by modifying the basic schema used in our discussion of universal laws. Instead of a universal law (1), we take as the first premiss a statistical law (1′), which says that the relative frequency (*rf*) of Q with respect to P is (say) .8. The second premiss (2) states, as before, that a certain individual *a* has the property P. The third statement (3) asserts that *a* has the property Q. This third statement, *Qa,* is the hypothesis we wish to consider on the basis of the two premises.

In symbolic form:

$$(1') \ rf(Q,P) = .8$$

$$(2) \ Pa$$

$$(3) \ Qa$$

What can we say about the logical relation of (3) to (1′) and (2)? In the previous case—the schema for a universal law—we could make the following logical statement:

(4) Statement (3) is logically implied by (1) and (2).

We cannot make such a statement about the schema given above because the new premiss (1′) is weaker than the former premiss (1); it states a relative frequency rather than a universal law. We *can,* however, make the following statement, which also asserts a logical relation, but in terms of logical probability or degree of confirmation, rather than in terms of implication:

(4′) Statement (3), on the basis of (1′) and (2), has a probability of .8.

Note that this statement, like statement (4), is not a logical inference from (1′) and (2). Both (4) and (4′) are statements in what is called a metalanguage; they are logical statements *about* three assertions: (1) [or (1′), respectively], (2), and (3).

It is important to understand precisely what is meant by such a statement as "The statistical probability of Q with respect to P is .8." When scientists make such statements, speaking of probability in the frequency sense, it is not always clear exactly what frequency they mean. Is it the frequency of Q in an observed sample? Is it the frequency of Q in the total population under consideration? Is it an *estimate* of the frequency in the total population? If the number of observed instances in the sample is very large, then the frequency of Q in the sample may not differ in any significant degree from the frequency of Q in the population or from an estimate of this frequency. Nevertheless, it is important to keep in mind the theoretical distinctions involved here.

Suppose that we wish to know what percentage of a hundred thousand men living in a certain city shave with electric razors. We decide to question one thousand of these men. To avoid a biased sample, we must select the thousand men in ways developed by workers in the field of modern polling techniques. Assume that we obtain an unbiased sample and that eight hundred men in the sample report that they use an electric razor. The observed relative frequency of this property is, therefore, .8. Since one thousand is a fairly large sample, we might conclude that the statistical probability of this property, in the total population, is .8. Strictly speaking, this is not a warranted conclusion. Only the value of the frequency in the sample is known. The value of the frequency in the population is not known. The best we can do is make an *estimate* of the frequency in the population. This estimate must not be confused with the value of the frequency in the sample. In general, such estimates should deviate in a certain direction from the observed relative frequency in a sample.[2]

Assume that (1′) is known: the statistical probability of *Q*, with respect to *P*, is .8. (How we know this is a question that need not be considered. We may have tested the entire population of a hundred thousand by interviewing every man in the city.) The statement of this probability is, of course, an empirical statement. Suppose, also, that the second premiss is known: (2) *Pa.* We can now make statement (4′), which says that the logical probability of (3) *Qa*, with respect to premisses (1′) and (2), is .8. If, however, the first premiss is not a statement of statistical probability, but the statement of an observed relative frequency in a sample, then we must take into consideration the size of the sample. We can still calculate the logical probability, or degree of confirmation, expressed in statement (4), but it will not be exactly .8. It will deviate in ways I have discussed in the monograph mentioned in the previous footnote.

When an inductive inference is made in this way, from a sample to the population, from one sample to an unknown future sample, or from one sample to an unknown future instance, I speak of it as "indirect probability inference" or "indirect inductive inference," as distinct from the inductive inference that goes from the population to a sample or an instance. As I have said earlier, *if* knowledge of the actual statistical probability in the population is given in (1′), it is correct to assert in (4) the same numerical value for the degree of confirmation. Such an inference is not deductive; it occupies a somewhat intermediate position between the other kinds of inductive and deductive inferences. Some writers have even called it a "deductive probability inference," but I prefer to speak of it as inductive rather than deductive. Whenever the statistical probability for a population is given and we wish to determine the probability for a sample, the values given by my inductive logic are the same as those a statistician would give. If, however, we make an indirect inference from a sample to the population or from a sample to a future single instance or a future finite sample (these two latter cases I call "predictive inferences"), then I believe that the methods used in statistics are not quite adequate. In my monograph on *The Continuum of Inductive Methods,* I give in detail the reasons for my scepticism.

The main points that I wish to stress here are these: Both types of probability—statistical and logical—may occur together in the same chain of reasoning. Statistical probability is part of the object language of science. To statements about statistical probability we can apply logical probability, which is part of the metalanguage of science. It is my conviction that this point of view gives a much clearer picture of statistical inference than is commonly found in books on statistics and that it provides an essential groundwork for the construction of an adequate inductive logic of science.

NOTES

[1] My general view, that both statistical and logical probability are legitimate, good scientific concepts that play different roles, is expressed in Chapter II of *Logical Foundations of Probability,* and in my 1945 paper, "The Two Concepts of Probability," reprinted in Herbert Feigl and Wilfrid Sellars, eds., *Readings in Philosophical Analysis* (New York: Appleton-Century-Crofts, 1949), pp. 330–348, and Herbert Feigl and May Brodbeck, eds., *Readings in the Philosophy of Science* (New York: Appleton-Century-Crofts, 1953), pp. 438–455. For a more popularly written defense of the same viewpoint, see my article "What is Probability?" *Scientific American,* 189 (September 1953).

[2] This question is not discussed in my *Logical Foundations of Probability;* but in a small monograph, *The Continuum of Inductive Methods* (University of Chicago Press, 1952), I have developed a number of techniques for estimating relative frequency on the basis of observed samples.

THEORIES AND NONOBSERVABLES

One of the most important distinctions between two types of laws in science is the distinction between what may be called (there is no generally accepted terminology for them) empirical laws and theoretical laws. Empirical laws are laws that can be confirmed directly by empirical observations. The term "observable" is often used for any phenomenon that can be directly observed, so it can be said that empirical laws are laws about observables.

Here, a warning must be issued. Philosophers and scientists have quite different ways of using the terms "observable" and "nonobservable." To a philosopher, "observable" has a very narrow meaning. It applies to such properties as "blue," "hard," "hot." These are properties directly perceived by the senses. To the physicist, the word has a much broader meaning. It includes any quantitative magnitude that can be measured in a relatively simple, direct way. A philosopher would not consider a temperature of, perhaps, 80 degrees centigrade, or a weight of 93½ pounds, an observable because there is no direct sensory perception of such magnitudes. To a physicist, both are observables because they can be measured in an extremely simple way. The object to be weighed is placed on a balance scale. The temperature is measured with a thermometer. The physicist would not say that the mass of a molecule, let alone the mass of an electron, is something observable, because here the procedures of measurement are much more complicated and indirect. But magnitudes that can be established by relatively simple procedures—length with a ruler, time with a clock, or frequency of light waves with a spectrometer—are called observables.

A philosopher might object that the intensity of an electric current is not really observed. Only a pointer position was observed. An ammeter was attached to the circuit and it was noted that the pointer pointed to a mark labeled 5.3. Certainly the current's intensity was not observed. It was *inferred* from what was observed.

The physicist would reply that this was true enough, but the inference was not very complicated. The procedure of measurement is so simple, so well established, that it could not be doubted that the ammeter would give an accurate measurement of current intensity. Therefore, it is included among what are called observables.

There is no question here of who is using the term "observable" in a right or proper way. There is a continuum which starts with direct sensory observations and proceeds to enormously complex, indirect methods of observation. Obviously no sharp line can be drawn across this continuum; it is a matter of degree. A philosopher is sure that the sound of his wife's voice, coming from across the room, is an observable. But suppose he listens to her on the telephone. Is her voice an observable or isn't it? A physicist would certainly say that when he looks at something through an ordinary microscope, he is observing it directly. Is this also the case when he looks into an electron microscope? Does he observe the path of a particle when he sees the track it makes in a bubble chamber? In general, the physicist speaks of observables in a very wide sense compared with the narrow sense of the philosopher, but, in both cases, the line separating observable from nonobservable is highly arbitrary. It is well to keep this in mind whenever these terms are encountered in a book by a philosopher or scientist. Individual authors will draw the line where it is most convenient, depending on their points of view, and there is no reason why they should not have this privilege.

Empirical laws, in my terminology, are laws containing terms either directly observable by the senses or measurable by relatively simple techniques. Sometimes such laws are called empirical generalizations, as a reminder that they have been obtained by generalizing results found by observations and measurements. They include not only simple qualitative laws (such as, "All ravens are black") but also quantitative laws that arise from simple measurements. The laws relating pressure, volume, and temperature of gases are of this type. Ohm's law, connecting the electric potential difference, resistance, and intensity of current, is another familiar example. The scientist makes repeated measurements, finds certain regularities, and expresses them in a law. These are the empirical laws. As indicated in earlier chapters, they are used for explaining observed facts and for predicting future observable events.

There is no commonly accepted term for the second kind of laws, which I call *theoretical laws*. Sometimes they are called abstract or hypothetical laws. "Hypothetical" is perhaps not suitable because it suggests that the distinction between the two types of laws is based on the degree to which the laws are confirmed. But an empirical law, if it is a tentative hypothesis, confirmed only to a low degree, would still be an empirical law although it might be said that it was rather hypothetical. A theoretical law is not to be distinguished from an empirical law by the fact that it is not well established, but by the fact that it contains terms of a different kind. The terms of a theoretical law do not refer to observables even when the physicist's wide meaning for what can be observed is adopted. They are laws about such entities as molecules, atoms, electrons, protons, electromagnetic fields, and others that cannot be measured in simple, direct ways.

If there is a static field of large dimensions, which does not vary from point to point, physicists call it an observable field because it can be measured with a simple apparatus. But if the field changes from point to point in very small distances, or varies very quickly in time, perhaps changing billions of times each second, then it cannot be directly measured by simple techniques. Physicists would not call such a field an observable. Sometimes a physicist will distinguish between observables and nonobservables in just this way. If the magnitude remains the same within large enough spatial distances, or large enough time intervals, so that an apparatus can be applied for a direct measurement of the magnitude, it is called a *macroevent*. If the magnitude changes within such extremely small intervals of space and time that it cannot be directly measured by simple apparatus, it is a *microevent*. (Earlier authors used the terms "microscopic" and "macroscopic," but today many authors have shortened these terms to "micro" and "macro.")

A microprocess is simply a process involving extremely small intervals of space and time. For example, the oscillation of an electromagnetic wave of visible light is a microprocess. No instrument can directly measure how its intensity varies. The distinction between macro- and microconcepts is sometimes taken to be parallel to observable and nonobservable. It is not exactly the same, but it is roughly so. Theoretical laws concern nonobservables, and very often these are microprocesses. If so, the laws are sometimes called microlaws. I use the term "theoretical laws" in a wider sense than this, to include all those laws that contain nonobservables, regardless of whether they are microconcepts or macroconcepts.

It is true, as shown earlier, that the concepts "observable" and "nonobservable" cannot be sharply defined because they lie on a continuum. In actual practice, however, the difference is usually great enough so there is not likely to be debate. All physicists would agree that the laws relating pressure, volume, and temperature of a gas, for example, are empirical laws. Here the amount of gas is large enough so that the magnitudes to be measured remain constant over a sufficiently large volume of space and period of time to permit direct, simple measurements which can then be generalized into laws. All physicists would agree that laws about the behavior of single molecules are theoretical. Such laws concern a microprocess about which generalizations cannot be based on simple, direct measurements.

Theoretical laws are, of course, more general than empirical laws. It is important to understand, however, that theoretical laws cannot be arrived at simply by taking the empirical laws, then generalizing a few steps further. How does a physicist arrive at an empirical law? He observes certain events in nature. He notices a certain regularity. He describes this regularity by making an inductive generalization. It might be supposed that he could now put together a group of empirical laws, observe some sort of pattern, make a wider inductive generalization, and arrive at a theoretical law. Such is not the case.

To make this clear, suppose it has been observed that a certain iron bar expands when heated. After the experiment has been repeated many times, always with the same result, the regularity is generalized by saying that this bar expands when heated. An empirical law has been stated, even though it has a narrow range and applies only to one particular iron bar. Now further tests are made of other iron objects with the ensuing discovery that every time an iron object is heated it expands. This permits a more general law to be formulated, namely that all bodies of iron expand when heated. In similar fashion, the still more general laws "All metals . . . ," then "All solid bodies . . . ," are developed. These are all simple generalizations, each a bit more general than the previous one, but they are all empirical laws. Why? Because in each case, the objects dealt with are observable (iron, copper, metal, solid bodies); in each case the increases in temperature and length are measurable by simple, direct techniques.

In contrast, a theoretical law relating to this process would refer to the behavior of molecules in the iron bar. In what way is the behavior of the molecules connected with the expansion of the bar when heated? You see at once that we are now speaking of nonobservables. We must introduce a theory—the atomic theory of matter—and we are quickly plunged into atomic laws involving concepts radically different from those we had before. It is true that these theoretical concepts differ from concepts of length and temperature only in the degree to which they are directly or indirectly observable, but the difference is so great that there is no debate about the radically different nature of the laws that must be formulated.

Theoretical laws are related to empirical laws in a way somewhat analogous to the way empirical laws are related to single facts. An empirical law helps to explain a fact that has been observed and to predict a fact not yet observed. In similar fashion, the theoretical law helps to explain empirical laws already formulated, and to permit the derivation of new empirical laws. Just as the single, separate facts fall into place in an orderly pattern when they are generalized in an empirical law, the single and separate empirical laws fit into the orderly pattern of a theoretical law. This raises one of the main problems in the methodology of science. How can the kind of knowledge that will justify the assertion of a theoretical law be obtained? An empirical law may be justified by making observations of single facts. But to justify a theoretical law, comparable observations cannot be made because the entities referred to in theoretical laws are nonobservables.

Before taking up this problem, some remarks made in an earlier chapter, about the use of the word "fact," should be repeated. It is important in the present context to be extremely careful in the use of this word because some authors, especially scientists, use "fact" or "empirical fact" for some propositions which I would call empirical laws. For example, many physicists will refer to the "fact" that the specific heat of copper is .090. I would call this a law because in its full formulation it is seen to be a universal conditional statement: "For any x, and any time t, if x is a solid body of copper, then the specific heat of x at t is .090." Some physicists may even speak of the law of thermal expansion, Ohm's law, and others, as facts. Of course, they can then say that theoretical laws help explain such facts. This sounds like my statement that empirical laws explain facts, but the word "fact" is being used here in two different ways. I restrict the word to particular, concrete facts that can be spatiotemporally specified, not thermal expansion in general, but *the* expansion of this iron bar observed this morning at ten o'clock when it was heated. It is important to bear in mind the restricted way in which I speak of facts. If the word "fact" is used in an ambiguous manner, the important difference between the ways in which empirical and theoretical laws serve for explanation will be entirely blurred.

How can theoretical laws be discovered? We cannot say: "Let's just collect more and more data, then generalize beyond the empirical laws until we reach theoretical ones." No theoretical law was ever found that way. We observe stones and trees and flowers, noting various regularities and describing them by empirical laws. But no matter how long or how carefully we observe such things, we never reach a point at which we observe a molecule. The term "molecule" never arises as a result of observations. For this reason, no amount of generalization from observations will ever produce a theory of molecular processes. Such a theory must arise in another way. It is stated not as a generalization of facts but as a hypothesis. The hypothesis is then tested in a manner analogous in certain ways to the testing of an empirical law. From the hypothesis, certain empirical laws are derived, and these empirical laws are tested in turn by observation of facts. Perhaps the empirical laws derived from the theory are already known and well confirmed. (Such laws may even have motivated the formulation of the theoretical law.) Regardless of whether the derived empirical laws are known and confirmed, or whether they are new laws confirmed by new observations, the confirmation of such derived laws provides indirect confirmation of the theoretical law.

The point to be made clear is this. A scientist does not start with one empirical law, perhaps Boyle's law for gases, and then seek a theory about molecules from which this law can be derived. The scientist tries to formulate a much more general theory from which a variety of empirical laws can be derived. The more such laws, the greater their variety and apparent lack of connection with one another, the stronger will be the theory that explains them. Some of these derived laws may have been known before, but the theory may also make it possible to derive new empirical laws which can be confirmed by new tests. If this is the case, it can be said that the theory made it possible to predict new empirical laws. The prediction is understood in a hypothetical way. If the theory holds, certain empirical laws will also hold. The predicted empirical law speaks about relations between observables, so it is now possible to make experiments to see if the empirical law holds. If the empirical law is confirmed, it provides indirect confirmation of the theory. Every confirmation of a law, empirical or theoretical, is, of course, only partial, never complete and absolute. But in the case of empirical laws, it is a more direct confirmation. The confirmation of a theoretical law is indirect, because it takes place only through the confirmation of empirical laws derived from the theory.

The supreme value of a new theory is its power to predict new empirical laws. It is true that it also has value in explaining known empirical laws, but this is a minor value. If a scientist proposes a new theoretical system, from which no new laws can be derived, then it is logically equivalent to the set of all known empirical laws. The theory may have a certain elegance, and it may simplify to some degree the set of all known laws, although it is not likely that there would be an essential simplification. On the other hand, every new theory in physics that has led to a great leap forward has been a theory from which new empirical laws could be derived. If Einstein had done no more than propose his theory of relativity as an elegant new theory that would embrace certain known laws—perhaps also simplify them to a certain degree— then his theory would not have had such a revolutionary effect.

Of course it was quite otherwise. The theory of relativity led to new empirical laws which explained for the first time such phenomena as the movement of the perihelion of Mercury, and the bending of light rays in the neighborhood of the sun. These predictions showed that relativity theory was more than just a new way of expressing the old laws. Indeed, it was a theory of great predictive power. The consequences that can be derived from Einstein's theory are far from being exhausted. These are consequences that could not have been derived from earlier theories. Usually a theory of such power does have an elegance, and a unifying effect on known laws. It is simpler than the total collection of known laws. But the great value of the theory lies in its power to suggest new laws that can be confirmed by empirical means.

CORRESPONDENCE RULES

An important qualification must now be added to the discussion of theoretical laws and terms given in the last [section]. The statement that empirical laws are derived from theoretical laws is an oversimplification. It is not possible to derive them directly because a theoretical law contains theoretical terms, whereas an empirical law contains only observable terms. This prevents any direct deduction of an empirical law from a theoretical one.

To understand this, imagine that we are back in the nineteenth century, preparing to state for the first time some theoretical laws about molecules in a gas. These laws are to describe the number of molecules per unit volume of the gas, the molecular velocities, and so forth. To simplify matters, we assume that all the molecules have the same velocity. (This was indeed the original assumption; later it was abandoned in favor of a certain probability distribution of velocities.) Further assumptions must be made about what happens when molecules collide. We do not know the exact shape of molecules, so let us suppose that they are tiny spheres. How do spheres collide? There are laws about colliding spheres, but they concern large bodies. Since we cannot directly observe molecules, we assume their collisions are analogous to those of large bodies; perhaps they behave like perfect billiard balls on a frictionless table. These are, of course, only assumptions; guesses suggested by analogies with known macrolaws.

But now we come up against a difficult problem. Our theoretical laws deal exclusively with the behavior of molecules, which cannot be seen. How, therefore, can we deduce from such laws a law about observable properties such as the pressure or temperature of a gas or properties of sound waves that pass through the gas? The theoretical laws contain only theoretical terms. What we seek are empirical laws containing observable terms. Obviously, such laws cannot be derived without having something else given in addition to the theoretical laws.

The something else that must be given is this: a set of rules connecting the theoretical terms with the observable terms. Scientists and philosophers of science have long recognized the need for such a set of rules, and their nature has been often discussed. An example of such a rule is: "If there is an electromagnetic oscillation of a specified frequency, then there is a visible greenish-blue color of a certain hue." Here something observable is connected with a nonobservable micro-process.

Another example is: "The temperature (measured by a thermometer and, therefore, an observable in the wider sense explained earlier) of a gas is proportional to the mean kinetic energy of its molecules." This rule connects a nonobservable in molecular theory, the kinetic energy of molecules, with an observable, the temperature of the gas. If statements of this kind did not exist, there would be no way of deriving empirical laws about observables from theoretical laws about nonobservables.

Different writers have different names for these rules. I call them "correspondence rules." P. W. Bridgman calls them operational rules. Norman R. Campbell speaks of them as the "Dictionary."[1] Since the rules connect a term in one terminology with a term in another terminology, the use of the rules is analogous to the use of a French-English dictionary. What does the French word "*cheval*" mean? You look it up in the dictionary and find that it means "horse." It is not really that simple when a set of rules is used for connecting nonobservables with observables; nevertheless, there is an analogy here that makes Campbell's "Dictionary" a suggestive name for the set of rules.

There is a temptation at times to think that the set of rules provides a means for defining theoretical terms, whereas just the opposite is really true. A theoretical term can never be explicitly defined on the basis of observable terms, although sometimes an observable can be defined in theoretical terms. For example, "iron" can be defined as a substance consisting of small crystalline parts, each having a certain arrangement of atoms and each atom being a configuration of particles of a certain type. In theoretical terms then, it is possible to express what is meant by the observable term "iron," but the reverse is not true.

There is no answer to the question: "Exactly what is an electron?" Later we shall come back to this question, because it is the kind that philosophers are always asking scientists. They want the physicist to tell them just what he means by "electricity," "magnetism," "gravity," "a molecule." If the physicist explains them in theoretical terms, the philosopher may be disappointed. "That is not what I meant at all," he will say. "I want you to tell me, in ordinary language, what those terms mean." Sometimes the philosopher writes a book in which he talks about the great mysteries of nature. "No one," he writes, "has been able so far, and perhaps no one ever will be able, to give us a straightforward answer to the question: 'What is electricity?' And so electricity remains forever one of the great, unfathomable mysteries of the universe."

There is no special mystery here. There is only an improperly phrased question. Definitions that cannot, in the nature of the case, be given, should not be demanded. If a child does not know what an elephant is, we can tell him it is a huge animal with big ears and a long trunk. We can show him a picture of an elephant. It serves admirably to define an elephant in observable terms that a child can understand. By analogy, there is a temptation to believe that, when a scientist introduces theoretical terms, he should also be able to define them in familiar terms. But this is not possible. There is no way a physicist can show us a picture of electricity in the way he can show his child a picture of an elephant. Even the cell of an organism, although it cannot be seen with the unaided eye, can be represented by a picture because the cell can be seen when it is viewed through a microscope. But we do not possess a picture of the electron. We cannot say how it looks or how it feels, because it cannot be seen or touched. The best we can do is to say that it is an extremely small body that behaves in a certain manner. This may seem to be analogous to our description of an elephant. We can describe an elephant as a large animal that behaves in a certain manner. Why not do the same with an electron?

The answer is that a physicist can describe the behavior of an electron only by stating theoretical laws, and these laws contain only theoretical terms. They describe the field produced by an electron, the reaction of an electron to a field, and so on. If an electron is in an electrostatic field, its velocity will accelerate in a certain way. Unfortunately, the electron's acceleration is an unobservable. It is not like the acceleration of a billiard ball, which can be studied by direct observation. There is no way that a theoretical concept can be defined in terms of observables. We must, therefore, resign ourselves to the fact that definitions of the kind that can be supplied for observable terms cannot be formulated for theoretical terms.

It is true that some authors, including Bridgman, have spoken of the rules as "operational definitions." Bridgman had a certain justification, because he used his rules in a somewhat different way, I believe, than most physicists use them. He was a great physicist and was certainly aware of his departure from the usual use of rules, but he was willing to accept certain forms of speech that are not customary, and this explains his departure. It was pointed out [earlier] that Bridgman preferred to say that there is not just one concept of intensity of electric current, but a dozen concepts. Each procedure by which a magnitude can be measured provides an operational definition for that magnitude. Since there are different procedures for measuring current, there are different concepts. For the sake of convenience, the physicist speaks of just one concept of current. Strictly speaking, Bridgman believed, he should recognize many different concepts, each defined by a different operational procedure of measurement.

We are faced here with a choice between two different physical languages. If the customary procedure among physicists is followed, the various concepts of current will be replaced by one concept. This means, however, that you place the concept in your theoretical laws, because the operational rules are just correspondence rules, as I call them, which connect the theoretical terms with the empirical ones. Any claim to possessing a definition—that is, an operational definition—of the theoretical concept must be given up. Bridgman could speak of having operational definitions for his theoretical terms only because he was not speaking of a general concept. He was speaking of partial concepts, each defined by a different empirical procedure.

Even in Bridgman's terminology, the question of whether his partial concepts can be adequately defined by operational rules is problematic. Reichenbach speaks often of what he calls "correlative definitions." (In his German publications, he calls them *Zuordnungsdefinitionen,* from *zuordnen,* which means to correlate.) Perhaps correlation is a better term than definition for what Bridgman's rules actually do. In geometry, for instance, Reichenbach points out that the axiom system of geometry, as developed by David Hilbert, for example, is an uninterpreted axiom system. The basic concepts of point, line, and plane could just as well be called "class alpha," "class beta," and "class gamma." We must not be seduced by the sound of familiar words, such as "point" and "line," into thinking they must be taken in their ordinary meaning. In the axiom system, they are uninterpreted terms. But when geometry is applied to physics, these terms must be connected with something in the physical world. We can say, for example, that the lines of the geometry are exemplified by rays of light in a vacuum or by stretched cords. In order to connect the uninterpreted terms with observable physical phenomena, we must have rules for establishing the connection.

What we call these rules is, of course, only a terminological question; we should be cautious and not speak of them as definitions. They are not definitions in any strict sense. We cannot give a really adequate definition of the geometrical concept of "line" by referring to anything in nature. Light rays, stretched strings, and so on are only approximately straight; moreover, they are not lines, but only segments of lines. In geometry, a line is infinite in length and absolutely straight. Neither property is exhibited by any phenomenon in nature. For that reason, it is not possible to give an operational definition, in the strict sense of the word, of concepts in theoretical geometry. The same is true of all the other theoretical concepts of physics.

Strictly speaking, there are no "definitions" of such concepts. I prefer not to speak of "operational definitions" or even to use Reichenbach's term "correlative definitions." In my publications (only in recent years have I written about this question), I have called them "rules of correspondence" or, more simply, "correspondence rules."

Campbell and other authors often speak of the entities in theoretical physics as mathematical entities. They mean by this that the entities are related to each other in ways that can be expressed by mathematical functions. But they are not mathematical entities of the sort that can be defined in pure mathematics. In pure mathematics, it is possible to define various kinds of numbers, the function of logarithm, the exponential function, and so forth. It is not possible, however, to define such terms as "electron" and "temperature" by pure mathematics. Physical terms can be introduced only with the help of nonlogical constants, based on observations of the actual world. Here we have an essential difference between an axiomatic system in mathematics and an axiomatic system in physics.

If we wish to give an interpretation to a term in a mathematical axiom system, we can do it by giving a definition in logic. Consider, for example, the term "number" as it is used in Peano's axiom system. We can define it in logical terms, by the Frege-Russell method, for example. In this way the concept of "number" acquires a complete, explicit definition on the basis of pure logic. There is no need to establish a connection between the number 5 and such observables as "blue" and "hot." The terms have only a logical interpretation; no connection with the actual world is needed. Sometimes an axiom system in mathematics is called a theory. Mathematicians speak of set theory, group theory, matrix theory, probability theory. Here the word "theory" is used in a purely analytic way. It denotes a deductive system that makes no reference to the actual world. We must always bear in mind that such a use of the word "theory" is entirely different from its use in reference to empirical theories such as relativity theory, quantum theory, psychoanalytical theory, and Keynesian economic theory.

A postulate system in physics cannot have, as mathematical theories have, a splendid isolation from the world. Its axiomatic terms—"electron," "field," and so on—must be interpreted by correspondence rules that connect the terms with observable phenomena. This interpretation is necessarily incomplete. Because it is always incomplete, the system is left open to make it possible to add new rules of correspondence. Indeed, this is what continually happens in the history of physics. I am not thinking now of a revolution in physics, in which an entirely new theory is developed, but of less radical changes that modify existing theories. Nineteenth-century physics provides a good example, because classical mechanics and electromagnetics had been established, and, for many decades, there was relatively little change in fundamental laws. The basic theories of physics remained unchanged. There was, however, a steady addition of new correspondence rules, because new procedures were continually being developed for measuring this or that magnitude.

Of course, physicists always face the danger that they may develop correspondence rules that will be incompatible with each other or with the theoretical laws. As long as such incompatibility does not occur, however, they are free to add new correspondence rules. The procedure is never-ending. There is always the possibility of adding new rules, thereby increasing the amount of interpretation specified for the theoretical terms; but no matter how much this is increased, the interpretation is never final. In a mathematical system, it is otherwise. There a logical interpretation of an axiomatic term *is* complete. Here we find another reason for reluctance in speaking of theoretical terms as "defined" by correspondence rules. It tends to blur the important distinction between the nature of an axiom system in pure mathematics and one in theoretical physics.

Is it not possible to interpret a theoretical term by correspondence rules so completely that no further interpretation would be possible? Perhaps the actual world is limited in its structure and laws. Eventually a point may be reached beyond which there will be no room for strengthening the interpretation of a term by new correspondence rules. Would not the rules then provide a final, explicit definition for the term? Yes, but then the term would no longer be theoretical. It would become part of the observation language. The history of physics has not yet indicated that physics will become complete; there has been only a steady addition of new correspondence rules and a continual modification in the interpretations of theoretical terms. There is no way of knowing whether this is an infinite process or whether it will eventually come to some sort of end.

It may be looked at this way. There is no prohibition in physics against making the correspondence rules for a term so strong that the term becomes explicitly defined and therefore ceases to be theoretical. Neither is there any basis for assuming that it will always be possible to add new correspondence rules. Because the history of physics has shown such a steady, unceasing modification of theoretical concepts, most physicists would advise against correspondence rules so strong that a theoretical term becomes explicitly defined. Moreover, it is a wholly unnecessary procedure. Nothing is gained by it. It may even have the adverse effect of blocking progress.

Of course, here again we must recognize that the distinction between observables and nonobservables is a matter of degree. We might give an explicit definition, by empirical procedures, to a concept such as length, because it is so easily and directly measured, and is unlikely to be modified by new observations. But it would be rash to seek such strong correspondence rules that "electron" would be explicitly defined. The concept "electron" is so far removed from simple, direct observations that it is best to keep it theoretical, open to modifications by new observations.

NOTE

[1] See Percy W. Bridgman, *The Logic of Modern Physics* (New York: Macmillan, 1927), and Norman R. Campbell, *Physics: The Elements* (Cambridge: Cambridge University Press, 1920). Rules of correspondence are discussed by Ernest Nagel, *The Structure of Science* (New York: Harcourt, Brace, & World, 1961), pp. 97–105.

KARL R. POPPER
SCIENCE: CONJECTURES AND REFUTATIONS

Mr. Turnbull had predicted evil consequences, . . . and was now doing the best in his power to bring about the verification of his own prophecies.

Anthony Trollope

I

When I received the list of participants in this course and realized that I had been asked to speak to philosophical colleagues I thought, after some hesitation and consultation, that you would probably prefer me to speak about those problems which interest me most, and about those developments with which I am most intimately acquainted. I therefore decided to do what I have never done before: to give you a report on my own work in the philosophy of science, since the autumn of 1919 when I first began to grapple with the problem, "*When should a theory be ranked as scientific?*" or "*Is there a criterion for the scientific character or status of a theory?*"

The problem which troubled me at the time was neither, "When is a theory true?" nor, "When is a theory acceptable?" My problem was different. I *wished to distinguish between science and pseudo-science;* knowing very well that science often errs, and that pseudo-science may happen to stumble on the truth.

I knew, of course, the most widely accepted answer to my problem: that science is distinguished from pseudo-science—or from "metaphysics"—by its *empirical method,* which is essentially *inductive,* proceeding from observation or experiment. But this did not satisfy me. On the contrary, I often formulated my problem as one of distinguishing between a genuinely empirical method and a non-empirical or even a pseudo-empirical method—that is to say, a method which, although it appeals to observation and experiment, nevertheless does not come up to scientific standards. The latter method may be exemplified by astrology, with its stupendous mass of empirical evidence based on observation—on horoscopes and on biographies.

But as it was not the example of astrology which led me to my problem I should perhaps briefly describe the atmosphere in which my problem arose and the examples by which it was stimulated. After the collapse of the Austrian Empire there had been a revolution in Austria: the air was full of revolutionary slogans and ideas, and new and often wild theories. Among the theories which interested me Einstein's theory of relativity was no doubt by far the most important. Three others were Marx's theory of history, Freud's psycho-analysis, and Alfred Adler's so-called "individual psychology."

There was a lot of popular nonsense talked about these theories, and especially about relativity (as still happens even today), but I was fortunate in those who introduced me to the study

---

A lecture given at Peterhouse, Cambridge, in Summer 1953, as part of a course on developments and trends in contemporary British philosophy, organized by the British Council; originally published under the title "Philosophy of Science: a Personal Report" in *British Philosophy in Mid-Century,* ed. C. A. Mace, 1957.

of this theory. We all—the small circle of students to which I belonged—were thrilled with the result of Eddington's eclipse observations which in 1919 brought the first important confirmation of Einstein's theory of gravitation. It was a great experience for us, and one which had a lasting influence on my intellectual development.

The three other theories I have mentioned were also widely discussed among students at that time. I myself happened to come into personal contact with Alfred Adler, and even to co-operate with him in his social work among the children and young people in the working-class districts of Vienna where he had established social guidance clinics.

It was during the summer of 1919 that I began to feel more and more dissatisfied with these three theories—the Marxist theory of history, psychoanalysis, and individual psychology; and I began to feel dubious about their claims to scientific status. My problem perhaps first took the simple form, "What is wrong with Marxism, psycho-analysis, and individual psychology? Why are they so different from physical theories, from Newton's theory, and especially from the theory of relativity?"

To make this contrast clear I should explain that few of us at the time would have said that we believed in the *truth* of Einstein's theory of gravitation. This shows that it was not my doubting the *truth* of those other three theories which bothered me, but something else. Yet neither was it that I merely felt mathematical physics to be more *exact* than the sociological or psychological type of theory. Thus what worried me was neither the problem of truth, at that stage at least, nor the problem of exactness or measurability. It was rather that I felt that these other three theories, though posing as sciences, had in fact more in common with primitive myths than with science; that they resembled astrology rather than astronomy.

I found that those of my friends who were admirers of Marx, Freud, and Adler, were impressed by a number of points common to these theories, and especially by their apparent *explanatory power*. These theories appeared to be able to explain practically everything that happened within the fields to which they referred. The study of any of them seemed to have the effect of an intellectual conversion or revelation, opening your eyes to a new truth hidden from those not yet initiated. Once your eyes were thus opened you saw confirming instances everywhere: the world was full of *verifications* of the theory. Whatever happened always confirmed it. Thus its truth appeared manifest; and unbelievers were clearly people who did not want to see the manifest truth; who refused to see it, either because it was against their class interest, or because of their repressions which were still "un-analysed" and crying aloud for treatment.

The most characteristic element in this situation seemed to me the incessant stream of confirmations, of observations which "verified" the theories in question; and this point was constantly emphasized by their adherents. A Marxist could not open a newspaper without finding on every page confirming evidence for his interpretation of history; not only in the news, but also in its presentation—which revealed the class bias of the paper—and especially of course in what the paper did *not* say. The Freudian analysts emphasized that their theories were constantly verified by their "clinical observations." As for Adler, I was much impressed by a personal experience. Once, in 1919, I reported to him a case which to me did not seem particularly Adlerian, but which he found no difficulty in analysing in terms of his theory of inferiority feelings, although he had not even seen the child. Slightly shocked, I asked him how he could be so sure. "Because of my thousandfold experience," he replied; whereupon I could not help saying: "And with this new case, I suppose, your experience has become thousand-and-one-fold."

What I had in mind was that his previous observations may not have been much sounder than this new one; that each in its turn had been interpreted in the light of "previous experience," and at the same time counted as additional confirmation. What, I asked myself, did it confirm? No more than that a case could be interpreted in the light of the theory. But this meant very little, I reflected, since every conceivable case could be interpreted in the light of Adler's theory, or equally of Freud's. I may illustrate this by two very different examples of human behaviour: that of a man who pushes a child into the water with the intention of drowning it; and that of a man who sacrifices his life in an attempt to save the child. Each of these two cases can be explained with equal ease in Freudian and in Adlerian terms. According to Freud the first man suffered from repression (say, of some component of his Oedipus complex), while the second man had achieved sublimation. According to Adler the first man suffered from feelings of inferiority (producing perhaps the need to prove to himself that he dared to commit some crime), and so did the second man (whose need was to prove to himself that he dared to rescue the child). I could not think of any human behaviour which could not be interpreted in terms of either theory. It was precisely this fact—that they always fitted, that they were always confirmed—which in the eyes of their admirers constituted the strongest argument in favour of these theories. It began to dawn on me that this apparent strength was in fact their weakness.

With Einstein's theory the situation was strikingly different. Take one typical instance—Einstein's prediction, just then confirmed by the findings of Eddington's expedition. Einstein's gravitational theory had led to the result that light must be attracted by heavy bodies (such as the sun), precisely as material bodies were attracted. As a consequence it could be calculated that light from a distant fixed star whose apparent position was close to the sun would reach the earth from such a direction that the star would seem to be slightly shifted away from the sun; or, in other words, that stars close to the sun would look as if they had moved a little away from the sun, and from one another. This is a thing which cannot normally be observed since such stars are rendered invisible in daytime by the sun's overwhelming brightness; but during an eclipse it is possible to take photographs of them. If the same constellation is photographed at night one can measure the distances on the two photographs, and check the predicted effect.

Now the impressive thing about this case is the *risk* involved in a prediction of this kind. If observation shows that the predicted effect is definitely absent, then the theory is simply refuted. The theory is *incompatible with certain possible results of observation*—in fact with results which everybody before Einstein would have expected.[1] This is quite different from the situation I have previously described, when it turned out that the theories in question were compatible with the most divergent human behaviour, so that it was practically impossible to describe any human behaviour that might not be claimed to be a verification of these theories.

These considerations led me in the winter of 1919–20 to conclusions which I may now reformulate as follows.

(1) It is easy to obtain confirmations, or verifications, for nearly every theory—if we look for confirmations.

(2) Confirmations should count only if they are the result of *risky predictions;* that is to say, if, unenlightened by the theory in question, we should have expected an event which was incompatible with the theory—an event which would have refuted the theory.

(3) Every "good" scientific theory is a prohibition: it forbids certain things to happen. The more a theory forbids, the better it is.

(4) A theory which is not refutable by any conceivable event is nonscientific. Irrefutability is not a virtue of a theory (as people often think) but a vice.

(5) Every genuine *test* of a theory is an attempt to falsify it, or to refute it. Testability is falsifiability; but there are degrees of testability: some theories are more testable, more exposed to refutation, than others; they take, as it were, greater risks.

(6) Confirming evidence should not count *except when it is the result of a genuine test of the theory;* and this means that it can be presented as a serious but unsuccessful attempt to falsify the theory. (I now speak in such cases of "corroborating evidence.")

(7) Some genuinely testable theories, when found to be false, are still upheld by their admirers—for example by introducing *ad hoc* some auxiliary assumption, or by reinterpreting the theory *ad hoc* in such a way that it escapes refutation. Such a procedure is always possible, but it rescues the theory from refutation only at the price of destroying, or at least lowering, its scientific status. (I later described such a rescuing operation as a "*conventionalist twist*" or a "*conventionalist stratagem.*")

One can sum up all this by saying that *the criterion of the scientific status of a theory is its falsifiability, or refutability, or testability.*

II

I may perhaps exemplify this with the help of the various theories so far mentioned. Einstein's theory of gravitation clearly satisfied the criterion of falsifiability. Even if our measuring instruments at the time did not allow us to pronounce on the results of the tests with complete assurance, there was clearly a possibility of refuting the theory.

Astrology did not pass the test. Astrologers were greatly impressed, and misled, by what they believed to be confirming evidence—so much so that they were quite unimpressed by any unfavourable evidence. Moreover, by making their interpretations and prophecies sufficiently vague they were able to explain away anything that might have been a refutation of the theory had the theory and the prophecies been more precise. In order to escape falsification they destroyed the testability of their theory. It is a typical soothsayer's trick to predict things so vaguely that the predictions can hardly fail: that they become irrefutable.

The Marxist theory of history, in spite of the serious efforts of some of its founders and followers, ultimately adopted this soothsaying practice. In some of its earlier formulations (for example in Marx's analysis of the character of the "coming social revolution") their predictions were testable, and in fact falsified.[2] Yet instead of accepting the refutations the followers of Marx re-interpreted both the theory and the evidence in order to make them agree. In this way they rescued the theory from refutation; but they did so at the price of adopting a device which made it irrefutable. They thus gave a "conventionalist twist" to the theory; and by this stratagem they destroyed its much advertised claim to scientific status.

The two psycho-analytic theories were in a different class. They were simply non-testable, irrefutable. There was no conceivable human behaviour which could contradict them. This does not mean that Freud and Adler were not seeing certain things correctly: I personally do not doubt that much of what they say is of considerable importance, and may well play its part one day in a psychological science which is testable. But it does mean that those 'clinical observations' which analysts naïvely believe confirm their theory cannot do this any more than the daily confirmations which astrologers find in their practice.[3] And as for Freud's epic of the Ego, the Super-ego, and the Id, no substantially stronger claim to scientific status can be made for it than for Homer's collected stories from Olympus. These theories describe some facts, but in the manner of myths. They contain most interesting psychological suggestions, but not in a testable form.

At the same time I realized that such myths may be developed, and become testable; that historically speaking all—or very nearly all—scientific theories originate from myths, and that a myth may contain important anticipations of scientific theories. Examples are Empedocles' theory of evolution by trial and error, or Parmenides' myth of the unchanging block universe in which nothing ever happens and which, if we add another dimension, becomes Einstein's block universe (in which, too, nothing ever happens, since everything is, four-dimensionally speaking, determined and laid down from the beginning). I thus felt that if a theory is found to be non-scientific, or "metaphysical" (as we might say), it is not thereby found to be unimportant, or insignificant, or "meaningless," or "nonsensical."[4] But it cannot claim to be backed by empirical evidence in the scientific sense—although it may easily be, in some genetic sense, the "result of observation."

(There were a great many other theories of this pre-scientific or pseudo-scientific character, some of them, unfortunately, as influential as the Marxist interpretation of history; for example, the racialist interpretation of history—another of those impressive and all-explanatory theories which act upon weak minds like revelations.)

Thus the problem which I tried to solve by proposing the criterion of falsifiability was neither a problem of meaningfulness or significance, nor a problem of truth or acceptability. It was the problem of drawing a line (as well as this can be done) between the statements, or systems of statements, of the empirical sciences, and all other statements—whether they are of a religious or of a metaphysical character, or simply pseudo-scientific. Years later—it must have been in 1928 or 1929—I called this first problem of mine the "*problem of demarcation.*" The criterion of falsifiability is a solution to this problem of demarcation, for it says that statements or systems of statements, in order to be ranked as scientific, must be capable of conflicting with possible, or conceivable, observations.

III

Today I know, of course, that this *criterion of demarcation*—the criterion of testability, or falsifiability, or refutability—is far from obvious; for even now its significance is seldom realized.

At that time, in 1920, it seemed to me almost trivial, although it solved for me an intellectual problem which had worried me deeply, and one which also had obvious practical consequences (for example, political ones). But I did not yet realize its full implications, or its philosophical significance. When I explained it to a fellow student of the Mathematics Department (now a distinguished mathematician in Great Britain), he suggested that I should publish it. At the time I thought this absurd for I was convinced that my problem, since it was so important for me, must have agitated many scientists and philosophers who would surely have reached my rather obvious solution. That this was not the case I learnt from Wittgenstein's work, and from its reception; and so I published my results thirteen years later in the form of a criticism of Wittgenstein's *criterion of meaningfulness.*

Wittgenstein, as you all know, tried to show in the *Tractatus* (see for example his propositions 6.53; 6.54; and 5) that all so-called philosophical or metaphysical propositions were actually non-propositions or pseudo-propositions: that they were senseless or meaningless. All genuine (or meaningful) propositions were truth functions of the elementary or atomic propositions which described "atomic facts," i.e.—facts which can in principle be ascertained by observation. In other words, meaningful propositions were fully reducible to elementary or atomic propositions which were simple statements describing possible states of affairs, and which could in principle be established or rejected by observation. If we call a statement an "observation statement" not only if it states an actual observation but also if it states anything that *may* be observed, we shall have to say (according to the *Tractatus,* 5 and 4.52) that every genuine proposition must be a truth-function of, and therefore deducible from, observation statements. All other apparent propositions will be meaningless pseudo-propositions; in fact they will be nothing but nonsensical gibberish.

This idea was used by Wittgenstein for a characterization of science, as opposed to philosophy. We read (for example in 4.11, where natural science is taken to stand in opposition to philosophy): "The totality of true propositions is the total natural science (or the totality of the natural sciences)." This means that the propositions which belong to science are those deducible from *true* observation statements; they are those propositions which can be *verified* by true observation statements. Could we know all true observation statements, we should also know all that may be asserted by natural science.

This amounts to a crude verifiability criterion of demarcation. To make it slightly less crude, it could be amended thus: "The statements which may possibly fall within the province of science are those which may possibly be verified by observation statements; and these statements, again, coincide with the class of *all* genuine or meaningful statements." For this approach, then, *verifiability, meaningfulness, and scientific character all coincide.*

I personally was never interested in the so-called problem of meaning; on the contrary, it appeared to me a verbal problem, a typical pseudo-problem. I was interested only in the problem of demarcation, i.e. in finding a criterion of the scientific character of theories. It was just this interest which made me see at once that Wittgenstein's verifiability criterion of meaning was intended to play the part of a criterion of demarcation as well; and which made me see that, as such, it was totally inadequate, even if all misgivings about the dubious concept of meaning were set aside. For Wittgenstein's criterion of demarcation—to use my own terminology in this context—is verifiability, or deducibility from observation statements. But this criterion is too narrow (*and* too wide): it excludes from science practically everything that is, in fact, characteristic of it (while failing in effect to exclude astrology). No scientific theory can ever be deduced from observation statements, or be described as a truth-function of observation statements.

All this I pointed out on various occasions to Wittgensteinians and members of the Vienna Circle. In 1931-2 I summarized my ideas in a largish book (read by several members of the Circle but never published; although part of it was incorporated in my *Logic of Scientific Discovery*); and in 1933 I published a letter to the Editor of *Erkenntnis* in which I tried to compress into two pages my ideas on the problems of demarcation and induction.[5] In this letter and elsewhere I described the problem of meaning as a pseudo-problem, in contrast to the problem of demarcation. But my contribution was classified by members of the Circle as a proposal to replace the verifiability criterion of *meaning* by a falsifiability criterion of *meaning*—which effectively made nonsense of my views.[6] My protests that I was trying to solve, not their pseudo-problem of meaning, but the problem of demarcation, were of no avail.

My attacks upon verification had some effect, however. They soon led to complete confusion in the camp of the verificationist philosophers of sense and nonsense. The original proposal of verifiability as the criterion of meaning was at least clear, simple, and forceful. The modifications and shifts which were now introduced were the very opposite.[7] This, I should say, is now seen even by the participants. But since I am usually quoted as one of them I wish to repeat that although I created this confusion I never participated in it. Neither falsifiability nor testability were proposed by me as criteria of meaning; and although I may plead guilty to having introduced both terms into the discussion, it was not I who introduced them into the theory of meaning.

Criticism of my alleged views was widespread and highly successful. I have yet to meet a criticism of my views.[8] Meanwhile, testability is being widely accepted as a criterion of demarcation.

IV

I have discussed the problem of demarcation in some detail because I believe that its solution is the key to most of the fundamental problems of the philosophy of science. I am going to give you later a list of some of these other problems, but only one of them—the *problem of induction*—can be discussed here at any length.

I had become interested in the problem of induction in 1923. Although this problem is very closely connected with the problem of demarcation, I did not fully appreciate the connection for about five years.

I approached the problem of induction through Hume. Hume, I felt, was perfectly right in pointing out that induction cannot be logically justified. He held that there can be no valid logical[9] arguments allowing us to establish "*that those instances, of which we have had no experience, resemble those, of which we have had experience.*" Consequently "*even after the observation of the frequent or constant conjunction of objects, we have no reason to draw any inference concerning any object beyond those of which we have had experience.*" For "shou'd it be said that we have experience" [10]—experience teaching us that objects constantly conjoined with certain other objects continue to be so conjoined—then, Hume says, "I wou'd renew my question, *why from this experience we form any conclusion beyond those past instances, of which we have had experience.*" In other words, an attempt to justify the practice of induction by an appeal to experience must lead to an *infinite regress.* As a result we can say that theories can never be inferred from observation statements, or rationally justified by them.

I found Hume's refutation of inductive inference clear and conclusive. But I felt completely dissatisfied with his psychological explanation of induction in terms of custom or habit.

It has often been noticed that this explanation of Hume's is philosophically not very satisfactory. It is, however, without doubt intended as a *psychological* rather than a philosophical theory; for it tries to give a causal explanation of a psychological fact—*the fact that we believe in laws,* in statements asserting regularities or constantly conjoined kinds of events—by asserting that this fact is due to (i.e. constantly conjoined with) custom or habit. But even this reformulation of Hume's theory is still unsatisfactory; for what I have just called a "psychological fact" may itself be described as a custom or habit—the custom or habit of believing in laws or regularities; and it is neither very surprising nor very enlightening to hear that such a custom or habit must be explained as due to, or conjoined with, a custom or habit (even though a different one). Only when we remember that the words "custom" and "habit" are used by Hume, as they are in ordinary language, not merely to *describe* regular behaviour, but rather to *theorize about its origin* (ascribed to frequent repetition), can we reformulate his psychological theory in a more satisfactory way. We can then say that, like other habits, *our habit of believing in laws is the product of frequent repetition*—of the repeated observation that things of a certain kind are constantly conjoined with things of another kind.

This genetico-psychological theory is, as indicated, incorporated in ordinary language, and it is therefore hardly as revolutionary as Hume thought. It is no doubt an extremely popular psychological theory—part of "common sense," one might say. But in spite of my love of both common sense and Hume, I felt convinced that this psychological theory was mistaken; and that it was in fact refutable on purely logical grounds.

Hume's psychology, which is the popular psychology, was mistaken, I felt, about at least three different things: (*a*) the typical result of repetition; (*b*) the genesis of habits; and especially (*c*) the character of those experiences or modes of behaviour which may be described as "believing in a law" or "expecting a law-like succession of events."

(**A**) The typical result of repetition—say, of repeating a difficult passage on the piano—is that movements which at first needed attention are in the end executed without attention. We might say that the process becomes radically abbreviated, and ceases to be conscious: it becomes "physiological." Such a process, far from creating a conscious expectation of law-like succession, or a belief in a law, may on the contrary begin with a conscious belief and destroy it by making it superfluous. In learning to ride a bicycle we may start with the belief that we can avoid falling if we steer in the direction in which we threaten to fall, and this belief may be useful for guiding our movements. After sufficient practice we may forget the rule; in any case, we do not need it any longer. On the other hand, even if it is true that repetition may create unconscious expectations, these become conscious only if something goes wrong (we may not have heard the clock tick, but we may hear that it has stopped).

(**B**) Habits or customs do not, as a rule, *originate* in repetition. Even the habit of walking, or of speaking, or of feeding at certain hours, *begins* before repetition can play any part whatever. We may say, if we like, that they deserve to be called "habits" or "customs" only after repetition has played its typical part; but we must not say that the practices in question originated as the result of many repetitions.

(**C**) Belief in a law is not quite the same thing as behaviour which betrays an expectation of a law-like succession of events; but these two are sufficiently closely connected to be treated together. They may, perhaps, in exceptional cases, result from a mere repetition of sense impressions (as in the case of the stopping clock). I was prepared to concede this, but I contended that normally, and in most cases of any interest, they cannot be so explained. As Hume admits, even a single striking observation may be sufficient to create a belief or an expectation—a fact which he tries to explain as due to an inductive habit, formed as the result of a vast number of long repetitive sequences which had been experienced at an earlier period of life.[11] But this, I contended, was merely his attempt to explain away unfavourable facts which threatened his theory; an unsuccessful attempt, since these unfavourable facts could be observed in very young animals and babies—as early, indeed, as we like. "A lighted cigarette was held near the noses of the young puppies," reports F. Bäge. "They sniffed at it once, turned tail, and nothing would induce them to come back to the source of the smell and to sniff again. A few days later, they reacted to the mere sight of a cigarette or even of a rolled piece of white paper, by bounding away, and sneezing."[12] If we try to explain cases like this by postulating a vast number of long repetitive sequences at a still earlier age we are not only romancing, but forgetting that in the clever puppies' short lives there must be room not only for repetition but also for a great deal of novelty, and consequently of non-repetition.

But it is not only that certain empirical facts do not support Hume; there are decisive arguments of a *purely logical* nature against his psychological theory.

The central idea of Hume's theory is that of *repetition, based upon similarity* (or "resemblance"). This idea is used in a very uncritical way. We are led to think of the water-drop that hollows the stone: of sequences of unquestionably like events slowly forcing themselves upon us, as does the tick of the clock. But we ought to realize that in a psychological theory such as Hume's, only repetition-for-us, based upon similarity-for-us, can be allowed to have any effect upon us. We must respond to situations as if they were equivalent; *take* them as similar; *interpret* them as repetitions. The clever puppies, we may assume, showed by their response, their way of acting or of reacting, that they recognized or interpreted the second situation as a repetition of the first: that they expected its main element, the objectionable smell, to be present. The situation was a repetition-for-them because they responded to it by *anticipating* its similarity to the previous one.

This apparently psychological criticism has a purely logical basis which may be summed up in the following simple argument. (It happens to be the one from which I originally started my criticism.) The kind of repetition envisaged by Hume can never be perfect; the cases he has in mind cannot be cases of perfect sameness; they can only be cases of similarity. Thus *they are repetitions only from a certain point of view*. (What has the effect upon me of a repetition may not have this effect upon a spider.) But this means that, for logical reasons, there must always be a point of view—such as a system of expectations, anticipations, assumptions, or interests—*before* there can be any repetition; which point of view, consequently, cannot be merely the result of repetition. (See now also appendix *x, (1), to my *L.Sc.D.*)

We must thus replace, for the purposes of a psychological theory of the origin of our beliefs, the naïve idea of events which *are* similar by the idea of events to which we react by *interpreting* them as being similar. But if this is so (and I can see no escape from it) then Hume's psychological theory of induction leads to an infinite regress, precisely analogous to that other infinite regress which was discovered by Hume himself, and used by him to explode the logical theory of induction. For what do we wish to explain? In the example of the puppies we wish to explain behaviour which may be described as *recognizing or interpreting* a situation as a repetition of another. Clearly, we cannot hope to explain this by an appeal to earlier repetitions, once we realize that the earlier repetitions must also have been repetitions-for-them, so that precisely the same problem arises again: that of *recognizing or interpreting* a situation as a repetition of another.

To put it more concisely, similarity-for-us is the product of a response involving interpretations (which may be inadequate) and anticipations or expectations (which may never be fulfilled). It is therefore impossible to explain anticipations, or expectations, as resulting from many repetitions, as suggested by Hume. For even the first repetition-for-us must be based upon similarity-for-us, and therefore upon expectations—precisely the kind of thing we wished to explain.

This shows that there is an infinite regress involved in Hume's psychological theory.

Hume, I felt, had never accepted the full force of his own logical analysis. Having refuted the logical idea of induction he was faced with the following problem: how do we actually obtain our knowledge, as a matter of psychological fact, if induction is a procedure which is logically invalid and rationally unjustifiable? There are two possible answers: (1) We obtain our knowledge by a non-inductive procedure. This answer would have allowed Hume to retain a form of rationalism. (2) We obtain our knowledge by repetition and induction, and therefore by a logically invalid and rationally unjustifiable procedure, so that all apparent knowledge is merely a kind of belief—belief based on habit. This answer would imply that even scientific knowledge is irrational, so that rationalism is absurd, and must be given up. (I shall not discuss here the age-old attempts, now again fashionable, to get out of the difficulty by asserting that though induction is of course logically invalid if we mean by "logic" the same as "deductive logic," it is not irrational by its own standards, as may be seen from the fact that every reasonable man applies it *as a matter of fact*: it was Hume's great achievement to break this uncritical identification of the question of fact—*quid facti?*—and the question of justification or validity—*quid juris?* . . .

It seems that Hume never seriously considered the first alternative. Having cast out the logical theory of induction by repetition he struck a bargain with common sense, meekly allowing the re-entry of induction by repetition, in the guise of a psychological theory. I proposed to turn the tables upon this theory of Hume's. Instead of explaining our propensity to expect regularities as the result of repetition, I proposed to explain repetition-for-us as the result of our propensity to expect regularities and to search for them.

Thus I was led by purely logical considerations to replace the psychological theory of induction by the following view. Without waiting, passively, for repetitions to impress or impose regularities upon us, we actively try to impose regularities upon the world. We try to discover similarities in it, and to interpret it in terms of laws invented by us. Without waiting for premises we jump to conclusions. These may have to be discarded later, should observation show that they are wrong.

This was a theory of trial and error—of *conjectures and refutations*. It made it possible to understand why our attempts to force interpretations upon the world were logically prior to the observation of similarities. Since there were logical reasons behind this procedure, I thought that it would apply in the field of science also; that scientific theories were not the digest of observations, but that they were inventions—conjectures boldly put forward for trial, to be eliminated if they clashed with observations; with observations which were rarely accidental but as a rule undertaken with the definite intention of testing a theory by obtaining, if possible, a decisive refutation.

V

The belief that science proceeds from observation to theory is still so widely and so firmly held that my denial of it is often met with incredulity. I have even been suspected of being insincere—of denying what nobody in his senses can doubt.

But in fact the belief that we can start with pure observations alone, without anything in the nature of a theory, is absurd; as may be illustrated by the story of the man who dedicated his life to natural science, wrote down everything he could observe, and bequeathed his priceless collection of observations to the Royal Society to be used as inductive evidence. This story should show us that though beetles may profitably be collected, observations may not.

Twenty-five years ago I tried to bring home the same point to a group of physics students in Vienna by beginning a lecture with the following instructions: "Take pencil and paper; carefully observe, and write down what you have ordered!" They asked, of course, *what* I wanted them to observe. Clearly the instruction, "Observe!" is absurd.[13] (It is not even idiomatic, unless the object of the transitive verb can be taken as understood.) Observation is always selective. It needs a chosen object, a definite task, an interest, a point of view, a problem. And its description presupposes a descriptive language, with property words; it presupposes similarity and classification, which in its turn presupposes interests, points of view, and problems. "A hungry animal," writes Katz,[14] "divides the environment into edible and inedible things. An animal in flight sees roads to escape and hiding places. . . . Generally speaking, objects change . . . according to the needs of the animal." We may add that objects can be classified, and can become similar or dissimilar, *only* in this way—by being related to needs and interests. This rule applies not only to animals but also to scientists. For the animal a point of view is provided by its needs, the task of the moment, and its expectations; for the scientist by his theoretical interests, the special problem under investigation, his conjectures and anticipations, and the theories which he accepts as a kind of background: his frame of reference, his "horizon of expectations."

The problem "Which comes first, the hypothesis (H) or the observation (O)," is soluble; as is the problem, "Which comes first, the hen (H) or the egg (O)." The reply to the latter is, "An earlier kind of egg"; to the former, "An earlier kind of hypothesis." It is quite true that any particular hypothesis we choose will have been preceded by observations—the observations, for example, which it is designed to explain. But these observations, in their turn, presupposed the adoption of a frame of reference: a frame of expectations: a frame of theories. If they were significant, if they created a need for explanation and thus gave rise to the invention of a hypothesis, it was because they could not be explained within the old theoretical framework, the old horizon of expectations. There is no danger here of an infinite regress. Going back to more and more primitive theories and myths we shall in the end find unconscious, *inborn* expectations.

The theory of inborn *ideas* is absurd, I think; but every organism has inborn *reactions* or *responses;* and among them, responses adapted to impending events. These responses we may describe as "expectations" without implying that these "expectations" are conscious. The newborn baby "expects," in this sense, to be fed (and, one could even argue, to be protected and loved). In view of the close relation between expectation and knowledge we may even speak in quite a reasonable sense of "inborn knowledge." This "knowledge" is not, however, *valid a priori;* an inborn expectation, no matter how strong and specific, may be mistaken. (The newborn child may be abandoned, and starve.)

Thus we are born with expectations; with "knowledge" which, although not *valid a priori,* is *psychologically or genetically a priori,* i.e. prior to all observational experience. One of the most important of these expectations is the expectation of finding a regularity. It is connected with an inborn propensity to look out for regularities, or with a *need* to *find* regularities, as we may see from the pleasure of the child who satisfies this need.

This "instinctive" expectation of finding regularities, which is psychologically *a priori,* corresponds very closely to the "law of causality" which Kant believed to be part of our mental outfit and to be *a priori* valid. One might thus be inclined to say that Kant failed to distinguish between psychologically *a priori* ways of thinking or responding and *a priori* valid beliefs. But I do not think that his mistake was quite as crude as that. For the expectation of finding regularities is not only psychologically *a priori,* but also logically *a priori:* it is logically prior to all observational experience, for it is prior to any recognition of similarities, as we have seen; and all observation involves the recognition of similarities (or dissimilarities). But in spite of being logically *a priori* in this sense the expectation is not valid *a priori.* For it may fail: we can easily construct an environment (it would be a lethal one) which, compared with our ordinary environment, is so chaotic that we completely fail to find regularities. (All natural laws could remain valid: environments of this kind have been used in the animal experiments mentioned in the next section.)

Thus Kant's reply to Hume came near to being right; for the distinction between an *a priori* valid expectation and one which is both genetically *and* logically prior to observation, but not *a priori* valid, is really somewhat subtle. But Kant proved too much. In trying to show how knowledge is possible, he proposed a theory which had the unavoidable consequence that our quest for knowledge must necessarily succeed, which is clearly mistaken. When Kant said, "Our intellect does not draw its laws from nature but imposes its laws upon nature," he was right. But in thinking that these laws are necessarily true, or that we necessarily succeed in imposing them upon nature, he was wrong.[15] Nature very often resists quite successfully, forcing us to discard our laws as refuted; but if we live we may try again.

To sum up this logical criticism of Hume's psychology of induction we may consider the idea of building an induction machine. Placed in a simplified "world" (for example, one of sequences of coloured counters) such a machine may through repetition "learn," or even "formulate," laws of succession which hold in its "world." If such a machine can be constructed (and I have no doubt that it can) then, it might be argued, my theory must be wrong; for if a machine is capable of performing inductions on the basis of repetition, there can be no logical reasons preventing us from doing the same.

The argument sounds convincing, but it is mistaken. In constructing an induction machine we, the architects of the machine, must decide *a priori* what constitutes its "world"; what things are to be taken as similar or equal; and what *kind* of "laws" we wish the machine to be able to "discover" in its "world." In other words we must build into the machine a framework determining what is relevant or interesting in its world: the machine will have its "inborn" selection principles. The problems of similarity will have been solved for it by its makers who thus have interpreted the "world" for the machine.

VI

Our propensity to look out for regularities, and to impose laws upon nature, leads to the psychological phenomenon of *dogmatic thinking* or, more generally, dogmatic behaviour: we expect regularities everywhere and attempt to find them even where there are none; events which do not yield to these attempts we are inclined to treat as a kind of "background noise"; and we stick to our expectations even when they are inadequate and we ought to accept defeat. This dogmatism is to some extent necessary. It is demanded by a situation which can only be dealt with by forcing our conjectures upon the world. Moreover, this dogmatism allows us to approach a good theory in stages, by way of approximations: if we accept defeat too easily, we may prevent ourselves from finding that we were very nearly right.

It is clear that this *dogmatic attitude,* which makes us stick to our first impressions, is indicative of a strong belief; while a *critical attitude,* which is ready to modify its tenets, which admits doubt and demands tests, is indicative of a weaker belief. Now according to Hume's theory, and to the popular theory, the strength of a belief should be a product of repetition; thus it should always grow with experience, and always be greater in less primitive persons. But dogmatic thinking, an uncontrolled wish to impose regularities, a manifest pleasure in rites and in repetition as such, are characteristic of primitives and children; and increasing experience and maturity sometimes create an attitude of caution and criticism rather than of dogmatism.

I may perhaps mention here a point of agreement with psycho-analysis. Psycho-analysts assert that neurotics and others interpret the world in accordance with a personal set pattern which is not easily given up, and which can often be traced back to early childhood. A pattern or scheme which was adopted very early in life is maintained throughout, and every new experience is interpreted in terms of it; verifying it, as it were, and contributing to its rigidity. This is a description of what I have called the dogmatic attitude, as distinct from the critical attitude, which shares with the dogmatic attitude the quick adoption of a schema of expectations—a myth, perhaps, or a conjecture or hypothesis—but which is ready to modify it, to correct it, and even to give it up. I am inclined to suggest that most neuroses may be due to a partially arrested development of the critical attitude; to an arrested rather than a natural dogmatism; to resistance to demands for the modification and adjustment of certain schematic interpretations and responses. This resistance in its turn may perhaps be explained, in some cases, as due to an injury or shock, resulting in fear and in an increased need for assurance or certainty analogous to the way in which an injury to a limb makes us afraid to move it, so that it becomes stiff. (It might even be argued that the case of the limb is not merely analogous to the dogmatic response, but an instance of it.) The explanation of any concrete case will have to take into account the weight of the difficulties involved in making the necessary adjustments—difficulties which may be considerable, especially in a complex and changing world: we know from experiments on animals that varying degrees of neurotic behaviour may be produced at will by correspondingly varying difficulties.

I found many other links between the psychology of knowledge and psychological fields which are often considered remote from it—for example the psychology of art and music; in fact, my ideas about induction originated in a conjecture about the evolution of Western polyphony. But you will be spared this story.

VII

My logical criticism of Hume's psychological theory, and the considerations connected with it (most of which I elaborated in 1926-7, in a thesis entitled "On Habit and Belief in Laws" [16]) may seem a little removed from the field of the philosophy of science. But the distinction between dogmatic and critical thinking, or the dogmatic and the critical attitude, brings us right back to our central problem. For the dogmatic attitude is clearly related to the tendency to *verify* our laws and schemata by seeking to apply them and to confirm them, even to the point of neglecting refutations, whereas the critical attitude is one of readiness to change them—to test them; to refute them; to *falsify* them, if possible. This suggests that we may identify the critical attitude with the scientific attitude, and the dogmatic attitude with the one which we have described as pseudo-scientific.

It further suggests that genetically speaking the pseudo-scientific attitude is more primitive than, and prior to, the scientific attitude: that it is a prescientific attitude. And this primitivity or priority also has its logical aspect. For the critical attitude is not so much opposed to the dogmatic attitude as super-imposed upon it: criticism must be directed against existing and influential beliefs in need of critical revision—in other words, dogmatic beliefs. A critical attitude needs for its raw material, as it were, theories or beliefs which are held more or less dogmatically.

Thus science must begin with myths, and with the criticism of myths; neither with the collection of observations, nor with the invention of experiments, but with the critical discussion of myths, and of magical techniques and practices. The scientific tradition is distinguished from the pre-scientific tradition in having two layers. Like the latter, it passes on its theories; but it also passes on a critical attitude towards them. The theories are passed on, not as dogmas, but rather with the challenge to discuss them and improve upon them. This tradition is Hellenic: it may be traced back to Thales, founder of the first *school* (I do not mean "of the first *philosophical* school," but simply "of the first school") which was not mainly concerned with the preservation of a dogma.[17]

The critical attitude, the tradition of free discussion of theories with the aim of discovering their weak spots so that they may be improved upon, is the attitude of reasonableness, of rationality. It makes far-reaching use of both verbal argument and observation—of observation in the interest of argument, however. The Greeks' discovery of the critical method gave rise at first to the mistaken hope that it would lead to the solution of all the great old problems; that it would establish certainty; that it would help to *prove* our theories, to *justify* them. But this hope was a residue of the dogmatic way of thinking; in fact nothing can be justified or proved (outside of mathematics and logic). The demand for rational proofs in science indicates a failure to keep distinct the broad realm of rationality and the narrow realm of rational certainty: it is an untenable, an unreasonable demand.

Nevertheless, the role of logical argument, of deductive logical reasoning, remains all-important for the critical approach; not because it allows us to prove our theories, or to infer them from observation statements, but because only by purely deductive reasoning is it possible for us to discover what our theories imply, and thus to criticize them effectively. Criticism, I said, is an attempt to find the weak spots in a theory, and these, as a rule, can be found only in the more remote logical consequences which can be derived from it. It is here that purely logical reasoning plays an important part in science.

Hume was right in stressing that our theories cannot be validly inferred from what we can know to be true—neither from observations nor from anything else. He concluded from this that our belief in them was irrational. If "belief" means here our inability to doubt our natural laws, and the constancy of natural regularities, then Hume is again right: this kind of dogmatic belief has, one might say, a physiological rather than a rational basis. If, however, the term "belief" is taken to cover our critical acceptance of scientific theories—a *tentative* acceptance combined with an eagerness to revise the theory if we succeed in designing a test which it cannot pass—then Hume was wrong. In such an acceptance of theories there is nothing irrational. There is not even anything irrational in relying for practical purposes upon well-tested theories, for no more rational course of action is open to us.

Assume that we have deliberately made it our task to live in this unknown world of ours; to adjust ourselves to it as well as we can; to take advantage of the opportunities we can find in it; and to explain it, *if* possible (we need not assume that it is), and as far as possible, with the help of laws and explanatory theories. *If we have made this our task, then there is no more rational procedure than the method of trial and error—of conjecture and refutation:* of boldly proposing theories; of trying our best to show that these are erroneous; and of accepting them tentatively if our critical efforts are unsuccessful.

From the point of view here developed all laws, all theories, remain essentially tentative, or conjectural, or hypothetical, even when we feel unable to doubt them any longer. Before a theory has been refuted we can never know in what way it may have to be modified. That the sun will always rise and set within twenty-four hours is still proverbial as a law "established by induction beyond reasonable doubt." It is odd that this example is still in use, though it may have served well enough in the days of Aristotle and Pytheas of Massalia—the great traveller who for centuries was called a liar because of his tales of Thule, the land of the frozen sea and the *midnight sun.*

The method of trial and error is not, of course, simply identical with the scientific or critical approach—with the method of conjecture and refutation. The method of trial and error is applied not only by Einstein but, in a more dogmatic fashion, by the amoeba also. The difference lies not so much in the trials as in a critical and constructive attitude towards errors; errors which the scientist consciously and cautiously tries to uncover in order to refute his theories with searching arguments, including appeals to the most severe experimental tests which his theories and his ingenuity permit him to design.

The critical attitude may be described as the conscious attempt to make our theories, our conjectures, suffer in our stead in the struggle for the survival of the fittest. It gives us a chance to survive the elimination of an inadequate hypothesis—when a more dogmatic attitude would eliminate it by eliminating us. (There is a touching story of an Indian community which disappeared because of its belief in the holiness of life, including that of tigers.) We thus obtain the fittest theory within our reach by the elimination of those which are less fit. (By "fitness" I do not mean merely "usefulness" but truth; see chapters 3 and 10 of the present work.) I do not think that this procedure is irrational or in need of any further rational justification.

VIII

Let us now turn from our logical criticism of the *psychology of experience* to our real problem—the problem of *the logic of science.* Although some of the things I have said may help us here, in so far as they may have eliminated certain psychological prejudices in favour of induction, my treatment of the *logical problem of induction* is completely independent of this criticism, and of all psychological considerations. Provided you do not dogmatically believe in the alleged psychological fact that we make inductions, you may now forget my whole story with the exception of two logical points: my logical remarks on testability or falsifiability as the criterion of demarcation; and Hume's logical criticism of induction.

From what I have said it is obvious that there was a close link between the two problems which interested me at that time: demarcation, and induction or scientific method. It was easy to see that the method of science is criticism, i.e. attempted falsifications. Yet it took me a few years to notice that the two problems—of demarcation and of induction—were in a sense one.

Why, I asked, do so many scientists believe in induction? I found they did so because they believed natural science to be characterized by the inductive method—by a method starting from, and relying upon, long sequences of observations and experiments. They believed that the difference between genuine science and metaphysical or pseudo-scientific speculation depended solely upon whether or not the inductive method was employed. They believed (to put it in my own terminology) that only the inductive method could provide a satisfactory *criterion of demarcation.*

I recently came across an interesting formulation of this belief in a remarkable philosophical book by a great physicist—Max Born's *Natural Philosophy of Cause and Chance*.[18] He writes: "Induction allows us to generalize a number of observations into a general rule: that night follows day and day follows night . . . But while everyday life has no definite criterion for the validity of an induction, . . . science has worked out a code, or rule of craft, for its application." Born nowhere reveals the contents of this inductive code (which, as his wording shows, contains a "definite criterion for the validity of an induction"); but he stresses that "there is no logical argument" for its acceptance: "it is a question of faith"; and he is therefore "willing to call induction a metaphysical principle." But why does he believe that such a code of valid inductive rules must exist? This becomes clear when he speaks of the "vast communities of people ignorant of, or rejecting, the rule of science, among them the members of anti-vaccination societies and believers in astrology. It is useless to argue with them; I cannot compel them to accept the same criteria of valid induction in which I believe: the code of scientific rules." This makes it quite clear that *"valid induction" was here meant to serve as a criterion of demarcation between science and pseudo-science.*

But it is obvious that this rule or craft of "valid induction" is not even metaphysical: it simply does not exist. No rule can ever guarantee that a generalization inferred from true observations, however often repeated, is true. (Born himself does not believe in the truth of Newtonian physics, in spite of its success, although he believes that it is based on induction.) And the success of science is not based upon rules of induction, but depends upon luck, ingenuity, and the purely deductive rules of critical argument.

I may summarize some of my conclusions as follows:

(1) Induction, i.e. inference based on many observations, is a myth. It is neither a psychological fact, nor a fact of ordinary life, nor one of scientific procedure.

(2) The actual procedure of science is to operate with conjectures: to jump to conclusions—often after one single observation (as noticed for example by Hume and Born).

(3) Repeated observations and experiments function in science as *tests* of our conjectures or hypotheses, i.e. as attempted refutations.

(4) The mistaken belief in induction is fortified by the need for a criterion of demarcation which, it is traditionally but wrongly believed, only the inductive method can provide.

(5) The conception of such an inductive method, like the criterion of verifiability, implies a faulty demarcation.

(6) None of this is altered in the least if we say that induction makes theories only probable rather than certain. (See especially chapter 10, the present work.)

IX

If, as I have suggested, the problem of induction is only an instance or facet of the problem of demarcation, then the solution to the problem of demarcation must provide us with a solution to the problem of induction. This is indeed the case, I believe, although it is perhaps not immediately obvious.

For a brief formulation of the problem of induction we can turn again to Born, who writes: ". . . no observation or experiment, however extended, can give more than a finite number of repetitions"; therefore, "the statement of a law—B depends on A—always transcends experience. Yet this kind of statement is made everywhere and all the time, and sometimes from scanty material." [19]

In other words, the logical problem of induction arises from (*a*) Hume's discovery (so well expressed by Born) that it is impossible to justify a law by observation or experiment, since it "transcends experience"; (*b*) the fact that science proposes and uses laws "everywhere and all the time." (Like Hume, Born is struck by the "scanty material," i.e. the few observed instances upon which the law may be based.) To this we have to add (*c*) *the principle of empiricism* which asserts that in science, only observation and experiment may decide upon the *acceptance or rejection* of scientific statements, including laws and theories.

These three principles, (*a*), (*b*), and (*c*), appear at first sight to clash; and this apparent clash constitutes the *logical problem of induction.*

Faced with this clash, Born gives us (*c*), the principle of empiricism (as Kant and many others, including Bertrand Russell, have done before him), in favour of what he calls a "metaphysical principle"; a metaphysical principle which he does not even attempt to formulate; which he vaguely describes as a "code or rule of craft"; and of which I have never seen any formulation which even looked promising and was not clearly untenable.

But in fact the principles (*a*) to (*c*) do not clash. We can see this the moment we realize that the acceptance by science of a law or of a theory is *tentative only;* which is to say that all laws and theories are conjectures, or tentative *hypotheses* (a position which I have sometimes called "hypotheticism"); and that we may reject a law or theory on the basis of new evidence, without necessarily discarding the old evidence which originally led us to accept it. [20]

The principle of empiricism (*c*) can be fully preserved, since the fate of a theory, its acceptance or rejection, is decided by observation and experiment—by the result of tests. So long as a theory stands up to the severest tests we can design, it is accepted; if it does not, it is rejected. But it is never inferred, in any sense, from the empirical evidence. There is neither a psychological nor a logical induction. *Only the falsity of the theory can be inferred from empirical evidence, and this inference is a purely deductive one.*

Hume showed that it is not possible to infer a theory from observation statements; but this does not affect the possibility of refuting a theory by observation statements. The full appreciation of this possibility makes the relation between theories and observations perfectly clear.

This solves the problem of the alleged clash between the principles (*a*), (*b*), and (*c*), and with it Hume's problem of induction.

X

Thus the problem of induction is solved. But nothing seems less wanted than a simple solution to an age-old philosophical problem. Wittgenstein and his school hold that genuine philosophical problems do not exist; [21] from which it clearly follows that they cannot be solved. Others among my contemporaries do believe that there are philosophical problems, and respect them; but they seem to respect them too much; they seem to believe that they are insoluble, if not taboo; and they are shocked and horrified by the claim that there is a simple, neat, and lucid, solution to any of them. If there is a solution it must be deep, they feel, or at least complicated.

However this may be, I am still waiting for a simple, neat and lucid criticism of the solution which I published first in 1933 in my letter to the Editor of *Erkenntnis*,[22] and later in *The Logic of Scientific Discovery*.

Of course, one can invent new problems of induction, different from the one I have formulated and solved. (Its formulation was half its solution.) But I have yet to see any reformulation of the problem whose solution cannot be easily obtained from my old solution. I am now going to discuss some of these re-formulations.

One question which may be asked is this: how do we really jump from an observation statement to a theory?

Although this question appears to be psychological rather than philosophical, one can say something positive about it without invoking psychology. One can say first that the jump is not from an observation statement, but from a problem-situation, and that the theory must allow us *to explain* the observations which created the problem (that is, *to deduce* them from the theory strengthened by other accepted theories and by other observation statements, the so-called initial conditions). This leaves, of course, an immense number of possible theories, good and bad; and it thus appears that our question has not been answered.

But this makes it fairly clear that when we asked our question we had more in mind than, "How do we jump from an observation statement to a theory?" The question we had in mind was, it now appears, "How do we jump from an observation statement to a *good* theory?" But to this the answer is: by jumping first to *any* theory and then testing it, to find whether it is good or not; i.e. by repeatedly applying the critical method, eliminating many bad theories, and inventing many new ones. Not everybody is able to do this; but there is no other way.

Other questions have sometimes been asked. The original problem of induction, it was said, is the problem of *justifying* induction, i.e. of justifying inductive inference. If you answer this problem by saying that what is called an "inductive inference" is always invalid and therefore clearly not justifiable, the following new problem must arise: how do you justify your method of trial and error? Reply: the method of trial and error is a *method of eliminating false theories* by observation statements; and the justification for this is the purely logical relationship of deducibility which allows us to assert the falsity of universal statements if we accept the truth of singular ones.

Another question sometimes asked is this: why is it reasonable to prefer non-falsified statements to falsified ones? To this question some involved answers have been produced, for example pragmatic answers. But from a pragmatic point of view the question does not arise, since false theories often serve well enough: most formulae used in engineering or navigation are known to be false, although they may be excellent approximations and easy to handle; and they are used with confidence by people who know them to be false.

The only correct answer is the straightforward one: because we search for truth (even though we can never be sure we have found it), and because the falsified theories are known or believed to be false, while the non-falsified theories may still be true. Besides, we do not prefer *every* non-falsified theory—only one which, in the light of criticism, appears to be better than its competitors: which solves our problems, which is well tested, and of which we think, or rather conjecture or hope (considering other provisionally accepted theories), that it will stand up to further tests.

It has also been said that the problem of induction is, "Why is it *reasonable* to believe that the future will be like the past?," and that a satisfactory answer to this question should make it plain that such a belief is, in fact, reasonable. My reply is that it is reasonable to believe that the future will be very different from the past in many vitally important respects. Admittedly it is perfectly reasonable to *act* on the assumption that it will, in many respects, be like the past, and that well-tested laws will continue to hold (since we can have no better assumption to act upon); but it is also reasonable to believe that such a course of action will lead us at times into severe trouble, since some of the laws upon which we now heavily rely may easily prove unreliable. (Remember the midnight sun!) One might even say that to judge from past experience, and from our general scientific knowledge, the future will *not* be like the past, in perhaps most of the ways which those have in mind who say that it will. Water will sometimes not quench thirst, and air will choke those who breathe it. An apparent way out is to say that the future will be like the past *in the sense that the laws of nature will not change,* but this is begging the question. We speak of a "law of nature" only if we think that we have before us a regularity which does not change; and if we find that it changes then we shall not continue to call it a "law of nature." Of course our search for natural laws indicates that we hope to find them, and that we believe that there are natural laws; but our belief in any particular natural law cannot have a safer basis than our unsuccessful critical attempts to refute it.

I think that those who put the problem of induction in terms of the *reasonableness* of our beliefs are perfectly right if they are dissatisfied with a Humean, or post-Humean, sceptical despair of reason. We must indeed reject the view that a belief in science is as irrational as a belief in primitive magical practices—that both are a matter of accepting a "total ideology," a convention or a tradition based on faith. But we must be cautious if we formulate our problem, with Hume, as one of the reasonableness of our *beliefs*. We should split this problem into three—our old problem of demarcation, or of how to *distinguish* between science and primitive magic; the problem of the rationality of the scientific or critical *procedure,* and of the role of observation within it; and lastly the problem of the rationality of our *acceptance* of theories for scientific and for practical purposes. To all these three problems solutions have been offered here.

One should also be careful not to confuse the problem of the reasonableness of the scientific procedure and the (tentative) acceptance of the results of this procedure—i.e. the scientific theories—with the problem of the rationality or otherwise *of the belief that this procedure will succeed.* In practice, in practical scientific research, this belief is no doubt unavoidable and reasonable, there being no better alternative. But the belief is certainly unjustifiable in a theoretical sense, as I have argued (in section V). Moreover, if we could show, on general logical grounds, that the scientific quest is likely to succeed, one could not understand why anything like success has been so rare in the long history of human endeavours to know more about our world.

Yet another way of putting the problem of induction is in terms of probability. Let *t* be the theory and *e* the evidence: we can ask for *P(t,e)*, that is to say, the probability of *t*, given *e*. The problem of induction, it is often believed, can then be put thus: construct a *calculus of probability* which allows us to work out for any theory *t* what its probability is, relative to any given empirical evidence *e;* and show that *P(t,e)* increases with the accumulation of supporting evidence, and reaches high values—at any rate values greater than ½.

In *The Logic of Scientific Discovery* I explained why I think that this approach to the problem is fundamentally mistaken.[23] To make this clear, I introduced there the distinction between *probability* and *degree of corroboration or confirmation*. (The term "confirmation" has lately been so much used and misused that I have decided to surrender it to the verificationists and to use for my own purposes "corroboration" only. The term "probability" is best used in some of the many senses which satisfy the well-known calculus of probability, axiomatized, for example, by Keynes, Jeffreys, and myself; but nothing of course depends on the choice of words, as long as we do not *assume,* uncritically, that degree of corroboration must also be a probability—that is to say, that it must satisfy the calculus of probability.)

I explained in my book why we are interested in theories with a *high degree of corroboration*. And I explained why it is a mistake to conclude from this that we are interested in *highly probable* theories. I pointed out that the probability of a statement (or set of statements) is always the greater the less the statement says: it is inverse to the content or the deductive power of the statement, and thus to its explanatory power. Accordingly every interesting and powerful statement must have a low probability; and *vice versa:* a statement with a high probability will be scientifically uninteresting, because it says little and has no explanatory power. Although we seek theories with a high degree of corroboration, *as scientists we do not seek highly probable theories but explanations; that is to say, powerful and improbable theories.*[24] The opposite view—that science aims at high probability—is a characteristic development of verificationism: if you find that you cannot verify a theory, or make it certain by induction, you may turn to probability as a kind of "*Ersatz*" for certainty, in the hope that induction may yield at least that much.

I have discussed the two problems of demarcation and induction at some length. Yet since I set out to give you in this lecture a kind of report on the work I have done in this field I shall have to add, in the form of an Appendix, a few words about some other problems on which I have been working, between 1934 and 1953. I was led to most of these problems by trying to think out the consequences of the solutions to the two problems of demarcation and induction. But time does not allow me to continue my narrative, and to tell you how my new problems arose out of my old ones. Since I cannot even start a discussion of these further problems now, I shall have to confine myself to giving you a bare list of them, with a few explanatory words here and there. But even a bare list may be useful, I think. It may serve to give an idea of the fertility of the approach. It may help to illustrate what our problems look like; and it may show how many there are, and so convince you that there is no need whatever to worry over the question whether philosophical problems exist, or what philosophy is really about. So this list contains, by implication, an apology for my unwillingness to break with the old tradition of trying to solve problems with the help of rational argument, and thus for my unwillingness to participate wholeheartedly in the developments, trends, and drifts, of contemporary philosophy.

NOTES

[1] This is a slight oversimplification, for about half of the Einstein effect may be derived from the classical theory, provided we assume a ballistic theory of light.

[2] See, for example, my *Open Society and Its Enemies,* ch. 15, section iii, and notes 13–14.

[3] "Clinical observations," like all other observations, are *interpretations in the light of theories* . . . ; and for this reason alone they are apt to seem to support those theories in the light of which they were interpreted. But real support can be obtained only from observations undertaken as tests (by "attempted refutations"); and for this purpose *criteria of refutation* have to be laid down beforehand: it must be agreed which observable situations, if actually observed, mean that the theory is refuted. But what kind of clinical responses would refute to the satisfaction of the analyst not merely a particular analytic diagnosis but psycho-analysis itself? And have such criteria ever been discussed or agreed upon by analysts? Is there not, on the contrary, a whole family of analytic concepts, such as "ambivalence" (I do not suggest that there is no such thing as ambivalence), which would make it difficult, if not impossible, to agree upon such criteria? Moreover, how much headway has been made in investigating the question of the extent to which the (conscious or unconscious) expectations and theories held by the analyst influence the "clinical responses" of the patient? (To say nothing about the conscious attempts to influence the patient by proposing interpretations to him, etc.) Years ago I introduced the term "*Oedipus effect*" to describe the influence of a theory or expectation or prediction *upon the event which it predicts* or describes: it will be remembered that the causal chain leading to Oedipus' parricide was started by the oracle's prediction of this event. This is a characteristic and recurrent theme of such myths, but one which seems to have failed to attract the interest of the analysts, perhaps not accidentally. (The problem of confirmatory dreams suggested by the analyst is discussed by Freud, for example in *Gesammelte Schriften,* III, 1925, where he says on p. 314: "If anybody asserts that most of the dreams which can be utilized in an analysis . . . owe their origin to [the analyst's] suggestion, then no objection can be made from the point of view of analytic theory. Yet there is nothing in this fact," he surprisingly adds, "which would detract from the reliability of our results.")

[4] The case of astrology, nowadays a typical pseudo-science, may illustrate this point. It was attacked by Aristotelians and other rationalists, down to Newton's day, for the wrong reason—for its now accepted assertion that the planets had an "influence" upon terrestrial ("sublunar") events. In fact Newton's theory of gravity, and especially the lunar theory of the tides, was historically speaking an offspring of astrological lore. Newton, it seems, was most reluctant to adopt a theory which came from the same stable as for example the theory that "influenza" epidemics are due to an astral "influence." And Galileo, no doubt for the same reason, actually rejected the lunar theory of the tides; and his misgivings about Kepler may easily be explained by his misgivings about astrology.

[5] My *Logic of Scientific Discovery* (1959, 1960, 1961), here usually referred to as *L.Sc.D.,* is the translation of *Logik der Forschung* (1934), with a number of additional notes and appendices, including (on pp. 312–14) the letter to the Editor of *Erkenntnis* mentioned here in the text which was first published in *Erkenntnis,* 3, 1933, pp. 426 f.

Concerning my never published book mentioned here in the text, see R. Carnap's paper "*Ueber Protokollstäze*" (On Protocol-Sentences), *Erkenntnis,* 3, 1932, pp. 215–28 where he gives an outline of my theory on pp. 223–8, and accepts it. He calls my theory "procedure B," and says (p. 224, top): "Starting from a point of view different from Neurath's" (who developed what Carnap calls on p. 223 "procedure A"), "Popper developed procedure B as part of his system." And after describing in detail my theory of tests, Carnap sums up his views as follows (p. 228): "After weighing the various arguments here discussed, it appears to me that the second language form with procedure B—that is in the form here described—is the most adequate among the forms of scientific language at present advocated . . . in the . . . theory of knowledge." This paper of Carnap's contained the first published report of my theory of critical testing. (See also my critical remarks in *L.Sc.D.,* note 1 to section 29, p. 104, where the date "1933" should read "1932"; and ch. 11, below, text to note 39.)

[6] Wittgenstein's example of a nonsensical pseudo-proposition is: "Socrates is identical." Obviously, "Socrates is not identical" must also be nonsense. Thus the negation of any nonsense will be nonsense, and that of a meaningful statement will be meaningful. *But the negation of a testable (or falsifiable) statement need not*

be testable, as was pointed out, first in my *L.Sc.D.,* (e.g. pp. 38 f.) and later by my critics. The confusion caused by taking testability as a criterion of *meaning* rather than of *demarcation* can easily be imagined.

[7] The most recent example of the way in which the history of this problem is misunderstood is A. R. White's "Note on Meaning and Verification," *Mind,* 63, 1954, pp. 66 ff. J. L. Evans's article, *Mind,* 62, 1953, pp. 1 ff., which Mr. White criticizes, is excellent in my opinion, and unusually perceptive. Understandably enough, neither of the authors can quite reconstruct the story. (Some hints may be found in my *Open Society,* notes 46, 51 and 52 to ch. 11; and a fuller analysis in ch. 11 of the present volume.)

[8] In *L.Sc.D.* I discussed, and replied to, some likely objections which afterwards were indeed raised without reference to my replies. One of them is the contention that the falsification of a natural law is just as impossible as its verification. The answer is that this objection mixes two entirely different levels of analysis (like the objection that mathematical demonstrations are impossible since checking, no matter how often repeated, can never make it quite certain that we have not overlooked a mistake). On the first level, there is a logical asymmetry: one singular statement—say about the perihelion of Mercury—can formally falsify Kepler's laws; but these cannot be formally verified by any number of singular statements. The attempt to minimize this asymmetry can only lead to confusion. On another level, we may hesitate to accept any statement, even the simplest observation statement; and we may point out that every statement involves *interpretation in the light of theories,* and that it is therefore uncertain. This does not affect the fundamental asymmetry, but it is important: most dissectors of the heart before Harvey observed the wrong things—those, which they expected to see. There can never be anything like a completely safe observation, free from the dangers of misinterpretation. (This is one of the reasons why the theory of induction does not work.) The "empirical basis" consists largely of a mixture of *theories* of lower degree of universality (of "reproducible effects"). But the fact remains that, relative to whatever basis the investigator may accept (at his peril), he can test his theory only by trying to refute it.

[9] Hume does not say "logical" but "demonstrative," a terminology which, I think, is a little misleading. The following two quotations are from the *Treatise of Human Nature,* Book I, Part III, sections vi and xii. (The italics are all Hume's.)

[10] This and the next quotation are from *loc. cit.,* section vi. See also Hume's *Enquiry Concerning Human Understanding,* section IV, Part II, and his *Abstract,* edited 1938 by J. M. Keynes and P. Sraffa, p. 15, and quoted in *L.Sc.D.,* new appendix *VII, text to note 6.

[11] *Treatise,* section xiii; section xv, rule 4.

[12] F. Bäge, "Zur Entwicklung, etc.," *Zeitschrift f. Hundeforschung,* 1933; cp. D. Katz, *Animals and Men,* ch. VI, footnote.

[13] See section 30 of *L.Sc.D.*

[14] Katz, *loc. cit.*

[15] Kant believed that Newton's dynamics was *a priori* valid. (See his *Metaphysical Foundations of Natural Science,* published between the first and the second editions of the *Critique of Pure Reason.*) But if, as he thought, we can explain the validity of Newton's theory by the fact that our intellect imposes its laws upon nature, it follows, I think, that our intellect *must succeed* in this; which makes it hard to understand why *a priori* knowledge such as Newton's should be so hard to come by. A somewhat fuller statement of this criticism can be found in ch. 2, especially section ix, and chs. 7 and 8 of the present work.

[16] A thesis submitted under the title "*Gewohnheit und Gesetzerlebnis*" to the Institute of Education of the City of Vienna in 1927. (Unpublished.)

[17] Further comments on these developments may be found in chs. 4 and 5 of the present work.

[18] Max Born, *Natural Philosophy of Cause and Chance,* Oxford, 1949, p. 7.

[19] *Natural Philosophy of Cause and Chance,* p. 6.

[20] I do not doubt that Born and many others would agree that theories are accepted only tentatively. But the widespread belief in induction shows that the far-reaching implications of this view are rarely seen.

[21] Wittgenstein still held this belief in 1946.

[22] See note 5, above.

[23] *L.Sc.D.* (see note 5 above), ch. x, especially sections 80 to 83, also section 34 ff. See also my note "A Set of Independent Axioms for Probability," *Mind,* N.S. 47, 1938, p. 275. (This note has since been reprinted, with corrections, in the new appendix *ii of *L.Sc.D.*)

[24] A definition, in terms of probabilities (see the next note), of $C(t,e)$, i.e. of the degree of corroboration (of a theory t relative to the evidence e) satisfying the demands indicated in my *L.Sc.D.*, sections 82 to 83, is the following:

$$C(t,e) = E(t,e) (1 + P(t)P(t,e)),$$

where $E(t,e) = (P(e,t) - P(e))/(P(e,t) + P(e))$ is a (non-additive) measure of the explanatory power of t with respect to e. Note that $C(t,e)$ is not a probability: it may have values between -1 (refutation of t by e) and $C(t,t) \leq +1$. Statements t which are lawlike and thus non-verifiable cannot even reach $C(t,e) = C(t,t)$ upon empirical evidence e. $C(t,t)$ is the *degree of corroborability* of t, and is equal to the *degree of testability* of t, or to the *content* of t. Because of the demands implied in point (6) at the end of section I above, I do not think, however, that it is possible to give a complete formalization of the idea of corroboration (or, as I previously used to say, of confirmation).

(Added 1955 to the first proofs of this paper:)

See also my note "Degree of Confirmation," *British Journal for the Philosophy of Science,* 5, 1954, pp. 143 ff. (See also 5, pp. 334.) I have since simplified this definition as follows (*B.J.P.S.,* 1955, 5, p. 359:)

$$C(t,e) = (P(e,t) - P(e))/(P(e,t) - P(et) + P(e))$$

For a further improvement, see *B.J.P.S.* 6, 1955, p. 56.

IMRE LAKATOS
HISTORY OF SCIENCE AND ITS RATIONAL RECONSTRUCTIONS

INTRODUCTION

"Philosophy of science without history of science is empty; history of science without philosophy of science is blind." Taking its cue from this paraphrase of Kant's famous dictum, this [reading] intends to explain *how* the historiography of science should learn from the philosophy of science and *vice versa.* It will be argued that (a) philosophy of science provides normative methodologies in terms of which the historian reconstructs "internal history" and thereby provides a rational explanation of the growth of objective knowledge; (b) two competing methodologies can be evaluated with the help of (normatively interpreted) history; (c) any rational reconstruction of history needs to be supplemented by an empirical (socio-psychological) "external history."

The vital demarcation between normative-internal and empirical-external is different for each methodology. Jointly, internal and external historiographical theories determine to a very large extent the choice of problems for the historian. But some of external history's most crucial problems can be formulated only in terms of one's methodology; thus internal history, so defined, is primary, and external history only secondary. Indeed, in view of the autonomy of internal (but not of external) history, external history is irrelevant for the understanding of science.[1]

RIVAL METHODOLOGIES OF SCIENCE; RATIONAL RECONSTRUCTIONS AS GUIDES TO HISTORY

There are several methodologies afloat in contemporary philosophy of science; but they are all very different from what used to be understood by "methodology" in the seventeenth and even eighteenth century. Then it was hoped that methodology would provide scientists with a mechanical book of rules for solving problems. This hope has now been given up: modern methodologies or "logics of discovery" consist merely of a set of (possibly not even tightly knit, let alone mechanical) rules for the *appraisal* of ready, articulated theories.[2] Often these rules, or systems of appraisal, also serve as "theories of scientific rationality," "demarcation criteria" or "definitions of science."[3] Outside the legislative domain of these normative rules there is, of course, an empirical psychology and sociology of discovery.

I shall now sketch four different "logics of discovery." Each will be characterised by rules governing the (scientific) *acceptance* and *rejection* of theories or research programmes.[4] These rules have a double function. First, they function as *a code of scientific honesty* whose violation is intolerable; secondly, as hard cores of *(normative) historiographical research programmes.* It is their second function on which I should like to concentrate.

A. INDUCTIVISM

One of the most influential methodologies of science has been inductivism. According to inductivism only those propositions can be accepted into the body of science which either describe hard facts or are infallible inductive generalisations from them.[5] When the inductivist *accepts* a scientific proposition, he accepts it as provenly true; he *rejects* it if it is not. His scientific rigour is strict: a proposition must be either proven from facts, or—deductively or inductively—derived from other propositions already proven.

Each methodology has its specific epistemological and logical problems. For example, inductivism has to establish with certainty the truth of "factual" ("basic") propositions and the validity of inductive inferences. Some philosophers get so preoccupied with their epistemological and logical problems that they never get to the point of becoming interested in actual history; if actual history does not fit their standards they may even have the temerity to propose that we start the whole business of science anew. Some others take some crude solution of these logical and epistemological problems for granted and devote themselves to a rational reconstruction of history without being aware of the logico-epistemological weakness (or, even, untenability) of their methodology.[6]

Inductivist criticism is primarily sceptical: it consists in showing that a proposition is unproven, that is, pseudoscientific, rather than in showing that it is false.[7] When the inductivist historian writes the *prehistory* of a scientific discipline, he may draw heavily upon such criticisms. And he often explains the early dark age—when people were engrossed by "unproven ideas"—with the help of some "external," explanation, like the socio-psychological theory of the retarding influence of the Catholic Church.

The inductivist historian recognizes only two sorts of *genuine scientific discoveries: hard factual propositions* and inductive *generalisations.* These and only these constitute the backbone of his *internal history.* When writing history, he looks out for them—finding them is quite a problem. Only when he finds them, can he start the construction of his beautiful pyramids. Revolutions consist in unmasking [irrational] errors which then are exiled from the history of science into the history of pseudo-science, into the history of mere beliefs: genuine scientific progress starts with the latest scientific revolution in any given field.

Each internal historiography has its characteristic victorious paradigms.[8] The main paradigms of inductivist historiography were Kepler's generalisations from Tycho Brahe's careful observations; Newton's discovery of his law of gravitation by, in turn, inductively generalising Kepler's "phenomena" of planetary motion; and Ampère's discovery of his law of electrodynamics by inductively generalising his observations of electric currents. Modern chemistry too is taken by some inductivists as having really started with Lavoisier's experiments and his "true explanations" of them.

But the inductivist historian cannot offer a *rational* "internal" explanation for *why* certain facts rather than others were selected in the first instance. For him this is a *non-rational, empirical, external* problem. Inductivism as an "internal" theory of rationality is compatible with many different supplementary empirical or external theories of problem-choice. It is, for instance, compatible with the vulgar-Marxist view that problem-choice is determined by social needs;[9] indeed, some vulgar-Marxists identify major phases in history of science with the major phases of economic development.[10] But choice of facts need not be determined by social factors; it may be determined by extra-scientific intellectual influences. And inductivism is equally compatible with the "external" theory that the choice of problems is primarily determined by inborn, or by arbitrarily chosen (or traditional) theoretical (or "metaphysical") frameworks.

There is a radical brand of inductivism which condemns all external influences, whether intellectual, psychological or sociological, as creating impermissible bias: radical inductivists allow only a [random] selection by the empty mind. Radical inductivism is, in turn, a special kind of *radical internalism.* According to the latter once one establishes the existence of some external influence on the acceptance of a scientific theory (or factual proposition) one must withdraw one's acceptance: proof of external influence means invalidation:[11] but since external influences always exist, radical internalism is utopian, and, as a theory of rationality, self-destructive.[12]

When the radical inductivist historian faces the problem of why some great scientists thought highly of metaphysics and, indeed, why they thought that their discoveries were great for reasons which, in the light of inductivism, look very odd, he will refer these problems of "false consciousness" to psychopathology, that is, to external history.

B. CONVENTIONALISM

Conventionalism allows for the building of any system of pigeon holes which organises facts into some coherent whole. The conventionalist decides to keep the centre of such a pigeon-hole system intact as long as possible: when difficulties arise through an invasion of anomalies, he only changes and complicates the peripheral arrangements. But the conventionalist does not regard any pigeonhole system as provenly true, but only as "true by convention" (or possibly even as neither true nor false). In *revolutionary* brands of conventionalism one does not have to adhere forever to a given pigeonhole system: one may abandon it if it becomes unbearably clumsy and if a simpler one is offered to replace it.[13] This version of conventionalism is epistemologically, and especially logically, much simpler than inductivism: it is in no need of valid inductive inferences. Genuine *progress* of science is cumulative and takes place on the ground level of "proven" facts;[14] the *changes* on the theoretical level are merely instrumental. Theoretical "progress" is only in convenience ("simplicity"), and not in truth-content.[15] One may, of course, introduce revolutionary conventionalism also at the level of "factual" propositions, in which case one would accept "factual" propositions by decision rather than by experimental "proofs." But then, if the conventionalist is to retain the idea that the growth of "factual" science has anything to do with objective, factual truth, he must devise some metaphysical principle which he then has to superimpose on his rules for the game of science.[16] If he does not, he cannot escape scepticism or, at least, some radical form of instrumentalism.

(It is important to clarify the *relation between conventionalism and instrumentalism.* Conventionalism rests on the recognition that false assumptions may have true consequences; therefore false theories may have great predictive power. Conventionalists had to face the problem of comparing rival false theories. Most of them conflated truth with its signs and found themselves holding some version of the pragmatic theory of truth. It was Popper's theory of truth-content, verisimilitude and corroboration which finally laid down the basis of a philosophically flawless version of conventionalism. On the other hand some conventionalists did not have sufficient logical education to realise that some propositions may be true whilst being unproven; and others false whilst having true consequences, and also some which are both false and approximately true. These people opted for "instrumentalism": they came to regard theories as neither true nor false but merely as "instruments" for prediction. Conventionalism, as here defined, is a philosophically sound position; instrumentalism is a degenerate version of it, based on a mere philosophical muddle caused by lack of elementary logical competence.)

Revolutionary conventionalism was born as the Bergsonians' philosophy of science: free will and creativity were the slogans. The code of scientific honour of the conventionalist is less rigorous than that of the inductivist: it puts no ban on unproven speculation, and allows a pigeonhole system to be built around *any* fancy idea. Moreover, conventionalism does not brand discarded systems as unscientific: the conventionalist sees much more of the actual history of science as rational ('internal') than does the inductivist.

For the conventionalist historian, major discoveries are primarily inventions of new and simpler pigeonhole systems. Therefore he constantly compares for simplicity: the complications of pigeonhole systems and their revolutionary replacement by simpler ones constitute the backbone of his internal history.

The paradigmatic case of a scientific revolution for the conventionalist has been the Copernican revolution.[17] Efforts have been made to show that Lavoisier's and Einstein's revolutions too were replacements of clumsy theories by simple ones.

Conventionalist historiography cannot offer a *rational* explanation of why certain facts were selected in the first instance or of why certain particular pigeonhole systems were tried rather than others at a stage when their relative merits were yet unclear. Thus conventionalism, like inductivism, is compatible with various supplementary empirical-"externalist" programmes.

Finally, the conventionalist historian, like his inductivist colleague, frequently encounters the problem of "false consciousness." According to conventionalism, for example, it is a "matter of fact" that great scientists arrive at their theories by flights of their imaginations. Why then do they often claim that they derived their theories from facts? The conventionalist's rational reconstruction often differs from the great scientists' own reconstruction—the conventionalist historian relegates these problems of false consciousness to the externalist.[18]

C. METHODOLOGICAL FALSIFICATIONISM

Contemporary falsificationism arose as a logico-epistemological criticism of inductivism and of Duhemian conventionalism. Inductivism was criticised on the grounds that its two basic assumptions, namely, that factual propositions can be "derived" from facts and that there can be valid inductive (content-increasing) inferences, are themselves unproven and even demonstrably false. Duhem was criticised on the grounds that comparison of intuitive simplicity can only be a matter for subjective taste and that it is so ambiguous that no hard-hitting criticism can be based on it. Popper, in his *Logik der Forschung,* proposed a new "falsificationist" methodology.[19] This methodology is another brand of revolutionary conventionalism: the main difference is that it allows factual, spatio-temporally singular "basic statements," rather than spatio-temporally universal theories, to be accepted by convention. In the code of honour of the falsificationist a theory is scientific only if it can be *made* to conflict with a basic statement; and a theory must be eliminated if it conflicts with an accepted basic statement. Popper also indicated a further condition that a theory must satisfy in order to qualify as scientific: it must predict facts which are *novel,* that is, unexpected in the light of previous knowledge. Thus it is against Popper's code of scientific honour to propose unfalsifiable theories or "ad hoc" hypotheses (which imply no *novel* empirical predictions)—just as it is against the [classical] inductivist code of scientific honour to propose unproven ones.

The great attraction of Popperian methodology lies in its clarity and force. Popper's deductive model of scientific criticism contains empirically falsifiable spatio-temporally universal propositions, initial conditions and their consequences. The weapon of criticism is the *modus tollens:* neither inductive logic nor intuitive simplicity complicate the picture.[20]

(Falsificationism, though logically impeccable, has epistemological difficulties of its own. In its "dogmatic" proto-version it assumes the provability of propositions from facts and thus the disprovability of theories—a false assumption.[21] In its Popperian "conventionalist" version it needs some (extra-methodological) "inductive principle" to lend epistemological weight to its decisions to accept "basic" statements, and in general to connect its rules of the scientific game with verisimilitude.[22])

The Popperian historian looks for great, "bold," falsifiable theories and for great negative crucial experiments. These form the skeleton of his rational reconstruction. The Popperians' favourite paradigms of great falsifiable theories are Newton's and Maxwell's theories, the radiation formulas of Rayleigh, Jeans and Wien, and the Einsteinian revolution; their favourite paradigms for crucial experiments are the Michelson-Morley experiment, Eddington's eclipse experiment, and the experiments of Lummer and Pringsheim. It was Agassi who tried to turn this naive falsificationism into a systematic historiographical research programme.[23] In particular he predicted (or "postdicted," if you wish) that behind each great experimental discovery lies a theory which the discovery contradicted; the importance of a factual discovery is to be measured by the importance of the theory refuted by it. Agassi seems to accept at face value the value judgments of the scientific community concerning the importance of factual discoveries like Galvani's, Oersted's, Priestley's, Roentgen's and Hertz's; but he denies the "myth" that they were chance discoveries (as the first four were said to be) or confirming instances (as Hertz first thought his discovery was).[24] Thus Agassi arrives at a bold prediction: all these five experiments were successful refutations—in some cases even *planned* refutations—of theories which he proposes to unearth, and, indeed, in most cases, claims to have unearthed.[25]

Popperian internal history, in turn, is readily supplemented by external theories of history. Thus Popper himself explained that [on the positive side] (1) the main *external* stimulus of scientific theories comes from unscientific "metaphysics," and even from myths (this was later beautifully illustrated mainly by Koyré); and that [on the negative side] (2) facts do *not* consti-tute such external stimulus—factual discoveries belong completely to internal history, emerg-ing as refutations of some scientific theory, so that facts are only noticed if they conflict with some previous expectation. Both theses are cornerstones of Popper's *psychology* of discov-ery.[26] Feyerabend developed another interesting *psychological* thesis of Popper, namely, that proliferation of rival theories may—*externally*—speed up *internal* Popperian falsification.[27]

But the external supplementary theories of falsificationism need not be restricted to purely intellectual influences. It has to be emphasized (*pace* Agassi) that falsificationism is no less com-patible with a vulgar-Marxist view of what makes science progress than is inductivism. The only difference is that while for the latter Marxism might be invoked to explain the discovery of *facts,* for the former it might be invoked to explain the invention of *scientific theories;* while the choice of facts (that is, for the falsificationist, the choice of "potential falsifiers") is primarily determined internally by the theories.

"False awareness"—"false" from the point of view of *his* rationality theory—creates a prob-lem for the falsificationist historian. For instance, why do some scientists believe that crucial experiments are positive and verifying rather than negative and falsifying? It was the falsifica-tionist Popper who, in order to solve these problems, elaborated better than anybody else be-fore him the cleavage between objective knowledge (in his "third world") and its distorted reflections in individual minds.[28] Thus he opened up the way for my demarcation between in-ternal and external history.

D. METHODOLOGY OF SCIENTIFIC RESEARCH PROGRAMMES

According to my methodology the greatest scientific achievements are research programmes which can be evaluated in terms of progressive and degenerating problemshifts; and scientific revolutions consist of one research programme superseding (overtaking in progress) an-other.[29] This methodology offers a new rational reconstruction of science. It is best presented by contrasting it with falsificationism and conventionalism, from both of which it borrows es-sential elements.

From conventionalism, this methodology borrows the licence rationally to accept by con-vention not only spatio-temporally singular "factual statements" but also spatio-temporally uni-versal theories: indeed, this becomes the most important clue to the continuity of scientific growth.[30] The basic unit of appraisal must be not an isolated theory or conjunction of theories but rather a "*research programme*," with a conventionally accepted (and thus by provisional decision "irrefutable") "*hard core*" and with a "*positive heuristic*" which defines problems, outlines the construction of a belt of auxiliary hypotheses, foresees anomalies and turns them victoriously into examples, all according to a preconceived plan. The scientist lists anomalies, but as long as his research programme sustains its momentum, he may freely put them aside. *It is primarily the positive heuristic of his programme, not the anomalies, which dictate the choice of his problems.*[31] Only when the driving force of the positive heuristic weakens, may more attention be given to anomalies. The methodology of research programmes can explain in this way *the high degree of autonomy of theoretical science;* the naive falsificationist's disconnected chains of conjectures and refutations cannot. What for Popper, Watkins and Agassi is *external,* influential metaphysics, here turns into the *internal* "hard core" of a programme.[32]

The methodology of research programmes presents a very different picture of the game of science from the picture of the methodological falsificationist. The best opening gambit is not a falsifiable (and therefore consistent) hypothesis, but a research programme. Mere "falsification" (in Popper's sense) must not imply rejection.[33] Mere "falsifications" (that is, anomalies) are to be recorded but need not be acted upon. Popper's great negative crucial experiments disappear; "crucial experiment" is an honorific title, which may, of course, be conferred on certain anomalies, but only *long after the event,* only when one programme has been defeated by another one. According to Popper a crucial experiment is described by an accepted basic statement which is inconsistent with a theory—according to the methodology of scientific research programmes no accepted basic statement *alone* entitles the scientist to reject a theory. Such a clash may present a problem (major or minor), but in no circumstance a "victory." Nature may shout *no,* but human ingenuity—contrary to Weyl and Popper[34]—may always be able to shout louder. With sufficient resourcefulness and some luck, any theory can be defended "progressively" for a long time, even if it is false. The Popperian pattern of "conjectures and refutations," that is the pattern of trial-by-hypothesis followed by error-shown-by-experiment, is to be abandoned: no experiment is crucial at the time—let alone before—it is performed (except, possibly, psychologically).

It should be pointed out, however, that the methodology of scientific research programmes has more teeth than Duhem's conventionalism: instead of leaving it to Duhem's unarticulated common sense[35] to judge when a "framework" is to be abandoned, I inject some hard Popperian elements into the appraisal of whether a programme progresses or degenerates or of whether one is overtaking another. That is, I give criteria of progress and stagnation within a programme and also rules for the "elimination" of whole research programmes. A research programme is said to be *progressing* as long as its theoretical growth anticipates its empirical growth, that is, as long as it keeps predicting novel facts with some success ("*progressive problemshift*"); it is *stagnating* if its theoretical growth lags behind its empirical growth, that is, as long as it gives only *post-hoc* explanations either of chance discoveries or of facts anticipated by, and discovered in, a rival programme ("*degenerating problemshift*").[36] If a research programme progressively explains more than a rival, it "supersedes" it, and the rival can be eliminated (or, if you wish, "shelved").[37]

(*Within* a research programme a theory can only be eliminated by a better theory, that is, by one which has excess empirical content over its predecessors, some of which is subsequently confirmed. And for this replacement of one theory by a better one, the first theory does not even have to be "falsified" in Popper's sense of the term. Thus progress is marked by instances verifying excess content rather than by falsifying instances;[38] empirical "falsification" and actual "rejection" become independent.[39] Before a theory has been modified we can never know in what way it had been "refuted," and some of the most interesting modifications are motivated by the "positive heuristic" of the research programme rather than by anomalies. This difference alone has important consequences and leads to a rational reconstruction of scientific change very different from that of Popper's.[40])

It is very difficult to decide, especially since one must not demand progress at each single step, when a research programme has degenerated hopelessly or when one of two rival programmes has achieved a decisive advantage over the other. In this methodology, as in Duhem's conventionalism, there can be no instant—let alone mechanical—rationality. *Neither the logician's proof of inconsistency nor the experimental scientist's verdict of anomaly can defeat a research programme in one blow.* One can be "wise" only after the event.[41]

In this code of scientific honour modesty plays a greater role than in other codes. One *must* realise that one's opponent, even if lagging badly behind, may still stage a comeback. No advantage for one side can ever be regarded as absolutely conclusive. There is never anything inevitable about the triumph of a programme. Also, there is never anything inevitable about its defeat. Thus pigheadedness, like modesty, has more "rational" scope. *The scores of the rival sides, however, must be recorded*[42] *and publicly displayed at all times.*

(We should here at least refer to the main epistemological problem of the methodology of scientific research programmes. As it stands, like Popper's methodological falsificationism, it represents a very radical version of conventionalism. One needs to posit some extra-methodological inductive principle to relate—even if tenuously—the scientific gambit of pragmatic acceptances and rejections to verisimilitude.[43] Only such an "inductive principle" can turn science from a mere game into an epistemologically rational exercise; from a set of light-hearted sceptical gambits pursued for intellectual fun into a—more serious—fallibilist venture of approximately the Truth about the Universe.[44])

The methodology of scientific research programmes constitutes, like any other methodology, a historiographical research programme. The historian who accepts this methodology as a guide will look in history for rival research programmes, for progressive and degenerating problem shifts. Where the Duhemian historian sees a revolution merely in simplicity (like that of Copernicus), he will look for a large scale progressive programme overtaking a degenerating one. Where the falsificationist sees a crucial negative experiment, he will "predict" that there was none, that behind any alleged crucial experiment, behind any alleged single battle between theory and experiment, there is a hidden war of attrition between two research programmes. The outcome of the war is only later linked in the falsificationist reconstruction with some alleged single "crucial experiment."

The methodology of research programmes—like any other theory of scientific rationality—must be supplemented by empirical-external history. No rationality theory will ever solve problems like why Mendelian genetics disappeared in Soviet Russia in the 1950's, or why certain schools of research into genetic racial differences or into the economics of foreign aid came into disrepute in the Anglo-Saxon countries in the 1960's. Moreover, to explain different speeds of development of different research programmes we may need to invoke external history. Rational reconstruction of science (in the sense in which I use the term) cannot be comprehensive since human beings are not *completely* rational animals; and even when they act rationally they may have a false theory of their own rational actions.[45]

But the methodology of research programmes draws a demarcation between internal and external history which is markedly different from that drawn by other rationality theories. For instance, what for the falsificationist looks like the (regrettably frequent) phenomenon of irrational adherence to a "refuted" or to an inconsistent theory and which he therefore relegates to *external* history, may well be explained in terms of my methodology *internally* as a rational defence of a promising research programme. Or, the successful *pre*dictions of novel facts which constitute serious evidence for a research programme and therefore vital parts of internal history, are irrelevant both for the inductivist and for the falsificationist.[46] For the inductivist and the falsificationist it does not really matter whether the discovery of a fact preceded or followed a theory: only their logical relation is decisive. The "irrational" impact of the historical coincidence that a theory happened to have *anticipated* a factual discovery, has no internal significance. Such anticipations constitute "not proof but [mere] propaganda."[47] Or again, take Planck's discontent with his own 1900 radiation formula, which he regarded as "arbitrary." For the falsificationist the formula was a bold, falsifiable hypothesis and Planck's dislike of it a non-rational mood, explicable only in terms of psychology. However, in my view, Planck's discontent can be explained internally: it was a rational condemnation of an "*ad hoc$_3$*" theory.[48] To mention yet another example: for falsificationism irrefutable "metaphysics" is an external intellectual influence, in my approach it is a vital part of the rational reconstruction of science.

Most historians have hitherto tended to regard the solution of some problems as being the monopoly of externalists. One of these is the problem of the high frequency of *simultaneous discoveries.* For this problem vulgar-Marxists have an easy solution: a discovery is made by many people at the same time, once a social need for it arises.[49] Now what constitutes a "discovery," and especially a major discovery, depends on one's methodology. For the inductivist, the most important discoveries are factual, and, indeed, such discoveries are frequently made simultaneously. For the falsificationist a *major* discovery consists in the discovery of a theory rather than of a fact. Once a theory is discovered (or rather invented), it becomes public property; and nothing is more obvious than that several people will test it simultaneously and make, simultaneously, (minor) factual discoveries. Also, a published theory is a challenge to devise higher-level, independently testable explanations. For example, given Kepler's ellipses and Galileo's rudimentary dynamics, simultaneous "discovery" of an inverse square law is not so very surprising: a problem-situation being public, simultaneous solutions can be explained on *purely internal* grounds.[50] The discovery of a new problem however may not be so readily explicable. If one thinks of the history of science as one of rival research programmes, then most simultaneous discoveries, theoretical or factual, are explained by the fact that research programmes being public property, many people work on them in different corners of the world, possibly not knowing of each other. However, really *novel, major, revolutionary* developments are rarely invented simultaneously. Some alleged simultaneous discoveries of novel programmes are seen as having been simultaneous discoveries only with false hindsight: in fact they are *different* discoveries, merged only later into a single one.[51]

A favourite hunting ground of externalists has been the related problem of why so much importance is attached to—and energy spent on—*priority disputes.* This can be explained only *externally* by the inductivist, naive falsificationist, or the conventionalist; but in the light of the methodology of research programmes some priority disputes are vital *internal* problems, since in this methodology *it becomes all-important for rational appraisal which programme was first in anticipating a novel fact and which fitted in the by now old fact only later.* Some priority disputes can be explained by rational interest and not simply by vanity and greed for fame. It then becomes important that Tychonian theory, for instance, succeeded in explaining—only *post hoc*—the observed phases of, and the distance to, Venus which were originally precisely anticipated by Copernicans;[52] or that Cartesians managed to explain everything that the Newtonians *predicted*—but only *post hoc.* Newtonian optical theory explained *post hoc* many phenomena which were anticipated and first observed by Huyghensians.[53]

All these examples show how the methodology of scientific research programmes turns many problems which had been *external* problems for other historiographies into internal ones. But occasionally the borderline is moved in the opposite direction. For instance there may have been an experiment which was accepted *instantly*—in the absence of a better theory—as a negative crucial experiment. For the falsificationist such acceptance is part of internal history; for me it is not rational and has to be explained in terms of external history.

Note: The methodology of research programmes was criticised by Feyerabend and by Kuhn. According to Kuhn: "[Lakatos] must specify criteria which can be used *at the time* to distinguish a degenerative from a progressive research programme; and so on. Otherwise, *he has told us nothing at all.*"[54] Actually, I *do* specify such criteria. But Kuhn probably meant that "[my] standards have practical force only if they are combined with a *time limit* (what looks like a degenerating problemshift may be the beginning of a much longer period of advance)."[55] Since I specify no such time limit, Feyerabend concludes that my standards are no more than "*verbal ornaments.*"[56] A related point was made by Musgrave in a letter containing some major constructive criticisms of an earlier draft, in which he demanded that I specify, for instance, at what point dogmatic adherence to a programme ought to be explained "externally" rather than "internally."

Let me try to explain why such objections are beside the point. One may rationally stick to a degenerating programme until it is overtaken by a rival *and even after.* What one must *not* do is to deny its poor public record. Both Feyerabend and Kuhn conflate *methodological* appraisal of a programme with firm *heuristic* advice about what to do.[57] It is perfectly rational to play a risky game: what is irrational is to deceive oneself about the risk.

This does not mean as much licence as might appear for those who stick to a degenerating programme. For they can do this mostly only in private. Editors of scientific journals should refuse to publish their papers which will, in general, contain either solemn reassertions of their position or absorption of counterevidence (or even of rival programmes) by *ad hoc,* linguistic adjustments. Research foundations, too, should refuse money.[58]

These observations also answer Musgrave's objection by separating rational and irrational (or honest and dishonest) adherence to a degenerating programme. They also throw further light on the demarcation between internal and external history. They show that internal history is self-sufficient for the presentation of the history of disembodied science, including degenerating problemshifts. External history explains why some people have false beliefs about scientific progress, and how their scientific activity may be influenced by such beliefs.

E. INTERNAL AND EXTERNAL HISTORY

Four theories of the rationality of scientific progress—or logics of scientific discovery—have been briefly discussed. It was shown how each of them provides a theoretical framework for the rational reconstruction of the history of science.

Thus the internal history of *inductivists* consists of alleged discoveries of hard facts and of so-called inductive generalisations. The internal history of *conventionalists* consists of factual discoveries and of the erection of pigeonhole systems and their replacement by allegedly simpler ones.[59] The internal history of *falsificationists* dramatises bold conjectures, improvements which are said to be *always* content-increasing and, above all, triumphant "negative crucial experiments." The *methodology of research programmes,* finally, emphasizes long-extended theoretical and empirical rivalry of major research programmes, progressive and degenerating problemshifts, and the slowly emerging victory of one programme over the other.

Each rational reconstruction produces some characteristic pattern of rational growth of scientific knowledge. But all of these *normative* reconstructions may have to be supplemented by *empirical* external theories to explain the residual non-rational factors. The history of science is always richer than its rational reconstruction. *But rational reconstruction or internal history is primary, external history only secondary, since the most important problems of external history are defined by internal history.* External history either provides non-rational explanation of the speed, locality, selectiveness etc. of historic events *as interpreted* in terms of internal history; or, when history differs from its rational reconstruction, it provides an empirical explanation of why it differs. But the *rational* aspect of scientific growth is fully accounted for by one's logic of scientific discovery.

Whatever problem the historian of science wishes to solve, he has first to reconstruct the relevant section of the growth of objective scientific knowledge, that is, the relevant section of "internal history." As it has been shown, what constitutes for him internal history, depends on his philosophy, whether he is aware of this fact or not. Most theories of the growth of knowledge are theories of the growth of disembodied knowledge: whether an experiment is crucial or not, whether a hypothesis is highly probable in the light of the available evidence or not, whether a problemshift is progressive or not, is not dependent in the slightest on the scientists' beliefs, personalities or authority. These subjective factors are of no interest for any internal history. For instance, the "internal historian" records the Proutian programme with its hard core (that atomic weights of pure chemical elements are whole numbers) and its positive heuristic (to overthrow, and replace, the contemporary false observational theories applied in measuring atomic weights). This programme was later carried through.[60] The internal historian will waste little time on Prout's *belief* that if the "experimental techniques" *of his time* were "carefully" applied, and the experimental findings properly interpreted, the anomalies would *immediately* be seen as mere illusions. The internal historian will regard this historical fact as a fact in the second world which is only a caricature of its counterpart in the third world.[61] *Why* such caricatures come about is none of his business; he might—in a footnote—pass on to the externalist the problem of why certain scientists had "false beliefs" about what they were doing.[62]

Thus in constructing internal history the historian will be highly selective: he will omit everything that is irrational in the light of his rationality theory. But this normative selection still does not add up to a fully fledged rational reconstruction. For instance, Prout never articulated the "Proutian programme": the Proutian programme is not Prout's programme. *It is not only the ("internal") success or the ("internal") defeat of a programme which can only be judged with hindsight: it is frequently also its content.* Internal history is not just a *selection* of methodologically interpreted facts: it may be, on occasion, their *radically improved version.* One may illustrate this using the Bohrian programme. Bohr, in 1913, may not have even thought of the possibility of electron spin. He had more than enough on his hands without the spin. Nevertheless, the historian, describing with hindsight the Bohrian programme, should include electron spin in it, since electron spin fits naturally in the original outline of the programme. Bohr might have referred to it in 1913. Why Bohr did not do so, is an interesting problem which deserves to be indicated in a footnote.[63] (Such problems might then be solved either internally by pointing to rational reasons in the growth of objective, impersonal knowledge; or externally by pointing to psychological causes in the development of Bohr's personal beliefs.)

One way to indicate discrepancies between history and its rational reconstruction is to relate the internal history *in the text,* and indicate *in the footnotes* how actual history "misbehaved" in the light of its rational reconstruction.[64]

Many historians will abhor the idea of *any* rational reconstruction. They will quote Lord Bolingbroke: "History is philosophy teaching by example." They will say that before philosophising "we need a lot more examples."[65] But such an inductivist theory of historiography is utopian.[66] *History without some theoretical "bias" is impossible.*[67] Some historians look for the discovery of hard facts, inductive generalisations, others for bold theories and crucial negative experiments, yet others for great simplifications, or for progressive and degenerating problemshifts; all of them have *some* theoretical "bias." This bias, of course, may be obscured by an eclectic variation of theories or by theoretical confusion: but neither eclecticism nor confusion amounts to an atheoretical outlook. What a historian regards as an external problem is often an excellent guide to his implicit methodology: some will ask why a "hard fact" or a "bold theory" was discovered exactly when and where it actually was discovered; others will ask why a "degenerating problemshift" could have wide popular acclaim over an incredibly long period or why a "progressive problemshift" was left "unreasonably" unacknowledged.[68] Long texts have been devoted to the problem of whether, and if so, why, the emergence of science was a purely European affair; but such an investigation is bound to remain a piece of confused rambling until one clearly defines "science" according to some normative philosophy of science. One of the most interesting problems of external history is to specify the psychological, and indeed, social conditions which are necessary (but, of course, never sufficient) to make scientific progress possible; but in the very formulation of this "external" problem *some* methodological theory, *some* definition of science is bound to enter. History of *science* is a history of events which are selected and interpreted in a normative way.[69] This being so, the hitherto neglected problem of appraising rival logics of scientific discovery and, hence, rival reconstructions of history, acquires paramount importance. . . .

NOTES

* Earlier versions of this paper were read and criticized by Colin Howson, Alan Musgrave, John Watkins, Elie Zahar, and especially John Worrall.

The present paper further develops some of the theses proposed in my "Falsification and the Methodology of Scientific Research Programmes" (1970). I have tried, at the cost of some repetition, to make it self-contained.

[1] "Internal history" is usually defined as intellectual history; "external history" as social history (cf. e.g. Kuhn [1968]). My unorthodox, new demarcation between "internal" and "external" history constitutes a considerable problemshift and may sound dogmatic. But my definitions form the hard core of a historiographical research programme; their evaluation is part and parcel of the evaluation of the fertility of the whole programme.

[2] This is an all-important shift in the problem of normative philosophy of science. The term "normative" no longer means rules for arriving at solutions, but merely directions for the appraisal of solutions already there. Thus *methodology* is separated from *heuristics,* rather as value judgments are from ought statements. (I owe this analogy to John Watkins.)

[3] This profusion of synonyms has proved to be rather confusing.

[4] The epistemological significance of scientific "acceptance" and "rejection" is, as we shall see, far from being the same in the four methodologies to be discussed.

[5] "*Neo*-inductivism" demands only (provably) highly probable generalisations. In what follows I shall only discuss classical inductivism; but the watered down neo-inductivist variant can be similarly dealt with.

[6] Cf. p. 107.

[7] For a detailed discussion of inductivist (and, in general, justificationist) criticism cf. my "Popkin on Skepticism" (1966).

[8] I am now using the term "paradigm" in its pre-Kuhnian sense.

[9] This compatibility was pointed out by Agassi on pp. 23–27 of his *Towards an Historiography of Science* (1963). But he did not point out the analogous compatibility within his own falsificationist historiography; cf. above, pp. 98–9.

[10] Cf. e.g. Bernal (1965), p. 377.

[11] Some logical positivists belonged to this set: one recalls Hempel's horror at Popper's casual praise of certain external metaphysical influences upon science (Hempel, 1937).

[12] When German obscurantists scoff at "positivism," they frequently mean radical internalism, and in particular, radical inductivism.

[13] For what I here call *revolutionary conventionalism*, see my "Falsification and the Methodology" (1970), pp. 105–6 and 187–9.

[14] I mainly discuss here only one version of revolutionary conventionalism, the one which Agassi, in his "Sensationalism" (1966), called "unsophisticated": the one which assumes that factual propositions—unlike pigeonhole systems—can be "proven." (Duhem, for instance, draws no clear distinction between facts and factual propositions.)

[15] It is important to note that most conventionalists are reluctant to give up inductive generalisations. They distinguish between the "*floor of facts*," the "*floor of laws*" (i.e. inductive generalisations from "facts") and the "*floor of theories*" (or of pigeonhole systems) which classify, conveniently, both facts and inductive laws. (Whewell, the conservative conventionalist and Duhem, the revolutionary conventionalist, differ less than most people imagine.)

[16] One may call such metaphysical principles "inductive principles." For an "inductive principle" which—roughly speaking—makes Popper's "degree of corroboration" (a conventionalist appraisal) the measure of Popper's verisimilitude (truth-content minus falsity-content) see my "Changes in the Problems of Inductive Logic" (1968a), pp. 390–408 and my "Popper on Demarcation and Induction" (1971a), §2. (Another widely spread "inductive principle" may be formulated like this: "What the group of trained—or up-to-date, or suitably purged—scientists decide to *accept* as 'true', is true.")

[17] Most historical accounts of the Copernican revolution are written from the conventionalist point of view. Few claimed that Copernicus' theory was an "inductive generalisation" from some "factual discovery"; or that it was proposed as a bold theory to replace the Ptolemaic theory which had been "refuted" by some celebrated "crucial" experiment.

For a further discussion of the historiography of the Copernican revolution, cf. my "A Note on the Historiography of the Copernican Revolution" (1971b).

[18] For example, for non-inductivist historians Newton's "*Hypotheses non fingo*" represents a major problem. Duhem, who unlike most historians did not over-indulge in Newton-worship, dismissed Newton's inductivist methodology as logical nonsense; but Koyré, whose many strong points did not include logic, devoted long chapters to the "hidden depths" of Newton's muddle.

[19] In this paper I use this term to stand exclusively for one version of falsificationism, namely for "naive methodological falsificationism," as defined in my "Falsification and the Methodology" (1970), pp. 93–116.

[20] Since in his methodology the *concept* of intuitive simplicity has no place, Popper was able to use the term "simplicity" for "degree of falsifiability." But there is more to simplicity than this: cf. my "Falsification and the Methodology" (1970), pp. 131ff.

[21] For a discussion cf. my "Falsification and the Methodology" (1970), especially pp. 99–100.

[22] For further discussion cf. my "Falsification and the Methodology" (1970), pp. 108–09.

[23] Agassi (1963).

[24] An experimental discovery is *a chance discovery in the objective sense* if it is neither a confirming nor a refuting instance of some theory in the objective body of knowledge of the time; it is *a chance discovery in the subjective sense* if it is made (or recognised) by the discoverer neither as a confirming nor as a refuting instance of some theory he personally had entertained at the time.

[25] Agassi (1963), pp. 64–74.

[26] Within the Popperian circle, it was Agassi and Watkins who particularly emphasized the importance of unfalsifiable or barely testable *"empirical"* theories in providing *external* stimulus to later properly *scientific* developments. (Cf. Agassi, 1964 and Watkins, 1958.) This idea, of course, is already there in Popper's *Logik der Forschung* (1935) and "Philosophy and Physics" (1960). Cf. my "Falsification and Methodology" (1970), p. 184; but the new formulation of the difference between their approach and mine which I am going to give in this paper will, I hope, be much clearer.

[27] Popper occasionally—and Feyerabend systematically—stressed the catalytic (*external*) role of alternative theories in devising so-called "crucial experiments." But alternatives are not merely catalysts, which can be later removed in the rational reconstruction, they are *necessary* parts of the falsifying process. Cf. Popper (1940) and Feyerabend (1965); but cf. also Lakatos (1970), especially p. 121, footnote 4.

[28] Cf. Popper (1968a) and (1968b).

[29] The terms "progressive" and "degenerating problemshifts," "research programmes," "superseding" will be crudely defined in what follows—for more elaborate definitions see Lakatos (1968b) and especially (1970).

[30] Popper does not permit this: "There is a vast difference between my views and conventionalism. I hold that what characterises the empirical method is just this: our conventions determine the acceptance of the *singular,* not of the *universal* statements" (Popper, 1935, Section 30).

[31] The falsificationist hotly denies this: "Learning from experience is learning from a refuting instance. The refuting instance then becomes a problematic instance." (Agassi, 1964, p. 201). In his "Popper on Learning from Experience" (1969), Agassi attributed to Popper the statement that "we learn from experience by refutations" (p. 169), and adds that according to Popper one can learn *only* from refutation but not from corroboration (p. 167). Feyerabend, even in his "A Note on Two 'Problems' of Induction" (1969), says that *"negative instances suffice in science."* But these remarks indicate a very one-sided theory of learning from experience. (Cf. my "Falsification and the Methodology" (1970), p. 121, footnote 1, and p. 123.)

[32] Duhem, as a staunch positivist within philosophy of science, would, no doubt, exclude most "metaphysics" as unscientific and would not allow it to have any influence on science proper.

[33] Cf. Lakatos (1968a), pp. 383–6, (1968b), pp. 162–7, and (1970), pp. 116ff. and pp. 155ff.

[34] Cf. Popper (1935), Section 85.

[35] Cf. Duhem (1906), Part II, Chapter VI, §10.

[36] In fact, I define a research programme as degenerating even if it anticipates novel facts but does so in a patched-up development rather than by a coherent, pre-planned positive heuristic. I distinguish three types of *ad hoc* auxiliary hypotheses: those which have no excess empirical content over their predecessor ("*ad hoc$_1$*"), those which do have such excess content but none of it is corroborated ("*ad hoc$_2$*") and finally those which are not *ad hoc* in these two senses but do not form an integral part of the positive heuristic ("*ad hoc$_3$*"). Examples for an *ad hoc$_1$* hypothesis are provided by the linguistic prevarications of pseudosciences, or by the conventionalist stratagems discussed in my "Proofs and Refutations" (1963–4), like "monsterbarring," "exception-barring," "monsteradjustment," etc. A famous example of an *ad hoc$_2$* hypothesis is provided by the Lorentz-Fitzgerald contraction hypothesis; an example of an *ad hoc$_3$* hypothesis is Planck's first correction of the Lummer-Pringsheim formula. Some of the cancerous growth in contemporary social "sciences" consists of a cobweb of such *ad hoc$_3$* hypotheses, as shown by Meehl and Lykken. (For references, cf. my "Falsification and the Methodology" (1970), p. 175, footnotes 2 and 3.)

[37] The rivalry of two research programmes is, of course, a protracted process during which it is rational to work in either (*or, if one can, in both*). The latter pattern becomes important, for instance, when one of the rival programmes is vague and its opponents wish to develop it in a sharper form in order to show up its weak-

ness. Newton elaborated Cartesian vortex theory in order to show that it is inconsistent with Kepler's laws. (Simultaneous work on rival programmes, of course, undermines Kuhn's thesis of the psychological incommensurability of rival paradigms.)

The progress of one programme is a vital factor in the degeneration of its rival. If programme P_1 constantly produces "novel facts" these, by definition, will be anomalies for the rival programme P_2. If P_2 accounts for these novel facts only in an *ad hoc* way, it is degenerating by definition. Thus the more P_1 progresses, the more difficult it is for P_2 to progress.

[38] Cf. especially my "Falsification and the Methodology" (1970), pp. 120–1.

[39] Cf. especially my "Changes in the Problem of Inductive Logic" (1968a), p. 385 and "Falsification and the Methodology" (1970), p. 121.

[40] For instance, a rival theory, which acts as an *external* catalyst for the Popperian falsification of a theory, here becomes an *internal* factor. In Popper's (and Feyerabend's) reconstruction such a theory, after the falsification of the theory under test, can be removed from the rational reconstruction; in my reconstruction it has to stay within the internal history lest the falsification be undone. (Cf. note 27.)

Another important consequence is the difference between Popper's discussion of the Duhem-Quine argument and mine; cf. on the one hand Popper (1935), last paragraph of Section 18 and Section 19, footnote 1; Popper (1957), pp. 131–3; Popper (1963a), p. 112, footnote 26, pp. 238–9 and p. 243; and on the other hand, my "Falsification and the Methodology" (1970), pp. 184–9.

[41] For the falsificationist this is a repulsive idea; cf. e.g. Agassi (1963), pp. 48ff.

[42] Feyerabend seems now to deny that even this is a possibility; cf. his "Consolations for the Specialist" (1970a) and especially "Against Method" (1970b) and *Against Method* (1971).

[43] I use "verisimilitude" here in Popper's technical sense, as the difference between the truth content and falsity content of a theory. Cf. his *Conjectures and Refutations* (1963a), Chapter 10.

[44] For a more general discussion of this problem, cf. my "Falsification and the Methodology" (1970), pp. 108–09.

[45] Also cf. my "Falsification and the Methodology" (1970), pp. 94, 96, 98, 106.

[46] The reader should remember that in this paper I discuss only naive falsificationism; cf. note 19.

[47] This is Kuhn's comment on Galileo's successful *prediction* of the phases of Venus (Kuhn, 1957, p. 224). Like Mill and Keynes before him, Kuhn cannot understand why the historic order of theory and evidence should count, and he cannot see the importance of the fact that Copernicans *predicted* the phases of Venus, while Tychonians only explained them by *post hoc* adjustments. Indeed, since he does not see the importance of the fact, he does not even care to mention it.

[48] Cf. note 36.

[49] For a statement of this position and an interesting critical discussion cf. Polanyi (1951), pp. 4ff and pp. 78ff.

[50] Popper (1963b) and Musgrave (1969).

[51] This was illustrated convincingly by Elkana for the case of the so-called simultaneous discovery of the conservation of energy; cf. his "The Conservation of Energy" (1971).

[52] Also cf. note 47.

[53] For the Mertonian brand of functionalism—as Alan Musgrave pointed out to me—priority disputes constitute a *prima facie* disfunction and therefore an anomaly for which Merton has been labouring to give a general socio-psychological explanation. (Cf. e.g. Merton 1957, 1963 and 1969.) According to Merton "scientific *knowledge* is not the richer or the poorer for having credit given where credit is due: it is the social *institution* of science and individual men of science that would suffer from repeated failures to allocate credit justly" (Merton, 1957, p. 648). But Merton overdoes his point: in important cases (like in some of Galileo's priority fights) there was more at stake than institutional interests: the problem was whether the Copernican research programme was progressive or not. (Of course, not all priority disputes have scientific relevance. For instance, the priority dispute between Adams and Leverrier about who was first to discover Neptune had no such relevance: whoever discovered it, the discovery strengthened the same (Newtonian) programme. In such cases Merton's external explanation may well be true.)

54 Kuhn (1970), p. 239; my italics.

55 Feyerabend (1970a), p. 215.

56 *Ibid.*

57 Cf. note 2.

58 I do, of course, *not* claim that such decisions are necessarily uncontroversial. In such decisions one has to use also one's *common sense*. Common sense (that is, judgment in *particular* cases which is not made according to mechanical rules but only follows general principles which leave some *Spielraum*) plays a role in all brands of non-mechanical methodologies. The Duhemian conventionalist needs common sense to decide when a theoretical framework has become sufficiently cumbersome to be replaced by a "simpler" one. The Popperian falsificationist needs common sense to decide when a basic statement is to be "accepted," or to which premise the *modus tollens* is to be directed. (Cf. my "Falsification and the Methodology" (1970), pp. 106ff.) But neither Duhem, nor Popper gives a blank cheque to "common sense." They give very definite guidance. The Duhemian judge directs the jury of common sense to agree on comparative simplicity; the Popperian judge directs the jury to look out primarily for, and agree upon, accepted basic statements which clash with accepted theories. My judge directs the jury to agree on appraisals of progressive and degenerating research programmes. But, for example, there may be conflicting views about whether an accepted basic statement expresses a *novel* fact or not. Cf. my "Falsification and the Methodology" (1970), p. 156.

   Although it is important to reach agreement on such verdicts, there must also be the possibility of appeal. In such appeals inarticulated common sense is questioned, articulated and criticised. (The criticism may even turn from a criticism of law interpretation into a criticism of the law itself.)

59 Most conventionalists have also an intermediate inductive layer of "laws" between facts and theories; cf. note 15.

60 The proposition "the Proutian programme was carried through" looks like a "factual" proposition. But there are no "factual" propositions: the phrase only came into ordinary language from dogmatic empiricism. *Scientific "factual" propositions* are theory-laden: the theories involved are "observational theories." *Historiographical "factual" propositions* are also theory-laden: the theories involved are methodological theories. In the decision about the truth-value of the "factual" proposition, "the Proutian programme was carried through," two methodological theories are involved. First, the theory that the units of scientific appraisal are research programmes; secondly, some *specific* theory of how to judge whether a programme was "in fact" carried through. For all these considerations a Popperian internal historian will not need to take any interest whatsoever in the *persons* involved, or in their beliefs about their own activities.

61 The "first world" is that of matter, the "second" the world of feelings, beliefs, consciousness, the "third" the world of objective knowledge, articulated in propositions. This is an age-old and vitally important trichotomy; its leading contemporary proponent is Popper. Cf. Popper (1968a), (1968b) and Musgrave (1969) and (1971).

62 Of course what, in this context, constitutes "false belief" (or "false consciousness"), depends on the rationality theory of the critic: But no rationality theory can ever succeed in leading to "true consciousness."

63 If the publication of Bohr's programme had been delayed by a few years, further speculation might even have led to the spin problem without the previous observation of the anomalous Zeeman effect. Indeed, Compton raised the problem in the context of the Bohrian programme in his "The Size and Shape of the Electron" (1919).

64 I first applied this expositional device in my "Proofs and Refutations" (1963–4); I used it again in giving a detailed account of the Proutian and the Bohrian programmes; cf. my "Falsification and the Methodology" (1970), pp. 138, 140, 146. This practice was criticised at the 1969 Minneapolis conference by some historians. McMullin, for instance, claimed that this presentation may illuminate a *methodology,* but certainly not real *history:* the text tells the reader what ought to have happened and the footnotes what in fact happened (cf. McMullin, 1970). Kuhn's criticism of my exposition ran essentially on the same lines: he thought that it was a specifically *philosophical* exposition: "a *historian* would not include *in his narrative* a factual report which he knows to be false. If he had done so, he would be so sensitive to the offence that he could not conceivably compose a footnote calling attention to it." (Cf. Kuhn, 1970, p. 256.)

[65] Cf. L. P. Williams (1970).

[66] Perhaps I should emphasize the difference between on the one hand, *inductivist historiography of science,* according to which *science* proceeds through discovery of hard facts (in nature) and (possibly) inductive generalisations, and, on the other hand, the *inductivist theory of historiography of science* according to which *historiography of science* proceeds through discovery of hard facts (in history of science) and (possibly) inductive generalisations. "Bold conjectures," "crucial negative experiments," and even "progressive and degenerating research programmes" may be regarded as "hard historical facts" by some inductivist historiographers. One of the weaknesses of Agassi (1963) is that he omitted to emphasize this distinction between scientific and historiographical inductivism.

[67] Cf. Popper (1957), Section 31.

[68] This thesis implies that the work of those "externalists" (mostly trendy "sociologists of science") who claim to do social history of some scientific discipline without having mastered the discipline itself, and its internal history, is worthless. Also cf. Musgrave (1971).

[69] Unfortunately there is only one single word in most languages to denote history$_1$ (the set of historical events) and history$_2$ (a set of historical propositions). Any history$_2$ is a theory and value-laden reconstruction of history$_1$.

REFERENCES

Agassi, J. (1963), *Towards an Historiography of Science.*

Agassi, J. (1964), "Scientific Problems and their Roots in Metaphysics," in *The Critical Approach to Science and Philosophy* (ed. by M. Bunge), pp. 189–211.

Agassi, J. (1966), "Sensationalism," *Mind* 75, 1–24.

Agassi, J. (1969), "Popper on Learning from Experience," in *Studies in the Philosophy of Science* (ed. by N. Rescher), pp. 162–71.

Bernal, J. D. (1965), *Science in History,* 3rd Edition.

Compton, A. H. (1919), "The Size and Shape of the Electron," *Physical Review* 14, 20–43.

Duhem, P. (1905), *La théorie physique, son objet et sa structure* (English transl. of 2nd (1914) edition: *The Aim and Structure of Physical Theory,* 1954).

Elkana, Y. (1971), "The Conservation of Energy: a Case of Simultaneous Discovery?" *Archives Internationales d'Histoire des Sciences* 24, 31–60.

Feyerabend, P. K. (1965), "Reply to Criticism," in *Boston Studies in the Philosophy of Science* 2 (ed. by R. S. Cohen and M. Wartofsky), pp. 223–61.

Feyerabend, P. K. (1969), "A Note on Two 'Problems' of Induction," *British Journal for the Philosophy of Science* 19, 251–3.

Feyerabend, P. K. (1970a), "Consolations for the Specialist," in *Criticism and the Growth of Knowledge* (ed. by I. Lakatos and A. Musgrave), pp. 197–230.

Feyerabend, P. K. (1970b), "Against Method," in *Minnesota Studies for the Philosophy of Science* 4.

Hempel, C. G. (1937), Review of Popper (1934), *Deutsche Literaturzeitung,* pp. 309–14.

Kuhn, T. S. (1957), *The Copernican Revolution.*

Kuhn, T. S. (1968), "Science: The History of Science," in *International Encyclopedia of the Social Sciences* (ed. by D. L. Sills), Vol. 14, pp. 74–83.

Kuhn, T. S. (1970), "Reflections on my Critics," in *Criticism and the Growth of Knowledge* (ed. by I. Lakatos and A. Musgrave), pp. 237–78.

Lakatos, I. (1963–4), "Proofs and Refutations," *The British Journal for the Philosophy of Science* 14, 1–25, 120–39, 221–43, 296–342.

Lakatos, I. (1966), "Popkin on Skepticism," in *Logic, Physics and History* (ed. by W. Yourgrau and A. D. Breck), 1970, pp. 220–3.

Lakatos, I. (1968a), "Changes in the Problem of Inductive Logic," in *The Problem of Inductive Logic* (ed. by I. Lakatos), pp. 315–417.

Lakatos, I. (1968b), "Criticism and the Methodology of Scientific Research Programmes," *Proceedings of the Aristotelian Society* 69, 149–86.

Lakatos, I. (1970), "Falsification and the Methodology of Scientific Research Programmes," in *Criticism and the Growth of Knowledge* (ed. by I. Lakatos and A. Musgrave).

Lakatos, I. (1971a), "Popper on Demarcation and Induction" in *The Philosophy of Sir Karl Popper* (ed. by P. A. Schilpp), forthcoming. (Available in German in *Neue Aspekte der Wissenschaftstheorie* ed. by H. Lenk.)

Lakatos, I. (1971b), "A Note on the Historiography of the Copernican Revolution," forthcoming.

Lakatos, I. and Musgrave, A. (1970), *Criticism and the Growth of Knowledge.*

McMullin, E. (1970), "The History and Philosophy of Science: a Taxonomy," *Minnesota Studies in the Philosophy of Science* 5, 12–67.

Merton, R. (1957), "Priorities in Scientific Discovery," *American Sociological Review* 22, 635–59.

Merton, R. (1963), "Resistance to the Systematic Study of Multiple Discoveries in Science," *European Journal of Sociology* 4, 237–82.

Merton R. (1969), "Behaviour Patterns of Scientists," *American Scholar* 38, 197–225.

Musgrave, A. (1969), *Impersonal Knowledge: A Criticism of Subjectivism,* Ph.D. thesis, University of London.

Musgrave, A. (1971), "The Objectivism of Popper's Epistemology," in *The Philosophy of Sir Karl Popper* (ed. by P. A. Schilpp), forthcoming.

Polanyi, M. (1951), *The Logic of Liberty.*

Popper, K. R. (1935), *Logik der Forschung.*

Popper, K. R. (1940), "What is Dialectic?," *Mind* 49, 403–26; reprinted in Popper (1963), pp. 312–35.

Popper, K. R. (1957), *The Poverty of Historicism.*

Popper, K. R. (1959), *The Logic of Scientific Discovery.*

Popper, K. R. (1960), "Philosophy and Physics," *Atti del XII Congresso Internazionale di Filosofia* 2, 363–74.

Popper, K. R. (1963a), *Conjectures and Refutations.*

Popper, K. R. (1963b), "Science: Problems, Aims, Responsibilities," *Federation Proceedings* 22, 961–72.

Popper, K. R. (1968a), "Epistemology Without a Knowing Subject," in *Proceedings of the Third International Congress for Logic, Methodology and Philosophy of Science* (ed. by B. Rootselaar and J. Staal), Amsterdam, pp. 333–73.

Popper, K. R. (1968b), "On the Theory of the Objective Mind," in *Proceedings of the XIV International Congress of Philosophy,* Vol. 1, pp. 25–33.

Watkins, J. W. N. (1958), "Influential and Confirmable Metaphysics," *Mind* 67, 344–65.

Williams, L. P. (1970), "Normal Science and its Dangers," in *Criticism and the Growth of Knowledge* (ed. by I. Lakatos and A. Musgrave), pp. 49–50.

N O R W O O D   R U S S E L L   H A N S O N
OBSERVATION

Were the eye not attuned to the Sun,
The Sun could never be seen by it.

Goethe[1]

A

Consider two microbiologists. They look at a prepared slide; when asked what they see, they may give different answers. One sees in the cell before him a cluster of foreign matter: it is an artefact, a coagulum resulting from inadequate staining techniques. This clot has no more to do with the cell, *in vivo,* than the scars left on it by the archaeologist's spade have to do with the original shape of some Grecian urn. The other biologist identifies the clot as a cell organ, a "Golgi body." As for techniques, he argues: "The standard way of detecting a cell organ is by fixing and staining. Why single out this one technique as producing artefacts, while others disclose genuine organs?"

The controversy continues.[2] It involves the whole theory of microscopical technique; nor is it an obviously experimental issue. Yet it affects what scientists say they see. Perhaps there is a sense in which two such observers do not see the same thing, do not begin from the same data, though their eyesight is normal and they are visually aware of the same object.

Imagine these two observing a Protozoon—*Amoeba.* One sees a one-celled animal, the other a non-celled animal. The first sees *Amoeba* in all its analogies with different types of single cells: liver cells, nerve cells, epithelium cells. These have a wall, nucleus, cytoplasm, etc. Within this class *Amoeba* is distinguished only by its independence. The other, however, sees *Amoeba*'s homology not with single cells, but with whole animals. Like all animals *Amoeba* ingests its food, digests and assimilates it. It excretes, reproduces and is mobile—more like a complete animal than an individual tissue cell.

This is not an experimental issue, yet it can affect experiment. What either man regards as significant questions or relevant data can be determined by whether he stresses the first or the last term in 'unicellular animal.'[3]

Some philosophers have a formula ready for such situations: "Of course they see the same thing. They make the same observation since they begin from the same visual data. But they interpret what they see differently. They construe the evidence in different ways."[4] The task is then to show how these data are moulded by different theories or interpretations or intellectual constructions.

Considerable philosophers have wrestled with this task. But in fact the formula they start from is too simple to allow a grasp of the nature of observation within physics. Perhaps the scientists cited above do not begin their inquiries from the same data, do not make the same observations, do not even see the same thing? Here many concepts run together. We must proceed carefully, for wherever it makes sense to say that two scientists looking at *x* do not see the same thing, there must always be a prior sense in which they do see the same thing. The issue is, then, "Which of these senses is most illuminating for the understanding of observational physics?"

These biological examples are too complex. Let us consider Johannes Kepler: imagine him on a hill watching the dawn. With him is Tycho Brahe. Kepler regarded the sun as fixed: it was the earth that moved. But Tycho followed Ptolemy and Aristotle in this much at least: the earth was fixed and all other celestial bodies moved around it. *Do Kepler and Tycho see the same thing in the east at dawn?*

We might think this an experimental or observational question, unlike the questions "Are there Golgi bodies?" and "Are Protozoa one-celled or non-celled?" Not so in the sixteenth and seventeenth centuries. Thus Galileo said to the Ptolemaist ". . . neither Aristotle nor you can prove that the earth is *de facto* the centre of the universe. . . ."[5] "Do Kepler and Tycho see the same thing in the east at dawn?" is perhaps not a *de facto* question either, but rather the beginning of an examination of the concepts of seeing and observation.

The resultant discussion might run:

"Yes, they do."

"No, they don't."

"Yes, they do!"

"No, they don't!" . . .

That this is possible suggests that there may be reasons for both contentions.[6] Let us consider some points in support of the affirmative answer.

The physical processes involved when Kepler and Tycho watch the dawn are worth noting. Identical photos are emitted from the sun; these traverse solar space, and our atmosphere. The two astronomers have normal vision; hence these photons pass through the cornea, aqueous humour, iris, lens and vitreous body of their eyes in the same way. Finally their retinas are affected. Similar electro-chemical changes occur in their selenium cells. The same configuration is etched on Kepler's retina as on Tycho's. So they see the same thing.

Locke sometimes spoke of seeing in this way: a man sees the sun if his is a normally-formed retinal picture of the sun. Dr. Sir W. Russell Brain speaks of our retinal sensations as indicators and signals. Everything taking place behind the retina is, as he says, "an intellectual operation based largely on non-visual experience. . . ."[7] What we *see* are the changes in the *tunica retina*. Dr. Ida Mann regards the macula of the eye as itself "seeing details in bright light," and the rods as "seeing approaching motor-cars." Dr. Agnes Arber speaks of the eye as itself seeing.[8] Often, talk of seeing can direct attention to the retina. Normal people are distinguished from those for whom no retinal pictures can form: we may say of the former that they can see whilst the latter cannot see. Reporting when a certain red dot can be seen may supply the occulist with direct information about the condition of one's retina.[9]

This need not be pursued, however. These writers speak carelessly: seeing the sun is not seeing retinal pictures of the sun. The retinal images which Kepler and Tycho have are four in number, inverted and quite tiny.[10] Astronomers cannot be referring to these when they say they see the sun. If they are hypnotized, drugged, drunk or distracted they may not see the sun, even though their retinas register its image in exactly the same way as usual.

Seeing is an experience. A retinal reaction is only a physical state—a photochemical excitation. Physiologists have not always appreciated the differences between experiences and physical states.[11] People, not their eyes, see. Cameras, and eye-balls, are blind. Attempts to locate within the organs of sight (or within the neurological reticulum behind the eyes) some nameable called "seeing" may be dismissed. That Kepler and Tycho do, or do not, see the same thing cannot be supported by reference to the physical states of their retinas, optic nerves or visual cortices: there is more to seeing than meets the eyeball.

Naturally, Tycho and Kepler see the same physical object. They are both visually aware of the sun. If they are put into a dark room and asked to report when they see something—anything at all—they may both report the same object at the same time. Suppose that the only object to be seen is a certain lead cylinder. Both men see the same thing: namely this object—whatever it is. It is just here, however, that the difficulty arises, for while Tycho sees a mere pipe, Kepler will see a telescope, the instrument about which Galileo has written to him.

Unless both are visually aware of the same object there can be nothing of philosophical interest in the question whether or not they see the same thing. Unless they both see the sun in this prior sense our question cannot even strike a spark.

Nonetheless, both Tycho and Kepler have a common visual experience of some sort. This experience perhaps constitutes their seeing the same thing. Indeed, this may be a seeing logically more basic than anything expressed in the pronouncement "I see the sun" (where each means something different by "sun"). If what they meant by the word "sun" were the only clue, then Tycho and Kepler could not be seeing the same thing, even though they were gazing at the same object.

If, however, we ask, not "Do they see the same thing?" but rather "What is it that they both see?", an unambiguous answer may be forthcoming. Tycho and Kepler are both aware of a brilliant yellow-white disc in a blue expanse over a green one. Such a "sense-datum" picture is single and uninverted. To be unaware of it is not to have it. Either it dominates one's visual attention completely or it does not exist.

If Tycho and Kepler are aware of anything visual, it must be of some pattern of colours. What else could it be? We do not touch or hear with our eyes, we only take in light.[12] This private pattern is the same for both observers. Surely if asked to sketch the contents of their visual fields they would both draw a kind of semicircle on a horizon-line.[13] They say they see the sun. But they do not see every side of the sun at once; so what they really see is discoid to begin with. It is but a visual aspect of the sun. In any single observation the sun is a brilliantly luminescent disc, a penny painted with radium.

So something about their visual experiences at dawn is the same for both: a brilliant yellow-white disc centred between green and blue colour patches. Sketches of what they both see could be identical—congruent. In this sense Tycho and Kepler see the same thing at dawn. The sun appears to them in the same way. The same view, or scene, is presented to them both.

In fact, we often speak in this way. Thus the account of a recent solar eclipse:[14] "Only a thin crescent remains; white light is now completely obscured; the sky appears a deep blue, almost purple, and the landscape is a monochromatic green . . . there are the flashes of light on the disc's circumference and now the brilliant crescent to the left. . . ." Newton writes in a similar way in the *Opticks:* "These Arcs at their first appearance were of a violent and blue Colour, and between them were white Arcs of Circles, which . . . became a little tinged in their inward Limbs with red and yellow. . . ."[15] Every physicist employs the language of lines, colour patches, appearances, shadows. In so far as two normal observers use this language of the same event, they begin from the same data: they are making the same observation. Differences between them must arise in the interpretations they put on these data.

Thus, to summarize, saying that Kepler and Tycho see the same thing at dawn just because their eyes are similarly affected is an elementary mistake. There is a difference between a physical state and a visual experience. Suppose, however, that it is argued as above—that they see the same thing because they have the same sense-datum experience. Disparities in their accounts arise in *ex post facto* interpretations of what is seen, not in the fundamental visual data. If this is argued, further difficulties soon obtrude.

B

Normal retinas and cameras are impressed similarly by fig. 1.[16] Our visual sense-data will be the same too. If asked to draw what we see, most of us will set out a configuration like fig. 1.

Do we all see the same thing?[17] Some will see a perspex cube viewed from below. Others will see it from above. Still others will see it as a kind of polygonally-cut gem. Some people see only criss-crossed lines in a plane. It may be seen as a block of ice, an aquarium, a wire frame for a kite—or any of a number of other things.

Do we, then, all see the same thing? If we do, how can these differences be accounted for?

Here the "formula" re-enters: "These are different *interpretations* of what all observers see in common. Retinal reactions to fig. 1 are virtually identical; so too are our visual sense-data, since our drawings of what we see will have the same content. There is no place in the seeing for these differences, so they must lie in the interpretations put on what we see."

This sounds as if I do two things, not one, when I see boxes and bicycles. Do I put different interpretations on fig. 1 when I see it now as a box from below, and now as a cube from above? I am aware of no such thing. I mean no such thing when I report that the box's perspective has snapped back into the page.[18] If I do not mean this, then the concept of seeing which is natural in this connexion does not designate two diaphanous components, one optical, the other interpretative. Fig. 1 is simply seen now as a box from below, now as a cube from above; one does not first soak up an optical pattern and then clamp an interpretation on it. Kepler and Tycho just see the sun. That is all. That is the way the concept of seeing works in this connexion.

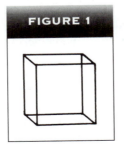

FIGURE 1

"But," you say, "seeing fig. 1 first as a box from below, then as a cube from above, involves interpreting the lines differently in each case." Then for you and me to have a different interpretation of fig. 1 just *is* for us to see something different. This does not mean we see the same thing and then interpret it differently. When I suddenly exclaim "Eureka—a box from above," I do not refer simply to a different interpretation. (Again, there is a logically prior sense in which seeing fig. 1 as from above and then as from below is seeing the same thing differently, i.e. being aware of the same diagram in different ways. We can refer just to this, but we need not. In this case we do not.)

Besides, the word "interpretation" is occasionally useful. We know where it applies and where it does not. Thucydides presented the facts objectively; Herodotus put an interpretation on them. The word does not apply to everything—it has a meaning. Can interpreting always be going on when we see? Sometimes, perhaps, as when the hazy outline of an agricultural machine looms up on a foggy morning and, with effort, we finally identify it. Is this the "interpretation" which is active when bicycles and boxes are clearly seen? Is it active when the perspective of fig. 1 snaps into reverse? There was a time when Herodotus was half-through with his interpretation of the Graeco-Persian wars. Could there be a time when one is half-through interpreting fig. 1 as a box from above, or as anything else?

"But the interpretation takes very little time—it is instantaneous." Instantaneous interpretation hails from the Limbo that produced unsensed sensibilia, unconscious inference, incorrigible statements, negative facts and *Objektive*. These are ideas which philosophers force on the world to preserve some pet epistemological or metaphysical theory.

Only in contrast to "Eureka" situations (like perspective reversals, where one cannot interpret the data) is it clear what is meant by saying that though Thucydides could have put an interpretation on history, he did not. Moreover, whether or not an historian is advancing an interpretation is an empirical question: we know what would count as evidence one way or the other. But whether we are employing an interpretation when we see fig. 1 in a certain way is not empirical. What could count as evidence? In no ordinary sense of "interpret" do I interpret fig. 1 differently when its perspective reverses for me. If there is some extraordinary sense of word it is not clear, either in ordinary language, or in extraordinary (philosophical) language. To insist that different reactions to fig. 1 *must* lie in the interpretations put on a common visual experience is just to reiterate (without reasons) that the seeing of *x must* be the same for all observers looking at *x*.

"But 'I see the figure as a box' means: I am having a particular visual experience which I always have when I interpret the figure as a box, or when I look at a box. . . ." ". . . if I meant this, I ought to know it. I ought to be able to refer to the experience directly and not only indirectly. . . ."[19]

Ordinary accounts of the experiences appropriate to fig. 1 do not require visual grist going into an intellectual mill: theories and interpretations are "there" in the seeing from the outset. How can interpretations "be there" in the seeing? How is it possible to see an object according to an interpretation? "The question represents it as a queer fact; as if something were being forced into a form it did not really fit. But no squeezing, no forcing took place here."[20]

Consider now the reversible perspective figures which appear in textbooks on Gestalt psychology: the tea-tray, the shifting (Schröder) staircase, the tunnel. Each of these can be seen as concave, as convex, or as a flat drawing.[21] Do I really see something different each time, or do I only interpret what I see in a different way? To interpret is to think, to do something; seeing is an experiential state.[22] The different ways in which these figures are seen are not due to different thoughts lying behind the visual reactions. What could "spontaneous" mean if these reactions are not spontaneous? When the staircase "goes into reverse" it does so spontaneously. One does not think of anything special; one does not think at all. Nor does one interpret. One just sees, now a staircase as from above, now a staircase as from below.

The sun, however, is not an entity with such variable perspective. What has all this to do with suggesting that Tycho and Kepler may see different things in the east at dawn? Certainly the cases are different. But these reversible perspective figures are examples of different things being seen in the same configuration, where this difference is due neither to differing visual pictures, nor to any "interpretation" superimposed on the sensation.

Some will see in fig. 2 an old Parisienne, others a young woman (à la Toulouse-Lautrec).[23] All normal retinas "take" the same picture; and our sense-datum pictures must be the same, for even if you see an old lady and I a young lady, the pictures we draw of what we see may turn out to be geometrically indistinguishable. (Some can see this *only* in one way, not both. This is like the difficulty we have after finding a face in a tree-puzzle; we cannot thereafter see the tree without the face.)

When what is observed is characterized so differently as "young woman" or "old woman," is it not natural to say that the observers see different things? Or must "see different things" mean only "see different objects"? This is a primary sense of the expression, to be sure. But is there not also a sense in which one who cannot see the young lady in fig. 2 sees something different from me, who sees the young lady? Of course there is.

Similarly, in Köhler's famous drawing of the Goblet-and-Faces[24] we "take" the same retinal/cortical/sense-datum picture of the configuration; our drawings might be indistinguishable. I see a goblet, however, and you see two men staring at one another. Do we see the same thing? Of course we do. But then again we do not. (The sense in which we *do* see the same thing begins to lose its philosophical interest.)

FIGURE 2

I draw my goblet. You say "That's just what I saw, two men in a staring contest." What steps must be taken to get you to see what I see? When attention shifts from the cup to the faces does one's visual picture change? How? What is it that changes? What could change? Nothing optical or sensational is modified. Yet one sees different things. The organization of what one sees changes.[25]

How does one describe the difference between the *jeune fille* and the *vieille femme* in fig. 2? Perhaps the difference is not describable: it may just show itself.[26] That two observers have not seen the same things in fig. 2 could show itself in their behaviour. What is the difference between us when you see the zebra as black with white stripes and I see it as white with black stripes? Nothing optical. Yet there might be a context (for instance, in the genetics of animal pigmentation), where such a difference could be important.

A third group of figures will stress further this organizational element of seeing and observing. They will hint at how much more is involved when Tycho and Kepler witness the dawn than "the formula" suggests.

What is portrayed in fig. 3? Your retinas and visual cortices are affected much as mine are; our sense-datum pictures would not differ. Surely we could all produce an accurate sketch of fig. 3. Do we see the same thing?

I see a bear climbing up the other side of a tree. Did the elements "pull together"/cohere/organize, when you learned this?[27] You might even say with Wittgenstein "it has not changed, and yet I see it differently. . . ."[28] Now, does it not have ". . . a quite particular 'organization'"?

Organization is not itself seen as are the lines and colours of a drawing. It is not itself a line, shape, or a colour. It is not an element in the visual field, but rather the way in which elements are appreciated. Again, the plot is not another detail in the story. Nor is the tune just one more

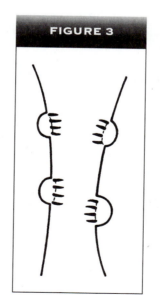

FIGURE 3

note. Yet without plots and tunes details and notes would not hang together. Similarly the organization of fig. 3 is nothing that registers on the retina along with other details. Yet it gives the lines and shapes a pattern. Were this lacking we would be left with nothing but an unintelligible configuration of lines.

How do visual experiences become organized? How is seeing possible?

Consider fig. 4 in the context of fig. 5.

The context gives us the clue. Here, some people could not see the figure as an antelope. Could people who had never seen an antelope, but only birds, see an antelope in fig. 4?

In the context of fig. 6 the figure may indeed stand out as an antelope. It might even be urged that the figure seen in fig. 5 has no similarity to the one in fig. 6 although the two are congruent. Could anything be more opposed to a sense-datum account of seeing?

Of a figure similar to the Necker cube (fig. 1) Wittgenstein writes, "You could imagine [this] appearing in several places in a text-book. In the relevant text something different is in question every time: here a glass cube, there an inverted open box, there a wire frame of that shape, there three boards forming a solid angle. Each time the text supplies the interpretation of the illustration. But we can also see the illustration now as one thing, now as another. So we interpret it, and see it as we interpret it." [29]

Consider now the head-and-shoulders in fig. 7.

The upper margin of the picture cuts the brow, thus the top of the head is not shown. The point of the jaw, clean shaven and brightly illuminated, is just above the geometric center of the picture. A white mantle . . . covers the right shoulder. The right upper sleeve is exposed as the rather black area at the lower left. The hair and beard are after the manner of a late mediaeval representation of Christ.[30]

The appropriate aspect of the illustration is brought out by the verbal context in which it appears. It is not an illustration of anything determinate unless it appears in some such context.

FIGURE 4   FIGURE 5

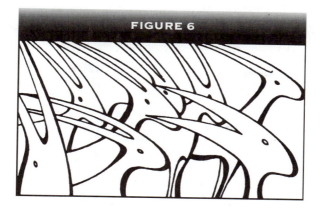

FIGURE 6

In the same way, I must talk and gesture around fig. 4 to get you to see the antelope when only the bird has revealed itself. I must provide a context. The context is part of the illustration itself.

Such a context, however, need not be set out explicitly. Often it is "built into" thinking, imagining and picturing. We are set[31] to appreciate the visual aspect of things in certain ways. Elements in our experience do not cluster at random.

A trained physicist could see one thing in fig. 8: an X-ray tube viewed from the cathode. Would Sir Lawrence Bragg and an Eskimo baby see the same thing when looking at an X-ray tube? Yes, and no. Yes—they are visually aware of the same object. No—the *ways* in which they are visually aware are profoundly different. Seeing is not only the having of a visual experience; it is also the way in which the visual experience is had.

At school the physicist had gazed at this glass-and-metal instrument. Returning now, after years in University and research, his eye lights upon the same object once again. Does he see

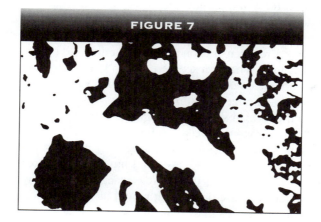

FIGURE 7

FIGURE 8

the same thing now as he did then? Now he sees the instrument in terms of electrical circuit theory, thermodynamic theory, the theories of metal and glass structure, thermionic emission, optical transmission, refraction, diffraction, atomic theory, quantum theory and special relativity.

Contrast the freshman's view of college with that of his ancient tutor. Compare a man's first glance at the motor of his car with a similar glance ten exasperating years later.

"Granted, one learns all these things," it may be countered, "but it all figures in the interpretation the physicist puts on what he sees. Though the layman sees exactly what the physicist sees, he cannot interpret it in the same way because he has not learned so much."

Is the physicist doing more than just seeing? No; he does nothing over and above what the layman does when he sees an X-ray tube. What are you doing over and above reading these words? Are you interpreting marks on a page? When would this ever be a natural way of speaking? Would an infant see what you see here, when you see words and sentences and he sees but marks and lines? One does nothing beyond looking and seeing when one dodges bicycles, glances at a friend, or notices a cat in the garden.

"The physicist and the layman see the same thing," it is objected, "but they do not make the same thing of it." The layman can make nothing of it. Nor is that just a figure of speech. I can make nothing of the Arab word for *cat,* though my purely visual impressions may be indistinguishable from those of the Arab who can. I must learn Arabic before I can see what he sees. The layman must learn physics before he can see what the physicist sees.

If one must find a paradigm case of seeing it would be better to regard as such not the visual apprehension of colour patches but things like seeing what time it is, seeing what key a piece of music is written in, and seeing whether a wound is septic.[32]

Pierre Duhem writes:

Enter a laboratory; approach the table crowded with an assortment of apparatus, an electric cell, silk-covered copper wire, small cups of mercury, spools, a mirror mounted on an iron bar; the experimenter is inserting into small openings the metal ends of ebony-headed pins; the iron os-cillates, and the mirror attached to it throws a luminous band upon a celluloid scale; the forward-backward motion of this spot enables the physicist to observe the minute oscillations of the iron bar. But ask him what he is doing. Will he answer "I am studying the oscillations of an iron bar which carries a mirror"? No, he will say that he is measuring the electric resistance of the spools. If you are astonished, if you ask him what his words mean, what relation they have with the phe-nomena he has been observing and which you have noted at the same time as he, he will answer that your question requires a long explanation and that you should take a course in electricity.[33]

The visitor must learn some physics before he can see what the physicist sees. Only then will the context throw into relief those features of the objects before him which the physicist sees as indicating resistance.

This obtains in all seeing. Attention is rarely directed to the space between the leaves of a tree, save when a Keats brings it to our notice.[34] (Consider also what was involved in Crusoe's seeing a vacant space in the sand as a footprint.) Our attention most naturally rests on objects and events which dominate the visual field. What a blooming, buzzing, undifferentiated con-fusion visual life would be if we all arose tomorrow without attention capable of dwelling only on what had heretofore been overlooked.[35]

The infant and the layman can see: they are not blind. But they cannot see what the physi-cist sees; they are blind to what he sees.[36] We may not hear that the oboe is out of tune, though this will be painfully obvious to the trained musician. (Who, incidentally, will not hear the tones and *interpret* them as being out of tune, but will simply hear the oboe to be out of tune.[37] We simply see what time it is; the surgeon simply sees a wound to be septic; the physicist sees the X-ray tube's anode overheating.) The elements of the visitor's visual field, though identical with those of the physicist, are not organized for him as for the physicist; the same lines, colours, shapes are apprehended by both, but not in the same way. There are indefinitely many ways in which a constellation of lines, shapes, patches, may be seen. *Why* a visual pattern is seen differently is a question for psychology, but *that* it may be seen differently is important in any examination of the concepts of seeing and observation. Here, as Wittgenstein might have said, the psychological is a symbol of the logical.

You see a bird, I see an antelope; the physicist sees an X-ray tube, the child a complicated lamp bulb; the microscopist sees coelenterate mesoglea, his new student sees only a gooey, formless stuff. Tycho and Simplicius see a mobile sun, Kepler and Galileo see a static sun.[38]

It may be objected, "Everyone, whatever his state of knowledge, will see fig. 1 as a box or cube, viewed as from above or as from below." True; almost everyone, child, layman, physicist, will see the figure as box-like one way or another. But could such observations be made by people ignorant of the construction of box-like objects? No. This objection only shows that most of us—the blind, babies, and dimwits excluded—have learned enough to be able to see this figure as a three-dimensional box. This reveals something about the sense in which Simpli-cius and Galileo do see the same thing (which I have never denied): they both see a brilliant heavenly body. The schoolboy and the physicist both see that the X-ray tube will smash if dropped. Examining how observers see different things in x marks something important about their seeing the same thing when looking at x. If seeing different things involves having different knowledge and theories about x, then perhaps the sense in which they see the same thing involves their sharing knowledge and theories about x. Bragg and the baby share no knowledge of X-ray tubes. They see the same thing only in that if they are looking at x they are both having some visual experience of it. Kepler and Tycho agree on more: they see the same thing in a stronger sense. Their visual fields are organized in much the same way. Neither sees the sun about to break out in a grin, or about to crack into ice cubes. (The baby is not "set" even against these eventualities.) Most people today see the same thing at dawn in an even stronger sense: we share much knowledge of the sun. Hence Tycho and Kepler see different things, and yet they see the same thing. That these things can be said depends on their knowledge, experience, and theories.

Kepler and Tycho are to the sun as we are to fig. 4, when I see the bird and you see only the antelope. The elements of their experiences are identical; but their conceptual organization is vastly different. Can their visual fields have a different organization? Then they can see different things in the east at dawn.

It is the sense in which Tycho and Kepler do not observe the same thing which must be grasped if one is to understand disagreement within microphysics. Fundamental physics is primarily a search for intelligibility—it is philosophy of matter. Only secondarily is it a search for objects and facts (though the two endeavours are as hand and glove). Microphysicists seek new modes of conceptual organization. If that can be done the finding of new entities will follow. Gold is rarely discovered by one who has not got the lay of the land.

To say that Tycho and Kepler, Simplicius and Galileo, Hooke and Newton, Priestley and Lavoisier, Soddy and Einstein, De Broglie and Born, Heisenberg and Bohm all make the same observations but use them differently is too easy.[39] It does not explain controversy in research science. Were there no sense in which they were different observations they could not be used differently. This may perplex some: that researchers sometimes do not appreciate data in the same way is a serious matter. It is important to realize, however, that sorting out differences about data, evidence, observation, may require more than simply gesturing at observable objects. It may require a comprehensive reappraisal of one's subject matter. This may be difficult, but it should not obscure the fact that nothing less than this may do.

c

There is a sense, then, in which seeing is a "theory-laden" undertaking. Observation of x is shaped by prior knowledge of x. Another influence on observation rests in the language or notation used to express what we know, and without which there would be little we could recognize as knowledge. This will be examined.[40]

I do not mean to identify seeing with *seeing as*. Seeing an X-ray tube is not seeing a glass-and-metal object as an X-ray tube.[41] However, seeing an antelope and seeing an object as an antelope have much in common. Something of the concept of seeing can be discerned from tracing uses of "seeing . . . as . . . ." Wittgenstein is reluctant[42] to concede this, but his reasons are not clear to me. On the contrary, the logic of "seeing as" seems to illuminate the general perceptual case.[43] Consider again the footprint in the sand. Here all the organizational features of *seeing as* stand out clearly, in the absence of an *"object."* One can even imagine cases where "He sees it as a footprint" would be a way of referring to another's apprehension of what actually is a footprint. So, while I do not identify, for example, Hamlet's seeing of a camel in the clouds with his seeing of Yorick's skull, there is still something to be learned about the latter from noting what is at work in the former.

There is, however, a further element in seeing and observation. If the label "seeing as" has drawn out certain features of these concepts, "seeing that . . ." may bring out more. Seeing a bear in fig. 3 was to see that were the "tree" circled we should come up behind the beast. Seeing the dawn was for Tycho and Simplicius to see that the earth's brilliant satellite was beginning its diurnal circuit around us, while for Kepler and Galileo it was to see that the earth was spinning them back into the light of our local star. Let us examine "seeing that" in these examples. It may be the logical element which connects observing with our knowledge, and with our language.

Of course there are cases where the data are confused and where we may have no clue to guide us. In microscopy one often reports sensations in a phenomenal, lustreless way: "it is green in this light; darkened areas mark the broad end. . . ." So too the physicist may say: "the needle oscillates, and there is a faint streak near the neon parabola. Scintillations appear on the periphery of the cathodescope. . . ." To deny that these are genuine cases of seeing, even observing, would be unsound, just as is the suggestion that they are the *only* genuine cases of seeing.

These examples are, however, overstressed. The language of shapes, colour patches, oscillations and pointer-readings is appropriate to the unsettled experimental situation, where confusion and even conceptual muddle may dominate. The observer may not know what he is seeing: he aims only to get his observations to cohere against a background of established knowledge. This seeing is the goal of observation. It is in these terms, and not in terms of "phenomenal" seeing, that new inquiry proceeds. Every physicist forced to observe his data as in an oculist's office finds himself in a special, unusual situation. He is obliged to forget what he knows and to watch events like a child. These are non-typical cases, however spectacular they may sometimes be.

First registering observations and then casting about for knowledge of them gives a simple model of how the mind and the eye fit together. The relationship between seeing and the corpus of our knowledge, however, is not a simple one.

What is it to see boxes, staircases, birds, antelopes, bears, goblets, X-ray tubes? It is (at least) to have knowledge of certain sorts. (Robots and electric eyes are blind, however efficiently they react to light. Cameras cannot see.) It is to see that, were certain things done to objects before our eyes, other things would result. How should we regard a man's report that he sees x if we know him to be ignorant of all x-ish things? Precisely as we would regard a four-year-old's report that he sees a meson shower. "Smith sees x" suggests that Smith could specify some things pertinent to x. To see an X-ray tube is at least to see that, were it dropped on stone, it would smash. To see a goblet is to see something with concave interior. We may be wrong, but not always—not even usually. Besides, deceptions proceed in terms of what is normal, ordinary. Because the world is not a cluster of conjurer's tricks, conjurers can exist. Because the logic of "seeing that" is an intimate part of the concept of seeing, we sometimes rub our eyes at illusions.

"Seeing as" and "seeing that" are not components of seeing, as rods and bearings are parts of motors: seeing is not composite. Still, one *can* ask logical questions. What must have occurred, for instance, for us to describe a man as having found a collar stud, or as having seen a bacillus? Unless he had had a visual sensation and knew what a bacillus was (and looked like) we would not say that he had seen a bacillus, except in the sense in which an infant could see a bacillus. "Seeing as" and "seeing that," then, are not psychological components of seeing. They are logically distinguishable elements in seeing-talk, in our concept of seeing.

To see fig. 1 as a transparent box, an ice-cube, or a block of glass is to see that it is six-faced, twelve-edged, eight-cornered. Its corners are solid right angles; if constructed it would be of rigid, or semi-rigid material, not of liquescent or gaseous stuff like oil, vapour or flames. It would be tangible. It would take up space in an exclusive way, being locatable here, there, but at least somewhere. Nor would it cease to exist when we blinked. Seeing it as a cube is just to see that all these things would obtain.

This is knowledge: it is knowing what kind of a thing "box" or "cube" denotes and something about what materials can make up such an entity. "Transparent box" or "glass cube" would not express what was seen were any of these further considerations denied. Seeing a bird in the sky involves seeing that it will not suddenly do vertical snap rolls; and this is more than marks the retina. We could be wrong. But to see a bird, even momentarily, is to see it in all these connexions. As Wisdom would say, every perception involves an aetiology and a prognosis.[44]

Sense-datum theorists stress how we can go wrong in our observations, as when we call aeroplanes "birds." Thus they seek what we are right about, even in these cases. Preoccupation with this problem obscures another one, namely, that of describing what is involved when we are right about what we say we see; and after all this happens very often. His preoccupation with mistakes leads the phenomenalist to portray a world in which we are usually deceived; but the world of physics is not like that. Were a physicist in an ordinary laboratory situation to react to his visual environment with purely sense-datum responses—as does the infant or the idiot—we would think him out of his mind. We would think him *not* to be seeing what was around him.

"Seeing that" threads knowledge into our seeing; it saves us from re-identifying everything that meets our eye; it allows physicists to observe new data as physicists, and not as cameras. We do not ask "What's that?" of every passing bicycle. The knowledge is there in the seeing and not an adjunct of it. (The pattern of threads is there in the cloth and not tacked on to it by ancillary operations.) We rarely catch ourselves tacking knowledge on to what meets the eye. Seeing this page as having an opposite side requires no squeezing or forcing, yet nothing optical guarantees that when you turn the sheet it will not cease to exist. This is but another way of saying that ordinary seeing is corrigible, which everybody would happily concede.

The search for incorrigible seeing has sometimes led some philosophers to deny that anything less than the incorrigible is seeing at all.

Seeing an object x is to see that it may behave in the ways we know x's do behave: if the object's behaviour does not accord with what we expect of x's we may be blocked from seeing it as a straightforward x any longer. Now we rarely see dolphin as fish, the earth as flat, the heavens as an inverted bowl or the sun as our satellite. ". . . what I perceive as the dawning of an aspect is not a property of the object, but an internal relation between it and other objects."[45] To see in fig. 8 an X-ray tube is to see that a photo-sensitive plate placed below it will be irradiated. It is to see that the target will get extremely hot, and as it has no water-jacket it must be made of metal with a high melting-point—molybdenum or tungsten. It is to see that at high voltages green fluorescence will appear at the anode. Could a physicist see an X-ray tube without seeing that these other things would obtain? Could one see something as an incandescent light bulb and fail to see that it is the wire filament which "lights up" to a white heat? The answer may sometimes be "yes," but this only indicates that different things can be meant by "X-ray tube" and "incandescent bulb." Two people confronted with an x may mean different things by x. Must their saying "I see x" mean that they see the same thing? A child could parrot "X-ray tube," or "Kentucky" or "Winston," when confronted with the figure above, but he would not see that these other things followed. And this is what the physicist does see.

If in the brilliant disc of which he is visually aware Tycho sees only the sun, then he cannot but see that it is a body which will behave in characteristically "Tychonic" ways. These serve as the foundation for Tycho's general geocentric-geostatic theories about the sun. They are not imposed on his visual impressions as a tandem interpretation: they are "there" in the seeing. (So too the interpretation of a piece of music is there in the music. Where else could it be? It is not something superimposed upon pure, unadulterated sound.)

Similarly we see fig. 1 as from underneath, as from above, or as a diagram of a rat maze or a gem-cutting project. However construed, the construing is there in the seeing. One is tempted to say "the construing *is* the seeing." The thread and its arrangement *is* the fabric, the sound and its composition *is* the music, the colour and its disposition *is* the painting. There are not two operations involved in my seeing fig. 1 as an ice-cube; I simply see it as an ice-cube. Analogously, the physicist sees an X-ray tube, not by first soaking up reflected light and then clamping on interpretations, but just as you see this page before you.

Tycho sees the sun beginning its journey from horizon to horizon. He sees that from some celestial vantage point the sun (carrying with it the moon and planets) could be watched circling our fixed earth. Watching the sun at dawn through Tychonic spectacles would be to see it in something like this way.

Kepler's visual field, however, has a different conceptual organization. Yet a drawing of what he sees at dawn could be a drawing of exactly what Tycho saw,[46] and could be recognized as such by Tycho. But Kepler will see the horizon dipping, or turning away, from our fixed local star. The shift from sunrise to horizon-turn is analogous to the shift-of-aspect phenomena already considered; it is occasioned by differences between what Tycho and Kepler think they know.

These logical features of the concept of seeing are inextricable and indispensable to observation in research physics. Why indispensable? That men do see in a way that permits analysis into "seeing as" and "seeing that" factors is one thing; "indispensable," however, suggests that the world must be seen thus. This is a stronger claim, requiring a stronger argument. Let us put it differently: that observation in physics is not an encounter with unfamiliar and unconnected flashes, sounds and bumps, but rather a calculated meeting with these as flashes, sounds and bumps of a particular kind—this might figure in an account of what observation is. It would not secure the point that observation could not be otherwise. This latter type of argument is now required: it must establish that an alternative account would be not merely false, but absurd. . . .

NOTES

[1]　Wär' nicht das Auge sonnenhaft,
　　Die Sonne könnt' es nie erblicken;
Goethe, *Zahme Xenien* (Werke, Weimar, 1887–1918), Bk. 3, 1805.

[2]　Cf. the papers by Baker and Gatonby in *Nature,* 1949–present.

[3]　This is not a *merely* conceptual matter, of course. Cf. Wittgenstein, *Philosophical Investigations* (Blackwell, Oxford, 1953), p. 196.

[4]　(1) G. Berkeley, *Essay Towards a New Theory of Vision* (in *Works,* vol. I (London, T. Nelson, 1948–56)), pp. 51ff. (2) James Mill, *Analysis of the Phenomena of the Human Mind* (Longmans, London, 1869), vol. I, p. 97. (3) J. Sully, *Outlines of Psychology* (Appleton, New York, 1885). (4) William James, *The Principles of Psychology* (Holt, New York, 1890–1905), vol. II, pp. 4, 78, 80 and 81; vol. I, p. 221. (5) A. Schopenhauer, *Satz vom Grunde* (in *Sämmtliche Werke,* Leipzig, 1888), ch. IV. (6) H. Spencer, *The Principles of Psychology* (Appleton, New York, 1897), vol. IV, chs. IX, X. (7) E. von Hartmann, *Philosophy of the Unconscious* (K. Paul, London, 1931), B, chs. VII, VIII. (8) W. M. Wundt, *Vorlesungen über die Menschen und Thierseele* (Voss, Hamburg, 1892), IV, XIII. (9) H. L. F. von Helmholtz, *Handbuch der Physiologischen Optik* (Leipzig, 1867), pp. 430, 447. (10) A. Binet, *La psychologie du raisonnement, recherches expérimentales par l'hypnotisme* (Alcan, Paris, 1886), chs. III, V. (11) J. Grote, *Exploratio Philosophica* (Cambridge, 1900), vol. II, pp. 201 ff. (12) B. Russell, in *Mind* (1913), p. 76. *Mysticism and Logic* (Longmans, New York, 1918), p. 209. *The Problems of Philosophy* (Holt, New York, 1912), pp. 73, 92, 179, 203. (13) Dawes Hicks, *Arist. Soc. Sup.* vol. II (1919), pp. 176–8. (14) G. F. Stout, *A Manual of Psychology* (Clive, London, 1907, 2nd ed.), vol. II, 1 and 2, pp. 324, 561–4. (15) A. C. Ewing, *Fundamental Questions of Philosophy* (New York, 1951), pp. 45 ff. (16) G. W. Cunningham, *Problems of Philosophy* (Holt, New York, 1924), pp. 96–7.

[5]　Galileo, *Dialogue Concerning the Two Chief World Systems* (California, 1953), "The First Day," p. 33.

[6]　"'Das ist doch kein Sehen!'—'Das ist doch ein Sehen!' Beide müssen sich begrifflich rechtfertigen lassen" (Wittgenstein, *Phil. Inv.* p. 203).

[7]　Brain, *Recent Advances in Neurology* (with Strauss) (London, 1929), p. 88. Compare Helmholtz: "The sensations are signs to our consciousness, and it is the task of our intelligence to learn to understand their meaning" (*Handbuch der Physiologischen Optik* [Leipzig, 1867], vol. III, p. 433).
　　See also Husserl, "Ideen zu einer Reinen Phaenomenologie," in *Jahrbuch für Philosophie,* vol. I (1913), pp. 75, 79, and Wagner's *Handwörterbuch der Physiologie,* vol. III, section I (1846), p. 183.

[8]　Mann, *The Science of Seeing* (London, 1949), pp. 48–9. Arber, *The Mind and the Eye* (Cambridge, 1954). Compare Müller: "In any field of vision, the retina sees only itself in its spatial extension during a state of affection. It perceives itself as . . . etc." (*Zur vergleichenden Physiologie des Gesichtesinnes des Menschen und der Thiere* [Leipzig, 1826], p. 54).

[9]　Kolin: "An astigmatic eye when looking at millimeter paper can accommodate to see sharply either the vertical lines or the horizontal lines" (*Physics* [New York, 1950], pp. 570 ff.).

[10]　Cf. Whewell, *Philosophy of Discovery* (London, 1860), "The Paradoxes of Vision."

[11] Cf. e.g. J. Z. Young, *Doubt and Certainty in Science* (Oxford, 1951, The Reith Lectures), and Gary Walter's article in *Aspects of Form,* ed. by L. L. Whyte (London, 1953). Compare Newton: "Do not the Rays of Light in falling upon the bottom of the Eye excite Vibrations in the Tunica Retina? Which Vibrations, being propagated along the solid Fibres of the Nerves into the Brain, cause the Sense of seeing" (*Opticks* [London, 1769], Bk. III, part I).

[12] "Rot und grün kann ich nur sehen, aber nicht hören" (Wittgenstein, *Phil. Inv.* p. 209).

[13] Cf. "An appearance is the same whenever the same eye is affected in the same way" (Lambert, *Photometria* [Berlin, 1760]); "We are justified, when different perceptions offer themselves to us, to infer that the underlying real conditions are different" (Helmholtz, *Wissenschaftliche Abhandlungen* [Leipzig, 1882], vol. II, p. 656), and Hertz: "We form for ourselves images or symbols of the external objects; the manner in which we form them is such that the logically necessary (*denknotwendigen*) consequences of the images in thought are invariably the images of materially necessary (*naturnotwendigen*) consequences of the corresponding objects" (*Principles of Mechanics* [London, 1889], p. 1).

Broad and Price make depth a feature of the private visual pattern. However, Weyl (*Philosophy of Mathematics and Natural Science* [Princeton, 1949], p. 125) notes that a single eye perceives qualities spread out in a *two*-dimensional field, since the latter is dissected by any one-dimensional line running through it. But our conceptual difficulties remain even when Kepler and Tycho keep one eye closed.

Whether or not two observers are having the same visual sense-data reduces directly to the question of whether accurate pictures of the contents of their visual fields are identical, or differ in some detail. We can then discuss the publicly observable pictures which Tycho and Kepler draw of what they see, instead of those private, mysterious entities locked in their visual consciousness. The accurate picture and the sense-datum must be identical; how could they differ?

[14] From the B.B.C. report, 30 June 1954.

[15] Newton, *Opticks,* Bk. II, part I. The writings of Claudius Ptolemy sometimes read like a phenomenalist's textbook. Cf. e.g. *The Almagest* (Venice, 1515), VI, section II, "On the Directions in the Eclipses," "When it touches the shadow's circle from within," "When the circles touch each other from without." Cf. also VII and VIII, IX (section 4). Ptolemy continually seeks to chart and predict "the appearances"—the points of light on the celestial globe. *The Almagest* abandons any attempt to explain the machinery behind these appearances.

Cf. Pappus: "The (circle) dividing the milk-white portion which owes its colour to the sun, and the portion which has the ashen colour natural to the moon itself is indistinguishable from a great circle" (*Mathematical Collection* [Hultsch, Berlin and Leipzig, 1864], pp. 554–60).

[16] This famous illusion dates from 1832, when L. A. Necker, the Swiss naturalist, wrote a letter to Sir David Brewster describing how when certain rhomboidal crystals were viewed on end the perspective could shift in the way now familiar to us. Cf. *Phil. Mag.* III, no. 1 (1832), 329–37, especially p. 336. It is important to the present argument to note that this observational phenomenon began life not as a psychologist's trick, but at the very frontiers of observational science.

[17] Wittgenstein answers: "Denn wir sehen eben wirklich zwei verschiedene Tatsachen" (*Tractatus,* 5. 5423).

[18] "Auf welche Vorgänge spiele ich an?" (Wittgenstein, *Phil. Inv.* p. 214).

[19] *Ibid.* p. 194 (top).

[20] *Ibid.* p. 200.

[21] This is *not* due to eye movements, or to local retinal fatigue. Cf. Flugel, *Brit. J. Psychol.* VI (1913), 60; *Brit. J. Psychol.* V (1913), 357. Cf. Donahue and Griffiths, *Amer. J. Psychol.* (1931), and Luckiesh, *Visual Illusions and Their Applications* (London, 1922). Cf. also Peirce, *Collected Papers* (Harvard, 1931), 5, 183. References to psychology should not be misunderstood; but as one's acquaintance with the psychology of perception deepens, the character of the conceptual problems one regards as significant will deepen accordingly. Cf. Wittgenstein, *Phil. Inv.* p. 206 (top). Again, p. 193: "Its causes are of interest to psychologists. We are interested in the concept and its place among the concepts of experience."

[22] Wittgenstein, *Phil. Inv.* p. 212.

[23] From Boring, *Amer. J. Psychol.* XLII (1930), 444 and cf. Allport, *Brit. J. Psychol.* XXI (1930), 133; Leeper, *J. Genet. Psychol.* XLVI (1935), 41; Street, *Gestalt Completion Test* (Columbia Univ., 1931); Dees and Grindley, *Brit. J. Psychol.* (1947).

[24] Köhler, *Gestalt Psychology* (London, 1929). Cf. his *Dynamics in Psychology* (London, 1939).

[25] "Mein Gesichtseindruck hat sich geändert;—wie war er früher; wie ist er jetzt?—Stelle ich ihn durch eine genaue Kopie dar—und ist das keine gute Darstellung?—so zeigt sich keine Änderung" (Wittgenstein, *Phil. Inv.* p. 196).

[26] "Was gezeigt werden kann, kann nicht gesagt werden" (Wittgenstein, *Tractatus,* 4. 1212).

[27] This case is different from fig. 1. Now I can help a "slow" percipient by tracing in the outline of the bear. In fig. 1 a percipient either gets the perspectival arrangement, or he does not, though even here Wittgenstein makes some suggestions as to how one might help; cf. *Tractatus,* 5. 5423, last line.

[28] Wittgenstein, *Phil. Inv.* p. 193. Helmholtz speaks of the "integrating" function which converts the figure into the appearance of an object hit by a visual ray (*Phys. Optik,* vol. III, p. 239). This is reminiscent of Aristotle, for whom seeing consisted in emanations from our eyes. They reach out, tentacle-fashion, and touch objects whose shapes are "felt" in the eye. (Cf. *De Caelo* [Oxford, 1928], 290a, 18; and *Meteorologica* [Oxford, 1928], III, iv, 373b, 2. [Also Plato, *Meno,* London, 1869] 76c–d.) But he controverts this in *Topica* (Oxford, 1928), 105b, 6.) Theophrastus argues that "Vision is due to the gleaming . . . which [in the eye] reflects to the object" (*On the Senses,* 26, trans. G. M. Stratton). Hero writes: "Rays proceeding from our eyes are reflected by mirrors . . . that our sight is directed in straight lines proceeding from the organ of vision may be substantiated as follows" (*Catoptrics,* 1–5, trans. Schmidt in *Heronis Alexandrini Opera* (Leipzig, 1899–1919)). Galen is of the same opinion. So too is Leonardo: "The eye sends its image to the object . . . the power of vision extends by means of the visual rays . . ." (*Notebooks,* C.A. 135 v.b. and 270 v.c.). Similarly Donne in *The Ecstasy* writes: "Our eyebeams twisted and . . . pictures in our eyes to get was all *our* propagation."

This is the view that all perception is really a species of touching, e.g. Descartes' *impressions,* and the analogy of the wax. Compare: "[Democritus] explains [vision] by the air between the eye and the object [being] compressed . . . [it] thus becomes imprinted . . . 'as if one were to take a mould in wax' . . ." Theophrastus (*op. cit.* 50–3). Though it lacks physical and physiological support, the view is attractive in cases where lines seem suddenly to be forced into an intelligible pattern—by us.

[29] *Ibid.* p. 193. Cf. Helmholtz, *Phys. Optik,* vol. III, pp. 4, 18, and Fichte (*Bestimmung des Menschen,* ed. Medicus [Bonn, 1834], vol. III, p. 326). Cf. also Wittgenstein, *Tractatus,* 2. 0123.

[30] P. B. Porter, *Amer. J. Psychol.* LXVII (1954), 550.

[31] Writings by Gestalt psychologists on "set" and "Aufgabe" are many. Yet they are overlooked by most philosophers. A few fundamental papers are: Külpe, *Ber. I Kongress Exp. Psychol., Giessen* (1904); Bartlett, *Brit. J. Psychol.* VIII (1916), 222; George, *Amer. J. Psychol.* XXVIII (1917), I; Fernberger, *Psychol. Monogr.* XXVI (1919), 6; Zigler, *Amer. J. Psychol.* XXXI (1920), 273; Boring, *Amer. J. Psychol.* XXXV (1924), 301; Wilcocks, *Amer. J. Psychol.* XXXVI (1925), 324; Gilliland, *Psychol. Bull.* XXIV (1927), 622; Gottschaldt, *Psychol. Forsch.* XII (1929), I; Boring, *Amer. J. Psychol.* XLII (1930), 444; Street, *Gestalt Completion Test* (Columbia University, 1931); Ross and Schilder, *J. Gen. Psychol.* X (1934), 152; Hunt, *Amer. J. Psychol.* XLVII (1935), I; Süpola, *Psychol. Monogr.* XLVI (1935), 210, 27; Gibson, *Psychol. Bull.* XXXVIII (1941), 781; Henle, *J. Exp. Psychol.* XXX (1942), I; Luchins, *J. Soc. Psychol.* XXI (1945), 257; Wertheimer, *Productive Thinking* (1945); Russell Davis and Sinha, *Quart. J. Exp. Psychol.* (1950); Hall, *Quart. J. Exp. Psychol.* II (1950), 153.

Philosophy has no concern with fact, only with conceptual matters (cf. Wittgenstein, *Tractatus,* 4. 111); but discussions of perception could not but be improved by the reading of these twenty papers.

[32] Often "What do you see?" only poses the question "Can you identify the object before you?" This is calculated more to test one's knowledge than one's eyesight.

[33] Duhem, *La théorie physique* (Paris, 1914), p. 218.

[34] Chinese poets felt the significance of "negative features" like the hollow of a clay vessel or the central vacancy of the hub of a wheel (cf. Waley, *Three Ways of Thought in Ancient China* [London, 1939], p. 155).

[35] Infants are indiscriminate; they take in spaces, relations, objects and events as being of equal value. They still must learn to organize their visual attention. The camera-clarity of their visual reactions is not by itself sufficient to differentiate elements in their visual fields. Contrast Mr. W. H. Auden who recently said of the poet that he is "bombarded by a stream of varied sensations which would drive him mad if he took them all in. It is impossible to guess how much energy we have to spend every day in not-seeing, not-hearing, not-smelling, not-reacting."

36 Cf. "He was blind to the *expression* of a face. Would his eyesight on that account be defective?" (Wittgenstein, *Phil. Inv.* p. 210) and "Because they seeing see not; and hearing they hear not, neither do they understand" (Matt. xiii. 10 – 13).

37 "Es hört doch jeder nur, was er versteht" (Goethe, *Maxims* [*Werke,* Weimar, 1887 – 1918]).

38 Against this Professor H. H. Price has argued: "Surely it appears to both of them to be rising, to be moving upwards, across the horizon . . . they both see a moving sun: they both see a round bright body which appears to be rising." Philip Frank retorts: "Our sense observation shows only that in the morning the distance between horizon and sun is increasing, but it does not tell us whether the sun is ascending or the horizon is descending . . ." (*Modern Science and its Philosophy* [Harvard, 1949], p. 231). Precisely. For Galileo and Kepler the horizon drops; for Simplicius and Tycho the sun rises. This is the difference Price misses, and which is central to this essay.

39 This parallels the too-easy epistemological doctrine that all normal observers see the same things in *x,* but interpret them differently.

40 Cf. the important paper by Carmichael, Hogan and Walter, "An Experimental Study of the Effect of Language on the Reproduction of Visually Perceived Form," *J. Exp. Psychol.* XV (1932), 73 – 86. (Cf. also Wulf, *Beiträge zur Psychologie der Gestalt.* VI. "Über die Veränderung von Vorstellungen [Gedächtnis und Gestalt]." *Psychol. Forsch.* I (1921), 333 – 73.) Cf. also Wittgenstein, *Tractatus,* 5. 6; 5. 61.

41 Wittgenstein, *Phil. Inv.* p. 206.

42 "'Seeing as . . .' is not part of perception. And for that reason it is like seeing and again not like" (*ibid.* p. 197).

43 "All seeing is seeing as . . . if a person sees something at all it must look like something to him . . ." (G. N. A. Vesey, "Seeing and Seeing As," *Proc. Aristotelian Soc.* (1956), p. 114.)

44 "Is the pinning on of a medal merely the pinning on of a bit of metal?" (Wisdom, "Gods," *Proc. Aristotelian Soc.* (1944 – 5)).

45 Wittgenstein, *Phil. Inv.* p. 212. Cf. *Tractatus* 2. 0121. Cf. Also Helmholtz, *Phys. Optik,* vol. III, p. 18.

46 Drawn on grid paper the two visual pictures could be geometrically identical. Cf. "If the two different 'appearances' of a reversible figure were indeed things ('pictures') we could conceive of them projected out from our minds, on to a screen, side by side, and distinguishable. But the only images on a screen which could serve as projections of the two different 'appearances' would be identical" (G. N. A. Vesey, "Seeing and Seeing As," *Proc. Aristotelian Soc.* (1956)).

H I L A R Y   P U T N A M
WHAT THEORIES ARE NOT

In this paper I consider the role of *theories* in empirical science, and attack what may be called the "received view"—that theories are to be thought of as "partially interpreted calculi" in which only the "observation terms" are "directly interpreted" (the theoretical terms being only "partially interpreted," or, some people even say, "partially understood").

To begin, let us review this received view. The view divides the nonlogical vocabulary of science into two parts:

OBSERVATION TERMS	**THEORETICAL TERMS**
such terms as	such terms as
"red"	"electron"
"touches"	"dream"
"stick," etc.	"gene," etc.

The basis for the division appears to be as follows: the observation terms apply to what may be called publicly observable things and signify observable qualities of these things, while the theoretical terms correspond to the remaining unobservable qualities and things.

This division of terms into two classes is then allowed to generate a division of statements into two[1] classes as follows:

OBSERVATIONAL STATEMENTS	**THEORETICAL STATEMENTS**
statements containing only observation terms and logical vocabulary	statements containing theoretical terms

Lastly, a scientific theory is conceived of as an axiomatic system which may be thought of as initially uninterpreted, and which gains "empirical meaning" as a result of a specification of meaning *for the observation terms alone*. A kind of partial meaning is then thought of as drawn up to the theoretical terms, by osmosis, as it were.

THE OBSERVATIONAL–THEORETICAL DICHOTOMY

One can think of many distinctions that are crying out to be made ("new" terms vs. "old" terms, technical terms vs. non-technical ones, terms more-or-less peculiar to one science vs. terms common to many, for a start). My contention here is simply:

(1) The *problem* for which this dichotomy was invented ("how is it possible to interpret theoretical terms?") does not exist.

(2) A basic reason some people have given for introducing the dichotomy is false: namely, justification in science does *not* proceed "down" in the direction of observation

terms. In fact, justification in science proceeds in any direction that may be handy—
more observational assertions sometimes being justified with the aid of more theoretical ones, and vice versa. Moreover, as we shall see, while the notion of an *observation
report* has some importance in the philosophy of science, such reports cannot be
identified on the basis of the vocabulary they do or do not contain.

(3) In any case, whether the reasons for introducing the dichotomy were good ones or
bad ones, the double distinction (observation terms – theoretical terms, observation
statements – theoretical statements) presented above is, in fact, completely broken-
backed. This I shall try to establish now.

In the first place, it should be noted that the dichotomy under discussion was intended as
an explicative and not merely a stipulative one. That is, the words "observational" and "theoretical" are not having arbitrary new meanings bestowed upon them; rather, pre-existing uses
of these words (especially in the philosophy of science) are presumably being sharpened and
made clear. And, in the second place, it should be recalled that we are dealing with a double,
not just a single, distinction. That is to say, part of the contention I am criticizing is that, once
the distinction between observational and theoretical *terms* has been drawn as above, the distinction between theoretical statements and observational reports or assertions (in something
like the sense usual in methodological discussions) can be drawn in terms of it. What I mean
when I say that the dichotomy is "completely broken-backed" is this:

(A) If an "observation term" is one that cannot apply to an unobservable, then there are
no observation terms.[2]

(B) Many terms that refer primarily to what Carnap would class as "unobservables"
are not theoretical terms; and at least some theoretical terms refer primarily to
observables.

(C) Observational reports can and frequently do contain theoretical terms.

(D) A scientific theory, properly so-called, may refer only to observables. (Darwin's theory
of evolution, as originally put forward, is one example.)

To start with the notion of an "observation term": Carnap's formulation in *Testability and
Meaning* (Carnap, 1955) was that for a term to be an observation term not only must it correspond to an observable quality, but the determination whether the quality is present or not
must be able to be made by the observer in a relatively short time, and with a high degree of
confirmation. In his most recent authoritative publication (Carnap, 1956), Carnap is rather
brief. He writes, "the terms of V_O [the 'observation vocabulary'] are predicates designating observable properties of events or things (e.g. 'blue', 'hot', 'large', etc.) or observable relations
between them (e.g. 'x is warmer than y', 'x is contiguous to y', etc.)" (Carnap, 1956, p. 41). The
only other clarifying remarks I could find are the following: "The name 'observation language'
may be understood in a narrower or in a wider sense; the observation language in the wider
sense includes the disposition terms. In this article I take the observation language L_O in the
narrower sense" (Carnap, 1956, p. 63). "An observable property may be regarded as a simple

special case of a testable disposition: for example, the operation for finding out whether a thing is blue or hissing or cold, consists simply in looking or listening or touching the thing, respectively. Nevertheless, *in the reconstruction of the language* [italics mine] it seems convenient to take some properties for which the test procedure is extremely simple (as in the examples given) as directly observable, and use them as primitives in L_O" (Carnap, 1956, p. 63).

These paragraphs reveal that Carnap, at least, thinks of observation terms as corresponding to qualities that can be detected without the aid of instruments. But always so detected? Or can an observation term refer sometimes to an observable thing and sometimes to an unobservable? While I have not been able to find any explicit statement on this point, it seems to me that writers like Carnap must be *neglecting* the fact that *all* terms—including the "observation terms"—have at least the possibility of applying to unobservables. Thus their problem has sometimes been formulated in quasi-historical terms—"How could theoretical terms have been introduced into the language?" And the usual discussion strongly suggests that the following puzzle is meant: if we imagine a time at which people could only talk about observables (had not available any theoretical terms), how did they ever manage to *start* talking about unobservables?

It is possible that I am here doing Carnap and his followers an injustice. However, polemics aside, the following points must be emphasized.

(1) Terms referring to unobservables are *invariably* explained, in the actual history of science, with the aid of already present locutions referring to unobservables. There never was a stage of language at which it was impossible to talk about unobservables. Even a three-year-old child can understand a story about "people too little to see"[3] and not a single "theoretical term" occurs in this phrase.

(2) There is not even a single *term* of which it is true to say that it *could not* (without changing or extending its meaning) be used to refer to unobservables. "Red," for example, was so used by Newton when he postulated that red light consists of *red corpuscles.*[4]

In short: if an "observation term" is a term which *can,* in principle, only be used to refer to observable things, then *there are no observation terms.* If, on the other hand, it is granted that locutions consisting of just observation terms can refer to unobservables, there is no longer any reason to maintain *either* that theories and speculations about the unobservable parts of the world must contain "theoretical (= non-observation) terms" *or* that there is any general problem as to how one can introduce terms referring to unobservables. Those philosophers who find difficulty in how we understand theoretical terms should find an equal difficulty in how we understand "red" and "smaller than."

So much for the notion of an "observation term." Of course, one may recognize the point just made—that the "observation terms" also apply, in some contexts, to unobservables—and retain the class (with a suitable warning as to how the label "observational term" is to be understood). But can we agree that the complementary class—what should be called the "nonobservable terms"—is to be labelled "theoretical terms"? No, for the identification of "theoretical term" with "term (other than the 'disposition terms,' which are given a special place in Carnap's scheme) designating an unobservable quality" is unnatural and misleading. On the one hand, it is clearly an enormous (and, I believe, insufficiently motivated) extension of common usage to classify such terms as "angry," "loves," and so forth, as "theoretical terms" simply because they allegedly do not refer to public observables. A theoretical term, properly so-called, is one which comes from a scientific *theory* (and the almost untouched problem, in thirty years of writing about "theoretical terms" is what is *really* distinctive about such terms). In this sense (and I think it the sense important for discussions of science) "satellite" is, for example, a theoretical term (although the things it refers to are quite observable [5]) and "dislikes" clearly is not.

Our criticisms so far might be met by re-labelling the first dichotomy (the dichotomy of terms) "observation vs. non-observation," and suitably "hedging" the notion of "observation." But more serious difficulties are connected with the identification upon which the second dichotomy is based—the identification of "theoretical statements" with statements containing nonobservation ("theoretical" terms) and "observation statements" with "statements in the observational vocabulary."

That observation statements may contain theoretical terms is easy to establish. For example, it is easy to imagine a situation in which the following sentence might occur: "We also *observed* the creation of two electron-positron pairs."

This objection is sometimes dealt with by proposing to "relativize" the observation-theoretical dichotomy to the context. (Carnap, however, rejects this way out in the article we have been citing.) This proposal to "relativize" the dichotomy does not seem to me to be very helpful. In the first place, one can easily imagine a context in which "electron" would occur, in the same text, in *both* observational reports and in theoretical conclusions from those reports. (So that one would have distortions if one tried to put the term in either the "observational term" box or in the "theoretical term" box.) In the second place, for what philosophical problem or point does one require even the relativized dichotomy?

The usual answer is that sometimes a statement A (observational) is offered in support of a statement B (theoretical). Then, in order to explain why A is not itself questioned in the context, we need to be able to say that A is functioning, in that context, as an observation report. But this misses the point I have been making! I do not deny the need for some such notion as "observation report." What I deny is that the distinction between observation reports and, among other things, theoretical statements, can or should be drawn on the basis of vocabulary. In addition, a relativized dichotomy will not serve Carnap's purposes. One can hardly maintain that theoretical terms are only partially interpreted, whereas observation terms are completely interpreted, if no sharp line exists between the two classes. (Recall that Carnap takes his problem to be "reconstruction of the language," not of some isolated scientific context.)

NOTES

[1] Sometimes a *tripartite* division is used: observation statements, theoretical statements (containing *only* theoretical terms), and "mixed" statements (containing both kinds of terms). This refinement is not considered here, because it avoids none of the objections presented below.

[2] I neglect the possibility of trivially constructing terms that refer only to observables: namely, by conjoining "and is an observable thing" to terms that would otherwise apply to some unobservables. "Being an observable thing" is, in a sense, highly theoretical and yet applies only to observables!

[3] Von Wright has suggested (in conversation) that this is an *extended* use of language (because we first learn words like "people" in connection with people we *can* see). This argument from "the way we learn to use the word" appears to be unsound, however (cf. Fodor, 1961).

[4] Some authors (although not Carnap) explain the intelligibility of such discourse in terms of logically possible submicroscopic observers. But (a) such observers could not see single photons (or light corpuscles) even on Newton's theory; and (b) once such physically impossible (though logically possible) "observers" are introduced, why not go further and have observers with sense organs for electric charge, or the curvature of space, etc.! Presumably because *we* can see *red*, but not *charge*. But then, this just makes the point that we *understand* "red" even when applied outside our normal "range," even though we learn it ostensively, without *explaining* that fact. (The explanation lies in this: that understanding any term—even "red"—involves at least two elements: internalizing the syntax of a natural language, and acquiring a background of ideas. Overemphasis on the way "red" is *taught* has led some philosophers to misunderstand how it is *learned*.)

[5] Carnap might exclude "satellite" as an observation term, on the ground that it takes a comparatively long time to verify that something is a satellite with the naked eye, even if the satellite is close to the parent body (although this could be debated). However, "satellite" cannot be excluded on the quite different ground that many satellites are too far away to see (which is the ground that first comes to mind) since the same is true of the huge majority of all *red* things.

REFERENCES

Carnap, R. 1955. "Testability and Meaning" in H. Feigl and M. Brodbeck (eds.), *Readings in the Philosophy of Science,* Appleton-Century-Crofts. Reprinted from *Philosophy of Science 3* (1939) and *4* (1937).

Carnap, R. 1956. "The Methodological Character of Theoretical Concepts" in H. Feigl *et al.* (eds.), *Minnesota Studies in the Philosophy of Science,* Minneapolis, 1–74.

Fodor, J. A. 1961. "Of Words and Uses," *Inquiry* 4:3 (Autumn), 190–208.

F R E D E R I C K   S U P P E
WHAT'S WRONG WITH THE RECEIVED VIEW ON THE STRUCTURE OF SCIENTIFIC THEORIES?

For many years the *Received View on Scientific Theories* has been that theories are to be construed as axiomatic calculi in which theoretical terms are given a partial observational interpretation by means of correspondence rules. Underlying this analysis is a strict bifurcation of the nonlogical terms of the theory into an observational vocabulary and a theoretical vocabulary. Putnam, Achinstein, and others have urged the rejection of the Received View because (i) the notion of partial interpretation it employs cannot be given a precise formulation adequate for the purposes of the Received View, and (ii) the observational/theoretical distinction cannot be drawn satisfactorily.[1] It is my contention that the Received View is unsatisfactory and ought to have been rejected, but not for these reasons. Section I of this chapter (based on my 1971 article, "On Partial Interpretation") argues that reason (i) is false. Section II goes on to argue that it is virtually impossible to establish reason (ii). Section III attempts to show that the Received View nonetheless ought to be rejected because its reliance on the observational/theoretical distinction causes it to obscure a number of epistemologically important and revealing features of the structure of scientific theories. In the process of arguing for this latter claim, a more adequate account of the epistemological structure of scientific theories is presented—it is a version of the *Semantic Conception of Theories.*

I. ON PARTIAL INTERPRETATION

Achinstein and Putnam argue in support of reason (i) for rejecting the Received View by observing that its advocates have not made the notion of partial interpretation clear. They consider a number of possible explications of the notion, then show that they are inadequate for the purposes of the Received View (Achinstein 1968, 85–91; Putnam 1962, 244–48).

In this section I attempt to present an analysis of partial interpretation compatible with the rest of the Received View. My interests in presenting this analysis do not lie in the direction of attempting to rescue the Received View from its critics—for I am convinced that ultimately it must be rejected as unsatisfactory—but rather are grounded in the belief that a clear understanding of the notion of partial interpretation employed by the Received View will bring to light a number of important characteristics about scientific theories and scientific meaning.

A. AN EXPLICATION OF THE RECEIVED VIEW

Explication of the notion of partial interpretation requires a precise formulation of the Received View, and since Carnap and Hempel have given its most extensive and sophisticated development, their formulation will be used.[2] Since their position has undergone considerable revision over the years, and because they have published no single comprehensive account of their ultimate formulation, I have reconstructed it from their various recent writings on the subject.

The reconstruction is as follows: Scientific theories are such that they can be given a canonical reformulation which satisfies the following conditions:

(1) There is a first-order language L in terms of which the theory is formulated, and a calculus K defined in terms of L.

(2) The nonlogical or descriptive primitive constants (i.e., the "terms") of L are bifurcated into two disjoint classes:

    (A) V_O, which contains just the observation terms, and

    (B) V_T, which contains the nonobservation or theoretical terms.

    V_O must contain at least one individual constant.

(3) The language L is divided into the following sublanguages, and the calculus K is divided into the following subcalculi:

    (A) The *observation language, L_O,* is a sublanguage of L which contains no quantifiers or modalities and contains the terms of V_O, but none from V_T. The associated calculus K_O is the restriction of K to L_O and must be such that any non–V_O-terms (i.e., nonprimitive terms) in L_O are explicitly defined in K_O. Furthermore, K_O must admit of at least one finite model.

    (B) The *logically extended observation language, L'_O,* contains no V_T-terms. It may be regarded as being formed from L_O by adding the quantifiers, modalities, etc., of L to L_O. Its associated calculus, K'_O, is the restriction of K to L'_O.

    (C) The *theoretical language, L_T,* is that sublanguage of L which does not contain V_O-terms; its associated calculus, K_T, is the restriction of K to L_T.

These sublanguages together do not exhaust L, for L also contains *mixed sentences,* i.e., those in which at least one V_T- and one V_O-term occur. In addition, it is assumed that each of the sublanguages above has its own stock of predicate or functional variables and the L_O and L'_O have the same stock, which is distinct from that of L_T.

(4) L_O and its associated calculi are given a *semantic interpretation* which meets the following conditions:

    (A) The domain of interpretation consists of concrete observable entities such as observable events, things, or thing-moments; the relations and properties of the interpretation must be directly observable.

    (B) Every value of any variable in L_O must be designated by an expression in L_O.

It follows that any such interpretation of L_O and K_O, when augmented by appropriate additional rules of truth, will become an interpretation of L'_O and K'_O. We may construe interpretations of L_O and K_O as being *partial semantic interpretations of L and K,* and we require that L and K be given no empirical semantic interpretation other than that provided by such partial semantic interpretations.

(5) A *partial interpretation* of the theoretical terms and of the sentences of L containing them is provided by the following two kinds of postulates: the *theoretical postulates T* (i.e., the axioms of the theory) in which only terms of V_T occur, and the

correspondence rules or postulates C which are mixed sentences. The correspondence rules C must satisfy the following conditions:

(A) The set of rules C must be finite.

(B) The set of rules C must be logically compatible with T.

(C) C contains no extralogical term that does not belong to V_O or V_T.

(D) Each rule in C must contain at least one V_O-term and at least one V_T-term essentially or nonvacuously.[3]

Let T be the conjunction of the theoretical postulates and C be the conjunction of the correspondence rules. Then the scientific theory based on L, T, and C consists of the conjunction of T and C and is designated by 'TC'.

Note that condition (4) allows the possibility of alternative semantical systems (or interpretations) for L_O which may differ in the designata of V_O-terms. The Received View intends, however, that there be a fixed set of designata for the terms of V_O, and so restrictions must be imposed on the class of admissible interpretations. Let us assume that a fixed set of rules of designation has been specified for these V_O-terms; then let us say that the class of semantical systems that use these rules are *permissible semantical systems* for L_O, and the class of interpretations they specify are *permissible interpretations* for L_O and K_O. Notice that different permissible interpretations are possible, since the rules of designation for predicate variables may differ. The classes of permissible semantical systems and interpretations for L_O' and K_O' are defined analogously.

. . .

III. THE RECEIVED VIEW VERSUS THE SEMANTIC CONCEPTION

Our consideration of the observational/theoretical distinction makes it clear that if the distinction can be drawn in a manner satisfactory for the purposes of the Received View, things will be exceedingly complex. The fact that science manages to go about its business without involving itself in such complexities suggests that the distinction is not really required or presupposed by science, and so is extraneous to an adequate analysis of scientific theories. The question, then, is whether the observational/theoretical distinction is required for an adequate analysis of the epistemological structure of theories. More specifically, is it possible to give an analysis of the structure of theories which does not employ the observational/theoretical distinction, yet is epistemologically more revealing than the Received View? If such an analysis can be shown possible, then I think we have sufficient reason for rejecting the Received View.

Those who claim that the observational/theoretical distinction is an essential ingredient of an adequate analysis of scientific theories apparently justify their contention with the following implicit line of argument:

Scientific theories are developed to explain or predict events which can be observed: however, for reasons of simplicity, scope, and economy, such theories typically must employ theoretical entities or constructs in providing these explanations or predictions; these theoretical constructs are not directly observable. Accordingly, in any theoretical explanation or prediction one finds two sorts of sentences: (a) various premises the truth of which is nonproblematic in virtue of their being confirmed by direct observation; (b) various laws the truth of which is problematic since they cannot be confirmed by direct observation. And the observational-theoretical distinction is needed to keep distinct the different statuses of these two kinds of sentences.[18]

This picture is partially correct. Evidently it is the case that in theoretical explanation and prediction the truth of the laws used often is problematic, (especially when predictions are made in order to test the theory), whereas the truth of the evidential premises used in conjunction with the laws is assumed to be nonproblematic. Thus far the dichotomist's argument is satisfactory; but to infer from this that the premises are nonproblematic by virtue of being observational statements and that the laws are problematic by virtue of being nonobservational is unwarranted, for it amounts to assuming an additional premise in the argument—that to be nonproblematic is to be an observational statement.

Not only does this premise beg the question, it also seems false. For the purposes of explanation and prediction all that is required is that the data premises used with the theory be considered nonproblematic relative to the theory or law which provides the prediction or explanation. This is, in applying a theory (or law) to phenomena, what we do is collect data about phenomena; the process of collecting the data often involves recourse to rather sophisticated bodies of theory. If accepted standards of experimental design, control, instrumentation—and possibly involved reliability checks—are carried out, a body of "hard" data is obtained from experimentation and is taken to be relatively nonproblematic; sometimes generally accepted laws or theories are also employed in obtaining these "hard" data.[19] It is to this body of "hard" data that the theory is applied.

If the purpose of the application of a theory is explanation, then the theory explains the event under the description provided by this "hard" data by relating it to other "hard" data which function as descriptions of other features which were the cause of the event so described.[20] If the point of the application of the theory is prediction, then the initial "hard" data are used as premises from which to obtain predictions as to the "hard" data one subsequently would obtain. And these "hard" data may be quite theory-laden, hence nondirectly observable. In addition, what counts as "hard" or nonproblematic data is relative—for should the theory's predictions fail, we may come to treat the data as problematic again.[21] Thus the relevant distinction is between "hard" data and the more problematic theories, and not between the directly observable and the nondirectly observable. Accordingly, the correspondence rules for a theory should not correlate direct-observation statements with theoretical statements, but rather should correlate "hard" data with theoretical statements. Thus it seems that the observational/theoretical distinction is not essential to an adequate analysis of the structure of scientific theories.

Suggestive as this may be, this line of argument does not establish the inadequacy of the Received View. For an advocate of it could accept such an argument and still deny the conclusion, arguing as follows: "It is true that in actual scientific practice theories are pitted against 'hard' data. But what makes them 'hard' is that they ultimately rest on directly observable evidence; and in the Received View reconstruction of theories, that dependence of 'hard' data on the direct evidence of the senses is reflected in the correspondence rules. In fact, even the relativity of 'hard' data can be accommodated in terms of changes in the correspondence rules." There is little doubt that this can be built into the correspondence rules, but the relevant question is whether this can be done without obscuring important epistemological features of scientific theorizing. However, when one reflects that the theory's reliance on the results and procedures of related branches of science, the design of experiments, the interpretation of theories, calibration procedures, and so on, are all being lumped into the correspondence rules, there is reason to suspect that a number of epistemologically important and revealing aspects of scientific theorizing are being obscured.

I maintain that this is indeed so: Because of its reliance on the observational/theoretical distinction, the Received View's account of correspondence rules must combine together a number of widely disparate aspects of the scientific enterprise in such a manner as to obscure a number of epistemologically important and revealing aspects of scientific theorizing. To support this contention it will be necessary to sketch a more adequate alternative account of scientific theories, the Semantic Conception, which reveals what the Received View's treatment of correspondence rules obscures.

The notion of a *physical system* provides us with a convenient starting point for sketching and motivating this alternative account. A science does not deal with phenomena in all of their complexity; rather, it is concerned with certain kinds of phenomena only insofar as their behavior is determined by, or characteristic of, a small number of parameters abstracted from those phenomena.[22] Thus in characterizing falling bodies, classical particle mechanics is concerned with only those aspects of falling-body behavior which depend upon mass, velocity, distance traveled over time, and so on. The color of the object and such are aspects of the phenomena that are ignored; but the process of abstraction from the phenomena goes one step further: We are not concerned with, say, actual velocities, but with velocity under idealized conditions (e.g., in a frictionless environment, with the mass the object would have if it were concentrated at an extensionless point). Thus, for example, classical particle mechanics is concerned with the behavior of isolated systems of extensionless point-masses which interact in a vacuum, where the behavior of these point-masses depends only on their positions and momenta at a given time. A physical system for classical particle mechanics consists of such a system of point-masses undergoing a particular behavior over time. Physical systems, then, are highly abstract and idealized replicas of phenomena, being characterizations of how the phenomena *would have* behaved *had* the idealized conditions been met. Looking at classical particle mechanics again for an illustration, the phenomena within its scope are characterized in terms of the physical systems corresponding to the phenomena.

In arguing that scientific theories are concerned with characterizing the behavior of physical systems, and not phenomena, I may seem to be making the case too easy for myself by using the example of classical particle mechanics—which is what Quine has called a "limit myth" and thus is particularly susceptible of my treatment. However, a brief consideration of some examples will indicate that this is not so and will display the generality of my treatment.

First, consider classical thermodynamics, statistical mechanics, and quantum mechanics. These embody essentially the same "limit myth" and easily can be shown susceptible of my treatment (see Suppe 1967, ch. 3, for details). Second, observe that the gas laws (e.g., Boyle's law and Charles' law) describe the behavior of ideal gases, not real gases; yet they are used in work with actual gases. Here, the ideal gases described by the laws are the physical systems. Subject to appropriate experimental design, and so on, they correspond to actual gases as idealized replicas.

The third example, the valence theory of chemical reactions, is similar. It describes the way theoretically pure chemical substances react together. However, such pure substances are fictional ideals, and the substances in actual chemical reactions are always only approximations of them. The theory describes physical systems, which are chemical reactions theoretically pure substances undergo in this case, and with appropriate experimental and quality controls we can approximate the fiction that our actual substances are pure substances and thereby treat the actual chemical reactions (phenomena) as if they were idealized reactions between pure substances (physical systems).

The fourth example concerns the genetic theory of natural selection which characterizes evolutionary phenomena in terms of changes in the distributions of genotypes in populations as a function of reproductive rates, reproductive barriers, crossover frequencies, and so on. As such, the theory treats populations of individuals (phenomena) as if they were idealized populations of genotypes (physical systems) whose changes in genotypic distributions are functions of only a few selected factors.[23]

A fifth example is the body of stimulus-response behavioral theories which attempts to characterize various kinds of behavior as functions of selected stimulus and response parameters. Such theories describe the behavior of populations of idealized individuals whose behavior is only a function of the specified stimulus and response patterns, reinforcement schedules, and so on (physical systems). On the contrary, the behavior of individuals in actual populations of, say, rats or humans (phenomena) is not simply a function of these selected parameters, and only under the most strictly controlled laboratory conditions can this fiction be approximated. The stimulus and response theories thus describe the behavior of physical systems, not phenomena.

In addition to the above examples, one may include grammatical theories of linguistic competence, kinship system theories, theories in animal physiology, and so on, which also describe the behavior of idealized systems or mechanisms, whose actual systems or mechanisms are, to varying degrees, only idealized approximations. Although brief and sketchy, the examples suffice to illustrate the variety of theories susceptible of my treatment. Further, their variety strongly suggests that scientific theories in general describe the behavior of physical systems, which are idealized replicas of actual phenomena. . . .

In general, a scientific theory has the task of describing, predicting, and (possibly) explaining a class of phenomena. It does so by selecting and abstracting certain idealized parameters from the phenomena, then characterizing a class of abstract replicas of the phenomena which are characterized in terms of the selected idealized parameters (see note 22). These abstract replicas are physical systems. The theory thus provides a comprehensive characterization of the behavior of phenomena under the idealized conditions characteristic of the physical systems corresponding to the phenomena; typically, this characterization enables one to predict the behavior of physical systems over time.[24] When coupled with an appropriate experimental methodology, the theory can also predict or explain phenomena which do not meet these idealized conditions by displaying how these phenomena *would have* behaved *had* the idealized conditions been met.

A central task of a theory, then, is to present descriptive, predictive, and possibly explanatory accounts of the behavior of physical systems which correspond to phenomena. The theory is not concerned merely with providing such an account for just the phenomena we do in fact observe, but also with providing one for any phenomena of the sort we *might* encounter in *any* causally possible universe.[25] Further, it must provide a predictive, and possibly explanatory, characterization of all those physical systems which correspond (as abstract replicas) to phenomena of the latter sort. Let us call this class of physical systems the class of *causally possible physical systems*. A central task of any scientific theory is to provide a precise characterization of the set of causally possible physical systems for the theory.

How does the theory provide such a characterization? Once the relevant parameters for the theory have been abstracted and selected from the phenomena, the physical systems for the theory can be specified in terms of these parameters (a physical system being a possible behavior pattern specifiable in terms of these parameters). For example, in classical particle mechanics we might specify a particular state of a physical system in terms of the values of position and momentum parameters at a given time, and then characterize a physical system as a possible sequence of states over time. Of all logically possible physical systems capable of being specified in terms of the chosen parameters, only some will be empirically possible. For example, some of them will not be compatible with accepted existing bodies of theory. Of those which are, only some will be causally possible—in the sense that they correspond (as abstract idealized replicas) to phenomena which could be observed in some causally possible universe.

The theory, then, must specify which logically possible physical systems are causally possible—typically, by providing general laws which are claimed to describe the behavior patterns characteristic of just the causally possible physical systems. These laws are designed to yield predictions of subsequent system states when used together with specifications of initial states and boundary conditions. For example, in classical particle mechanics the equations of motion provide a general description of the class of causally possible physical systems. The characterization of a particular causally possible physical system can be obtained by solving the equations of motion relative to specified boundary conditions and an initial state; the solution can then be manipulated to yield predictions of subsequent system states.[26]

The account of theories just sketched seems to cohere closely with the actual formulations of many theories in the physical sciences. If it is substantially correct, then an observational/theoretical distinction is not required in an adequate analysis of the structure of scientific theories; this is so because theories are not concerned primarily with applying laws directly to phenomena, but rather with using laws to predict and explain the behavior of physical systems abstracted from phenomena in such a manner that their behavior can be correlated with phenomena. These conclusions obviously have important implications for the Received View's notion of a correspondence rule.

We now explore these implications, beginning with a look at how the "hard" data relate to physical systems and their corresponding phenomena. The observation reports or "hard" data to which the theory is applied are partial descriptions of the behavior of some physical system, the physical system being an abstract replica of the phenomena from which the data were collected. Data collection not only involves performing measurements upon the phenomena, which determine the "actual" values of the chosen parameters at different times, but it also involves employing various correction procedures (such as using friction coefficients, and the like) to alter the observed data into data representing the measurement results which *would have been* obtained *had* the defining features of the idealized parameters of the physical system been met by the phenomena.

Thus, in classical particle mechanics our data do not represent, for example, the velocity with which the milk bottle actually fell, but rather the velocity with which it *would have* fallen *had* it fallen in a vacuum, *had* it been a point-mass, and so on. That is, in a typical predictive or explanatory application of a theory, the "hard" data employed are data about the behavior of a physical system at certain times rather than about the actual behavior of the corresponding phenomena. As such, the "hard" data will be expressed in terms of the basic parameters common to the physical system and the theory—which is to say, in terms of what might be called the "theoretical" vocabulary.

Once these "hard" data are obtained, perhaps together with "hard" data about boundary conditions, and so forth, they are used in conjunction with the laws of the theory to deduce various predictions or explanations about the physical system. These deductions typically are "calculational" in nature. For example, in classical particle mechanics they might encompass solving the basic equations of motion for special case solutions, and then "plugging in" values of the parameters to calculate subsequent states of the physical system. Typically the predicted data about these subsequent states of the physical system are then converted into data about the corresponding phenomena by reversing the procedures used originally to convert the data about the phenomena to data about their corresponding physical system.

What we have here, then, is a two-stage move from raw phenomena to statements of the theory—first a move from phenomena to "hard" data about the physical system in question, and then a second move from the physical system to the postulates, and so on, of the theory.[27] The two sorts of moves are qualitatively quite different, the former being essentially empirical or experimental (being, in effect, a "translation" from the phenomena to an idealized description of it in the vocabulary of the theory's formalism), and the latter being essentially mathematical or computational in nature.

This perspective—together with the observation that theories have "hard"-data reports as their primary subject matter rather than direct-observation reports—invites reassessment of the Received View's account of the correspondence rules. For the rules of correspondence lump together the two sorts of moves just discussed so as to eliminate the physical system. It is tempting to reject the Received View's treatment of correspondence rules on the ground that most paradigmatic exact theories in physics and chemistry do work in terms of physical systems in the manner just explained, and then conclude that the Received View is inadequate since it fails to take them into account. While this is a somewhat appealing line, given the explicative character of the Received View analysis, it is not clear how far the criticism cuts. However, if important epistemological features of scientific theorizing are obscured by the failure to countenance physical systems, then it is justifiable to insist that the Received View is defective and epistemologically misleading by failing to include them.

The second-stage movement from data about the physical system to the theory (e.g., the various predictions, etc., about subsequent behavior of the physical system calculated on the basis of these data and the laws or postulates of the theory) is essentially computational in nature. If the theory is quantitative, the theory will be essentially mathematical, involving the solution of equations of motion, various auxiliary definitions and the hypotheses, and so on;[28] and at no time are counterfactual inferences involved. On the other hand, the transition from phenomena to a physical system (or vice versa) involves processes of measurement, equipment design, experimental techniques, interpretation and correction of raw data, the employment of theory from other branches of science, inter alia. And the transition from phenomena to physical system is, as I said before, fundamentally counterfactual—being a characterization of what the phenomena *would have been* under idealized circumstances.

From these characteristics it follows that the ways a transition from a physical system to theory can go wrong will be quite different from the ways that the transition from phenomena to a physical system can go wrong. And in the case of a disconfirming experiment, if the source of the difficulty can be isolated as occurring in the transition from phenomena to physical system (i.e., the data proved to be less "hard" than thought), the resolution of the disconfirmation does not require alteration of the theory. In this case, the theory was not at fault; rather, poor experimental procedure was followed (e.g., the instrumentation was miscalibrated, the wrong corrective factors were applied to the raw data, etc.). Only when the disconfirmation cannot be attributed to the transition from the phenomena to a physical system (i.e., the data are as "hard" as we had first supposed), will resolution of the defects require alteration or modification of the theory itself.[29]

It seems amply clear from these observations that there is considerable epistemic difference between the two transitions, and that attention to these differences exposes some rather characteristic features of the relations holding between theory and phenomena. The correspondence rules of the Received View obscure these differences by agglomerating all these various aspects of the relations holding between theory and phenomena into the one correspondence-rule transition. This, in particular, means that experimental errors, and so on, which result in disconfirming instances of a theory will require modification of the correspondence rules and hence of the theory itself, for the correspondence rules are part of the theory and embody a complete specification of all allowable experimental procedures. Another related problem is that the Received View's treatment of correspondence rules gives one little reason to suppose that an exhaustive explicit specification of allowable experimental procedures of the sort required can be given for most theories.[30]

It seems quite obvious, then, that the Received View's characterization of the correspondence rules gives a quite misleading account of the ways in which theories correlate with phenomena, thus obscuring a number of characteristic and important epistemic features of scientific theorizing. Using my characterization of physical systems and the two- (or more) stage transition between phenomena and theory, we obtain an epistemologically more revealing picture of scientific theorizing. Indeed, the need for an observational/theoretical dichotomy disappears, for at no point in that picture is such a dichotomy needed. Replacing it is the distinction between nonproblematic "hard" data about physical systems and boundary conditions, and so on, and the more problematic theoretically obtained assertions about these systems.[31]

And in place of the correspondence rules providing a bridge between theory and phenomena, we now have a two-stage transition: (a) the transition from phenomena to physical systems (which reduces to problems of measurement, experimental design, counterfactuals, and the like) and (b) the connection between the theory and physical systems, which are deductively determined by the (often mathematical) apparatus of the theory without requiring additional correspondence rules or postulates other than boundary conditions and data about the initial state of the physical system. The former transition is not part of the theoretical apparatus of the theory, but rather belongs to the experimental procedures used in applying the theory to phenomena; the latter transition is essentially computational in nature.

This suggested alternative account of the structure of scientific theories enables us to see another flaw in the Received View. If it is correct that the subject matter of a theory is the behavior of physical systems and that the "hard" data include experimental data about the behavior of physical systems, then the central distinction between the nonproblematic "hard" data and the more problematic theoretical assertions about physical systems cannot be drawn on the basis of language. This is because the defining parameters of the physical systems (e.g., position and momentum coordinates in classical particle mechanics) are the basic parameters of the theory, and so the same "theoretical" terms will be used to provide linguistic characterizations of both the theory and the "hard" data. That is, the relevant distinction here is not a linguistic one, but rather an epistemological one. The fact that the key distinction here is not a linguistic one indicates that a number of epistemologically revealing features of the structure of scientific theories are not reflected in their linguistic formulations, and so they cannot be characterized adequately by an analysis of the language of theories—herein lies the ultimate inadequacy of the Received View.

IV. SUMMARY AND CONCLUSION

To summarize, in section I of this chapter my primary aim has been to make the nature of partial interpretation as employed in the Received View reasonably precise for two reasons. First, I feel that this analysis can lead to a number of interesting criticisms of the Received View. In particular, it would appear that the sort of semantic interpretation provided by partial interpretation is insufficient to make Carnap's treatment of inductive logic and degree of confirmation applicable to *TC*. Second, although ultimately the Received View is unsatisfactory and must be rejected, a number of facts about the meaning of scientific terms revealed in the discussion of partial interpretation will prove useful in developing an alternative analysis to the Received View. In particular I suggest that an adequate analysis of theories in the exact or formalized sciences will have to treat the relationships between ordinary scientific language and mathematical formalism along the lines presented here, albeit in a manner that does not make recourse to an observable/theoretical distinction.

I also have tried to show that the sort of criticisms against the Received View raised by Achinstein and Putnam do not succeed in showing its inadequacy. Nonetheless, the Received View is unsatisfactory, since its reliance on the observational/theoretical distinction obscures much that is epistemologically important and revealing about how theories relate to, or connect with, phenomena. To demonstrate this, I have sketched an alternative analysis of the structure of theories and used it to show the following: how the Received View obscures the role of physical systems, the way in which extratheoretical postulates provide nonexhaustive characterizations of the admissible transitions between phenomena and physical systems, and wherein lies the role of counterfactuals in connecting theories with phenomena. These epistemic revelations do not exhaust the potential of this alternative account. To indicate just some of its potential, further development of the analysis (e.g., along the lines of Suppes 1962) will reveal much more about the experimental relations holding between phenomena and physical systems. In addition, the isolation of the counterfactual component of scientific theorizing in the transition between phenomena and physical systems provides a perspective which conceivably could advance us toward a breakthrough on the problem of laws and counterfactuals. For the exact sciences, there is ample evidence that this sort of account can be expanded and developed so as to give a particularly revealing account of exact theories (e.g., the sorts of revelations about phase spaces, the connection between deterministic and indeterministic theories, and so on, found in van Fraassen 1970; Suppe 1967, ch. 2; and parts II and III of [the present work]).

What's wrong with the Received View? It obscures much of epistemic importance other analyses can reveal. For this reason it should be rejected in favor of such an alternative analysis, which I have tried to sketch. . . .

NOTES

[1] Cf. Putnam 1962 and Achinstein 1968, 85–91, 157–58, 197–202. Achinstein's 1968 book incorporates his earlier writings on the subject with minor changes. Putnam 1962 also urges that the observational/theoretical distinction is untenable. He argues that it is misleading both to label the class of nonobservational terms "theoretical terms" and to characterize sentences formulated solely in terms of the observational vocabulary as observational sentences, and those formulated solely in terms of the theoretical vocabulary as theoretical sentences. However, while this is true, it hardly necessitates rejection of the Received View.

Although Achinstein (1968, 199–201) suggests that it would be epistemologically more revealing if we avoided reliance on an observational/theoretical distinction in our analysis of theories, this is only a corollary to his main arguments against the observational/theoretical distinction. The strength of Putnam's and Achinstein's contention that the Received View should be rejected lies in the establishment of (i) and (ii), and I shall confine my attention to those arguments.

[2] Versions of the Received View have been advanced by a number of authors, including Braithwaite (1953, 22 ff.), Campbell (1920, ch. 6), Carnap, (e.g., 1956, 43), Duhem (1954, 19), Hempel (1952, 1958), Hesse (1962, 1966), Kaplan (1964, 298–99), Margenau (1950), Nagel (1961, 90), Northrop (1947), Ramsay (1931, 212–36),

and Reichenbach (1962, ch. 8). Although a number of differences exist (some significant) between these various versions of the Received View, there is a substantial core of agreement among them.

The primary disagreements among them are about the form of the correspondence rules: Various authors refer to the rules as coordinating definitions, dictionaries, interpretative systems, operational definitions, epistemic correlations, and rules of interpretation. Campbell, Nagel, Hesse, and Kaplan maintain that (in addition to satisfying conditions [1] through [6] of my reformulation of Carnap's and Hempel's version) the theory also must possess realizable or concrete models. Kaplan deviates from the others in that he claims that the analysis only works for one type of theory. Hempel (1974) no longer adheres to the Received View and later adopted a similar position in which the observational/theoretical distinction was replaced by a different bifurcation of terms.

My discussion of the Received View and of partial interpretation will require recourse to a fair amount of symbolic logic. I assume that the reader is familiar with first-order languages, their alphabets, predicate calculi based on first-order languages, theories formulated in a first-order predicate calculus, semantic systems for languages, rules of designation, rules of truth, interpretation of first-order theories via semantic systems, true interpretations or models of first-order theories, and validity. Those readers requiring further details on these notions may skip the more technical portions of section I-B, relying on the informational summaries of their technical results. For further comprehension, one can consult Carnap 1942 and also the relevant portions of Mates 1965.

[3] This formulation of the Received View is extracted from Carnap 1956, 1959, 1963, and 1966 and Hempel 1958 and 1963. Conditions (2), (3), and (4) are more explicit in certain respects than either Carnap or Hempel specifically requires, but this is necessary if Carnap's restrictions on the sublanguages L_O and L'_O (Carnap 1956, 41–42) are to be satisfied. To meet these restrictions different additional conditions could have been imposed, but I have selected the most conservative ones. My particular choice in no way affects the analysis of partial interpretation given here.

Carnap and Hempel disagree as to the requirements to be imposed on the rules of correspondence. Hempel would replace clause (5)(d) with the following: "C contains every element V_O and V_T essentially—i.e., C is not logically equivalent to some set of sentences in which at least one term of V_O or V_T does not occur at all" (1963, 692). His version thus is more restrictive than Carnap's. Carnap also would require that the theory be cognitively significant, whereas Hempel doubts that a satisfactory criterion of cognitive significance can be given. These minor differences between Carnap's and Hempel's formulations need not concern us here.

. . .

[18] At one time proponents of the Received View also might have justified introducing the dichotomy by appealing to considerations of cognitive significance and using a thesis about language acquisition. The apparent failure of the positivistic account of cognitive significance and the falsity of the thesis about language acquisition make it both unlikely and undesirable that Received View advocates would argue it on these grounds.

[19] This discussion has benefited from my conversations with Professor Don E. Dulany. See Suppe 1974, 424–33, for Putnam's treatment of the use of such auxiliary hypotheses; see also van Fraassen 1970 for a related discussion.

[20] This rough characterization of the role of data in explanation turns on an observation—insufficiently considered in the literature on explanation—that explanations do not explain events simpliciter, but rather explain *events under a particular description*. . . . While it is beyond the scope of this [paper] to argue it, this observation apparently can be exploited to show that the alleged symmetry between explanation and prediction collapses.

[21] See the introduction to Quine 1959 for a discussion of this point.

[22] I use the term "parameter" rather than "variable" to mark the fact that the state "variables" need not be measurable on my quasi-realistic version of the Semantic Conception. This fact will be crucial in my treatment of measurement [later in the present work]. I am not using "parameter" in the statistical sense, where it means a variable set to a fixed or constant value.

[23] [Later in the present work] the applicability of the analysis of theories presented here to the genetic theory of natural selection is worked out in some detail. . . .

[24] For brevity, I confine my attention here only to theories which describe the behavior of physical systems in terms of changes in state over time. In addition to working for such theories with laws of succession, the analysis also will work for theories with laws of coexistence, laws of interaction, functional laws, and laws of quasi-succession. Also, it makes no difference whether the laws are deterministic or statistical. . . .

[25] The problems of characterizing causally possible universes are many, but they can be viewed roughly as the class of universes in which all the laws assumed nonproblematic relative to the theory in question hold. For a detailed characterization of the notion of a causally possible universe, see Burks 1977, ch. 10. My purpose in employing the notion is to use it to introduce the concept of a causally possible physical system later on. Since the rough characterization given meets the limited purposes set for it here, the difficult problem of providing an adequate characterization of causally possible universes can be avoided for the time being. I offer a detailed analysis of the notion in a book in progress, *Facts, Theories, and Scientific Observation.* . . .

[26] On this account, a theory may be construed as defining a class of theoretically possible physical systems; the theory will be empirically true just in case this class is identical with the class of causally possible physical systems. The account of empirical truth just specified is essentially a generalization of that introduced in section I of this chapter. In both cases the idea is that there exists a class of systems determined theoretically and a class determined empirically, the theory being empirically true just in case the classes are coextensive. Thus, intuitively, the class of causally possible physical systems is the class of physical systems which are empirically possible. . . .

[27] Actually this is still an oversimplification, the former move involving many more steps. . . .

[28] For an illuminating discussion of what is involved in this sort of move, see Putnam's discussion in Suppe, 1974, 424–33.

[29] For a detailed discussion of this point, see Suppe 1967, ch. 3.

[30] For a more detailed discussion of this last point, see Kuhn 1974, where he discusses the role of exemplars in the application of theories to phenomena; see also my commentary (1974a) on Kuhn 1974.

[31] Hempel now rejects the Received View, and in his 1969, 1970, and 1974 works he advances an analysis based on a distinction similar to this. He distinguishes between a *theoretical vocabulary* and *an antecedently available vocabulary,* where the latter may include theoretical terms from generally accepted theories. His proposal differs from mine in that he thinks the relevant distinction can be drawn on linguistic grounds, whereas I explicitly deny that it can. His analysis differs in other respects as well—especially on the nature of the transition between the "hard" data and the theory (his so-called *bridge principles*).

The "hard" data notion proves to be an overly simple heuristic notion. . . .

REFERENCES

Unpublished manuscripts not in press cited in the reading endnotes usually have not been included in the references.

Achinstein, P. 1968. *Concepts of Science.* Baltimore: Johns Hopkins University Press.

Braithwaite, R. B. 1953. *Scientific Explanation.* New York: Harper Torchbooks.

Burks, A. W. 1977. *Chance, Cause, Reason.* Chicago: University of Chicago Press.

Campbell, N. R. 1920. *Physics: The Elements.* Cambridge: Cambridge University Press. Republished as *Foundations of Science.* New York: Dover, 1957.

Carnap, R. 1942. *Introduction to Semantics.* Cambridge, Mass.: Harvard University Press.

———. 1956. The Methodological Character of Theoretical Concepts. In Feigl and Scriven 1956, 33–76.

———. 1959. Beobachtungssprache und theoretische Sprache. In *Logic: Studia Paul Bernays Dedicata,* vol. 34 of Bibliothèque Scientifique, 32–44. Neuchâtel: Editiones du Griffon.

———. 1963. Carl G. Hempel on Scientific Theories. In Schlipp 1963, 958–66.

———. 1966. *Philosophical Foundation of Physics.* New York: Basic Books.

Duhem, P. 1954. *The Aim and Structure of Physical Theory.* New York: Atheneum. Originally published in French in 1906.

Feigl, H., and M. Scriven, eds. 1958. *Minnesota Studies in the Philosophy of Science.* Vol. I. Minneapolis: University of Minnesota Press.

Feigl, H., M. Scriven, and G. Maxwell, eds. 1958. *Minnesota Studies in the Philosophy of Science.* Vol. II. Minneapolis: University of Minnesota Press.

Hempel, C. 1952. *Fundamentals of Concept Formation in Empirical Science.* Chicago: University of Chicago Press.

————. 1958. The Theoretician's Dilemma: Studies in the Logic of Theory Construction. In Feigl, Scriven, and Maxwell 1958, 37–98. Reprinted in Hempel 1965, 173–226.

————. 1963. Implications of Carnap's Work for the Philosophy of Science. In Schlipp 1963, 685–709.

————. 1969. On the Structure of Scientific Theories. In the *Isenberg Memorial Lecture Series, 1965–1966,* 11–39. East Lansing: Michigan State University Press.

————. 1970. On the "Standard Conception" of Scientific Theories. In Radner and Winokur 1970, 142–63.

Hesse, M. 1962. *Forces and Fields.* New York: Philosophical Library.

————. 1966. *Models and Analogies in Science.* Notre Dame, Ind.: University of Notre Dame Press.

Kaplan, A. 1964. *The Conduct of Inquiry.* San Francisco: Chandler Publications.

Kuhn, T. S. 1974. Second Thoughts on Paradigms. In Suppe 1974, 459–82.

Margenau, H. 1950. *The Nature of Physical Reality.* New York: McGraw-Hill.

Mates, B. 1965. *Elementary Logic.* New York: Oxford University Press.

Nagel, E. 1961. *The Structure of Science.* New York: Harcourt Brace.

Nagel, E., P. Suppes, and A. Tarski, eds. 1962. *Logic, Methodology and the Philosophy of Science: Proceedings of the 1960 International Congress.* Stanford: Stanford University Press.

Northrop, F. S. C. 1947. *The Logic of the Sciences and the Humanities.* New York: Macmillan.

Putnam, H. 1962. What Theories Are Not. In Nagel, Suppes, and Tarski 1962, 240–51.

Quine, W. V. O. 1959. *Methods of Logic.* Rev. ed. New York: Holt, Rinehart, and Winston.

Radner, M., and S. Winokur, eds. 1970. *Minnesota Studies in the Philosophy of Science.* Vol. IV. Minneapolis: University of Minnesota Press.

Ramsey, F. P. 1931. *The Foundations of Mathematics and Other Logical Essays.* London: Kegan Paul; New York: Harcourt Brace.

Reichenbach, H. 1962. *Rise of Scientific Philosophy.* Berkeley: University of California Press.

Schlipp, P., ed. 1963. *The Philosophy of Rudolf Carnap.* LaSalle, Ill.: Open Court Publishing Co.

Suppe, F. 1967. The Meaning and Use of Models in Mathematics and the Exact Sciences. Ph.D. dissertation, University of Michigan.

————. 1971. On Partial Interpretation. *Journal of Philosophy* 68:57–76.

————. 1973. Facts and Empirical Truth. *Canadian Journal of Philosophy* 3:197–212.

————. 1974. *The Structure of Scientific Theories.* Urbana: University of Illinois Press.

————. 1974a. Exemplars, Theories and Disciplinary Matrixes. In Suppe 1974, 483–99.

Suppes, P. 1962. Models of Data. In Nagel, Suppes, and Tarski 1962, 252–61.

van Fraassen, B. 1970. On the Extension of Beth's Semantics of Physical Theories. *Philosophy of Science* 37:325–39.

STUDY QUESTIONS FOR TOPIC I

1. In past centuries scholars argued that a theory can be demonstrated to be true entirely from the use of rational thought, and that the scientific method is grounded on pure reason without any need for experimental tests. But what exactly is wrong with such a methodology for the goal of demonstrating the truth of a theory about the world?

2. Imagine that at one moment you are the only person watching a squirrel resting under a tree, less than ten yards from the location of your observation. The next moment you close your eyes, seeing and hearing nothing. Based on Hume's theory of observation, is it possible to have genuine knowledge of the squirrel's presence under the tree during the time when you have no direct means of detecting the squirrel?

3. According to Carnap, when a theory is subjected to experimental tests, contradictory evidence leads to the conclusive refutation of a theory, but supporting evidence can never lead to the conclusive verification of the theory. Why is refutation conclusive, but confirmation only probable?

4. Does Popper agree with Hume's critique of induction?

5. Kepler's first law of planetary motion is as follows: Every planet orbits the sun in an elliptical path. In addition to planets in our solar system, this law correctly describes the path of many asteroids and comets. Based on Popper's conception of rational science, do we have any rational grounds to believe that this law is true?

6. Our use of a modern technology rests on our rational expectation that the technology will probably, but not necessarily, function as expected. For example, when we board an aircraft, we expect that the aircraft will transport its passengers, assuming of course no mechanical malfunction, pilot error, and so on. Based on Popper's principles for scientific inquiry, (a) is such an expectation about the future operation of the aircraft rational and (b) can Popper adequately explain the use of science in the design of a new technology?

7. Popper argues that any statement about the world must be falsifiable, which means that there must be some *possible event* in nature that would render the statement false. Which of the following statement(s), if any, is falsifiable in this sense? Defend your answer.

   (A) There is a 5% chance that snow will be falling on your house tomorrow at 2:00 P.M.
   (B) There is a 95% chance that snow will be falling on your house tomorrow at 2:00 P.M.
   (C) There is a 100% chance that snow will be falling on your house tomorrow at 2:00 P.M.

8. Hanson argues that all observation reports reflect some theoretical influences. Does this influence mean that all observation reports are completely biased, and therefore useless as a means to test a theory?

9. What exactly is Putnam's objection to the apparent distinction between observation statements and theoretical statements?

10. What reasons does Suppe give for rejecting the "Received View" conception of a theory?

11. What is Suppe's notion of a physical system? Why are physical systems so important for science in his view?

12. In his conception of a theory does Suppe resort to a distinction between an observation term and a nonobservation term?

BIBLIOGRAPHY

Ackermann, R. *Data, Instruments, and Theory.* Princeton: Princeton University Press, 1985.

Achinstein, P. *Concepts of Science.* Baltimore: Johns Hopkins UP, 1968.

Bogen, J., and J. Woodward. "Saving the Phenomena." *The Philosophical Review* 97 (1988): 303–52.

Churchland, P. M. *Scientific Realism and the Plasticity of Mind.* Cambridge: Cambridge UP, 1979.

Dretske, F. *Knowledge and the Flow of Information.* Cambridge: MIT Press, 1981.

Feyerabend, P. *Against Method.* London: Verso Press, 1978.

Franklin, A. *The Neglect of Experiment.* Cambridge: Cambridge UP, 1986.

Glymour, C. *Theory and Evidence.* Princeton: Princeton UP, 1980

Gooding, D., T. Pinch, S. Schaffer, eds. *The Uses of Experiment.* Cambridge: Cambridge UP, 1989.

Goodman, N. *Fact, Fiction, and Forecast.* Cambridge: Harvard UP, 1955.

Grandy, R., ed. *Theories and Observation in Science.* Englewood Cliffs: Prentice-Hall, 1973.

Hacking, I. "Do We See Through a Microscope?" *Images of Science: Essays on Realism and Empiricism with a Reply from Bas C. van Fraassen.* Ed. P. M. Churchland and C. W. Hooker. Chicago: U Chicago P, 1985.

Hanson, N. R. *Observation and Explanation: A Guide to Philosophy of Science.* New York: Harper & Row, 1971.

Harré, R. *The Philosophies of Science.* Oxford: Oxford UP, 1972, chaps 2 and 3.

———. *Great Scientific Experiments.* Oxford: Oxford UP, 1981.

Hempel, C. "The Test of a Hypothesis: Its Logic and Its Force." *Philosophy of Natural Science.* Englewood Cliffs: Prentice-Hall, 1966, chap 3.

Hesse, M. *The Structure of Scientific Inference.* Berkeley: U California P, 1974.

Pickering, A. "Living in the Material World: On Realism and Experimental Practice." *The Uses of Experiment.* Ed. Gooding, Pinch, and Schaffer. Cambridge: Cambridge UP, 1989.

Popper, K. *The Logic of Scientific Discovery.* New York: Basic Books, 1959.

———. *Conjectures and Refutations: The Growth of Scientific Knowledge.* London: Routledge & Kegan Paul, 1963.

———. Objective Knowledge: An Evolutionary Approach. Oxford: Clarendon P, 1972.

Putnam, H. "The 'Corroboration' of Theories." *The Philosophy of Karl Popper,* Book I. Ed. P. Schlipp. LaSalle: Open Court, 1971, pp. 221–40.

Reichenbach, H. *Experience and Prediction: An Analysis of the Foundations and the Structure of Knowledge.* Chicago: U Chicago P, 1939.

Rothbart, D. "Popper Against Inductivism." *Dialectica: International Review of Philosophy of Knowledge* 34 (1980): 121–27.

Rothbart, D., and S. Slayden. "The Epistemology of a Spectrometer," *Philosophy of Science* 61: (1994): 25–38.

Scheffler, I. *Science and Subjectivity.* Indianapolis: Bobbs-Merrill, 1967.

Shapere, D. "The Concept of Observation in Science and Philosophy." *Philosophy of Science* 49 (1982): 485–525.

TOPIC II

RIVAL CONCEPTIONS OF SCIENTIFIC EXPLANATION

INTRODUCTION

On January 17, 1994, at 4:31 A.M., a severe earthquake struck the Los Angeles area, causing water lines to burst, gas lines to rupture, and elevated highways to collapse. Thousands of buildings were destroyed and dozens of people were killed. Geologists immediately located the epicenter at a point under a shallow crust in the San Fernando Valley; the intensity was measured as 6.6 on the Richter scale. Why did this event occur? Geologists are continually faced with such questions in their attempts to explain natural disasters.

The search for explanations is not simply a useful by-product of doing science, but a major goal of scientific inquiry—one of its defining missions. The success of a theory is measured, in part, by its capacity to explain known events. Scientists are routinely asked to explain earthquakes, hurricanes, evolutionary patterns of a species, and illnesses, to give a few examples.

The topic of scientific explanation has provoked intense debate among philosophers. They address the following question: What are the defining elements that constitute a genuine explanation in science? Notice at the outset that an explanation must provide information about the event in question, information that augments such specific details as that the event occurred in a certain place, at a certain time. For example, the explanation of the earthquake in the San Fernando Valley must be more than simply a statement that the earthquake occurred at 4:31 A.M., January 17, 1994, and so on. What exactly might this information be?

A major point of contention in this philosophical debate centers on the goal of an explanation. Some philosophers believe that every explanation must show that the explained event fits perfectly into a general pattern of events, so that the event would have been expected to occur based on such a pattern. Once we apply our knowledge of the general pattern of events to the specific circumstances under investigation, we should not be surprised that the explained event occurred. Of course, a vital element of this proposal is knowledge of the general patterns of events. Such patterns are conveyed through laws of nature. For example, geologists explain why the 1994 earthquake struck Los Angeles by applying the relevant laws of geophysics to the specific circumstances of this event. As long as geologists have enough detailed information about the situation at hand, and as long as the relevant laws of geophysics are valid, the geologists could show that the particular earthquake conforms to the general pattern of earthquakes, as understood by the best scientific principles.

This conception can be called the explanation-as-argument conception, because all the vital information of an explanation can be conveyed by an argument. An argument is a sequence of statements in which one or more statement(s) are used to demonstrate (presumably) the truth of another statement. So, every argument must have at least one premise and exactly one conclusion. For example, how should we explain the occurrence of an eclipse of the moon? We must show that the eclipse would be expected to occur based on the application of relevant laws of astronomy and geometry to the positions of the sun, earth, and moon. We should be able to express all of this information in the form of a single argument.

But many critics object that the explanation-as-argument conception is much too restrictive to account for all genuine explanations in science. While some explanations can be conveyed by arguments, others cannot. The goal of an explanation is not always to show how an event being explained fits a general pattern of nature. We need an explanation to show how the event in question was caused by some underlying processes of nature. This view is called the causal conception of explanation, because an explanation is intended to provide information about the causal processes for the production of the event in question. Such processes are typically unseen mechanisms, such as unobservable forces, which generate observable events. What are the causal processes underlying the occurrence of the 1994 earthquake in Los Angeles? According to plate tectonic theory, the earth's surface consists of slowly moving plates, constantly changing the configuration of the continents and oceans. As the pressure between the plates builds, a sudden "jolting" movement of the plates occurs, generating earthquakes on the surface. So, the movement of tectonic plates comprises part of the physical process under the earth's crust, causing earthquakes. Advocates of the causal conception of explanation propose that the goal of an explanation is not always fulfilled by an argument.

In response to the causal conception, advocates of explanation-as-argument conception do not object necessarily to the value of revealing the causal mechanism for the production of the explained event. In fact, some arguments from an explanation provide information about the causal factors which generated the event. But such information is neither the defining goal nor the primary purpose of explanations, according to these advocates. Again, every explanation is intended to show that the event in question fits a general pattern of events, known to scientists as laws of nature.

SUMMARY OF READINGS

A well-known advocate of the explanation-as-argument view is Carl Hempel (selection #8). He believes that every explanation must show how a known event conforms to a specific universal pattern of events. This goal of an explanation can be fulfilled by something called an explanatory argument pattern. This argument pattern must include three types of statements: First, one statement in the argument pattern must describe the event being explained. This statement is identified as E in figure 1 below. Second, the argument pattern must include statements of the relevant laws of nature, indicated in figure 1 by $L_1, L_2, \ldots, L_n$. The precise definition of a law of nature is quite controversial, but at least we can say that a law is a statement describing a general pattern of events. (Hempel addresses this question in the reading.) Third, certain descriptive statements are needed to apply these laws to the particular topic of interest. These statements are depicted as $C_1, C_2, \ldots, C_k$ in figure 1. So, every explanation is associated with the following argument structure:

FIGURE 1

Statements expressing laws of nature: $L_1, L_2, \ldots, L_n$ (Premises)

Statements applying the laws to specific circumstances: $C_1, C_2, \ldots, C_k$ (Premises)

———

Statement describing the explained event: E (Conclusion)

For example, how should we explain why a reddish-brown haze covers a particular city during a sunny afternoon at a particular time? Following the covering law model, we need a statement E describing the exact place and time when this occurs. We need to show how this event fits the general patterns from laws of biochemistry, environmental science, and physics. Briefly, the relevant laws provide information about a chemical reaction between the oxygen of the natural environment and a by-product of fossil fuels that are burned for the purpose of generating energy. After fossil fuels are burned, nitrogen is released, producing a nitrogen dioxide gas. If this gas is enhanced by the ultraviolet light of the sun, a reddish-brown gas results, commonly known as smog. In principle, the explanation must include statements depicting a universal pattern of events, conveyed by laws of nature, $L_1, L_2, \ldots, L_n$ above, and statements applying these laws to the specific circumstance under examination, $C_1, C_2, \ldots, C_k$ above.

Hempel then claims that the argument pattern underlying each explanation has the same structure as the argument pattern underlying a prediction. The only difference is that in an explanation the event in question is known to have already occurred while in a prediction the event in question has not yet occurred. So, every prediction assumes that the predicted event is subsumed under the generalizing pattern of certain laws of nature, familiar to scientists at a given time.

But can the covering law model satisfactorily account for all explanations in every scientific context? Michael Scriven strongly objects to the explanation-as-argument view in general, and to Hempel's covering law model of explanation in particular. The wide range of explanations in science cannot all be reduced to the covering law model, according to Scriven (selection #9). The covering law model incorrectly presupposes that much more information is provided by an explanation than is provided by a description of the event in question. But many descriptions convey as much information as an explanation, according to Scriven. For example, a full description of the Los Angeles earthquake of 1994 may be just as informative as the (covering law) explanation: both description and explanation show how the earthquake centered in the San Fernando Valley over a fault line between two tectonic plates, and so on. Moreover, Hempel is wrong to claim that explanations and predictions convey the same logical structure, expressed by an argument pattern. Many genuine predictions in science lack the kind of argument pattern suggested by the covering law model of explanation, since a prediction needs nothing more than a bare description of some (possible) future event.

Nancy Cartwright takes a different line of attack against the covering law model (selection #10). Although scientists try to unify our knowledge of events by discovering universal laws of nature, they are continually blocked by the tremendous diversity of patterns found in nature. In many contexts, laws of universal generality are simply unavailable to scientists, who must then resort to laws that hold only in special circumstances. Events can be explained by appeal to laws of limited generality, applicable under special circumstances. Thus, Cartwright concludes that Hempel's covering law model is too demanding for many genuine explanations.

From another perspective, Philip Kitcher rejects the covering law model on the grounds that the tremendous diversity of explanations across all disciplines cannot be captured by a few argument patterns (selection #11). He believes that each scientific theory comes equipped with its own ingredients for an explanatory argument pattern. Rather than reduce all explanations to a few argument patterns, as Hempel proposes, the structure of an explanation will differ from one theory to another. This difference depends on the specific doctrines of the theory in question. For example, an eclipse of the moon can be explained by the laws of Newtonian physics. But these laws do not work well for explaining large-scale events, such as the transmission of light from distant stars. Such cosmic events require the use of Einsteinian general relativity theory. According to Kitcher, the argument pattern underlying the explanation of a lunar eclipse would be quite different from the argument pattern underlying the transmission of light from a distant star. The reason for this difference centers on the use of different theories, each of which is linked to a particular type of argument pattern.

But why must the information conveyed by an explanation be expressible in an argument form at all? Wesley Salmon challenges the explanation-as-argument conception on the grounds that many genuine explanations are not arguments (selection #12). Salmon is a well-known advocate of the causal conception of explanation. Under the causal conception, the primary goal of an explanation is to show how the event in question was generated by some underlying causal process of nature. Every scientific explanation provides knowledge of such a process. Again, why did the Los Angeles earthquake occur? The explanation for this event is given by information about the pressure between tectonic plates, the release of such pressure, and the resulting movement on the earth's surface. Such information need not be conveyed by an argument.

How exactly are such causal factors formulated in a complete explanation? To answer this, we must examine certain analogical relationships between the subject matter under investigation and a physical system that is already familiar to scientists, according to Rom Harré (selection #13). To explain how an event came into being, we must draw on the categories, relations, and causal processes embedded in analogous explanations from another subject of scientific study. For example, throughout the history of science color has been explained as the physical effects of wavelengths of light. The very notion of a wavelength and associated properties were drawn by analogy from wavelike properties of water. Through such analogical relations, scientists can construct the conceptual apparatus that is needed to explain how the event was causally generated.

Harré's conception of explanation rests on articulating the analogical relations between different physical systems. But what exactly is an analogical relation? As Mary Hesse argues (selection #14), two physical systems are analogous to one another if they exhibit known similarities (positive analogies), known differences (negative analogies), and unknown relations (neutral analogies). A neutral analogy arises when scientists lack sufficient information to determine whether or not a given property is shared by both systems. Nevertheless, the neutral analogies can provide clues to some previously unresolved controversy. Certain causal properties from a known physical system may be projected as a reasonable guess to another system in ways that overcome an obstacle to scientific progress. Such a project may assist scientists in formulating plausible models for explaining the occurrence of phenomena, according to Hesse.

CARL G. HEMPEL
LAWS AND THEIR ROLE IN SCIENTIFIC EXPLANATION

TWO BASIC REQUIREMENTS
FOR SCIENTIFIC EXPLANATIONS

To explain the phenomena of the physical world is one of the primary objectives of the natural sciences. Indeed, almost all of the scientific investigations that served as illustrations [earlier] were aimed not at ascertaining some particular fact but at achieving some explanatory insight; they were concerned with questions such as how puerperal fever is contracted, why the water-lifting capacity of pumps has its characteristic limitation, why the transmission of light conforms to the laws of geometrical optics, and so forth. In this chapter and the next one, we will examine in some detail the character of scientific explanations and the kind of insight they afford.

That man has long and persistently been concerned to achieve some understanding of the enormously diverse, often perplexing, and sometimes threatening occurrences in the world around him is shown by the manifold myths and metaphors he has devised in an effort to account for the very existence of the world and of himself, for life and death, for the motions of the heavenly bodies, for the regular sequence of day and night, for the changing seasons, for thunder and lightning, sunshine and rain. Some of these explanatory ideas are based on anthropomorphic conceptions of the forces of nature, others invoke hidden powers or agents, still others refer to God's inscrutable plans or to fate.

Accounts of this kind undeniably may give the questioner a sense of having attained some understanding; they may resolve his perplexity and in this sense "answer" his question. But however satisfactory these answers may be psychologically, they are not adequate for the purposes of science, which, after all, is concerned to develop a conception of the world that has a clear, logical bearing on our experience and is thus capable of objective test. Scientific explanations must, for this reason, meet two systematic requirements, which will be called the requirement of explanatory relevance and the requirement of testability.

The astronomer Francesco Sizi offered the following argument to show why, contrary to what his contemporary, Galileo, claimed to have seen through his telescope, there could be no satellites circling around Jupiter:

> There are seven windows in the head, two nostrils, two ears, two eyes and a mouth; so in the heavens there are two favorable stars, two unpropitious, two luminaries, and Mercury alone undecided and indifferent. From which and many other similar phenomena of nature such as the seven metals, etc., which it were tedious to enumerate, we gather that the number of planets is necessarily seven. . . . Moreover, the satellites are invisible to the naked eye and therefore can have no influence on the earth and therefore would be useless and therefore do not exist.[1]

The crucial defect of this argument is evident: the "facts" it adduces, even if accepted without question, are entirely irrelevant to the point at issue; they do not afford the slightest reason for the assumption that Jupiter has no satellites; the claim of relevance suggested by the barrage of words like 'therefore,' 'it follows,' and 'necessarily' is entirely spurious.

Consider by contrast the physical explanation of a rainbow. It shows that the phenomenon comes about as a result of the reflection and refraction of the white light of the sun in spherical droplets of water such as those that occur in a cloud. By reference to the relevant optical laws, this account shows that the appearance of a rainbow is to be expected whenever a spray or mist of water droplets is illuminated by a strong white light behind the observer. Thus, even if we happened never to have seen a rainbow, the explanatory information provided by the physical account would constitute good grounds for expecting or believing that a rainbow will appear under the specified circumstances. We will refer to this characteristic by saying that the physical explanation meets the *requirement of explanatory relevance:* the explanatory information adduced affords good grounds for believing that the phenomenon to be explained did, or does, indeed occur. This condition must be met if we are to be entitled to say: "That explains it—the phenomenon in question was indeed to be expected under the circumstances!"

The requirement represents a necessary condition for an adequate explanation, but not a sufficient one. For example, a large body of data showing a red-shift in the spectra of distant galaxies provides strong grounds for believing *that* those galaxies recede from our local one at enormous speeds, yet it does not explain *why*.

To introduce the second basic requirement for scientific explanations, let us consider once more the conception of gravitational attraction as manifesting a natural tendency akin to love. As we noted earlier, this conception has no test implications whatever. Hence, no empirical finding could possibly bear it out or disconfirm it. Being thus devoid of empirical content, the conception surely affords no grounds for expecting the characteristic phenomena of gravitational attraction: it lacks objective explanatory power. Similar comments apply to explanations in terms of an inscrutable fate: to invoke such an idea is not to achieve an especially profound insight, but to give up the attempt at explanation altogether. By contrast, the statements on which the physical explanation of a rainbow is based do have various test implications; these concern, for example, the conditions under which a rainbow will be seen in the sky, and the order of the colors in it; the appearance of rainbow phenomena in the spray of a wave breaking on the rocks and in the midst of a lawn sprinkler; and so forth. These examples illustrate a second condition for scientific explanations, which we will call the *requirement of testability:* the statements constituting a scientific explanation must be capable of empirical test.

It has already been suggested that since the conception of gravitation in terms of an underlying universal affinity has no test implications, it can have no explanatory power: it cannot provide grounds for expecting that universal gravitation will occur, nor that gravitational attraction will show such and such characteristic features; for if it did imply such consequences either deductively or even in a weaker, inductive-probabilistic sense, then it would be testable by reference to those consequences. As this example shows, the two requirements just considered are interrelated: a proposed explanation that meets the requirement of relevance also meets the requirement of testability. (The converse clearly does not hold.)

Now let us see what forms scientific explanations take, and how they meet the two basic requirements.

DEDUCTIVE-NOMOLOGICAL EXPLANATION

Consider once more Périer's finding in the Puy-de-Dôme experiment, that the length of the mercury column in a Torricelli barometer decreased with increasing altitude. Torricelli's and Pascal's ideas on atmospheric pressure provided an explanation for this phenomenon; somewhat pedantically, it can be spelled out as follows:

(A) At any location, the pressure that the mercury column in the closed branch of the Torricelli apparatus exerts upon the mercury below equals the pressure exerted on the surface of the mercury in the open vessel by the column of air above it.

(B) The pressures exerted by the columns of mercury and of air are proportional to their weights; and the shorter the columns, the smaller their weights.

(C) As Périer carried the apparatus to the top of the mountain, the column of air above the open vessel became steadily shorter.

(D) (Therefore), the mercury column in the closed vessel grew steadily shorter during the ascent.

Thus formulated, the explanation is an argument to the effect that the phenomenon to be explained, as described by the sentence (d), is just what is to be expected in view of the explanatory facts cited in (a), (b), and (c); and that, indeed, (d) follows deductively from the explanatory statements. The latter are of two kinds: (a) and (b) have the character of general laws expressing uniform empirical connections; whereas (c) describes certain particular facts. Thus, the shortening of the mercury column is here explained by showing that it occurred in accordance with certain laws of nature, as a result of certain particular circumstances. The explanation fits the phenomenon to be explained into a pattern of uniformities and shows that its occurrence was to be expected, given the specified laws and the pertinent particular circumstances.

The phenomenon to be accounted for by an explanation will henceforth also be referred to as the *explanandum phenomenon;* the sentence describing it, as the *explanandum sentence.* When the context shows which is meant, either of them will simply be called the explanandum. The sentences specifying the explanatory information—(a), (b), and (c) in our example—will be called the *explanans sentences;* jointly they will be said to form the *explanans.*

As a second example, consider the explanation of a characteristic of image formation by reflection in a spherical mirror; namely, that generally $1/u + 1/v = 2/r$, where u and v are the distances of object-point and image-point from the mirror, and r is the mirror's radius of curvature. In geometrical optics, this uniformity is explained with the help of the basic law of reflection in a plane mirror, by treating the reflection of a beam of light at any one point of a spherical mirror as a case of reflection in a plane tangential to the spherical surface. The resulting explanation can be formulated as a deductive argument whose conclusion is the explanandum sentence, and whose premises include the basic laws of reflection and of rectilinear propagation, as well as the statement that the surface of the mirror forms a segment of a sphere.[2]

A similar argument, whose premises again include the law for reflection in a plane mirror, offers an explanation of why the light of a small light source placed at the focus of a paraboloidal mirror is reflected in a beam parallel to the axis of the paraboloid (a principle technologically applied in the construction of automobile headlights, searchlights, and other devices).

The explanations just considered may be conceived, then, as deductive arguments whose conclusion is the explanandum sentence, E, and whose premiss-set, the explanans, consists of general laws, $L_1, L_2, \ldots, L_r$ and of other statements, $C_1, C_2, \ldots, C_k$, which make assertions about particular facts. The form of such arguments, which thus constitute one type of scientific explanation, can be represented by the following schema:

$$\left.\begin{array}{c} L_1, L_2, \ldots, L_r \\[4pt] C_1, C_2, \ldots, C_k \end{array}\right\} \text{Explanans sentences}$$

D-N]

$$E \qquad \text{Explanandum sentence}$$

Explanatory accounts of this kind will be called explanations by deductive subsumption under general laws, or *deductive-nomological explanations*. (The root of the term "nomological" is the Greek word "nomos," for law.) The laws invoked in a scientific explanation will also be called *covering laws* for the explanandum phenomenon, and the explanatory argument will be said to subsume the explanandum under those laws.

The explanandum phenomenon in a deductive-nomological explanation may be an event occurring at a particular place and time, such as the outcome of Périer's experiment. Or it may be some regularity found in nature, such as certain characteristics generally displayed by rainbows; or a uniformity expressed by an empirical law such as Galileo's or Kepler's laws. Deductive explanations of such uniformities will then invoke laws of broader scope, such as the laws of reflection and refraction, or Newton's laws of motion and of gravitation. As this use of Newton's laws illustrates, empirical laws are often explained by means of theoretical principles that refer to structures and processes underlying the uniformities in question. We will return to such explanations in the next chapter.

Deductive-nomological explanations satisfy the requirement of explanatory relevance in the strongest possible sense: the explanatory information they provide implies the explanandum sentence deductively and thus offers logically conclusive grounds why the explanandum phenomenon is to be expected. (We will soon encounter other scientific explanations, which fulfill the requirement only in a weaker, inductive, sense.) And the testability requirement is met as well, since the explanans implies among other things that under the specified conditions, the explanandum phenomenon occurs.

Some scientific explanations conform to the pattern (D-N) quite closely. This is so, particularly, when certain quantitative features of a phenomenon are explained by mathematical derivation from covering general laws, as in the case of reflection in spherical and paraboloidal mirrors. Or take the celebrated explanation, propounded by Leverrier (and independently by Adams), of peculiar irregularities in the motion of the planet Uranus, which on the current Newtonian theory could not be accounted for by the gravitational attraction of the other planets then known. Leverrier conjectured that they resulted from the gravitational pull of an as yet undetected outer planet, and he computed the position, mass, and other characteristics which that planet would have to possess to account in quantitative detail for the observed irregularities. His explanation was strikingly confirmed by the discovery, at the predicted location, of a new planet, Neptune, which had the quantitative characteristics attributed to it by Leverrier. Here again, the explanation has the character of a deductive argument whose premisses include general laws—specifically, Newton's laws of gravitation and of motion—as well as statements specifying various quantitative particulars about the disturbing planet.

Not infrequently, however, deductive-nomological explanations are stated in an elliptical form: they omit mention of certain assumptions that are presupposed by the explanations but are simply taken for granted in the given context. Such explanations are sometimes expressed in the form 'E because C,' where E is the event to be explained and C is some antecedent or concomitant event or state of affairs. Take, for example, the statement: "The slush on the sidewalk remained liquid during the frost because it had been sprinkled with salt." This explanation does not explicitly mention any laws, but it tacitly presupposes at least one: that the freezing point of water is lowered whenever salt is dissolved in it. Indeed, it is precisely by virtue of this law that the sprinkling of salt acquires the explanatory, and specifically causative, role that the elliptical because-statement ascribes to it. That statement, incidentally, is elliptical also in other respects; for example, it tacitly takes for granted, and leaves unmentioned, certain assumptions about the prevailing physical conditions, such as the temperature's not dropping to a very low point. And if nomic and other assumptions thus omitted are added to the statement that salt had been sprinkled on the slush, we obtain the premisses for a deductive-nomological explanation of the fact that the slush remained liquid.

Similar comments apply to Semmelweis's explanation that childbed fever was caused by decomposed animal matter introduced into the bloodstream through open wound surfaces. Thus formulated, the explanation makes no mention of general laws; but it presupposes that such contamination of the bloodstream generally leads to blood poisoning attended by the characteristic symptoms of childbed fever, for this is implied by the assertion that the contamination *causes* puerperal fever. The generalization was no doubt taken for granted by Semmelweis, to whom the cause of Kolletschka's fatal illness presented no etiological problem: given that infectious matter was introduced into the bloodstream, blood poisoning would result. (Kolletschka was by no means the first one to die of blood poisoning resulting from a cut with an infected scalpel. And by a tragic irony, Semmelweis himself was to suffer the same fate.) But once the tacit premiss is made explicit, the explanation is seen to involve reference to general laws.

As the preceding examples illustrate, corresponding general laws are always presupposed by an explanatory statement to the effect that a particular event of a certain kind G (e.g., expansion of a gas under constant pressure; flow of a current in a wire loop) was *caused* by an event of another kind, F (e.g., heating of the gas; motion of the loop across a magnetic field). To see this, we need not enter into the complex ramifications of the notion of cause; it suffices to note that the general maxim "Same cause, same effect," when applied to such explanatory statements, yields the implied claim that whenever an event of kind F occurs, it is accompanied by an event of kind G.

To say that an explanation rests on general laws is not to say that its discovery required the discovery of the laws. The crucial new insight achieved by an explanation will sometimes lie in the discovery of some particular fact (e.g., the presence of an undetected outer planet; infectious matter adhering to the hands of examining physicians) which, by virtue of antecedently accepted general laws, accounts for the explanandum phenomenon. In other cases, such as that of the lines in the hydrogen spectrum, the explanatory achievement does lie in the discovery of a covering law (Balmer's) and eventually of an explanatory theory (such as Bohr's); in yet other cases, the major accomplishment of an explanation may lie in showing that, and exactly how, the explanandum phenomenon can be accounted for by reference to laws and data about particular facts that are already available: this is illustrated by the explanatory derivation of the reflection laws for spherical and paraboloidal mirrors from the basic law of geometrical optics in conjunction with statements about the geometrical characteristics of the mirrors.

An explanatory problem does not by itself determine what kind of discovery is required for its solution. Thus, Leverrier discovered deviations from the theoretically expected course also in the motion of the planet Mercury; and as in the case of Uranus, he tried to explain these as resulting from the gravitational pull of an as yet undetected planet, Vulcan, which would have to be a very dense and very small object between the sun and Mercury. But no such planet was found, and a satisfactory explanation was provided only much later by the general theory of relativity, which accounted for the irregularities not by reference to some disturbing particular factor, but by means of a new system of laws.

UNIVERSAL LAWS AND ACCIDENTAL GENERALIZATIONS

As we have seen, laws play an essential role in deductive-nomological explanations. They provide the link by reason of which particular circumstances (described by $C_1, C_2, \ldots, C_k$) can serve to explain the occurrence of a given event. And when the explanandum is not a particular event, but a uniformity such as those represented by characteristics mentioned earlier of spherical and paraboloidal mirrors, the explanatory laws exhibit a system of more comprehensive uniformities, of which the given one is but a special case.

The laws required for deductive-nomological explanations share a basic characteristic: they are, as we shall say, statements of universal form. Broadly speaking, a statement of this kind asserts a uniform connection between different empirical phenomena or between different aspects of an empirical phenomenon. It is a statement to the effect that whenever and wherever conditions of a specified kind F occur, then so will, always and without exception, certain conditions of another kind, G. (Not all scientific laws are of this type. In the sections that follow, we will encounter laws of probabilistic form, and explanations based on them.)

Here are some examples of statements of universal form: whenever the temperature of a gas increases while its pressure remains constant, its volume increases; whenever a solid is dissolved in a liquid, the boiling point of the liquid is raised; whenever a ray of light is reflected at a plane surface, the angle of reflection equals the angle of incidence; whenever a magnetic iron rod is broken in two, the pieces are magnets again; whenever a body falls freely from rest in a vacuum near the surface of the earth, the distance it covers in t seconds is $16t^2$ feet. Most of the laws of the natural sciences are quantitative: they assert specific mathematical connections between different quantitative characteristics of physical systems (e.g., between volume, temperature, and pressure of a gas) or of processes (e.g., between time and distance in free fall in Galileo's law; between the period of revolution of a planet and its mean distance from the sun, in Kepler's third law; between the angles of incidence and refraction in Snell's law).

Strictly speaking, a statement asserting some uniform connection will be considered a law only if there are reasons to assume it is true: we would not normally speak of false laws of nature. But if this requirement were rigidly observed, then the statements commonly referred to as Galileo's and Kepler's laws would not qualify as laws; for according to current physical knowledge, they hold only approximately; and as we shall see later, physical theory explains why this is so. Analogous remarks apply to the laws of geometrical optics. For example, even in a homogeneous medium, light does not move strictly in straight lines: it can bend around corners. We shall therefore use the word "law" somewhat liberally, applying the term also to certain statements of the kind here referred to, which, on theoretical grounds, are known to hold only approximately and with certain qualifications. We shall return to this point when, in the next chapter, we consider the explanation of laws by theories.

We saw that the laws invoked in deductive-nomological explanations have the basic form: "In all cases when conditions of kind F are realized, conditions of kind G are realized as well." But, interestingly, not all statements of this universal form, even if true, can qualify as laws of nature. For example, the sentence "All rocks in this box contain iron" is of universal form (F is the condition of being a rock in the box, G that of containing iron); yet even if true, it would not be regarded as a law, but as an assertion of something that "happens to be the case," as an "accidental generalization." Or consider the statement: "All bodies consisting of pure gold have a mass of less than 100,000 kilograms." No doubt all bodies of gold ever examined by man conform to it; thus, there is considerable confirmatory evidence for it and no disconfirming instances are known. Indeed, it is quite possible that never in the history of the universe has there been or will there be a body of pure gold with a mass of 100,000 kilograms or more. In this case, the proposed generalization would not only be well confirmed, but true. And yet, we would presumably regard its truth as accidental, on the ground that nothing in the basic laws of nature as conceived in contemporary science precludes the possibility of there being—or even the possibility of our producing—a solid gold object with a mass exceeding 100,000 kilograms.

Thus, a scientific law cannot be adequately defined as a true statement of universal form: this characterization expresses a necessary, but not a sufficient, condition for laws of the kind here under discussion.

What distinguishes genuine laws from accidental generalizations? This intriguing problem has been intensively discussed in recent years. Let us look briefly at some of the principal ideas that have emerged from the debate, which is still continuing.

One telling and suggestive difference, noted by Nelson Goodman,[3] is this: a law can, whereas an accidental generalization cannot, serve to support *counterfactual conditionals,* i.e., statements of the form "If A were (had been) the case, then B would be (would have been) the case," where in fact A is not (has not been) the case. Thus, the assertion "If this paraffin candle had been put into a kettle of boiling water, it would have melted" could be supported by adducing the law that paraffin is liquid above 60 degrees centigrade (and the fact that the boiling point of water is 100 degrees centigrade). But the statement "All rocks in this box contain iron" could not be used similarly to support the counterfactual statement "If this pebble had been put into the box, it would contain iron." Similarly, a law, in contrast to an accidentally true generalization, can support *subjunctive conditionals,* i.e., sentences of the type "If *A* should come to pass, then so would *B*," where it is left open whether or not *A* will in fact come to pass. The statement "If this paraffin candle should be put into boiling water then it would melt" is an example.

Closely related to this difference is another one, which is of special interest to us: a law can, whereas an accidental generalization cannot, serve as a basis for an explanation. Thus, the melting of a particular paraffin candle that was put into boiling water can be explained, in conformity with the schema (D-N), by reference to the particular facts just mentioned and to the law that paraffin melts when its temperature is raised above 60 degrees centigrade. But the fact that a particular rock in the box contains iron cannot be analogously explained by reference to the general statement that all rocks in the box contain iron.

It might seem plausible to say, by way of a further distinction, that the latter statement simply serves as a conveniently brief formulation of a finite conjunction of this kind: "Rock r_1 contains iron, and rock r_2 contains iron, . . . , and rock r_{63} contains iron"; whereas the generalization about paraffin refers to a potentially infinite set of particular cases and therefore cannot be paraphrased by a finite conjunction of statements describing individual instances. This distinction is suggestive, but it is overstated. For to begin with, the generalization "All rocks in this box contain iron" does not in fact tell us how many rocks there are in the box, nor does it name any particular rocks r_1, r_2, etc. Hence, the general sentence is not logically equivalent to a finite conjunction of the kind just mentioned. To formulate a suitable conjunction, we need additional information, which might be obtained by counting and labeling the rocks in the box. Besides, our generalization "All bodies of pure gold have a mass of less than 100,000 kilograms" would not count as a law even if there were infinitely many bodies of gold in the world. Thus, the criterion we have under consideration fails on several grounds.

Finally, let us note that a statement of universal form may qualify as a law even if it actually has no instances whatever. As an example, consider the sentence: "On any celestial body that has the same radius as the earth but twice its mass, free fall from rest conforms to the formula $s = 32t^2$." There might well be no celestial object in the entire universe that has the specified size and mass, and yet the statement has the character of a law. For it (or rather, a close approximation of it, as in the case of Galileo's law) follows from the Newtonian theory of gravitation and of motion in conjunction with the statement that the acceleration of free fall on the earth is 32 feet per second per second; thus, it has strong theoretical support, just like our earlier law for free fall on the moon.

A law, we noted, can support subjunctive and counterfactual conditional statements about potential instances, i.e., about particular cases that might occur, or that might have occurred but did not. In similar fashion, Newton's theory supports our general statement in a subjunctive version that suggests its lawlike status, namely: "On any celestial body that there may be which has the same size as the earth but twice its mass, free fall would conform to the formula $s = 32t^2$." By contrast, the generalization about the rocks cannot be paraphrased as asserting that any rock that might be in this box would contain iron, nor of course would this latter claim have any theoretical support.

Similarly, we would not use our generalization about the mass of gold bodies—let us call it H—to support statements such as this: "Two bodies of pure gold whose individual masses add up to more than 100,000 kilograms cannot be fused to form one body; or if fusion should be possible, then the mass of the resulting body will be less than 100,000 kg," for the basic physical and chemical theories of matter that are currently accepted do not preclude the kind of fusion here considered, and they do not imply that there would be a mass loss of the sort here referred to. Hence, even if the generalization H should be true, i.e., if no exceptions to it should ever occur, this would constitute a mere accident or coincidence as judged by current theory, which permits the occurrence of exceptions to H.

Thus, whether a statement of universal form counts as a law will depend in part upon the scientific theories accepted at the time. This is not to say that "empirical generalizations"— statements of universal form that are empirically well confirmed but have no basis in theory— never qualify as laws: Galileo's, Kepler's, and Boyle's laws, for example, were accepted as such before they received theoretical grounding. The relevance of theory is rather this: a statement of universal form, whether empirically confirmed or as yet untested, will qualify as a law if it is implied by an accepted theory (statements of this kind are often referred to as theoretical laws); but even if it is empirically well confirmed and presumably true in fact, it will not qualify as a law if it rules out certain hypothetical occurrences (such as the fusion of two gold bodies with a resulting mass of more than 100,000 kilograms, in the case of our generalization H) which an accepted theory qualifies as possible.[4]

PROBABILISTIC EXPLANATION: FUNDAMENTALS

Not all scientific explanations are based on laws of strictly universal form. Thus, little Jim's getting the measles might be explained by saying that he caught the disease from his brother, who had a bad case of the measles some days earlier. This account again links the explanandum event to an earlier occurrence, Jim's exposure to the measles; the latter is said to provide an explanation because there is a connection between exposure to the measles and contracting the disease. That connection cannot be expressed by a law of universal form, however; for not every case of exposure to the measles produces contagion. What can be claimed is only that persons exposed to the measles will contract the disease with high probability, i.e., in a high percentage of all cases. General statements of this type, which we shall soon examine more closely, will be called *laws of probabilistic form* or *probabilistic laws,* for short.

In our illustration, then, the explanans consists of the probabilistic law just mentioned and the statement that Jim was exposed to the measles. In contrast to the case of deductive-nomological explanation, these explanans statements do not deductively imply the explanandum statement that Jim got the measles; for in deductive inferences from true premisses, the conclusion is invariably true, whereas in our example, it is clearly possible that the explanans statement might be true and yet the explanandum statement false. We will say, for short, that the explanans implies the explanandum, not with "deductive certainty," but only with near-certainty or with high probability.

The resulting explanatory argument may be schematized as follows . . .

The probability for persons exposed to the measles
to catch the disease is high.

Jim was exposed to the measles.
————————————————— [makes highly probable]
Jim caught the measles.

In the customary presentation of a deductive argument, which was used, for example, in the schema (D-N) above, the conclusion is separated from the premises by a single line, which serves to indicate that the premises logically imply the conclusion. The double line used in our latest schema is meant to indicate analogously that the "premises" (the explanans) make the "conclusion" (the explanandum sentence) more or less probable; the degree of probability is suggested by the notation in brackets.

Arguments of this kind will be called *probabilistic explanations.* As our discussion shows, a probabilistic explanation of a particular event shares certain basic characteristics with the corresponding deductive-nomological type of explanation. In both cases, the given event is explained by reference to others, with which the explanandum event is connected by laws. But in one case, the laws are of universal form; in the other, of probabilistic form. And while a deductive explanation shows that, on the information contained in the explanans, the explanandum was to be expected with "deductive certainty," an inductive explanation shows only that, on the information contained in the explanans, the explanandum was to be expected with high probability, and perhaps with "practical certainty"; it is in this manner that the latter argument meets the requirement of explanatory relevance.

STATISTICAL PROBABILITIES AND PROBABILISTIC LAWS

We must now consider more closely the two differentiating features of probabilistic explanation that have just been noted: the probabilistic laws they invoke and the peculiar kind of probabilistic implication that connects the explanans with the explanandum.

Suppose that from an urn containing many balls of the same size and mass, but not necessarily of the same color, successive drawings are made. At each drawing, one ball is removed, and its color is noted. Then the ball is returned to the urn, whose contents are thoroughly mixed before the next drawing takes place. This is an example of a so-called random process or random experiment, a concept that will soon be characterized in more detail. Let us refer to the procedure just described as experiment *U,* to each drawing as one performance of *U,* and to the color of the ball produced by a given drawing as the result, or the outcome, of that performance.

If all the balls in an urn are white, then a statement of strictly universal form holds true of the results produced by the performance of *U:* every drawing from the urn yields a white ball, or yields the result *W*, for short. If only some of the balls—say, 600 of them—are white, whereas the others—say 400—are red, then a general statement of probabilistic form holds true of the experiment: the probability for a performance of *U* to produce a white ball, or outcome *W*, is .6; in symbols:

5a] $P(W,U) = .6$

Similarly, the probability of obtaining heads as a result of the random experiment *C* of flipping a fair coin is given by

5b] $P(H,C) = .5$

and the probability of obtaining an ace as a result of the random experiment *D* of rolling a regular die is

5c] $P(A,D) = 1/6$

What do such probability statements mean? According to one familiar view, sometimes called the "classical" conception of probability, the statement (5a) would have to be interpreted as follows: each performance of the experiment *U* effects a choice of one from among 1,000 basic possibilities, or basic alternatives, each represented by one of the balls in the urn; of these possible choices, 600 are "favorable" to the outcome *W;* and the probability of drawing a white ball is simply the ratio of the number of favorable choices available to the number of all possible choices, i.e., 600/1,000. The classical interpretation of the probability statements (5b) and (5c) follows similar lines.

Yet this characterization is inadequate; for if before each drawing, the 400 red balls in the urn were placed on top of the white ones, then in this new kind of urn experiment—let us call it *U'*—the ratio of favorable to possible basic alternatives would remain the same, but the probability of drawing a white ball would be smaller than in the experiment *U*, in which the balls are thoroughly mixed before each drawing. The classical conception takes account of this difficulty by requiring that the basic alternatives referred to in its definition of probability must be "equipossible" or "equiprobable"—a requirement presumably violated in the case of experiment *U'*.

This added proviso raises the question of how to define equipossibility or equiprobability. We will pass over this notoriously troublesome and controversial issue, because—even assuming that equiprobability can be satisfactorily characterized—the classical conception would still be inadequate, since probabilities are assigned also to the outcomes of random experiments for which no plausible way is known of marking off equiprobable basic alternatives. Thus, for the random experiment *D* of rolling a regular die, the six faces might be regarded as representing such equiprobable alternatives; but we attribute probabilities to such results as rolling an ace, or an odd number of points, etc., also in the case of a loaded die, even though no equiprobable basic outcomes can be marked off here.

Similarly—and this is particularly important—science assigns probabilities to the outcomes of certain random experiments or random processes encountered in nature, such as the step-by-step decay of the atoms of radioactive substances, or the transition of atoms from one energy state to another. Here again, we find no equiprobable basic alternatives in terms of which such probabilities might be classically defined and computed.

To arrive at a more satisfactory construal of our probability statements, let us consider how one would ascertain the probability of the rolling of an ace with a given die that is not known to be regular. This would obviously be done by making a large number of throws with the die and ascertaining the *relative frequency,* i.e., the proportion, of those cases in which an ace turns up. If, for example, the experiment D' of rolling the given die is performed 300 times and an ace turns up in 62 cases, then the relative frequency, 62/300, would be regarded as an approximate value of the probability $p(A,D')$ of rolling an ace with the given die. Analogous procedures would be used to estimate the probabilities associated with the flipping of a given coin, the spinning of a roulette wheel, and so on. Similarly, the probabilities associated with radioactive decay, with the transitions between different atomic energy states, with genetic processes, etc., are determined by ascertaining the corresponding relative frequencies; however, this is often done in highly indirect ways rather than by simply counting individual atomic or other events of the relevant kinds.

The interpretation in terms of relative frequencies applies also to probability statements such as (5b) and (5c), which concern the results of flipping a fair (i.e., homogeneous and strictly cylindrical) coin or tossing a regular (homogeneous and strictly cubical) die: what the scientist (or the gambler, for that matter) is concerned with in making a probability statement is the relative frequency with which a certain outcome O can be expected in long series of repetitions of some random experiment R. The counting of "equiprobable" basic alternatives and of those among them which are "favorable" to O may be regarded as a heuristic device for guessing at the relative frequency of O. And indeed when a regular die or a fair coin is tossed a large number of times, the different faces tend to come up with equal frequency. One might expect this on the basis of symmetry considerations of the kind frequently used in forming physical hypotheses, for our empirical knowledge affords no grounds on which to expect any of the faces to be favored over any other. But while such considerations often are heuristically useful, they must not be regarded as certain or as self-evident truths: some very plausible symmetry assumptions, such as the principle of parity, have been found not to be generally satisfied at the subatomic level. Assumptions about equiprobabilities are therefore always subject to correction in the light of empirical data concerning the actual relative frequencies of the phenomena in question. This point is illustrated also by the statistical theories of gases developed by Bose and Einstein and by Fermi and Dirac, respectively, which rest on different assumptions concerning what distributions of particles over a phase space are equiprobable.

The probabilities specified in the probabilistic laws, then, represent relative frequencies. They cannot, however, be strictly defined as relative frequencies in long series of repetitions of the relevant random experiment. For the proportion, say, of aces obtained in throwing a given die will change, if perhaps only slightly, as the series of throws is extended; and even in two series of exactly the same length, the number of aces will usually differ. We do find, however, that as the number of throws increases, the relative frequency of each of the different outcomes tends to change less and less, even though the results of successive throws continue to vary in an irregular and practically unpredictable fashion. This is what generally characterizes a random experiment R with outcomes $O_1, O_2, \ldots O_n$: successive performance of R yield one or another of those outcomes in an irregular manner; but the relative frequencies of the outcomes tend to become stable as the number of performances increases. And the probabilities of the outcomes, $p(O_1,R)$, $p(O_2,R)$, $\ldots$, $p(O_n,R)$, may be regarded as ideal values that the actual frequencies tend to assume as they become increasingly stable. For mathematical convenience, the probabilities are sometimes defined as the mathematical *limits* toward which the relative frequencies converge as the number of performances increases indefinitely. But this definition has certain conceptual shortcomings, and in some more recent mathematical studies of the subject, the intended empirical meaning of the concept of probability is deliberately, and for good reasons, characterized more vaguely by means of the following so-called *statistical interpretation of probability:*[5]

The statement

$$p(O,R) = r$$

means that in a long series of performances of random experiment R, the proportion of cases with outcome O is almost certain to be close to r.

The concept of *statistical probability* thus characterized must be carefully distinguished from the concept of *inductive or logical probability,* which we considered in section 4.5. Logical probability is a quantitative logical relation between definite *statements;* the sentence

$$c(H,K) = r$$

asserts that the hypothesis H is supported, or made probable, to degree r by the evidence formulated in statement K. Statistical probability is a quantitative relation between repeatable *kinds of events:* a certain kind of outcome, O, and a certain kind of random process, R; it represents, roughly speaking, the relative frequency with which the result O tends to occur in a long series of performances of R.

What the two concepts have in common are their mathematical characteristics: both satisfy the basic principles of mathematical probability theory:

a]   The possible numerical values of both probabilities range from 0 to 1:

$$0 \leqslant p(O,R) \leqslant 1$$

$$0 \leqslant c(H,K) \leqslant 1$$

b]   The probability for one of two mutually exclusive outcomes of R to occur is the sum of the probabilities of the outcomes taken separately; the probability, on any evidence K, for one or the other of two mutually exclusive hypotheses to hold is the sum of their respective probabilities:

If O_1, O_2 are mutually exclusive, then
$$p(O_1 \text{ or } O_2,R) = p(O_1,R) + p(O_2,R)$$

If H_1, H_2 are logically exclusive hypotheses, then
$$c(H_1 \text{ or } H_2,K) = c(H_1,K) + c(H_2,K)$$

c]   The probability of an outcome that necessarily occurs in all cases—such as *O* or not *O*—is 1; the probability, on any evidence, of a hypothesis that is logically (and in this sense necessarily) true, such as *H* or not *H,* is 1:

$$p(O \text{ or not } O,R) = 1$$

$$c(H \text{ or not } H,K) = 1$$

Scientific hypotheses in the form of statistical probability statements can be, and are, tested by examining the long-run relative frequencies of the outcomes concerned; and the confirmation of such hypotheses is then judged, broadly speaking, in terms of the closeness of the agreement between hypothetical probabilities and observed frequencies. The logic of such tests, however, presents some intriguing special problems, which call for at least brief examination.

Consider the hypothesis, *H,* that the probability of rolling an ace with a certain die is .15; or briefly, that $p(A,D) = .15$, where *D* is the random experiment of rolling the given die. The hypothesis *H* does not deductively imply any test implications specifying how many aces will occur in a finite series of throws of the die. It does not imply, for example, that exactly 75 among the first 500 throws will yield an ace, nor even that the number of aces will lie between 50 and 100, say. Hence, if the proportion of aces actually obtained in a large number of throws differs considerably from .15, this does not refute *H* in the sense in which a hypothesis of strictly universal form, such as "All swans are white," can be refuted, in virtue of the *modus tollens* argument, by reference to one counter-instance, such as a black swan. Similarly, if a long run of throws of the given die yields a proportion of aces very close to .15, this does not confirm *H* in the sense in which a hypothesis is confirmed by the finding that a test sentence *I* that it logically implies is in fact true. For in this latter case, the hypothesis asserts *I* by logical implication, and the test result is thus confirmatory in the sense of showing that a certain part of what the hypothesis asserts is indeed true; but nothing strictly analogous is shown for *H* by confirmatory frequency data; for *H* does *not* assert by implication that the frequency of aces in some long run will definitely be very close to .15.

But while *H* does not logically preclude the possibility that the proportion of aces obtained in a long series of throws of the given die may depart widely from .15, it does logically imply that such departures are highly improbable in the statistical sense; i.e., that if the experiment of performing a long series of throws (say, 1,000 of them per series) is repeated a large number of times, then only a tiny proportion of those long series will yield a proportion of aces that differs considerably from .15. For the case of rolling a die, it is usually assumed that the results of successive throws are "statistically independent"; this means roughly that the probability of obtaining an ace in a throw of the die does not depend on the result of the preceding throw. Mathematical analysis shows that in conjunction with this independence assumption, our hypothesis *H* deductively determines the statistical probability for the proportion of aces obtained in *n* throws to differ from .15 by no more than a specified amount. For example, *H* implies that for a series of 1,000 throws of the die here considered, the probability is about .976 that the proportion of aces will lie between .125 and .175; and similarly, that for a run of

10,000 throws the probability is about .995 that the proportion of aces will be between .14 and .16. Thus, we may say that if H is true, then it is practically certain that in a long trial run the observed proportion of aces will differ by very little from the hypothetical probability value .15. Hence, if the observed long-run frequency of an outcome is not close to the probability assigned to it by a given probabilistic hypothesis, then that hypothesis is very likely to be false. In this case, the frequency data count as disconfirming the hypothesis, or as reducing its credibility; and if sufficiently strong disconfirming evidence is found, the hypothesis will be considered as practically, though not logically, refuted and will accordingly be rejected. Similarly, close agreement between hypothetical probabilities and observed frequencies will tend to confirm a probabilistic hypothesis and may lead to its acceptance.

If probabilistic hypotheses are to be accepted or rejected on the basis of statistical evidence concerning observed frequencies, then appropriate standards are called for. These will have to determine (*a*) what deviations of observed frequencies from the probability stated by a hypothesis are to count as grounds for rejecting the hypothesis, and (*b*) how close an agreement between observed frequencies and hypothetical probability is to be required as a condition for accepting the hypothesis. The requirements in question can be made more or less strict, and their specification is a matter of choice. The stringency of the chosen standards will normally vary with the context and the objectives of the research in question. Broadly speaking, it will depend on the importance that is attached, in the given context, to avoiding two kinds of error that might be made: rejecting the hypothesis under test although it is true, and accepting it although it is false. The importance of this point is particularly clear when acceptance or rejection of the hypothesis is to serve as a basis for practical action. Thus, if the hypothesis concerns the probable effectiveness and safety of a new vaccine, then the decision about its acceptance will have to take into account not only how well the statistical test results accord with the probabilities specified by the hypothesis, but also how serious would be the consequences of accepting the hypothesis and acting on it (e.g. by inoculating children with the vaccine) when in fact it is false, and of rejecting the hypothesis and acting accordingly (e.g. by destroying the vaccine and modifying or discontinuing the process of manufacture) when in fact the hypothesis is true. The complex problems that arise in this context form the subject matter of the theory of statistical tests and decisions, which has been developed in recent decades on the basis of the mathematical theory of probability and statistics.[6]

Many important laws and theoretical principles in the natural sciences are of probabilistic character, though they are often of more complicated form than the simple probability statements we have discussed. For example, according to current physical theory, radioactive decay is a random phenomenon in which the atoms of each radioactive element possess a characteristic probability of disintegrating during a specified period of time. The corresponding probabilistic laws are usually formulated as statements giving the "half-life" of the element concerned. Thus, the statements that the half-life of radium[226] is 1,620 years and that of polonium[218] is 3.05 minutes are laws to the effect that the probability for a radium[226] atom to decay within 1,620 years, and for an atom of polonium[218] to decay within 3.05 minutes, are both one-half. According to the statistical interpretation cited earlier these laws imply that of a large number of radium[226] atoms or of polonium[218] atoms given at a certain time, very close to one-half will still exist 1,620 years, or 3.05 minutes, later; the others having disintegrated by radio-active decay.

Again, in the kinetic theory various uniformities in the behavior of gases, including the laws of classical thermodynamics, are explained by means of certain assumptions about the constituent molecules; and some of these are probabilistic hypotheses concerning statistical regularities in the motions and collisions of those molecules.

A few additional remarks concerning the notion of a probabilistic law are indicated. It might seem that all scientific laws should be qualified as probabilistic since the supporting evidence we have for them is always a finite and logically inconclusive body of findings, which can confer upon them only a more or less high probability. But this argument misses the point that the distinction between laws of universal form and laws of probabilistic form does not refer to the strength of the evidential support for the two kinds of statements, but to their form, which reflects the logical character of the claim they make. A law of universal form is basically a statement to the effect that in *all* cases where conditions of kind F are realized, conditions of kind G are realized as well; a law of probabilistic form asserts, basically, that under certain conditions, constituting the performance of a random experiment R, a certain kind of outcome will occur in a specified percentage of cases. No matter whether true or false, well supported or poorly supported, these two types of claims are of a logically different character, and it is on this difference that our distinction is based.

As we saw earlier, a law of the universal form "Whenever F then G" is by no means a brief, telescoped equivalent of a report stating for each occurrence of F so far examined that it was associated with an occurrence of G. Rather, it implies assertions also for all unexamined cases of F, past as well as present and future; also, it implies counterfactual and hypothetical conditionals which concern, so to speak "possible occurrences" of F: and it is just this characteristic that gives such laws their explanatory power. Laws of probabilistic form have an analogous status. The law stating that the radioactive decay of radium[226] is a random process with an associated half-life of 1,620 years is plainly not tantamount to a report about decay rates that have been observed in certain samples of radium[226]. It concerns the decaying process of any body of radium[226]—past, present, or future; and it implies subjunctive and counterfactual conditionals, such as: if two particular lumps of radium[226] were to be combined into one, the decay rates would remain the same as if the lumps had remained separate. Again, it is this characteristic that gives probabilistic laws their predictive and their explanatory force.

THE INDUCTIVE CHARACTER OF PROBABILISTIC EXPLANATION

One of the simplest kinds of probabilistic explanation is illustrated by our earlier example of Jim's catching the measles. The general form of that explanatory argument may be stated thus:

$p(O,R)$ is close to 1

i is a case of R

————————————— [makes highly probable]

i is a case of O

Now the high probability which, as indicated in brackets, the explanans confers upon the explanandum is surely not a statistical probability, for it characterizes a relation between sentences, not between (kinds of) events. Using a term introduced earlier, we might say that the probability in question represents the rational credibility of the explanandum, given the information provided by the explanans; and as we noted earlier, in so far as this notion can be construed as a probability, it represents a logical or inductive probability.

In some simple cases, there is a natural and obvious way of expressing that probability in numerical terms. In an argument of the kind just considered, if the numerical value of $p(O,R)$ is specified, then it is reasonable to say that the inductive probability that the explanans confers upon the explanandum has the same numerical value. The resulting probabilistic explanation has the form:

$$p(O,R) = r$$
$$i \text{ is a case of } R$$
$$\overline{\phantom{i \text{ is a case of } R}} \quad [r]$$
$$i \text{ is a case of } O$$

If the explanans is more complex, the determination of corresponding inductive probabilities for the explanandum raises difficult problems, which in part are still unsettled. But whether or not it is possible to assign definite numerical probabilities to all such explanations, the preceding considerations show that when an event is explained by reference to probabilistic laws, the explanans confers upon the explanandum only more or less strong inductive support. Thus, we may distinguish deductive-nomological from probabilistic explanations by saying that the former effect a deductive subsumption under laws of universal form, the latter an inductive subsumption under laws of probabilistic form.

It is sometimes said that precisely because of its inductive character, a probabilistic account does not explain the occurrence of an event, since the explanans does not logically preclude its nonoccurrence. But the important, steadily expanding role that probabilistic laws and theories play in science and its applications, makes it preferable to view accounts based on such principles as affording explanations as well, though of a less stringent kind than those of deductive-nomological form. Take, for example, the radioactive decay of a sample of one milligram of polonium[218]. Suppose that what is left of this initial amount after 3.05 minutes is found to have a mass that falls within the interval from .499 to .501 milligrams. This finding can be explained by the probabilistic law of decay for polonium[218]; for that law, in combination with the principles of mathematical probability, deductively implies that given the huge number of atoms in a milligram of polonium[218], the probability of the specified outcome is overwhelmingly large, so that in a particular case its occurrence may be expected with "practical certainty."

Or consider the explanation offered by the kinetic theory of gases for an empirically established generalization called Graham's law of diffusion. The law states that at fixed temperature and pressure, the rates at which different gases in a container escape, or diffuse, through a thin porous wall are inversely proportional to the square roots of their molecular weights; so that the amount of a gas that diffuses through the wall per second will be the greater, the lighter its molecules. The explanation rests on the consideration that the mass of a given gas that diffuses through the wall per second will be proportional to the average velocity of its molecules, and that Graham's law will therefore have been explained if it can be shown that the average molecular velocities of different pure gases are inversely proportional to the square roots of their molecular weights. To show this, the theory makes certain assumptions broadly to the effect that a gas consists of a very large number of molecules moving in random fashion at different speeds that frequently change as a result of collisions, and that this random behavior shows certain probabilistic uniformities—in particular, that among the molecules of a given gas at specified temperature and pressure, different velocities will occur with definite, and different, probabilities. These assumptions make it possible to compute the probabilistically expected values—or, as we might briefly say, the "most probable" values—that the average velocities of different gases will possess at equal temperatures and pressures. These most probable average values, the theory shows, are indeed inversely proportional to the square roots of the molecular weights of the gases. But the actual diffusion rates, which are measured experimentally and are the subject of Graham's law, will depend on the actual values that the average velocities have in the large but finite swarms of molecules constituting the given bodies of gas. And the actual average values are related to the corresponding probabilistically estimated, or "most probable," values in a manner that is basically analogous to the relation between the proportion of aces occurring in a large but finite series of tossings of a given die and the corresponding probability of rolling an ace with that die. From the theoretically derived conclusion concerning the probabilistic estimates, it follows only that in view of the very large number of molecules involved, it is overwhelmingly *probable* that at any given time the actual average speeds will have values very close to their probability estimates and that, therefore, it is *practically certain* that they will be, like the latter, inversely proportional to the square roots of their molecular masses, thus satisfying Graham's law.[7]

It seems reasonable to say that this account affords an explanation, even though "only" with very high associated probability, of why gases display the uniformity expressed by Graham's law; and in physical texts and treatises, theoretical accounts of this probabilistic kind are indeed very widely referred to as explanations.

NOTES

[1] From Holton and Roller, *Foundations of Modern Physical Science,* p. 160.
[2] The derivation of the laws of reflection for the curved surfaces referred to in this example and in the next one is simply and lucidly set forth in Chap. 17 of Morris Kline, *Mathematics and the Physical World* (New York: Thomas Y. Crowell Company, 1959).
[3] In his essay, "The Problem of Counterfactual Conditionals," reprinted as the first chapter of his book, *Fact, Fiction, and Forecast,* 2nd ed. (Indianapolis: The Bobbs-Merrill Co., Inc., 1965). This work raises fascinating basic problems concerning laws, counterfactual statements, and inductive reasoning, and examines them from an advanced analytic point of view.
[4] For a fuller analysis of the concept of law, and for further bibliographic references, see E. Nagel, *The Structure of Science* (New York: Harcourt, Brace & World, Inc., 1961), Chap. 4.
[5] Further details on the concept of statistical probability and on the limit-definition and its shortcomings will be found in E. Nagel's monograph, *Principles of the Theory of Probability* (Chicago: University of Chicago Press, 1939). Our version of the statistical interpretation follows that given by H. Cramér on pp. 148–49 of his book, *Mathematical Methods of Statistics* (Princeton: Princeton University Press, 1946).

[6] On this subject, see R. D. Luce and H. Raiffa, *Games and Decisions* (New York: John Wiley & Sons, Inc., 1957).

[7] The "average" velocities here referred to are technically defined as root-mean-square velocities. Their values do not differ very much from those of average velocities in the usual sense of the arithmetic mean. A succinct outline of the theoretical explanation of Graham's law can be found in Chap. 25 of Holton and Roller, *Foundations of Modern Physical Science*. The distinction, not explicitly mentioned in that presentation, between the average value of a quantity for some finite number of cases and the probabilistically estimated or expected value of that quantity is briefly discussed in Chap. 6 (especially section 4) of R. P. Feynman, R. B. Leighton, and M. Sands, *The Feynman Lectures on Physics* (Reading, Mass.: Addison-Wesley Publishing Co., 1963).

MICHAEL SCRIVEN
EXPLANATIONS, PREDICTIONS, AND LAWS

1. PREFACE

There are two distinct kinds of problem encountered by the logician in studying the physical sciences. In certain areas of theoretical physics the current problems *for the physicist* are of an essentially logical kind, so that the logician's technical skills are immediately relevant. The contribution he makes, if successful, is to the solution of the exact difficulty the physicist faces. To do this he requires considerable ability in both fields; and when successful he earns a double accolade. There is another kind of problem, however, of a less spectacular but no less interesting kind. Rather than selecting the logical difficulties out of the physicist's collection, one may consider those difficulties in the logician's bundle of problems which have some relevance to physics. The discussion of these with detailed reference to physics is often viewed with suspicion by the physicist; but it may prove enlightening to the philosopher, and the path between fundamental physics and such logical problems has proved startlingly short.

Examples of the first kind are the relativity of simultaneity, the idea of identity for fundamental particles, the existence of subquantum particles, the reversibility of temporal processes, the measurement of the dimensions of the universe, the existence of temperatures below absolute zero, the conventionality of the (one-way) velocity of light, etc. These are problems concerned with the substance of physics, and I shall refer to them as problems of *applied logic in the physical sciences* or *problems in the substantial logic of the physical sciences*. If this has an honorific connotation, it is well deserved. It would require a form of theory-be-damned bigotry virtually unknown among physicists today to deny the importance of these issues. A more common position is to deny that these are problems of "an essentially logical kind." By this phrase I mean to exclude issues which are entirely "decided by the facts," or by calculation, or which could be so decided, and by "the facts" I mean undisputed (not indisputable) observations. I believe these definitions make the issues mentioned unexceptionable examples of logical issues; put positively, they are issues where the very criteria for interpreting observational evidence and the very meaning of the fundamental concepts are in dispute. Such disputes cannot be settled entirely within the subject of physics as it is usually conceived; they are necessarily in the province of logic itself, where modes of reasoning and the presuppositions of concepts are themselves the object of study. And to the extent that a physicist is concerned with such issues, he is playing logician, just as in other cases he must perforce play mathematician or writer or recording instrument. He is no less a theoretical physicist for this; a theoretical physicist is one who combines these roles in treating a certain

---

Note: The present paper has benefited greatly from helpful criticisms of my fellow contributors, and my students and colleagues at Indiana, and is based in part on work done with support from the National Science Foundation and the Hill Foundation; to them I am most grateful.

range of problem. Some of these problems are essentially logical, others essentially experimental or mathematical; and some are mixtures of all these. But as I have previously said, even the ones that are "essentially" of one of these kinds usually require considerable knowledge of physics itself for their solution. A student of comparative linguistics may have an essentially logical problem on his hands but it does not follow that a logician can solve it without knowing the language under consideration, for translating the problem into the appropriate logical terms is very often the really difficult step, and requires understanding both the terms of the original problem and those of logic.

The second kind of problem is exemplified by discussions of the frequency (and other) analyses of probability, the testability of indeterminism, the role of simplicity in evaluating theories, the status of unobservable entities, the definitional element in fundamental laws, the notions of "significant results" and "crucial experiments," the relation between explanation and prediction, the connection between dispositional properties, states, and laws, the utility of idealization, etc. These are problems about the structure of physical theories, language, and experiments, and I shall refer to them as those problems of *pure* logic with a bearing on the physical sciences, or *as problems in the structural logic of the physical sciences*. This volume contains papers dealing with topics of both kinds, examples of the first and second kind respectively being those by Professor Grünbaum on geometry and Professor Putnam on analyticity. This paper represents an attempt to handle some of the closely connected problems of the second kind. It is in no sense a comprehensive study, being chiefly concerned with explanations and predictions and to a lesser extent with causes, laws, determinism, and probability. The general approach can be very crudely indicated as claiming that problems of structural logic can only be solved by reference to concepts previously condemned by many logicians as "psychological, not logical," e.g., understanding, belief, and judgment.

2. OUTLINE

I shall pay special attention to an account of scientific explanation and prediction given by Hempel and Braithwaite, and attempt to improve on it. In so doing I shall be led to comment on the notion of physical law (since this is said to be involved in all explanations), and this will introduce the problematic notion of universally law-governed behavior, i.e., determinism. Comments on reductionism and causation follow from these considerations. A second necessity in studying explanations is some reference to the notion of probability (for, in the absence of general law, we may find that statistical laws provide a basis for a weaker notion of "probability explanation"). As the discussion of law brings in determinism, so the discussion of probability will lead me to say something about the nature of physical knowledge and understanding.

It is perhaps worth mentioning that this paper has a twin, devoted to the corresponding problems in the social sciences and, especially, history;[1] and they both stand on the shoulders of the treatment of certain logical problems in "Definitions, Explanations, and Theories," in Volume II of this series.

3. PRELIMINARY ISSUES

3.1. EXPLANATIONS: INTRODUCTION.

I am going to take a series of suggested analytical claims about the logic of explanation and gradually develop a general idea of what is lacking in them, or too restrictive about them. I shall at each stage try to formulate criteria which will survive the difficulties while retaining the virtues of the current candidate. Eventually I shall try to draw the surviving criteria together into an outline of a new account of both explanation and understanding; but this will not be possible until I have encompassed the whole field of topics envisioned above. The questions with which I begin will seem quite unimportant; but they are in fact more significant than they appear because of the cumulative error in the standard answers to them.

3.2. EXPLANATIONS AS ANSWERS TO "WHY" QUESTIONS.

"To explain the phenomena in the world of our experience, to answer the question 'Why?' rather than only the question 'What?' . . ." With these words, Hempel and Oppenheim begin their monograph on scientific explanation.[2] Braithwaite says, "Any proper answer to a 'Why?' question may be said to be an explanation of a sort. So the different kinds of explanation can best be appreciated by considering the different sorts of answers that are appropriate to the same or to different 'Why?' questions."[3]

This happens to be a *non sequitur,* but it is the conclusion that I particularly wish to consider. The "answer-to-a-why-question" criterion could have been proposed in the absence of a serious attempt to think of counterexamples. "How can a neutrino be detected, when it has zero mass and zero charge?" is a perfectly good request for a perfectly standard scientific explanation. "What is it about cepheid variables that makes them so useful for the determination of interstellar distances?" Likewise, and the same can be said of suitable Which, Whither, and When questions. Not all, perhaps not even most, of the answers to such questions involve explanations, whereas it is perhaps true that most answers to Why questions are explanations. (But not all, as for example an answer that rebuts a presupposition of the question "Why do you persist in lying?" "I have *never* lied about this affair.") But explanations are also given when no questions are asked at all, as in the course of a lecture, or in correcting or supporting an assertion. The identifying feature of an explanation cannot, therefore, be the grammatical form of the question which (sometimes) produces it. Indeed, it is fairly clear that one does not teach a foreigner or a child the word "explanation" simply by reference to Why questions; so the authors quoted presumably had some prior (or at least alternative) notion of explanation in mind which enabled them to identify answers to Why questions as explanations. Should we not look for the meaning of that notion?

It is sometimes replied that our common notion of explanation is excessively vague, and it is therefore quite unrewarding to seek its exact meaning; far better to concentrate on some substantial concept which clearly does occur. This is a very good reply and represents a sensible approach, if only it can be shown to be true. This requires showing (a) that the ordinary notion *is* excessively vague, and (b) that the "substantial" alternative occurs often enough to justify any general conclusions about explanations which are inferred from studying it. I shall be arguing that neither of these seemingly innocuous premises can be established, and in consequence the analysis suggested by the reconstructionist authors is fundamentally unsatisfactory.

Explanation is undoubtedly a notion whose analysis must be sought in the practical foundation of language; but it is too much to hope one can identify explanations by such a simple linguistic device as the one suggested. Nor will it do to suppose that explanations are such that they are answers to *potential* Why questions; for then they are also potentially answers to What-about questions, How-possibly questions, etc. Thus, to take an example quoted by Hempel and Oppenheim, the question "Why does a stick half-immersed in water appear bent?" can readily be rephrased as "What makes a stick (in such circumstances) seem to be bent?" Indeed, such a question as "How can the sun possibly continue to produce so much energy with a negligible loss of mass?" is only with some difficulty rephrased as a Why question.[4] In sum, the grammatical indicators of explanations are complicated and none of them are necessary; some more illuminating and reliable criteria must be sought.

3.3. EXPLANATIONS AS "MORE THAN" DESCRIPTIONS.

Another common remark in the literature is that explanations are more than descriptions. This is put by Hempel and Oppenheim in the following words: ". . . especially, scientific research in its various branches strives to go beyond a mere description of its subject matter by providing an explanation of the phenomena it investigates."[5] But if one goes on to examine their own examples of explanations one finds what seem to be simply complex descriptions.[6] Thus they offer an explanation of the fact that when "a mercury thermometer is rapidly immersed in hot water, there occurs a temporary drop of the mercury column, which is then followed by a swift rise." And the explanation consists of the following account: "The increase in temperature affects at first only the glass tube of the thermometer; it expands and thus provides a larger space for the mercury inside, whose surface therefore drops. As soon as by heat conduction the rise in temperature reaches the mercury, however, the latter expands, and as its coefficient of expansion is considerably larger than that of glass, a rise of the mercury level results."[7]

This is surely intended to be a narrative description of exactly what happens. The one feature which might suggest a difference from a "mere description" is the occurrence of such words as "thus," "however," and "results." These are *reminiscent* of an argument or demonstration, and I think partially explain the analysis proposed by Hempel and Oppenheim, and others. But they are not part of an argument or demonstration here, simply of an explanation; and they or their equivalents occur in some of the simplest descriptions. "The curtains knocked over the vase" is a description which includes a causal claim and it could equally well be put, style aside, as "The curtains brushed against the vase, *thus* knocking it over" (or ". . . *resulting* in it being knocked over"). The fact that it is an explanatory account is therefore not in any way a ground for saying it is not a descriptive account (cf. "historical narrative"). Indeed, if it was not descriptive of what happens, it could hardly be explanatory. The question we have to answer is how and when certain descriptions count as explanations. Explaining how fusion processes enable the sun to maintain its heat output consists exactly in describing these processes and their products. Explaining therefore sometimes consists simply in giving the *right* description. What counts as the right description? Tentatively we can consider the vague hypothesis that the right description is the one which fills in a particular gap in the understanding of the person or people to whom the explanation is directed. That there is a gap in understanding, or a mis-understanding, seems plausible since whatever an explanation *actually* does, in order to be called an explanation at all it must be *capable* of making clear something not previously clear, i.e., of increasing or producing understanding of something. The difference between explain-ing and "merely" informing, like the difference between explaining and describing, does not, I shall argue, consist in explaining being something "more than" or even something intrinsically different from informing or describing, but in its being the appropriate piece of informing or describing, the appropriateness being a matter of its *relation to a particular context.* Thus, what would in one context be "a mere description" can in another be "a full explanation." The distinguishing features will be found, not in a verbal form of the question or answer, but in the known or inferred state of understanding and the proposed explanation's relation to it. To these, of course, the form of the question and answer are often important clues, though not the only clues. But this is only a rough indication of the *direction* of the solution to be proposed in this paper, and it may be that the notion of understanding will present us with substantial difficulties, quite apart from the problem of identifying the criteria for "closing the gap" in understanding (or rectifying the misunderstanding). However, let me remind the reader that understanding is *not* a subjectively appraised state any more than knowing is; both are objec-tively testable and are, in fact, tested in examinations. We may first benefit from examining the relation between explanation and another important scientific activity.

3.4. EXPLANATIONS AS "ESSENTIALLY SIMILAR" TO PREDICTIONS.

The next suggestion to be considered is a much more penetrating one, and although it cannot be regarded as satisfactory, the reasons for dissatisfaction are more involved. Quoting from Hempel and Oppenheim once more: ". . . the same formal analysis . . . applies to scientific pre-diction as well as to explanation. The difference between the two is of a pragmatic character . . . It may be said, therefore, that an explanation is not fully adequate unless . . . if taken account of in time, [it] could have served as a basis for predicting the phenomenon under consideration."[8]

(3.41)   The full treatment of this view will require some points that will only be made later in the paper; but we can begin with several rather weighty objections. First, there certainly seem to be occasions when we can predict some phenomenon with the greatest success, but cannot provide any explanation of it. For example, we may discover that whenever cows lie down in the open fields by day, it always rains within a few hours. We are in an excellent posi-tion for prediction, but we could scarcely offer the earlier event as an explanation of the latter. It appears that explanation requires something "more than" prediction; and my suggestion would be that, whereas an understanding of a phenomenon often enables us to forecast it, the ability to forecast it does not constitute an understanding of a phenomenon.

(3.42)   Indeed, the forecast is simply a description of an event (or condition, etc.) given prior to its occurrence and identified as referring to a future time; whereas an explanation will have to do more than merely describe *those features of the thing to be explained that identify it.* (In this sense, it is more than a (particular) description.[9]) At the very least some other features of it must be mentioned, and often some reference is made to previous or (other) concurrent events and/or laws. Since none of this is required of a prediction, it seems rather extraordinary to suppose that the *contents* of a prediction are logically identified to those of an explanation. And our first point showed that the *grounds* for the two are often quite different, in that one can be inferred from a mere correlation and the other not.

Such cases also demonstrate that explaining something is by no means the same as showing it was to be expected, since the latter task can be accomplished without any explanation being given.[10] For our purpose, however, the crucial point is that, however achieved, a prediction is what it is, simply because it is produced in advance of the event it predicts; it is *intrinsically* nothing but a bare description of that event. Whereas an explanation of the event must be more than the *identifying* description of it, else to request an explanation of X (where "X" is a description, not a name) is to give an explanation of X. Of course, there is usually a difference of tense, but we could agree to this as a pragmatic difference. However, it is the *least* and not the *only* difference between explanations and predictions.

(3.43)   There also seem to be cases where explanation is not in terms of temporally ordered and causally related events, and we are consequently never able to make predictions. These cases are common enough outside the physical sciences, e.g., in explaining the rules of succession in an Egyptian dynasty, or the symbolism of a tribal dance. Within science there are of course all the cases of explaining a theory or mechanism or proof; these are normally dismissed by supporters of the Hempel and Oppenheim position, on the grounds that they are clearly a different kind of explanation, the explanation of *meaning,* not at all related to *scientific* explanation. While there is no doubt about the difference in procedure between explaining a theory and explaining some phenomenon in terms of the theory, it is not enough to appeal to intuition for support of the claim that they are not "fundamentally," i.e., for all logical purposes, the same except for subject matter, much as definition in mathematics might be said to be fundamentally the same as definition in the empirical sciences except for subject matter. In fact, it seems clear enough that one important element is held in common between the two "kinds" of explanation, viz., the provision of understanding. But is there not a great deal of difference between the kinds of understanding provided in the two cases?

Now, *not* understanding a theory may be due to not understanding what its assumptions are, to not understanding the meaning of some of its terms, or to not understanding how the derivations said to be possible from it are to be made. One might suppose this to be quite unlike not understanding why a stick half-immersed in water appears bent.

But instead of asking how we go about explaining a natural phenomenon, let us ask how we come to ask for an explanation, i.e., what it is that we think *needs* explanation. It may seem that science is committed to the view that *everything* needs to be explained. Now it is clear that *everything* cannot be explained *every time* we give an explanation of some particular thing (or set of things) which is all we ever do in a given context. So we can rephrase our question as, What is it that needs explanation in a given context? It seems clear that it is those things which are not properly understood (by whomever the explanation is addressed to). Now, lack of understanding of a natural phenomenon may be due to the absence of certain information about the situation, to the presence of false beliefs about it, or to an inability to see the connections between what is understood and what is not understood. These are much the same kinds of difficulty as occur in not understanding a theory, although the information will be in one case about a verbal construction out of our knowledge and in the other about, for example, a mechanical construction out of our raw materials. However important the differences of subject may be, it is not obvious that the notion of understanding or explanation involved is in any important way different; and it *is* quite obvious that no predictions are possible on the basis of an explanation of the meaning of a theory except, irrelevantly, those which the theory makes possible, if any—and it may be a theory whose advantages lie solely in its unifying powers). Certainly one should feel uneasy about any general claims of common logical structure for explanation and prediction which have to be defended by rejecting clear cases of explanation as "essentially different," without detailed examination. I shall argue that the differences are much less important than the similarities: in effect we are in both cases providing a series of comprehensible statements that have some of a wide range of logical relations to other statements. Lest this seem to be a proof of similarity by simply weakening the definition of "similar," I also try to show that the narrower definition is independently unsatisfactory.

(3.44)   Again, we often talk of *explaining laws:* indeed half of Hempel and Oppenheim's examples are of this kind. Now, when we offer an explanation of Newton's Law of Cooling (that a body cools at a rate proportional to the difference between its temperature and that of its surroundings), we do so—according to Hempel and Oppenheim—by deriving this law from more general laws.[11] What predictions could be made which would have "the same formal structure" as this kind of explanation? The "pragmatic" difference between the two as they see it is essentially that explanation occurs after the phenomenon, and prediction before. But in the case of laws, which are presumably believed to hold at all times, what does it mean to talk of predicting the phenomenon? It is surely the case that the truth of Newton's law is *simultaneous* with that of the more general laws from which it is derivable. We cannot speak of being able to predict the inclusion of the class of A's in the class of C's if we already know that A's are B's and B's are C's.

It may seem that this argument can only be countered by saying that a law is a generalization about a number of events and that to "predict a law" is to predict the outcome of experiments done to determine the pattern of these events. It is true that this is different from predicting an eclipse, where the actual event to which the prediction refers is in the future, not merely the discovery of its nature. However, (i) it is certainly true that *some*—but not all— events governed by most laws lie entirely in the future, and its truth depends on these and these are predictable in the usual sense. (ii) Certainly, too, we want to say that inferences about the past, which *generate* predictions about what archaeologists or geologists will discover, have exactly the same logical structure as inferences about the future, a fact well brought out by the practice of calling them postdictions or retrodictions. So, if *explaining a law* consists in explaining the over-all pattern of events, past, present, and future, *predicting a law,* as it seems we might interpret it, could be regarded as compounded out of such predictions and postdictions. This interpretation represents at the very least an *extension of meaning* since we cannot in the usual sense call inferences about the activities of the earth's crust in Jurassic times (which will be covered by geological laws) predictions. Although we could quite properly apply this term to inferences about what will be found by geologists upon searching in certain areas, this is not what the law is about (for else we must say that the law asserts something different every time something new is discovered by the geologists, there being that much less for them still to discover). Indeed, we land in a well-known swamp if we make this move; for the same argument makes all historical statements into statements about contemporary evidence and all statements about distant places into statements about local evidence, etc. It is the argument which confuses the *reference of* a statement with the *evidence for* a statement. So explanations of laws only have a correlate among predictions if we *extend* the meaning of the notion of prediction to include postdiction.

Now this extension may not seem very significant until one reminds oneself that the whole significance of the term "prediction" resides in the temporal relation of its utterance to the event it mentions. "Prediction" is a term defining a category of sentences, in the same way as "command," "argument," "description," etc.; it defines descriptive sentences in the future tense made when the tense is appropriate. The sentence uttered or written in making any given prediction can be repeated after the event has occurred as a perfectly good historical description, provided only that the tense of the verbs (or the corresponding construction) is changed, i.e., *apart from tense,* predictions are not identifiable. So this extension of meaning amounts to an *elimination* of the meaning with which one began. We may agree that one procedure of inferring past events is essentially the same as one procedure of inferring future events, but we cannot possibly conclude that the *results* in the first case are essentially the same as predictions. This is like saying that analytic statements are essentially the same as synthetic statements since both can be inferred syllogistically. If the *only* way of inferring to such different kinds of statement was syllogistic, one *might* be more inclined to call them logically identical. One would still not be very impressed, since their logical character is written on their face, and appealing to their common ancestry cannot prove that all siblings are twins; it cannot eliminate the obvious differences. But it is clear that there is nothing unique about the type of inference suggested here; predictions and postdictions can be obtained from arguments of virtually any logical form and also without any argument at all, as in the case of the expert but inarticulate diagnostician or the precognitive. I conclude that the explanation of laws has no proper counterpart among predictions, since there is no general concept of predicting laws; for (i) if what can be predicted is said to be the *discovery* of a law, this fails because the counterpart to explaining an *event* is predicting *it,* not its *discovery* (which would require laws about discovering laws); (ii) in the only other possible interpretation, a large number of the conclusions inferred are simply not predictions at all; (iii) even ignoring the first two points, nothing is more obvious than the difference in logical structure between the "prediction" "All A's are (or even, will be found to be) C's" and anything that might conceivably be said to be an explanation of it.

(3.45)   I think little can be salvaged from the impact of this set of four points (3.41 through 3.44) against the 3.4 thesis, but I wish to indicate another series of difficulties which will help us to develop a constructive alternative position. The first involves a rather lengthy example, but the same example is of some assistance in dealing with the notion of cause as well as those of explanation and prediction. Suppose we are in a position to explain the collapse of a bridge as due to the fatigue of the metal in one of the thrust members. This is not an unusual kind of situation, and it is, of course, one where no prediction was *in fact* made. According to Hempel and Oppenheim, if this is a satisfactory explanation, then, if taken account of in time, it could have formed the basis for a prediction. (We can abandon the idea—presumably but incorrectly taken to be equivalent by Hempel and Oppenheim—that it would actually have the same logical structure as the prediction.) Let us examine in a little detail how this could be so.

We begin our search for the explanation with an eyewitness account that locates a particular girder as the first to go. We already know that there is a substantial deterioration in the elastic properties of carbon steel as it ages and is subjected to repeated compressions; we also know that the amount of this deterioration is not predictable with great reliability since it depends on the conditions in the original welding, casting, and annealing processes, the size and frequency of subsequent temperature changes to which the formed metal is subjected, the special stresses to which it may have been subjected, e.g., by lightning discharges which put heavy currents through it, and, of course, irregularities in and perhaps violations of the design load. The only way to deal with these sources of error is to "over-design," i.e., to make an allowance for the unpredictables and provide a safety factor on top of that. But the cost of materials and the pressure of competitive tenders puts limits on the size of such safety margins, and every now and then, as in the spectacular case of the Launceston Bridge, where the wind set up resonant vibrations, a failure occurs. In the present case, where internal rather than external circumstances are the significant factor in the failure, we obtain samples of the metal from the girder in question and discover that its elastic properties have substantially deteriorated. But as we do not have any exact data about the load at the time of failure, we cannot immediately prove that such a load would definitely have produced failure.

Now we go over the rest of the bridge carefully, searching for other possible causes of failure and find none. The bridge is of standard design, sited on good bedrock, and well built. We do have good reason to suppose that the load-causing failure was no greater than the bridge had withstood on many previous occasions, though greater than the static load (assume standard traffic and moderate wind); so we are forced to look for the cause in the structural changes. In the light of all this information, we can have great confidence in our explanation of the failure as due to fatigue in the particular beam; but we simply do not have the data required for a prediction that the failure would take place on a certain date.

It is perfectly true that *if* we *also* had exact data about the load when the failure occurred, could obtain some exact and reliable elastic coefficients from the fatigued sample, were in no doubt about our theory, and found on calculation with the revised elastic coefficients that the load exceeded the residual strength, we could be *even more confident* of our explanation. But I have described a much more realistic situation in which we can still have a very high level of rational confidence in our explanation, a level which places it beyond reasonable doubt.

Now, in both cases—with and without the exact details—we can make some kind of a *conditional* prediction—that the bridge will fail *if* the load goes over a certain point, for obviously we can give some load which exceeds any known bridge's capacity. It must be noticed first that such a prediction has no practical interest at all except in so far as we can predict the occurrence of such loads. It is a conditional prediction not a categorical prediction, and if the only kind of prediction which is associated with explanations is conditional prediction, especially if they are of this "upper limit" kind, this is of very little interest indeed for scientists or engineers who cannot predict when the conditions are met, or who know they are very rarely met.

These considerations make us realize that the crucial element in the "duality thesis" about explanations and predictions is the existence of a specific correlative prediction for each explanation. Naturally, we can make a number of conditional predictions as soon as, or indeed *before,* we have any data about the material and form of the bridge; but these are independent of the particular circumstances of the failure. The "duality" claim presumably implies that to every different good explanation there corresponds a different prediction relating to precisely those circumstances to which the explanation applies. But it is easy enough to see that we can attain all reasonable certainty about an explanation with less evidence than is required to justify even a conditional prediction with the same *specific* reference.

In the bridge example, we have so far been much too profligate of our investigator's time. In fact, he knows very well that the only causes of failure other than a load in excess of anything for which the structure was originally designed are metal fatigue or external damage by, for example, corrosion, abrasion, or explosion. It is easy to check for the symptoms of external damage, it is relatively easy to judge that the load was not beyond the design limits. Consequently, he can almost certainly identify the cause of failure immediately as fatigue. In suitable circumstances, i.e., with suitable evidence for the above statements, it is only a formality to go through with testing samples of the structural steel. Suppose, however, as a final check, we do a rough computation of Young's modulus for material in the beam and find it has substantially decreased and by much more than for the other beams; but we take no exact measurements of it, and none at all of the other elastic coefficients (which normally vary in the same direction as Young's modulus). Our hypothesized explanation has been very strongly confirmed. It is now beyond reasonable doubt. Now what conditional prediction can we make? It seems there is only the extremely weak one that if sufficient substantial fatiguing takes place, and a somewhat higher load than normal is imposed, failure will take place.[12] Not only does such a "prediction" correspond to an indefinitely large number of explanations and hence fail to meet the uniqueness condition previously mentioned, but it is couched in such vague terms as to be almost wholly uninformative. Yet, I wish to maintain that such a prediction is all that can be said to be correlated with some very well-established explanations.

Let us examine the most natural counterargument. This would consist in saying that no such explanation could ever be regarded as certain in view of its lack of precise support. Imagine an attorney for the steel company attacking this explanation in court. "How can you be sure that the metal fatigue was *enough* to produce a failure? You make no calculation and no measurements from which you could in any way infer that a bridge built of that same steel, in the same condition you found it, would fail even under *twice* the load impressed on it that windy night. Hence, I submit that no evidence for blaming the steel has been produced, and hence no evidence that the steel was at fault."

The weakness of this argument as far as *our* considerations are concerned is twofold. First, there is not the least difference between direct and indirect evidence for establishing a conclusion beyond reasonable doubt; indirect evidence is often more reliable and the distinction between the two is largely arbitrary. If only A, B, or C can cause X, and A and B are ruled out, it is unnecessary to show C is present; in this case, however, it was *also* shown that C was present, and the only debate is over whether *sufficient* C was present. The reply to such doubts is simply "What else, then?" A redoubtable prima-facie case has been made, and if not rebutted, it must be accepted.

Second, there are some grounds for doubting the significance of any "direct" test, which do not apply to the indirect evidence. Suppose we take all the exact measurements we can and make all the calculations we can, and they indicate that a bridge made of the metal tested would *not* collapse under any stress that seems likely to have occurred in the circumstances at the time of failure. Here we have *two conflicting* indications. Far from it being the case that the "direct" test affords the crucial test, we find it substantially less reliable than the other evidence. First the sample of metal tested is not known to be identical with that which failed: we take a sample adjacent to the *fracture,* but it is a very difficult matter to determine where the fracture *begins,* i.e., where the *failure* occurs. It is quite certain that different spots on the same girder—and along the same fracture—are under very different stresses and hence at very different stages of fatigue. Second, the steps involved in going from the data on materials to conclusions about bridge strength involve a vast number of assumptions of various kind, few of them more than approximations whose errors may in sum be fatal to the argument. For example, it is *possible* that exceptional conditions did prevail in local areas around the bridge structure, producing strains such as would not normally be associated with a moderate storm—a typical example is provided by the random development of wind resonance, which can build up a considerable, though not precisely known, extra force from a mild breeze that happens to be blowing in the right direction at the right velocity. Hence our "direct" calculations by no means settle the matter; and the recent examples of wing failure in the Electra airliner show that fatigue can be identified as the cause of failure even when exact theory is wholly inapplicable. The moral of this example is that explanations can be supported by assertions about qualitative *necessary* conditions whereas even a conditional prediction requires quantitative *sufficient* conclusions. (This point would of course be completely lost if one proceeds on the common assumption that causes are simply sufficient conditions: see 4.9.)

We have thus discovered that the "direct test" of the indirectly supported hypothesis is by no means immune to rejection. But the general issues about confirmation are not important here; it is the existence of *some* cases where we can have every confidence in an explanation and yet be in no position to make a prediction, even an applicable conditional prediction. This counterexample to the "duality" view is the analogue of the counterexamples already mentioned where we are in an excellent position to make a prediction but cannot produce an explanation. A simple and somewhat rough way of putting the point of the last example would be to say that a prediction has to say *when* something will happen, or *what* will (sometime) happen, a causal explanation only *what made it* happen. The first requires either attaching a time or range of times (unconditional prediction), or a value of some other variable (conditional prediction), to the description of an event, whereas the second often requires only giving a cause, i.e., picking out (not estimating the size of) a variable, or another event.

Naturally there are some cases where more than these minimum requirements are available. Sometimes the nature of the problem is such that when the explanation is certain the prediction is possible: the Farnborough research into the fuselage fatigue of the De Havilland Comet airliners is a case in point. This was possibly only because they had excellent data on the circumstances of the failure (from service records plus recovered instruments). The first type of case we have described is of central importance in the social sciences, because most of our knowledge of human behavior can be expressed only in necessary condition propositions or judgment propositions. Hence it enables us to explain but not predict with equal accuracy. We can confidently explain the migration of the Okies to California in terms of the drought in Oklahoma, though we could not have predicted it with any reliability. For we know (i) that there must have been a reason for migrating and (ii) that drought produces economic conditions which can provide such a reason, and (iii) that nothing else with such effects was present. But we do *not* know *how much* of a drought is required to produce a migration and hence could not have predicted this with any confidence. Hempel mistakenly regards this as grounds for doubting the explanation.[13] We must insist on making a distinction between a *dubious* explanation and one for which further confirmation—in the technical sense—is still possible: every empirical claim has the latter property.

(3.46) To summarize, in part. The idea that a causal explanation can only be justified by direct test of the conditions from which a prediction could be made is a root notion in the Hempel and Oppenheim treatment of explanation, and they try to give it a precise formulation. It is said that an explanation must have the form of a deduction from (a) causal laws (L_v) connecting certain antecedent conditions (C_v) to certain consequent conditions (E_v), plus (b) assertions that the conditions C_v obtained in the case under consideration, where we are trying to explain X, which is the sum of the conditions E_v. In the bridge example, we would have to show (by appeal to connections involving L_v) that material with the properties of the sample taken ($C_1, C_2, \ldots, C_{n-1}$) under the ambient conditions of the failure ($C_n, C_{n+1}, \ldots, C_{m-1}$) would lead to the behavior described, i.e., X, the collapse of the bridge (the bridge's design and state prior to failure being described in terms of $C_m, C_{m+1}, \ldots, C_p$). I have been arguing that an indirect approach may be just as effective, i.e., one showing fatigue (C_1) to be a necessary condition for X under the circumstances ($C_2, \ldots, C_p$). This would involve appealing to a proposition of the form "If X occurs, then either A_1, B_1, or C_1 caused it" and showing that $C_2, \ldots, C_p$ rule out A_1 and B_1. The main trouble with such laws for the thesis of Hempel and Oppenheim is that they do not permit any predictions of X, since the occurrence of X is required for their application. Nor can such laws be reformulated for predictive use, for they are quite different from "If A_1 or B_1 or C_1 occur, they will produce X," not just because one states necessary and the other sufficient conditions, but because the first does not and the second does require quantitative formulation if it is to be true—for it is obviously false that *any* degree of fatigue produces failure. These laws incidentally demonstrate that the duality thesis about explanation and prediction was actually a separate, fifth condition and not a consequence of the four conditions R_1-R_4.

(3.47) In concluding this discussion of the prediction criterion for explanations, I think it is worth mentioning some points which are neither wholly independent of those discussed above nor, it seems to me, quite so strong. First, it is a consequence of Hempel and Oppenheim's analysis that whatever we explain must be a true statement, since they explicitly require all statements in an explanation to be true. Now it is certainly not the case that all the predictions we make must be true: we often err in predicting the behavior of the stock market, the weather, and the ponies. This point is thought by Scheffler to show that explanations and predictions are different in this respect; but I take it to be mainly a difficulty with Hempel and Oppenheim's analysis of explanation. For one can talk of explaining things that do not happen, just as one can talk of the consequences of things that do not happen. "If you hadn't got here on time, I know who would have been responsible," the irate parent says to the almost-wayward daughter; "If the fourth stage had failed to (ever fails to) fire, you may be sure it would have been (will be) because of a valve failure in the fuel-line," the missile technician may say. This use is *derivative,* i.e., it can be explained by reference to the commonest use; and in the commonest use I think we can agree that to say something is an explanation of X is to presuppose (in Strawson's sense) that X occurred. But this is not to say that in *all proper* uses, this can be inferred.

Apart from the case just cited, where it is known that X did not occur, known even by the giver of the explanation, and apart from explanations of events in fiction, there are other cases where this condition does not hold. In the modified phlogiston theory of about 1785, the explanation of the limited phlogistication of air when calcination occurs in a closed vessel was in terms of the finite capacity of a finite volume of air for absorbing phlogiston. The very phenomenon here explained does not exist, although even Cavendish thought it did. The explanation given is within the theory, of something described in *theoretical* terms. This is not to be confused with the case where we quite commonly put single quotation marks around the term "explanation," meaning that the term is not properly applicable, as when Conant says "an 'explanation' of metallury was at hand: Metallic ore (an oxide) + Phlogiston from charcoal → Metal." [14] For here we are referring to an incorrect explanation of something we know *does* occur, viz., smelting, and we know this *not* to be the correct explanation: compare the previous cases discussed where we know the phenomenon *does not* occur. I am therefore unwilling to agree that all proper uses of the term "explanation" presuppose that the phenomenon explained occurs; though I would agree that in the primary use this is so. [15] I shall say something about the necessity for the truth of the body of the explanation itself in the next section.

In the primary use of explanation, then, we know something when we are called on for an explanation that we do not know when called on for a prediction, viz., that the event referred to has occurred. This is sometimes a priceless item of information since it may demonstrate the existence or absence of a hitherto unknown strength of a certain power. Thus, to take a simpler example than the bridge case, a man in charge of an open-hearth furnace may be suspiciously watching a roil on the surface of the liquid steel, wondering if it is a sign of a "boil" (an occasionally serious destructive reaction) on the furnace lining down below or just due to some normal oxidizing of the additives in the mixture. Suddenly, a catastrophe: the whole charge drops through the furnace lining into the basement. It is now absolutely clear that there was a boil which has eaten through the lining: apart from sabotage (easily disproved by examination) there's no other possibility. But no prediction is possible to the event, using the data then available. This renders almost empty Hempel and Oppenheim's (and even Scheffler's) conclusion that explanations provide a basis for predictions. For "Had we known what was going to happen, we could have predicted it" is a vacuous claim. One might mutter something about "If the furnace was in exactly the same state *again* we could predict it would dump," but I have already pointed out that this is a virtually empty remark since we usually can't identify "exactly the same state"; it is simply a dubious determinist slogan, not even a genuine conditional prediction. Since it is technically entirely impossible to rebuild the furnace to the point where it is identical down to the temperature distribution in the mixture (a crucial factor) and the shape of the irregularities in the floor (also crucial), even if we knew these specifications, it will be pure chance if the conditions ever recur and when they do they won't be identifiable. Thus our grounds for thinking the determinist's slogan to be true—if we do—are entirely indirect, and the explanation certainly does not rest on subsumption under the slogan since we cannot even tell when the latter applies, whereas we can be sure the explanation is correct.

The problem of direct vs. indirect confirmation which arises here is of great importance throughout structural logic. To say that "same cause, same effect" is a determinist's slogan is not to say it has *no* empirical content. It has, and it is actually false, as far as present evidence goes, though only to a small extent for macroscopic observations. (It is also not equivalent to the idea of determinism as universal law-governed behavior.) What it lacks is single-case applicability and hence direct confirmability when complex systems are involved—for it is often impossible to specify what counts as the "same conditions." It may still be felt on general grounds that unless we *do* know what counts as the "same conditions" in a given case, we cannot be sure of the proposed causal explanation in that case. The opposite thesis will be defended in a later section of this paper, and to prepare for it I shall need to make several further distinctions and points. At this stage, however, let me summarize by saying that any prediction specifically associated with an explanation is (i) often conditional, and (ii) either so general as to be almost empty or so specific as to refer to no other case, and (iii) often not assertible until it is known the event occurred, i.e., not a true prediction.

3.5. EXPLANATIONS AS SETS OF TRUE STATEMENTS.

It is not possible to claim that explanations can only be offered for events that actually occur or have occurred. They can be given for events in the future (Scheffler), for events in fiction, for events known not to occur, and for events wrongly believed to occur—and also for some laws, states, and relationships which are timeless (see above). Assuming Hempel and Oppenheim's analysis to be in other respects correct, it follows that in such cases some of the propositions comprising the explanation itself cannot be true, contrary to one of their explicit conditions.[16]

The reason they give for this condition is a very plausible one, however, and it is of interest to see if a more general account can be given which will contain allowance for their point. They say: ". . . it might seem more appropriate to stipulate that the (explanation) has to be highly confirmed by all the relevant evidence rather than that it should be true. This stipulation, however, leads to awkward consequences. Suppose that a certain phenomenon was explained at an earlier stage of science by means of an (explanation) which was well supported by the evidence then at hand, but which had been highly disconfirmed by more recent empirical findings. In such a case, we would have to say that originally the explanatory account was a correct explanation, but that it ceased to be one later, when unfavorable evidence was discovered. This does not appear to accord with sound common usage, which directs us to say that . . . the account in question was not—and had never been—a correct explanation." [17]

It is roughly on these grounds that Conant puts the term "explanation" in quotes when he is referring to the phlogiston theory's account of calcination. For much the same reason we refer to an astrologer's remarks as an "explanation" of Henry Ford's successful business career.

But notice we can talk perfectly well about "two competing explanations" of some phenomenon in contemporary physics without feeling it improper to refer to both as explanations although only one can be true. And there certainly seem to be cases where we want to say, for example, that the Babylonian explanation of the origin of the universe was basically naturalistic, without using inverted commas. The best treatment of these cases, it seems to me, is to regard them as secondary uses which have become fairly standard, the notion of a secondary use being defined in terms of the fact that understanding it depends logically on understanding the primary use. But these are definitely proper uses and the term "explanation" is hence perhaps less a "success word" or "achievement word" than, for example, "knowledge" and "perception." We cannot say of two contradictory claims that both are *known* since this implies both are true. And this suggests a solution to our present problem.

The proper way of avoiding Hempel and Oppenheim's powerful argument is, I think, very simple; the secondary uses of "explanation" are legitimate but there are no such secondary uses of "correct explanation," the term which they substitute halfway through the argument. Remove the qualifying adjective "correct" and you will see that the argument is no longer persuasive. For consistency, this term must be and can be added to the occurrences of "explanation" in the premises. Overwhelming counterevidence does not necessarily lead us to abandon or even to put quotes around "explanation," but, as the argument rightly says, it does lead us to abandon the application of the term "correct explanation" (or "*the* explanation" which is often used equivalently). Hence we should regard Hempel and Oppenheim's analysis as an analysis of "correct explanation" rather than of "explanation," or "*an* explanation," and this is surely what they were most interested in. "Explanations," or "an explanation," or "his explanation," or "a possible explanation," do not *always* have to be true (or of the appropriate type, or adequate); they only need high confirmation, at some stage.

Doesn't the notion of confirmation come into the analysis of "correct explanation" at all? It is not part of the *analysis,* which only involves truth; but it is our only *means of access* to the truth. We have not got the correct explanation unless it contains only true assertions, but if we want to know which explanation is most likely to meet that condition, we must select the one with the highest degree of confirmation. Good evidence does not guarantee true conclusions but it is the best indicator, so we need no excuse for appealing to degree of confirmation. Moreover, we have no need to adopt the skeptic's position that all possibility of knowing when we have a correct explanation is by now beyond reasonable doubt, and to restrict "knowing" to cases of absolute logical necessity is to mistake the empty glitter of definitional truth for the fallible flame of knowledge. The notion of reasonable doubt is highly dependent on context, but highly unambiguous in a given context, and it sets the threshold level which distinguishes knowledge from likelihood. Anything that is to be called the "correct explanation" of something that is known to have happened must contain only statements from the domain of knowledge.

Now among the things we know are some statements about the probability of certain events under certain circumstances, e.g., about the probability of throwing a six with a die that passes various specifiable tests. Could we not use such propositions as part of an explanation? Hempel and Oppenheim—in the papers cited—countenance the possibility that what they call statistical explanations may be of great importance but they neither undertake to discuss them nor, more significantly, restrict most of their conclusions about explanation in general in the way that would be appropriate if we do take seriously the claims of statistical explanations (which I include in the broader class of explanations based on probability statements). In the present volume, Hempel sets out an account of statistical explanation on which I comment later. Such explanations cannot be subsumed under Hempel and Oppenheim's original analysis as it stands, because no *deduction* of a nonprobability statement from them is possible, and it is hence impossible for them to explain any actual occurrence, since actual occurrences have to be described by nonprobability statements. In particular we could make a (probable) prediction from such 'laws,' but could not—using the same premises—be said to explain the event predicted, if it does come about.

(3.51)   It is of some importance to notice that Hempel and Oppenheim's analysis of explanation absolutely presupposes a descriptive language. For them there can be nothing to explain if there is no language, since the thing-to-be-explained is dealt with *only* via the "explanandum" which is its description in the relevant language. One suspects such a restriction immediately because there are clearly cases where we can explain without language, e.g., when we explain to the mechanic in a Yugoslav garage what has gone wrong with the car. Now this is hardly a scientific explanation, but it seems reasonable to suppose that the scientific explanation represents a refinement on, rather than a totally different kind of entity from, the ordinary explanation. In our terms, it is the *understanding* which is the essential part of an explanation and the *language* which is a useful accessory for the process of communicating the understanding. By completely eliminating consideration of the step from the phenomenon to the description of the phenomenon, Hempel and Oppenheim make it much easier to convince us that deducibility is a criterion of explanation. In fact, within the language there is only one other relation possible, viz., inducibility. We shall argue that good inductive inferribility is the only required relation involved in explanations, deduction being a dispensable and overrestrictive requirement which may of course sometimes be met. But a source of both error and understanding is left out of account in such a debate; for unexplained things are sometimes such that we do not describe them in asking for an explanation and such that they are explained *merely* by being described in the correct way regardless of deduction from laws.[18] (And on the other hand, sometimes a *true* description and deduction is not enough.)

3.6. EXPLANATIONS AS INVOLVING DESCRIPTIONS OF WHAT IS TO BE EXPLAINED.

Once we have realized the extraordinary difficulty there is in supposing that explanations and predictions have a common structure, it is natural to ask what the structure of an explanation really is. The "structure" of a prediction, we noticed, is simply that of a declarative statement using an appropriate future tense and any kind of descriptive language. It *may* indeed be of the form "C will bring about X" but is more usually of the form "X will occur" or "X, at time t." The structure of an argument, to take a further example, is such as to involve several statements which are put forward as bearing upon each other or upon some other statements in the relation of premises to conclusions. Now what is the structure of an explanation? A bridge's failure may have as its explanation the fatigue of the metal in a particular member of the overload due to a bomb blast. These appear to be a state and an event which could be held to be the cause of the event to be explained. A different account will have to be given of the explanation of laws, but for the moment we can profitably concentrate on the explanation of events, to which Hempel and Oppenheim devote a good deal of space, and which has some claim to be epistemologically prior to the explanation of laws.

Now there is a further apparent ambiguity about "explanation": it can either refer to the linguistic structure which describes certain states or events or to the states (or events) themselves. This kind of ambiguity even occurs in connection with such terms as "consequence," "concept," "cause," "inference," and "argument"; it is common throughout logic and best illustrated, perhaps, by the very term "fact." We shall usually be referring to the linguistic entity when we use the term "explanation," but clearly *neither* this entity nor its referents include whatever it is that is to be explained. In the simple but standard examples just given, the explanation, in this sense, is an assertion about a state or event that is entirely different from (assertions about) the state or event to be explained. But Hempel and Oppenheim say, "We divide an explanation into two major constituents . . . the sentence describing the phenomenon to be explained . . . [and] the class of those sentences which are adduced to account for the phenomenon."[19] The former is plainly not a constituent of the explanation at all (except where it is all of the explanation—see 3.5). Only if we find its consequences very confusing or inconvenient should we abandon such a clear distinction as this.

The first difficulty that strikes us about this version of the Hempel and Oppenheim account, then, is that it asserts all explanations of a phenomenon X consist in a deductive argumentlike structure, with a statement about X as the conclusion, whereas our simple examples above are merely statements about something or other that is held to be the *cause* of whatever is to be explained. And are there not occasions, on which one is going over—demonstrating—an explanation, when one does finish off by giving as the last step the description of what is to be explained? It is certainly not a common practice, scientifically or ordinarily, and even when it occurs, it only shows that part of a proof *that* something is an explanation of X may involve a description of X. The *explanation* of the photoelectric effect does not involve the description of the effect—this is presupposed by the explanation. The point may be minor, but it puts us on our guard, for we cannot be sure whether it may not have unfortunate consequences, analogous to those involved in saying that predictions have the same logical structure as explanations. In fact, we have already seen one error that results from this incautious amalgamation of (i) phenomena, (ii) their description, and (iii) their explanation, in 3.5. We could state part of it by saying that a sixth requirement is actually implicit in their account, viz., the requirement of accuracy and relevance of the description of X, which for them is part of the explanation of X.

In fact, the most serious error of all those I believe to be involved in Hempel and Oppenheim's analysis also springs from the very same innocuous-seeming oversimplification: the requirement of the deducibility itself, plausible only if we forget that our concern is fundamentally with a phenomenon, not a statement. It may seem unjust to suggest that Hempel and Oppenheim amalgamate the phenomenon and its description (though certainly they do amalgamate the description and the explanation) when they make clear that the "conclusion" of the explanation is "a sentence describing the phenomenon (not that phenomenon itself)."[20] The justice of my complaint rests, not on their failure *ever* to make this distinction, but on their failure to be consistent in dealing with its consequences. For it is a consequence of this distinction that a nondeductive step is involved between the statements in an explanation and the phenomenon explained. And we may then ask why they should suppose deducibility to be the only logical relation in a good explanation. They never address themselves to this question directly, chiefly, I think, because they do *not* realize the consequences of the distinction they do once make. Attention to it would surely have led them to notice (i) cases of explanatory description (see 3.5), (ii) cases where the completeness or (iii) the uniqueness of the description are crucial in assessing the explanation (see 6.2). Only if we assume that getting as far as the description is getting to the phenomenon, i.e., doing what an explanation is supposed to do, could we overlook such interesting cases. (I think the fact that "description" can be taken to *mean* "accurate description" also led them to overlook the independent importance of this requirement.)

3.7. THE LAST TWO CONDITIONS AND A SUMMARY OF DIFFICULTIES.

It is stated that the explanation "must contain general laws, and these must actually be required for the derivation . . ." And finally, it is said that the derivation must be deductive, ". . . for otherwise the (explanation) would not constitute adequate grounds for (the proposition describing the phenomenon)."[21] We now have a general idea of Hempel and Oppenheim's model of explanation, which I have elsewhere christened, for obvious reasons, "the deductive model."[22] I wish to maintain against it the following criticisms in particular, and some others incidentally;

(1) It fails to make the crucial logical distinctions between explanations, grounds for explanations, predictions, things to be explained, and the description of these things.

(2) It is too restrictive in that it excludes their own examples and almost every ordinary scientific one.

(3) It is too inclusive and admits entirely nonexplanatory schema.

(4) It requires an account of cause, law, and probability which are basically unsound.

(5) It leaves out of account three notions that are in fact essential for an account of scientific explanation: context, judgment, and understanding.

These objections are not wholly independent, and I have already dealt with some of them.

NOTES

[1] "Truisms as the Grounds for Historical Explanations" in *Theories of History,* P. L. Gardiner, ed. (Glencoe, Ill.: Free Press, 1959).

[2] "The Logic of Explanation" in *Readings in the Philosophy of Science,* H. Feigl and M. Brodbeck, eds. (New York: Appleton-Century-Crofts, 1953), p. 319. This is an abridgment of "Studies in the Logic of Explanation," *Philosophical of Science,* 15: 135–175 (1948). All page references hereafter are to the later version.

[3] *Scientific Explanation* (Cambridge: Cambridge University Press, 1953), p. 319.

[4] The discussion of How-possibly questions has been initiated and sustained by William Dray. See his *Laws and Explanation in History* (London: Oxford University Press, 1957), especially pp. 164ff.

[5] *Op. cit.,* p. 319.

[6] For an alternative and acceptable interpretation of their remark, see 3.4 below.

[7] *Op. cit.,* p. 320.

[8] *Op. cit.,* pp. 322–323.

[9] And this salvages the theme which forms the title of 3.3—but at the expense of making that of 3.4 untenable. I am thus uncertain which interpretation to accept.

[10] See also "Explanation, Prediction, and the Abstraction" by Israel Scheffler, *British Journal for the Philosophy of Science,* 7: 293–309 (1957), where several of the points in this section are discussed.

[11] The reader may be worried by the fact that his law is known to be only an approximation. This is true of almost all "laws," but we do give explanations of them, e.g., of Kepler's laws, Snell's law. Now, for any such law, deducing *it* from any premises would simply show the premises to be inaccurate. Hence, explanation cannot require deduction from true premises. We must substitute a weaker requirement; there are several possibilities which appear to retain much of the Hempel analysis (but see 3.5, . . .).

[12] Hempel, replying to this point in the present volume, suggests another, more specific candidate. I comment on this later.

[13] "The Function of General Laws in History," *Journal of Philosophy,* 39: 35–48 (1942).

[14] *Harvard Case Histories in Experimental Science,* Vol. I (Cambridge, Mass.: Harvard University Press, 1958), pp. 70, 110.

[15] There are of course a number of terms besides "explanation" (e.g., description [see 3.6], observation, insight) that are used in such a way that the description "incorrect (explanation)" can be synonymous with "not an (explanation) at all." The points just made do not, however, depend on this ambiguity.

[16] *Op. cit.,* pp. 321–322

[17] *Op. cit.,* pp. 322.

[18] A common case is that when someone, greatly puzzled, asks What on earth is this? or What's going on here? and is told, for example, that it is an initiation ceremonial on which he has stumbled. Analogous cases in particle physics, engineering, and astronomy are obvious. The point of these examples is that understanding is roughly the perception of relationships and hence may be conveyed by any process which locates the puzzling phenomenon in a system of relations. When we supply a law, we supply part of the system; but a description may enable us to supply a whole framework which we already understand, but of whose *relevance* we had been unaware. We deduce nothing; our understanding comes because we see the phenomenon for what it is, and are *in a position* to make other inferences from this realization.

[19] *Op. cit.,* p. 321.

[20] *Op. cit.,* p. 321.

[21] *Op. cit.,* p. 321.

[22] "Certain Weaknesses in the Deductive Model of Explanation," paper read at the Midwestern Division of the American Philosophical Association, May 1955.

N A N C Y   C A R T W R I G H T
THE TRUTH DOESN'T EXPLAIN MUCH

0. INTRODUCTION

Scientific theories must tell us both what is true in nature, and how we are to explain it. I shall argue that these are entirely different functions and should be kept distinct. Usually the two are conflated. The second is commonly seen as a by-product of the first. Scientific theories are thought to explain by dint of the descriptions they give of reality. Once the job of describing is done, science can shut down. That is all there is to do. To describe nature—to tell its laws, the values of its fundamental constants, its mass distributions—is *ipso facto* to lay down how we are to explain it.

This is a mistake, I shall argue; a mistake that is fostered by the covering-law model of explanation. The covering-law model supposes that all we need to know are the laws of nature—and a little logic, perhaps a little probability theory—and then we know which factors can explain which others. For example, in the simplest deductive-nomological version,[1] the covering-law model says that one factor explains another just in case the occurrence of the second can be deduced from the occurrence of the first given the laws of nature.

But the D-N model is just an example. In the sense which is relevant to my claims here, most models of explanation offered recently in the philosophy of science are covering-law models. This includes not only Hempel's own inductive statistical model,[2] but also Patrick Suppes's probabilistic model of causation,[3] Wesley Salmon's statistical relevance model,[4] and even Bengt Hanson's contextualistic model.[5] All these accounts rely on the laws of nature, and just the laws of nature, to pick out which factors we can use in explanation.

A good deal of criticism has been aimed at Hempel's original covering-law models. Much of the criticism objects that these models let in too much. On Hempel's account it seems we can explain Henry's failure to get pregnant by his taking birth control pills, and we can explain the storm by the falling barometer. My objection is quite the opposite. Covering-law models let in too little. With a covering-law model we can explain hardly anything, even the things of which we are most proud—like the role of DNA in the inheritance of genetic characteristics, or the formation of rainbows when sunlight is refracted through raindrops. We cannot explain these phenomena with a covering-law model, I shall argue, because we do not have laws that cover them. Covering laws are scarce.

Many phenomena which have perfectly good scientific explanations are not covered by any laws. No true laws, that is. They are at best covered by *ceteris paribus* generalizations—generalizations that hold only under special conditions, usually ideal conditions. The literal translation is "other things being equal"; but it would be more apt to read "*ceteris paribus*" as "other things being *right*."

Sometimes we act as if this does not matter. We have in the back of our minds an "understudy" picture of *ceteris paribus* laws: *ceteris paribus* laws are real laws; they can stand in when the laws we would like to see are not available and they can perform all the same functions, only not quite so well. But this will not do. *Ceteris paribus* generalizations, read literally without the "*ceteris paribus*" modifier, are false. They are not only false, but held by us to be false; and there is no ground in the covering-law picture for false laws to explain anything. On the other hand, with the modifier the *ceteris paribus* generalizations may be true, but they cover only those few cases where the conditions are right. For most cases, either we have a law that purports to cover, but cannot explain because it is acknowledged to be false, or we have a law that does not cover. Either way, it is bad for the covering-law picture.

1. *CERTERIS PARIBUS* LAWS

When I first started talking about the scarcity of covering laws, I tried to summarize my view by saying "There are no exceptionless generalizations." Then a friend asked, "How about 'All men are mortal'?" She was right. I had been focusing too much on the equations of physics. A more plausible claim would have been that there are no exceptionless quantitative laws in physics. Indeed not only are there no exceptionless laws, but in fact our best candidates are known to fail. This is something like the Popperian thesis that *every theory is born refuted.* Every theory we have proposed in physics, even at the time when it was most firmly entrenched, was known to be deficient in specific and detailed ways. I think this is also true for every precise quantitative law within a physics theory.

But this is not the point I had wanted to make. Some laws are treated, at least for the time being, as if they were exceptionless, whereas others are not, even though they remain "on the books." Snell's law (about the angle of incidence and the angle of refraction for a ray of light) is a good example of this latter kind. In the optics text I use for reference (Miles V. Klein, *Optics*),[6] it first appears on page 21, and without qualification:

> *Snell's Law:* At an interface between dielectric media, there is (also) *a refracted ray* in the second medium, lying in the plane of incidence, making an angle θ_t with the normal, and obeying Snell's law:
>
> $$\sin \theta / \sin \theta_t = n_2/n_1$$
>
> where v_1 and v_2 are the velocities of propagation in the two media, and $n_1 = (c/v_1)$, $n_2 = (c/v_2)$ are the indices of refraction.

It is only some 500 pages later, when the law is derived from the "full electromagnetic theory of light," that we learn that Snell's law as stated on page 21 is true only for media whose optical properties are *isotropic.* (In anisotropic media, "there will generally be *two* transmitted waves.") So what is deemed true is not really Snell's law as stated on page 21, but rather a refinement of Snell's law:

> *Refined Snell's Law: For any two media which are optically isotropic,* at an interface between dielectrics there is a refracted ray in the second medium, lying in the plane of incidence, making an angle θ_t with the normal, such that:
>
> $$\sin \theta / \sin \theta_t = n_2/n_1.$$

The Snell's law of page 21 in Klein's book is an example of a *ceteris paribus* law, a law that holds only in special circumstances—in this case when the media are both isotropic. Klein's statement on page 21 is clearly not to be taken literally. Charitably, we are inclined to put the modifier "*ceteris paribus*" in front to hedge it. But what does this *ceteris paribus* modifier do? With an eye to statistical versions of the covering law model (Hempel's I-S picture, or Salmon's statistical relevance model, or Suppes's probabilistic model of causation) we may suppose that the unrefined Snell's law is not intended to be a universal law, as literally stated, but rather some kind of statistical law. The obvious candidate is a crude statistical law: *for the most part,* at an interface between dielectric media there is *a* refracted ray . . . But this will not do. For *most* media are optically anisotropic, and in an anisotropic medium there are *two* rays. I think there are no more satisfactory alternatives. If *ceteris paribus* laws are to be true laws, there are no statistical laws with which they can generally be identified.

2. WHEN LAWS ARE SCARCE

Why do we keep Snell's law on the books when we both know it to be false and have a more accurate refinement available? There are obvious pedagogic reasons. But are there serious scientific ones? I think there are, and these reasons have to do with the task of explaining. Specifying which factors are explanatorily relevant to which others is a job done by science over and above the job of laying out the laws of nature. Once the laws of nature are known, we still have to decide what kinds of factors can be cited in explanation.

One thing that *ceteris paribus* laws do is to express our explanatory commitments. They tell what kinds of explanations are permitted. We know from the refined Snell's law that in any isotropic medium, the angle of refraction can be explained by the angle of incidence, according to the equation $\sin \theta / \sin \theta_t = n_2/n_1$. To leave the unrefined Snell's law on the books is to signal that the same kind of explanation can be given even for some anisotropic media. The pattern of explanation derived from the ideal situation is employed even where the conditions are less than ideal; and we assume that we can understand what happens in *nearly* isotropic media by rehearsing how light rays behave in pure isotropic cases.

This assumption is a delicate one. It fits far better with the simulacrum account of explanation that I will urge in Essay 8 than it does with any covering-law model. For the moment I intend only to point out that it *is* an assumption, and an assumption which (prior to the "full electromagnetic theory") goes well beyond our knowledge of the facts of nature. We *know* that in isotropic media, the angle of refraction is due to the angle of incidence under the equation $\sin \theta / \sin \theta_t = n_2/n_1$. We *decide* to explain the angles for the two refracted rays in anisotropic media in the same manner. We may have good reasons for the decision; in this case if the media are nearly isotropic, the two rays will be very close together, and close to the angle predicted by Snell's law; or we believe in continuity of physical processes. But still this decision is not forced by our knowledge of the laws of nature.

Obviously this decision could not be taken if we also had on the books a second refinement of Snell's law, implying that in any anisotropic media the angles are quite different from those given by Snell's law. But laws are scarce, and often we have no law at all about what happens in conditions that are less than ideal.

Covering-law theorists will tell a different story about the use of *ceteris paribus* laws in explanation. From their point of view, *ceteris paribus* explanations are elliptical for genuine covering law explanations from true laws which we do not yet know. When we use a *ceteris paribus* "law" which we know to be false, the covering-law theorist supposes us to be making a bet about what form the true law takes. For example, to retain Snell's unqualified law would be to bet that the (at the time unknown) law for anisotropic media will entail values "close enough" to those derived from the original Snell law.

I have two difficulties with this story. The first arises from an extreme metaphysical possibility, in which I in fact believe. Covering-law theorists tend to think that nature is well-regulated; in the extreme, that there is a law to cover every case. I do not. I imagine that natural objects are much like people in societies. Their behaviour is constrained by some specific laws and by a handful of general principles, but it is not determined in detail, even statistically. What happens on most occasions is dictated by no law at all. This is not a metaphysical picture that I urge. My claim is that this picture is as plausible as the alternative. God may have written just a few laws and grown tired. We do not know whether we are in a tidy universe or an untidy one. Whichever universe we are in, the ordinary commonplace activity of giving explanations ought to make sense.

The second difficulty for the ellipsis version of the covering-law account is more pedestrian. Elliptical explanations are not explanations: they are at best assurances that explanations are to be had. The law that is supposed to appear in the complete, correct D-N explanation is not a law we have in our theory, not a law that we can state, let alone test. There may be covering-law explanations in these cases. But those explanations are not our explanations; and those unknown laws cannot be our grounds for saying of a nearly isotropic medium, "$\sin \theta_t \approx k(n_2/n_1)$ *because* $\sin \theta = k$."

What then are our grounds? I assert only what they are not: they are not the laws of nature. The laws of nature that we know at any time are not enough to tell us what kinds of explanations can be given at that time. That requires a decision; and it is just this decision that covering-law theorists make when they wager about the existence of unknown laws. We may believe in these unknown laws, but we do so on no ordinary grounds: they have not been tested, nor are they derived from a higher level theory. Our grounds for believing in them are only as good as our reasons for adopting the corresponding explanatory strategy, and no better.

3. WHEN LAWS CONFLICT

I have been maintaining that there are not enough covering laws to go around. Why? The view depends on the picture of science that I mentioned earlier. Science is broken into various distinct domains: hydrodynamics, genetics, laser theory, . . . We have many detailed and sophisticated theories about what happens within the various domains. But we have little theory about what happens in the intersection of domains.

Diagramatically, we have laws like

$$\textit{ceteris paribus, } (x)\, (S(x) \hookrightarrow I(x))$$

and

$$\textit{ceteris paribus, } (x)\, (A(x) \hookrightarrow \neg I(x)).$$

For example, (*ceteris paribus*) adding salt to water decreases the cooking time of potatoes; taking the water to higher altitudes increases it. Refining, if we speak more carefully we might say instead, "Adding salt to water while keeping the altitude constant decreases the cooking time; whereas increasing the altitude while keeping the saline content fixed increases it"; or

$$(x)\ (S(x)\ \&\ \neg\ A(x)\ \hookrightarrow I(x))$$

and

$$(x)\ (A(x)\ \&\ \neg\ S(x)\ \hookrightarrow \neg\ I(x))$$

But neither of these tells what happens when we both add salt to the water and move to higher altitudes.

Here we think that probably there is a precise answer about what would happen, even though it is not part of our common folk wisdom. But this is not always the case. I discuss this in detail in the next essay. More real life cases involve some combination of causes; and general laws that describe what happens in these complex cases are not always available. Although both quantum theory and relativity are highly developed, detailed, and sophisticated, there is no satisfactory theory of relativistic quantum mechanics. . . . The general lesson is this: where theories intersect, laws are usually hard to come by.

4. WHEN EXPLANATIONS CAN BE GIVEN ANYWAY

So far, I have only argued half the case. I have argued that covering laws are scarce, and that *ceteris paribus* laws are no true laws. It remains to argue that, nevertheless, *ceteris paribus* laws have a fundamental explanatory role. But this is easy, for most of our explanations are explanations from *ceteris paribus* laws.

Let me illustrate with a humdrum example. Last year I planted camellias in my garden. I know that camellias like rich soil, so I planted them in composted manure. On the other hand, the manure was still warm, and I also know that camellia roots cannot take high temperatures. So I did not know what to expect. But when many of my camellias died, despite otherwise perfect care, I knew what went wrong. The camellias died because they were planted in hot soil.

This is surely the right explanation to give. Of course, I cannot be absolutely certain that this explanation is the correct one. Some other factor may have been responsible, nitrogen deficiency or some genetic defect in the plants, a factor that I did not notice, or may not even have known to be relevant. But this uncertainty is not peculiar to cases of explanation. It is just the uncertainty that besets all of our judgements about matters of fact. We must allow for oversight; still, since I made a reasonable effort to eliminate other menaces to my camellias, we may have some confidence that this is the right explanation.

So we have an explanation for the death of my camellias. But it is not an explanation from any true covering law. There is no law that says that camellias just like mine, planted in soil which is both hot and rich, die. To the contrary, they do not all die. Some thrive; and probably those that do, do so *because* of the richness of the soil they are planted in. We may insist that there must be some differentiating factor which brings the case under a covering law: in soil which is rich and hot, camellias of one kind die; those of another thrive. I will not deny that there may be such a covering law. I merely repeat that our ability to give this humdrum explanation precedes our knowledge of that law. On the Day of Judgment, when all laws are known, these may suffice to explain all phenomena. But in the meantime we do give explanations; and it is the job of science to tell us what kinds of explanations are admissible.

In fact I want to urge a stronger thesis. If, as is possible, the world is not a tidy deterministic system, this job of telling how we are to explain will be a job which is still left when the descriptive task of science is complete. Imagine for example (what I suppose actually to be the case) that the facts about camellias are irreducibly statistical. Then it is possible to know all the general nomological facts about camellias which there are to know—for example, that 62 per cent of all camellias in just the circumstances of my camellias die, and 38 per cent survive.[7] But one would not thereby know how to explain what happened in my garden. You would still have to look to the *Sunset Garden Book* to learn that the *heat* of the soil explains the perishing, and the *richness* explains the plants that thrive.

5. CONCLUSION

Most scientific explanations use *ceteris paribus* laws. These laws, read literally as descriptive statements, are false, not only false but deemed false even in the context of use. This is no surprise: we want laws that unify; but what happens may well be varied and diverse. We are lucky that we can organize phenomena at all. There is no reason to think that the principles that best organize will be true, nor that the principles that are true will organize much.

NOTES

[1] See C. G. Hempel, "Scientific Explanation," in C. G. Hempel (ed.), *Aspects of Scientific Explanation* (New York: Free Press, 1965).
[2] See C. G. Hempel, "Scientific Explanation," ibid.
[3] See Patrick Suppes, *A Probabilistic Theory of Causality* (Amsterdam: North-Holland Publishing Co., 1970).
[4] See Wesley Salmon, "Statistical Explanation," in Wesley Salmon (ed.), *Statistical Explanation and Statistical Relevance* (Pittsburgh: University of Pittsburgh Press, 1971).
[5] See Bengt Hanson, "Explanations—Of What?" (mimeograph, Stanford University, 1974).
[6] Miles V. Klein. *Optics* (New York: John Wiley and Sons, 1970), p. 21, italics added. θ is the angle of incidence.
[7] Various writers, especially Suppes (note 3) and Salmon (note 4), have urged that knowledge of more sophisticated statistical facts will suffice to determine what factors can be used in explanation. I do not believe that this claim can be carried out, as I have argued [elsewhere].

PHILIP KITCHER
EXPLANATORY UNIFICATION

1. THE DECLINE AND FALL OF THE COVERING LAW MODEL

One of the great apparent triumphs of logical empiricism was its official theory of explanation. In a series of lucid studies (Hempel 1965, Chapters 9, 10, 12; Hempel 1962; Hempel 1966), C. G. Hempel showed how to articulate precisely an idea which had received a hazy formulation from traditional empiricists such as Hume and Mill. The picture of explanation which Hempel presented, the *covering law model,* begins with the idea that explanation is derivation. When a scientist explains a phenomenon, he derives (deductively or inductively) a sentence describing that phenomenon (the *explanandum* sentence) from a set of sentences (the *explanans*) which must contain at least one general law.

Today the model has fallen on hard times. Yet it was never the empiricists' whole story about explanation. Behind the official model stood an unofficial model, a view of explanation which was not treated precisely, but which sometimes emerged in discussions of theoretical explanation. In contrasting scientific explanation with the idea of reducing unfamiliar phenomena to familiar phenomena, Hempel suggests this unofficial view: "What scientific explanation, especially theoretical explanation, aims at is not [an] intuitive and highly subjective kind of understanding, but an objective kind of insight that is achieved by a systematic unification, by exhibiting the phenomena as manifestations of common, underlying structures and processes that conform to specific, testable, basic principles" (Hempel 1966, p. 83; see also Hempel 1965, pp. 345, 444). Herbert Feigl makes a similar point: "The aim of scientific explanation throughout the ages has been *unification,* that is, the comprehending of a maximum of facts and regularities in terms of a minimum of theoretical concepts and assumptions" (Feigl 1970, p. 12).

This unofficial view, which regards explanation as unification, is, I think, more promising than the official view. My aim in this [reading] is to develop the view and to present its virtues. Since the picture of explanation which results is rather complex, my exposition will be programmatic, but I shall try to show that the unofficial view can avoid some prominent shortcomings of the covering law model.

Why should we want an account of scientific explanation? Two reasons present themselves. Firstly, we would like to understand and to evaluate the popular claim that the natural sciences do not merely pile up unrelated items of knowledge of more or less practical significance, but that they increase our understanding of the world. A theory of explanation should show us *how* scientific explanation advances our understanding. (Michael Friedman cogently presents this demand in his [1974]). Secondly, an account of explanation ought to enable us to comprehend and to arbitrate disputes in past and present science. Embryonic theories are often defended by appeal to their explanatory power. A theory of explanation should enable us to judge the adequacy of the defense.

The covering law model satisfies neither of these *desiderata.* Its difficulties stem from the fact that, when it is viewed as providing a set of necessary *and sufficient* conditions for explanation, it is far too liberal. Many derivations which are intuitively non-explanatory meet the conditions of the model. Unable to make relatively gross distinctions, the model is quite powerless to adjudicate the more subtle considerations about explanatory adequacy which are the focus of scientific debate. Moreover, our ability to derive a description of a phenomenon from a set of premises *containing a law* seems quite tangential to our understanding of the phenomenon. Why should it be that exactly those derivations which employ laws advance our understanding?

The unofficial theory appears to do better. As Friedman points out, we can easily connect the notion of unification with that of understanding. (However, as I have argued in my [1976], Friedman's analysis of unification is faulty; the account of unification offered below is indirectly defended by my diagnosis of the problems for his approach.) Furthermore, as we shall see below, the acceptance of some major programs of scientific research—such as, the Newtonian program of eighteenth-century physics and chemistry, and the Darwinian program of nineteenth-century biology—depended on recognizing promises for unifying, and thereby explaining, the phenomena. Reasonable skepticism may protest at this point that the attractions of the unofficial view stem from its unclarity. Let us see.

2. EXPLANATION: SOME PRAGMATIC ISSUES

Our first task is to formulate the problem of scientific explanation clearly, filtering out a host of issues which need not concern us here. The most obvious way in which to categorize explanation is to view it as an activity. In this activity we answer the actual or anticipated questions of an actual or anticipated audience. We do so by presenting reasons. We draw on the beliefs we hold, frequently using or adapting arguments furnished to us by the sciences.

Recognizing the connection between explanations and arguments, proponents of the covering law model (and other writers on explanation) have identified explanations as special types of arguments. But although I shall follow the covering law model in employing the notion of argument to characterize that of explanation, I shall not adopt the ontological thesis that explanations are arguments. Following Peter Achinstein's thorough discussion of ontological issues concerning explanation in his (1977), I shall suppose that an explanation is an ordered pair consisting of a proposition and an act type.[1] The relevance of arguments to explanation resides in the fact that what makes an ordered pair (p, explaining q) an explanation is that a sentence expressing p bears an appropriate relation to a particular argument. (Achinstein shows how the central idea of the covering law model can be viewed in this way.) So I am supposing that there are acts of explanation which draw on arguments supplied by science, reformulating the traditional problem of explanation as the question: What features should a scientific argument have if it is to serve as the basis for an act of explanation?[2]

The complex relation between scientific explanation and scientific argument may be illuminated by a simple example. Imagine a mythical Galileo confronted by a mythical fusilier who wants to know why his gun attains maximum range when it is mounted on a flat plain, if the barrel is elevated at 45° to the horizontal. Galileo reformulates this question as the question of why an ideal projectile, projected with fixed velocity from a perfectly smooth horizontal plane and subject only to gravitational acceleration, attains maximum range when the angle of elevation of the projection is 45°. He defends this reformulation by arguing that the effects of air resistance in the case of the actual projectile, the cannonball, are insignificant, and that the curvature of the earth and the unevenness of the ground can be neglected. He then selects a kinematical argument which shows that, for fixed velocity, an ideal projectile attains maximum range when the angle of elevation is 45°. He adapts this argument by explaining to the fusilier some unfamiliar terms ("uniform acceleration," let us say), motivating some problematic principles (such as the law of composition of velocities), and by omitting some obvious computational steps. Both Galileo and the fusilier depart satisfied.

The most general problem of scientific explanation is to determine the conditions which must be met if science is to be used in answering an explanation-seeking question Q. I shall restrict my attention to explanation-seeking why-questions, and I shall attempt to determine the conditions under which an argument whose conclusion is S can be used to answer the question "Why is it the case that S?" More colloquially, my project will be that of deciding when an argument explains why its conclusion is true.[3]

We leave on one side a number of interesting, and difficult issues. So, for example, I shall not discuss the general relation between explanation-seeking questions and the arguments which can be used to answer them, nor the pragmatic conditions governing the idealization of questions and the adaptation of scientific arguments to the needs of the audience. (For illuminating discussions of some of these issues, see Bromberger 1962.) Given that so much is dismissed, does anything remain?

In a provocative article, (van Fraassen 1977) Bas van Fraassen denies, in effect, that there are any issues about scientific explanation other than the pragmatic questions I have just banished. After a survey of attempts to provide a theory of explanation he appears to conclude that the idea that explanatory power is a special virtue of theories is a myth. We accept scientific theories on the basis of their empirical adequacy and simplicity, and, having done so, we use the arguments with which they supply us to give explanations. This activity of applying scientific arguments in explanation accords with extra-scientific, "pragmatic," conditions. Moreover, our views about these extra-scientific factors are revised in the light of our acceptance of new theories: ". . . science schools our imagination so as to revise just those prior judgments of what satisfies and eliminates wonder" (van Fraassen 1977, p. 150). Thus there are no context-independent conditions, beyond those of simplicity and empirical adequacy which distinguish arguments for use in explanation.

Van Fraassen's approach does not fit well with some examples from the history of science—such as the acceptance of Newtonian theory of matter and Darwin's theory of evolution—examples in which the explanatory promise of a theory was appreciated in advance of the articulation of a theory with predictive power. (See section 3 below.) Moreover, the account I shall offer provides an answer to skepticism that no "global constraints" (van Fraassen 1977, p. 146) on explanation can avoid the familiar problems of asymmetry and irrelevance, problems which bedevil the covering law model. I shall try to respond to van Fraassen's challenge by showing that there are certain context-independent features of arguments which distinguish them for application in response to explanation-seeking why-questions, and that we can assess theories (including embryonic theories) by their ability to provide us with such arguments. Hence I think that it is possible to defend the thesis that historical appeals to the explanatory power of theories involve recognition of a virtue over and beyond considerations of simplicity and predictive power.

Resuming our main theme, we can use the example of Galileo and the fusilier to achieve a further refinement of our problem. Galileo selects and adapts an argument from his new kinematics—that is, he draws an argument from a set of arguments available for explanatory purposes, a set which I shall call the *explanatory store.* We may think of the sciences not as providing us with many unrelated individual arguments which can be used in individual acts of explanation, but as offering a reserve of explanatory arguments, which we may tap as need arises. Approaching the issue in this way, we shall be led to present our problem as that of specifying the conditions which must be met by the explanatory store.

The set of arguments which science supplies for adaptation acts of explanation will change with our changing beliefs. Therefore the appropriate *analysandum* is the notion of the store of arguments relative to a set of accepted sentences. Suppose that, at the point in the history of inquiry which interests us, the set of accepted sentences is *K.* (I shall assume, for simplicity's sake, that *K* is consistent. Should our beliefs be inconsistent then it is more appropriate to regard *K* as some tidied version of our beliefs.) The general problem I have set is that of specifying *E(K)*, the *explanatory store over K,* which is the set of arguments acceptable as the basis for acts of explanation by those whose beliefs are exactly the members of *K.* (For the purposes of this paper I shall assume that, for each *K* there is exactly one *E(K)*.)

The unofficial view answers the problem: for each *K, E(K)* is the set of arguments which best unifies *K.* My task is to articulate the answer. I begin by looking at two historical episodes in which the desire for unification played a crucial role. In both cases, we find three important features: (i) prior to the articulation of a theory with high predictive power, certain proposals for theory construction are favored on grounds of their explanatory promise; (ii) the explanatory power of embryonic theories is explicitly tied to the notion of unification; (iii) particular features of the theories are taken to support their claims to unification. Recognition of (i) and (ii) will illustrate points that have already been made, while (iii) will point towards an analysis of the concept of unification.

3. A NEWTONIAN PROGRAM

Newton's achievements in dynamics, astronomy and optics inspired some of his successors to undertake an ambitious program which I shall call "dynamic corpuscularianism."[4] *Principia* had shown how to obtain the motions of bodies from a knowledge of the forces acting on them, and had also demonstrated the possibility of dealing with gravitational systems in a unified way. The next step would be to isolate a few basic force laws, akin to the law of universal gravitation, so that, applying the basic laws to specifications of the dispositions of the ultimate parts of bodies, all of the phenomena of nature could be derived. Chemical reactions, for example, might be understood in terms of the rearrangement of ultimate parts under the action of cohesive and repulsive forces. The phenomena of reflection, refraction and diffraction of light might be viewed as resulting from a special force of attraction between light corpuscles and ordinary matter. These speculations encouraged eighteenth-century Newtonians to construct very general hypotheses about inter-atomic forces—even in the absence of any confirming evidence for the existence of such forces.

In the preface to *Principia,* Newton had already indicated that he took dynamic corpuscularianism to be a program deserving the attention of the scientific community:

> I wish we could derive the rest of the phenomena of Nature by the same kind of reasoning from mechanical principles, for I am induced by many reasons to suspect that they may all depend upon certain forces by which the particles of bodies, by some causes hitherto unknown, are either mutually impelled towards one another, and cohere in regular figures, or are repelled and recede from one another (Newton 1962, p. xviii. See also Newton 1952, pp. 401–2).

This, and other influential passages, inspired Newton's successors to try to complete the unification of science by finding further force laws analogous to the law of universal gravitation. Dynamic corpuscularianism remained popular so long as there was promise of significant unification. Its appeal began to fade only when repeated attempts to specify force laws were found to invoke so many different (apparently incompatible) attractive and repulsive forces that the goal of unification appeared unlikely. Yet that goal could still motivate renewed efforts to implement the program. In the second half of the eighteenth century Boscovich revived dynamic corpuscularian hopes by claiming that the whole of natural philosophy can be reduced to "one law of forces existing in nature."[5]

The passage I have quoted from Newton suggests the nature of the unification that was being sought. *Principia* had exhibited how one style of argument, one "kind of reasoning from mechanical principles," could be used in the derivation of descriptions of many, diverse, phenomena. The unifying power of Newton's work consisted in its demonstration that one *pattern* of argument could be used again and again in the derivation of a wide range of accepted sentences. (I shall give a representation of the Newtonian pattern in Section 5.) In searching for force laws analogous to the law of universal gravitation, Newton's successors were trying to generalize the pattern of argument presented in *Principia,* so that one "kind of reasoning" would suffice to derive all phenomena of motion. If, furthermore, the facts studied by chemistry, optics, physiology and so forth, could be related to facts about particle motion, then one general pattern of argument would be used in the derivation of all phenomena. I suggest that this is the ideal of unification at which Newton's immediate successors aimed, which came to seem less likely to be attained as the eighteenth century wore on, and which Boscovich's work endeavored, with some success, to reinstate.

4. THE RECEPTION OF DARWIN'S EVOLUTIONARY THEORY

The picture of unification which emerges from the last section may be summarized quite simply: a theory unifies our beliefs when it provides one (or more generally, a few) pattern(s) of argument which can be used in the derivation of a large number of sentences which we accept. I shall try to develop this idea more precisely in later sections. But first I want to show how a different example suggests the same view of unification.

In several places, Darwin claims that his conclusion that species evolve through natural selection should be accepted because of its explanatory power, that ". . . the doctrine must sink or swim according as it groups and explains phenomena" (F. Darwin 1887; vol. 2, p. 155, quoted in Hull 1974, p. 292). Yet, as he often laments, he is unable to provide any complete derivation of any biological phenomenon—our ignorance of the appropriate facts and regularities is "profound." How, then, can he contend that the primary virtue of the new theory is its explanatory power?

The answer lies in the fact that Darwin's evolutionary theory promises to unify a host of biological phenomena (C. Darwin 1964, pp. 243–44). The eventual unification would consist in derivations of descriptions of these phenomena which would instantiate a common pattern. When Darwin expounds his doctrine what he offers us is the pattern. Instead of detailed explanations of the presence of some particular trait in some particular species, Darwin presents two "imaginary examples" (C. Darwin 1964, pp. 90–96) and a diagram, which shows, in a general way, the evolution of species *represented by schematic letters* (1964, pp. 116–26). In doing so, he exhibits a pattern of argument, which, he maintains, can be instantiated, *in principle,* by a complete and rigorous derivation of descriptions of the characteristics of any current species. The derivation would employ the principle of natural selection—as well as premises describing ancestral forms and the nature of their environment and the (unknown) laws of variation and inheritance. In place of detailed evolutionary stories, Darwin offers *explanation-sketches.* By showing how a particular characteristic would be advantageous to a particular species, he indicates an explanation of the emergence of that characteristic in the species, suggesting the outline of an argument instantiating the general pattern.

From this perspective, much of Darwin's argumentation in the *Origin* (and in other works) becomes readily comprehensible. Darwin attempts to show how his pattern can be applied to a host of biological phenomena. He claims that, by using arguments which instantiate the pattern, we can account for analogous variations in kindred species, for the greater variability of specific (as opposed to generic) characteristics, for the facts about geographical distribution, and so forth. But he is also required to resist challenges that the pattern cannot be applied in some cases, that premises for arguments instantiating the pattern will not be forthcoming. So, for example, Darwin must show how evolutionary stories, fashioned after his pattern, can be told to account for the emergence of complex organs. In both aspects of his argument, whether he is responding to those who would limit the application of his pattern or whether he is campaigning for its use within a realm of biological phenomena, Darwin has the same goal. He aims to show that his theory should be accepted because it unifies and explains.

5. ARGUMENT PATTERNS

Our two historical examples[6] have led us to the conclusion that the notion of an argument pattern is central to that of explanatory unification. Quite different considerations could easily have pointed us in the same direction. If someone were to distinguish between the explanatory worth of two arguments instantiating a common pattern, then we would regard that person as an explanatory deviant. To grasp the concept of explanation is to see that if one accepts an argument as explanatory, one is thereby committed to accepting as explanatory other arguments which instantiate the same pattern.

To say that members of a set of arguments instantiate a common pattern is to recognize that the arguments in the set are similar in some interesting way. With different interests, people may fasten on different similarities, and may arrive at different notions of argument pattern. Our enterprise is to characterize the concept of argument pattern which plays a role in the explanatory activity of scientists.

Formal logic, ancient and modern, is concerned in one obvious sense with patterns of argument. The logician proceeds by isolating a small set of expressions (the logical vocabulary), considers the schemata formed from sentences by replacing with dummy letters all expressions which do not belong to this set, and tries to specify which sequences of these schemata are valid patterns of argument. The pattern of argument which is taught to students of Newtonian dynamics is not a pattern of the kind which interests logicians. It has instantiations with different logical structures. (A rigorous derivation of the equations of motion of different dynamical systems would have a logical structure depending on the number of bodies involved and the mathematical details of the integration.) Moreover, an argument can only instantiate the Newtonian pattern if particular *non*-logical terms, "force," "mass," and "acceleration," occur in it in particular ways. However, the logician's approach can help us to isolate the notion of argument pattern which we require.

Let us say that a *schematic sentence* is an expression obtained by replacing some, but not necessarily all, the non-logical expressions occurring in a sentence with dummy letters. A set of *filling instructions* for a schematic sentence is a set of directions for replacing the dummy letters of the schematic sentence, such that, for each dummy letter, there is a direction which tells us how it should be replaced. A *schematic argument* is a sequence of schematic sentences. A *classification* for a schematic argument is a set of sentences which describe the inferential characteristics of the schematic argument: its function is to tell us which terms in the sequence are to be regarded as premises, which are to be inferred from which, what rules of inference are to be used, and so forth.

We can use these ideas to define the concept of a *general argument pattern*. A general argument pattern is a triple consisting of a schematic argument, a set of sets of filling instructions containing one set of filling instructions for each term of the schematic argument, and a classification for the schematic argument. A sequence of sentences instantiates the general argument pattern just in case it meets the following conditions:

(I) The sequence has the same number of terms as the schematic argument of the general argument pattern.

(II) Each sentence in the sequence is obtained from the corresponding schematic sentence in accordance with the appropriate set of filling instructions.

(III) It is possible to construct a chain of reasoning which assigns to each sentence the status accorded to the corresponding schematic sentence by the classification.

We can make these definitions more intuitive by considering the way in which they apply to the Newtonian example. Restricting ourselves to the basic pattern used in treating systems which contain one body (such as the pendulum and the projectile) we may represent the schematic argument as follows:

(1) The force on α is β.
(2) The acceleration of α is γ.
(3) Force = mass $\cdot$ acceleration.
(4) (Mass of α) $\cdot$ (γ) = β
(5) $\delta = \theta$

The filling instructions tell us that all occurrences of 'α' are to be replaced by an expression referring to the body under investigation; occurrences of 'β' are to be replaced by an algebraic expression referring to a function of the variable coordinates and of time; 'γ' is to be replaced by an expression which gives the acceleration of the body as a function of its coordinates and their time-derivatives (thus, in the case of a one-dimensional motion along the x-axis of a Cartesian coordinate system, 'γ' would be replaced by the expression 'd^2x/dt^2'); 'δ' is to be replaced by an expression referring to the variable coordinates of the body, and 'θ' is to be replaced by an explicit function of time, (thus the sentences which instantiate (5) reveal the dependence of the variable coordinates on time, and so provide specifications of the positions of the body in question throughout the motion). The classification of the argument tells us that (1)–(3) have the status of premises, that (4) is obtained from them by substituting identicals, and that (5) follows from (4) using algebraic manipulation and the techniques of the calculus.

Although the argument patterns which interest logicians are general argument patterns in the sense just defined, our example exhibits clearly the features which distinguish the kinds of patterns which scientists are trained to use. Whereas logicians are concerned to display all the schematic premises which are employed and to specify exactly which rules of inference are used, our example allows for the use of premises (mathematical assumptions) which do not occur as terms of the schematic argument, and it does not give a complete description of the way in which the route from (4) to (5) is to go. Moreover, our pattern does not replace all non-logical expressions by dummy letters. Because some non-logical expressions remain, the pattern imposes special demands on arguments which instantiate it. In a different way, restrictions are set by the instructions for replacing dummy letters. The patterns of logicians are very liberal in both these latter respects. The conditions for replacing dummy letters in Aristotelian syllogisms, or first-order schemata, require only that some letters be replaced with predicates, others with names.

Arguments may be similar either in terms of their logical structure or in terms of the non-logical vocabulary they employ at corresponding places. I think that the notion of similarity (and the corresponding notion of pattern) which is central to the explanatory activity of scientists results from a compromise in demanding these two kinds of similarity. I propose that scientists are interested in *stringent* patterns of argument, patterns which contain some non-logical expressions and which are fairly similar in terms of logical structure. The Newtonian pattern cited above furnishes a good example. Although arguments instantiating this pattern do not have exactly the same logical structure, the classification imposes conditions which ensure that there will be similarities in logical structure among such arguments. Moreover, the presence of the non-logical terms sets strict requirements on the instantiations and so ensures a different type of kinship among them. Thus, without trying to provide an exact analysis of the notion of stringency, we may suppose that the stringency of a pattern is determined by two different constraints: (1) the conditions on the substitution of expressions for dummy letters, jointly imposed by the presence of non-logical expressions in the pattern and by the filling instructions; and, (2) the conditions on the logical structure, imposed by the classification. If both conditions are relaxed completely then the notion of pattern degenerates so as to admit *any* argument. If both conditions are simultaneously made as strict as possible, then we obtain another degenerate case, a "pattern" which is its own unique instantiation. If condition (2) is tightened at the total expense of (1), we produce the logician's notion of pattern. The use of condition (1) requires that arguments instantiating a common pattern draw on a common non-logical vocabulary. We can glimpse here that ideal of unification through the use of a few theoretical concepts which the remarks of Hempel and Feigl suggest.

Ideally, we should develop a precise account of how these two kinds of similarity are weighted against one another. The best strategy for obtaining such an account is to see how claims about stringency occur in scientific discussions. But scientists do not make explicit assessments of the stringency of argument patterns. Instead they evaluate the ability of a theory to explain and to unify. The way to a refined account of stringency lies through the notions of explanation and unification.

6. EXPLANATION AS UNIFICATION

As I have posed it, the problem of explanation is to specify which set of arguments we ought to accept for explanatory purposes given that we hold certain sentences to be true. Obviously this formulation can encourage confusion: we must not think of a scientific community as *first* deciding what sentences it will accept and *then* adopting the appropriate set of arguments. The Newtonian and Darwinian examples should convince us that the promise of explanatory power enters into the modification of our beliefs. So, in proposing that $E(K)$ is a function of K, I do not mean to suggest that the acceptance of K must be temporally prior to the adoption of $E(K)$.

$E(K)$ is to be that set of arguments which best unifies K. There are, of course, usually many ways of deriving some sentences in K from others. Let us call a set of arguments which derives some members of K from other members of K a *systematization* of K. We may then think of $E(K)$ as the best systematization of K.

Let us begin by making explicit an idealization which I have just made tacitly. A set of arguments will be said to be *acceptable relative* to K just in case every argument in the set consists of a sequence of steps which accord with elementary valid rules of inference (deductive or inductive) and if every premise of every argument in the set belongs to K. When we are considering ways of systematizing K we restrict our attention to those sets of arguments which are acceptable relative to K. This is an idealization because we sometimes use as the basis of acts of explanation arguments furnished by theories whose principles we no longer believe. I shall not investigate this practice nor the considerations which justify us in engaging in it. The most obvious way to extend my idealized picture to accommodate it is to regard the explanatory store over K, as I characterize it here, as being supplemented with an extra class of arguments meeting the following conditions: (a) from the perspective of K, the premises of these arguments are approximately true; (b) these arguments can be viewed as approximating the structure of (parts of) arguments in $E(K)$; (c) the arguments are simpler than the corresponding arguments in $E(K)$. Plainly, to spell out these conditions precisely would lead into issues which are tangential to my main goal in this paper.

    The moral of the Newtonian and Darwinian examples is that unification is achieved by using similar arguments in the derivation of many accepted sentences. When we confront the set of possible systematizations of K we should therefore attend to the *patterns* of argument which are employed in each systematization. Let us introduce the notion of a *generating set:* if Σ is a set of arguments then a generating set for Σ is a set of argument patterns Π such that each argument in Σ is an instantiation of some pattern in Π. A generating set for Σ will be said to be *complete with respect to K* if and only if every argument which is acceptable relative to K and which instantiates a pattern in Π belongs to Σ. In determining the explanatory store $E(K)$ we first narrow our choice to those sets of arguments which are acceptable relative to K, the systematizations of K. Then we consider, for each such set of arguments, the various generating sets of argument patterns which are complete with respect to K. (The importance of the requirement of completeness is to debar explanatory deviants who use patterns selectively.) Among these latter sets we select that set with the greatest unifying power (according to criteria shortly to be indicated) and we call the selected set the *basis* of the set of arguments in question. The explanatory store over K is that systematization whose basis does best by the criteria of unifying power.

    This complicated picture can be made clearer, perhaps, with the help of a diagram.

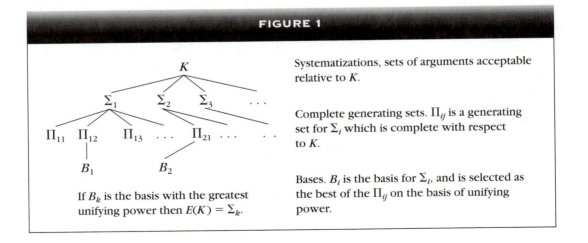

FIGURE 1

Systematizations, sets of arguments acceptable relative to K.

Complete generating sets. Π_{ij} is a generating set for Σ_i which is complete with respect to K.

Bases. B_i is the basis for Σ_i, and is selected as the best of the Π_{ij} on the basis of unifying power.

If B_k is the basis with the greatest unifying power then $E(K) = \Sigma_k$.

The task which confronts us is now formulated as that of specifying the factors which determine the unifying power of a set of argument patterns. Our Newtonian and Darwinian examples inspire an obvious suggestion: unifying power is achieved by generating a large number of accepted sentences as the conclusions of acceptable arguments which instantiate a few, stringent patterns. With this in mind, we define the *conclusion set* of a set of arguments Σ, $C(\Sigma)$, to be the set of sentences which occur as conclusions of some argument in Σ. So we might propose that the unifying power of a basis B_i with respect to K varies directly with the size of $C(\Sigma_i)$, varies directly with the stringency of the patterns which belong to B_i, and varies inversely with the number of members of B_i. This proposal is along the right lines, but it is, unfortunately, too simple.

The pattern of argument which derives a specification of the positions of bodies as explicit functions of time from a specification of the forces acting on those bodies is, indeed, central to Newtonian explanations. But not every argument used in Newtonian explanations instantiates this pattern. Some Newtonian derivations consist of an argument instantiating the pattern followed by further derivations from the conclusion. Thus, for example, when we explain why a pendulum has the period it does we may draw on an argument which *first* derives the equation of motion of the pendulum and *then* continues by deriving the period. Similarly, in explaining why projectiles projected with fixed velocity obtain maximum range when projected at 45° to the horizontal, we first show how the values of the horizontal and vertical coordinates can be found as functions of time and the angle of elevation, use our results to compute the horizontal distance traveled by the time the projectile returns to the horizontal, and then show how this distance is a maximum when the angle of elevation of projection is 45°. In both cases we take further steps beyond the computation of the explicit equations of motion—and the further steps in each case are different.

If we consider the entire range of arguments which Newtonian dynamics supplies for explanatory purposes, we find that these arguments instantiate a number of different patterns. Yet these patterns are not entirely distinct, for all of them proceed by using the computation of explicit equations of motion as a prelude to further derivation. It is natural to suggest that the pattern of computing equations of motion is the *core* pattern provided by Newtonian theory, and that the theory also shows how conclusions generated by arguments instantiating the core pattern can be used to derive further conclusions. In some Newtonian explanations, the core pattern is supplemented by a *problem-reducing pattern,* a pattern of argument which shows how to obtain a further type of conclusion from explicit equations of motion.

This suggests that our conditions on unifying power should be modified, so that, instead of merely counting the number of different patterns in a basis, we pay attention to similarities among them. All the patterns in the basis may contain a common core pattern, that is, each of them may contain some pattern as a subpattern. The unifying power of a basis is obviously increased if some (or all) of the patterns it contains share a common core pattern.

As I mentioned at the beginning of this [reading], the account of explanation as unification is complicated. The explanatory store is determined on the basis of criteria which pull in different directions, and I shall make no attempt here to specify precisely the ways in which these criteria are to be balanced against one another. Instead, I shall show that some traditional problems of scientific explanation can be solved without more detailed specification of the conditions on unifying power. For the account I have indicated has two important corollaries.

(A) Let Σ, Σ' be sets of arguments which are acceptable relative to K and which meet the following conditions:

  (I) the basis of Σ' is as good as the basis of Σ in terms of the criteria of stringency of patterns, paucity of patterns, presence of core patterns and so forth.
  (II) $C(\Sigma)$ is a proper subset of $C(\Sigma')$.

Then $\Sigma \neq E(K)$.

(B) Let Σ, Σ' be sets of arguments which are acceptable relative to K and which meet the following conditions:

  (I) $C(\Sigma) = C(\Sigma')$
  (II) the basis of Σ' is a proper subset of the basis of Σ.

Then $\Sigma \neq E(K)$.

(A) and (B) tell us that sets of arguments which do equally well in terms of some of our conditions are to be ranked according to their relative ability to satisfy the rest. I shall try to show that (A) and (B) have interesting consequences.

7. ASYMMETRY, IRRELEVANCE AND ACCIDENTAL GENERALIZATION

Some familiar difficulties beset the covering law model. The *asymmetry problem* arises because some scientific laws have the logical form of equivalences. Such laws can be used "in either direction." Thus a law asserting that the satisfaction of a condition C_1 is equivalent to the satisfaction of a condition C_2 can be used in two different kinds of argument. From a premise asserting that an object meets C_1, we can use the law to infer that it meets C_2; conversely, from a premise asserting that an object meets C_2, we can use the law to infer that it meets C_1. The asymmetry problem is generated by noting that in many such cases one of these derivations can be used in giving explanations while the other cannot.

Consider a hoary example. (For further examples, see Bromberger 1966.) We can explain why a simple pendulum has the period it does by deriving a specification of the period from a specification of the length and the law which relates length and period. But we cannot explain the length of the pendulum by deriving a specification of the length from a specification of the period and the same law. What accounts for our different assessment of these two arguments? Why does it seem that one is explanatory while the other "gets things backwards"? The covering law model fails to distinguish the two, and thus fails to provide answers.

The *irrelevance problem* is equally vexing. The problem arises because we can sometimes find a lawlike connection between an accidental and irrelevant occurrence and an event or state which would have come about independently of that occurrence. Imagine that Milo the magician waves his hands over a sample of table salt, thereby "hexing" it. It is true (and I shall suppose, lawlike) that all hexed samples of table salt dissolve when placed in water. Hence we can construct a derivation of the dissolving of Milo's hexed sample of salt by citing the circumstances of the hexing. Although this derivation fits the covering law model, it is, by our ordinary lights, non-explanatory. (This example is given by Wesley Salmon in his (1970); Salmon attributes it to Henry Kyburg. For more examples, see Achinstein 1971.)

The covering law model explicitly debars a further type of derivation which any account of explanation ought to exclude. Arguments whose premises contain no laws, but which make essential use of accidental generalizations are intuitively non-explanatory. Thus, if we derive the conclusion that Horace is bald from premises stating that Horace is a member of the Greenbury School Board and that all members of the Greenbury School Board are bald, we do not thereby explain why Horace is bald. (See Hempel 1965, p. 339.) We shall have to show that our account does not admit as explanatory derivations of this kind.

I want to show that the account of explanation I have sketched contains sufficient resources to solve these problems.[7] In each case we shall pursue a common strategy. Faced with an argument we want to exclude from the explanatory store we endeavor to show that any set of arguments containing the unwanted argument could not provide the best unification of our beliefs. Specifically, we shall try to show either that any such set of arguments will be more limited than some other set with an equally satisfactory basis, or that the basis of the set must fare worse according to the criterion of using the smallest number of most stringent patterns. That is, we shall appeal to the corollaries (A) and (B) given above. In actual practice, this strategy for exclusion is less complicated than one might fear, and, as we shall see, its applications to the examples just discussed brings out what is intuitively wrong with the derivations we reject.

Consider first the irrelevance problem. Suppose that we were to accept as explanatory the argument which derives a description of the dissolving of the salt from a description of Milo's act of hexing. What will be our policy for explaining the dissolving of samples of salt which have not been hexed? If we offer the usual chemical arguments in these latter cases then we shall commit ourselves to an inflated basis for the set of arguments we accept as explanatory. For, unlike the person who explains *all* cases of dissolving of samples of salt by using the standard chemical pattern of argument, we shall be committed to the use of two different patterns of argument in covering such cases. Nor is the use of the extra pattern of argument offset by its applicability in explaining other phenomena. Our policy employs one extra pattern of argument without extending the range of things we can derive from our favored set of arguments. Conversely, if we eschew the standard chemical pattern of argument (just using the pattern which appeals to the hexing) we shall find ourselves unable to apply our favored pattern to cases in which the sample of salt dissolved has not been hexed. Moreover, the pattern we use will not fall under the more general patterns we employ to explain chemical phenomena such as solution, precipitation and so forth. Hence the unifying power of the basis for our preferred set of arguments will be less than that of the basis for the set of arguments we normally accept as explanatory.[8]

If we explain the dissolving of the sample of salt which Milo has hexed by appealing to the hexing then we are faced with the problems of explaining the dissolving of unhexed samples of salt. We have two options: (a) to adopt two patterns of argument corresponding to the two kinds of case; (b) to adopt one pattern of argument whose instantiations apply just to the cases of hexed salt. If we choose (a) then we shall be in conflict with (B), whereas choice of (b) will be ruled out by (A). The general moral is that appeals to hexing fasten on a local and accidental feature of the cases of solution. By contrast our standard arguments instantiate a pattern which can be generally applied.[9]

A similar strategy succeeds with the asymmetry problem. We have general ways of explaining why bodies have the dimensions they do. Our practice is to describe the circumstances leading to the formation of the object in question and then to show how it has since been modified. Let us call explanations of this kind "origin and development derivations." (In some cases, the details of the original formation of the object are more important; with other objects, features of its subsequent modification are crucial.) Suppose now that we admit as explanatory a derivation of the length of a simple pendulum from a specification of the period. Then we shall either have to explain the lengths of *non*-swinging bodies by employing quite a different style of explanation (an origin and development derivation) or we shall have to forego explaining the lengths of such bodies. The situation is exactly parallel to that of the irrelevance problem. Admitting the argument which is intuitively non-explanatory saddles us with a set of arguments which is less good at unifying our beliefs than the set we normally choose for explanatory purposes.

Our approach also solves a more refined version of the pendulum problem (given by Paul Teller in his ["On Why-Questions"] [1974]). Many bodies which are not currently executing pendulum motion *could* be making small oscillations, and, were they to do so, the period of their motion would be functionally related to their dimensions. For such bodies we can specify the *dispositional period* as the period which the body would have if it were to execute small oscillations. Someone may now suggest that we can construct derivations of the dimensions of bodies from specifications of their dispositional periods, thereby generating an argument pattern which can be applied as generally as that instantiated in origin and development explanations. This suggestion is mistaken. There are some objects—such as the Earth and the Crab Nebula—which *could not* be pendulums, and for which the notion of a dispositional period makes no sense. Hence the argument pattern proposed cannot entirely supplant our origin and development derivations, and, in consequence, acceptance of it would fail to achieve the best unification of our beliefs.

The problem posed by accidental generalizations can be handled in parallel fashion. We have a general pattern of argument, using principles of physiology, which we apply to explain cases of baldness. This pattern is generally applicable, whereas that which derives ascriptions of baldness using the principle that all members of the Greenbury School Board are bald is not. Hence, as in the other cases, sets which contain the unwanted derivation be ruled out by one of the conditions (A), (B).

Of course, this does not show that an account of explanation along the lines I have suggested would sanction only derivations which satisfy the conditions imposed by the covering law model. For I have not argued that an explanatory derivation need contain *any* sentence of universal form. What *does* seem to follow from the account of explanation as unification is that explanatory arguments must not use accidental generalization, and, in this respect, the new account appears to underscore and generalize an important insight of the covering law model. Moreover, our success with the problems of asymmetry and irrelevance indicates that, even in the absence of a detailed account of the notion of stringency and of the way in which generality of the consequence set is weighed against paucity and stringency of the patterns in the basis, the view of explanation as unification has the resources to solve some traditional difficulties for theories of explanation.

8. SPURIOUS UNIFICATION

Unfortunately there is a fly in the ointment. One of the most aggravating problems for the covering law model has been its failure to exclude certain types of self-explanation. (For a classic source of difficulties see Eberle, Kaplan and Montague 1961.) As it stands, the account of explanation as unification seems to be even more vulnerable on this score. The problem derives from a phenomenon which I shall call *spurious unification*.

Consider, first, a difficulty which Hempel and Oppenheim noted in a seminal article (Hempel 1965, Chapter 10). Suppose that we conjoin two laws. Then we can derive one of the laws from the conjunction, and the derivation conforms to the covering law model (unless, of course, the model is restricted to cover only the explanation of singular sentences; Hempel and Oppenheim do, in fact, make this restriction). To quote Hempel and Oppenheim:

> The core of the difficulty can be indicated briefly by reference to an example: Kepler's laws, *K,* may be conjoined with Boyle's law, *B,* to a stronger law $K \cdot B$; but derivation of *K* from the latter would not be considered as an explanation of the regularities stated in Kepler's laws; rather it would be viewed as representing, in effect, a pointless "explanation" of Kepler's laws by themselves. (Hempel 1965, p. 273, fn. 33)

This problem is magnified for our account. For, why may we not unify our beliefs *completely* by deriving all of them using arguments which instantiate the one pattern?

$$\frac{\alpha \text{ and } B}{\alpha} \qquad [\text{``}\alpha\text{'' is to be replaced by any sentence we accept.}]$$

Or, to make matters even more simple, why should we not unify our beliefs by using the most trivial pattern of self-derivation?

$$\alpha \qquad [\text{``}\alpha\text{'' is to be replaced by any sentence we accept.}]$$

There is an obvious reply. The patterns just cited may succeed admirably in satisfying our criteria of using a few patterns of argument to generate many beliefs, but they fail dismally when judged by the criterion of stringency. Recall that the stringency of a pattern is assessed by adopting a compromise between two constraints: stringent patterns are not only to have instantiations with similar logical structures; their instantiations are also to contain similar non-logical vocabulary at similar places. Now both of the above argument patterns are very lax in allowing any vocabulary whatever to appear in the place of "α." Hence we can argue that, according to our intuitive concept of stringency, they should be excluded as non-stringent.

Although this reply is promising, it does not entirely quash the objection. A defender of the unwanted argument patterns may *artificially* introduce restrictions on the pattern to make it more stringent. So, for example, if we suppose that one of *our* favorite patterns (such as the Newtonian pattern displayed above) is applied to generate conclusions meeting a particular condition *C,* the defender of the patterns just cited may propose that 'α' is to be replaced, not by any sentence, but by a sentence which meets *C*. He may then legitimately point out that his newly contrived pattern is as stringent as our favored pattern. Inspired by this partial success, he may adopt a general strategy. Wherever we use an argument pattern to generate a particular type of conclusion, he may use some argument pattern which involves self-derivation, placing an appropriate restriction on the sentences to be substituted for the dummy letters. In this way, he will mimic whatever unification we achieve. His "unification" is obviously spurious. How do we debar it?

The answer comes from recognizing the way in which the stringency of the unwanted patterns was produced. Any condition on the substitution of sentences for dummy letters would have done equally well, provided only that it imposed constraints comparable to those imposed by acceptable patterns. Thus the stringency of the restricted pattern seems accidental to it. This accidental quality is exposed when we notice that we can vary the filling instructions, while retaining the same syntactic structure, to obtain a host of other argument patterns with equally many instantiations. By contrast, the constraints imposed on the substitution of non-logical vocabulary in the Newtonian pattern (for example) cannot be amended without destroying the stringency of the pattern or without depriving it of its ability to furnish us with many instantiations. Thus the constraints imposed in the Newtonian pattern are essential to its functioning; those imposed in the unwanted pattern are not.

Let us formulate this idea as an explicit requirement. If the filling instructions associated with a pattern P could be replaced by different filling instructions, allowing for the substitution of a class of expressions of the same syntactic category, to yield a pattern P' and if P' would allow the derivation *any* sentence, then the unification achieved by P is spurious. Consider, in this light, any of the patterns which we have been trying to debar. In each case, we can vary the filling instructions to produce an even more "successful" pattern. So, for example, given the pattern:

$$\alpha \qquad [\text{``}\alpha\text{''} \text{ is to be replaced by a sentence meeting condition } C]$$

we can generalize the filling instructions to obtain

$$\alpha \qquad [\text{``}\alpha\text{''} \text{ is to be replaced by any sentence}].$$

Thus, under our new requirement, the unification achieved by the original pattern is spurious.

In a moment I shall try to show how this requirement can be motivated, both by appealing to the intuition which underlies the view of explanation as unification and by recognizing the role that something like my requirement has played in the history of science. Before I do so, I want to examine a slightly different kind of example which initially appears to threaten my account. Imagine that a group of religious fanatics decides to argue for the explanatory power of some theological doctrines by claiming that these doctrines unify their beliefs about the world. They suggest that their beliefs can be systematized by using the following pattern:

God wants it to be the case that α.
What God wants to be the case is the case.

$$\alpha$$

["α" is to be replaced by any accepted sentence describing the physical world.]

The new requirement will also identify as spurious the pattern just presented, and will thus block the claim that the theological doctrines that God exists and has the power to actualize his wishes have explanatory power. For it is easy to see that we can modify the filling instructions to obtain a pattern that will yield any sentence whatsoever.

Why should patterns whose filling instructions can be modified to accommodate any sentence be suspect? The answer is that, in such patterns, the non-logical vocabulary which remains is idling. The presence of that non-logical vocabulary imposes no constraints on the expressions we can substitute for the dummy symbols, so that, beyond the specification that a place be filled by expressions of a particular syntactic category, the structure we impose by means of filling instructions is quite incidental. Thus the patterns in question do not genuinely reflect the contents of our beliefs. The explanatory store should present the order of natural phenomena which is exposed by what we think we know. To do so, it must exhibit connections among our beliefs beyond those which could be found among any beliefs. Patterns of self-derivation and the type of pattern exemplified in the example of the theological community merely provide trivial, omnipresent connections, and, in consequence, the unification they offer is spurious.

My requirement obviously has some kinship with the requirement that the principles put forward in giving explanations be testable. As previous writers have insisted that genuine explanatory theories should not be able to cater to all possible evidence, I am demanding that genuinely unifying patterns should not be able to accommodate all conclusions. The requirement that I have proposed accords well with some of the issues which scientists have addressed in discussing the explanatory merits of particular theories. Thus several of Darwin's opponents complain that the explanatory benefits claimed for the embryonic theory of evolution are illusory, on the grounds that the style of reasoning suggested could be adapted to any conclusion. (For a particularly acute statement of the complaint, see the review by Fleeming Jenkin, printed in Hull 1974, especially p. 342.) Similarly, Lavoisier denied that the explanatory power of the phlogiston theory was genuine, accusing that theory of using a type of reasoning which could adapt itself to any conclusion (Lavoisier 1862, vol. II, p. 233). Hence I suggest that some problems of spurious unification can be solved in the way I have indicated, and that the solution conforms both to our intuitions about explanatory unification and to the considerations which are used in scientific debate.

However, I do not wish to claim that my requirement will debar all types of spurious unification. It may be possible to find other unwanted patterns which circumvent my requirement. A full characterization of the notion of a stringent argument pattern should provide a criterion for excluding the unwanted patterns. My claim in this section is that it will do so by counting as spurious the unification achieved by patterns which adapt themselves to any conclusion and by patterns which accidentally restrict such universally hospitable patterns. I have also tried to show how this claim can be developed to block the most obvious cases of spurious unification.

9. CONCLUSIONS

I have sketched an account of explanation as unification, attempting to show that such an account has the resources to provide insight into episodes in the history of science and to overcome some traditional problems for the covering law model. In conclusion, let me indicate very briefly how my view of explanation as unification suggests how scientific explanation yields understanding. By using a few patterns of argument in the derivation of many beliefs we minimize the number of *types* of premises we must take as underived. That is, we reduce, in so far as possible, the number of types of facts we must accept as brute. Hence we can endorse something close to Friedman's view of the merits of explanatory unification (Friedman 1974, pp. 18–19).

Quite evidently, I have only *sketched* an account of explanation. To provide precise analyses of the notions I have introduced, the basic approach to explanation offered here must be refined against concrete examples of scientific practice. What needs to be done is to look closely at the argument patterns favored by scientists and attempt to understand what characteristics they share. If I am right, the scientific search for explanation is governed by a maxim, once formulated succinctly by E. M. Forster. Only connect.

NOTES

A distant ancestor of this paper was read to the Dartmouth College Philosophy Colloquium in the Spring of 1977. I would like to thank those who participated, especially Merrie Bergmann and Jim Moor, for their helpful suggestions. I am also grateful to two anonymous referees for *Philosophy of Science* whose extremely constructive criticisms have led to substantial improvements. Finally, I want to acknowledge the amount I have learned from the writing and the teaching of Peter Hempel. The present essay is a token payment on an enormous debt.

[1] Strictly speaking, this is one of two views which emerge from Achinstein's discussion and which he regards as equally satisfactory. As Achinstein goes on to point out, either of these ontological theses can be developed to capture the central idea of the covering law model.

[2] To pose the problem in this way we may still invite the charge that *arguments* should not be viewed as the bases for acts of explanation. Many of the criticisms leveled against the covering law model by Wesley Salmon in his seminal paper on statistical explanation (Salmon 1970) can be reformulated to support this charge. My discussion in section 7 will show how some of the difficulties raised by Salmon for the covering law model do not bedevil my account. However, I shall not respond directly to the points about statistical explanation and statistical inference advanced by Salmon and by Richard Jeffrey in his ["Statistical Explanation"] (1970). I believe that Peter Railton has shown how these specific difficulties concerning statistical explanation can be accommodated by an approach which takes explanations to be (or be based on) arguments (see Railton 1978), and that the account offered in section 4 of his paper can be adapted to complement my own.

[3] Of course, in restricting my attention to why-questions I am following the tradition of philosophical discussion of scientific explanation: as Bromberger notes in section IV of his ["Why-Questions"] (1966) not all explanations are directed at why-questions, but attempts to characterize explanatory responses to why-questions have a special interest for the philosophy of science because of the connection to a range of methodological issues. I believe that the account of explanation offered in the present [reading] could be extended to cover explanatory answers to some other kinds of questions (such as how-questions). But I do want to disavow the claim that unification is relevant to all types of explanation. If one believes that explanations are sometimes offered in response to what-questions (for example), so that it is correct to talk of someone explaining what a gene is, then one should allow that some types of explanation can be characterized independently of the notions of unification or of argument. I ignore these kinds of explanation in part because they lack the methodological

significance of explanations directed at why-questions and in part because the problem of characterizing explanatory answers to what-questions seems so much less recalcitrant than that of characterizing explanatory answers to why-questions (for a similar assessment, see Belnap and Steel 1976, pp. 86–87). Thus I would regard a full account of explanation as a heterogeneous affair, because the conditions required of adequate answers to different types of questions are rather different, and I intend the present essay to make a proposal about how *part* of this account (the most interesting part) should be developed.

[4] For illuminating accounts of Newton's influence on eighteenth-century research see Cohen (1956) and Schofield (1969). I have simplified the discussion by considering only *one* of the programs which eighteenth-century scientists derived from Newton's work. A more extended treatment would reveal the existence of several different approaches aimed at unifying science, and I believe that the theory of explanation proposed in this [reading] may help in the historical task of understanding the diverse aspirations of different Newtonians. (For the problems involved in this enterprise, see Heimann and McGuire 1971.)

[5] See Boscovich (1966) Part III, especially p. 134. For an introduction to Boscovich's work, see the essays by L. L. Whyte and Z. Markovic in Whyte (1961). For the influence of Boscovich on British science, see the essays of Pearce Williams and Schofield in the same volume, and Schofield (1969).

[6] The examples could easily be multiplied. I think it is possible to understand the structure and explanatory power of such theories as modern evolutionary theory, transmission genetics, plate tectonics, and sociobiology in the terms I develop here.

[7] More exactly, I shall try to show that my account can solve some of the principal versions of these difficulties which have been used to discredit the covering law model. I believe that it can also overcome more refined versions of the problems than I consider here, but to demonstrate that would require a more lengthy exposition.

[8] There is an objection to this line of reasoning. Can't we view the arguments $\langle(x)((Sx \text{ and } Hx) \to Dx)$, Sa and $Ha, Da\rangle$, $\langle(x)((Sx \text{ and } {\sim}Hx) \to Dx)$, Sb and ${\sim}Hb, Db\rangle$ as instantiating a common pattern? I reply that, insofar as we can view these arguments as instantiating a common pattern, the standard pair of comparable (low-level) derivations — $\langle(x)(Sx \to Dx)$, $Sa, Da\rangle$, $\langle(x)(Sx \to Dx)$, $Sb, Db\rangle$ — share a more stringent common pattern. Hence incorporating the deviant derivations in the explanatory store would give us an inferior basis. We can justify the claim that the pattern instantiated by the standard pair of derivations is more stringent than that shared by the deviant derivations, by noting that representation of the deviant pattern would compel us to broaden our conception of schematic sentence, and, even were we to do so, the deviant pattern would contain a "degree of freedom" which the standard pattern lacks. For a representation of the deviant "pattern" would take the form $\langle(x)((Sx \text{ and } \alpha Hx) \to Dx)$, Sa and $\alpha Ha, Da\rangle$, where "α" is to be replaced uniformly either with the null symbol or with "${\sim}$". Even if we waive my requirement that, in schematic sentences, we substitute for *non*-logical vocabulary, it is evident that this "pattern" is more accommodating than the standard pattern.

[9] However, the strategy I have recommended will not avail with a different type of case. Suppose that a deviant wants to explain the dissolving of the salt by appealing to some property which holds universally. That is, the "explanatory" arguments are to begin from some premise such as "$(x)((x$ is a sample of salt and x does not violate conservation of energy) $\to x$ dissolves in water)" or "$(x)((x$ is a sample of salt and $x = x) \to x$ dissolves in water)." I would handle these cases somewhat differently. If the deviant's explanatory store were to be as unified as our own, then it would contain arguments corresponding to ours in which a redundant conjunct systematically occurred, and I think it would be plausible to invoke a criterion of simplicity to advocate dropping that conjunct.

REFERENCES

Achinstein, P., *Law and Explanation*. Oxford: Oxford University Press, 1971.

Achinstein, P., "What Is an Explanation?," *American Philosophical Quarterly* 14(1977), pp. 1–15.

Belnap, N. and Steel, T. B., *The Logic of Questions and Answers*. New Haven: Yale University Press, 1976.

Boscovich, R. J., *A Theory of Natural Philosophy* (trans. J. M. Child). Cambridge: M.I.T. Press, 1966.

Bromberger, S., "An Approach to Explanation," in R. J. Butler (ed.), *Analytical Philosophy* (First Series). Oxford: Blackwell, 1962.

Bromberger, S., "Why-Questions," in R. Colodny (ed.), *Mind and Cosmos.* Pittsburgh: University of Pittsburgh Press, 1966.

Cohen, I. B., *Franklin and Newton.* Philadelphia: American Philosophical Society, 1956.

Darwin, C., *On the Origin of Species,* Facsimile of the First Edition, ed. E. Mayr. Cambridge: Harvard University Press, 1964.

Darwin, F., *The Life and Letters of Charles Darwin.* London: John Murray, 1987.

Eberle, R., Kaplan, D., and Montague, R., "Hempel and Oppenheim on Explanation," *Philosophy of Science* 28(1961), pp. 418–28.

Feigl, H., "The 'Orthodox' View of Theories: Remarks in Defense as Well as Critique," in M. Radner and S. Winokur (eds.), *Minnesota Studies in the Philosophy of Science,* vol. IV. Minneapolis: University of Minnesota Press, 1970.

Friedman, M., "Explanation and Scientific Understanding," *Journal of Philosophy,* vol. LXXI(1974), pp. 5–19.

Heimann, P., and McGuire, J. E. "Newtonian Forces and Lockean Powers," *Historical Studies in the Physical Sciences* 3(1971), pp. 233–306.

Hempel, C. G., *Aspects of Scientific Explanation.* New York: The Free Press, 1965.

——, "Deductive-Nonlogical vs. Statistical Explanation," in H. Feigl and G. Maxwell (eds.) *Minnesota Studies in the Philosophy of Science,* vol. III. Minneapolis: University of Minnesota Press, 1962.

——, *Philosophy of Natural Science.* Englewood Cliffs, N.J.: Prentice-Hall, 1966.

Hull, D. (ed.), *Darwin and His Critics.* Cambridge: Harvard University Press, 1974.

Jeffrey, R., "Statistical Explanation vs. Statistical Inference," in N. Rescher (ed.), *Essays in Honor of Carl G. Hempel.* Dordrecht: D. Reidel, 1970.

Kitcher, P. S., "Explanation, Conjunction and Unification," *Journal of Philosophy,* vol. LXXIII(1976), pp. 207–12.

Lavoisier, A., *Oeuvres.* Paris, 1862.

Newton, I., *The Mathematical Principles of Natural Philosophy* (trans. A. Motte and F. Cajori). Berkeley: University of California Press, 1962.

Newton, I., *Opticks.* New York: Dover, 1952.

Railton, P., "A Deductive-Nomological Model of Probabilistic Explanation," *Philosophy of Science* 45(1978), pp. 206–26.

Salmon, W., "Statistical Explanation," in R. Colodny (ed.), *The Nature and Function of Scientific Theories.* Pittsburgh: University of Pittsburgh Press, 1970.

Schofield, R. E., *Mechanism and Materialism.* Princeton: Princeton University Press, 1969.

Teller, P., "On Why-Questions," *Noûs,* vol. VIII(1974), pp. 371–80.

van Fraassen, B., "The Pragmatics of Explanation," *American Philosophical Quarterly* 14(1977), pp. 143–50.

Whyte, L. L. (ed.), *Roger Joseph Boscovich.* London: Allen and Unwin, 1961.

W E S L E Y   C .   S A L M O N
WHY ASK, "WHY?"?
AN INQUIRY CONCERNING SCIENTIFIC EXPLANATION [1]

Concerning the first order question "Why?" I have raised the second order question "Why ask, 'Why?'?" to which you might naturally respond with the third order question "Why ask, 'Why ask, "Why?"?'?" But this way lies madness, to say nothing of an infinite regress. While an infinite sequence of nested intervals may converge upon a point, the series of nested questions just initiated has no point to it, and so we had better cut it off without delay. The answer to the very natural third order question is this: the question "Why ask, 'Why?'?" expresses a deep philosophical perplexity which I believe to be both significant in its own right and highly relevant to certain current philosophical discussions. I want to share it with you.

The problems I shall be discussing pertain mainly to scientific explanation, but before turning to them, I should remark that I am fully aware that many—perhaps most—why-questions are requests for some sort of *justification* (Why did one employee receive a larger raise than another? Because she had been paid less than a male colleague for doing the same kind of job) or *consolation* (Why, asked Job, was I singled out for such extraordinary misfortune and suffering?). Since I have neither the time nor the talent to deal with questions of this sort, I shall not pursue them further, except to remark that the seeds of endless philosophical confusion can be sown by failing carefully to distinguish them from requests for scientific explanation.

Let me put the question I do want to discuss to you this way. Suppose you had achieved the epistemic status of Laplace's demon—the hypothetical superintelligence who knows all of nature's regularities, and the precise state of the universe full in detail at some particular moment (say now, according to some suitable simultaneity slice of the universe). Possessing the requisite logical and mathematical skill, you would be able to predict any future occurrence, and you would be able to retrodict any past event. Given this sort of apparent omniscience, would your scientific knowledge be complete, or would it still leave something to be desired? Laplace asked no more of his demon; should we place further demands upon ourselves? And if so, what should be the nature of the additional demands?

If we look at most contemporary philosophy of science texts, we find an immediate *affirmative* answer to this question. Science, the majority say, has at least two principal aims—prediction (construed broadly enough to include inference from the observed to the unobserved, regardless of temporal relations) and explanation. The first of these provides knowledge of *what* happens; the second is supposed to furnish knowledge of *why* things happen as they do. This is not a new idea. In the *Posterior Analytics,* Aristotle distinguishes syllogisms which provide scientific understanding from those which do not.[2] In the Port Royal Logic, Arnauld distinguishes demonstrations which merely convince the mind from those which also enlighten the mind.[3]

Presidential Address delivered before the Fifty-second Annual Pacific Meeting of the American Philosophical Association in San Francisco, California, March 24, 1978.

This view has not been universally adopted. It was not long ago that we often heard statements to the effect that the business of science is to predict, not to explain. Scientific knowledge is descriptive—it tell us *what* and *how.* If we seek explanations—if we want to know why—we must go outside of science, perhaps to metaphysics or theology. In his Preface to the Third Edition (1911) of *The Grammar of Science,* Karl Pearson wrote, "Nobody believes now that science *explains* anything; we all look upon it as a shorthand description, as an economy of thought."[4] This doctrine is not very popular nowadays. It is now fashionable to say that science aims not merely at describing the world—it also provides *understanding, comprehension,* and *enlightenment.* Science presumably accomplishes such high-sounding goals by supplying scientific explanations.

The current attitude leaves us with a deep and perplexing question, namely, if explanation does involve something over and above mere description, just what sort of thing is it? The use of such honorific near-synonyms as "understanding," "comprehension," and "enlightenment" makes it sound important and desirable, but does not help at all in the philosophical analysis of explanation—scientific or other. What, over and above its complete descriptive knowledge of the world, would Laplace's demon require in order to achieve understanding? I hope you can see that this is a real problem, especially for those who hold what I shall call "the inferential view" of scientific explanation, for Laplace's demon can infer every fact about the universe, past, present, and future. If the problem does not seem acute, I would quote a remark made by Russell about Zeno's paradox of the flying arrow—"The more the difficulty is meditated, the more real it becomes."[5]

It is not my intention this evening to discuss the details of the various formal models of scientific explanation which have been advanced in the last three decades.[6] Instead, I want to consider the general conceptions which lie beneath the most influential theories of scientific explanation. Two powerful intuitions seem to have guided much of the discussion. Although they have given rise to disparate basic conceptions and considerable controversy, both are, in my opinion, quite sound. Moreover, it seems to me, both can be incorporated into a single overall theory of scientific explanation.

(1) The first of these intuitions is the notion that the explanation of a phenomenon essentially involves *locating and identifying its cause or causes.* This intuition seems to arise rather directly from common sense, and from various contexts in which scientific knowledge is applied to concrete situations. It is strongly supported by a number of paradigms, the most convincing of which are explanations of particular occurrences. To explain a given airplane crash, for example, we seek "the cause"—a mechanical failure, perhaps, or pilot error. To explain a person's death again we seek the cause—strangulation or drowning, for instance. I shall call the general view of scientific explanation which comes more or less directly from this fundamental intuition *the causal conception;* Michael Scriven has been one of its chief advocates.[7]

(2) The second of these basic intuitions is the notion that all scientific explanation involves *subsumption under laws.* This intuition seems to arise from consideration of developments in theoretical science. It has led to the general "covering law" conception of explanation, as well as to several formal "models" of explanation. According

to this view, a fact is subsumed under one or more general laws if the assertion of its occurrence follows, either deductively or inductively, from statements of the laws (in conjunction, in some cases, with other premises). Since this view takes explanations to be arguments, I shall call it *the inferential conception;* Carl G. Hempel has been one of its ablest champions.[8]

Although the proponents of this inferential conception have often chosen to illustrate it with explanations of particular occurrences—e.g., why did the bunsen flame turn yellow on this particular occasion?—the paradigms which give it strongest support are explanations of general regularities. When we look to the history of science for the most outstanding cases of scientific explanations, such examples as Newton's explanation of Kepler's laws of planetary motion or Maxwell's electromagnetic explanation of optical phenomena come immediately to mind.

It is easy to guess how Laplace might have reacted to my question about his demon, and to the two basic intuitions I have just mentioned. The super-intelligence would have everything needed to provide scientific explanations. When, to mention one of Laplace's favorite examples, a seemingly haphazard phenomenon, such as the appearance of a comet, occurs, it can be explained by showing that it actually conforms to natural laws.[9] On Laplace's assumption of determinism, the demon possesses explanations of all happenings in the entire history of the world—past, present, and future. Explanation, for Laplace, seemed to consist in showing how events conform to the laws of nature, and these very laws provide the causal connections among the various states of the world. The Laplacian version of explanation thus seems to conform both to the causal conception and to the inferential conception.

Why, you might well ask, is not the Laplacian view of scientific explanation basically sound? Why do twentieth century philosophers find it necessary to engage in lengthy disputes over this matter? There are, I think, three fundamental reasons: (1) the causal conception faces the difficulty that no adequate treatment of causation has yet been offered; (2) the inferential conception suffers from the fact that it seriously misconstrues the nature of subsumption under laws; and (3) both conceptions have overlooked a central explanatory principle.

The inferential view, as elaborated in detail by Hempel and others, has been the dominant theory of scientific explanation in recent years—indeed, it has become virtually "the received view." From that standpoint, anyone who had attained the epistemic status of Laplace's demon could use the known laws and initial conditions to predict a future event, and when the event comes to pass, the argument which enabled us to predict it would ipso facto constitute an explanation of it. If, as Laplace believed, determinism is true, then every *future* event would thus be amenable to deductive-nomological explanation.

When, however, we consider the explanation of past events—events which occurred earlier than our initial conditions—we find a strange disparity. Although, by applying known laws, we can reliably *retrodict* any past occurrence on the basis of facts subsequent to the event, our intuitions rebel at the idea that we can *explain* events in terms of subsequent conditions. Thus, although our inferences to future events qualify as explanations according to the inferential conception, our inferences to the past do not. Laplace's demon can, of course, construct explanations of past events by inferring the existence of still earlier conditions and, with the aid of the known laws, deducing the occurrence of the events to be explained from these conditions which held in the more remote past. But if, as the inferential conception maintains, explanations are essentially inferences, such as approach to explanation of past events seems strangely roundabout. Explanations demand an asymmetry not present in inferences.

When we drop the fiction of Laplace's demon, and relinquish the assumption of determinism, the asymmetry becomes even more striking. The demon can predict the future and retrodict the past with complete precision and reliability. We cannot. When we consider the comparative difficulty of prediction vs. retrodiction, it turns out that retrodiction enjoys a tremendous advantage. We have records of the past—tree rings, diaries, fossils—but none of the future. As a result, we can have extensive and detailed knowledge of the past which has no counterpart in knowledge about the future. From a newspaper account of an accident, we can retrodict all sorts of details which could not have been predicted an hour before the collision. But the newspaper story—even though it may *report* the explanation of the accident—surely does not *constitute* the explanation. We see that *inference* has a preferred temporal direction, and that *explanation* also has a preferred temporal direction. The fact that these two are opposite to each other is one thing which makes me seriously doubt that explanations are essentially arguments.[10] As we shall see, however, denying that explanations are arguments does not mean that we must give up the *covering law* conception. Subsumption under laws can take a different form.

Although the Laplacian conception bears strong similarities to the received view, there is a fundamental difference which must be noted. Laplace evidently believed that the explanations provided by his demon would be *causal explanations,* and the laws invoked would be *causal laws.* Hempel's deductive-nomological explanations are often casually called "causal explanations," but this is not accurate.[11] Hempel explicitly notes that some laws, such as the ideal gas law

$$PV = nRT$$

are non-causal. This law states a mathematical functional relationship among several quantities—pressure P, volume V, temperature T, number of moles of gas n, universal gas constant R—but gives no hint as to how a change in one of the values would lead causally to changes in others. As far as I know, Laplace did not make any distinction between causal and non-causal laws; Hempel has recognized the difference, but he allows non-causal as well as causal laws to function as covering laws in scientific explanations.

This attitude toward noncausal laws is surely too tolerant. If someone inflates an air mattress of a given size to a certain pressure under conditions which determine the temperature, we can deduce the value of n—the amount of air blown into it. The *subsequent* values of pressure, temperature, and volume are thus taken to explain the quantity of air *previously* introduced. Failure to require covering laws to be causal laws leads to a violation of the temporal requirement on explanations. This is not surprising. The asymmetry of explanation is inherited from the asymmetry of causation—namely, that causes precede their effects. At this point, it seems to me, we experience vividly the force of the intuitions underlying the causal conception of scientific explanation.

There is another reason for maintaining that non-causal laws cannot bear the burden of covering laws in scientific explanations. Non-causal regularities, instead of having explanatory force which enables them to provide understanding of events in the world, cry out to be explained. Mariners, long before Newton, were fully aware of the correlation between the behavior of the tides and the position and phase of the moon. But inasmuch as they were totally ignorant of the causal relations involved, they rightly believed that they did not understand why the tides ebb and flow. When Newton provided the gravitational links, understanding was achieved. Similarly, I should say, the ideal gas law had little or no explanatory power until its causal underpinnings were furnished by the molecular-kinetic theory of gases. Keeping this consideration in mind, we realize that we must give at least as much attention to the explanations of regularities as we do to explanations of particular facts. I will argue, moreover, that these regularities demand causal explanation. Again, we must give the causal conception its due.

Having considered a number of preliminaries, I should now like to turn my attention to an attempt to outline a general theory of causal explanation. I shall not be trying to articulate a formal model; I shall be focusing upon general conceptions and fundamental principles rather than technical details. I am not suggesting, of course, that the technical details are dispensable—merely that this is not the time or place to try to go into them. Let me say at the outset that I shall be relying very heavily upon works by Russell (especially *The Analysis of Matter* and *Human Knowledge, Its Scope and Limits*) and Reichenbach (especially *The Direction of Time*). Although, to the best of my knowledge, neither of these authors ever published an article, or a book, or a chapter of a book devoted explicitly to scientific explanation, nevertheless it seems to me that a rather appealing theory of causal explanation can be constructed by putting together the insights expressed in the aforementioned works.

Developments in twentieth-century science should prepare us for the eventuality that some of our scientific explanations will have to be statistical—not merely because our knowledge is incomplete (as Laplace would have maintained), but rather, because nature itself is inherently statistical. Some of the laws used in explaining particular events will be statistical, and some of the regularities we wish to explain will also be statistical. I have been urging that causal considerations play a crucial role in explanation; indeed, I have just said that regularities—and this certainly includes statistical regularities—require causal explanation. I do not believe there is any conflict here. It seems to me that, by employing a statistical conception of causation along the lines developed by Patrick Suppes and Hans Reichenbach,[12] it is possible to fit together harmoniously the causal and statistical factors in explanatory contexts. Let me attempt to illustrate this point by discussing a concrete example.

A good deal of attention has recently been given in the press to cases of leukemia in military personnel who witnessed an atomic bomb test (code name "Smokey") at close range in 1957.[13] Statistical studies of the survivors of the bombings of Hiroshima and Nagasaki have established the fact that exposure to high levels of radiation, such as occur in an atomic blast, is statistically relevant to the occurrence of leukemia—indeed, that the probability of leukemia is closely correlated with the distance from the explosion.[14] A clear pattern of statistical relevance relations is exhibited here. If a particular person contracts leukemia, this fact may be explained by citing the fact that he was, say, 2 kilometers from the hypocenter at the time of the explosion. This relationship is further explained by the fact that individuals located at specific distances from atomic blasts of specified magnitude receive certain high doses of radiation.

This tragic example has several features to which I should like to call special attention:

(1) The location of the individual at the time of the blast is statistically relevant to the occurrence of leukemia; the probability of leukemia for a person located 2 kilometers from the hypocenter of an atomic blast is radically different from the probability of the disease in the population at large. Notice that the probability of such an individual contracting leukemia is not high; it is much smaller than one-half—indeed, in the case of Smokey it is much less than 1/100. But it is markedly higher than for a random member of the entire human population. It is the *statistical relevance* of exposure to an atomic blast, not a high probability, which has explanatory force.[15] Such examples defy explanation according to an inferential view, which requires high inductive probability for statistical explanation.[16] The case of leukemia is subsumed under a statistical regularity, but it does not "follow inductively" from the explanatory facts.

(2) There is a *causal process* which connects the occurrence of the bomb blast with the physiological harm done to people at some distance from the explosion. High energy radiation, released in the nuclear reactions, traverses the space between the blast and the individual. Although some of the details may not yet be known, it is a well-established fact that such radiation does interact with cells in a way which makes them susceptible to leukemia at some later time.

(3) At each end of the causal process—i.e., the transmission of radiation from the bomb to the person—there is a *causal interaction*. The radiation is emitted as a result of a nuclear interaction when the bomb explodes, and it is absorbed by cells in the body of the victim. Each of these interactions may well be irreducibly statistical and indeterministic, but that is no reason to deny that they are causal.

(4) The causal processes begin at a central place, and they travel outward at a finite velocity. A rather complex set of statistical relevance relations is explained by the propagation of a process, or set of processes, from a common central event.

In undertaking a general characterization of causal explanation, we must begin by carefully distinguishing between causal processes and causal interactions. The transmission of light from one place to another, and the motion of a material particle, are obvious examples of causal processes. The collision of two billiard balls, and the emission or absorption of a photon, are standard examples of causal interactions. Interactions are the sorts of things we are inclined to identify as events. Relative to a particular context, an event is comparatively small in its spatial and temporal dimensions; processes typically have much larger durations, and they may be more extended in space as well. A light ray, traveling to earth from a distant star, is a process which covers a large distance and lasts for a long time. What I am calling a "causal process" is similar to what Russell called a "causal line."[17]

When we attempt to identify causal processes, it is of crucial importance to distinguish them from such pseudo-processes as a shadow moving across the landscape. This can best be done, I believe, by invoking Reichenbach's *mark criterion*.[18] Causal processes are capable of propagating marks or modifications imposed upon them; pseudo-processes are not. An automobile traveling along a road is an example of a causal process. If a fender is scraped as a result of a collision with a stone wall, the mark of that collision will be carried on by the car long after the interaction with the wall occurred. The shadow of a car moving along the shoulder is a pseudo-process. If it is deformed as it encounters a stone wall, it will immediately resume its former shape as soon as it passes by the wall. It will not transmit a mark or modification. For this reason, we say that a causal process can transmit information or causal influence; a pseudo-process cannot.[19]

When I say that a causal process has the capability of transmitting a causal influence, it might be supposed that I am introducing precisely the sort of mysterious power Hume warned us against. It seems to me that this danger can be circumvented by employing an adaptation of the "at-at" theory of motion, which Russell used so effectively in dealing with Zeno's paradox of the flying arrow.[20] The flying arrow—which is, by the way, a causal process—gets from one place to another by being at the appropriate intermediate points of space at the appropriate instants of time. Nothing more is involved in getting *from* one point *to* another. A mark, analogously, can be said to be propagated from the point of interaction at which it is imposed to later stages in the process if it appears *at* the appropriate intermediate stages in the process *at* the appropriate times without additional interactions which regenerate the mark. The precise formulation of this condition is a bit tricky, but I believe the basic idea is simple, and that the details can be worked out.[21]

If this analysis of causal processes is satisfactory, we have an answer to the question, raised by Hume, concerning the connection between cause and effect. If we think of a cause as one event, and of an effect as a distinct event, then the connection between them is simply a spatio-temporally continuous causal process. This sort of answer did not occur to Hume because he did not distinguish between causal processes and causal interactions. When he tried to analyze the connections between distinct events, he treated them as if they were chains of events with discrete links, rather than processes analogous to continuous filaments. I am inclined to attribute considerable philosophical significance to the fact that each link in a chain has adjacent links, while the points in a continuum do not have next-door neighbors. This consideration played an important role in Russell's discussion of Zeno's paradoxes.[22]

After distinguishing between causal interactions and causal processes, and after introducing a criterion by means of which to discriminate the pseudo-processes from the genuine causal processes, we must consider certain configurations of processes which have special explanatory import. Russell noted that we often find similar structures grouped symmetrically about a center—for example, concentric waves moving across an otherwise smooth surface of a pond, or sound waves moving out from a central region, or perceptions of many people viewing a stage from different seats in a theatre. In such cases, Russell postulates the existence of a central event—a pebble dropped into the pond, a starter's gun going off at a race track, or a play being performed upon the stage—from which the complex array emanates.[23] It is noteworthy that Russell never suggests that the central event is to be explained on the basis of convergence of influences from remote regions upon that locale.

Reichenbach articulated a closely related idea in his *principle of the common cause.* If two or more events of certain types occur at different places, but occur at the same time more frequently than is to be expected if they occurred independently, then this apparent coincidence is to be explained in terms of a common causal antecedent.[24] If, for example, all of the electric lights in a particular area go out simultaneously, we do not believe that they just happened by chance to burn out at the same time. We attribute the coincidence to a common cause such as a blown fuse, a downed transmission line, or trouble at the generating station. If all of the students in a dormitory fall ill on the same night, it is attributed to spoiled food in the meal which all of them ate. Russell's similar structures arranged symmetrically about a center obviously qualify as the sorts of coincidences which require common causes for their explanations.[25]

In order to formulate his common cause principle more precisely, Reichenbach defined what he called a *conjunctive fork.* Suppose we have events of two types, A and B, which happen in conjunction more often than they would if they were statistically independent of one another. For example, let A and B stand for colorblindness in two brothers. There is a certain probability that a male, selected from the population at random, will have that affliction, but since it is hereditary, occurrences in male siblings are not independent. The probability that both will have it is greater than the product of the two respective probabilities. In cases of such statistical dependencies, we invoke a common cause, C, which accounts for them; in this case, it is a genetic factor carried by the mother. In order to satisfy the conditions for a conjunctive fork, events of the types A and B must occur independently in the absence of the common cause C—that is, for two unrelated males, the probability of both being colorblind is equal to the product of the two separate probabilities. Furthermore, the probabilities of A and B must each be increased above their overall values if C is present. Clearly the probability of colorblindness is greater in sons of mothers carrying the genetic factor than it is among all male children regardless of the genetic make-up of their mothers. Finally, Reichenbach stipulates, the dependency between A and B is absorbed into the occurrence of the common cause C, in the sense that the probability of A and B given C equals the product of the probability of A given C and the probability of B given C. This is true in the colorblindness case. Excluding pairs of identical twins, the question of whether a male child inherits colorblindness from the mother who carries the genetic trait depends only upon the genetic relationship between that child and his mother, not upon whether other sons happened to inherit the trait.[26] Note that screening-off occurs here.[27] While the colorblindness of a brother is statistically relevant to colorblindness in a boy, it becomes irrelevant if the genetic factor is known to be present in the mother.

Reichenbach obviously was not the first philosopher to notice that we explain coincidences in terms of common causal antecedents. Leibniz postulated a pre-established harmony for his windowless monads which mirror the same world, and the occasionalists postulated God as the coordinator of mind and body. Reichenbach was, to the best of my knowledge, the first to give a precise characterization of the conjunctive fork, and to formulate the general principle that conjunctive forks are open only to the future, not to the past.[28] The result is that we cannot explain coincidences on the basis of future effects, but only on the basis of antecedent causes. A widespread blackout is explained by a power failure, not by the looting which occurs as a consequence. (A common effect, E, may form a conjunctive fork with A and B, but only if there is also a common cause, C.) The principle that conjunctive forks are not open to the past accounts for Russell's principle that symmetrical patterns emanate from a central source—they do not converge from afar upon the central point. It is also closely related to the operation of the second law of thermodynamics and the increase of entropy in the physical world.

The common cause principle has, I believe, deep explanatory significance. Bas van Fraassen has recently subjected it to careful scrutiny, and he has convinced me that Reichenbach's formulation in terms of the conjunctive fork, as he defined it, is faulty.[29] (We do not, however, agree about the nature of the flaw.) There are, it seems, certain sorts of causal *interactions* in which the resulting effects are more strongly correlated with one another than is allowed in Reichenbach's conjunctive forks. If, for example, an energetic photon collides with an electron in a Compton scattering experiment, there is a certain probability that a photon with a given smaller energy will emerge, and there is a certain probability that the electron will be kicked out with a given kinetic energy (see Figure 1). However, because of the law of conservation of energy, there is a strong correspondence between the two energies—their sum must be close to the energy of the incident photon. Thus, the probability of getting a photon with energy E_1 and an electron with energy E_2, where $E_1 + E_2$ is approximately equal to

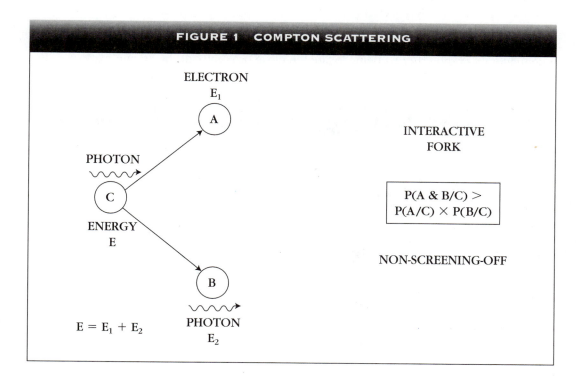

FIGURE 1   COMPTON SCATTERING

ELECTRON
E_1

A

PHOTON

C

ENERGY
E

INTERACTIVE
FORK

$$P(A \& B/C) > P(A/C) \times P(B/C)$$

NON-SCREENING-OFF

B

PHOTON
E_2

$E = E_1 + E_2$

E (the energy of the incident photon), is much greater than the product of the probabilities of each energy occurring separately. Assume, for example, that there is a probability of 0.1 that a photon of energy E_1 will emerge if a photon of energy *E* impinges on a given target, and assume that there is a probability of 0.1 that an electron with kinetic energy E_2 will emerge under the same circumstances (where E, E_1, and E_2 are related as the law of conservation of energy demands). In this case the probability of the joint result is not 0.01, the product of the separate probabilities, but 0.1, for each result will occur if and only if the other does.[30] The same relationships could be illustrated by such macroscopic events as collisions of billiard balls, but I have chosen Compton scattering because there is good reason to believe that events of that type are irreducibly statistical. Given a high energy photon impinging upon the electron in a given atom, there is no way, even in principle, of predicting with certainty the energies of the photon and electron which result from the interaction.

This sort of interaction stands in sharp contrast with the sort of statistical dependency we have in the leukemia example (see Figure 2, which also represents the relationships in the colorblindness case). In the absence of a strong source of radiation, such as the atomic blast, we may assume that the probability of next-door neighbors contracting the disease equals the product of the probabilities for each of them separately. If, however, we consider two next-door neighbors who lived at a distance of 2 kilometers from the hypocenter of the atomic explosion, the probability of both of them contracting leukemia is much greater than it would be for any two randomly selected members of the population at large. This apparent dependency between the two leukemia cases is not a direct physical dependency between them; it is merely a statistical result of the fact that the probability for each of them has been enhanced independently of the other by being located in close proximity to the atomic explosion. But

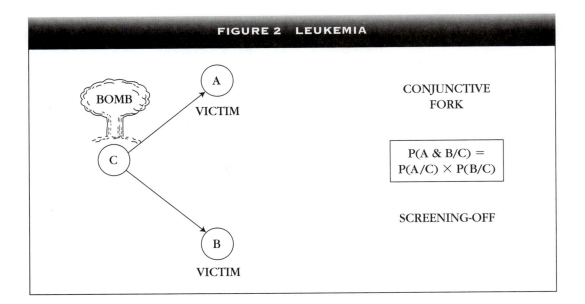

FIGURE 2   LEUKEMIA

CONJUNCTIVE FORK

$$P(A \ \& \ B/C) = P(A/C) \times P(B/C)$$

SCREENING-OFF

the individual photons of radiation which impinge upon the two victims are emitted independently, travel independently, and damage living tissues independently.

It thus appears that there are two kinds of causal forks: (1) Reichenbach's *conjunctive forks,* in which the common cause screens-off the one effect from the other, which are exemplified by the colorblindness and leukemia cases, and (2) *interactive forks,* exemplified by the Compton scattering of a photon and an electron. In forks of the interactive sort, the common cause does not screen-off the one effect from the other. The probability that the electron will be ejected with kinetic energy E_2 given an incident photon of energy E is *not equal* to the probability that the electron will emerge with energy E_2 given an incident photon of energy E and a scattered photon of energy E_1. In the conjunctive fork, the common cause C absorbs the dependency between the effects A and B, for the probability of A and B given C is *equal to* the product of the probability of A given C and the probability of B given C. In the interactive fork, the common cause C does not absorb the dependency between the effects A and B, for the probability of A and B given C is *greater than* the product of the two separate conditional probabilities.[31]

Recognition and characterization of the interactive fork enables us to fill a serious lacuna in the treatment up to this point. I have discussed causal processes, indicating roughly how they are to be characterized, and I have mentioned causal interactions, but have said nothing about their characterization. Indeed, the criterion by which we distinguished causal processes from pseudo-processes involved the use of marks, and marks are obviously results of causal interactions. Thus, our account stands in serious need of a characterization of causal interactions, and the interactive fork enables us, I believe, to furnish it.

There is a strong temptation to think of events as basic types of entities, and to construe processes—real or pseudo—as collections of events. This viewpoint may be due, at least in part, to the fact that the space-time interval between events is a fundamental invariant of the special theory of relativity, and that events thus enjoy an especially fundamental status. I suggest, nevertheless, that we reverse the approach. Let us begin with processes (which have not yet been sorted out into causal and pseudo) and look at their intersections. We can be reassured about the legitimacy of this new orientation by the fact that the basic spacetime structure of both special relativity and general relativity can be built upon processes without direct recourse to events.[32] An electron traveling through space is a process, and so is a photon; if they collide, that is an intersection. A light pulse traveling from a beacon to a screen is a process, and a piece of red glass standing in the path is another; the light passing through the glass is an intersection. Both of these intersections constitute interactions. If two light beams cross one another, we have an intersection without an interaction—except in the extremely unlikely event of a particle-like collision between photons. What we want to say, very roughly, is that when two processes intersect, and both are modified in such ways that the changes in one are correlated with changes in the other—in the manner of an interactive fork (see Figure 3)—we have a causal interaction. There are technical details to be worked out before we can claim to have a satisfactory account, but the general idea seems clear enough.[33]

I should like to commend the principle of the common cause—so construed as to make reference to both conjunctive forks and interactive forks—to your serious consideration.[34] Several of its uses have already been mentioned and illustrated. *First,* it supplies a schema for

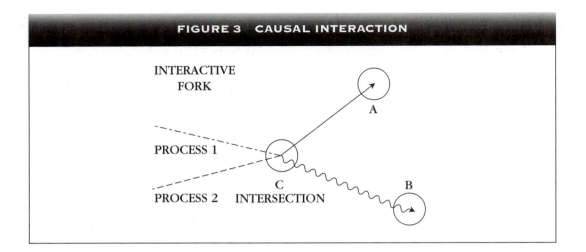

FIGURE 3   CAUSAL INTERACTION

the straightforward explanations of everyday sorts of otherwise improbable coincidences. *Second,* it is the source of the fundamental temporal asymmetry of causality, and it accounts for the temporal asymmetry we impose upon scientific explanations. *Third,* it provides the key to the explication of the concept of causal interaction. These considerations certainly testify to its philosophical importance.

There are, however, two additional applications to which I should like to call attention. *Fourth,* as Russell showed, the principle plays a fundamental role in the causal theory of perception. When various observers (including cameras as well as human beings) arranged around a central region, such as a stage in theatre-in-the-round, have perceptions that correspond systematically with one another in the customary way, we may infer, with reasonable reliability, that they have a common cause—namely, a drama being performed on the stage.[35] This fact has considerable epistemological import.

Fifth, the principle of the common cause can be invoked to support scientific realism.[36] Suppose, going back to a previous example, we have postulated the existence of molecules to provide a causal explanation of the phenomena governed by the ideal gas law. We will naturally be curious about their properties—how large they are, how massive they are, how many there are. An appeal to Brownian motion enables us to infer such things. By microscopic examination of smoke particles suspended in a gas, we can ascertain their average kinetic energies, and since the observed system can be assumed to be in a state of thermal equilibrium, we can immediately infer the average kinetic energies of the molecules of the gas in which the particles are suspended. Since average velocities of the molecules are straightforwardly ascertainable by experiment, we can easily find the masses of the individual molecules, and hence, the number of molecules in a given sample of gas. If the sample consists of precisely one mole (gram molecular weight) of the particular gas, the number of molecules in the sample is Avogadro's number—a fundamental physical constant. Thus, the causal explanation of Brownian motion yields detailed quantitative information about the microentities of which the gas is composed.

Now, consider another phenomenon which appears to be of an altogether different sort. If an electric current is passed through an electrolytic solution—for example, one containing a silver salt—a certain amount of metallic silver is deposited on the cathode. The amount deposited is proportional to the amount of electric charge which passes through the solution. In constructing a causal explanation of this phenomenon (known as electrolysis), we postulate that charged ions travel through the solution, and that the amount of charge required to deposit a singly charged ion is equal to the charge on the electron. The magnitude of the electron charge was empirically determined through the work of J. J. Thomson and Robert Millikan. The amount of electric charge required to deposit one mole of a monovalent metal is known as the Faraday, and by experimental determination, it is equal to 96,487 coulombs. When this number is divided by the charge on the electron (-1.602×10^{-19} coulombs), the result is Avogadro's number. Indeed, the Faraday is simply Avogadro's number of electron charges.

The fundamental fact to which I wish to call attention is that the value of Avogadro's number ascertained from the analysis of Brownian motion agrees, within the limits of experimental error, with the value obtained by electrolytic measurement. Without a common causal antecedent, such agreement would constitute a remarkable coincidence. The point may be put in this way. From the molecular kinetic theory of gases we can derive the statement form, "The number of molecules in the mole of gas is _____ ." From the electrochemical theory of electrolysis, we can derive the statement form, "The number of electron charges in a Faraday is _____ ." The astonishing fact is that the same number fills both blanks. In my opinion, the instrumentalist cannot, with impunity, ignore what must be an amazing correspondence between what happens when one scientist is watching smoke particles dancing in a container of gas while another scientist in a different laboratory is observing the electroplating of silver. Without an underlying causal mechanism—of the sort involved in the postulation of atoms, molecules, and ions—the coincidence would be as miraculous as if the number of grapes harvested in California in any given year were equal, up to the limits of observational error, to the number of coffee beans produced in Brazil in the same year. Avogadro's number, I must add, can be ascertained in a variety of other ways as well—e.g., X-ray diffraction from crystals—which also appear to be entirely different unless we postulate the existence of atoms, molecules, and ions. The principle of the common cause thus seems to apply directly to the explanation of observable regularities by appeal to unobservable entities. In this instance, to be sure, the common cause is not some sort of event; it is rather a common constant underlying structure which manifests itself in a variety of different situations.

Let me now summarize the picture of scientific explanation I have tried to outline. If we wish to explain a particular event, such as death by leukemia of GI Joe, we begin by assembling the factors statistically relevant to that occurrence—for example, his distance from the atomic explosion, the magnitude of the blast, and the type of shelter he was in. There will be many others, no doubt, but these will do for purposes of illustration. We must also obtain the probability values associated with the relevancy relations. The statistical relevance relations are statistical regularities, and we proceed to explain them. Although this differs substantially from things I have said previously, I no longer believe that the assemblage of relevant factors provides a complete explanation—or much of anything in the way of an explanation.[37] We do, I believe, have a bona fide explanation of an event if we have a complete set of statistically relevant factors, the pertinent probability values, *and* causal explanations of the relevance relations. Subsumption of a particular occurrence under statistical regularities—which, we recall, does not imply anything about the construction of deductive or inductive arguments—is a necessary part of any adequate explanation of its occurrence, but it is not the whole story. The causal explanation of the regularity is also needed. This claim, it should be noted, is in direct conflict with the received view, according to which the mere subsumption—deductive or inductive—of an event under a lawful regularity constitutes a complete explanation. One can, according to the received view, go on to ask for an explanation of any law used to explain a given event, but that is a different explanation. I am suggesting, on the contrary, that if the regularity invoked is not a causal regularity, then a causal explanation of that very regularity must be made part of the explanation of the event.

If we have events of two types, *A* and *B,* whose respective members are not spatiotemporally contiguous, but whose occurrences are correlated with one another, the causal explanation of this regularity may take either of two forms. Either there is a direct causal connection from *A* to *B* or from *B* to *A,* or there is a common cause, *C,* which accounts for the statistical dependency. In either case, those events which stand in the cause-effect relation to one another are joined by a causal process.[38] The distinct events *A, B,* and *C* which are thus related constitute interactions—as defined in terms of an interactive fork—at the appropriate places in the respective causal processes. The interactions *produce* modifications in the causal processes, and the causal processes *transmit* the modifications. Statistical dependency relations arise out of local interactions—there is no action-at-a-distance (as far as macrophenomena are concerned, at least)—and they are propagated through the world by causal processes. In our leukemia example, a slow neutron, impinging upon a uranium atom, has a certain probability of inducing nuclear fission, and if fission occurs, gamma radiation is emitted. The gamma ray travels through space, and it may interact with a human cell, producing a modification which may leave the cell open to attack by the virus associated with leukemia. The fact that many such interactions of neutrons with fissionable nuclei are occurring in close spatio-temporal proximity, giving rise to processes which radiate in all directions, produces a pattern of statistical dependency relations. After initiation, these processes go on independently of one another, but they do produce relationships which can be described by means of the conjunctive fork.

Causal processes and causal interactions are, of course, governed by various laws—e.g., conservation of energy and momentum. In a causal process, such as the propagation of a light wave or the free motion of a material particle, energy is being transmitted. The distinction between causal processes and pseudo-processes lies in the distinction between the transmission of energy from one space-time locale to another and the mere appearance of energy at various space-time locations. When causal interactions occur—not merely intersections of processes—we have energy and/or momentum transfer. Such laws as conservation of energy and momentum are causal laws in the sense that they are regularities exhibited by causal processes and interactions.

Near the beginning, I suggested that deduction of a restricted law from a more general law constitutes a paradigm of a certain type of explanation. No theory of scientific explanation can hope to be successful unless it can handle cases of this sort. Lenz's law, for example, which governs the direction of flow of an electric current generated by a changing magnetic field, can be deduced from the law of conservation of energy. But this deductive relation shows that the more restricted regularity is simply part of a more comprehensive physical pattern expressed by the law of conservation of energy. Similarly, Kepler's laws of planetary motion describe a restricted subclass of the class of all motions governed by Newtonian mechanics. The deductive relations *exhibit* what amounts to a part–whole relationship, but it is, in my opinion, the physical relationship between the more comprehensive physical regularity and the less comprehensive physical regularity which has explanatory significance. I should like to put it this way. An explanation may sometimes provide the materials out of which an argument, deductive or inductive, can be constructed; an argument may sometimes exhibit explanatory relations. It does not follow, however, that explanations are arguments.

Earlier in this discussion, I mentioned three shortcomings in the most widely held theories of scientific explanation. I should now like to indicate the ways in which the theory I have been outlining attempts to cope with these problems. (1) The causal conception, I claimed, has lacked an adequate analysis of causation. The foregoing explications of causal processes and causal interactions were intended to fill that gap. (2) The inferential conception, I claimed, had misconstrued the relation of subsumption under law. When we see how statistical relevance relations can be brought to bear upon facts-to-be-explained, we discover that it is possible to have a *covering law conception* of scientific explanation without regarding explanations as arguments. The recognition that subsumption of narrower regularities under broader regularities can be viewed as a part-whole relation reinforces that point. At the same time, it suggests a reason for the tremendous appeal of the inferential conception in the first place. (3) Both of the popular conceptions, I claimed, overlooked a fundamental explanatory principle. That principle, obviously, is the principle of the common cause. I have tried to display its enormous explanatory significance. The theory outlined above is designed to overcome all three of these difficulties.

On the basis of the foregoing characterization of scientific explanation, how should we answer the question posed at the outset? What does Laplace's demon lack, if anything, with respect to the explanatory aim of science? Several items may be mentioned. The demon *may* lack an adequate recognition of the distinction between causal laws and non-causal regularities; it *may* lack adequate knowledge of causal processes and of their ability to propagate causal influence; and it *may* lack adequate appreciation of the role of causal interactions in *producing* changes and regularities in the world. None of these capabilities was explicitly demanded by Laplace, for his analysis of causal relations in general was rather superficial.

What does scientific explanation offer, over and above the inferential capacity of prediction and retrodiction, at which the Laplacian demon excelled? It provides knowledge of the mechanisms of *production* and *propagation* of structure in the world. That goes some distance beyond mere recognition of regularities, and of the possibility of subsuming particular phenomena thereunder. It is my view that knowledge of the mechanisms of production and propagation of structure in the world yields scientific understanding, and that this is what we seek when we pose explanation-seeking why questions. The answers are well worth having. That is why we ask not only "What?" but "Why?"

NOTES

1 The author wishes to express his gratitude to the National Science Foundation for support of research on scientific explanation.

2 Book 1.2, 71b, 17-24.

3 Antoine Arnauld, *The Art of Thinking* (Indianapolis: Bobbs-Merrill, 1964), p. 330. "Such demonstrations may convince the mind, but they do not enlighten it; and enlightenment ought to be the principal fruit of true knowledge. Our minds are unsatisfied unless they know not only *that* a thing is but *why* it is."

4 Karl Pearson, *The Grammar of Science,* 3rd ed. (New York: Meridian Books, 1957), p. xi. The first edition appeared in 1892, the second in 1899, and the third was first published in 1911. In the Preface to the Third Edition, Pearson remarked, just before the statement quoted in the text, "Reading the book again after many years, it was surprising to find how the heterodoxy of the eighties had become the commonplace and accepted doctrine of today." Since the "commonplace and accepted doctrine" of 1911 has again become heterodox, one wonders to what extent such changes in philosophic doctrine are mere matters of changing fashion.

5 Bertrand Russell, *Our Knowledge of the External World* (London: George Allen & Unwin Ltd, 1922), p. 179.

6 The classic paper by Carl G. Hempel and Paul Oppenheim, "Studies in the Logic of Explanation," which has served as the point of departure for almost all subsequent discussion was first published just thirty years ago in 1948 in *Philosophy of Science,* Vol. 15, pp. 135-175.

7 See, for example, his recent paper, "Causation as Explanation," *Noûs,* Vol. 9 (1975), pp. 3-16.

8 Hempel's conceptions have been most thoroughly elaborated in his monographic essay, "Aspects of Scientific Explanation," in *Aspects of Scientific Explanation and Other Essays in the Philosophy of Science* (New York: Free Press, 1965), pp. 331-496.

9 P. S. Laplace, *A Philosophical Essay on Probabilities* (New York: Dover Publications, 1951), pp. 3-6.

10 In "A Third Dogma of Empiricism" in Robert Butts and Jaakko Hintikka, eds., *Basic Problems in Methodology and Linguistics* (Dordrecht: D. Reidel Publishing Co., 1977), pp. 149-166, I have given an extended systematic critique of the thesis (dogma?) that scientific explanations are arguments.

11 Hempel, "Aspects of Scientific Explanation," pp. 352-354.

12 Patrick Suppes, *A Probabilistic Theory of Causation* (Amsterdam: North-Holland Publishing Co., 1970); Hans Reichenbach, *The Direction of Time* (Berkeley & Los Angeles: University of California Press 1956), Chap. IV.

13 See *Nature,* Vol. 271 (2 Feb. 1978), p. 399.

14 Irving Copi, *Introduction to Logic,* 4th ed. (New York: Macmillan Publishing Co., 1972), pp. 396-397, cites this example from *No More War* by Linus Pauling.

15 According to the article in *Nature* (note 13), "the eight reported cases of leukemia among 2235 [soldiers] was 'out of the normal range.'" Dr. Karl Z. Morgan "had 'no doubt whatever' that [the] radiation had caused the leukemia now found in those who had taken part in the maneuvers."

16 Hempel's inductive-statistical model, as formulated in "Aspects of Scientific Explanation" (1965), embodied such a high probability requirement, but in "Nachwort 1976"—inserted into a German translation of this article (*Aspekte wissenschaftlicher Erklärung,* Walter de Gruyter, 1977)—this requirement is retracted.

17 Bertrand Russell, *Human Knowledge, Its Scope and Limits* (New York: Simon and Schuster, 1948), p. 459.

18 Hans Reichenbach, *The Philosophy of Space and Time* (New York: Dover Publications, 1958), Sec. 21.

19 See my "Theoretical Explanation," Sec. 3, pp. 129-134, in Stephan Körner, ed., *Explanation* (Oxford: Basil Blackwell, 1975), for a more detailed discussion of this distinction. It is an unfortunate lacuna in Russell's

discussion of causal lines—though one which can easily be repaired—that he does not notice the distinction between causal processes and pseudo-processes.

[20] See Wesley C. Salmon, ed., *Zeno's Paradoxes* (Indianapolis: Bobbs-Merrill, 1970), p. 23, for a description of this "theory."

[21] I have made an attempt to elaborate this idea in "An 'At-At' Theory of Causal Influence," *Philosophy of Science*, Vol. 44, No. 2 (June 1977), pp. 215–224. Because of a criticism due to Nancy Cartwright, I now realize that the formulation given in this article is not entirely satisfactory, but I think the difficulty can be repaired.

[22] Russell, *Our Knowledge of the External World*, Lecture VI, "The Problem of Infinity Considered Historically." The relevant portions are reprinted in my anthology, *Zeno's Paradoxes*.

[23] Russell, *Human Knowledge*, pp. 460–475.

[24] Reichenbach, *The Direction of Time*, Sec. 19.

[25] In "Theoretical Explanation" I discuss the explanatory import of the common cause principle in greater detail.

[26] Reichenbach offers the following formal definition of a conjunctive fork *ACB*

$$P(A\&B/C) = P(A/C) \times P(B/C)$$
$$P(A\&B/\bar{C}) = P(A/\bar{C}) \times P(B/\bar{C})$$
$$P(A/C) > P(A/\bar{C})$$
$$P(A/C) > P(B/\bar{C})$$

in *The Direction of Time*, p. 159. I have changed these formulas from Reichenbach's notation into a more standard one.

[27] *C* screens-off *A* from *B* if

$$P(A/C\&B) = P(A/C) \neq P(A/B)$$

[28] *The Direction of Time*, pp. 162–163.

[29] Bas C. van Fraassen, "The Pragmatics of Explanation," *American Philosophical Quarterly*, Vol. 14, No. 2 (April 1977), pp. 143–150. This paper was presented at the 51st Annual Meeting of the American Philosophical Association, Pacific Division, March 1977.

[30] The relation between $E_1 + E_2$ and E is an approximate rather than a precise equality because the ejected electron has some energy of its own before scattering, but this energy is so small compared with the energy of the incident X-ray or γ-ray photon that it can be neglected. When I refer to the probability that the scattered photon and electron will have energies E_1 and E_2, respectively, this should be taken to mean that these energies fall within some specified interval, not that they have exact values.

[31] As the boxed formulas in Figures 1 and 2 indicate, the difference between a conjunctive fork and an interactive fork lies in the difference between

$$P(A\&B/C) = P(A/C) \times P(B/C)$$

and

$$P(A\&B/C) > P(A/C) \times P(B/C)$$

The remaining formulas given in Note 26 may be incorporated into the definitions of both kinds of forks. One reason why Reichenbach may have failed to notice the interactive fork is that, in the special case in which

$$P(A/C) = P(B/C) = 1$$

the conjunctive fork shares a fundamental property of the interactive fork, namely, a perfect correlation between *A* and *B* given *C*. Many of his illustrative examples are instances of this special case.

[32] For the special theory of relativity, this has been shown by John Winnie in "The Causal Theory of Space-time," in John S. Earman, Clark N. Glymour, and John J. Stachel, eds., *Foundations of Space-Time Theories, Minnesota Studies in the Philosophy of Science*, Vol. VIII (Minneapolis: University of Minnesota Press, 1977),

pp. 134–205, which utilizes much earlier results of A. A. Robb. For general relativity, the approach is discussed under the heading "The Geodesic Method" in Adolf Grünbaum, *Philosophical Problems of Space and Time,* 2nd ed. (Dordrecht: D. Reidel Publishing Co., 1973), pp. 735–750.

[33] The whole idea of characterizing causal interactions in terms of forks was suggested by Philip von Bretzel in "Concerning a Probabilistic Theory of Causation Adequate for the Causal Theory of Time," *Synthese,* Vol. 35, No. 2 (June 1977), pp. 173–190, especially Note 13.

[34] It strikes me as an unfortunate fact that this important principle seems to have gone largely unnoticed by philosophers ever since its publication in Reichenbach's *The Direction of Time* in 1956.

[35] Russell, *Human Knowledge,* pp. 491–492.

[36] Scientific realism is a popular doctrine nowadays, and most contemporary philosophers of science probably do not feel any pressing need for additional arguments to support this view. Although I am thoroughly convinced (in my heart) that scientific realism is correct, I am largely dissatisfied with the arguments usually brought in support of it. The argument I am about to outline seems to me more satisfactory than others.

[37] Compare Wesley C. Salmon et al., *Statistical Explanation and Statistical Relevance* (Pittsburgh: University of Pittsburgh Press, 1971), p. 78. There I ask, "What more could one ask of an explanation?" The present [reading] attempts to present at least part of the answer.

[38] Reichenbach believed that various causal relations, including conjunctive forks, could be explicated entirely in terms of the statistical relations among the events involved. I do not believe this is possible; it seems to me that we must also establish the appropriate connections via causal processes.

R O M   H A R R É
EXPLANATION

We have been feeling our way, from several different directions, towards the culmination of our study, the elucidation of the ideal form for theories. Theories are the crown of science, for in them our understanding of the world is expressed. The function of theories is to explain. We have already identified some of the forms of explanation.

Two important paradigms of theory have appeared upon which we can base our ideas of what a theory should be. Here I refer back to our discussion [earlier]. The science of mechanics with its central concept of force is one, and the science of medicine with such concepts as the virus is another. They are opposing paradigms. . . . They present two different kinds of theory as seen from a logical, epistemological, and metaphysical point of view. Must we accept both paradigms? Does each have a particular role to play? Can the one be reduced to the other? We shall come some way to settling these questions in this [reading].

The concept of force and the concept of virus seem to play similar roles since each is used to explain observations, on the one hand concerning motion, and on the other concerning the course and development of disease in plants and animals. In the normal course of events neither a force nor a virus is observable in the way in which the happenings which they are designed to explain are observable. Finally, both the conception of force and the conception of the virus are concepts devised by analogy. They are descriptive of entities analogous to certain things with which we are familiar. Forces are analogous to the efforts that people make in shifting things against a resistance, and viruses are analogous to the bacteria which had been found to be the causes of many diseases. We have looked already at some of the detail in the development of these analogies. But if we look a little further at the science of mechanics, and compare it with pathology, a deep difference appears. The concept "force," and with it the analogy with human effort, is inessential to the science of mechanics, as has been shown by the several ways in which that science can be reformulated without this concept. Its function is entirely "pragmatic." It serves the function of an aid to understanding, a device by which intuition is engaged in the business of understanding motion. But it is perfectly possible to understand motion without the concept of force. It is possible to understand all the phenomena of motion using, say, the concept of "energy," and its redistribution among the bodies involved in a system of moving particles according to certain laws. The analogies are quite inessential to mechanics. But compare this situation with that in pathology. Without the concept of the virus as micro-organism the whole theory of the transmission and cause of a wide range of diseases would be quite different. The theory is an essential part of the understanding of the observations. A description of a disease is one thing, its pathology is quite another. This shows up for example in the difference between bad doctoring, in which the symptoms only are treated, and good doctoring, where a diagnosis of the cause of the disease is made and that cause is treated. Finally, and it is this which explains all the other differences between the concept of force and the concept of the virus, it makes sense to ask whether or not there are viruses, and it makes a tremendous difference to medicine which way that question is answered. But though it makes sense to *ask* whether or not there are forces, whether or not individual things exert efforts as people do in bringing about motion, it makes not the slightest difference to the science of mechanics whether there *are* or *are not* forces. The science would be differently formulated no doubt, but there would be not the slightest difference in the predictions of future states of moving systems which could be made by means of it.

Each of the paradigms marks an important ingredient of theory, at least one of which must be present for a theory to be satisfactory. The science of mechanics is organized by the use of a mathematical mode of expression into a logical system, where there are certain fundamental principles and the practical laws of motion are deduced from these in a logical and rigorous way. It is obvious that there are certain great practical advantages in being able to express a theory in a logical system. A great many particular laws and even particular facts can be comprehended in a very economical way in the principles of the theory. Systematization has considerable pragmatic value. But a theory would still be a theory and would still explain the facts it did explain if its laws did not fit easily or at all into a logical system. The laws might only hang together because they were the laws of the same subject matter, that is the laws describing the behaviour of the same kind of things or materials. We have a great deal of knowledge about human behaviour for instance. But this knowledge cannot be formulated in such a way as to fit into a deductive, logical structure. One theory of human behaviour is a rag-bag of principles united by virtue of the fact that they all concern the same subject matter, namely, the behaviour of people. We may never find a systematic formulation of these laws. We may never achieve the pragmatic advantages of system.

A scientific explanation of happenings, whether individual happenings or sequences of events, consists in describing the mechanism which produces them. Only in the most minimal sense does the science of mechanics explain any course of motion. The laws of mechanics are descriptive laws, not explanatory laws. Apart from the tenuous and rather feeble concept of "force" there is no attempt in that science to advance any account of the mechanisms of motion, of why the laws of impact, of momentum conservation, and so on are what they are. So far as I know the only attempt that has ever been made at this is the grotesque set of explanations offered by Descartes in Book II of his *Principles*.[1] But the virus theory has exactly what is required for a scientific explanation of the course of the disease with which it is concerned. The presence of the virus explains what is described in the syndrome or course of the disease, and the more we know about the nature and behaviour of viruses, the more we know about the disease. It is the interaction between body as host and virus as parasite that produces the symptoms of the disease and explains the course of it. The virus theory of poliomyelitis is truly a scientific explanation, where the beautifully systematized laws of mechanics are not. Of course in certain cases the mechanics of particles in motion explains other phenomena, because then the laws of mechanics serve as perfect descriptions of the causal mechanism at work. Such for example, is the often quoted example of the kinetic theory of gases, where the mechanics of the molecules of the gas sample serves as a causal mechanism which explains how samples of the gas behave under various conditions. The kinetic theory is an explanation, and a scientific explanation at that, of the behaviour of gases, but it follows the paradigm of the virus explanation of poliomyelitis, and not the paradigm of the force formulation of mechanics. The fact that mathematical means of expression are used in the kinetic theory and in mechanics, and are not used in the virus theory should not blind us, as philosophers of science, to the essential difference of the former and the essential likeness of the latter.

The generation of the concept at the heart of a theory, what Whewell called the Idea of the theory is, as we have seen in the many examples that were discussed [earlier], a matter of analogy. Building a theory is a matter of developing an appropriate concept by analogy. This is the essential heart of science, because it is the basis of explanation. Why is it that we cannot just go out and find out what the basic mechanisms are? Why can we not eliminate the need for analogy, and go directly to nature? The answer is that science proceeds by a sort of leap-frogging process of discovery. As soon as a field of the phenomena is identified as worth studying and comes under scrutiny we can find all sorts of regularities and patterns among phenomena, but we do not find among these phenomena their causes, nor do we find the mechanisms responsible for the patterns of behaviour we have found. Chemistry proceeds both in the study of the chemical behaviour of different substances and materials, and in the discovery of the mechanisms of these reactions. In studying the reactions we do not study the mechanism of reaction. In many, many cases a great many facts about a certain kind of phenomenon can be found out without it ever being possible to study the mechanisms of the phenomena directly. In such circumstances the necessary mechanisms have to be thought out, to be imagined, and to be the subject of hypotheses. And once they have been thought out, then we know what sort of observations would lead to their independent discovery. Sometimes a wholly different line of investigation leads indirectly to the discovery of the causal mechanisms underlying some phenomena. Such, for example, was the case with the study of radioactivity and chemistry, where the examination of the disintegration of certain rather unusual materials led to discoveries of the greatest importance about the structure of the elementary parts of materials, the chemical atoms. These discoveries were turned by Lewis and Langmuir into a theory of chemical reaction, a description of the mechanism of chemical bonding and the circumstances under which chemical change took place. When we do not know what are the mechanisms underlying the processes we are studying, then we must imagine them, and they must be plausible, reasonable, and possible mechanisms. To achieve this we proceed by the method of analogy, supposing that they are like something about which we all ready know a good deal, and upon the basis of our knowledge of which we can imagine similar mechanisms at work behind the phenomena we are investigating.

What is an analogy? An analogy is a relationship between two entities, processes, or what you will, which allows inferences to be made about one of the things, usually that about which we know least, on the basis of what we know about the other. If two things are alike in some respects we can reasonably expect them to be alike in other respects, though there may be still others in which they are unlike. In general between any two things there will be some likenesses and some unlikenesses. The art of using analogy is to balance up what we know of the likenesses against the unlikenesses between two things, and then on the basis of this balance make an inference as to what is called the neutral analogy, that about which we do not know. Suppose we compare a horse with a car. There are certain likenesses in that both are used as means of transport, both cost a certain amount to buy and to maintain. There are unlikenesses in that one is wholly an artefact, and only in the choice of breeding partners does the hand of man interfere in the production of horses. Horses are organisms, cars are machines. Cars can be repaired by replacing worn-out parts from an external source, but this technique is of limited application for the horse. Suppose we learn that a certain city uses only horse transport, but we know nothing else about their system. We can make certain inferences about the traffic density from what we know about cities which use mechanical transport on the basis of the likeness between horse and car as means of transport, and we can make other inferences about the air pollution based upon what we know of the unlikenesses between them. In this way, by the use of analogy, we penetrate our area of ignorance about a city whose transport is by horse.

In many cases in science we are operating from one term of an analogy only. Molecules are analogous to particles in motion, but we cannot examine molecules directly to see how far they are analogous. Since the molecule is an entity which we imagine as being like a particle in motion, we are free to give it just such characteristics as are required for it to fulfil its function as a possible explanatory mechanism for the behaviour of gases. The neutral analogy is just that part of what we know about particles that we do not yet transpose to our imagined thing, the molecule. The molecule is analogous to the particle not because we find it so but because we make it so. And there is another analogy which completes the theory. A swarm of molecules must be analogous to the gas, otherwise we should not be able to use the molecule concept as an explanatory device. These distinctions are not really well brought out in terms of the simple notion of analogy. From the point of view of the notion of analogy, the relation of molecules to material particles, and the relation of the laws describing their behaviour to the laws of mechanics, and the relation between a swarm of molecules confined in a vessel and a gas, are analogies. But whereas a gas sample might really be a swarm of molecules and molecules might really be material particles, the relationships are, from an epistemological point of view, quite different.

The distinctions which we are looking for can best be made by introducing a new concept, which allows us to analyse analogy relationships a good deal more carefully and finely. This is the concept of the *model*. In the technical literature of logic there are two distinct meanings to the "model," or perhaps it might be better to say two different kinds of model. In certain formal sciences such as logic and mathematics a model for, or of a theory is a set of sentences which can be matched with the sentences in which the theory is expressed, according to some matching rule. We shall not be concerned with such formal, sentential models here. The other meaning of "model" is that of some real or imagined thing, or process, which behaves similarly to some other thing or process, or in some other way than in its behaviour is similar to it. Such a model has been called a real or *iconic model*. It is with iconic models that we are mostly concerned in science, that is, with real or imagined things and processes which are similar to other things and processes in various ways, and whose function is to further our understanding. Toys, for example, are often iconic models, that is things which are similar to other things in some respects, and can indeed play something of their role. For example, dolls are often models of babies, that is, a doll is a thing which is like a baby, and can be treated for certain purposes as a baby. And baby-models can be used quite seriously in training mothers and midwives in baby-handling where it is inconvenient or even dangerous to employ a real baby for the purpose. A toy car is often a model car, a toy plane a model plane.

Models are used for certain definite purposes, and in the sciences these purposes are (i) logical: they enable certain inferences, which would not otherwise be possible, to be made; and (ii) epistemological: that is they express, and enable us to extend, our knowledge of the world. To sort out these purposes rationally yet another idea is needed, that is, the difference between the source of a model and the subject of a model. A doll is a model *of* a baby, and also modelled *on* a baby. Its source is the real thing, the baby, while its subject is, in this case also the baby. Its source and its subject are the same. Such models are called *homoeomorphs*. But when one is using the idea of the molecules as the basis of a model of gas, the molecule is not modelled on gas in any way at all. The molecule is modelled on something quite different, namely the solid, material particles whose laws of motion are the science of mechanics. Such a model for which the source and subject differ is called a *paramorph.*

Science employs both homoeomorphs and paramorphs, and indeed the proper use of models is the very basis of scientific thinking.[2] A theory is often nothing but the description and exploitation of some model. The kinetic theory of gases is nothing but the exploitation of the molecule model of gas, and that model is itself conceived by reference to the mechanics of material particles. We have seen how our lack of knowledge of the real mechanisms at work in nature is supplemented by our imagining something analogous to mechanisms we know, which could perhaps exist in nature and be responsible for the phenomena we observe. Such imagined mechanisms are models, modelled *on* the things and processes we know, and being models *of* the unknown processes and things which are responsible for the phenomena we are studying. This important fact leads to our having to acknowledge that a theory has a very complicated structure, one in which there are at least two major connections which are not strictly logical in the formal sense, but are relations of analogy. The gas molecule is analogous to the material particle, and the swarm of molecules is analogous to whatever a gas really is, and both these analogies are tested by the degree to which the model can replicate the behaviour of real gases. Gas molecules are only like material particles (in some versions of the theory they do not have volume, for instance), and a swarm of them is only like a gas, since even the most sophisticated molecular theories do not quite catch all the nuances of the behaviour of real gases.

But there is a further and final point of the utmost importance. Since we do not know the constituents of a gas independently of our model, we can scarcely be in a position to declare any negative analogy between the model and the gas of which it is a model. Any defects in the molecule concept can be made good so long as we can change its properties without contradiction. We can make and remake the molecule so that in swarms it behaves as near as we like to the gas. When we are considering a model of something we wish to understand we are presented with a neutral analogy and a positive analogy only. The fact that our model may be modelled on something with which it has, in addition to its positive and neutral analogy, a strong negative analogy is of no consequence, since it simply means that the model does express the concept of a new kind of entity or process, different from the one upon which it is modelled. Now as a model of some process or mechanism or material responsible for the phenomenon we are studying becomes more and more refined, a new question gradually presents itself. During the process of refinement we were concerned only with so adjusting our model that it behaved in a way which *would* account for the phenomena. Gradually we are brought to consider the question as to the reality of what had previously been only a model of the real mechanism of nature. Perhaps, we might say to ourselves, gas molecules are not just models of the unknown mechanism of the behaviour of the gases, perhaps there really are gas molecules, and perhaps gases really are nothing but swarms of these things.

I want to present some examples now to show the different ways in which this deeply penetrating question of the reality of an iconic model can be pursued. Darwin's Theory of Natural Selection provides an excellent example of the use of iconic model building to devise a hypothetical mechanism to account for the facts which were known to naturalists. Students of nature had come to see that the populations of animals and plants that at present existed on the earth were different from those that had existed previously. They had also come to see that in nature there was a great variety of forms of many plants and animals closely similar to each other. Many people were very familiar with the possibilities of breeding, particularly gardeners, and stock-breeders of various animals. How are we to explain the variety of species that had existed, and to explain the distribution of that variety of species which now exists? What process in nature is responsible for these striking facts? Now whatever process it is works very slowly, so slowly that Aristotle, one of the greatest biologists of all time, had been deceived into thinking that the species of animals and plants were fixed, so impressed had he been by the similarity between plants and offspring. But there are also minute differences, and it was upon these that Darwin's theory was fixed. Darwin did not know what were the processes by which change in the animals and plants of nature came about, so he constructed a model. He knew very well that there is change in domestic animals and plants and he knew that that change is due to the fact that the breeder *selects* those plants and animals from which he wishes to breed, which are more suited to whatever purpose he has in mind, and that after several repetitions of selection a quite different-appearing creature can be derived from appropriately chosen individuals solely by breeding. There is a variation in nature, and Darwin conceived of a process analogous to domestic selection which could be a model of whatever process was really taking place in nature. He called this process, modelled on domestic selection, *natural selection.*

Had Darwin proceeded with the same model source, for filling out the details of his imaginary process of natural selection, he might have posited the active intervention of a breeder, who like the gardener or stock-breeder had some purpose in mind in bringing together those particular plants and animals which did breed, and which produce the subsequent generation. Now Darwin was looking for a process which was wholly natural and which did not involve divine intervention as a part of the model. He found another source which contributed to his model process. This was the theory of population pressure, originated by Malthus, and elaborated by Herbert Spencer, who had coined the term "Survival of the Fittest," as a brief description of the outcome of the competition for space, light, food, and so on, which by analogy with the conditions which Malthus reckoned to detect in human society, could be projected on to nature. Darwin's Theory of Natural Selection became in effect the elaboration of the various ways in which different varieties of animals and plants were caused to breed at different rates, and so to explain why, in each generation certain individuals were favoured and bred more freely than others. All this was an elaboration of a basic model of whatever process was really responsible for change and development of animal and plant forms in nature. Did the things that Darwin's model suggested really happen in nature? By this question I do not mean "Did evolution occur?" Rather I mean, "Is it the case that some individuals are able to breed more freely because they are more suited to their environment, and do they therefore transmit to their offspring whatever characteristics favoured them?" The reality of the mechanisms of evolution as proposed by Darwin is a separate question from the reality of the evolution process, that is the gradual change of species. Nowadays it is hardly conceived by most biologists that Darwin's theory began as a model of the real processes in nature, so much is it taken for granted that Darwin's model is real. I suppose that it is still just possible, though extremely unlikely, that it may eventually turn out that quite different mechanisms are responsible for the evolution of species.

Recently an interesting example of model building has taken place in the theory of electrical conduction. Somehow the electrons that are in metals are responsible for the conduction of electricity in metal. Drude produced a very successful model of the mechanism of conduction by supposing that there were free electrons in the metal which behaved like the swarm of molecules which we have seen as a most successful model of gas. From supposing that the electrons were like a gas confined within a container, he was able, with very few supplementary assumptions, to work out an explanation of the known laws of conduction, that is he showed that a swarm of electrons obeying the gas laws would behave analogously to a conductor. Here the model is modelled on another model, and is a model of a truly unknown mechanism, the unknown mechanism of the conduction of electricity in metals.

To explain a phenomenon, to explain some pattern of happenings, we must be able to describe the causal mechanism which is responsible for it. To explain the catalytic action of platinum we must not only know in which cases platinum does catalyse a chemical reaction, but what the mechanism of catalysis is. To explain the fact of catalysis we need to know or to be able to imagine a plausible mechanism for the action of catalysis. Ideally a theory should describe what really is responsible for whatever process we are trying to understand. But this ideal can rarely be fulfilled. In practice it becomes this: ideally a theory should contain the description of a plausible iconic model, modelled on some thing, material, or process which is already well understood, as a model of the unknown mechanism, capable of standing in for it in all situations.

Finally this ideal of explanation is complemented by another and final demand. The ideal model will be one which not only allows us to reason by the complex structure of double analogy which I have described, but is one which might be conceived to be a hypothetical mechanism which might really be responsible for the phenomena to be explained. This is what prompts that deepest of all scientific questions, "What is there really in the world? Are those hypothetical mechanisms which we believe might exist really there?"

If knowledge is pursued according to this method it will tend to be stratified. Perhaps this can be seen best if we look at the way causes are elaborated. There are two conditions which have to be fulfilled for there to be truly said to be a causal relation among happenings or phenomena. The first condition, ensuring that there is prima facie evidence, is that there should seem to be some pattern or structure in what we observe to be happening. This might be that simple kind of pattern which we call regularity or repetition, when we find one sort of happening followed regularly by happenings of a certain, definite other kind, when for instance those who are deprived of fresh fruit and vegetables develop scurvy, and those who have plenty of the above commodities do not. We have prima facie evidence that there is a causal relation between the deprivation and the disease. But to eliminate all possibility that something else, some third factor, might be responsible both for the shortage of vegetables and for the scurvy, we must find out what is the mechanism involved, and that involves us in a study of the chemistry of the food materials and of the physiology and chemistry of the body. That study supplies an idea of the mechanism which explains the pattern of happenings involving presence and absence of fresh vegetables, and the onset and cure of scurvy. Satisfying this second condition, that is, describing the causal mechanisms, completes one causal study. Our knowledge falls out into two strata as it were: in one stratum the facts to be explained are set out and their pattern described; in the underlying stratum we may imagine or describe the causal mechanism.

Now, that mechanism is described in terms of chemical reactions and physiological mechanisms. These exhibit their own characteristic patterns and regularities, and these call again for causal explanation. But now a new kind of fact must be adduced. Chemical reactions are explained by the theory of atoms and molecules and chemical valency. By means of this model we can describe a causal mechanism for chemical reactions, and similar considerations apply to the explanation of the physiological and biochemical facts. We have reached another stratum. Then that stratum itself becomes the occasion for prima facie hypotheses that there too are causal relations, that there is some mechanism which explains the combining powers of chemical atoms, and some model of the chemical atom which would explain the diversity of chemical elements. Such a model is to hand in the electron–proton–neutron picture of the atom and the electronic theory of valency. This forms another stratum. Finally, and this is where we are today, if we are to be true to our scientific ideals, we must ask what is responsible for the behaviour of protons, neutrons, electrons, and the other subatomic particles, and we must try to penetrate to yet another stratum. As we have seen in this chapter, this must first be a work of the disciplined imagination, working according to the principles of model building, the method which has enabled us to proceed to such depths in uncovering the strata of the mechanisms and processes which make up the natural world.

In each era scientists find themselves at a loss, incapable of proceeding deeper into nature. And in each era scientists explain this temporary ending of scientific penetration by a metaphysical theory in which what is basic for one time and one limited scientific culture is elevated to the status of the ultimate. As we saw in the chapter on metaphysics, the metaphysical theories of the past have presented forms of explanation as ideals, and those ideals, expressing the ultimately conceivable models for that culture, end with a seemingly impenetrable stratum, that closes the layers of knowledge. But we have also seen that metaphysical systems are not systems of facts. They are systems of concepts which we invent, and which we adopt if we will. Without them we could not think at all, but we must not allow any particular one to stand in the way of scientific progress. Perhaps science may come to an end for us, by reaching a stratum beyond which we have neither the imagination nor the technical resources to penetrate. But that end will not be the end of nature, it will be the projection upon nature of our own limitations. In the meantime we have no alternative but to follow the methods of science as we know them.

SUMMARY OF THE ARGUMENT

(1) Since the function of theories is to explain, an examination of the structure of acceptable theories will yield the forms of explanation.

(*a*) Two paradigms of theory:

(i) The mechanical theory of force introduces an entity which is not observable, which is supposed to cause the mechanical phenomena, *but which can be eliminated from mechanics,* without radically changing the theory. The function of the "force" concept is easily seen to be "pragmatic," serving only to enlist intuition in the understanding of certain abstract relations.

(ii) The virus theory of disease introduces an entity which was unobservable when first introduced, and which is supposed to cause the observed phenomena, but which cannot be eliminated from the theory without entailing a radically different conception of illness, cure, and so on.

(*b*) Consequential differences between the paradigms:

(i) When we understand mechanics we come to see that the question of whether there are or are not forces does not arise, but when we understand the virus theory of disease we do so by accepting the putative existence of viruses, and commit ourselves to the hazard of having to abandon the theory if it is shown by later developments that there are no such things.

(ii) Mechanics is capable of a high degree of organization according to the principles of mathematics and deductive logic. The virus theory is united around the central entity "virus" whose contingent features are not deducible from some set of first principles. For such sciences as social psychology there is not even, in principle, a way in which the general feature of human behaviour could be united into a system with only logical connections.

(iii) Reflection on the virus example leads one to say that a scientific explanation is characterized by the fact that it describes the causal mechanism which produces the phenomena.

(*c*) The origin of the concept at the heart of a theory:

(i) In general the hypothetical entities which constitute the causal mechanisms referred to in scientific explanations are not discovered initially by observation.

(ii) They are first imagined, and their attributes are derived by analogy with entities already known, either by observation, or as the hypothetical entities enshrined in another explanation.

(2) (*a*) Analogies have the following structure:

(i) Positive analogy, that in which A and B are *alike.*

(ii) Negative analogy, that in which A and B are *unlike.*

(iii) Neutral analogy, those attributes of either A or B about which we have no information as to their being matched in the analogue.

(iv) In conceiving hypothetical entities we can examine only one of the entities entering into the analogy, namely that form which the analogy derives, i.e. its source.

(v) The behaviour of the hypothetical entity must be analogous to the behaviour of the real thing which is really causing the phenomena under study.

(b) The technical concept of "model" allows a ready codification of these conditions. In science we are concerned with "iconic" models, that is analogues of things and processes.

(c) The two main uses of models in science are

(i) Heuristic, to simplify a phenomenon, or to make it more readily handlable, as e.g. hydraulic models of electrical networks.

(ii) Explanatory, as described above where the model is a model of the real causal mechanism, then unknown.

(d) Models can be classified by whether their source and subject are identical (*homoeomorphs*) or different (*paramorphs*). In explanatory theories source and subject must be different, so these theories use paramorphic models.

(e) Creative use of paramorphs involves no negative analogy, since disanalogies simply disappear from the definition of the model.

(f) Successful use of an iconic model begins to prompt "reality" questions:

(i) It may be supposed that the iconic model is a true or good representation of the real causal mechanism.

(ii) Provided that it depicts a plausible hypothetical mechanism, it may be possible to inaugurate a search for the entities involved. This, in itself, may stimulate the invention both of sense-extending instruments, and of new forms of detector. As an example of the former consider the electron microscope, and of the latter, the Geiger counter.

(3) This conception of a model as paramorph can be used in the analysis of theories:

(a) Darwin's evolutionary theory can be looked upon as the description of an iconic model of the unknown processes of evolution through

(i) the analogy between natural selection and artificial selection as explanations of natural variation and domestic variation respectively.

(ii) the analogy between plants and animals in the world and the competition for resources among an ever-expanding human population.

(b) Drude's explanation of the relations between electrical and thermal conductivity depends on the invention of a model of the causal mechanism of these phenomena derived through an analogy between the electrons in a metal and the molecules in a gas, that latter itself the product of a famous analogy between the particles of a gas and ordinary material things in motion.

(4) Organized in this way, knowledge is stratified.

  (*a*) In the stratum of observation non-random patterns are discovered which call for explanation.

  (*b*) Their explanation is provided by the description of causal mechanisms, in general unobservable, whose behaviour generates the observed pattern.

  (*c*) This process of stratification continues until the most fundamental relations recognized in each era are reached.

NOTES

[1] R. Descartes, *Principles of Philosophy,* Bk. II, xxxvii, xxxix, xl; in *Descartes, Philosophical Writings,* trans. E. Anscombe and P. T. Geach (London: Nelson, 1954), pp. 216–19.

[2] For the full development of this idea, see R. Harré, *The Principles of Scientific Thinking* (London: Macmillan, and Chicago, Ill.: University of Chicago Press, 1970).

MARY HESSE
MATERIAL ANALOGY

Two questions raised in our dialogue now require more detached investigation:

(1) What is an analogy?

(2) When is an argument from analogy valid?

It is characteristic of modern, as opposed to classical and medieval logic, that the answer to the first question is taken to be either obvious or unanalyzable, while the second is taken to be a question involving induction, and therefore highly problematic. In classical and medieval logic, on the other hand, there is a certain amount of analysis of types of analogy, but practically no attempt at justification of the validity of analogical arguments, although such arguments are frequently used. And since neither the classical types of analogy nor the sketchily defined analogies of modern logic bear much resemblance to analogy as used in reasoning from scientific models,[1] we need to examine the relation of this problem to the traditional discussions. I shall, then, put forward a definition of the analogy *relation* in this [reading], and go on to consider the justification of analogical *argument* [elsewhere].

It is as well to begin by considering very briefly examples of various types of analogy from the literature in order to bring out the main issues.

Example A. An analogy may be said to exist between two objects in virtue of their common properties. Take, for example, the earth and the moon. Both are large, solid, opaque, spherical bodies, receiving heat and light from the sun, revolving on their axes, and gravitating toward other bodies. These properties may be said to constitute their positive analogy. On the other hand, the moon is smaller than the earth, more volcanic, and has no atmosphere and no water. In these respects there is negative analogy between them. Thus the question of what the analogy is in this case is fully answered by pointing to the positive and negative analogies, and the discussion passes immediately to the second question. Under what circumstances can we argue from, for example, the presence of human beings on the earth to their presence on the moon? The validity of such an argument will depend, first, on the extent of the positive analogy compared with the negative (for example, it is stronger for Venus than for the moon, since Venus is more similar to the earth) and, second, on the relation between the new property and the properties already known to be parts of the positive or negative analogy, respectively. If we have reason to think that the properties in the positive analogy are causally related, in a favorable sense, to the presence of humans on the earth, the argument will be strong. If, on the other hand, the properties of the moon which are parts of the negative analogy tend causally to *prevent* the presence of humans on the moon the argument will be weak or invalid.

I shall return to this type of argument later, but meanwhile two features of the analogy should be noted. First, there is a one-to-one relation of identity or difference between a property of one of the analogues and a corresponding property of the other and, second, the relation between properties of the same analogue is that of being properties of the same object, together with causal relations between these properties. Schematically:

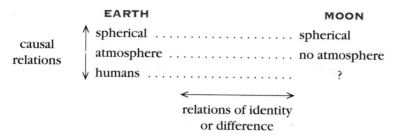

We shall find that a common feature of all the analogies we discuss will be the appearance of two sorts of dyadic relation, and I shall call these *horizontal* and *vertical relations,* respectively. Thus, horizontal relations will be concerned with identity and difference, as in this case, or in general with *similarity,* and vertical relations will, in most cases, be *causal.*

Example B. Consider next the scientific analogy [referred to elsewhere], between the properties of light and of sound. Here again we have two lists of properties, with some members of one list corresponding to some members of the other:

	PROPERTIES OF SOUND	PROPERTIES OF LIGHT
↑	echoes	reflection
	loudness	brightness
causal relations	pitch	color
	detected by ear	detected by eye
↓	propagated in air	propagated in "ether"
	⋮	⋮

similarity relations

In this example, unlike *A,* there is no clear division of the two lists into identities and differences, since the pairs of corresponding terms are never identical but only *similar.* There are, of course, some terms on both sides that have no corresponding term on the other, but I shall regard these as special cases of "similars," where the similarity relation is defined so as to include identities and differences. The vertical relations between members of the same list are, as in example *A,* causal relations.

It has been suggested in the previous chapter that this analogy, like *A,* can be used in arguments from similarities in some respects to similarity in respect of a property known to belong to one analogue but not yet known to belong to the other. For example, known similarities in properties of reflection, refraction, and intensity may lead to a prediction regarding color from properties involving pitch or from the properties of air to those of "ether." Here, however, the situation is more complicated than in example *A,* in that it may not be initially obvious *which* property of light corresponds with which property of sound (why do we make color correspond with pitch?), or it may be that a particular property of sound has *no* correlate among the properties of light, in which case one may be invented ("ether" is initially not *ob-served* as the obvious correlate of air, it is rather *postulated* to fill the place of a missing correlate among the properties of light). Thus in this example, unlike the first, the question of defining the analogy relation and hence identifying its terms must come before the question of justification of the analogical argument.

Example C. Consider next an analogy in a classification system, of a kind first stated explicitly by Aristotle:

GENERA	BIRD	FISH
	wing	fin
	lungs	gills
	feathers	scales
	⋮	⋮

Here the horizontal relation may be one or more or several similarities of structure or of function, and each list may contain some items which have no, or no obvious, correspondent in the older list; for example, without anatomical investigation it is not clear that birds' legs correspond to anything in the structure of fish. The vertical relations may be conceived as no more than that of whole to its parts, or they may be regarded as causal relations depending on some theory or interrelation of parts determined by evolutionary origin or adaptation to environment. In this latter case, the analogy may be used predictively as in the previous example — to argue, for instance, from the known structure of a bird's skeleton to missing parts of a fish skeleton. But again the nature of the analogy relation itself requires elucidation before considering the validity of the argument.

Example D. Finally, an example of a kind used and misused in political rhetoric brings out by contrast some important characteristics of the three previous examples:

$$\frac{\text{father}}{\text{children}} :: \frac{\text{state}}{\text{citizens}}$$

An analogy of this kind is apparently an assertion that the relation between father and child is the same in many respects as that between state and citizens, for example, in that the father is responsible for the maintenance, welfare, and defense of the child; and it is further implied that it follows from this that other relations should also be the same, for example that the citizen owes respect and obedience to the state. There are several differences between this example and the previous ones. First of all, its purpose is persuasive rather than predictive. It is not arguing from three known terms to one unknown, as is the case in the first three examples; it is rather pointing out the consequences, of a moral or normative character, which follow from the relations of four terms already known. Second, the vertical relation is not specifically causal. There are in fact several vertical relations, provider-for, protector-of, and so on; and the argument implicitly passes from asserting some such relations which are already recognized to persuading the hearer that other relations (obedient-to, etc.) follow from these. Third, there does not seem to be any horizontal relation of similarity between the terms, except in virtue of the fact that the two pairs are related by the same vertical relation. That is to say, there is no horizontal relation *independent* of the vertical relations, and here this example differs from all the other three types, where the horizontal relations of similarity were independent of the vertical and could be recognized before the vertical relations were known. It seems to be exclusively analogies of this kind that Richard Robinson is thinking of when he asserts that analogy in any sense other than mathematical proportionality "is merely the fact that some relations have more than one example,"[2] that is that "*a* is to *b* as *c* is to *d*" is merely equivalent to asserting the existence of a relation *R* such that *aRb* and *cRd*. But Robinson overlooks analogies of the other kinds we have mentioned, where there are similarity relations *aSc* and *bS'd* independent of the vertical relations.

ANALOGY AND MATHEMATICAL PROPORTION

At this point we can usually draw a distinction between the types of analogy we are concerned with and the relation of mathematical proportionality. The two kinds of relation have often been thought to be closely connected, as is indicated by the fact that the Greek word for "proportion" is *analogia*. And the relations do indeed have some formal resemblances, which have been presupposed in the notation for the four-term relation already adopted in the previous chapter.

Let us represent the relation "*a* is to *b* as *c* is to *d*" by $\frac{a}{b} :: \frac{c}{d}$, where *a* and *b* are any two terms taken from a list representing one analogue in examples *A*, *B*, or *C*, including the heading, and *c* and *d* are the corresponding terms taken from the other list. For example, "pitch is to sound as color is to light," "wing is to bird as fin is to fish," or "wing is to feathers as fin is to scales":

$$\frac{\text{pitch}}{\text{sound}} :: \frac{\text{color}}{\text{light}}, \quad \frac{\text{wing}}{\text{bird}} :: \frac{\text{fin}}{\text{fish}}, \quad \frac{\text{wing}}{\text{feathers}} :: \frac{\text{fin}}{\text{scales}}.$$

This generalized analogy relation has the following formal characteristics in common with numerical proportionality:

(1) We wish to say that the analogy relation is *reflexive*, that is to say $\frac{a}{b} :: \frac{a}{b}$, although this is a trivial case of the general relation.

(2) We wish to say that the analogy relation is *symmetrical*, for if $\frac{a}{b} :: \frac{c}{d}$, then $\frac{c}{d} :: \frac{a}{b}$.

(3) We wish to say that the analogy relation can be *inverted*, for if $\frac{a}{b} :: \frac{c}{d}$, then $\frac{b}{a} :: \frac{d}{c}$.

(4) We can compare the additive property of numerical proportion with the results of taking the *logical sum* of terms of an analogy. Just as we have in numerical proportion that if $\frac{a}{b} = \frac{c}{d}$ then $\frac{a+b}{b} = \frac{c+d}{d}$, so it is convenient to say, for example, that

$$\frac{\text{properties of sound}}{\text{pitch}} :: \frac{\text{properties of light}}{\text{color}}$$

where "properties of sound" and "properties of light" are taken to be just logical sums of terms in their respective lists.

(5) Locating a corresponding term in an analogy has some resemblance to finding the fourth term of a proportionality, given the other three terms. Suppose we are given three terms of an analogy, say *a, b, c,* where *a* and *b* specify a vertical relation, say *aRb,* and *c* is the term corresponding to *a* in another analogue. Location of a fourth term can then occur in two different ways. If we know the relations between terms of this other analogue, we may locate *d* such that *cRd* from the given *c* and *R.* This will be the case in example *B* when we already know the wave-theory relations between pitch and other properties of sound, and between color and other properties of light. The analogy will then tell us that color corresponds to pitch. Or we may not know the causal relations in the second set of terms, and then we have to look for a *d* related to *b* by similarity. This will be the case in the pretheoretic use of example *B,* where we look for that property of light which has some similarity with pitch (for example, has similar effects on our sense organs). Or again, in example *C,* wing and fin are similar in structure and function, therefore the required term corresponding to lungs will be similar to one or both of these respects to lungs.

Here, however, the resemblance between proportion and analogy ends. Even the resemblance just discussed under (5) is not complete, for it may not be the case that the analogy relation gives a *unique* fourth term. For example, we may think that birds' legs or birds' tails are equally good analogues for fishes' tails, so that both would provide a fourth term in "fish is to fishtail as bird is to . . . ," each corresponding to similarities in different respects. Another difference between proportion and analogy arises from the fact that the horizontal and vertical relations are relations of the same kind in proportion, but not in analogy. This means, among other things, that the terms of an analogy cannot be alternated without producing a relation of a different kind, for if $\frac{a}{b}::\frac{c}{d}$ is replaced by $\frac{a}{c}::\frac{b}{d}$, the relation no longer conforms to the convention that horizontal relations are relations of similarity, and vertical relations are causal. Finally, in analogy, unlike proportion, there is not, in general, transitivity between three pairs of terms, for if $\frac{a}{b}::\frac{c}{d}$ and $\frac{c}{d}::\frac{e}{f}$, there may be no analogy relation at all, or anyway not such a close one, between $\frac{a}{b}$ and $\frac{e}{f}$. This is due to the dependence of analogy on similarity, for it is not in general the case that two things which are each similar to a third thing are similar to each other. They may be similar to the third thing in different respects, or, if in the same respect, their respective similarities to the third thing may be much greater than their similarity to each other.

THE SIMILARITY RELATION

The examples *A* to *D* do not by any means exhaust all possible types of analogy and analogical argument, but they are sufficient to indicate the boundaries that can be drawn round the present enquiry into analogical reasoning from scientific models. We have seen that analogy is used in two senses in physical theories—there is the one-to-one correspondence between different interpretations of the same formal theory, which we may call *formal analogy,* and there are pretheoretic analogies between observables such as

$$\frac{\text{properties of sound}}{\text{pitch}} :: \frac{\text{properties of light}}{\text{color}}$$

which enable predictions to be made from a model. Let us call this second sense *material analogy.*

It is clearly the notion of material analogy which causes most of the difficulties, and it is this type of analogy which is required if prediction from models is to be possible in the strong sense of the last chapter. One of the questions left unanswered there was whether the above example about sound and light can be counted as an analogy at all, except in the formal posttheoretic sense. It is already clear that if there is a sense of analogy other than the formal here, this must be in virtue of some kind of similarity between the horizontal terms. Examples *A* to *D* include two extreme cases of the similarity relation, both of which are instructive. Example *D* is a case of no horizontal similarity independent of the vertical relation, and in this respect it is paralleled exactly by *formal* analogy in science, for there two terms related by analogy need have no similarity other than that of both being interpretations of the same term in a formal theory, that is, of being corresponding *relata* in the *vertical* causal network of relations constituting the theory. An example of such an analogy was given in our first chapter—the formal analogy between elliptic membranes and the acrobat's equilibrium, both of which are described by Mathieu's Equation. This analogy is useless for prediction precisely because there is no similarity between corresponding terms. At the other extreme in respect of similarity is example *A*. Here there is not merely *similarity* between the properties related horizontally in the positive analogy, for they are the *same* property. This contrasts with the pairs of terms in the other examples—"wing" and "fin," and "pitch" and "color"—in which members of a pair are not only not identical, but it is often not clear in what their similarity consists or what term of a given analogue should be paired with what in virtue of their similarity. The fact that most modern logical accounts of analogy have been carried out only with examples like *A* or *D* in mind, explains why the *nature* of the analogical relation has not been thought to be problematic.

It should be noticed that if material analogies between models and explicanda are to do the predictive job required of them, they must be *observable* similarities between corresponding terms and must not depend on a theory of the explicandum. Thus, the colliding-elastic-ball model for gases suggests itself in the first place because of observable similarities between, for example, the behavior of bouncing balls and bouncing balloons, and between the effects of pressure on a surface due to a hail of particles and those due to an expanding gas. The pretheoretic similarities between pitch and color are rather less obvious, but a good deal of support can be gathered from the history of theories of sound and light for the assertion that such similarities were recognized before any theory having the same formal characteristics for both sound and light was known. Aristotle, for instance, based his conjecture of the analogy between pitch and color on the observed facts that certain combinations of sounds and certain mixtures of colors are pleasant to the senses and others unpleasant, and that excess of brightness or darkness, or of sharp or flat, destroys the senses.

These examples suggest that when similarities are recognized they are described in some such way as, "Both analogues have property B, but whereas the first has property A, the second has instead property C."[3] It may be that when the nature of the similarity is pressed, it will be admitted that the analogues do not both have the *identical* property B, but two *similar* properties, say B and B', in which case the analysis of the similarity of B and B' repeats the same pattern. But if we suppose that at some point this analysis stops, with the open or tacit assumption that further consideration of difference between otherwise identical properties can be ignored, we have an analysis of similarity into relations of identity and difference. And only if this is the case can we assimilate arguments from similarities between model and explicandum to what traditional logic has called "argument from analogy," of which a classic example is A, and which depends only on identities and differences.

In terms of such an analysis the general schema for the four examples we have considered becomes:

$$
\begin{array}{ll}
\textbf{ANALOGUE } X & \textbf{ANALOGUE } Y \\
A_1(x)B_1(x) & B_1(y)C_1(y) \\
A_2(x)B_2(x) & B_2(y)C_2(y) \\
\quad\vdots\quad\vdots & \quad\vdots\quad\vdots
\end{array}
$$

Let us call the predicates A_1, A_2, B_1 etc., *characters*. Example A of analogy now becomes the special case in which there are no characters such as the A's and C's, which occur in one list and not in the other, and example D is the special case in which there are no characters as the B's which occur in both lists.

But why place the characters in groups rather than list them singly as identities or differences between the two analogues as in example A? The reason for this formulation is not fundamental but is connected with the way in which the characters present themselves at a given stage of empirical enquiry. Let us consider the earth-moon example, in which the characters are listed as simple identities or differences.

If it is said (as by Mill) that the validity of the analogical argument depends on the known causal relations between the properties of both analogues, two situations may arise. Either (as in the case of the conditions for human life) the causal relations are known *independently* of either of the analogues, in which case the argument for or against human life on the moon is an ordinary causal argument from universal laws of nature applied in a particular instance, the moon, and the earth is irrelevant to the argument; or else the only causal relations known are those implied by the co-occurrence of certain properties on the earth, in which case the argument looks like an enumerative induction which is very weak because based on only one instance. But neither of these alternatives is a satisfactory analysis of analogical argument; the first because it does away with the argument derived from the similarity of the analogues altogether; the other because it represents analogical argument merely as a weak induction from a single instance.

But analogical argument is not just inductive generalization, and any account which reduces it to this is misleading. Expressing the matter more formally, the analogical argument consists in the following: given two analogues x and y which resemble each other in a number of characters $B_1 \ldots B_m$, and are dissimilar in that x also has $A_1 \ldots A_n$ and y has not, and y has also $C_1 \ldots Cl$ and x has not, we want to know whether another character D of x is likely to belong also to y. This will be called the *logical problem* of analogy. (For brevity we refer to the characters in intensional notation and leave their arguments x and y to be understood. The translation to extensional notation is obvious throughout.)

If the casual relations of $A_1 \ldots A_n$ with D, and $B_1 \ldots B_m$ with D are known independently of each other, and, in particular, independently of x, then the inference to possession of D by y is purely causal and need make no reference to x. This is the situation in the earth-moon example, since in that case enough is known of the causal relation of, for example, atmosphere to life, to make this relation a universal law, independent of the particular co-occurrence of atmosphere and human life on the earth. Hence the inference that human life cannot occur on the moon follows simply from the absence on the moon of one of its causally necessary conditions. But this is not always the situation, and in particular is not the situation in analogical reasoning from scientific models. In a system x which is to be used as a model for a theory about an explicandum y, we do not generally know the causal relations of the A's with D and the B's with D *separately,* we only know that D is related to the A's and B's as they occur together in the model. For example, if an elastic ball is taken as a model for sound, we know that when a ball is thrown against a wall it rebounds, but we cannot empirically separate the characteristics which are in common between the throwing of a ball and the uttering of a sound, and those which are different, in order to infer a general causal relation applicable also to sound: "throwing is correlated with rebound," in such a way that this is independent of the occurrence of the other characters of the ball. It is this practical impossibility of empirically separating some of the characters from others that has dictated the form in which characters have been listed for each analogue in the table just given.

Another point should be made here about the relations of induction and analogical argument. There is a well-known chicken-and-egg paradox which can be expressed as follows: argument from analogy depends on induction from known laws connecting the properties of each analogue; hence all such argument is inductive. On the other hand, inductive argument depends on recognizing similarities between instances, none of which is in practice exactly the same as the others; hence all such argument is analogical. The regress may be stopped, however, if we agree to admit characters between which we recognize identities or differences which we take to be not further analyzable. Then an inductive argument will be one from a large number of instances of which a typical one may be represented by $B_1 \ldots B_m C_{r1} \ldots C_{rl}$, where $B_1 \ldots B_m$ are identical for all instances, and $C_{r1} \ldots C_{rl}$ is a set of characters which differentiates the rth instance from the others. When $B_1 \ldots B_m$ have been found to occur together in a large number of instances, each containing different sets of C's, we conclude that we can ignore the C's in forming inductive arguments about the B's. In an analogical argument, however, we have *one* set of B's and *one* set of C's presented together, and we do not know, and are not in a position to find out, whether the relations between the B's remain the same in the absence of the C's. Thus inductive argument is more fundamental than analogical. But this does not mean that inductive argument requires instances to repeat themselves exactly, which never happens; it merely requires us to be able to discriminate among characters which are presented together those which are relevant to the argument (because they have retained constant mutual relations in many otherwise different instances), and those which are not (because they have varied from instance to instance).

This point also helps to answer another objective. It may be said that it is impossible to discriminate characters which are always presented together, as is assumed to be the case in analogical argument. But if this were so, it would never be possible to recognize more than one instance of the same inductive generalization, for we should never recognize $B_1 \ldots B_m$ in association with $C_{11} \ldots C_{1l}$ as the same $B_1 \ldots B_m$ that we next find in association with $C_{21} \ldots C_{2k}$. It is essential for both inductive and analogical arguments that the characters are separately *recognizable* although they may never be separately presented. The difference between the two types of argument is due to the amount of information available, and analogical argument is necessary only in situations where it has not been possible to observe or to produce experimentally a large number of instances in which sets of characters are differently associated. In other words, it is necessary in situations where Bacon's or Mill's methods of agreement and difference cannot be applied. Thus, in a sense analogical argument is "weaker" than inductive, but on the other hand it has the advantage of being applicable where straightforward generalization is not.

Of course the description of similarities and differences between two analogues is a notoriously inaccurate, incomplete, and inconclusive procedure. Although we often feel some confidence in asserting the existence of a similarity and that some things are more similar to each other than to other things, we cannot usually locate discrete characteristics in one object which are positively and finally identifiable with or differentiable from those in another object. But the inconclusive nature of the procedure is not fatal here, because we are not looking for incorrigible inductive methods, but only for methods of selecting *hypotheses*. Analogical argument is inconclusive, both for the usual inductive reasons and also because it may rest on incomplete location of similarities; nevertheless, . . . it does provide a method of hypothesis-selection which is justifiable on at least some of the recognized criteria for such selection. Further, we shall see that even if it were possible accurately to *weight* the similarities between an explicandum and different models which are compared with it, this would not strengthen the analogical argument according to any of its acceptable justifications, and so it is pointless even to seek to define *degrees* of similarity among the sets of characters.

THE CAUSAL RELATION

An argument from analogy requires a certain kind of similarity relation between the horizontal terms of the analogy, and also a certain kind of vertical relation. The examples C and D indicate the existence of analogies where the dyadic vertical relation or relations may be of many different kinds: whole-to-part, organism-to-organ, protector-of-, obedient-to, and so on; most of which are not obviously causal in the sense in which the relation of "atmosphere" to "humans" or "wave-motion" to "reflection" is causal. But what, more precisely, is this sense? It is at least a tendency to co-occurrence. In the case of the relation "atmosphere" to "humans," the first term is, or is claimed to be, a necessary condition of the second; that is to say, the occurrence of one of the terms is a causal condition of the occurrence of the other.

The same can be said of the relations between the properties of a model such as elastic balls or sound waves. Certain properties are necessary or sufficient conditions for other properties, and the network of causal relations thus established will make the occurrence of one property at least tend, subject to the presence of other properties, to promote or inhibit the occurrence of another. Arguments from models involve those analogies which can be used to predict the *occurrence* of certain properties or events, and hence the relevant relations are causal, at least in the sense of implying a tendency to co-occur. Dyadic relations in which the empirical occurrence of one of the relata implies nothing about the occurrence of the other will not justify analogical inference. For example, it may be said that "man is to woman as boy is to girl," but the occurrence of a man, a woman, and a boy, gives in itself no grounds for expecting the occurrence of a girl. And, as we shall see, it can be argued that the mere placing of terms in a classification system, as in example *C,* gives a sense to the relation of analogy, but gives in itself no grounds for inferring from the existence of entities represented by three of the terms to the existence of an entity represented by the fourth.

Within the requirement of tendency to co-occurrence, the causal relation may be analyzed in a number of ways. It may be represented in terms of a Humean relative frequency of co-occurrence in which closeness of causal connection between A and B corresponds to a high proportion of occurrences of A and B together as compared with their occurrences apart. (Some restrictions will be placed on this interpretation later.) Or the analysis of cause may be carried out in terms of a hypothetico-deductive theory, in which the causal relation between A and B follows as a law from some higher-level hypothesis. Or a cause A may be interpreted modally, as in some sense *necessary* for $B,$ or even ontologically, as in some sense *productive* of $B.$ It is not my purpose here to go into the difficulties involved in these interpretations of cause, because in analyzing the nature of analogical argument in general, it is only necessary to point out that the argument, if valid, carries over the *same* sense of causal relation from model to explicandum, in virtue of the relations between the characters which model and explicandum share.

In whatever way the causal relation is interpreted, it is necessary to stress again that in the logical problem of analogy, the characters we are concerned with are not hidden causes or theoretical entities but *observables.* This is because, as well as being causally related within one analogue, they must, as we have seen, also be the characters in virtue of which similarities are recognized between superficially distinct causal systems. An analogical argument from models may lead to the discovery of hidden causes or to the postulation of theoretical entities, but the similarities from which it starts must be observable. Again, it should not be supposed that the characters are necessarily some kind of atomic constituents, combining to form the system by connection of parts, although they may sometimes be this. But in general we are not in a position observably to identify the atomic constituents of the systems we investigate, and, in any case, the characters in many of the examples we have discussed are not parts or constituents, and the systems are not constructed by connecting them. Thus sound is not *composed of* reflection, loudness, pitch, etc. But the whole-part relationship is not in general implied by the representation of a system by means of characters. All that is implied in representing a system as, for example *ABD,* is that the characters *A, B, D* are causally related according to some acceptable interpretation of causality, which may be a relation of whole-part, as in the case of an organism and its organs, or may be co-occurrence and concomitant variation described by a set of empirical laws, as in such cases as elastic balls, gases, sound, and light.

The requirement of "an acceptable interpretation of causality" raises another point. This acceptability is not only a question of the philosophical analysis of causality, but also of the correctness of the assertion of a causal relation of given type between the actual terms of the analogy. Analogical arguments may be attacked not only on the grounds that they depend on superficial similarities, but also on the grounds that the causal relations assumed are inappropriate to the subject matter. These two forms of objection must be carefully distinguished. The second form of attack is based on disagreement about whether the connections asserted in the model do after all deserve to be called causal, or perhaps whether, though they may be appropriately causal for the model, they are proper to the subject matter of the explicandum. This is not specifically a disagreement about analogical argument, but about what kinds of theories or laws are to be admitted into different branches of science.

One form of this problem is illustrated by example *C.* In nineteenth-century biology definitions were elaborated of *homologies* and *analogies* in different species and groups of species. Roughly, organs in different species are *homologous* when they are structurally the same organ, that is, correspond in position and connections relative to the whole organism and are made up of corresponding parts, whatever difference there may be between their functions. In this sense the human hand and the bat's wing are homologous. Parts or organs are said to be *analogous* when they have the same function, whether or not they are also homologous; for example, the bat's wing and the bird's wing are analogous but are not structurally the same, and therefore are not homologous. Both "homology" and "analogy" can be said to be analogies in the sense of our material taken from its parts. Again, this is not a dispute about the logical validity of analogical argument as such, but about the acceptability of certain causal relations.

The same kind of problem arises in a more extreme form in the attempts to draw analogies between human and divine, created and creator, which were the motive for a large part of medieval discussion of analogy. The suggested relation

$$\frac{\text{sculptor}}{\text{statue}} :: \frac{\text{God}}{\text{world}}$$

for example, has been objected to on the grounds (among others) that the causal relation asserted between God and the world *cannot,* in principle, be identical with that between sculptor and statue. And if this is the case, then it follows that this is not an analogy relation in the sense defined here, because it means that whatever similarity relations may be asserted between the terms in horizontal pairs, they do not carry causal relations from one analogue to the other.

CONDITIONS FOR A MATERIAL ANALOGY

The conditions for a material analogy between scientific model$_2$ and explicandum may now be summarized as follows.

(1) The horizontal dyadic relations between terms are relations of similarity, where similarity can, at least for purposes of analysis, be reduced to identities and differences between sets of characters making up the terms.

(2) The vertical relations in the model are causal relations in some acceptable scientific sense, where there are no compelling a priori reasons for denying that causal relations *of the same kind* may hold between terms of the explicandum.

These conditions have been suggested by analysis of examples of the use of models which make the theories strongly predictive in the sense defined in the first chapter. The question now arises, are these conditions *necessary* and *sufficient* for this predictive use of models? Three kinds of counter-examples suggest themselves, the first to the assertion that the conditions are necessary, and the others to the assertion that they are sufficient. . . .

MEANING OF THEORETICAL TERMS

This chapter has so far been concerned wholly with analogies with *observables* in the explicandum, but in conclusion let us look briefly at another use of analogy in connection with scientific models. The analysis of analogy in terms of relations of similarity and causality has been directed to answering questions such as: What is meant by the analogical relation

$$\frac{\text{properties of sound}}{\text{pitch}} :: \frac{\text{observable properties of light}}{\text{color}} ?$$

If the arguments of this chapter are accepted, it will be agreed that there is a material, pretheoretic analogy here, and that it is in virtue of this analogy that we use sound as a model for light and make predictions about color *before* we have any theory of color. The suggestion immediately arises, however, that there are also analogical relations in which one term is *unobservable,* that is, is a theoretical term. An example would be:

$$\frac{\text{elastic balls}}{\text{bouncing}} :: \frac{\text{gas molecules}}{\text{pressure}}$$

or as an example from sound and light:

$$\frac{\text{air}}{\text{sound}} :: \frac{\text{ether}}{\text{light}}$$

where "gas molecules" and "ether" are theoretical terms.

It is clearly possible to interpret these last two examples as *formal analogies,* that is to say, terms in the same horizontal row are interpretations of the same symbol or set of symbols of the formal kinetic theory in the first example, or the formal wave theory in the second. This, however, says nothing about the theoretical terms "gas molecules" or "ether" except that they *are* such interpretations—and any other form of words would have done just as well to name the interpretations. But, given the formal analogy, we can also regard these examples as *material analogies* in the sense defined. In this case the vertical causal relations are shown by the position of the terms in the deductive systems of the theories, and the horizontal similarity relations between the *observables* in the lower row are given by an overlap of observable characters as before. Now consider the relation between "air" and "ether" in the second example. "Air" in this analogy must be interpreted as a complex of characters; to say "sound travels in air" is to ascribe an indefinitely long list of characters to air of which some of the relevant ones of this analogy are "air is a chemical substance capable of oscillation having a certain density, a certain elasticity . . . ," and so on. Thus air might be represented by the sum of characters $A_1 \ldots A_n B_1 \ldots B_m D_1 \ldots D_k$. Let us suppose that $B_1 \ldots B_m$ represent the *known positive analogy* between sound and light, including characters associated with wave motion, and $D_1 \ldots D_k$ represent the neutral analogy, including the density, elasticity, and chemical composition of the medium of the waves. Then the theoretical term "ether," corresponding to "air," may be interpreted in one of two ways, either as including the positive and negative analogies only, as $B_1 \ldots B_m C_1 \ldots C_l$, or including also the neutral analogy, as $B_1 \ldots B_m C_1 \ldots C_l D_1 \ldots D_k$. The second interpretation of "ether" represents the analogy between what I have called model₂ (in this case sound) and model₁ (in this case the wave theory of light); the first represents that between model₂ and the known positive analogy between light and sound. It will be noticed that the first alternative introduces no terms not already in the formal analogy between model₂ and the accepted theory, whereas the second alternative introduces also the growing points of the theory. The two interpretations can be illustrated as follows:

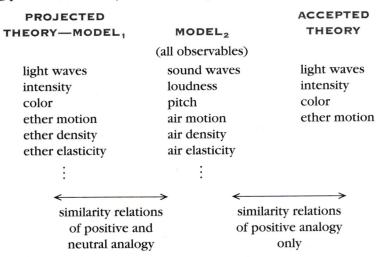

PROJECTED THEORY—MODEL₁	MODEL₂ (all observables)	ACCEPTED THEORY
light waves	sound waves	light waves
intensity	loudness	intensity
color	pitch	color
ether motion	air motion	ether motion
ether density	air density	
ether elasticity	air elasticity	

similarity relations of positive and neutral analogy   similarity relations of positive analogy only

The difference between the material analogies, containing only observables, which have been previously discussed, and the material analogies containing at least one theoretical term, lies in their use rather than in their nature. In the first case we have been concerned with the use of analogy to infer from three or more given observable terms to another predicted observable; in the second case the scientific use of the analogy is rather to pass from three given observables to the *definition* of a theoretical term, and hence to hypotheses about the theoretical term. The theoretical term may be regarded as a convenient way of summarizing the positive and neutral analogy at any given stage of investigation, and hence of suggesting new, observable predictions by means of the neutral analogy. *Justification* of the postulate of the theoretical term will depend on the success of these predictions, but the *meaning* of the term is clarified by showing how it is partially defined by the characters (the B's) which it shares with the corresponding term in model$_2$.

There need be no conflict between this way of regarding theoretical terms and the more usual account of their meaning as partially defined by their deductive relations with observables. It has already been argued that this "partial definition" is not sufficient, and the account now given supplements it in just the way required. This account depends on the assumption that the identity of formal structure between the model$_2$ and the theory of the explicandum is due to identities between characters (the B's) in one, and corresponding characters in the other. In model$_2$ these characters when combined with the A's may represent observables; in the theory they are combined with the C's and represent theoretical terms or "unobservables." Definition of the theoretical terms as containing the B's is more satisfactory than their partial definition in terms of the observables of the explicandum only. Looked at in this way it might be said that argument from models presupposes identity of characters between model$_2$ and theory in *essential* respects, where "essential" means those respects which are relevant to the causal structure of both model$_2$ and theory. The known differences, or negative analogies, can be regarded as *accidental* to the causal structure. Thus the definition of a theoretical term by means of a model$_2$ is a definition of its essential characters, and if the neutral analogy is included in the definition, as in the second alternative above, this presupposes that the characters in the neutral analogy are also essential rather than accidental. That this may be in fact false, and that the theory will then be false, does not affect our understanding of the *meaning* of the theoretical term.

It may now be asked whether this account of the meaning of theoretical terms is necessary to the general account of the use of models for prediction. We were able to describe the reasoning which led to such predictions apparently without mentioning the nonobservable terms occurring in the theory of the explicandum. Can we not regard the predictive process as consisting wholly of reasoning by analogy from the observed behavior of the model$_2$ to observable behavior of the explicandum, without going via the theory in either case?[4] Thus, some observed analogies of behavior between sound and light may lead to further predictions about light, without any theory of either sound or light.

This would not, however, be in general a sufficient account of the matter. First, it is the theory of model$_2$ which defines the causal relations of that model, and hence shows what are its essential properties and also what kind of causal relation is involved. As we have seen in several examples, it is not justifiable to pass by analogy from model$_2$ to explicandum in respect either of properties which are not essential to the model or of causal relations of a kind which are not appropriate to model or explicandum. Second, it is model$_2$ which supplies suggestions for extensions of the theory of the explicandum, and in seeing how this theory can yield new predictions in the domain of the explicandum it is often necessary to take account of differences as well as similarities. This will involve reasoning by analogy about the theoretical terms as well as about analogous observables. Sometimes there may be only a question of numerical constants, as when the scale of model$_2$ is greater than that of the explicandum, and the effect of the scale on the observables has to be calculated in terms of the theories of both model$_2$ and explicandum. Or the difference may be more fundamental, as, for example, in the case of the effect on the velocities of light and sound of passage into a denser medium. The wave theory of sound then has to be generalized to take account of velocities which are diminished instead of increased under these circumstances. As soon as model$_2$ gives way to model$_1$ in the reasoning, by the conscious exclusion of the known negative analogy, it is not sufficient to say that reasoning by analogy consists merely in passing from the observable model$_2$ to the observable explicandum. Third, and finally, if we regard a valid argument by analogy from models as essentially a transfer of causal relations between some characters from one side of the analogy relation to the other, it follows that the interpretation of theoretical terms we have just given is *presupposed* in the argument, even if not explicitly referred to, for if there is a theory about the causal relations in model$_2$, then the same theory holds for the relevant characters in model$_1$, and hence for the explanatory theory being sought.

To summarize the discussion so far: We have found the distinction between *formal* and *material* analogy to be crucial to the predictive use of scientific models, and in this chapter material analogy has been characterized by two types of dyadic relation, those of *similarity* and *causality.* Analogical arguments from models have been formulated in terms of *characters* which are independently observable but not also experimentally separable. In connection with the justification of analogical argument, a distinction has been made between the *logical* problem of justifying inference from similarity and the *causal* problem of deciding whether the type of vertical relation implied in the analogy is acceptable as causal for either or both of the analogues. Finally, the problem of the meaning of theoretical terms has been elucidated in terms of the analogy relation defined. We now go on to study the logical problem of analogical inference.

NOTES

[1] In this [reading], the sense of "model" will always be model$_2$ of [an earlier passage not included here].
[2] *Rev. Metaphysics,* V, 1952, 466.
[3] "Having a property *A*" is here regarded as an *intensional* characteristic of an analogue. No attempt is made to give a purely extensional analysis either of the properties or of relations of identity and difference between them. But once objects have been sorted into classes by recognition of their intensional properties, these classes can, as far as the *logical* discussion is concerned, be regarded as defining the properties, and extensional interpretation applied throughout.
[4] I owe this suggestion to Mr. John Richard Thomson, of King's College, Cambridge.

STUDY QUESTIONS FOR TOPIC II

1. According to Hempel's covering law model of explanation, must every explanatory argument be deductive? Is it possible for an explanatory argument to be nondeductive? Defend your answer.

2. What is the conception of law of nature that Hempel advocates in his covering law model?

3. Identify all the requirements for a genuine explanation according to Hempel's covering law model.

4. Hempel requires that every explanation include at least one law of nature, but critics object that many explanations in science are given without such laws. For example, the occurrence of an earthquake is explained without repeating the relevant laws of nature from geology. What exactly is Hempel's answer to this objection, based on his discussion of explanation?

5. According to Scriven, what precisely is wrong with Hempel's conception of a scientific prediction? Provide at least one example on behalf of Scriven's argument.

6. Kitcher raises objections to Hempel's covering law model of explanation. Does this imply that Kitcher rejects all forms of the explanation-as-argument conception of explanation?

7. What is the primary purpose of an explanation, according to Salmon's causal conception of explanation?

8. What are the similarities and differences between Harré's conception of explanation and Salmon's conception?

9. As discussed in the introduction to this topic, earthquakes are explained by a theory concerning the movement of tectonic plates. Following Harré's conception of explanation, what precisely are the analogical relations between tectonic plates and other types of plates, such as a thin sheet of metal, that are relevant in this context? In other words, what properties of a thin sheet of metal are extended by analogy to tectonic plates in the context of explaining earthquakes?

BIBLIOGRAPHY

Achinstein, P. *Law and Explanation.* Oxford: Clarendon P, 1971.

Armstrong, D. *What Is a Law of Nature?* Cambridge: Cambridge UP, 1983.

Boyd, R. "Observations, Explanatory Power, and Simplicity: Toward a Non-Human Account." *Observation, Experiment, and Hypothesis in Modern Physical Science.* Ed. P. Achinstein and O. Hannaway. Cambridge: MIT P, 1985, pp. 47–94.

Braithwaite, R. *Scientific Explanation.* Cambridge: Cambridge UP, 1959.

Brody, B. "Towards an Aristotelian Theory of Scientific Explanation." *Philosophy of Science* 39 (1972): 20–31.

Causey, R. *Unity of Science.* Dordrecht-Holland: Reidel, 1977.

Duhem, P. *Aim and Structure of Physical Theories.* New York: Atheneum, 1954, pp. 7–30.

Feyerabend, P. "Explanation, Reduction, and Empiricism." *Minnesota Studies in the Philosophy of Science.* Volume 3, *Scientific Explanation, Space, and Time.* Ed. H. Feigl and G. Maxwell. Minneapolis: U Minnesota P, 1962, pp. 28–97.

Friedman, M., "Explanation and Scientific Understanding," *Journal of Philosophy* 71 (1974): 5–19.

Garfinkel, A. *Forms of Explanation: Rethinking the Questions in Social Theory.* New Haven: Yale UP, 1981.

Giere, R. *Explaining Science.* Chicago: U Chicago P, 1988.

Glymour, C. "Explanation and Realism," *Images of Science: Essays on Realism and Empiricism with a Reply from Bas C. Van Fraassen.* Ed. P. M. Churchland and C. Hooker. Chicago: U Chicago P, 1985.

Hempel, C. *Aspects of Scientific Explanation.* New York: Free Press, 1965.

Hesse, M. *Forces and Fields*. New York: Littlefield, Adams, 1965.

Kitcher, P. and W. C. Salmon, eds. *Minnesota Studies in the Philosophy of Science*. Volume 13, *Scientific Explanation*. Minneapolis: U Minnesota P, 1990.

McMullin, E. "Structural Explanation," *American Philosophical Quarterly* 15 (1978): 139–147.

Nagel, E. *The Structure of Science*. New York: Harcourt, Brace and World, 1961, pp. 15–46.

Pitt, J., ed. *Theories of Explanation*. New York: Oxford UP, 1988.

Salmon, W. *Scientific Explanation and the Causal Structure of the World*. Princeton: Princeton UP, 1984.

Schaffner, K. *Discovery and Explanation in Biology and Medicine*. Chicago: U Chicago P, 1994.

Shapere, D. "Scientific Theories and Their Domains." *The Structure of Scientific Theories,* 2nd edition. Ed. F. Suppe. Champaign-Urbana: U Illinois P, 1977, pp. 518–65.

Suppe, F. *The Semantic Conception of Theories*. Champaign-Urbana: U Illinois P, 1989.

Van Fraassen, B. "The Pragmatics of Explanation." *The Scientific Image*. Oxford: Clarendon P, 1980, pp. 97–157.

Wright, L. *Teleological Explanations*. Berkeley: U California P, 1976.

PARADIGMS AND THE GROWTH OF SCIENTIFIC KNOWLEDGE

INTRODUCTION

The common assumption that scientists produce fixed doctrines, lodged forever in the journals and textbooks, is historically naive and intellectually arrogant. Many "truths" discovered in past generations have been overthrown. For example, in the 1860s a fierce debate in Europe focused on the scientific study of intelligence, as many anthropologists argued that a person's intelligence is revealed by the size of the brain. At that time Paul Broca, a professor of medicine, carried out extensive studies on behalf of the claim that the volume of a person's brain is closely correlated to mental capacities. But such views have been thoroughly discredited in contemporary science. Broca could not explain the extensive counterexamples, such as small-brained individuals who were, presumably, highly intelligent (Gould 1981). Even though the nature of intelligence continues to evoke serious debate, the scientific understanding of the brain has advanced tremendously since the nineteenth century.

The fact that science does progress suggests a pivotal philosophical question: What exactly is scientific progress? How can we be reasonably sure that new ideas represent improvements over preceding beliefs? Should scientific changes be understood as all-or-nothing affairs in which every aspect of theories are replaced, or as incremental replacements of smaller elements of theories?

S U M M A R Y   O F   R E A D I N G S

One philosopher who addressed the issue of scientific change is Thomas Kuhn (selection #15). He dismisses the view that scientific research is driven entirely by the rational use of evidence to justify the truth of a theory. Research centers on the commitment to exemplary cases of success, which Kuhn calls "paradigms." A paradigm can be a theory, principle, law, normative rule for research, empirical evidence, instrument, and even a machine. For example, during the seventeenth century some scientists were so impressed with the mechanism of a clock that they believed that the entire universe was driven by a similar mechanism forming a cosmic machine, as Galileo called it. For these scientists, the understanding of the clock motivated scientific research at that time. This means that the commitment to the paradigm was strong enough to influence all facets of research, such as the content of theories, rules for performing experiments, assumptions about reality, and even the character of experimental evidence. Kuhn describes such periods as eras of "normal science" and, during them, no serious challenge to the monolithic rule of the current paradigm may be tolerated.

Eventually, some scientists will identify certain problems which the paradigm cannot resolve, leading to an era of "crisis." Potential rivals to the paradigm are then explored, leading to a period called "extraordinary science," when scientists reexamine some of their most fundamental beliefs about nature. Among these rivals, one achievement gains prominence, having solved the problems facing the old paradigm. The endorsement of the new paradigm is associated with a radical transformation in most aspects of research, ushering in another era of "normal science." All doctrines, theories, and even standards for evaluation are subject to change from a paradigm shift. In this respect the transition from one era of normal science to another potentially constitutes an all-encompassing, monolithic change of scientific research, according to Kuhn.

Kuhn's ideas generated a firestorm of controversy. Some objections center on the apparently elusive nature of Kuhn's concepts. The notion of paradigm appears to be so broadly defined that almost any product of scientific inquiry falls within its scope. Also, Kuhn's stages of scientific development, such as the era of normal science, are so vague that the application of these stages to actual cases of science is at best tenuous, and at worst impossible.

Another criticism is that Kuhn failed to articulate the conditions for *rational* science, and in so doing, avoided an explanation of *progressive* changes of ideas. Kuhn describes the commitment to a new paradigm in political terms, through the challenge of young renegades, the resistance of powerful scientists, and the revolutionary upheaval that results. The debate between advocates of rival paradigms is settled more from power politics and the rhetoric of persuasion than the rationality of argument. Commitment to a new paradigm involves a personal conversion experience, similar to an experience of religious rebirth. Kuhn's theory seems to suggest that scientific change is inherently irrational, or at least arational.

Kuhn responds by charging that his critics grossly misread his work (selection #16). Of course, science is guided by rational criteria of theory appraisal, even though such criteria are extremely imprecise and typically inconsistent with one another. The competition between rival paradigms can be settled rationally by appeal to the following criteria (or values): (1) The theory must conform to all experimental evidence available to scientists; (2) the theory must be internally consistent as well as consistent with currently accepted theories; (3) it must extend far beyond its intended domain of application; (4) the theory should promote simplicity; (5) it should disclose new phenomena beyond those already known.

Kuhn's central doctrine of a paradigm-driven science is, however, hopelessly flawed, writes Larry Laudan (selection #17). A paradigm shift presumably requires that scientists abandon all fundamental assumptions underlying scientific inquiry, including beliefs about physical reality, guidelines for performing experiments, and scientific values. Laudan argues that scientific change is gradually continuous, rather than radically discontinuous. Global and monolithic dominance of a paradigm is extremely rare. Typically, the fundamental doctrines accepted at any given time are individually replaceable in a piecemeal fashion, without a universal transformation of all philosophical and scientific commitments. Scientific change appears to be discontinuous only when we erroneously telescope the intricate and gradualistic history of science into a few major traditions, writes Laudan.

The character of scientific change is not revealed by the metaphor of political revolution, but is analogous to the survival of a species under conditions of evolutionary pressures, writes Karl Popper (selection #18). According to evolutionary theory, a species evolves by adapting to an environmental niche through a genetically inherited structure. Species which cannot adapt to these environmental conditions will be eliminated, leaving only well-adapted species whose genetic instructions are then inherited in the next generation. Similarly, scientific progress begins when a dominant scientific theory is transmitted to a younger generation. The exposure of this theory to severe experimental scrutiny may result in its elimination. An alternative theory is needed, one that addresses the deficiencies of its predecessors, but that must also be subject to severe testing. The shift in theories is revolutionary only if the surviving theory explains all the successes of the failed conjectures and leads to new predictions.

THOMAS KUHN
SELECTIONS FROM *THE STRUCTURE OF SCIENTIFIC REVOLUTIONS*

I. INTRODUCTION: A ROLE FOR HISTORY

History, if viewed as a repository for more than anecdote or chronology, could produce a decisive transformation in the image of science by which we are now possessed. That image has previously been drawn, even by scientists themselves, mainly from the study of finished scientific achievements as these are recorded in the classics and, more recently, in the textbooks from which each new scientific generation learns to practice its trade. Inevitably, however, the aim of such books is persuasive and pedagogic; a concept of science drawn from them is no more likely to fit the enterprise that produced them than an image of a national culture drawn from a tourist brochure or a language text. This essay attempts to show that we have been misled by them in fundamental ways. Its aim is a sketch of the quite different concept of science that can emerge from the historical record of the research activity itself.

Even from history, however, that new concept will not be forthcoming if historical data continue to be sought and scrutinized mainly to answer questions posed by the unhistorical stereotype drawn from science texts. Those texts have, for example, often seemed to imply that the content of science is uniquely exemplified by the observations, laws, and theories described in their pages. Almost as regularly, the same books have been read as saying that scientific methods are simply the ones illustrated by the manipulative techniques used in gathering textbook data, together with the logical operations employed when relating those data to the textbook's theoretical generalizations. The result has been a concept of science with profound implications about its nature and development.

If science is the constellation of facts, theories, and methods collected in current texts, then scientists are the men who, successfully or not, have striven to contribute one or another element to that particular constellation. Scientific development becomes the piecemeal process by which these items have been added, singly and in combination, to the ever growing stockpile that constitutes scientific technique and knowledge. And history of science becomes the discipline that chronicles both these successive increments and the obstacles that have inhibited their accumulation. Concerned with scientific development, the historian then appears to have two main tasks. On the one hand, he must determine by what man and at what point in time each contemporary scientific fact, law, and theory was discovered or invented. On the other, he must describe and explain the congeries of error, myth, and superstition that have inhibited the more rapid accumulation of the constituents of the modern science text. Much research has been directed to these ends, and some still is.

In recent years, however, a few historians of science have been finding it more and more difficult to fulfil the functions that the concept of development-by-accumulation assigns to them. As chroniclers of an incremental process, they discover that additional research makes it harder, not easier, to answer questions like: When was oxygen discovered? Who first conceived of energy conservation? Increasingly, a few of them suspect that these are simply the wrong sorts of questions to ask. Perhaps science does not develop by the accumulation of individual discoveries and inventions. Simultaneously, these same historians confront growing difficulties in distinguishing the "scientific" component of past observation and belief from what their predecessors had readily labeled "error" and "superstition." The more carefully they study, say, Aristotelian dynamics, phlogistic chemistry, or caloric thermodynamics, the more certain they feel that those once current views of nature were, as a whole, neither less scientific nor more the product of human idiosyncrasy than those current today. If these out-of-date beliefs are to be called myths, then myths can be produced by the same sorts of methods and held for the same sorts of reasons that now lead to scientific knowledge. If, on the other hand, they are to be called science, then science has included bodies of belief quite incompatible with the ones we hold today. Given these alternatives, the historian must choose the latter. Out-of-date theories are not in principle unscientific because they have been discarded. That choice, however, makes it difficult to see scientific development as a process of accretion. The same historical research that displays the difficulties in isolating individual inventions and discoveries gives ground for profound doubts about the cumulative process through which these individual contributions to science were thought to have been compounded.

The result of all these doubts and difficulties is a historiographic revolution in the study of science, though one that is still in its early stages. Gradually, and often without entirely realizing they are doing so, historians of science have begun to ask new sorts of questions and to trace different, and often less than cumulative, developmental lines for the sciences. Rather than seeking the permanent contributions of an older science to our present vantage, they attempt to display the historical integrity of that science in its own time. They ask, for example, not about the relation of Galileo's views to those of modern science, but rather about the relationship between his views and those of his group, i.e., his teachers, contemporaries, and immediate successors in the sciences. Furthermore, they insist upon studying the opinions of that group and other similar ones from the viewpoint—usually very different from that of modern science—that gives those opinions the maximum internal coherence and the closest possible fit to nature. Seen through the works that result, works perhaps best exemplified in the writings of Alexandre Koyré, science does not seem altogether the same enterprise as the one discussed by writers in the older historiographic tradition. By implication, at least, these historical studies suggest the possibility of a new image of science. This essay aims to delineate that image by making explicit some of the new historiography's implications.

What aspects of science will emerge to prominence in the course of this effort? First, at least in order of presentation, is the insufficiency of methodological directives, by themselves, to dictate a unique substantive conclusion to many sorts of scientific questions. Instructed to examine electrical or chemical phenomena, the man who is ignorant of these fields but who knows what it is to be scientific may legitimately reach any one of a number of incompatible conclusions. Among those legitimate possibilities, the particular conclusions he does arrive at are probably determined by his prior experience in other fields, by the accidents of his investigation, and by his own individual makeup. What beliefs about the stars, for example, does he bring to the study of chemistry or electricity? Which of the many conceivable experiments relevant to the new field does he elect to perform first? And what aspects of the complex phenomenon that then results strike him as particularly relevant to an elucidation of the nature of chemical change or of electrical affinity? For the individual, at least, and sometimes for the scientific community as well, answers to questions like these are often essential determinants of scientific development. We shall note, for example . . . , that the early developmental stages of most sciences have been characterized by continual competition between a number of distinct views of nature, each partially derived from, and all roughly compatible with, the dictates of scientific observation and method. What differentiated these various schools was not one or another failure of method—they were all "scientific"—but what we shall come to call their incommensurable ways of seeing the world and of practicing science in it. Observation and experience can and must drastically restrict the range of admissible scientific belief, else there would be no science. But they cannot alone determine a particular body of such belief. An apparently arbitrary element, compounded of personal and historical accident, is always a formative ingredient of the beliefs espoused by a given scientific community at a given time.

That element of arbitrariness does not, however, indicate that any scientific group could practice its trade without some set of received beliefs. Nor does it make less consequential the particular constellation to which the group, at a given time, is in fact committed. Effective research scarcely begins before a scientific community thinks it has acquired firm answers to questions like the following: What are the fundamental entities of which the universe is composed? How do these interact with each other and with the senses? What questions may legitimately be asked about such entities and what techniques employed in seeking solutions? At least in the mature sciences, answers (or full substitutes for answers) to questions like these are firmly embedded in the educational initiation that prepares and licenses the student for professional practice. Because that education is both rigorous and rigid, these answers come to exert a deep hold on the scientific mind. That they can do so does much to account both for the peculiar efficiency of the normal research activity and for the direction in which it proceeds at any given time. When examining normal science . . . , we shall want finally to describe that research as a strenuous and devoted attempt to force nature into the conceptual boxes supplied by professional education. Simultaneously, we shall wonder whether research could proceed without such boxes, whatever the element of arbitrariness in their historic origins and, occasionally, in their subsequent development.

Yet that element of arbitrariness is present, and it too has an important effect on scientific development. . . . Normal science, the activity in which most scientists inevitably spend almost all their time, is predicated on the assumption that the scientific community knows what the world is like. Much of the success of the enterprise derives from the community's willingness to defend that assumption, if necessary at considerable cost. Normal science, for example, often suppresses fundamental novelties because they are necessarily subversive of its basic commitments. Nevertheless, so long as those commitments retain an element of the arbitrary, the very nature of normal research ensures that novelty shall not be suppressed for very long. Sometimes a normal problem, one that ought to be solvable by known rules and procedures, resists the reiterated onslaught of the ablest members of the group within whose competence it falls. On other occasions a piece of equipment designed and constructed for the purpose of normal research fails to perform in the anticipated manner, revealing an anomaly that cannot, despite repeated effort, be aligned with professional expectation. In these and other ways besides, normal science repeatedly goes astray. And when it does—when, that is, the profession can no longer evade anomalies that subvert the existing tradition of scientific practice—then begin the extraordinary investigations that lead the profession at last to a new set of commitments, a new basis for the practice of science. The extraordinary episodes in which that shift of professional commitments occurs are the ones known in this essay as scientific revolutions. They are the tradition-shattering complements to the tradition-bound activity of normal science.

The most obvious examples of scientific revolutions are those famous episodes in scientific development that have often been labeled revolutions before. . . . More clearly than most other episodes in the history of at least the physical sciences, [Copernicus, Newton, Lavoisier, and Einstein] display what all scientific revolutions are about. Each of them necessitated the community's rejection of one time-honored scientific theory in favor of another incompatible with it. Each produced a consequent shift in the problems available for scientific scrutiny and in the standards by which the profession determined what should count as an admissible problem or as a legitimate problem-solution. And each transformed the scientific imagination in ways that we shall ultimately need to describe as a transformation of the world within which scientific work was done. Such changes, together with the controversies that almost always accompany them, are the defining characteristics of scientific revolutions.

These characteristics emerge with particular clarity from a study of, say, the Newtonian or the chemical revolution. It is, however, a fundamental thesis of this [reading] that they can also be retrieved from the study of many other episodes that were not so obviously revolutionary. For the far smaller professional group affected by them, Maxwell's equations were as revolutionary as Einstein's, and they were resisted accordingly. The invention of other new theories regularly, and appropriately, evokes the same response from some of the specialists on whose area of special competence they impinge. For these men the new theory implies a change in the rules governing the prior practice of normal science. Inevitably, therefore, it reflects upon much scientific work they have already successfully completed. That is why a new theory, however special its range of application, is seldom or never just an increment to what is already known. Its assimilation requires the reconstruction of prior theory and the re-evaluation of prior fact, an intrinsically revolutionary process that is seldom completed by a single man and never overnight. No wonder historians have had difficulty in dating precisely this extended process that their vocabulary impels them to view as an isolated event.

Nor are new inventions of theory the only scientific events that have revolutionary impact upon the specialists in whose domain they occur. The commitments that govern normal science specify not only what sorts of entities the universe does contain, but also, by implication, those that it does not. It follows, though the point will require extended discussion, that a discovery like that of oxygen or X-rays does not simply add one more item to the population of the scientist's world. Ultimately it has that effect, but not until the professional community has re-evaluated traditional experimental procedures, altered its conception of entities with which it has long been familiar, and, in the process, shifted the network of theory through which it deals with the world. Scientific fact and theory are not categorically separable, except perhaps within a single tradition of normal-scientific practice. That is why the unexpected discovery is not simply factual in its import and why the scientist's world is qualitatively transformed as well as quantitatively enriched by fundamental novelties of either fact or theory.

. . .

Undoubtedly, some readers will already have wondered whether historical study can possibly effect the sort of conceptual transformation aimed at here. An entire arsenal of dichotomies is available to suggest that it cannot properly do so. History, we too often say, is a purely descriptive discipline. The theses suggested [here] are, however, often interpretive and sometimes normative. Again, many of my generalizations are about the sociology or social psychology of scientists; yet at least a few of my conclusions belong traditionally to logic or epistemology. [Elsewhere] I may even seem to have violated the very influential contemporary distinction between "the context of discovery" and "the context of justification." Can anything more than profound confusion be indicated by this admixture of diverse fields and concerns?

Having been weaned intellectually on these distinctions and others like them, I could scarcely be more aware of their import and force. For many years I took them to be about the nature of knowledge, and I still suppose that, appropriately recast, they have something important to tell us. Yet my attempts to apply them, even *grosso modo,* to the actual situations in which knowledge is gained, accepted, and assimilated have made them seem extraordinarily problematic. Rather than being elementary logical or methodological distinctions, which would thus be prior to the analysis of scientific knowledge, they now seem integral parts of a traditional set of substantive answers to the very questions upon which they have been deployed. That circularity does not at all invalidate them. But it does make them parts of a theory and, by doing so, subjects them to the same scrutiny regularly applied to theories in other fields. If they are to have more than pure abstraction as their content, then that content must be discovered by observing them in application to the data they are meant to elucidate. How could history of science fail to be a source of phenomena to which theories about knowledge may legitimately be asked to apply?

. . .

III. THE NATURE OF NORMAL SCIENCE

What then is the nature of the more professional and esoteric research that a group's reception of a single paradigm permits? If the paradigm represents work that has been done once and for all, what further problems does it leave the united group to resolve? Those questions will seem even more urgent if we now note one respect in which the terms used so far may be misleading. In its established usage, a paradigm is an accepted model or pattern, and that aspect of its meaning has enabled me, lacking a better word, to appropriate "paradigm" here. But it will shortly be clear that the sense of "model" and "pattern" that permits the appropriation is not quite the one usual in defining "paradigm." In grammar, for example, "*amo, amas, amat*" is a paradigm because it displays the pattern to be used in conjugating a large number of other Latin verbs, e.g., in producing "*laudo, laudas, laudat.*" In this standard application, the paradigm functions by permitting the replication of examples any one of which could in principle serve to replace it. In a science, on the other hand, a paradigm is rarely an object for replication. Instead, like an accepted judicial decision in the common law, it is an object for further articulation and specification under new or more stringent conditions.

To see how this can be so, we must recognize how very limited in both scope and precision a paradigm can be at the time of its first appearance. Paradigms gain their status because they are more successful than their competitors in solving a few problems that the group of practitioners has come to recognize as acute. To be more successful is not, however, to be either completely successful with a single problem or notably successful with any large number. The success of a paradigm—whether Aristotle's analysis of motion, Ptolemy's computations of planetary position, Lavoisier's application of the balance, or Maxwell's mathematization of the electromagnetic field—is at the start largely a promise of success discoverable in selected and still incomplete examples. Normal science consists in the actualization of that promise, an actualization achieved by extending the knowledge of those facts that the paradigm displays as particularly revealing, by increasing the extent of the match between those facts and the paradigm's predictions, and by further articulation of the paradigm itself.

Few people who are not actually practitioners of a mature science realize how much mop-up work of this sort a paradigm leaves to be done or quite how fascinating such work can prove in the execution. And these points need to be understood. Mopping-up operations are what engage most scientists throughout their careers. They constitute what I am here calling normal science. Closely examined, whether historically or in the contemporary laboratory, that enterprise seems an attempt to force nature into the preformed and relatively inflexible box that the paradigm supplies. No part of the aim of normal science is to call forth new sorts of phenomena; indeed those that will not fit the box are often not seen at all. Nor do scientists normally aim to invent new theories, and they are often intolerant of those invented by others.[1] Instead, normal-scientific research is directed to the articulation of those phenomena and theories that the paradigm already supplies.

Perhaps these are defects. The areas investigated by normal science are, of course, minuscule; the enterprise now under discussion has drastically restricted vision. But those restrictions, born from confidence in a paradigm, turn out to be essential to the development of science. By focusing attention upon a small range of relatively esoteric problems, the paradigm forces scientists to investigate some part of nature in a detail and depth that would otherwise be unimaginable. And normal science possesses a built-in mechanism that ensures the relaxation of the restrictions that bound research whenever the paradigm from which they derive ceases to function effectively. At that point scientists begin to behave differently, and the nature of their research problems changes. In the interim, however, during the period when the paradigm is successful, the profession will have solved problems that its members could scarcely have imagined and would never have undertaken without commitment to the paradigm. And at least part of that achievement always proves to be permanent.

To display more clearly what is meant by normal or paradigm-based research, let me now attempt to classify and illustrate the problems of which normal science principally consists. For convenience I postpone theoretical activity and begin with fact-gathering, that is, with the experiments and observations described in the technical journals through which scientists inform their professional colleagues of the results of their continuing research. On what aspects of nature do scientists ordinarily report? What determines their choice? And, since most scientific observation consumes much time, equipment, and money, what motivates the scientist to pursue that choice to a conclusion?

There are, I think, only three normal foci for factual scientific investigation, and they are neither always nor permanently distinct. First is that class of facts that the paradigm has shown to be particularly revealing of the nature of things. By employing them in solving problems, the paradigm has made them worth determining both with more precision and in a larger variety of situations. At one time or another, these significant factual determinations have included: in astronomy—stellar position and magnitude, the periods of eclipsing binaries and of planets; in physics—the specific gravities and compressibilities of materials, wave lengths and spectral intensities, electrical conductivities and contact potentials; and in chemistry—composition and combining weights, boiling points and acidity of solutions, structural formulas and optical activities. Attempts to increase the accuracy and scope with which facts like these are known occupy a significant fraction of the literature of experimental and observational science. Again and again complex special apparatus has been designed for such purposes, and the invention, construction, and deployment of that apparatus have demanded first-rate talent, much time, and considerable financial backing. Synchrotrons and radiotelescopes are only the most recent examples of the lengths to which research workers will go if a paradigm assures them that the facts they seek are important. From Tycho Brahe to E. O. Lawrence, some scientists have acquired great reputations, not from any novelty of their discoveries, but from the precision, reliability, and scope of the methods they developed for the redetermination of a previously known sort of fact.

A second usual but smaller class of factual determinations is directed to those facts that, though often without much intrinsic interest, can be compared directly with predictions from the paradigm theory. As we shall see shortly, when I turn from the experimental to the theoretical problems of normal science, there are seldom many areas in which a scientific theory, particularly if it is cast in a predominantly mathematical form, can be directly compared with nature. No more than three such areas are even yet accessible to Einstein's general theory of relativity.[2] Furthermore, even in those areas where application is possible, it often demands theoretical and instrumental approximations that severely limit the agreement to be expected. Improving that agreement or finding new areas in which agreement can be demonstrated at all presents a constant challenge to the skill and imagination of the experimentalist and observer. Special telescopes to demonstrate the Copernican prediction of annual parallax; Atwood's machine, first invented almost a century after the *Principia,* to give the first unequivocal demonstration of Newton's second law; Foucault's apparatus to show that the speed of light is greater in air than in water; or the gigantic scintillation counter designed to demonstrate the existence of the neutrino—these pieces of special apparatus and many others like them illustrate the immense effort and ingenuity that have been required to bring nature and theory into closer and closer agreement.[3] That attempt to demonstrate agreement is a second type of normal experimental work, and it is even more obviously dependent than the first upon a paradigm. The existence of the paradigm sets the problem to be solved; often the paradigm theory is implicated directly in the design of apparatus able to solve the problem. Without the *Principia,* for example, measurements made with the Atwood machine would have meant nothing at all.

A third class of experiments and observations exhausts, I think, the fact-gathering activities of normal science. It consists of empirical work undertaken to articulate the paradigm theory, resolving some of its residual ambiguities and permitting the solution of problems to which it had previously only drawn attention. This class proves to be the most important of all, and its description demands its subdivision. In the more mathematical sciences, some of the experiments aimed at articulation are directed to the determination of physical constants. Newton's work, for example, indicated that the force between two unit masses at unit distance would be the same for all types of matter at all positions in the universe. But his own problems could be solved without even estimating the size of this attraction, the universal gravitational constant; and no one else devised apparatus able to determine it for a century after the *Principia* appeared. Nor was Cavendish's famous determination in the 1790's the last. Because of its central position in physical theory, improved values of the gravitational constant have been the object of repeated efforts ever since by a number of outstanding experimentalists.[4] Other examples of the same sort of continuing work would include determinations of the astronomical unit, Avogadro's number, Joule's coefficient, the electronic charge, and so on. Few of these elaborate efforts would have been conceived and none would have been carried out without a paradigm theory to define the problem and to guarantee the existence of a stable solution.

Efforts to articulate a paradigm are not, however, restricted to the determination of universal constants. They may, for example, also aim at quantitative laws: Boyle's Law relating gas pressure to volume, Coulomb's Law of electrical attraction, and Joule's formula relating heat generated to electrical resistance and current are all in this category. Perhaps it is not apparent that a paradigm is prerequisite to the discovery of laws like these. We often hear that they are found by examining measurements undertaken for their own sake and without theoretical commitment. But history offers no support for so excessively Baconian a method. Boyle's experiments were not conceivable (and if conceived would have received another interpretation or none at all) until air was recognized as an elastic fluid to which all the elaborate concepts of hydrostatics could be applied.[5] Coulomb's success depended upon his constructing special apparatus to measure the force between point charges. (Those who had previously measured electrical forces using ordinary pan balances, etc., had found no consistent or simple regularity at all.) But that design, in turn, depended upon the previous recognition that every particle of electric fluid acts upon every other at a distance. It was for the force between such particles— the only force which might safely be assumed a simple function of distance—that Coulomb was looking.[6] Joule's experiments could also be used to illustrate how quantitative laws emerge through paradigm articulation. In fact, so general and close is the relation between qualitative paradigm and quantitative law that, since Galileo, such laws have often been correctly guessed with the aid of a paradigm years before apparatus could be designed for their experimental determination.[7]

Finally, there is a third sort of experiment which aims to articulate a paradigm. More than the others this one can resemble exploration, and it is particularly prevalent in those periods and sciences that deal more with the qualitative than with the quantitative aspects of nature's regularity. Often a paradigm developed for one set of phenomena is ambiguous in its application to other closely related ones. Then experiments are necessary to choose among the alternative ways of applying the paradigm to the new area of interest. For example, the paradigm applications of the caloric theory were to heating and cooling by mixtures and by change of state. But heat could be released or absorbed in many other ways—e.g., by chemical combination, by friction, and by compression or absorption of a gas—and to each of these other phenomena the theory could be applied in several ways. If the vacuum had a heat capacity, for example, heating by compression could be explained as the result of mixing gas with void. Or it might be due to a change in the specific heat of gases with changing pressure. And there were several other explanations besides. Many experiments were undertaken to elaborate these various possibilities and to distinguish between them; all these experiments arose from the caloric theory as paradigm, and all exploited it in the design of experiments and in the interpretation of results.[8] Once the phenomenon of heating by compression had been established, all further experiments in the area were paradigm-dependent in this way. Given the phenomenon, how else could an experiment to elucidate it have been chosen?

Turn now to the theoretical problems of normal science, which fall into very nearly the same classes as the experimental and observational. A part of normal theoretical work, though only a small part, consists simply in the use of existing theory to predict factual information of intrinsic value. The manufacture of astronomical ephemerides, the computation of lens characteristics, and the production of radio propagation curves are examples of problems of this sort. Scientists, however, generally regard them as hack work to be relegated to engineers or technicians. At no time do very many of them appear in significant scientific journals. But these journals do contain a great many theoretical discussions of problems that, to the nonscientist, must seem almost identical. These are the manipulations of theory undertaken, not because the predictions in which they result are intrinsically valuable, but because they can be confronted directly with experiment. Their purpose is to display a new application of the paradigm or to increase the precision of an application that has already been made.

The need for work of this sort arises from the immense difficulties often encountered in developing points of contact between a theory and nature. These difficulties can be briefly illustrated by an examination of the history of dynamics after Newton. By the early eighteenth century those scientists who found a paradigm in the *Principia* took the generality of its conclusions for granted, and they had every reason to do so. No other work known to the history of science has simultaneously permitted so large an increase in both the scope and precision of research. For the heavens Newton had derived Kepler's Laws of planetary motion and also explained certain of the observed respects in which the moon failed to obey them. For the earth he had derived the results of some scattered observations on pendulums and the tides. With the aid of additional but *ad hoc* assumptions, he had also been able to derive Boyle's Law and an important formula for the speed of sound in air. Given the state of science at the time, the success of the demonstrations was extremely impressive. Yet given the presumptive generality of Newton's Laws, the number of these applications was not great, and Newton developed almost no others. Furthermore, compared with what any graduate student of physics can achieve with those same laws today, Newton's few applications were not even developed with precision. Finally, the *Principia* had been designed for application chiefly to problems of celestial mechanics. How to adapt it for terrestrial applications, particularly for those of motion under constraint, was by no means clear. Terrestrial problems were, in any case, already being attacked with great success by a quite different set of techniques developed originally by Galileo and

Huyghens and extended on the Continent during the eighteenth century by the Bernoullis, d'Alembert, and many others. Presumably their techniques and those of the *Principia* could be shown to be special cases of a more general formulation, but for some time no one saw quite how.[9]

Restrict attention for the moment to the problem of precision. We have already illustrated its empirical aspect. Special equipment—like Cavendish's apparatus, the Atwood machine, or improved telescopes—was required in order to provide the special data that the concrete applications of Newton's paradigm demanded. Similar difficulties in obtaining agreement existed on the side of theory. In applying his laws to pendulums, for example, Newton was forced to treat the bob as a mass point in order to provide a unique definition of pendulum length. Most of his theorems, the few exceptions being hypothetical and preliminary, also ignored the effect of air resistance. These were sound physical approximations. Nevertheless, as approximations they restricted the agreement to be expected between Newton's predictions and actual experiments. The same difficulties appear even more clearly in the application of Newton's theory to the heavens. Simple quantitative telescopic observations indicate that the planets do not quite obey Kepler's Laws, and Newton's theory indicates that they should not. To derive those laws, Newton had been forced to neglect all gravitational attraction except that between individual planets and the sun. Since the planets also attract each other, only approximate agreement between the applied theory and telescopic observation could be expected.[10]

The agreement obtained was, of course, more than satisfactory to those who obtained it. Excepting for some terrestrial problems, no other theory could do nearly so well. None of those who questioned the validity of Newton's work did so because of its limited agreement with experiment and observation. Nevertheless, these limitations of agreement left many fascinating theoretical problems for Newton's successors. Theoretical techniques were, for example, required for treating the motions of more than two simultaneously attracting bodies and for investigating the stability of perturbed orbits. Problems like these occupied many of Europe's best mathematicians during the eighteenth and early nineteenth century. Euler, Lagrange, Laplace, and Gauss all did some of their most brilliant work on problems aimed to improve the match between Newton's paradigm and observation of the heavens. Many of these figures worked simultaneously to develop the mathematics required for applications that neither Newton nor the contemporary Continental school of mechanics had even attempted. They produced, for example, an immense literature and some very powerful mathematical techniques for hydrodynamics and for the problem of vibrating strings. These problems of application account for what is probably the most brilliant and consuming scientific work of the eighteenth century. Other examples could be discovered by an examination of the post-paradigm period in the development of thermodynamics, the wave theory of light, electromagnetic theory, or any other branch of science whose fundamental laws are fully quantitative. At least in the more mathematical sciences, most theoretical work is of this sort.

But it is not all of this sort. Even in the mathematical sciences there are also theoretical problems of paradigm articulation; and during periods when scientific development is predominantly qualitative, these problems dominate. Some of the problems, in both the more quantitative and more qualitative sciences, aim simply at clarification by reformulation. The *Principia,* for example, did not always prove an easy work to apply, partly because it retained some of the clumsiness inevitable in a first venture and partly because so much of its meaning was only implicit in its applications. For many terrestrial applications, in any case, an apparently unrelated set of Continental techniques seemed vastly more powerful. Therefore, from Euler and Lagrange in the eighteenth century to Hamilton, Jacobi, and Hertz in the nineteenth, many of Europe's most brilliant mathematical physicists repeatedly endeavored to reformulate mechanical theory in an equivalent but logically and aesthetically more satisfying form. They wished, that is, to exhibit the explicit and implicit lessons of the *Principia* and of Continental mechanics in a logically more coherent version, one that would be at once more uniform and less equivocal in its application to the newly elaborated problems of mechanics.[11]

Similar reformulations of a paradigm have occurred repeatedly in all of the sciences, but most of them have produced more substantial changes in the paradigm than the reformulations of the *Principia* cited above. Such changes result from the empirical work previously described as aimed at paradigm articulation. Indeed, to classify that sort of work as empirical was arbitrary. More than any other sort of normal research, the problems of paradigm articulation are simultaneously theoretical and experimental; the examples given previously will serve equally well here. Before he could construct his equipment and make measurements with it, Coulomb had to employ electrical theory to determine how his equipment should be built. The consequence of his measurements was a refinement in that theory. Or again, the men who designed the experiments that were to distinguish between the various theories of heating by compression were generally the same men who had made up the versions being compared. They were working both with fact and with theory, and their work produced not simply new information but a more precise paradigm, obtained by the elimination of ambiguities that the original form which they worked had retained. In many sciences, most normal work is of this sort.

These three classes of problems—determination of significant fact, matching of facts with theory, and articulation of theory—exhaust, I think, the literature of normal science, both empirical and theoretical. They do not, of course, quite exhaust the entire literature of science. There are also extraordinary problems, and it may well be their resolution that makes the scientific enterprise as a whole so particularly worthwhile. But extraordinary problems are not to be had for the asking. They emerge only on special occasions prepared by the advance of normal research. Inevitably, therefore, the overwhelming majority of the problems undertaken by even the very best scientists usually fall into one of the three categories outlined above. Work under the paradigm can be conducted in no other way, and to desert the paradigm is to cease practicing the science it defines. We shall shortly discover that such desertions do occur. They are the pivots about which scientific revolutions turn. But before beginning the study of such revolutions, we require a more panoramic view of the normal-scientific pursuits that prepare the way.

. . . .

IX. THE NATURE AND NECESSITY OF SCIENTIFIC REVOLUTIONS

These remarks permit us at least to consider the problems that provide this essay with its title. What are scientific revolutions, and what is their function in scientific development? Much of the answer to these questions has been anticipated in earlier sections. In particular, the preceding discussion has indicated that scientific revolutions are here taken to be those noncumulative developmental episodes in which an older paradigm is replaced in whole or in part by an incompatible new one. There is more to be said, however, and an essential part of it can be introduced by asking one further question. Why should a change of paradigm be called a revolution? In the face of the vast and essential differences between political and scientific development, what parallelism can justify the metaphor that finds revolutions in both?

One aspect of the parallelism must already be apparent. Political revolutions are inaugurated by a growing sense, often restricted to a segment of the political community, that existing institutions have ceased adequately to meet the problems posed by an environment that they have in part created. In much the same way, scientific revolutions are inaugurated by a growing sense, again often restricted to a narrow subdivision of the scientific community, that an existing paradigm has ceased to function adequately in the exploration of an aspect of nature to which that paradigm itself had previously led the way. In both political and scientific development the sense of malfunction that can lead to crisis is prerequisite to revolution. Furthermore, though it admittedly strains the metaphor, that parallelism holds not only for the major paradigm changes, like those attributable to Copernicus and Lavoisier, but also for the far smaller ones associated with the assimilation of a new sort of phenomenon, like oxygen or X-rays. Scientific revolutions . . . need seem revolutionary only to those whose paradigms are affected by them. To outsiders they may, like the Balkan revolutions of the early twentieth century, seem normal parts of the developmental process. Astronomers, for example, could accept X-rays as a mere addition to knowledge, for their paradigms were unaffected by the existence of the new radiation. But for men like Kelvin, Crookes, and Roentgen, whose research dealt with radiation theory or with cathode ray tubes, the emergence of X-rays necessarily violated one paradigm as it created another. That is why these rays could be discovered only through something's first going wrong with normal research.

This genetic aspect of the parallel between political and scientific development should no longer be open to doubt. The parallel has, however, a second and more profound aspect upon which the significance of the first depends. Political revolutions aim to change political institutions in ways that those institutions themselves prohibit. Their success therefore necessitates the partial relinquishment of one set of institutions in favor of another, and in the interim, society is not fully governed by institutions at all. Initially it is crisis alone that attenuates the role of political institutions as we have already seen it attenuate the role of paradigms. In increasing numbers individuals become increasingly estranged from political life and behave more and more eccentrically within it. Then, as the crisis deepens, many of these individuals commit themselves to some concrete proposal for the reconstruction of society in a new institutional framework. At that point the society is divided into competing camps or parties, one seeking to defend the old institutional constellation, the others seeking to institute some new one. And, once that polarization has occurred, *political recourse fails.* Because they differ about the institutional matrix within which political change is to be achieved and evaluated, because they acknowledge no supra-institutional framework for the adjudication of revolutionary difference, the parties to a revolutionary conflict must finally resort to the techniques of mass persuasion, often including force. Though revolutions have had a vital role in the evolution of political institutions, that role depends upon their being partially extrapolitical or extra-institutional events.

The remainder of this [reading] aims to demonstrate that the historical study of paradigm change reveals very similar characteristics in the evolution of the sciences. Like the choice between competing political institutions, that between competing paradigms proves to be a choice between incompatible modes of community life. Because it has that character, the choice is not and cannot be determined merely by the evaluative procedures characteristic of normal science, for these depend in part upon a particular paradigm, and that paradigm is at issue. When paradigms enter, as they must, into a debate about paradigm choice, their role is necessarily circular. Each group uses its own paradigm to argue in that paradigm's defense.

The resulting circularity does not, of course, make the arguments wrong or even ineffectual. The man who premises a paradigm when arguing in its defense can nonetheless provide a clear exhibit of what scientific practice will be like for those who adopt the new view of nature. That exhibit can be immensely persuasive, often compellingly so. Yet, whatever its force, the status of the circular argument is only that of persuasion. It cannot be made logically or even probabilistically compelling for those who refuse to step into the circle. The premises and values shared by the two parties to a debate over paradigms are not sufficiently extensive for that. As in political revolutions, so in paradigm choice—there is no standard higher than the assent of the relevant community. To discover how scientific revolutions are effected, we shall therefore have to examine not only the impact of nature and of logic, but also the techniques of persuasive argumentation effective within the quite special groups that constitute the community of scientists.

To discover why this issue of paradigm choice can never be unequivocally settled by logic and experiment alone, we must shortly examine the nature of the differences that separate the proponents of a traditional paradigm from their revolutionary successors. That examination is the principal object of this section and the next. We have, however, already noted numerous examples of such differences, and no one will doubt that history can supply many others. What is more likely to be doubted than their existence—and what must therefore be considered first—is that such examples provide essential information about the nature of science. Granting that paradigm rejection has been a historic fact, does it illuminate more than human credulity and confusion? Are there intrinsic reasons why the assimilation of either a new sort of phenomenon or a new scientific theory must demand the rejection of an older paradigm?

First notice that if there are such reasons, they do not derive from the logical structure of scientific knowledge. In principle, a new phenomenon might emerge without reflecting destructively upon any part of past scientific practice. Though discovering life on the moon would today be destructive of existing paradigms (these tell us things about the moon that seem incompatible with life's existence there), discovering life in some less well-known part of the galaxy would not. By the same token, a new theory does not have to conflict with any of its predecessors. It might deal exclusively with phenomena not previously known, as the quantum theory deals (but, significantly, not exclusively) with subatomic phenomena unknown before the twentieth century. Or again, the new theory might be simply a higher level theory than those known before, one that linked together a whole group of lower level theories without substantially changing any. Today, the theory of energy conservation provides just such links between dynamics, chemistry, electricity, optics, thermal theory, and so on. Still other compatible relationships between old and new theories can be conceived. Any and all of them might be exemplified by the historical process through which science has developed. If they were, scientific development would be genuinely cumulative. New sorts of phenomena would simply disclose order in an aspect of nature where none had been seen before. In the evolution of science new knowledge would replace ignorance rather than replace knowledge of another and incompatible sort.

Of course, science (or some other enterprise, perhaps less effective) might have developed in that fully cumulative manner. Many people have believed that it did so, and most still seem to suppose that cumulation is at least the ideal that historical development would display if only it had not so often been distorted by human idiosyncrasy. There are important reasons for that belief. . . . Nevertheless, despite the immense plausibility of that ideal image, there is increasing reason to wonder whether it can possibly be an image of *science*. After the pre-paradigm period the assimilation of all new theories and of almost all new sorts of phenomena has in fact demanded the destruction of a prior paradigm and a consequent conflict between competing schools of scientific thought. Cumulative acquisition of unanticipated novelties proves to be an almost non-existent exception to the rule of scientific development. The man who takes historic fact seriously must suspect that science does not tend toward the ideal that our image of its cumulativeness has suggested. Perhaps it is another sort of enterprise.

If, however, resistant facts can carry us that far, then a second look at the ground we have already covered may suggest that cumulative acquisition of novelty is not only rare in fact but improbable in principle. Normal research, which *is* cumulative, owes its success to the ability of scientists regularly to select problems that can be solved with conceptual and instrumental techniques close to those already in existence. (That is why an excessive concern with useful problems, regardless of their relation to existing knowledge and technique, can so easily inhibit scientific development.) The man who is striving to solve a problem defined by existing knowledge and technique is not, however, just looking around. He knows what he wants to achieve, and he designs his instruments and directs his thoughts accordingly. Unanticipated novelty, the new discovery, can emerge only to the extent that his anticipations about nature and his instruments prove wrong. Often the importance of the resulting discovery will itself be proportional to the extent and stubbornness of the anomaly that foreshadowed it. Obviously, then, there must be a conflict between the paradigm that discloses anomaly and the one that later renders the anomaly law-like. The examples of discovery through paradigm destruction . . . did not confront us with mere historical accident. There is no other effective way in which discoveries might be generated.

The same argument applies even more clearly to the invention of new theories. There are, in principle, only three types of phenomena about which a new theory might be developed. The first consists of phenomena already well explained by existing paradigms, and these seldom provide either motive or point of departure for theory construction. When they do . . . , the theories that result are seldom accepted, because nature provides no ground for discrimination. A second class of phenomena consists of those whose nature is indicated by existing paradigms but whose details can be understood only through further theory articulation. These are the phenomena to which scientists direct their research much of the time, but that research aims at the articulation of existing paradigms rather than at the invention of new ones. Only when these attempts at articulation fail do scientists encounter the third type of phenomena, the recognized anomalies whose characteristic feature is their stubborn refusal to be assimilated to existing paradigms. This type alone gives rise to new theories. Paradigms provide all phenomena except anomalies with a theory-determined place in the scientist's field of vision.

But if new theories are called forth to resolve anomalies in the relation of an existing theory to nature, then the successful new theory must somewhere permit predictions that are different from those derived from its predecessor. That difference could not occur if the two were logically compatible. In the process of being assimilated, the second must displace the first. Even a theory like energy conservation, which today seems a logical superstructure that relates to nature only through independently established theories, did not develop historically without paradigm destruction. Instead, it emerged from a crisis in which an essential ingredient was the incompatibility between Newtonian dynamics and some recently formulated consequences of the caloric theory of heat. Only after the caloric theory had been rejected could energy conservation become part of science.[1] And only after it had been part of science for some time could it come to seem a theory of a logically higher type, one not in conflict with its predecessors. It is hard to see how new theories could arise without these destructive changes in beliefs about nature. Though logical inclusiveness remains a permissible view of the relation between successive scientific theories, it is a historical implausibility.

A century ago it would, I think, have been possible to let the case for the necessity of revolutions rest at this point. But today, unfortunately, that cannot be done because the view of the subject developed above cannot be maintained if the most prevalent contemporary interpretation of the nature and function of scientific theory is accepted. That interpretation, closely associated with early logical positivism and not categorically rejected by its successors, would restrict the range and meaning of an accepted theory so that it could not possibly conflict with any later theory that made predictions about some of the same natural phenomena. The best-known and the strongest case for this restricted conception of a scientific theory emerges in discussions of the relation between contemporary Einsteinian dynamics and the older dynamical equations that descend from Newton's *Principia.* From the viewpoint of this essay these two theories are fundamentally incompatible in the sense illustrated by the relation of Copernican to Ptolemaic astronomy: Einstein's theory can be accepted only with the recognition that Newton's was wrong. Today this remains a minority view.[2] We must therefore examine the most prevalent objections to it.

The gist of these objections can be developed as follows. Relativistic dynamics cannot have shown Newtonian dynamics to be wrong, for Newtonian dynamics is still used with great success by most engineers and, in selected applications, by many physicists. Furthermore, the propriety of this use of the older theory can be proved from the very theory that has, in other applications, replaced it. Einstein's theory can be used to show that predictions from Newton's equations will be as good as our measuring instruments in all applications that satisfy a small number of restrictive conditions. For example, if Newtonian theory is to provide a good approximate solution, the relative velocities of the bodies considered must be small compared with the velocity of light. Subject to this condition and a few others, Newtonian theory seems to be derivable from Einsteinian, of which it is therefore a special case.

But, the objection continues, no theory can possibly conflict with one of its special cases. If Einsteinian science seems to make Newtonian dynamics wrong, that is only because some Newtonians were so incautious as to claim that Newtonian theory yielded entirely precise results or that it was valid at very high relative velocities. Since they could not have had any evidence for such claims, they betrayed the standards of science when they made them. In so far as Newtonian theory was ever a truly scientific theory supported by valid evidence, it still is. Only extravagant claims for the theory—claims that were never properly parts of science—can have been shown by Einstein to be wrong. Purged of these merely human extravagances, Newtonian theory has never been challenged and cannot be.

Some variant of this argument is quite sufficient to make any theory ever used by a significant group of competent scientists immune to attack. The much-maligned phlogiston theory, for example, gave order to a large number of physical and chemical phenomena. It explained why bodies burned—they were rich in phlogiston—and why metals had so many more properties in common than did their ores. The metals were all compounded from different elementary earths combined with phlogiston, and the latter, common to all metals, produced common properties. In addition, the phlogiston theory accounted for a number of reactions in which acids were formed by the combustion of substances like carbon and sulphur. Also, it explained the decrease of volume when combustion occurs in a confined volume of air—the phlogiston released by combustion "spoils" the elasticity of the air that absorbed it, just as fire "spoils" the elasticity of a steel spring.[3] If these were the only phenomena that the phlogiston theorists had claimed for their theory, that theory could never have been challenged. A similar argument will suffice for any theory that has ever been successfully applied to any range of phenomena at all.

But to save theories in this way, their range of application must be restricted to those phenomena and to that precision of observation with which the experimental evidence in hand already deals.[4] Carried just a step further (and the step can scarcely be avoided once the first is taken), such a limitation prohibits the scientist from claiming to speak "scientifically" about any phenomenon not already observed. Even in its present form the restriction forbids the scientist to rely upon a theory in his own research whenever that research enters an area or seeks a degree of precision for which past practice with the theory offers no precedent. These prohibitions are logically unexceptionable. But the result of accepting them would be the end of the research through which science may develop further.

By now that point too is virtually a tautology. Without commitment to a paradigm there could be no normal science. Furthermore, that commitment must extend to areas and to degrees of precision for which there is no full precedent. If it did not, the paradigm could provide no puzzles that had not already been solved. Besides, it is not only normal science that depends upon commitment to a paradigm. If existing theory binds the scientist only with respect to existing applications, then there can be no surprises, anomalies, or crises. But these are just the signposts that point the way to extraordinary science. If positivistic restrictions on the range of a theory's legitimate applicability are taken literally, the mechanism that tells the scientific community what problems may lead to fundamental change must cease to function. And when that occurs, the community will inevitably return to something much like its pre-paradigm state, a condition in which all members practice science but in which their gross product scarcely resembles science at all. Is it really any wonder that the price of significant scientific advance is a commitment that runs the risk of being wrong?

More important, there is a revealing logical lacuna in the positivist's argument, one that will reintroduce us immediately to the nature of revolutionary change. Can Newtonian dynamics really be *derived* from relativistic dynamics? What would such a derivation look like? Imagine a set of statements, $E_1, E_2, \ldots, E_n$, which together embody the laws of relativity theory. These statements contain variables and parameters representing spatial position, time, rest mass, etc. From them, together with the apparatus of logic and mathematics, is deducible a whole set of further statements including some that can be checked by observation. To prove the adequacy of Newtonian dynamics as a special case, we must add to the E_1's additional statements, like $(v/c)^2 << 1$, restricting the range of the parameters and variables. This enlarged set of statements is then manipulated to yield a new set, $N_1, N_2, \ldots, N_m$, which is identical in form with Newton's laws of motion, the law of gravity, and so on. Apparently Newtonian dynamics has been derived from Einsteinian, subject to a few limiting conditions.

Yet the derivation is spurious, at least to this point. Though the N_1's are a special case of the laws of relativistic mechanics, they are not Newton's Laws. Or at least they are not unless those laws are reinterpreted in a way that would have been impossible until after Einstein's work. The variables and parameters that in the Einsteinian E_1's represented spatial position, time, mass, etc., still occur in the N_1's; and they there still represent Einsteinian space, time, and mass. But the physical referents of these Einsteinian concepts are by no means identical with those of the Newtonian concepts that bear the same name. (Newtonian mass is conserved; Einsteinian is convertible with energy. Only at low relative velocities may the two be measured in the same way, and even then they must not be conceived to be the same.) Unless we change the definitions of the variables in the N_1's, the statements we have derived are not Newtonian. If we do change them, we cannot properly be said to have *derived* Newton's Laws, at least not in any sense of "derive" now generally recognized. Our argument has, of course, explained why Newton's Laws ever seemed to work. In doing so it has justified, say, an automobile driver in acting as though he lived in a Newtonian universe. An argument of the same type is used to justify teaching earth-centered astronomy to surveyors. But the argument has still not done what it purported to do. It has not, that is, shown Newton's Laws to be a limiting case of Einstein's. For in the passage to the limit it is not only the forms of the laws that have changed. Simultaneously we have had to alter the fundamental structural elements of which the universe to which they apply is composed.

This need to change the meaning of established and familiar concepts is central to the revolutionary impact of Einstein's theory. Though subtler than the changes from geocentrism to heliocentrism, from phlogiston to oxygen, or from corpuscles to waves, the resulting conceptual transformation is no less decisively destructive of a previously established paradigm. We may even come to see it as a prototype for revolutionary reorientations in the sciences. Just because it did not involve the introduction of additional objects or concepts, the transition from Newtonian to Einsteinian mechanics illustrates with particular clarity the scientific revolution as a displacement of the conceptual network through which scientists view the world.

These remarks should suffice to show what might, in another philosophical climate, have been taken for granted. At least for scientists, most of the apparent differences between a discarded scientific theory and its successor are real. Though an out-of-date theory can always be viewed as a special case of its up-to-date successor, it must be transformed for the purpose. And the transformation is one that can be undertaken only with the advantages of hindsight, the explicit guidance of the more recent theory. Furthermore, even if that transformation were a legitimate device to employ in interpreting the older theory, the result of its application would be a theory so restricted that it could only restate what was already known. Because of its economy, that restatement would have utility, but it could not suffice for the guidance of research.

Let us, therefore, now take it for granted that the differences between successive paradigms are both necessary and irreconcilable. Can we then say more explicitly what sorts of differences these are? The most apparent type has already been illustrated repeatedly. Successive paradigms tell us different things about the population of the universe and about that population's behavior. They differ, that is, about such questions as the existence of subatomic particles, the materiality of light, and the conservation of heat or of energy. These are the substantive differences between successive paradigms, and they require no further illustration. But paradigms differ in more than substance, for they are directed not only to nature but also back upon the science that produced them. They are the source of the methods, problem-field, and standards of solution accepted by any mature scientific community at any given time. As a result, the reception of a new paradigm often necessitates a redefinition of the corresponding science. Some old problems may be relegated to another science or declared entirely "unscientific." Others that were previously non-existent or trivial may, with a new paradigm, become the very archetypes of significant scientific achievement. And as the problems change, so, often, does the standard that distinguishes a real scientific solution from a mere metaphysical speculation, word game, or mathematical play. The normal-scientific tradition that emerges from a scientific revolution is not only incompatible but often actually incommensurable with that which has gone before.

The impact of Newton's work upon the normal seventeenth-century tradition of scientific practice provides a striking example of these subtler effects of paradigm shift. Before Newton was born the "new science" of the century had at last succeeded in rejecting Aristotelian and scholastic explanations expressed in terms of the essences of material bodies. To say that a stone fell because its "nature" drove it toward the center of the universe had been made to look a mere tautological word-play, something it had not previously been. Henceforth the entire flux of sensory appearances, including color, taste, and even weight, was to be explained in terms of the size, shape, position, and motion of the elementary corpuscles of base matter. The attribution of other qualities to the elementary atoms was a resort to the occult and therefore out of bounds for science. Molière caught the new spirit precisely when he ridiculed the doctor who explained opium's efficacy as a soporific by attributing to it a dormitive potency. During the last half of the seventeenth century many scientists preferred to say that the round shape of the opium particles enabled them to sooth the nerves about which they moved.[5]

In an earlier period explanations in terms of occult qualities had been an integral part of productive scientific work. Nevertheless, the seventeenth century's new commitment to mechanico-corpuscular explanation proved immensely fruitful for a number of sciences, ridding them of problems that had defied generally accepted solution and suggesting others to replace them. In dynamics, for example, Newton's three laws of motion are less a product of novel experiments than of the attempt to reinterpret well-known observations in terms of the motions and interactions of primary neutral corpuscles. Consider just one concrete illustration. Since neutral corpuscles could act on each other only by contact, the mechanico-corpuscular view of nature directed scientific attention to a brand-new subject of study, the alteration of particulate motions by collisions. Descartes announced the problem and provided its first putative solution. Huyghens, Wren, and Wallis carried it still further, partly by experimenting with colliding pendulum bobs, but mostly by applying previously well-known characteristics of motion to the new problem. And Newton embedded their results in his laws of motion. The equal "action" and "reaction" of the third law are the changes in quantity of motion experienced by the two parties to a collision. The same change of motion supplies the definition of dynamical force implicit in the second law. In this case, as in many others during the seventeenth century, the corpuscular paradigm bred both a new problem and a large part of that problem's solution.[6]

Yet, though much of Newton's work was directed to problems and embodied standards derived from the mechanico-corpuscular world view, the effect of the paradigm that resulted from his work was a further and partially destructive change in the problems and standards legitimate for science. Gravity, interpreted as an innate attraction between every pair of particles of matter, was an occult quality in the same sense as the scholastics' "tendency to fall" had been. Therefore, while the standards of corpuscularism remained in effect, the search for a mechanical explanation of gravity was one of the most challenging problems for those who accepted the *Principia* as paradigm. Newton devoted much attention to it and so did many of his eighteenth-century successors. The only apparent option was to reject Newton's theory for its failure to explain gravity, and that alternative, too, was widely adopted. Yet neither of these views ultimately triumphed. Unable either to practice science without the *Principia* or to make that work conform to the corpuscular standards of the seventeenth century, scientists gradually accepted the view that gravity was indeed innate. By the mid-eighteenth century that interpretation had been almost universally accepted, and the result was a genuine reversion (which is not the same as a retrogression) to a scholastic standard. Innate attractions and repulsions joined size, shape, position, and motion as physically irreducible primary properties of matter.[7]

The resulting change in the standards and problem-field of physical science was once again consequential. By the 1740's, for example, electricians could speak of the attractive "virtue" of the electric fluid without thereby inviting the ridicule that had greeted Molière's doctor a century before. As they did so, electrical phenomena increasingly displayed an order different from the one they had shown when viewed as the effects of a mechanical effluvium that could act only by contact. In particular, when electrical action-at-a-distance became a subject for study in its own right, the phenomenon we now call charging by induction could be recognized as one of its effects. Previously, when seen at all, it had been attributed to the direct action of electrical "atmospheres" or to the leakages inevitable in any electrical laboratory. The new view of inductive effects was, in turn, the key to Franklin's analysis of the Leyden jar and thus to the emergence of a new and Newtonian paradigm for electricity. Nor were dynamics and electricity the only scientific fields affected by the legitimization of the search for forces innate to matter. The large body of eighteenth-century literature on chemical affinities and replacement series also derives from this supramechanical aspect of Newtonianism. Chemists who believed in these differential attractions between the various chemical species set up previously unimagined experiments and searched for new sorts of reactions. Without the data and the chemical concepts developed in that process, the later work of Lavoisier and, more particularly, of Dalton would be incomprehensible.[8] Changes in the standards governing permissible problems, concepts, and explanations can transform a science. . . .

Other examples of these nonsubstantive differences between successive paradigms can be retrieved from the history of any science in almost any period of its development. For the moment let us be content with just two other and far briefer illustrations. Before the chemical revolution, one of the acknowledged tasks of chemistry was to account for the qualities of chemical substances and for the changes these qualities underwent during chemical reactions. With the aid of a small number of elementary "principles"—of which phlogiston was one—the chemist was to explain why some substances are acidic, others metalline, combustible, and so forth. Some success in this direction had been achieved. We have already noted that phlogiston explained why the metals were so much alike, and we could have developed a similar argument for the acids. Lavoisier's reform, however, ultimately did away with chemical "principles," and thus ended by depriving chemistry of some actual and much potential explanatory power. To compensate for this loss, a change in standards was required. During much of the nineteenth century failure to explain the qualities of compounds was no indictment of a chemical theory.[9]

Or again, Clerk Maxwell shared with other nineteenth-century proponents of the wave theory of light the conviction that light waves must be propagated through a material ether. Designing a mechanical medium to support such waves was a standard problem for many of his ablest contemporaries. His own theory, however, the electromagnetic theory of light, gave no account at all of a medium able to support light waves, and it clearly made such an account harder to provide than it had seemed before. Initially, Maxwell's theory was widely rejected for those reasons. But, like Newton's theory, Maxwell's proved difficult to dispense with, and as it achieved the status of a paradigm, the community's attitude toward it changed. In the early decades of the twentieth century Maxwell's insistence upon the existence of a mechanical ether looked more and more like lip service, which it emphatically had not been, and the attempts to design such an ethereal medium were abandoned. Scientists no longer thought it unscientific to speak of an electrical "displacement" without specifying what was being displaced. The result, again, was a new set of problems and standards, one which, in the event, had much to do with the emergence of relativity theory.[10]

These characteristic shifts in the scientific community's conception of its legitimate problems and standards would have less significance to this essay's thesis if one could suppose that they always occurred from some methodologically lower to some higher type. In that case their effects, too, would seem cumulative. No wonder that some historians have argued that the history of science records a continuing increase in the maturity and refinement of man's conception of the nature of science.[11] Yet the case for cumulative development of science's problems and standards is even harder to make than the case for cumulation of theories. The attempt to explain gravity, though fruitfully abandoned by most eighteenth-century scientists, was not directed to an intrinsically illegitimate problem; the objections to innate forces were neither inherently unscientific nor metaphysical in some pejorative sense. There are no external standards to permit a judgment of that sort. What occurred was neither a decline nor a raising of standards, but simply a change demanded by the adoption of a new paradigm. Furthermore, that change has since been reversed and could be again. In the twentieth century Einstein succeeded in explaining gravitational attractions, and that explanation has returned science to a set of canons and problems that are, in this particular respect, more like those of Newton's predecessors than of his successors. Or again, the development of quantum mechanics has reversed the methodological prohibition that originated in the chemical revolution. Chemists now attempt, and with great success, to explain the color, state of aggregation, and other qualities of the substances used and produced in their laboratories. A similar reversal may even be underway in electromagnetic theory. Space, in contemporary physics, is not the inert and homogenous substratum employed in both Newton's and Maxwell's theories; some of its new properties are not unlike those once attributed to the ether; we may someday come to know what an electric displacement is.

By shifting emphasis from the cognitive to the normative functions of paradigms, the preceding examples enlarge our understanding of the ways in which paradigms give form to the scientific life. Previously, we had principally examined the paradigm's role as a vehicle for scientific theory. In that role it functions by telling the scientist about the entities that nature does and does not contain and about the ways in which those entities behave. That information provides a map whose details are elucidated by mature scientific research. And since nature is too complex and varied to be explored at random, that map is as essential as observation and experiment to science's continuing development. Through the theories they embody, paradigms prove to be constitutive of the research activity. They are also, however, constitutive of science in other respects, and that is now the point. In particular, our most recent examples show that paradigms provide scientists not only with a map but also with some of the directions essential for map-making. In learning a paradigm the scientist acquires theory, methods, and standards together, usually in an inextricable mixture. Therefore, when paradigms change, there are usually significant shifts in the criteria determining the legitimacy both of problems and of proposed solutions.

That observation returns us to the point from which this section began, for it provides our first explicit indication of why the choice between competing paradigms regularly raises questions that cannot be resolved by the criteria of normal science. To the extent, as significant as it is incomplete, that two scientific schools disagree about what is a problem and what a solution, they will inevitably talk through each other when debating the relative merits of their respective paradigms. In the partially circular arguments that regularly result, each paradigm will be shown to satisfy more or less the criteria that it dictates for itself and to fall short of a few of those dictated by its opponent. There are other reasons, too, for the incompleteness of logical contact that consistently characterizes paradigm debates. For example, since no paradigm ever solves all the problems it defines and since no two paradigms leave all the same problems unsolved, paradigm debates always involve the question: Which problems is it more significant to have solved? Like the issue of competing standards, that question of values can be answered only in terms of criteria that lie outside of normal science altogether, and it is that recourse to external criteria that most obviously makes paradigm debates revolutionary. Something even more fundamental than standards and values is, however, also at stake. . . .

NOTES

SECTION III

[1] Bernard Barber, "Resistance by Scientists to Scientific Discovery," *Science,* CXXXIV (1961), 596–602.

[2] The only long-standing check point still generally recognized is the precession of Mercury's perihelion. The red shift in the spectrum of light from distant stars can be derived from considerations more elementary than general relativity, and the same may be possible for the bending of light around the sun, a point now in some dispute. In any case, measurements of the latter phenomenon remain equivocal. One additional check point may have been established very recently: the gravitational shift of Mossbauer radiation. Perhaps there will soon be others in this now active but long dormant field. For an up-to-date capsule account of the problem, see L. I. Schiff, "A Report on the NASA Conference on Experimental Tests of Theories of Relativity," *Physics Today,* XIV (1961), 42–48.

[3] For two of the parallax telescopes, see Abraham Wolf, *A History of Science, Technology, and Philosophy in the Eighteenth Century* (2d ed.; London, 1952), pp. 103–5. For the Atwood machine, see N. R. Hanson, *Patterns of Discovery* (Cambridge, 1958), pp. 100–102, 207–8. For the last two pieces of special apparatus, see M. L. Foucault, "Méthode générale pour mesurer la vitesse de la lumière dans l'air et les milieux transparants. Vitesses relatives de la lumière dans l'air et dans l'eau . . . ," *Comptes rendus . . . de l'Académie des sciences,* XXX (1850), 551–60; and C. L. Cowan, Jr., *et al.,* "Detection of the Free Neutrino: A Confirmation," *Science,* CXXIV (1956), 103–4.

[4] J. H. P[oynting] reviews some two dozen measurements of the gravitational constant between 1741 and 1901 in "Gravitation Constant and Mean Density of the Earth," *Encyclopaedia Britannica* (11th ed.; Cambridge, 1910–11), XII, 385–89.

[5] For the full transplantation of hydrostatic concepts into pneumatics, see *The Physical Treatises of Pascal,* trans. I. H. B. Spiers and A. G. H. Spiers, with an introduction and notes by F. Barry (New York, 1937). Torricelli's original introduction of the parallelism ("We live submerged at the bottom of an ocean of the element air") occurs on p. 164. Its rapid development is displayed by the two main treatises.

[6] Duane Roller and Duane H. D. Roller, *The Development of the Concept of Electric Charge: Electricity from the Greeks to Coulomb* ("Harvard Case Histories in Experimental Science," Case 8; Cambridge, Mass., 1954), pp. 66–80.

[7] For examples, see T. S. Kuhn, "The Function of Measurement in Modern Physical Science," *Isis,* LII (1961), 161–93.

[8] T. S. Kuhn, "The Caloric Theory of Adiabatic Compression," *Isis,* XLIX (1958), 132–40.

[9] C. Truesdell, "A Program toward Rediscovering the Rational Mechanics of the Age of Reason," *Archive for History of the Exact Sciences,* I (1960), 3–36, and "Reactions of Late Baroque Mechanics to Success, Conjecture, Error, and Failure in Newton's *Principia,*" *Texas Quarterly,* X (1967), 281–97. T. L. Hankins, "The Reception of Newton's Second Law of Motion in the Eighteenth Century." *Archives internationales d'histoire des sciences,* XX (1967), 42–65.

[10] Wolf, *op. cit.,* pp. 75–81, 96–101; and William Whewell, *History of the Inductive Sciences* (rev. ed.; London, 1847), II, 213–71.

[11] René Dugas, *Histoire de la mécanique* (Neuchatel, 1950), Books IV–V.

SECTION IX

[1] Silvanus P. Thompson, *Life of William Thomson Baron Kelvin of Largs* (London, 1910), I, 266–81.

[2] See, for example, the remarks by P. P. Wiener in *Philosophy of Science,* XXV (1958), 298.

[3] James B. Conant, *Overthrow of the Phlogiston Theory* (Cambridge, 1950), pp. 13–16; and J. R. Partington, *A Short History of Chemistry* (2d ed.; London, 1951), pp. 85–88. The fullest and most sympathetic account of the phlogiston theory's achievements is by H. Metzger, *Newton, Stahl, Boerhaave et la doctrine chimique* (Paris, 1930), Part II.

[4] Compare the conclusions reached through a very different sort of analysis by R. B. Braithwaite, *Scientific Explanation* (Cambridge, 1953), pp. 50–87, esp. p. 76.

[5] For corpuscularism in general, see Marie Boas, "The Establishment of the Mechanical Philosophy," *Osiris,* X (1952), 412–541. For the effect of particle-shape on taste, see *ibid.,* p. 483.

[6] R. Dugas, *La mécanique au XVIIᵉ siècle* (Neuchatel, 1954), pp. 177–85, 284–98, 345–56.

[7] I. B. Cohen, *Franklin and Newton: An Inquiry into Speculative Newtonian Experimental Science and Franklin's Work in Electricity as an Example Thereof* (Philadelphia, 1956), chaps. vi–vii.

[8] For electricity, see *ibid,* chaps. viii–ix. For chemistry, see Metzger, *op. cit.,* Part I.

[9] E. Meyerson, *Identity and Reality* (New York, 1930), chap. x.

[10] E. T. Whittaker, *A History of the Theories of Aether and Electricity,* II (London, 1953), 28–30.

[11] For a brilliant and entirely up-to-date attempt to fit scientific development into this Procrustean bed, see C. C. Gillispie, *The Edge of Objectivity: An Essay in the History of Scientific Ideas* (Princeton, 1960).

T H O M A S   K U H N
OBJECTIVITY, VALUE JUDGMENT, AND THEORY CHOICE

In the penultimate chapter of a controversial book first published fifteen years ago, I considered the ways scientists are brought to abandon one time-honored theory or paradigm in favor of another. Such decision problems, I wrote, "cannot be resolved by proof." To discuss their mechanism is, therefore, to talk "about techniques of persuasion, or about argument and counterargument in a situation in which there can be no proof." Under these circumstances, I continued, "lifelong resistance [to a new theory] . . . is not a violation of scientific standards. . . . Though the historian can always find men—Priestley, for instance—who were unreasonable to resist for as long as they did, he will not find a point at which resistance becomes illogical or unscientific." [1] Statements of that sort obviously raise the question of why, in the absence of binding criteria for scientific choice, both the number of solved scientific problems and the precision of individual problem solutions should increase so markedly with the passage of time. Confronting that issue, I sketched in my closing chapter a number of characteristics that scientists share by virtue of the training which licenses their membership in one or another community of specialists. In the absence of criteria able to dictate the choice of each individual, I argued, we do well to trust the collective judgment of scientists trained in this way. "What better criterion could there be," I asked rhetorically, "than the decision of the scientific group?" [2]

A number of philosophers have greeted remarks like these in a way that continues to surprise me. My views, it is said, make of theory choice "a matter for mob psychology." [3] Kuhn believes, I am told, that "the decision of a scientific group to adopt a new paradigm cannot be based on good reasons of any kind, factual or otherwise." [4] The debates surrounding such choices must, my critics claim, be for me "mere persuasive displays without deliberative substance." [5] Reports of this sort manifest total misunderstanding, and I have occasionally said as much in papers directed primarily to other ends. But those passing protestations have had negligible effect, and the misunderstandings continue to be important. I conclude that it is past time for me to describe, at greater length and with greater precision, what has been on my mind when I have uttered statements like the ones with which I just began. If I have been reluctant to do so in the past, that is largely because I have preferred to devote attention to areas in which my views diverge more sharply from those currently received than they do with respect to theory choice.

What, I ask to begin with, are the characteristics of a good scientific theory? Among a number of quite usual answers I select five, not because they are exhaustive, but because they are individually important and collectively sufficiently varied to indicate what is at stake. First, a theory should be accurate: within its domain, that is, consequences deducible from a theory should be in demonstrated agreement with the results of existing experiments and observations. Second, a theory should be consistent, not only internally or with itself, but also with other currently accepted theories applicable to related aspects of nature. Third, it should have broad scope: in particular, a theory's consequences should extend far beyond the particular observations, laws, or subtheories it was initially designed to explain. Fourth, and closely related, it should be simple, bringing order to phenomena that in its absence would be individually isolated and, as a set, confused. Fifth—a somewhat less standard item, but one of special importance to actual scientific decisions—a theory should be fruitful of new research findings: it should, that is, disclose new phenomena or previously unnoted relationships among those already known.[6] These five characteristics—accuracy, consistency, scope, simplicity, and fruitfulness—are all standard criteria for evaluating the adequacy of a theory. If they had not been, I would have devoted far more space to them in my book, for I agree entirely with the traditional view that they play a vital role when scientists must choose between an established theory and an upstart competitor. Together with others of much the same sort, they provide *the* shared basis for theory choice.

Nevertheless, two sorts of difficulties are regularly encountered by the men who must use these criteria in choosing, say, between Ptolemy's astronomical theory and Copernicus's, between the oxygen and phlogiston theories of combustion, or between Newtonian mechanics and the quantum theory. Individually the criteria are imprecise: individuals may legitimately differ about their application to concrete cases. In addition, when deployed together, they repeatedly prove to conflict with one another; accuracy may, for example, dictate the choice of one theory, scope the choice of its competitor. Since these difficulties, especially the first, are also relatively familiar, I shall devote little time to their elaboration. Though my argument does demand that I illustrate them briefly, my views will begin to depart from those long current only after I have done so.

Begin with accuracy, which for present purposes I take to include not only quantitative agreement but qualitative as well. Ultimately it proves the most nearly decisive of all the criteria, partly because it is less equivocal than the others but especially because predictive and explanatory powers, which depend on it, are characteristics that scientists are particularly unwilling to give up. Unfortunately, however, theories cannot always be discriminated in terms of accuracy. Copernicus's system, for example, was not more accurate than Ptolemy's until drastically revised by Kepler more than sixty years after Copernicus's death. If Kepler or someone else had not found other reasons to choose heliocentric astronomy, those improvements in accuracy would never have been made, and Copernicus's work might have been forgotten. More typically, of course, accuracy does permit discriminations, but not the sort that lead regularly to unequivocal choice. The oxygen theory, for example, was universally acknowledged to account for observed weight relations in chemical reactions, something the phlogiston theory had previously scarcely attempted to do. But the phlogiston theory, unlike its rival, could account for the metals' being much more alike than the ores from which they were formed. One theory thus matched experience better in one area, the other in another. To choose between them on the basis of accuracy, a scientist would need to decide the area in which accuracy was more significant. About that matter chemists could and did differ without violating any of the criteria outlined above, or any others yet to be suggested.

However important it may be, therefore, accuracy by itself is seldom or never a sufficient criterion for theory choice. Other criteria must function as well, but they do not eliminate problems. To illustrate I select just two—consistency and simplicity—asking how they functioned in the choice between the heliocentric and geocentric systems. As astronomical theories both Ptolemy's and Copernicus's were internally consistent, but their relation to related theories in other fields was very different. The stationary central earth was an essential ingredient of received physical theory, a tight-knit body of doctrine which explained, among other things, how stones fall, how water pumps function, and why the clouds move slowly across the skies. Heliocentric astronomy, which required the earth's motion, was inconsistent with the existing scientific explanation of these and other terrestrial phenomena. The consistency criterion, by itself, therefore, spoke unequivocally for the geocentric tradition.

Simplicity, however, favored Copernicus, but only when evaluated in a quite special way. If, on the one hand, the two systems were compared in terms of the actual computational labor required to predict the position of a planet at a particular time, then they proved substantially equivalent. Such computations were what astronomers did, and Copernicus's system offered them no labor-saving techniques; in that sense it was not simpler than Ptolemy's. If, on the other hand, one asked about the amount of mathematical apparatus required to explain, not the detailed quantitative motions of the planets, but merely their gross qualitative features— limited elongation, retrograde motion, and the like—then, as every schoolchild knows, Copernicus required only one circle per planet, Ptolemy two. In that sense the Copernican theory was the simpler, a fact vitally important to the choices made by both Kepler and Galileo and thus essential to the ultimate triumph of Copernicanism. But that sense of simplicity was not the only one available, nor even the one most natural to professional astronomers, men whose task was the actual computation of planetary position.

Because time is short and I have multiplied examples elsewhere, I shall here simply assert that these difficulties in applying standard criteria of choice are typical and that they arise no less forcefully in twentieth-century situations than in the earlier and better-known examples I have just sketched. When scientists must choose between competing theories, two men fully committed to the same list of criteria for choice may nevertheless reach different conclusions. Perhaps they interpret simplicity differently or have different convictions about the range of fields within which the consistency criterion must be met. Or perhaps they agree about these matters but differ about the relative weights to be accorded to these or to other criteria when several are deployed together. With respect to divergences of this sort, no set of choice criteria yet proposed is of any use. One can explain, as the historian characteristically does, why particular men made particular choices at particular times. But for that purpose one must go beyond the list of shared criteria to characteristics of the individuals who make the choice. One must, that is, deal with characteristics which vary from one scientist to another without thereby in the least jeopardizing their adherence to the canons that make science scientific. Though such canons do exist and should be discoverable (doubtless the criteria of choice with which I began are among them), they are not by themselves sufficient to determine the decisions of individual scientists. For that purpose the shared canons must be fleshed out in ways that differ from one individual to another.

Some of the differences I have in mind result from the individual's previous experience as a scientist. In what part of the field was he at work when confronted by the need to choose?

How long had he worked there; how successful had he been; and how much of his work depended on concepts and techniques challenged by the new theory? Other factors relevant to choice lie outside the sciences. Kepler's early election of Copernicanism was due in part to his immersion in the Neoplatonic and Hermetic movements of his day; German Romanticism predisposed those it affected toward both recognition and acceptance of energy conservation; nineteenth-century British social thought had a similar influence on the availability and acceptability of Darwin's concept of the struggle for existence. Still other significant differences are functions of personality. Some scientists place more premium than others on originality and are correspondingly more willing to take risks; some scientists prefer comprehensive, unified theories to precise and detailed problem solutions of apparently narrower scope. Differentiating factors like these are described by my critics as subjective and are contrasted with the shared or objective criteria from which I began. Though I shall later question that use of terms, let me for the moment accept it. My point is, then, that every individual choice between competing theories depends on a mixture of objective and subjective factors, or of shared and individual criteria. Since the latter have not ordinarily figured in the philosophy of science, my emphasis upon them has made my belief in the former hard for my critics to see.

What I have said so far is primarily simply descriptive of what goes on in the sciences at times of theory choice. As description, furthermore, it has not been challenged by my critics, who reject instead my claim that these facts of scientific life have philosophic import. Taking up that issue, I shall begin to isolate some, though I think not vast, differences of opinion. Let me begin by asking how philosophers of science can for so long have neglected the subjective elements which, they freely grant, enter regularly into the actual theory choices made by individual scientists? Why have these elements seemed to them an index only of human weakness, not at all of the nature of scientific knowledge?

One answer to that question is, of course, that few philosophers, if any, have claimed to possess either a complete or an entirely well-articulated list of criteria. For some time, therefore, they could reasonably expect that further research would eliminate residual imperfections and produce an algorithm able to dictate rational, unanimous choice. Pending that achievement, scientists would have no alternative but to supply subjectively what the best current list of objective criteria still lacked. That some of them might still do so even with a perfected list at hand would then be an index only of the inevitable imperfection of human nature.

That sort of answer may still prove to be correct, but I think no philosopher still expects that it will. The search for algorithmic decision procedures has continued for some time and produced both powerful and illuminating results. But those results all presuppose that individual criteria of choice can be unambiguously stated and also that, if more than one proves relevant, an appropriate weight function is at hand for their joint application. Unfortunately, where the choice at issue is between scientific theories, little progress has been made toward the first of these desiderata and none toward the second. Most philosophers of science would, therefore, I think, now regard the sort of algorithm which has traditionally been sought as a not quite attainable ideal. I entirely agree and shall henceforth take that much for granted.

Even an ideal, however, if it is to remain credible, requires some demonstrated relevance to the situations in which it is supposed to apply. Claiming that such demonstration requires no recourse to subjective factors, my critics seem to appeal, implicitly or explicitly, to the well-known distinction between the contexts of discovery and of justification.[7] They concede, that is, that the subjective factors I invoke play a significant role in the discovery or invention of new theories, but they also insist that that inevitably intuitive process lies outside of the bounds of philosophy of science and is irrelevant to the question of scientific objectivity. Objectivity enters science, they continue, through the processes by which theories are tested, justified, or judged. Those processes do not, or at least need not, involve subjective factors at all. They can be governed by a set of (objective) criteria shared by the entire group competent to judge.

I have already argued that that position does not fit observations of scientific life and shall now assume that that much has been conceded. What is now at issue is a different point: whether or not this invocation of the distinction between contexts of discovery and of justification provides even a plausible and useful idealization. I think it does not and can best make my point by suggesting first a likely source of its apparent cogency. I suspect that my critics have been misled by science pedagogy or what I have elsewhere called textbook science. In science teaching, theories are presented together with exemplary applications, and those applications may be viewed as evidence. But that is not their primary pedagogic function (science students are distressingly willing to receive the word from professors and texts). Doubtless *some* of them were *part* of the evidence at the time actual decisions were being made, but they represent only a fraction of the considerations relevant to the decision process. The context of pedagogy differs almost as much from the context of justification as it does from that of discovery.

Full documentation of that point would require longer argument than is appropriate here, but two aspects of the way in which philosophers ordinarily demonstrate the relevance of choice criteria are worth noting. Like the science textbooks on which they are often modelled, books and articles on the philosophy of science refer again and again to the famous crucial experiments: Foucault's pendulum, which demonstrates the motion of the earth; Cavendish's demonstration of gravitational attraction; or Fizeau's measurement of the relative speed of sound in water and air. These experiments are paradigms of good reason for scientific choice; they illustrate the most effective of all the sorts of argument which could be available to a scientist uncertain which of two theories to follow; they are vehicles for the transmission of criteria of choice. But they also have another characteristic in common. By the time they were performed no scientist still needed to be convinced of the validity of the theory their outcome is now used to demonstrate. Those decisions had long since been made on the basis of significantly more equivocal evidence. The exemplary crucial experiments to which philosophers again and again refer would have been historically relevant to theory choice only if they had yielded unexpected results. Their use as illustrations provides needed economy to science pedagogy, but they scarcely illuminate the character of the choices that scientists are called upon to make.

Standard philosophical illustrations of scientific choice have another troublesome characteristic. The only arguments discussed are, as I have previously indicated, the ones favorable to the theory that, in fact, ultimately triumphed. Oxygen, we read, could explain weight relations, phlogiston could not; but nothing is said about the phlogiston theory's power or about the oxygen theory's limitations. Comparisons of Ptolemy's theory with Copernicus's proceed in the same way. Perhaps these examples should not be given since they contrast a developed theory with one still in its infancy. But philosophers regularly use them nonetheless. If the only result of their doing so were to simplify the decision situation, one could not object. Even historians do not claim to deal with the full factual complexity of the situations they describe. But these simplifications emasculate by making choice totally unproblematic. They eliminate, that is, one essential element of the decision situations that scientists must resolve if their field is to move ahead. In those situations there are always at least some good reasons for each possible choice. Considerations relevant to the context of discovery are then relevant to justification as well; scientists who share the concerns and sensibilities of the individual who discovers a new theory are ipso facto likely to appear disproportionately frequently among that theory's first supporters. That is why it has been difficult to construct algorithms for theory choice, and also why such difficulties have seemed so thoroughly worth resolving. Choices that present problems are the ones philosophers of science need to understand. Philosophically interesting decision procedures must function where, in their absence, the decision might still be in doubt.

That much I have said before, if only briefly. Recently, however, I have recognized another, subtler source for the apparent plausibility of my critics' position. To present it, I shall briefly describe a hypothetical dialogue with one of them. Both of us agree that each scientist chooses between competing theories by deploying some Bayesian algorithm which permits him to compute a value for $p(T,E)$, i.e., for the probability of a theory T on the evidence E available both to him and to the other members of his professional group at a particular period of time. "Evidence," furthermore, we both interpret broadly to include such considerations as simplicity and fruitfulness. My critic asserts, however, that there is only one such value of p, that corresponding to objective choice, and he believes that all rational members of the group must arrive at it. I assert, on the other hand, for reasons previously given, that the factors he calls objective are insufficient to determine in full any algorithm at all. For the sake of the discussion I have conceded that each individual has an algorithm and that all their algorithms have much in common. Nevertheless, I continue to hold that the algorithms of individuals are all ultimately different by virtue of the subjective considerations with which each must complete the objective criteria before any computations can be done. If my hypothetical critic is liberal, he may now grant that these subjective differences do play a role in determining the hypothetical algorithm on which each individual relies during the early stages of the competition between rival theories. But he is also likely to claim that, as evidence increases with the passage of time, the algorithms of different individuals converge to the algorithm of objective choice with which his presentation began. For him the increasing unanimity of individual choices is evidence for their increasing objectivity and thus for the elimination of subjective elements from the decision process.

So much for the dialogue, which I have, of course, contrived to disclose the non sequitur underlying an apparently plausible position. What converges as the evidence changes over time need only be the values of p that individuals compute from their individual algorithms. Conceivably those algorithms themselves also become more alike with time, but the ultimate unanimity of theory choice provides no evidence whatsoever that they do so. If subjective factors are required to account for the decisions that initially divide the profession, they may still be present later when the profession agrees. Though I shall not here argue the point, consideration of the occasions on which a scientific community divides suggests that they actually do so.

My argument has so far been directed to two points. It first provided evidence that the choices scientists make between competing theories depend not only on shared criteria—those my critics call objective—but also on idiosyncratic factors dependent on individual biography and personality. The latter are, in my critics' vocabulary, subjective, and the second part of my argument has attempted to bar some likely ways of denying their philosophic import. Let me now shift to a more positive approach, returning briefly to the list of shared criteria— accuracy, simplicity, and the like—with which I began. The considerable effectiveness of such criteria does not, I now wish to suggest, depend on their being sufficiently articulated to dictate the choice of each individual who subscribes to them. Indeed, if they were articulated to that extent, a behavior mechanism fundamental to scientific advance would cease to function. What the tradition sees as eliminable imperfections in its rules of choice I take to be in part responses to the essential nature of science.

As so often, I begin with the obvious. Criteria that influence decisions without specifying what those decisions must be are familiar in many aspects of human life. Ordinarily, however, they are called, not criteria or rules, but maxims, norms, or values. Consider maxims first. The individual who invokes them when choice is urgent usually finds them frustratingly vague and often also in conflict one with another. Contrast "He who hesitates is lost" with "Look before you leap," or compare "Many hands make light work" with "Too many cooks spoil the broth." Individually maxims dictate different choices, collectively none at all. Yet no one suggests that supplying children with contradictory tags like these is irrelevant to their education. Opposing maxims alter the nature of the decision to be made, highlight the essential issues it presents, and point to those remaining aspects of the decision for which each individual must take responsibility himself. Once invoked, maxims like these alter the nature of the decision process and can thus change its outcome.

Values and norms provide even clearer examples of effective guidance in the presence of conflict and equivocation. Improving the quality of life is a value, and a car in every garage once followed from it as a norm. But quality of life has other aspects, and the old norm has become problematic. Or again, freedom of speech is a value, but so is preservation of life and property. In application, the two often conflict, so that judicial soul-searching, which still continues, has been required to prohibit such behavior as inciting to riot or shouting fire in a crowded theater. Difficulties like these are an appropriate source for frustration, but they rarely result in charges that values have no function or in calls for their abandonment. That response is barred to most of us by an acute consciousness that there are societies with other values and that these value differences result in other ways of life, other decisions about what may and what may not be done.

I am suggesting, of course, that the criteria of choice with which I began function not as rules, which determine choice, but as values, which influence it. Two men deeply committed to the same values may nevertheless, in particular situations, make different choices as, in fact, they do. But that difference in 'outcome ought not to suggest that the values scientists share are less than critically important either to their decisions or to the development of the enterprise in which they participate. Values like accuracy, consistency, and scope may prove ambiguous in application, both individually and collectively; they may, that is, be an insufficient basis for a *shared* algorithm of choice. But they do specify a great deal: what each scientist must consider in reaching a decision, what he may and may not consider relevant, and what he can legitimately be required to report as the basis for the choice he has made. Change the list, for example by adding social utility as a criterion, and some particular choices will be different, more like those one expects from an engineer. Subtract accuracy of fit to nature from the list, and the enterprise that results may not resemble science at all, but perhaps philosophy instead. Different creative disciplines are characterized, among other things, by different sets of shared values. If philosophy and engineering lie too close to the sciences, think of literature or the plastic arts. Milton's failure to set *Paradise Lost* in a Copernican universe does not indicate that he agreed with Ptolemy but that he had things other than science to do.

Recognizing that criteria of choice can function as values when incomplete as rules has, I think, a number of striking advantages. First, as I have already argued at length, it accounts in detail for aspects of scientific behavior which the tradition has seen as anomalous or even irrational. More important, it allows the standard criteria to function fully in the earliest stages of theory choice, the period when they are most needed but when, on the traditional view, they function badly or not at all. Copernicus was responding to them during the years required to convert heliocentric astronomy from a global conceptual scheme to mathematical machinery for predicting planetary position. Such predictions were what astronomers valued; in their absence, Copernicus would scarcely have been heard, something which had happened to the idea of a moving earth before. That his own version convinced very few is less important than his acknowledgment of the basis on which judgments would have to be reached if heliocentricism were to survive. Though idiosyncrasy must be invoked to explain why Kepler and Galileo were early converts to Copernicus's system, the gaps filled by their efforts to perfect it were specified by shared values alone.

That point has a corollary which may be more important still. Most newly suggested theories do not survive. Usually the difficulties that evoked them are accounted for by more traditional means. Even when this does not occur, much work, both theoretical and experimental, is ordinarily required before the new theory can display sufficient accuracy and scope to generate widespread conviction. In short, before the group accepts it, a new theory has been tested over time by the research of a number of men, some working within it, others within its traditional rival. Such a mode of development, however, *requires* a decision process which permits rational men to disagree, and such disagreement would be barred by the shared algorithm which philosophers have generally sought. If it were at hand, all conforming scientists would make the same decision at the same time. With standards for acceptance set too low, they would move from one attractive global viewpoint to another, never giving traditional theory an opportunity to supply equivalent attractions. With standards set higher, no one satisfying the criterion of rationality would be inclined to try out the new theory, to articulate it in ways which showed its fruitfulness or displayed its accuracy and scope. I doubt that science would survive the change. What from one viewpoint may seem the looseness and imperfection of choice criteria conceived as rules may, when the same criteria are seen as values, appear an indispensable means of spreading the risk which the introduction or support of novelty always entails.

Even those who have followed me this far will want to know how a value-based enterprise of the sort I have described can develop as a science does, repeatedly producing powerful new techniques for prediction and control. To that question, unfortunately, I have no answer at all, but that is only another way of saying that I make no claim to have solved the problem of induction. If science did progress by virtue of some shared and binding algorithm of choice, I would be equally at a loss to explain its success. The lacuna is one I feel acutely, but its presence does not differentiate my position from the tradition.

It is, after all, no accident that my list of the values guiding scientific choice is, as nearly as makes any difference, identical with the tradition's list of rules dictating choice. Given any concrete situation to which the philosopher's rules could be applied, my values would function like his rules, producing the same choice. Any justification of induction, any explanation of why the rules worked, would apply equally to my values. Now consider a situation in which choice by shared rules proves impossible, not because the rules are wrong but because they are, as rules, intrinsically incomplete. Individuals must then still choose and be guided by the rules (now values) when they do so. For that purpose, however, each must first flesh out the rules, and each will do so in a somewhat different way even though the decision dictated by the variously completed rules may prove unanimous. If I now assume, in addition, that the group is large enough so that individual differences distribute on some normal curve, then any argument that justifies the philosopher's choice by rule should be immediately adaptable to my choice by value. A group too small, or a distribution excessively skewed by external historical pressures, would, of course, prevent the argument's transfer.[8] But those are just the circumstances under which scientific progress is itself problematic. The transfer is not then to be expected.

I shall be glad if these references to a normal distribution of individual differences and to the problem of induction make my position appear very close to more traditional views. With respect to theory choice, I have never thought my departures large and have been correspondingly startled by such charges as "mob psychology," quoted at the start. It is worth noting, however, that the positions are not quite identical, and for that purpose an analogy may be helpful. Many properties of liquids and gases can be accounted for on the kinetic theory by supposing that all molecules travel at the same speed. Among such properties are the regularities known as Boyle's and Charles's law. Other characteristics, most obviously evaporation, cannot be explained in so simple a way. To deal with them one must assume that molecular speeds differ, that they are distributed at random, governed by the laws of chance. What I have been suggesting here is that theory choice, too, can be explained only in part by a theory which attributes the same properties to all the scientists who must do the choosing. Essential aspects of the process generally known as verification will be understood only by recourse to the features with respect to which men may differ while still remaining scientists. The tradition takes it for granted that such features are vital to the process of discovery, which it at once and for that reason rules out of philosophical bounds. That they may have significant functions also in the philosophically central problem of justifying theory choice is what philosophers of science have to date categorically denied.

What remains to be said can be grouped in a somewhat miscellaneous epilogue. For the sake of clarity and to avoid writing a book, I have throughout this [reading] utilized some traditional concepts and locutions about the viability of which I have elsewhere expressed serious doubts. For those who know the work in which I have done so, I close by indicating three aspects of what I have said which would better represent my views if cast in other terms, simultaneously indicating the main directions in which such recasting should proceed. The areas I have in mind are: value invariance, subjectivity, and partial communication. If my views of scientific development are novel—a matter about which there is legitimate room for doubt—it is in areas such as these, rather than theory choice, that my main departures from tradition should be sought.

Throughout this paper I have implicitly assumed that, whatever their initial source, the criteria or values deployed in theory choice are fixed once and for all, unaffected by their participation in transitions from one theory to another. Roughly speaking, but only very roughly, I take that to be the case. If the list of relevant values is kept short (I have mentioned five, not all independent) and if their specification is left vague, then such values as accuracy, scope, and fruitfulness are permanent attributes of science. But little knowledge of history is required to suggest that both the application of these values and, more obviously, the relative weights attached to them have varied markedly with time and also with the field of application. Furthermore, many of these variations in value have been associated with particular changes in scientific theory. Though the experience of scientists provides no philosophical justification for the values they deploy (such justification would solve the problem of induction), those values are in part learned from that experience, and they evolve with it.

The whole subject needs more study (historians have usually taken scientific values, though not scientific methods, for granted), but a few remarks will illustrate the sort of variations I have in mind. Accuracy, as a value, has with time increasingly denoted quantitative or numerical agreement, sometimes at the expense of qualitative. Before early modern times, however, accuracy in that sense was a criterion only for astronomy, the science of the celestial region. Elsewhere it was neither expected nor sought. During the seventeenth century, however, the criterion of numerical agreement was extended to mechanics, during the late eighteenth and early nineteenth centuries to chemistry and such other subjects as electricity and heat, and in this century to many parts of biology. Or think of utility, an item of value not on my initial list. It too has figured significantly in scientific development, but far more strongly and steadily for chemists than for, say, mathematicians and physicists. Or consider scope. It is still an important scientific value, but important scientific advances have repeatedly been achieved at its expense, and the weight attributed to it at times of choice has diminished correspondingly.

What may seem particularly troublesome about changes like these is, of course, that they ordinarily occur in the aftermath of a theory change. One of the objections to Lavoisier's new chemistry was the roadblocks with which it confronted the achievement of what had previously been one of chemistry's traditional goals: the explanation of qualities, such as color and texture, as well as of their changes. With the acceptance of Lavoisier's theory such explanations ceased for some time to be a value for chemists; the ability to explain qualitative variation was no longer a criterion relevant to the evaluation of chemical theory. Clearly, if such value changes had occurred as rapidly or been as complete as the theory changes to which they related, then theory choice would be value choice, and neither could provide justification for the other. But, historically, value change is ordinarily a belated and largely unconscious concomitant of theory choice, and the former's magnitude is regularly smaller than the latter's. For the functions I have here ascribed to values, such relative stability provides a sufficient basis. The existence of a feedback loop through which theory change affects the values which led to that change does not make the decision process circular in any damaging sense.

About a second respect in which my resort to tradition may be misleading, I must be far more tentative. It demands the skills of an ordinary language philosopher, which I do not possess. Still, no very acute ear for language is required to generate discomfort with the ways in which the terms "objectivity" and, more especially, "subjectivity" have functioned in this paper. Let me briefly suggest the respects in which I believe language has gone astray. "Subjective" is a term with several established uses: in one of these it is opposed to "objective," in another to "judgmental." When my critics describe the idiosyncratic features to which I appeal as subjective, they resort, erroneously I think, to the second of these senses. When they complain that I deprive science of objectivity, they conflate that second sense of subjective with the first.

A standard application of the term "subjective" is to matters of taste, and my critics appear to suppose that that is what I have made of theory choice. But they are missing a distinction standard since Kant when they do so. Like sensation reports, which are also subjective in the sense now at issue, matters of taste are undiscussable. Suppose that, leaving a movie theater with a friend after seeing a western, I exclaim: "How I liked that terrible potboiler!" My friend, if he disliked the film, may tell me I have low tastes, a matter about which, in these circumstances, I would readily agree. But, short of saying that I lied, he cannot disagree with my report that I liked the film or try to persuade me that what I said about my reaction was wrong. What is discussable in my remark is not my characterization of my internal state, my exemplification of taste, but rather my *judgment* that the film was a potboiler. Should my friend disagree on that point, we may argue most of the night, each comparing the film with good or great ones we have seen, each revealing, implicitly or explicitly, something about how he *judges* cinematic merit, about his aesthetic. Though one of us may, before retiring, have persuaded the other, he need not have done so to demonstrate that our difference is one of judgment, not taste.

Evaluations or choices of theory have, I think, exactly this character. Not that scientists never say merely, I like such and such a theory, or I do not. After 1926 Einstein said little more than that about his opposition to the quantum theory. But scientists may always be asked to explain their choices, to exhibit the bases for their judgments. Such judgments are eminently discussable, and the man who refuses to discuss his own cannot expect to be taken seriously. Though there are, very occasionally, leaders of scientific taste, their existence tends to prove the rule. Einstein was one of the few, and his increasing isolation from the scientific community in later life shows how very limited a role taste alone can play in theory choice. Bohr, unlike Einstein, did discuss the bases for his judgment, and he carried the day. If my critics introduce the term "subjective" in a sense that opposes it to judgmental—thus suggesting that I make theory choice undiscussable, a matter of taste—they have seriously mistaken my position.

Turn now to the sense in which "subjectivity" is opposed to "objectivity," and note first that it raises issues quite separate from those just discussed. Whether my taste is low or refined, my report that I liked the film is objective unless I have lied. To my judgment that the film was a potboiler, however, the objective-subjective distinction does not apply at all, at least not obviously and directly. When my critics say I deprive theory choice of objectivity, they must, therefore, have recourse to some very different sense of subjective, presumably the one in which bias and personal likes or dislikes function instead of, or in the face of, the actual facts. But that sense of subjective does not fit the process I have been describing any better than the first. Where factors dependent on individual biography or personality must be introduced to make values applicable, no standards of factuality or actuality are being set aside. Conceivably my discussion of theory choice indicates some limitations of objectivity, but not by isolating elements properly called subjective. Nor am I even quite content with the notion that what I have been displaying are limitations. Objectivity ought to be analyzable in terms of criteria like accuracy and consistency. If these criteria do not supply all the guidance that we have customarily expected of them, then it may be the meaning rather than the limits of objectivity that my argument shows.

Turn, in conclusion, to a third respect, or set of respects, in which this paper needs to be recast. I have assumed throughout that the discussions surrounding theory choice are unproblematic, that the facts appealed to in such discussions are independent of theory, and that the discussions' outcome is appropriately called a choice. Elsewhere I have challenged all three of these assumptions, arguing that communication between proponents of different theories is inevitably partial, that what each takes to be facts depends in part on the theory he espouses, and that an individual's transfer of allegiance from theory to theory is often better described as conversion than as choice. Though all these theses are problematic as well as controversial, my commitment to them is undiminished. I shall not now defend them, but must at least attempt to indicate how what I have said here can be adjusted to conform with these more central aspects of my view of scientific development.

For that purpose I resort to an analogy I have developed in other places. Proponents of different theories are, I have claimed, like native speakers of different languages. Communication between them goes on by translation, and it raises all translation's familiar difficulties. That analogy is, of course, incomplete, for the vocabulary of the two theories may be identical, and most words function in the same ways in both. But some words in the basic as well as in the theoretical vocabularies of the two theories—words like "star" and "planet," "mixture" and "compound," or "force" and "matter"—do function differently. Those differences are unexpected and will be discovered and localized, if at all, only by repeated experience of communication breakdown. Without pursuing the matter further, I simply assert the existence of significant limits to what the proponents of different theories can communicate to one another. The same limits make it difficult or, more likely, impossible for an individual to hold both theories in mind together and compare them point by point with each other and with nature. That sort of comparison is, however, the process on which the appropriateness of any word like "choice" depends.

Nevertheless, despite the incompleteness of their communication, proponents of different theories can exhibit to each other, not always easily, the concrete technical results achievable by those who practice within each theory. Little or no translation is required to apply at least some value criteria to those results. (Accuracy and fruitfulness are most immediately applicable, perhaps followed by scope. Consistency and simplicity are far more problematic.) However incomprehensible the new theory may be to the proponents of tradition, the exhibit of impressive concrete results will persuade at least a few of them that they must discover how such results are achieved. For that purpose they must learn to translate, perhaps by treating already published papers as a Rosetta stone or, often more effective, by visiting the innovator, talking with him, watching him and his students at work. Those exposures may not result in the adoption of the theory; some advocates of the tradition may return home and attempt to adjust the old theory to produce equivalent results. But others, if the new theory is to survive, will find that at some point in the language-learning process they have ceased to translate and begun instead to speak the language like a native. No process quite like choice has occurred, but they are practicing the new theory nonetheless. Furthermore, the factors that have led them to risk the conversion they have undergone are just the ones this [reading] has underscored in discussing a somewhat different process, one which, following the philosophical tradition, it has labelled theory choice.

NOTES

[1] *The Structure of Scientific Revolutions*, 2d ed. (Chicago, 1970), pp. 148, 151–52, 159. All the passages from which these fragments are taken appeared in the same form in the first edition, published in 1962.

[2] Ibid., p. 170.

[3] Imre Lakatos, "Falsification and the Methodology of Scientific Research Programmes," in I. Lakatos and A. Musgrave, eds., *Criticism and the Growth of Knowledge* (Cambridge, 1970), pp. 91–195. The quoted phrase, which appears on p. 178, is italicized in the original.

[4] Dudley Shapere, "Meaning and Scientific Change," in R. G. Colodny, ed., *Mind and Cosmos: Essays in Contemporary Science and Philosophy,* University of Pittsburgh Series in the Philosophy of Science, vol. 3 (Pittsburgh, 1966), pp. 41–85. The quotation will be found on p. 67.

[5] Israel Scheffler, *Science and Subjectivity* (Indianapolis, 1967), p. 81.

[6] The last criterion, fruitfulness, deserves more emphasis than it has yet received. A scientist choosing between two theories ordinarily knows that his decision will have a bearing on his subsequent research career. Of course he is especially attracted by a theory that promises the concrete successes for which scientists are ordinarily rewarded.

[7] The least equivocal example of this position is probably the one developed in Scheffler, *Science and Subjectivity,* chap. 4.

[8] If the group is small, it is more likely that random fluctuations will result in its members' sharing an atypical set of values and therefore making choices different from those that would be made by a larger and more representative group. External environment—intellectual, ideological, or economic—must systematically affect

the value system of much larger groups, and the consequences can include difficulties in introducing the scientific enterprise to societies with inimical values or perhaps even the end of that enterprise within societies where it had once flourished. In this area, however, great caution is required. Changes in the environment where science is practiced can also have fruitful effects on research. Historians often resort, for example, to differences between national environments to explain why particular innovations were initiated and at first disproportionately pursued in particular countries, e.g., Darwinism in Britain, energy conservation in Germany. At present we know substantially nothing about the minimum requisites of the social milieux within which a sciencelike enterprise might flourish.

L A R R Y   L A U D A N
DISSECTING THE HOLIST PICTURE
OF SCIENTIFIC CHANGE

It is now more than twenty years since the appearance of Thomas Kuhn's *The Structure of Scientific Revolutions.* For many of us entering the field two decades ago, that book made a powerful difference. Not because we fully understood it; still less because we became converts to it. It mattered, rather, because it posed in a particularly vivid form some direct challenges to the empiricism we were learning from the likes of Hempel, Nagel, Popper, and Carnap.

Philosophers of science of that era had no doubts about whom and what the book was attacking. If Kuhn was right, all the then reigning methodological orthodoxies were simply wrong. It was a good deal less clear what Kuhn's positive message amounted to, and not entirely because many of Kuhn's philosophical readers were too shocked to read him carefully. Was he saying that theories were really and always incommensurable so that rival scientists invariably misunderstood one another, or did he mean it when he said that the problem-solving abilities of rival theories could be objectively compared? Did he really believe that accepting a new theory was a "conversion experience," subject only to the Gestalt-like exigencies of the religious life? In the first wave of reaction to Kuhn's bombshell, answers to such questions were not easy to find.

Since 1962 most of Kuhn's philosophical writings have been devoted to clearing up some of the ambiguities and confusions generated by the language of the first edition of *The Structure of Scientific Revolutions.* By and large, Kuhn's message has been an ameliorative and conciliatory one, to such an extent that some passages in his later writings make him sound like a closet positivist. More than one commentator has accused the later Kuhn of taking back much of what made his message interesting and provocative in the first place.[1]

But that is not entirely fair, for if many of Kuhn's clarifications have indeed taken the sting out of what we once thought Kuhn's position was, there are several issues about which the later Kuhn is both clear *and* controversial. Significantly, several of those are central to the themes of this [reading]. Because they are, I want to use Kuhn's work as a stalking-horse to show how the features of the reticulational model, proposed [earlier], can be used to produce a more satisfactory account than Kuhn offers of scientific debate in particular and scientific change in general.

Kuhn, then, will be my immediate target, but I would be less than candid if I did not quickly add that the views I discuss here have spread considerably beyond the Kuhnian corpus. To some degree, almost all of us who wrote about scientific change in the 1970s (present company included) fell prey to some of the confusions I describe. In trying to characterize the mechanisms of theory change, we have tended to lapse into sloppy language for describing change. However, because Kuhn's is the best-known account of scientific change, and because Kuhn most overtly makes several of the mistakes I want to discuss, this [reading] focuses chiefly on his views. Similar criticisms can be raised with varying degrees of severity against authors as diverse as Foucault, Lakatos, Toulmin, Holton, and Laudan.

KUHN ON THE UNITS OF SCIENTIFIC CHANGE

It is notorious that the key Kuhnian concept of a paradigm is multiply ambiguous. Among its most central meanings are the following three: First and foremost, a paradigm offers a conceptual framework for classifying and explaining natural objects. That is, it specifies in a generic way the sorts of entities which are thought to populate a certain domain of experience and it sketches out how those entities generally interact. In short, every paradigm will make certain claims about what populates the world. Such ontological claims mark that paradigm off from others, since each paradigm is thought to postulate entities and modes of interaction which differentiate it from other paradigms. Second, a paradigm will specify the appropriate methods, techniques, and tools of inquiry for studying the objects in the relevant domain of application. Just as different paradigms have different ontologies, so they involve substantially different methodologies. (Consider, for instance, the very different methods of research and theory evaluation associated with behaviorism and cognitive psychology respectively.) These methodological commitments are persistent ones, and they characterize the paradigm throughout its history. Finally, the proponents of different paradigms will, according to Kuhn, espouse different sets of cognitive goals or ideals. Although the partisans of two paradigms may (and usually do) share some aims in common, Kuhn insists that the goals are not fully overlapping between followers of rival paradigms. Indeed, to accept a paradigm is, for Kuhn, to subscribe to a complex of cognitive values which the proponents of no other paradigm accept fully.

Paradigm change, on this account, clearly represents a break of great magnitude. To trade in one paradigm for another is to involve oneself in changes at each of the three levels defined in chapter 2 above. We give up one ontology for another, one methodology for another, and one set of cognitive goals for another. Moreover, according to Kuhn, this change is *simultaneous* rather than *sequential*. It is worth observing in passing that, for all Kuhn's vitriol about the impoverishment of older models of scientific rationality, there are several quite striking similarities between the classical version of the hierarchical model and Kuhn's alternative to it. Both lay central stress on the justificatory interactions between claims at the factual, methodological, and axiological levels. Both emphasize the centrality of values and standards as providing criteria of choice between rival views lower in the hierarchy. Where Kuhn breaks, and breaks radically, with the tradition is in his insistence that rationality must be relativized to choices within a paradigm rather than choices between paradigms. Whereas the older account of the hierarchical model had generally supposed that core axiological and methodological commitments would typically be common property across the sciences of an epoch, Kuhn asserts that there are methodological and axiological discrepancies between any two paradigms. Indeed (as we shall see below), one of the core failings of Kuhn's position is that it so fully internalizes the classical hierarchical approach that, whenever the latter breaks down (as it certainly does in grappling with interparadigmatic debate, or any other sort of disagreement involving conflicting goals), Kuhn's approach has nothing more to offer concerning the possibility of rational choices.[2]

For now, however, the immediate point to stress is that Kuhn portrays paradigm changes in ways that make them seem to be abrupt and global ruptures in the life of a scientific community. So great is this supposed transition that several of Kuhn's critics have charged that, despite Kuhn's proclaimed intentions to the contrary, his analysis inevitably turns scientific change into a nonrational or irrational process. In part, but only in part, it is Kuhn's infelicitous terminology that produces this impression. Notoriously, he speaks of the acceptance of a new paradigm as a "conversion experience,"[3] conjuring up a picture of the scientific revolutionary as a born-again Christian, long on zeal and short on argument. At other times he likens paradigm change to an "irreversible Gestalt-shift."[4] Less metaphorically, he claims that there is never a point at which it is "unreasonable" to hold onto an old paradigm rather than to accept a new one.[5] Such language does not encourage one to imagine that paradigm change is exactly the result of a careful and deliberate weighing-up of the respective strengths of rival contenders. But impressions based on some of Kuhn's more lurid language can probably be rectified by cleaning up some of the vocabulary of *The Structure of Scientific Revolutions,* a task on which Kuhn has been embarked more or less since the book first appeared.[6] No changes of terminology, however, will alter the fact that some central features of Kuhn's model of science raise serious roadblocks to a rational analysis of scientific change. The bulk of this chapter is devoted to examining some of those impedimenta. Before we turn to that examination, however, I want to stress early on that my complaint with Kuhn is not merely that he has failed to give any normatively robust or rational account of theory change, serious as that failing is. As I show below, he has failed even at the descriptive or narrative task of offering an accurate story about the manner in which large-scale changes of scientific allegiance occur.

But there is a yet more fundamental respect in which Kuhn's approach presents obstacles to an understanding of the dynamics of theory change. Specifically, by insisting that individual paradigms have an integral and static character—that changes take place only between, rather than within, paradigms—Kuhn has missed the single feature of science which promises to mediate and rationalize the transition from one world view or paradigm to another. Kuhn's various writings on this subject leave the reader in no doubt that he thinks the parts of a paradigm go together as an inseparable package. As he puts it in *The Structure of Scientific Revolutions,* "In learning a paradigm the scientist acquires theory, methods, and standards together, usually in an *inextricable* mix."[7] This theme, of the inextricable and inseparable ingredients of a paradigm, is a persistent one in Kuhn's work. One key aim of this chapter is to show how drastically we need to alter Kuhn's views about how tightly the pieces of a paradigm's puzzle fit together before we can expect to understand how paradigmlike change occurs.

Loosening up the fit.—Without too heavy an element of caricature, we can describe world-view models such as Kuhn's along the following lines: one group or faction in the scientific community accepts a particular "big picture." That requires acquiescence in a certain ontology of nature, acceptance of a specific set of rules about how to investigate nature, and adherence to a set of cognitive values about the teleology of natural inquiry (i.e., about the goals that science seeks). On this analysis, large-scale scientific change involves the replacement of one such world view by another, a process that entails the simultaneous repudiation of the key elements of the old picture and the adoption of corresponding (but of course different) elements of the new. In short, scientific change looks something like figure 1.

FIGURE 1   KUHN'S PICTURE OF THEORY CHANGE

WV1 (ontology 1, methodology 1, values 1)

WV2 (ontology 2, methodology 2, values 2)

When scientific change is construed so globally, it is no small challenge to see how it could be other than a conversion experience. If different scientists not only espouse different theories but also subscribe to different standards of appraisal and ground those standards in different and conflicting systems of cognitive goals, then it is difficult indeed to imagine that scientific change could be other than a whimsical change of style or taste. There could apparently never be compelling grounds for saying that one paradigm is better than another, for one has to ask: Better relative to which standards and whose goals? To make matters worse— much worse—Kuhn often suggested that each paradigm is more or less automatically guaranteed to satisfy its own standards and to fail the standards of rival paradigms, thus producing a kind of self-reinforcing solipsism in science. As he once put it, "To the extent, as significant as it is incomplete, that two scientific schools disagree about what is a problem and what a solution, they will inevitably talk through each other when debating the merits of their respective paradigms. In the partially circular arguments that regularly result, *each* paradigm will be shown to satisfy more or less the criteria that it dictates for itself and to fall short of those dictated by its opponent."[8] Anyone who writes prose of this sort must think that scientific decision making is fundamentally capricious. Or at least so many of us thought in the mid- and late 1960s, as philosophers began to digest Kuhn's ideas. In fact, if one looks at several discussions of Kuhn's work dating from that period, one sees this theme repeatedly. Paradigm change, it was said, could not possibly be a reasoned or rational process. Kuhn, we thought, has made science into an irrational "monster."

Kuhn's text added fuel to the fire by seeming to endorse such a construal of his own work. In a notorious discussion of the shift from the chemistry of Priestley to that of Lavoisier and Dalton, for instance, Kuhn asserted that it was perfectly reasonable for Priestley to hold onto phlogiston theory, just as it was fully rational for most of his contemporaries to be converting to the oxygen theory of Lavoisier. According to Kuhn, Priestley's continued adherence to phlogiston was reasonable because—given Priestley's cognitive aims and the methods he regarded as appropriate—his own theory continued to look good. Priestley lost the battle with Lavoisier, not because Priestley's paradigm was objectively inferior to its rivals, but rather because most of the chemists of the day came to share Lavoisier's and Dalton's views about what was important and how it should be investigated.

The clear implication of such passages in Kuhn's writings is that interparadigmatic debate is necessarily inconclusive and thus can never be brought to rational closure. When closure does occur, it must therefore be imposed on the situation by such external factors as the demise of some of the participants or the manipulation of the levers of power and reward within the institutional structure of the scientific community. Philosophers of science, almost without exception, have found such implications troubling, for they directly confute what philosophers have been at pains for two millennia to establish: to wit, that scientific disputes, and more generally all disagreements about matters of fact, are in principle open to rational clarification and resolution. It is on the strength of passages such as those I have mentioned that Kuhn has been charged with relativism, subjectivism, irrationalism, and a host of other sins high on the philosopher's hit list.

There is some justice in these criticisms of Kuhn's work, for (as I suggest [earlier]) Kuhn has failed over the past twenty years to elaborate any coherent account of consensus formation, that is, of the manner in which scientists could ever agree to support one world view rather than another. But that flaw, serious though it is, can probably be remedied, for I want to suggest that the problem of consensus formation can be solved if we will make two fundamental amendments in Kuhn's position. First (as argued [earlier]), we must replace the hierarchical view of justification with the reticulated picture, thereby making cognitive values "negotiable." Second, we must simply drop Kuhn's insistence on the integral character of world views or paradigms. More specifically, we solve the problem of consensus once we realize that *the various components of a world view are individually negotiable and individually replaceable in a piecemeal fashion* (that is, in such a manner that replacement of one element need not require wholesale repudiation of all the other components), Kuhn himself grants, of course, that some components of a world view can be revised; that is what "paradigm articulation" is all about. But for Kuhn, as for such other world view theorists as Lakatos and Foucault, the central commitments of a world view, its "hard core" (to use Lakatos's marvelous phrase), are not revisable—short of rejecting the entire world view. The core ontology of a world view or paradigm, along with its methodology and axiology, comes on a take-it-or-leave-it basis. Where these levels of commitment are concerned, Kuhn (along with such critics of his as Lakatos) is an uncompromising holist. Consider, for instance, his remark: "Just because it is a transition between incommensurables, the transition between competing paradigms cannot be made a step at a time . . . like the Gestalt-switch, it must occur all at once or not at all."[9] Kuhn could hardly be less ambiguous on this point.

But paradigms or research programs need not be so rigidly conceived, and typically they are not so conceived by scientists; nor, if we reflect on it a moment, should they be so conceived. . . . [T]here are complex justificatory interconnections among a scientist's ontology, his methodology, and his axiology. If a scientist's methodology fails to justify his ontology; if his methodology fails to promote his cognitive aims; if his cognitive aims prove to be utopian—in all these cases the scientist will have compelling reasons for replacing one component or other of his world view with an element that does the job better. Yet he need not modify everything else.

To be more precise, the choice confronting a scientist whose world view is under strain in this manner need be nothing like as stark as the choice sketched in figure 1 (where it is a matter of sticking with what he knows best unchanged or throwing that over for something completely different), but rather a choice where the modification of one core element—while retaining the others—may bring a decided improvement. Schematically, the choice may be one between

(1) $\qquad\qquad\qquad$ $O^1 \,\&\, M^1 \,\&\, A^1$

and

(2) $\qquad\qquad\qquad$ $O^2 \,\&\, M^1 \,\&\, A^1$

Or, between (1) and

(3) $\qquad\qquad\qquad$ $O^1 \,\&\, M^2 \,\&\, A^1.$

Or, to exhaust the simple cases, it may be between (1) and

(4) $\qquad\qquad\qquad$ $O^1 \,\&\, M^1 \,\&\, A^2.$

As shown [earlier], choices like those between (1) and (2), or between (1) and (3), are subject to strong normative constraints. And we saw . . . that choices of the sort represented between (1) and (4) are also, under certain circumstances, equally amenable to rational analysis.

In all these examples there is enough common ground between the rivals to engender hope of finding an "Archimedean standpoint" which can rationally mediate the choice. When such commonality exists, there is no reason to regard the choice as just a matter of taste or whim; nor is there any reason to say of such choices, as Kuhn does (recall his characterization of the Priestley-Lavoisier exchange), that there can be no compelling grounds for one preference over another. Provided theory change occurs one level at a time, there is ample scope for regarding it as a thoroughly reasoned process.

But the crucial question is whether change actually does occur in this manner. If one thinks quickly of the great transitions in the history of science, they *seem* to preclude such a stepwise analysis. The shift from (say) an Aristotelian to a Newtonian world view clearly involved changes on all three levels. So, too, did the emergence of psychoanalysis from nineteenth-century mechanistic psychology. But before we accept this wholesale picture of scientific change too quickly, we should ask whether it might not acquire what plausibility it enjoys only because our characterizations of such historical revolutions make us compress or telescope a number of gradual changes (one level at a time, as it were) into what, at our distance in time, can easily appear as an abrupt and monumental shift.

By way of laying out the core features of a more gradualist (and, I argue, historically more faithful) picture of scientific change, I will sketch a highly idealized version of theory change. Once it is in front of us, I will show in detail how it makes sense of some real cases of scientific change. Eventually, we will want a model that can show how one might move from an initial state of disagreement between rival traditions or paradigms to consensus about which one is better. But, for purposes of exposition, I want to begin with a rather simpler situation, namely, one in which consensus in favor of one world view or tradition gives way eventually to consensus in favor of another, without scientists ever being faced with a choice as stark as that between two well-developed, and totally divergent, rival paradigms. My "tall tale," represented schematically in figure 2, might go like this: at any given time, there will be at least one set of values, methods, and theories which one can identify as operating in any field or subfield of science. Let us call this collective C_1, and its components, T_1, M_1, and A_1. These components typically stand in the complex justificatory relationships to one another described [earlier]; that is, A_1 will justify M_1 and harmonize with T_1; M_1 will justify T_1 and exhibit the realizability of A_1; and T_1 will constrain M_1 and exemplify A_1. Let us suppose that someone then proposes a new theory, T_2, to replace T_1. The rules M_1 will be consulted and they may well indicate grounds for preferring T_2 to T_1. Suppose that they do, and that we thereby replace T_1 with T_2. As time goes by, certain scientists may develop reservations about M_1 and propose a new and arguably superior methodology, M_2. Now a choice must be made between M_1 and M_2. As we have seen, that requires determining whether M_1 or M_2 offers more promise of realizing our aims. Since that determination will typically be an empirical matter, both A_1 and the then prevailing theory, T_2, will have to be consulted to ascertain whether M_1 or M_2 is optimal for securing A_1. Suppose that, in comparing the relative efficacy of achieving the shared values, A_1, cogent arguments can be made to show that M_2 is superior to M_1. Under the circumstances, assuming scientists behave rationally, M_2 will replace M_1. This means that as new theories, T_3, T_4, . . . , T_n, emerge later, they will be assessed by rules M_2 rather than M_1. Suppose, still further along in this fairy tale, we imagine a challenge to the basic values themselves. Someone may, for instance, point to new evidence suggesting that some element or other of A_1 is unrealizable. Someone else may point out that virtually none of the theories accepted by the scientific community as instances of good science exemplify the values expressed in A_1. (Or, it may be shown that A_1 is an inconsistent set in that its component aspirations are fundamentally at odds with one another.) Under such circumstances, scientists may rationally decide to abandon A_1 and to take up an alternative, consistent set of values, A_2, should it be available. (Although I have considered a temporal sequence of changes—first in theory, then in methods, and finally in aims—which superficially corresponds to the justificatory order of the hierarchical model, it is crucial to realize how unlike the hierarchical picture this sequence really is. That model would countenance no rational deliberation of the sort represented by the transition from $T_2M_2A_1$ to $T_2M_2A_2$. Equally, the hierarchical model, as noted [earlier], does not permit our beliefs at the level of theories to shape our views as to permissible methods, since justification in the hierarchical model is entirely downward from methods to theories.)

Now that we have this hypothetical sequence before us, let us imagine a historian called Tom, who decides many years later to study this episode. He will doubtless be struck by the fact that a group of scientists who once accepted values A_1, rules M_1, and theory T_1 came over the course of, say, a decade or two to abandon the whole lot and to accept a new complex, C_2, consisting of A_2, M_2, and T_2. Tom will probably note, and rightly too, that the partisans of C_2 have precious little in common with the devotees of C_1. Surely, Tom may well surmise, here was a scientific revolution if ever there was one, for there was dramatic change

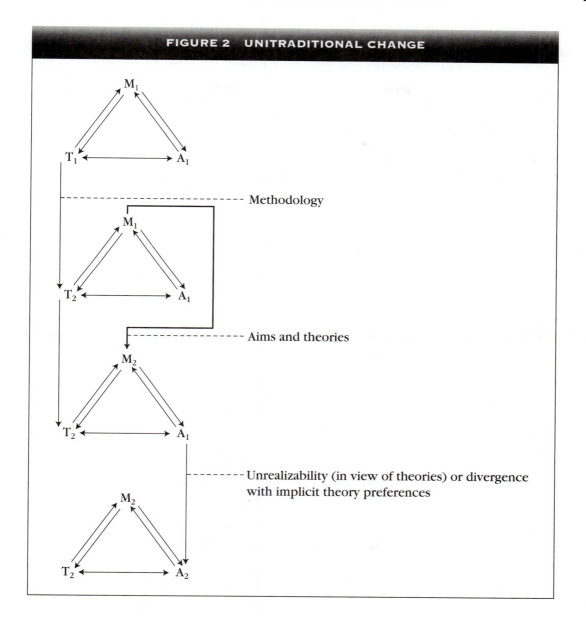

FIGURE 2   UNITRADITIONAL CHANGE

Methodology

Aims and theories

Unrealizability (in view of theories) or divergence with implicit theory preferences

at every level. If Tom decides to call the view that scientists eventually came to hold "Paradigm 2," and the view from which they began "Paradigm 1," then he will be able to document the existence of a massive paradigm shift between what (at our remoteness in time) appear to be conceptually distant and virtually incommensurable paradigms.

The point, of course, is that a sequence of belief changes which, described at the micro-level, appears to be a perfectly reasonable and rational sequence of events may appear, when represented in broad brushstrokes that drastically compress the temporal dimension, as a fundamental and unintelligible change of world view. This kind of tunnel vision, in which a sequence of gradual shifts is telescoped into one abrupt and mighty transformation, is a folly which every historian is taught to avoid. Yet knowing that one should avoid it and actually doing so are two different things. Once we recognize this fallacy for what it is, we should probably hesitate to accept too quickly the models of the holists and big-picture builders. For, if our fairy story has anything of the truth about it (that is, if change is, or more weakly even if it could be, more piecemeal than the holistic accounts imply), there may yet be room for incorporating changes of methods and of cognitive values into a rational account of scientific activity. My object in the rest of this [reading] is to offer some reasons to believe that the fairy tale is a good deal closer to the mark than its holistic rivals.

But before I present the evidence needed for demythologizing my story, we have to add a new twist to it. As I pointed out above, this story concerns what I call a "unitraditional paradigm shift." It reveals how it might be possible for scientists, originally advocates of one tradition or paradigm, to come around eventually to accept what appears to be a very different view of the world, not to say a very different view of what science is. I call such a change unitraditional because it is not prompted or provoked by the availability of a well-articulated rival world view. If you like, the unitraditional picture explains how one could get paradigm change by developments entirely internal to the dynamic of a particular paradigm. More interesting, and more challenging, is the problem of multitraditional paradigm shifts, that is, basic changes of world view which arise from competition between rival paradigms. To deal with such cases, we need to complicate our fairy story a bit.

Here, we need to imagine two of our complexes already well developed, and radically divergent (i.e., with different ontologies, different methodologies, and different axiologies). If we ask under what circumstances it would be reasonable for the partisans of C_1 to abandon it and accept C_2, some answers come immediately to mind. Suppose, for instance, it can be shown that the central theories of C_1 look worse than the theories of C_2, even by the standards of C_1. As we have seen, Kuhn denies that this is possible, since he says that the theories associated with a particular paradigm will always look better by its standards than will the theories of rival paradigms."[10] But as we have already seen, there is no way of guaranteeing in advance that the methods and standards of C_1 will always give the epistemic nod to theories associated with C_1, since it is always possible (and has sometimes happened) that rival paradigms to C_1 will develop theories that do a better job of satisfying the methodological demands of C_1 than do the theories developed within C_1 itself. Alternatively, suppose someone shows that there is a set of methods M_3 which is more nearly optimal than M_1 for achieving the aims of C_1, and that those methods give the epistemic nod to the theories of C_2 rather than those of C_1. Or, suppose that someone shows that the goals of C_1 are deeply at odds with the attributes of some of the major theories of science—theories that the partisans of C_1 themselves endorse—and that, by contrast, the cognitive values of C_2 are typified by those same theories. Again, new evidence might emerge which indicates the nonrealizability of some of the central cognitive aims of C_1 and the achievability of the aims of C_2. In all these circumstances (and several obvious ones which I shall not enumerate), the only reasonable thing for a scientist to do would be to give up C_1 and to embrace C_2.

But, once we begin to play around with the transformations permitted by the reticulational model, we see that the transition from one paradigm or world view to another can itself be a step-wise process, requiring none of the wholesale shifts in allegiance at every level required by Kuhn's analysis. The advocates of C_1 might, for instance, decide initially to accept many of the substantive theories of C_2, while still retaining for a time the methodology and axiology of C_1. At a later stage they might be led by a different chain of arguments and evidence to accept the methodology of C_2 while retaining C_1's axiology. Finally, they might eventually come to share the values of C_2. As William Whewell showed more than a century ago, precisely some such series of shifts occurred in the gradual capitulation of Cartesian physicists to the natural philosophy of Newton.[11]

In effect, I am claiming that the solution of the problem of consensus formation in the multiparadigm situation to be nothing more than a special or degenerate instance of unitraditional change. It follows that, if we can show that the unitraditional fairy tale has something going for it, then we will solve both forms of the consensus-formation problem simultaneously. The core question is whether the gradualist myth, which I have just sketched out, is better supported by the historical record than the holistic picture associated with Kuhn.

One striking way of formulating the contrast between the piecemeal and the holistic models, and thus designing a test to choose between them, is to ask a fairly straightforward question about the historical record: Is it true that the major historical shifts in the methodological rules of science and in the cognitive values of scientists have invariably been contemporaneous with one another *and* with shifts in substantive theories and ontologies? The holistic account is clearly committed to an affirmative answer to the question. Indeed, it is a straightforward corollary of Kuhn's analysis that changes in rules or values, when they occur, will occur only when a scientific revolution takes place, that is, only when there is a concomitant shift in theories, methods, and values. A change in values without an associated change in basic ontology is not a permissible variation countenanced in the Kuhnian scheme.[12] Nor is a change in methods possible for Kuhn without a paradigm change. Kuhn's analysis flatly denies that the values and norms of a "mature" science can shift in the absence of a revolution. Yet there are plenty of examples one may cite to justify the assertion made here that changes at the three levels do not always go together. I shall mention two such examples.

Consider, first, a well-known shift at the level of methodological rules. From the time of Bacon until the early nineteenth century most scientists subscribed to variants of the rules of inductive inference associated with Bacon, Hume, and Newton. The methods of agreement, difference, and concomitant variations were a standard part of the repertoire of most working scientists for two hundred years. These rules, at least as then understood, foreclosed the postulation of any theoretical or hypothetical entities, since observable bodies were the only sort of objects and properties to which one could apply traditional inductive methods. More generally (as shown [earlier]), thinkers of the Enlightenment believed it important to develop rules of inquiry which would exclude unobservable entities and bring to heel the tendency of scientists to indulge their *l'esprit de système*. Newton's famous third rule of reasoning in philosophy, the notorious "hypotheses non fingo," was but a particularly succinct and influential formulation of this trenchant empiricism.

It is now common knowledge that by the late nineteenth century this methodological orientation had largely vanished from the writings of major scientists and methodologists. Whewell, Peirce, Helmholtz, Mach, Darwin, Hertz, and a host of other luminaries had, by the 1860s and 1870s, come to believe that it was quite legitimate for science to postulate unobservable entities, and that most of the traditional rules of inductive reasoning had been superseded by the logic of hypothetico-deduction. Elsewhere I have described this shift in detail.[13] What is important for our purposes is both that it occurred and when it occurred. That it took place would be denied, I think, by no one who studies the record; determining precisely when it occurred is more problematic, although probably no scholar would quarrel with the claim that it comes in the period from 1800 to 1860. And a dating as fuzzy as that is sufficient to make out my argument.

For here we have a shift in the history of the explicit methodology of the scientific community as significant as one can imagine—from methods of enumerative and eliminative induction to the method of hypothesis—occurring across the spectrum of the theoretical sciences, from celestial mechanics to chemistry and biology.[14] Yet where is the larger and more global scientific revolution of which this methodological shift was the concomitant? There were of course revolutions, and important ones, in this period. Yet this change in methodology cannot be specifically linked to any of the familiar revolutions of the period. The method of hypothesis did not become the orthodoxy in science of the late nineteenth century because it rode on the coattails of any specific change in ontology or scientific values. So far as I can see, this methodological revolution was independent of any particular program of research in any one of the sciences, which is not to say that it did not reflect some very general tendencies appearing across the board in scientific research. The holist model, which would have us believe that changes in methodological orientation are invariably linked to changes in values and ontology, is patently mistaken here. Nor, if one reflects on the nature of methodological discussion, should we have expected otherwise. . . . [M]ethodological rules can reasonably be criticized and altered if one discovers that they fail optimally to promote our cognitive aims. If our aims shift, as they would in a Kuhnian paradigm shift, we would of course expect a reappraisal of our methods of inquiry in light of their suitability for promoting the new goals. But, even when our goals shift not at all, we sometimes discover arguments and evidence which indicate that the methods we have been using all along are not really suitable for our purposes. Such readjustments of methodological orientation, in the absence of a paradigm shift, are a direct corollary of the reticulational model as I described it earlier; yet they pose a serious anomaly for Kuhn's analysis.

What about changes in aims, as opposed to rules? Is it not perhaps more plausible to imagine, with Kuhn, that changes of cognitive values are always part of broader shifts of paradigm or world view? Here again, the historical record speaks out convincingly against this account. Consider, very briefly, one example: the abandonment of "infallible knowledge" as an epistemic aim for science. As before, my historical account will have to be "potted" for purposes of brevity; but there is ample serious scholarship to back up the claims I shall be making.[15]

That scholarship has established quite convincingly that, during the course of the nineteenth century, the view of science as aiming at certainty gave way among most scientists to a more modest program of producing theories that were plausible, probable, or well tested. As Peirce and Dewey have argued, this shift represents one of the great watersheds in the history of scientific philosophy: the abandonment of the quest for certainty. More or less from the time of Aristotle onward, scientists had sought theories that were demonstrable and apodictically certain. Although empiricists and rationalists disagreed about precisely how to certify knowledge as certain and incorrigible, all agreed that science was aiming exclusively at the production of such knowledge. This same view of science largely prevailed at the beginning of the nineteenth century. But by the end of that century this demonstrative and infallibilist ideal was well and truly dead. Scientists of almost every persuasion were insistent that science could, at most, aspire to the status of highly probable knowledge. Certainty, incorrigibility, and indefeasibility ceased to figure among the central aims of most twentieth-century scientists.

The full story surrounding the replacement of the quest for certainty by a thoroughgoing fallibilism is long and complicated; I have attempted to sketch out parts of that story elsewhere.[16] What matters for our purposes here is not so much the details of this epistemic revolution, but the fact that this profound transformation was not specifically associated with the emergence of any new scientific paradigms or research programs. The question of timing is crucial, for it is important to see that this deep shift in axiological sensibilities was independent of any specific change in scientific world view or paradigm. No new scientific tradition or paradigm in the nineteenth century was associated with a specifically fallibilist axiology. Quite the reverse, fallibilism came to be associated with virtually every major program of scientific research by the mid- to late nineteenth century. Atomists and antiatomists, wave theorists and particle theorists, Darwinians and Lamarckians, uniformitarians and catastrophists—all subscribed to the new consensus about the corrigibility and indemonstrability of scientific theories. A similar story could be told about other cognitive values which have gone the way of all flesh. The abandonment of intelligibility, of the requirement of picturable or mechanically constructible models of natural processes, of the insistence on "complete" descriptions of nature—all reveal a similar pattern. The abandonment of each of these cognitive ideals was largely independent of shifts in basic theories about nature.

Once again, the holistic approach leads to expectations that are confounded by the historical record. Changes in values and changes in substantive ontologies or methodologies show no neat isomorphism. Change certainly occurs at all levels, and sometimes changes are concurrent, but there is no striking covariance between the timing of changes at one level and the timing of those at any other. I conclude from such examples that scientific change is substantially more piecemeal than the holistic model would suggest. Value changes do not always accompany, nor are they always accompanied by, changes in scientific paradigm. Shifts in methodological rules may, but need not, be associated with shifts in either values or ontologies. The three levels, although unquestionably interrelated, do not come as an inseparable package on a take-it-or-leave-it basis.

This result is of absolutely decisive importance for understanding the processes of scientific change. Because these changes are not always concomitant, we are often in a position to hold one or two of the three levels fixed while we decide whether to make modifications at the disputed level. The existence of these (temporarily) fixed and thus shared points of perspective provides a crucial form of triangulation. Since theories, methodologies, and axiologies stand together in a kind of justificatory triad, we can use those doctrines about which there is agreement to resolve the remaining areas where we disagree. The uncontested levels will not always resolve the controversy, for underdetermination is an ever present possibility. But the fact that the levels of agreement are sometimes insufficient to terminate the controversy provides no comfort for Kuhn's subjectivist thesis that those levels of agreement are never sufficient to resolve the debate. As logicians say, we need to be very careful about our quantifiers here. Some writers have not always exercised the care they should. Kuhn, for instance, confusedly slides from (*a*) the correct claim that the shared values of scientists are, in certain situations, incapable of yielding unambiguously a preference between two rival theories to (*b*) the surely mistaken claim that the shared values of scientists are never sufficient to warrant a preference between rival paradigms. Manifestly in some instances, the shared rules and standards of methodology are unavailing. But neither Kuhn nor anyone else has established that the rules, evaluative criteria, and values to which scientists subscribe are generally so ambiguous in application that virtually any theory or paradigm can be shown to satisfy them. And we must constantly bear in mind the point that, even when theories are underdetermined by a set of rules or standards, many theories will typically be ruled out by the relevant rules; and if one party to a scientific debate happens to be pushing for a theory that can be shown to violate those rules, then the rules will eliminate that theory from contention.

What has led holistic theorists to misdescribe so badly the relations among these various sorts of changes? As one who was himself once an advocate of such an account, I can explain specifically what led me into thinking that change on the various levels was virtually simultaneous. If one focuses, as most philosophers of science have, on the processes of justification in science, one begins to see systemic linkages among what I earlier called factual, methodological, and axiological ideas. One notices further that beliefs at all three levels shift through time. Under the circumstances it is quite natural to conjecture that these various changes may be interconnected. Specifically, one can imagine that the changes might well be simultaneous, or at least closely dependent on one another. The suggestion is further borne out—at least to a first approximation—by an analysis of some familiar scientific episodes. It is clear, for instance, that the scientific revolution of the seventeenth century brought with it changes in theories, ontologies, rules, and values. Equally, the twentieth-century revolution in relativity theory and quantum mechanics brought in its wake a shift in both methodological and axiological orientations among theoretical physicists. But as I have already suggested, these changes came seriatim, not simultaneously. More to the point, it is my impression that the overwhelming majority of theory transitions in the history of science (including shifts as profound as that from creationist biology to evolution, from energeticist to atomistic views on the nature of matter, from catastrophism to uniformitarianism in geology, from particle to wave theories of light) have not taken place by means of Gestalt-like shifts at all levels concurrently. Often, change occurs on a single level only (e.g., the Darwinian revolution or the triumph of atomism, where it was chiefly theory or ontology that changed); sometimes it occurs on two levels simultaneously; rarely do we find an abrupt and wholesale shift of doctrines at all three levels.

This fact about scientific change has a range of important implications for our understanding of scientific debate and scientific controversy. Leaving aside the atypical case of simultaneous shifts at all three levels (discussed [earlier]), it means that most instances of scientific change—including most of the events we call scientific revolutions—occur amid a significant degree of consensus at a variety of levels among the contending parties. Scientists may, for instance, disagree about specific theories yet agree about the appropriate rules for theory appraisal. They may even disagree about both theories and rules but accept the same cognitive values. Alternatively, they may accept the same theories and rules yet disagree about the cognitive values they espouse. In all these cases there is no reason to speak (with Kuhn) of "incommensurable choices" or "conversion experiences," or (with Foucault) about abrupt "ruptures of thought," for there is in each instance the possibility of bringing the disagreement to rational closure. Of course, it may happen in specific cases that the mechanisms of rational adjudication are of no avail, for the parties may be contending about matters that are underdetermined by the beliefs and standards the contending parties share in common. But, even here, we can still say that there are rational rules governing the game being played, and that the moves being made (i.e., the beliefs being debated and the arguments being arrayed for and against them) are in full compliance with the rules of the game.

Above all, we must bear in mind that it has never been established that such instances of holistic change constitute more than a tiny fraction of scientific disagreements. Because such cases are arguably so atypical, it follows that sociologists and philosophers of science who predicate their theories of scientific change and cognition on the presumed ubiquity of irresolvable standoffs between monolithic world views (of the sort that Kuhn describes in *Structure of Scientific Revolutions*) run the clear risk of failing to recognize the complex ways in which rival theories typically share important background assumptions in common. To put it differently, global claims about the immunity of interparadigmatic disputes to rational adjudication (and such claims are central in the work of both Kuhn and Lakatos) depend for their plausibility on systematically ignoring the piecemeal character of most forms of scientific change and on a gross exaggeration of the impotence of rational considerations to bring such disagreements to closure. Beyond that, I have argued that, even if interparadigmatic clashes had the character Kuhn says they do (namely, of involving little or no overlap at any of the three levels), it still would not follow that there are no rational grounds for a critical and comparative assessment of the rival paradigms. In sum, no adequate support has been provided for the claim that clashes between rival scientific camps can never, or rarely ever, be resolved in an objective fashion. The problem of consensus formation, which I earlier suggested was the great Kuhnian enigma,[17] can be resolved, but only if we realize that science has adjudicatory mechanisms whose existence has gone unnoticed by Kuhn and the other holists.

But it would be misleading to conclude this treatment of Kuhn and the holist theory of theory change on such a triumphal note, for we have yet to confront directly and explicitly another relevant side of Kuhn's work: specifically, his claim, elaborated through a variety of arguments, that methodological rules and shared cognitive values (on which I have laid so much stress as instruments of closure and consensus formation) are impotent to resolve large-scale scientific disagreement. We must now turn to that task directly.

KUHN'S CRITIQUE OF METHODOLOGY

Several writers (e.g., Quine, Hesse, Goodman) have asserted that the rules or principles of scientific appraisal underdetermine theory choice. For reasons I have tried to spell out elsewhere,[18] such a view is badly flawed. Some authors, for instance, tend to confuse the logical underdetermination of theories by data with the underdetermination of theory choice by methodological rules. Others (e.g., Hesse and Bloor) have mistakenly taken the logical underdetermination of theories to be a license for asserting the causal underdetermination of our theoretical beliefs by the sensory evidence to which we are exposed.[19] But there is a weaker, and much more interesting, version of the thesis of underdetermination, which has been developed most fully in Kuhn's recent writings. Indeed, it is one of the strengths of Kuhn's challenge to traditional philosophy of science that he has "localized" and given flesh to the case for underdetermination, in ways that make it prima facie much more telling. In brief, Kuhn's view is this: if we examine situations where scientists are required to make a choice among the handful of paradigms that confront them at any time, we discover that the relevant evidence and appropriate methodological standards fail to pick out one contender as unequivocally superior to its extant rival(s). I call such situations cases of "local" underdetermination, by way of contrasting them with the more global forms of underdetermination (which say, in effect, that the rules are insufficient to pick out any theory as being uniquely supported by the data). Kuhn offers four distinct arguments for local underdetermination. Each is designed to show that, although methodological rules and standards do constrain and delimit a scientist's choices or options, those rules and standards are never sufficient to compel or unequivocally to warrant the choice of one paradigm over another.

1) *The "ambiguity of shared standards" argument.*—Kuhn's first argument for methodological underdetermination rests on the purported ambiguity of the methodological rules or standards that are shared by advocates of rival paradigms. The argument first appeared in *The Structure of Scientific Revolutions* (1962) and has been extended considerably in his later *The Essential Tension* (1977). As he put it in the earlier work, "lifelong resistance [to a new theory] . . . is not a violation of scientific standards . . . though the historian can always find men—Priestley, for instance—who were unreasonable to resist for as long as they did, he will not find a point at which resistance becomes illogical or unscientific."[20] Many of Kuhn's readers were perplexed by the juxtaposition of claims in such passages as these. On the one hand, we are told that Priestley's continued refusal to accept the theory of Lavoisier was "unreasonable"; but we are also told that Priestley's refusal was neither "illogical" nor "unscientific." To those inclined to think that being "scientific" (at least in the usual sense of that term) required one to be "reasonable" about shaping one's beliefs, Kuhn seemed to be talking gibberish. On a more sympathetic construal, Kuhn seemed to be saying that a scientist could always interpret the applicable standards of appraisal, whatever they might be, so as to "rationalize" his

own paradigmatic preferences, whatever they might be. This amounts to claiming that the methodological rules or standards of science never make a real or decisive difference to the outcome of a process of theory choice; if any set of rules can be used to justify any theory whatever, then methodology would seem to amount to just so much window dressing. But that construal, it turns out, is a far cry from what Kuhn intended. As he has made clear in later writings, he wants to bestow a positive, if (compared with the traditional view) much curtailed, role on methodological standards in scientific choice.

What Kuhn apparently has in mind is that the shared criteria, standards, and rules to which scientists explicitly and publicly refer in justifying their choices of theory and paradigm are typically "ambiguous" and "imprecise," so much so that "individuals [who share the same standards] may legitimately differ about their application to concrete cases." [21] Kuhn holds that, although scientists share certain cognitive values "and must do so if science is to survive, they do not all apply them in the same way. Simplicity, scope, fruitfulness, and even accuracy can be judged differently (which is not to say they may be judged arbitrarily) by different people." [22] Because, then, the shared standards are ambiguous, two scientists may subscribe to "exactly the same standard" (say, the rule of simplicity) and yet endorse opposing viewpoints.

Kuhn draws some quite large inferences from the presumed ambiguity of the shared standards or criteria. Specifically, he concludes that every case of theory choice must involve an admixture of objective and subjective factors, since (in Kuhn's view) the shared, and presumably objective, criteria are too amorphous and ambiguous to warrant a particular preference. He puts the point this way: "I continue to hold that the algorithms of individuals are all ultimately different by virtue of the subjective considerations with which each [scientist] must complete the objective criteria before any computations can be done." [23] As this passage makes clear, Kuhn believes that, because the shared criteria are too imprecise to justify a choice, and because—despite that imprecision—scientists do manage to make choices, those choices *must* be grounded in individual and subjective preferences different from those of his fellow scientists. As he says, "every individual choice between competing theories depends on a mixture of objective and subjective factors, or of shared and individual criteria." [24] And, the shared criteria "are not by themselves sufficient to determine the decisions of individual scientists." [25]

This very ambitious claim, if true, would force us to drastically rethink our views of scientific rationality. Among other things, it would drive us to the conclusion that every scientist has different reasons for his theory preferences from those of his fellow scientists. The view entails, among other things, that it is a category mistake to ask (say) why physicists think Einstein's theories are better than Newton's; for, on Kuhn's analysis, there must be as many different answers as there are physicists. We might note in passing that this is quite an ironic conclusion for Kuhn to reach. Far more than most writers on these subjects, he has tended to stress the importance of community and socialization processes in understanding the scientific enterprise. Yet the logic of his own analysis drives him to the radically individualistic position that every scientist has his own set of reasons for theory preferences and that there is no real consensus whatever with respect to the grounds for theory preference, not even among the advocates of the same paradigm. Seen from this perspective, Kuhn tackles what I earlier called the problem of consensus by a maneuver that trivializes the problem: for if we must give a separate and discrete explanation for the theory preferences of each member of the scientific community—which is what Kuhn's view entails—then we are confronted with a gigantic mystery at the collective level, to wit, why the scientists in a given discipline—each supposedly operating with his own individualistic and idiosyncratic criteria, each giving a different "gloss" to the criteria that are shared—are so often able to agree about which theories to bet on. But we can leave it to Kuhn to sort out how he reconciles his commitment to the social psychology of science with his views about the individual vagaries of theory preference. What must concern us is the question whether Kuhn has made a plausible case for thinking that the shared or collective criteria must be supplemented by individual and subjective criteria.

The first point to stress is that Kuhn's thesis purports to apply to all scientific rules or values that are shared by the partisans of rival paradigms, not just to a selected few, notoriously ambiguous ones. We can grant straightaway that some of the rules, standards, and values used by scientists ("simplicity" would be an obvious candidate) exhibit precisely that high degree of ambiguity which Kuhn ascribes to them. But Kuhn's general argument for the impotence of shared rules to settle disagreements between scientists working in different paradigms cannot be established by citing the occasional example. Kuhn must show us, for he claims as much, that there is something in the very nature of those methodological rules that come to be shared among scientists which makes the application of those rules or standards invariably inconclusive. He has not established this result, and there is a good reason why he has not: it is false. To see that it is, one need only produce a methodological rule widely accepted by scientists which can be applied to concrete cases without substantial imprecision or ambiguity. Consider, for instance, one of Kuhn's own examples of a widely shared scientific standard, namely, the requirement that an acceptable theory must be internally consistent and logically consistent with accepted theories in other fields. (One may or may not favor this methodological rule. I refer to it here only because it is commonly regarded, including by Kuhn, as a methodological rule that frequently plays a role in theory evaluation.)

I submit that we have a very clear notion of what it is for a theory to be internally consistent, just as we understand perfectly well what it means for a theory to be consistent with accepted beliefs. Moreover, on at least some occasions we can tell whether a particular theory has violated the standard of (internal or external) consistency. Kuhn himself, in a revealing passage, grants as much; for instance, when comparing the relative merits of geocentric and heliocentric astronomy, Kuhn says that "the consistency criterion, by itself, therefore, spoke unequivocally for the geocentric tradition."[26] (What he has in mind is the fact that heliocentric astronomy, when introduced, was inconsistent with the then reigning terrestrial physics, whereas the assumptions of geocentric astronomy were consistent with that physics.) Note that in this case we have a scientific rule or criterion "speaking unequivocally" in favor of one theory and against its rival. Where are the inevitable imprecision and ambiguity which are supposed by Kuhn to afflict all the shared values of the scientific community? What is ambiguous about the notion of consistency? The point of these rhetorical questions is to drive home the fact that, even by Kuhn's lights, some of the rules or criteria widely accepted in the scientific community do not exhibit that multiplicity of meanings which Kuhn has described as being entirely characteristic of methodological standards.

One could, incidentally, cite several other examples of reasonably clear and unambiguous methodological rules. For instance, the requirements that theories should be deductively closed or that theories should be subjected to controlled experiments have not generated a great deal of confusion or disagreement among scientists about what does and does not constitute closure or a control. Or, consider the rule that theories should lead successfully to the prediction of results unknown to their discoverer; so far as I am aware, scientists have not differed widely in their construal of the meaning of this rule. The significance of the nonambiguity of many methodological concepts and rules is to be found in the fact that such nonambiguity refutes one of Kuhn's central arguments for the incomparability of paradigms and for its corollary, the impotence of methodology as a guide to scientific rationality. There are at least some rules that are sufficiently determinate that one can show that many theories clearly fail to satisfy them. We need not supplement the shared content of these objective concepts with any private notions of our own in order to decide whether a theory satisfies them.

2) *The "collective inconsistency of rules" argument.* — As if the ambiguity of standards was not bad enough, Kuhn goes on to argue that the shared rules and standards, when taken as a collective, "repeatedly prove to conflict with one another." [27] For instance, two scientists may each believe that empirical accuracy and generality are desirable traits in a theory. But, when confronted with a pair of rival (and thus incompatible) theories, one of which is more accurate and the other more general, the judgments of those scientists may well differ about which theory to accept. One scientist may opt for the more general theory; the other, for the more accurate. They evidently share the same standards, says Kuhn, but they end up with conflicting appraisals. Kuhn puts it this way: ". . . in many concrete situations, different values, though all constitutive of good reasons, dictate different conclusions, different choices. In such cases of value-conflict (e.g., one theory is simpler but the other is more accurate) the relative weight placed on different values by different individuals can play a decisive role in individual choice." [28]

Because many methodological standards do pull in different directions, Kuhn thinks that the scientist can pretty well go whichever way he likes. Well, not quite any direction he likes, since — even by Kuhn's very liberal rules — it would be unreasonable for a scientist to prefer a theory (or paradigm) which failed to satisfy any of the constraints. In Kuhn's view, we should expect scientific disagreement or dissensus to emerge specifically in those cases where (*a*) no available theory satisfied all the constraints and (*b*) every extant theory satisfied some constraints not satisfied by its rivals. That scientists sometimes find themselves subscribing to contrary standards, I would be the first to grant. Indeed, . . . the discovery of that fact about oneself is often the first prod toward readjusting one's cognitive values. But Kuhn is not merely saying that this happens occasionally; he is asserting that such is the nature of any set of rules or standards which any group of reasonable scientists might accept. As before, our verdict has to be that Kuhn's highly ambitious claim is just that; he never shows us why families of methodological rules should always or even usually be internally inconsistent. He apparently expects us to take his word for it that he is just telling it as it is. [29] I see no reason why we should follow Kuhn in his global extrapolations from the tiny handful of cases he describes. On the contrary, there are good grounds for resisting, since there are plenty of sets of consistent methodological standards. Consider, for instance, one of the most influential documents of nineteenth-century scientific methodology, John Stuart Mill's *System of Logic.* Mill offered there a set of rules or canons for assessing the soundness of causal hypotheses. Nowadays those rules are still called "Mill's methods," and much research in the natural and social sciences utilizes them, often referring to them as the methods of agreement, difference, and concomitant variations. To the best of my knowledge, no one has ever shown that Mill's methods exhibit a latent tendency toward contradiction or conflict of the sort that Kuhn regards as typical of systems of methodological rules. To go back further in history, no one has ever shown that Bacon's or Descartes's or Newton's or Herschel's famous canons of reasoning are internally inconsistent. The fact that numerous methodologies of science may be cited which have never been shown to be inconsistent casts serious doubts on Kuhn's claim that any methodological standards apt to be shared by rival scientists will tend to exhibit mutual inconsistencies.

Kuhn could have strengthened his argument considerably if, instead of focusing on the purported tensions in sets of methodological rules, he had noted, rather, that whenever one has more than one standard in operation, it is conceivable that we will be torn in several directions. And this claim is true, regardless of whether the standards are strictly inconsistent with one another or not (just so long as there is not a complete covariance between their instances). If two scientists agree to judge theories by two standards, then it is trivially true that, depending upon how much weight each gives to the two standards, their judgments about theories may differ. Before we can make sense of how to work with several concurrent standards, we have to ask (as Kuhn never did) about the way in which these standards do (or should) control the selection of a preferred theory. Until we know the answer to that question, we will inevitably find that the standards are of little use in explaining scientific preferences. Kuhn simply assumes that all possible preference structures (i.e., all possible differential weightings of the applicable standards) are equally viable or equally likely to be exemplified in a working scientist's selection procedures. The analysis of cognitive values offered [earlier] shows that this assumption is ill advised.

To sum up the argument to this point: I have shown that Kuhn is wrong in claiming that all methodological rules are inevitably ambiguous and in claiming that scientific methodologies consisting of whole groups of rules always or even usually exhibit a high degree of internal "tension." Since these two claims were the linchpins in Kuhn's argument to the effect that shared criteria "are not by themselves sufficient to determine the decisions of individual scientists,"[30] we are entitled to say that Kuhn's effort to establish a general form of local underdetermination falls flat.

3) *The shifting standards argument.* — Equally important to Kuhn's critique of methodology is a set of arguments having to do with the manner in which standards are supposed to vary from one scientist to another. In treating Kuhn's views on this matter, I follow Gerald Doppelt's excellent and sympathetic explication of Kuhn's position.[31] In general, Kuhn's model of science envisages two quite distinct ways in which disagreements about standards might render scientific debate indeterminate or inconclusive. In the first place, the advocates of different paradigms may subscribe to different methodological rules or evaluative criteria. Indeed, "may" is too weak a term here, for, as we have seen, Kuhn evidently believes that associated

with each paradigm is a set of methodological orientations that are (at least partly) at odds with the methodologies of all rival paradigms. Thus, he insists that whenever a "paradigm shift" occurs, this process produces "changes in the standards governing permissible problems, concepts and explanations."[32] This is quite a strong claim. It implies, among other things, that the advocates of different paradigms invariably have different views about what constitutes a scientific explanation and even about what constitutes the relevant facts to be explained (viz., the "permissible problems"). If Kuhn is right about these matters, then debate between the proponents of two rival paradigms will involve appeal to different sets of rules and standards associated respectively with the two paradigms. One party to the dispute may be able to show that his theory is best by his standards, while his opponent may be able to claim superiority by his.

As I have shown in detail earlier in this [reading], Kuhn is right to say that scientists sometimes subscribe to different methodologies (including different standards for explanation and facticity). But he has never shown, and I believe him to be chronically wrong in claiming, that disagreements about matters of standards and rules neatly coincide with disagreements about substantive matters of scientific ontology. Rival scientists advocating fundamentally different theories or paradigms often have the same standards of assessment (and interpret them identically); on the other hand, adherents to the same paradigm will frequently espouse different standards. In short, methodological disagreements and factual disagreements about basic theories show no striking covariances of the kind required to sustain Kuhn's argument about the intrinsic irresolvability of interparadigmatic debate. It was the thrust of my earlier account of "piecemeal change" to show why Kuhn's claims about irresolvability will not work.

But, of course, a serious issue raised by Kuhn still remains before us. If different scientists sometimes subscribe to different standards of appraisal (and that much is surely correct), then how is it possible for us to speak of the resolution of such disagreements as anything other than an arbitrary closure? To raise that question presupposes a picture of science which I sought to demolish [earlier]. Provided there are mechanisms for rationally resolving disagreements about methodological rules and cognitive values . . . , the fact that scientists often disagree about such rules and values need not, indeed should not, be taken to show that there must be anything arbitrary about the resolution of such disagreements.

4) *The problem-weighting argument.*—As I have said earlier, Kuhn has another argument up his sleeve which he and others think is germane to the issue of the rationality of comparative theory assessment. Specifically, he insists that the advocates of rival paradigms assign differential degrees of importance to the solution of different sorts of problems. Because they do, he says that they will often disagree about which theory is better supported, since one side will argue that it is most important to solve a certain problem, while the other will insist on the centrality of solving a different problem. Kuhn poses the difficulty in these terms: "if there were but one set of scientific problems, one world within which to work on them, and one set of standards for their solution, paradigm competition might be settled more or less routinely by some process like counting the number of problems solved by each. But, in fact, these conditions are never met completely. The proponents of competing paradigms are always at least slightly at cross purposes . . . the proponents will often disagree about the list of problems that any candidate for paradigm must resolve."[33]

In this passage Kuhn runs together two issues which it is well to separate: one concerns the question (just addressed in the preceding section) about whether scientists have different standards of explanation or solution; the other (and the one that concerns us here) is the claim that scientists working in different paradigms want to solve different problems and that, because they do, their appraisals of the merits of theories will typically differ. So we must here deal with the case where scientists have the same standards for what counts as solving a problem but where they disagree about which problems are the most important to solve. As Kuhn puts it, "scientific controversies between the advocates of rival paradigms involve the question: which problems is it more significant to have solved? Like the issue of competing standards, that question of values can be answered only in terms of criteria that lie outside of normal science altogether."[34] Kuhn is surely right to insist that partisans of different global theories or paradigms often disagree about which problems it is most important to solve. But the existence of such disagreement does not establish that interparadigmatic debate about the epistemic support of rival paradigms is inevitably inconclusive or that it must be resolved by factors that lie outside the normal resources of scientific inquiry.

At first glance, Kuhn's argument seems very plausible: the differing weights assigned to the solution of specific problems by the advocates of rival paradigms may apparently lead to a situation in which the advocates of rival paradigms can each assert that their respective paradigms are the best because they solve precisely those problems they respectively believe to be the most important. No form of reasoning, insists Kuhn, could convince either side of the merits of the opposition or of the weakness of its own approach in such circumstances.

To see where Kuhn's argument goes astray in this particular instance, we need to dissect it at a more basic level. Specifically, we need to distinguish two quite distinct senses in which solving a problem may be said to be important. A problem may be important to a scientist just in the sense that he is particularly curious about it. Equally, it may be important because there is some urgent social or economic reason for solving it. Both sorts of considerations may explain why a scientist regards it as urgent to solve the problem. Such concerns are clearly relevant to explaining the motivation of scientists. But these senses of problem importance have no particular epistemic or probative significance. When we are assessing the evidential support for a theory, when we are asking how well supported or well tested that theory is by the available data, we are not asking whether the theory solves problems that are socially or personally important. Importance, in the sense chiefly relevant to this discussion, is what we might call epistemic or probative importance. One problem is of greater epistemic or probative significance than another if the former constitutes a more telling test of our theories than does the latter.

So, if Kuhn's point is to be of any significance for the epistemology of science (or, what amounts to the same thing, if we are asking how beliefworthy a theory is), then we must imagine a situation in which the advocates of different paradigms assign conflicting degrees of epistemic import to the solution of certain problems. Kuhn's thesis about such situations would be, I presume, that there is no rational machinery for deciding who is right about the assignment of epistemic weight to such problems. But that seems wrongheaded, or at least unargued, for philosophers of science have long and plausibly maintained that the primary function of scientific epistemology is precisely to ascertain the (epistemic) importance of any piece of confirming or disconfirming evidence. It is not open to a scientist simply to say that solving an arbitrarily selected problem (however great its subjective significance) is of high probative value. Indeed, it is often true that the epistemically most salient problems are ones with little or no prior practical or even heuristic significance. (Consider that Brownian motion was of decisive epistemic significance in discrediting classical thermodynamics, even though such motion had little intrinsic interest prior to Einstein's showing that such motion was anomalous for thermodynamics.) The whole point of the theory of evidence is to desubjectify the assignment of evidential significance by indicating the kinds of reasons that can legitimately be given for attaching a particular degree of epistemic importance to a confirming or refuting instance. Thus, if one maintains that the ability of a theory to solve a certain problem is much more significant epistemically than its ability to solve another, one must be able to give reasons for that epistemic preference. Put differently, one has to be able to show that the probative significance of the one problem for testing theories of a certain sort is indeed greater than that of the other. He might do so by showing that the former outcome was much more surprising than or more general than the latter. One may thus be able to motivate a claim for the greater importance of the first problem over the second by invoking relevant epistemic and methodological criteria. But if none of these options is open to him, if he can answer the question, "Why is solving this problem more important probatively than solving that one?" only by replying, in effect, "because I am interested in solving this rather than that," then he has surrendered any claim to be shaping his beliefs rationally in light of the available evidence.

We can put the point more generally: the rational assignment of any particular degree of probative significance to a problem must rest on one's being able to show that there are viable methodological and epistemic grounds for assigning that degree of importance rather than another. Once we see this, it becomes clear that the degree of empirical support which a solved problem confers on a paradigm is not simply a matter of how keenly the proponents of that paradigm want to solve the problem.

Let me expand on this point by using an example cited extensively by both Kuhn and Doppelt: the Daltonian "revolution" in chemistry. As Doppelt summarizes the Kuhnian position, ". . . the pre-Daltonian chemistry of the phlogiston theory and the theory of elective affinity achieved reasonable answers to a whole set of questions effectively abandoned by Dalton's new chemistry."[35] Because Dalton's chemistry failed to address many of the questions answered by the older chemical paradigm, Kuhn thinks that the acceptance of Dalton's approach deprived "chemistry of some actual and much potential explanatory power."[36] Indeed, Kuhn is right in holding that, during most of the nineteenth century, Daltonian chemists were unable to explain many things that the older chemical traditions could make sense of. On the other hand, as Kuhn stresses, Daltonian chemistry could explain a great deal that had eluded earlier chemical theories. In short, "the two paradigms seek to explain different kinds of observational data, in response to different agendas of problems."[37] This "loss" of solved problems during transitions from one major theory to another is an important insight of Kuhn's; in chapter 5 [of my *Science and Values,* op. cit.] I trace out some of the implications of noncumulative theory change for scientific epistemology. But this loss of problem-solving ability through paradigm change, although real enough, does not entail, as Kuhn claims, that proponents of old and new paradigms will necessarily be unable to make congruent assessments of how well tested or well supported their respective paradigms are.

What leads Kuhn and Doppelt to think otherwise is their assumption that the centrality of a problem on one's explanatory agenda necessarily entails one's assigning a high degree of epistemic or probative weight to that problem when it comes to determining how well supported a certain theory or paradigm is. But that assumption is usually false. In general, the observations to which a reasonable scientist attaches the most probative or epistemic weight are those instances that test a theory especially "severely" (to use Popper's splendid term). The instances of greatest probative weight in the history of science (e.g., the oblate shape of the "spherical" earth, the Arago disk experiment, the bending of light near the sun, the recession of Mercury's perihelion, the reconstitution of white light from the spectrum) have generally not been instances high on the list of problems that scientists developed their theories to solve. A test instance acquires high probative weight when, for example, it involves testing one of a theory's surprising or counterintuitive predictions, or when it represents a kind of crucial experiment between rival theories. The point is that a problem or instance does not generally acquire great probative strength in testing a theory simply because the advocates of that theory would like to be able to solve the problem. Quite the reverse, many scientists and philosophers would say. After all, it is conventional wisdom that a theory is not very acutely tested if its primary empirical support is drawn from the very sort of situations it was designed to explain. Most theories of experimental design urge—in sharp contrast with Kuhn—that theories should not be given high marks simply because they can solve the problems they were invented to solve. In arguing that the explanatory agenda a scientist sets for himself automatically dictates that scientist's reasoned judgments about well-testedness, Kuhn and Doppelt seem to have profoundly misconstrued the logic of theory appraisal.

Let us return for a moment to Kuhn's Dalton example. If I am right, Dalton might readily have conceded that pre-Daltonian chemistry solved a number of problems that his theory failed to address. Judged as theories about the qualitative properties of chemical reagents, those theories could even be acknowledged as well supported *of their type*. But Dalton's primary interests lie elsewhere, for he presumably regarded those earlier theories as failing to address what he considered to be the central problems of chemistry. But this is not an epistemic judgment; it is a pragmatic one. It amounts to saying: "These older theories are well-tested and reliable theories for explaining certain features of chemical change; but those features happen not to interest me very much." In sum, Kuhn and Doppelt have failed to offer us any grounds for thinking that a scientist's judgment about the degree of evidential support for a paradigm should or does reflect his personal views about the problems he finds most interesting. That, in turn, means that one need not share an enthusiasm for a certain paradigm's explanatory agenda in order to decide whether the theories that make up that paradigm are well tested or ill tested. It appears to me that what the Kuhn-Doppelt point really amounts to is the truism that scientists tend to invest their efforts exploring paradigms that address problems those scientists find interesting. That is a subjective and pragmatic matter which can, and should, be sharply distinguished from the question whether one paradigm or theory is better tested or better supported than its rivals. Neither Kuhn nor Doppelt has made plausible the claim that, because two scientists have different degrees of interest in solving different sorts of problems, it follows that their epistemic judgments of which theories are well tested and which are not will necessarily differ.

We are thus in a position to conclude that the existence of conflicting views among scientists about which problems are interesting apparently entails nothing about the *incompatibility* or *incommensurability* of the epistemic appraisals those scientists will make. That in turn means that these real differences of problem-solving emphasis between advocates of rival paradigms do nothing to undermine the viability of a methodology of comparative theory assessment, insofar as such a methodology is epistemically rather than pragmatically oriented. It seems likely that Kuhn and Doppelt have fallen into this confusion because of their failure to see that acknowledged differences in the motivational appeal of various problems to various scientists constitutes no rationale for asserting the existence of correlative differences in the probative weights properly assigned to those problems by those same scientists.

The appropriate conclusion to draw from the features of scientific life to which Kuhn and Doppelt properly direct our attention is that the pursuit of (and doubtless the recruitment of scientists into) rival paradigms is influenced by pragmatic as well as by epistemic considerations. That is an interesting thesis, and probably a sound one, but it does nothing to undermine the core premise of scientific epistemology: that there are principles of empirical or evidential support which are neither paradigm-specific, hopelessly vague, nor individually idiosyncratic. More important, these principles are sometimes sufficient to guide our preferences unambiguously.[38]

NOTES

[1] Alan Musgrave spoke for many of Kuhn's readers when he noted, apropos of the second edition of *The Structure of Scientific Revolutions,* that in "his recent writings, then, Kuhn disowns most of the challenging ideas ascribed to him by his critics . . . the new, more real Kuhn who emerges . . . [is] but a pale reflection of the old, revolutionary Kuhn" (Musgrave, 1980, p. 51).

[2] It has been insufficiently noted just how partial Kuhn's break with positivism is, so far as cognitive goals and values are concerned. As I show in detail below, most of his problems about the alleged incomparability of theories arise because Kuhn accepts without argument the positivist claim that cognitive values or standards at the top of the hierarchy are fundamentally immune to rational negotiation.

[3] Kuhn, 1962.

[4] Ibid.

[5] Ibid., p. 159.

[6] As Kuhn himself remarks, he has been attempting "to eliminate misunderstandings for which my own past rhetoric is doubtless partially responsible" (1970, pp. 259–260).

[7] Kuhn, 1962, p. 108; my italics.

[8] Ibid., pp. 108–109.

[9] Ibid., p. 149.

[10] [L. Lauden, *Science and Values,* Berkeley, California: University of California Press, 1984.]

[11] See Whewell's remarkably insightful essay of 1851, where he remarks, apropos the transition from one global theory to another: "the change . . . is effected by a transformation, or series of transformations, of the earlier hypothesis, by means of which it is brought nearer and nearer to the second [i.e., later]" (1851, p. 139).

[12] Some amplification of this point is required. Kuhn evidently believes that there are some values that transcend specific paradigms. He mentions such examples as the demand for accuracy, consistency, and simplicity.

The fortunes of these values are not linked to specific paradigms. Thus, if they were to change, such change would presumably be independent of shifts in paradigms. In Kuhn's view, however, these values have persisted unchanged since the seventeenth century. Or, rather, scientists have invoked these values persistently since that time; strictly speaking, on Kuhn's analysis, these values are changing constantly, since each scientist interprets them slightly differently. For a detailed discussion of Kuhn's handling of these quasi-shared values, see the final section of this [reading].

[13] See Laudan, 1981.

[14] For a discussion of the difference between explicit and implicit methodology, see [L. Laudan, *Science and Values, op cit.,*] chap. 3, pp. 53 ff.

[15] For an extensive bibliography on this issue, see Laudan, 1968.

[16] See Laudan, 1981.

[17] See [Laudan, *Science and Values, op. cit.,*] chap. 1.

[18] See Laudan, forthcoming.

[19] See ibid. for a lengthy treatment of some issues surrounding underdetermination of theories.

[20] Kuhn, 1962, p. 159.

[21] Kuhn, 1977, p. 322.

[22] Ibid., p. 262.

[23] Ibid., p. 329.

[24] Ibid., p. 325; see also p. 324.

[25] Ibid., p. 325.

[26] Ibid., p. 323.

[27] Ibid., p. 322.

[28] Kuhn, 1970, p. 262.

[29] "What I have said so far is primarily simply descriptive of what goes on in the sciences at times of theory choice" (Kuhn, 1977, p. 325).

[30] Kuhn, 1977, p. 325.

[31] Doppelt, 1978. Whereas Kuhn's own discussion of these questions in *The Structure of Scientific Revolutions* rambles considerably, Doppelt offers a succinct and perspicacious formulation of what is, or at least what should have been, Kuhn's argument. Although I quarrel with Doppelt's analysis at several important points, my own thoughts about these issues owe a great deal to his writings.

[32] Kuhn, 1962, p. 104.

[33] Ibid., pp. 147–148.

[34] Ibid., p. 110.

[35] Doppelt, 1978, p. 42.

[36] Kuhn, 1962, p. 107.

[37] Ibid., p. 43.

[38] Even on the pragmatic level, however, it is not clear that the Doppeltian version of Kuhn's relativistic picture of scientific change will stand up, for Doppelt is at pains to deny that there can be any short-term resolution between the advocates of rival axiologies. If the arguments of the preceding chapter have any cogency, it seems entirely possible that pragmatic relativism, every bit as much as its epistemic counterpart, is question begging.

REFERENCES

Doppelt, Gerald (1978). "Kuhn's Epistemological Relativism: An Interpretation and Defense," *Inquiry* 21:33–86.

Gutting, Gary, ed. (1980). *Paradigms and Revolutions.* Notre Dame: University of Notre Dame Press.

Kuhn, Thomas (1962). *The Structure of Scientific Revolutions.* Chicago: University of Chicago Press.

——— (1970). "Reflections on My Critics." In I. Lakatos and A. Musgrave, *Criticism and the Growth of Knowledge.* Cambridge: Cambridge University Press.

——— (1977). *The Essential Tension.* Chicago: University of Chicago Press.
Laudan, Larry (1968). "Theories of Scientific Method from Plato to Mach," *History of Science* 7:1–63.
——— (1981). *Science and Hypothesis.* Dordrecht: Reidel.
——— (forthcoming). *Science and Method.*
Musgrave, Alan (1980). "Kuhn's Second Thoughts." In Gutting, 1980.
Whewell, William (1851). "Of the Transformation of Hypotheses in the History of Science," *Transactions of the Cambridge Philosophical Society* 9:139–147.

K A R L   P O P P E R
THE RATIONALITY OF SCIENTIFIC REVOLUTIONS

The title of this series of Spencer lectures, *Progress and Obstacles to Progress in the Sciences,* was chosen by the organizers of the series. The title seems to me to imply that progress in science is a good thing, and that an obstacle to progress is a bad thing, a position held by almost everybody, until quite recently. Perhaps I should make clear at once that I accept this position, although with some slight and fairly obvious reservations to which I shall briefly allude later. Of course, obstacles which are due to the inherent difficulty of the problems tackled are welcome challenges. (Indeed, many scientists were greatly disappointed when it turned out that the problem of tapping nuclear energy was comparatively trivial, involving no new revolutionary change of theory.) But stagnation in science would be a curse. Still, I agree with Professor Bodmer's suggestion that scientific advance is only a *mixed* blessing.[1] Let us face it: Blessings *are* mixed, with some exceedingly rare exceptions.

My talk will be divided into two parts. The first part (Sections I–VIII) is devoted to progress in science, and the second part (Sections IX–XIV) to some of the social obstacles to progress. [Sections V–VII are not reprinted here.]

Remembering Herbert Spencer, I shall discuss progress in science largely *from an evolutionary point of view*—more precisely, from the point of view of the theory of natural selection. Only the end of the first part (that is, Section VIII), will be spent in discussing the progress of science *from a logical point of view,* and in proposing *two rational criteria* of progress in science, which will be needed in the second part of my talk.

In the second part I shall discuss a few obstacles to progress in science, more especially ideological obstacles; and I shall end (Sections XI–XIV) by discussing the distinction between, on the one hand, *scientific revolutions,* which are subject to rational criteria of progress, and on the other hand, *ideological revolutions,* which are only rarely rationally defensible. It appeared to me that this distinction was sufficiently interesting to call my lecture "The Rationality of Scientific Revolutions." The emphasis here must be, of course, on the word "scientific."

I

I now turn to progress in science. I will be looking at progress in science from a biological or evolutionary point of view. I am far from suggesting that this is the most important point of view for examining progress in science. But the biological approach offers a convenient way of introducing the two leading ideas of the first half of my talk. They are the ideas of *instruction* and of *selection.*

From a biological or evolutionary point of view, science, or progress in science, may be regarded as a means used by the human species to adapt itself to the environment: to invade

I wish to thank Troels Eggers Hansen, The Rev. Michael Sharratt, Dr. Herbert Spengler, and Dr. Martin Wenham for critical comments on this lecture.

new environmental niches, and even to invent new environmental niches.[2] This leads to the following problem.

We can distinguish between three levels of adaptation: genetic adaptation; adaptive behavioral learning; and scientific discovery, which is a special case of adaptive behavioral learning. My main problem in this part of my talk will be to enquire into the similarities and dissimilarities between the strategies of progress or adaptation on the *scientific* level and on those two other levels: the *genetic* level and the *behavioral* level. And I will compare the three levels of adaptation by investigating the role played on each level by *instruction* and by *selection*.

II

In order not to lead you blindfolded to the result of this comparison I will anticipate at once my main thesis. It is a thesis asserting the *fundamental similarity of the three levels,* as follows.

On all three levels—genetic adaptation, adaptive behavior, and scientific discovery—the mechanism of adaptation is fundamentally the same.

This can be explained in some detail.

Adaptation starts from an inherited *structure* which is basic for all three levels: *the gene structure of the organism.* To it corresponds, on the behavioral level, *the innate repertoire* of the types of behavior which are available to the organism, and on the scientific level, *the dominant scientific conjectures or theories.* These *structures* are always transmitted by *instruction,* on all three levels: by the replication of the coded genetic instruction on the genetic and the behavioral levels, and by social tradition and imitation on the behavioral and the scientific levels. On all three levels, the *instruction* comes from *within the structure.* If mutations or variations or errors occur, then these are new instructions, which also arise *from within the structure,* rather than *from without,* from the environment.

These inherited structures are exposed to certain pressures, or challenges, or problems: to selection pressures; to environmental challenges; to theoretical problems. In response, variations of the genetically or traditionally inherited *instructions* are produced[3] *by* methods which are at least partly *random.* On the genetic level, these are mutations and recombinations[4] of the coded instruction; on the behavioral level, they are tentative variations and recombinations within the repertoire; on the scientific level, they are new and revolutionary tentative theories. On all three levels we get new tentative trial instructions, or, briefly, tentative trials.

It is important that these tentative trials are changes that originate *within* the individual structure in a more or less random fashion—on all three levels. The view that they are *not* due to instruction from without, from the environment, is supported (if only weakly) by the fact that very similar organisms may sometimes respond in very different ways to the same new environmental challenge.

The next stage is that of *selection* from the available mutations and variations: those of the new tentative trials which are badly adapted are eliminated. *This is the stage of the elimination of error.* Only the more or less well adapted trial instructions survive and are inherited in their turn. Thus we may speak of *adaptation by "the method of trial and error"* or better, by "the method of trial and the elimination of error." The elimination of error, or of badly adapted trial instructions, is also called *natural selection:* it is a kind of "negative feedback." It operates on all three levels.

It is to be noted that in general *no equilibrium state of adaptation* is reached by any one application of the method of trial and the elimination of error, or by natural selection. First, because no perfect or optimal trial solutions to the problem are likely to be offered; secondly—and this is more important—because the emergence of new structures, or of new instructions, involves a change in the environmental situation. New elements of the environment may become relevant; and in consequence, new pressures, new challenges, new problems may arise, as a result of the structural changes which have arisen from within the organism.

On the genetic level the change may be a mutation of a gene, with a consequent change of an enzyme. Now the network of enzymes forms the more intimate environment of the gene structure. Accordingly, there will be a change in this intimate environment; and with it, new relationships between the organism and the more remote environment may arise; and further, new selection pressures.

The same happens on the behavioral level, for the adoption of a new kind of behavior can be equated in most cases with the adoption of a new ecological niche. As a consequence, new selection pressures will arise, and new genetic changes.

On the scientific level, the tentative adoption of a new conjecture or theory may solve one or two problems, but it invariably opens up many *new* problems; for a new revolutionary theory functions exactly like a new and powerful sense organ. If the progress is significant then the new problems will differ from the old problems: The new problems will be on a radically different level of depth. This happened, for example, in relativity; it happened in quantum mechanics; and it happens right now, most dramatically, in molecular biology. In each of these cases, new horizons of unexpected problems were opened up by the new theory.

This, I suggest, is the way in which science progresses. And our progress can best be gauged by comparing our old problems with our new ones. If the progress that has been made is great, then the new problems will be of a character undreamt of before. There will be deeper problems, and, besides, there will be more of them. The further we progress in knowledge, the more clearly we can discern the vastness of our ignorance.[5]

I will now sum up my thesis.

On all the three levels which I am considering—the genetic, the behavioral, and the scientific levels—we are operating with inherited structures which are passed on by instruction, either through the genetic code or through tradition. On all the three levels, new structures and new instructions arise by trial changes from *within the structure:* by tentative trials which are subject to natural selection or the elimination of error.

III

So far I have stressed the *similarities* in the working of the adaptive mechanism on the three levels. This raises an obvious problem: What about the *differences?*

The main difference between the genetic and the behavioral level is this. Mutations on the genetic level are not only random but completely "blind," in two senses.[6] First, they are in no way goal directed. Secondly, the survival of a mutation cannot influence the further mutations, not even the frequencies or probabilities of their occurrence; though admittedly, the *survival* of a mutation may sometimes determine what kind of mutations may possibly *survive* in future cases. On the behavioral level, trials are also more or less random, but they are no longer completely "blind" in either of the two senses mentioned. First, they are goal directed; and secondly, animals may learn from the outcome of a trial: They may learn to avoid the type of trial behavior which has led to a failure. (They may even avoid it in cases in which it could have succeeded.) Similarly, they may also learn from success; and successful behavior may be repeated, even in cases in which it is not adequate. However, a certain degree of "blindness" is inherent in all trials.[7]

Behavioral adaptation is usually an intensely active process: The animal—especially the young animal at play—and even the plant, are actively investigating the environment.[8]

This activity, which is largely genetically programmed, seems to me to mark an important difference between the genetic level and the behavioral level. I may here refer to the experience which the Gestalt psychologists call "insight"; an experience that accompanies many behavioral discoveries.[9] However, it must not be overlooked that even a discovery accompanied by "insight" may be *mistaken:* Every trial, even one with "insight," is of the nature of a conjecture or a hypothesis. Köhler's apes, it will be remembered, sometimes hit with "insight" on what turns out to be a mistaken attempt to solve their problem; and even great mathematicians are sometimes misled by intuition. Thus animals and men have to try out their hypotheses; they have to use the method of trial and of error elimination.

On the other hand I agree with Köhler and Thorpe[10] that the trials of problem-solving animals are in general not completely blind. Only in extreme cases, when the problem which confronts the animal does not yield to the making of hypotheses, will the animal resort to more or less blind and random attempts in order to get out of a disconcerting situation. Yet even in these attempts, goal-directedness is usually discernible, in sharp contrast to the blind randomness of genetic mutations and recombinations.

Another difference between genetic change and adaptive behavioral change is that the former *always* establishes a rigid and almost invariable genetic structure. The latter, admittedly, leads *sometimes* also to a fairly rigid behavior pattern which is dogmatically adhered to; radically so in the case of "imprinting" (Konrad Lorenz); but in other cases it leads to a flexible pattern which allows for differentiation or modification—for example, it may lead to exploratory behavior, or to what Pavlov called the "freedom reflex."[11]

On the scientific level, discoveries are revolutionary and creative. Indeed, a certain creativity may be attributed to all levels, even to the genetic level: New trials, leading to new environments and thus to new selection pressures, create new and revolutionary results on all levels, even though there are strong conservative tendencies built into the various mechanisms of instruction.

Genetic adaptation can of course operate only within the time span of a few generations— at the very least, say, one or two generations. In organisms which replicate very quickly this may be a short time span, and there may be simply no room for behavioral adaptation. More slowly reproducing organisms are compelled to invent behavioral adaptation in order to adjust themselves to quick environmental changes. They thus need a behavioral repertoire, with types of behavior of greater or lesser latitude or range. The repertoire, and the latitude of the available types of behavior can be assumed to be genetically programmed; and since, as indicated, a new type of behavior may be said to involve the choice of a new environmental niche, new types of behavior may indeed be genetically creative, for they may in their turn determine new selection pressures and thereby indirectly decide upon the future evolution of the genetic structure.[12]

On the level of scientific discovery two new aspects emerge. The most important one is that scientific theories can be formulated linguistically, and that they can even be published. Thus they become objects outside ourselves: objects open to investigation. As a consequence, they are now open to *criticism*. Thus we can get rid of a badly fitting theory before the adoption of the theory makes us unfit to survive: By criticizing our theories we can let our theories die in our stead. This is of course immensely important.

The other aspect is also connected with language. It is one of the novelties of human language that it encourages story telling, and thus *creative imagination*. Scientific discovery is akin to explanatory story telling, to myth making and to poetic imagination. The growth of imagination enhances of course the need for some control, such as, in science, inter-personal criticism—the friendly hostile cooperation of scientists which is partly based on competition and partly on the common aim to get nearer to the truth. This, and the role played by instruction and tradition, seems to me to exhaust the main sociological elements inherently involved in the progress of science; though more could be said of course about the social obstacles to progress, or the social dangers inherent in progress.

IV

I have suggested that progress in science, or scientific discovery, depends on *instruction* and *selection:* on a conservative or traditional or historical element, and on a revolutionary use of trial and the elimination of error by criticism, which includes severe empirical examinations or tests; that is, attempts to probe into the possible weaknesses of theories, attempts to refute them.

Of course, the individual scientist may wish to establish his theory rather than to refute it. But from the point of view of progress in science, this wish can easily mislead him. Moreover, if he does not himself examine his favorite theory critically, others will do so for him. The only results which will be regarded by them as supporting the theory will be the failures of interesting attempts to refute it; failures to find counter-examples where such counter-examples would be most expected, in the light of the best of the competing theories. Thus it need not create a great obstacle to science if the individual scientist is biased in favor of a pet theory. Yet I think that Claude Bernard was very wise when he wrote: "Those who have an excessive faith in their ideas are not well fitted to make discoveries."[13]

All this is part of the critical approach to science, as opposed to the inductivist approach; or of the Darwinian or eliminationist or selectionist approach, as opposed to the Lamarckian approach, which operates with the idea of *instruction from without,* or from the environment, while the critical or selectionist approach only allows *instruction from within*—from within the structure itself.

In fact, I contend that *there is no such thing as instruction from without the structure,* or the passive reception of a flow of information which impresses itself on our sense organs. All observations are theory impregnated: There is no pure, disinterested, theory-free observation. (To see this, we may try, using a little imagination, to compare human observation with that of an ant or a spider.)

Francis Bacon was rightly worried about the fact that our theories may prejudice our observations. This led him to advise scientists that they should avoid prejudice by purifying their minds of all theories. Similar recipes are still given.[14] But to attain objectivity we cannot rely on the empty mind: Objectivity rests on criticism, on critical discussion, and on the critical examination of experiments.[15] And we must recognize, particularly, that our very sense organs incorporate what amount to prejudices. I have stressed before (in Section II) that theories are like sense organs. Now I wish to stress that our sense organs are like theories. They *incorporate* adaptive theories (as has been shown in the case of rabbits and cats). And these theories are the result of natural selection. . . .

VIII

So far I have considered progress in science mainly from a biological point of view; however, it seems to me that the following two logical points are crucial.

First, in order that a new theory should constitute a discovery or a step forward it should conflict with its predecessor; that is to say, it should lead to at least some conflicting results. But this means, from a logical point of view, that it should contradict[25] its predecessor: It should overthrow it.

In this sense, progress in science—or at least striking progress—is always revolutionary.

My second point is that progress in science, although revolutionary rather than merely cumulative,[26] is in a certain sense always conservative: A new theory, however revolutionary, must always be able to explain fully the success of its predecessor. In all those cases in which its predecessor was successful, it must yield results at least as good as those of its predecessor and, if possible, better results. Thus in these cases the predecessor theory must appear as a good approximation to the new theory, while there should be, preferably, other cases where the new theory yields different and better results than the old theory.[27]

The important point about the two logical criteria which I have stated is that they allow us to decide of any new theory, even before it has been tested, whether it will be better than the old one, provided it stands up to tests. But this means that, in the field of science, we have something like a criterion for judging the quality of a theory as compared with its predecessor, and therefore a criterion of progress. And so it means that progress in science can be assessed rationally.[28] This possibility explains why, in science, only progressive theories are regarded as interesting; and it thereby explains why, as a matter of historical fact, the history of science is, by and large, a history of progress. (Science seems to be the only field of human endeavor of which this can be said.)

As I have suggested before, scientific progress is revolutionary. Indeed, its motto could be that of Karl Marx: "Revolution in permanence." However, scientific revolutions are rational in the sense that, in principle, it is rationally decidable whether or not a new theory is better than its predecessor. Of course, this does not mean that we cannot blunder. There are many ways in which we can make mistakes.

An example of a most interesting mistake is reported by Dirac.[29] Schrödinger found, but did not publish, a relativistic equation of the electron, later called the Klein–Gordon equation, before he found and published the famous non-relativistic equation which is now called by his name. He did not publish the relativistic equation because it did not seem to agree with the experimental results as interpreted by the preceding theory. However, the discrepancy was due to a faulty interpretation of empirical results, and not to a fault in the relativistic equation. Had Schrödinger published it, the problem of the equivalence between his wave mechanics and the matrix mechanics of Heisenberg and Born might not have arisen, and the history of modern physics might have been very different.

It should be obvious that the objectivity and the rationality of progress in science is not due to the personal objectivity and rationality of the scientist.[30] Great science and great scientists, like great poets, are often inspired by non-rational intuitions. So are great mathematicians. As Poincaré and Hadamard have pointed out,[31] a mathematical proof may be discovered by unconscious trials, guided by an inspiration of a decidedly aesthetic character, rather than by rational thought. This is true, and important. But obviously, it does not make the result, the mathematical proof, irrational. In any case, a proposed proof must be able to stand up to critical discussion, to its examination by competing mathematicians. And this may well induce the mathematical inventor to check, rationally, the results which he reached unconsciously or intuitively. Similarly, Kepler's beautiful Pythagorean dreams of the harmony of the world system did not invalidate the objectivity, the testability, the rationality of his three laws, nor the rationality of the problem which these laws posed for an explanatory theory.

With this, I conclude my two logical remarks on the progress of science; and I now move on to the second part of my lecture, and with it to remarks which may be described as partly sociological, and which bear on *obstacles* to progress in science.

IX

I think that the main obstacles to progress in science are of a social nature and that they may be divided into two groups: economic obstacles and ideological obstacles.

On the economic side poverty may, trivially, be an obstacle (although great theoretical and experimental discoveries have been made in spite of poverty). In recent years, however, it has become fairly clear that affluence may also be an obstacle: Too many dollars may chase too few ideas: Admittedly, even under such adverse circumstances progress *can* be achieved. But the spirit of science is in danger. Big Science may destroy great science, and the publication explosion may kill ideas: Ideas, which are only too rare, may become submerged in the flood. The danger is very real, and it is hardly necessary to enlarge upon it, but I may perhaps quote Eugene Wigner, one of the early heroes of quantum mechanics, who sadly remarks, "The spirit of science has changed." [32]

This is indeed a sad chapter. But since it is all too obvious I shall not say more about the economic obstacles to progress in science; instead, I will turn to discuss some of the ideological obstacles.

<h1 style="text-align:center">X</h1>

The most widely recognized of the ideological obstacles is ideological or religious intolerance, usually combined with dogmatism and lack of imagination. Historical examples are so well known that I need not dwell upon them. Yet it should be noted that even suppression may lead to progress. The martyrdom of Giordano Bruno and the trial of Galileo may have done more in the end for the progress of science than the Inquisition could do against it.

The strange case of Aristarchus and the original heliocentric theory opens perhaps a different problem. Because of his heliocentric theory Aristarchus was accused of impiety by Cleanthes, a Stoic. But this hardly explains the obliteration of the theory. Nor can it be said that the theory was too bold. We know that Aristarchus's theory was supported, a century after it was first expounded, by at least one highly respected astronomer (Seleucus).[33] And yet, for some obscure reason, only a few brief reports of the theory have survived. Here is a glaring case of the only too frequent failure to keep alternative ideas alive.

Whatever the details of the explanation, the failure was probably due to dogmatism and intolerance. But new ideas should be regarded as precious, and should be carefully nursed, especially if they seem to be a bit wild. I do not suggest that we should be eager to accept new ideas *just* for the sake of their newness. But we should be anxious not to suppress a new idea even if it does not appear to us to be very good.

There are many examples of neglected ideas, such as the idea of evolution before Darwin, or Mendel's theory. A great deal can be learned about obstacles to progress from the history of these neglected ideas. An interesting case is that of the Viennese physicist Arthur Haas who in 1910 partly anticipated Niels Bohr. Haas published a theory of the hydrogen spectrum based on a quantization of J. J. Thomson's atom model: Rutherford's model did not yet exist. Haas appears to have been the first to introduce Planck's quantum of action into atomic theory with a view to deriving the spectral constants. In spite of his use of Thomson's atom model, Haas almost succeeded in his derivation; and as Max Jammer explains in detail, it seems quite possible that the theory of Haas (which was taken seriously by Sommerfeld) indirectly influenced Niels Bohr.[34] In Vienna, however, the theory was rejected out of hand; it was ridiculed and decried as a silly joke by Ernst Lecher (whose early experiments had impressed Heinrich Hertz[35]), one of the professors of physics at the University of Vienna, whose somewhat pedestrian and not very inspiring lectures I attended some eight or nine years later.

A far more surprising case, also described by Jammer,[36] is the rejection in 1913 of Einstein's photon theory, first published in 1905, for which he was to receive the Nobel prize in 1921. This rejection of the photon theory formed a passage within a petition recommending

Einstein for membership of the Prussian Academy of Science. The document, which was signed by Max Planck, Walther Nernst, and two other famous physicists, was most laudatory and asked that a slip of Einstein's (such as they obviously believed his photon theory to be) should not be held against him. This confident manner of rejecting a theory which, in the same year, passed a severe experimental test undertaken by Millikan, has no doubt a humorous side; yet it should be regarded as a glorious incident in the history of science, showing that even a somewhat dogmatic rejection by the greatest living experts can go hand in hand with a most liberal-minded appreciation: These men did not dream of suppressing what they believed was mistaken. Indeed, the wording of the apology for Einstein's slip is most interesting and enlightening. The relevant passage of the petition says of Einstein: "That he may sometimes have gone too far in his speculations, as for example in his hypothesis of light quanta, should not weigh too heavily against him. For nobody can introduce, even into the most exact of the natural sciences, ideas which are really new, without sometimes taking a risk."[37] This is well said, but it is an understatement. One has always to take the risk of being mistaken and also the less important risk of being misunderstood or misjudged.

However, this example shows, drastically, that even great scientists sometimes fail to reach that self-critical attitude which would prevent them from feeling very sure of themselves while gravely misjudging things.

Yet a limited amount of dogmatism is necessary for progress: Without a serious struggle for survival in which the old theories are tenaciously defended, none of the competing theories can show their mettle, that is, their explanatory power and their truth content. Intolerant dogmatism, however, is one of the main obstacles to science. Indeed, we should not only keep alternative theories alive by discussing them, but we should systematically look for new alternatives; and we should be worried whenever there are no alternatives—whenever a dominant theory becomes too exclusive. The danger to progress in science is much increased if the theory in question obtains something like a monopoly.

XI

But there is even a greater danger: A theory, even a scientific theory, may become an intellectual fashion, a substitute for religion, an entrenched ideology. And with this I come to the main point of this second part of my lecture—the part that deals with obstacles to progress in science, to the distinction between scientific revolutions and ideological revolutions.

For in addition to the always important problem of dogmatism and the closely connected problem of ideological intolerance, there is a different and, I think, a more interesting problem. I mean the problem which arises from certain links between science and ideology, links which do exist but which have led some people to conflate science and ideology and to muddle the distinction between scientific and ideological revolutions.

I think that this is quite a serious problem at a time when intellectuals, including scientists, are prone to fall for ideologies and intellectual fashions. This may well be due to the decline of religion, to the unsatisfied and unconscious religious needs of our fatherless society.[38] During my lifetime I have witnessed, quite apart from the various totalitarian movements, a considerable number of intellectually highbrow and avowedly nonreligious movements with aspects whose religious character is unmistakable once your eyes are open to it.[39] The best of these many movements was that which was inspired by the father figure of Einstein. It was the best, because of Einstein's always modest and highly self-critical attitude and his humanity and tolerance. Nevertheless, I shall later have a few words to say about what seem to me the less satisfactory aspects of the Einsteinian ideological revolution.

I am not an essentialist, and I shall not discuss here the essence or nature of "ideologies." I will merely state very generally and vaguely that I am going to use the term "ideology" for *any non-scientific* theory or creed or view of the world which proves attractive, and which interests people, including scientists. (Thus there may be very helpful and also very destructive ideologies from, say, a humanitarian or a rationalist point of view.[40]) I need not say more about ideologies in order to justify the sharp distinction which I am going to make between science[41] and "ideology," and further, between *scientific revolutions* and *ideological revolutions*. But I will elucidate this distinction with the help of a number of examples.

These examples will show, I hope, that it is important to distinguish between a scientific revolution in the sense of a rational overthrow of an established scientific theory by a new one and all processes of "social entrenchment" or perhaps "social acceptance" of ideologies, including even those ideologies which incorporate some scientific results.

XII

As my first example I choose the Copernican and Darwinian revolutions, because in these two cases a scientific revolution gave rise to an ideological revolution. Even if we neglect here the ideology of "Social Darwinism,"[42] we can distinguish a scientific and an ideological component in both these revolutions.

The Copernican and Darwinian revolutions were *ideological* insofar as they both changed man's view of his place in the Universe. They clearly were *scientific* insofar as each of them overthrew a dominant scientific theory: a dominant astronomical theory and a dominant biological theory.

It appears that the ideological impact of the Copernican and also of the Darwinian theory was so great because each of them clashed with a religious dogma. This was highly significant for the intellectual history of our civilization, and it had repercussions on the history of science (for example, because it led to a tension between religion and science). And yet, the historical and sociological fact that the theories of both Copernicus and Darwin clashed with religion is completely irrelevant for the rational evaluation of the scientific theories proposed by them. Logically it has nothing whatsoever to do with the *scientific* revolution started by each of the two theories.

It is therefore important to distinguish between scientific and ideological revolutions particularly in those cases in which the ideological revolutions interact with revolutions in science.

The example, more especially, of the Copernican ideological revolution may show that even an ideological revolution might well be described as "rational." However, while we have a logical criterion of progress in science—and thus of rationality—we do not seem to have anything like general criteria of progress or of rationality outside science (although this should not be taken to mean that outside science there are no such things as standards of rationality). Even a highbrow intellectual ideology which bases itself on accepted scientific results may be irrational, as is shown by the many movements of modernism in art (and in science), and also of archaism in art, movements which in my opinion are intellectually insipid since they appeal to values which have nothing to do with art (or science). Indeed, many movements of this kind are just fashions which should not be taken too seriously.[43]

Proceeding with my task of elucidating the distinction between scientific and ideological revolutions, I will now give several examples of major scientific revolutions which did not lead to any ideological revolution.

The revolution of Faraday and Maxwell was, from a scientific point of view, just as great as that of Copernicus, and possibly greater: It dethroned Newton's central dogma—the dogma of central forces. Yet it did *not* lead to an ideological revolution, though it inspired a whole generation of physicists.

J. J. Thomson's discovery (and theory) of the electron was also a major revolution. To overthrow the age-old theory of the indivisibility of the atom constituted a scientific revolution easily comparable to Copernicus's achievement: When Thomson announced it, physicists thought he was pulling their legs. But it did not create an ideological revolution. And yet, it overthrew both of the two rival theories which for 2400 years had been fighting for dominance in the theory of matter—the theory of indivisible atoms, and that of the continuity of matter. To assess the revolutionary significance of this breakthrough it will be sufficient to remind you that it introduced structure as well as electricity into the atom, and thus into the constitution of matter. Also, the quantum mechanics of 1925 and 1926 of Heisenberg and of Born, of de Broglie, of Schrödinger and of Dirac, was essentially a quantization of the theory of the Thomson electron. And yet Thomson's scientific revolution did not lead to a new ideology.

Another striking example is Rutherford's overthrow in 1911 of the model of the atom proposed by J. J. Thomson in 1903. Rutherford had accepted Thomson's theory that the positive charge must be distributed over the whole space occupied by the atom. This may be seen from his reaction to the famous experiment of Geiger and Marsden. They found that when they shot alpha particles at a very thin sheet of gold foil, a few of the alpha particles—about one in twenty thousand—were reflected by the foil rather than merely deflected. Rutherford was incredulous. As he said later, "It was quite the most incredible event that has ever happened to me in my life. It was almost as incredible as if you fired a fifteen-inch shell at a piece of tissue paper and it came back and hit you."[44] This remark of Rutherford's shows the utterly revolutionary character of the discovery. Rutherford realized that the experiment refuted Thomson's model of the atom, and he replaced it by his nuclear model of the atom. This was the beginning of nuclear science. Rutherford's model became widely known, even among non-physicists. But it did not trigger off an ideological revolution.

One of the most fundamental scientific revolutions in the history of the theory of matter has never even been recognized as such. I mean the refutation of the electromagnetic theory of matter which had become dominant after Thomson's discovery of the electron. Quantum mechanics arose as part of this theory, and it was essentially this theory whose "completeness" was defended by Bohr against Einstein in 1935, and again in 1949. Yet in 1934 Yukawa had outlined a new quantum-theoretical approach to nuclear forces which resulted in the overthrow of the electromagnetic theory of matter after forty years of unquestioned dominance.[45]

There are many other major scientific revolutions which failed to trigger off any ideological revolution; for example, Mendel's revolution (which later saved Darwinism from extinction). Others are X-rays, radioactivity, the discovery of isotopes, and the discovery of superconductivity. To all these, there was no corresponding ideological revolution. Nor do I see as yet an ideological revolution resulting from the breakthrough of Crick and Watson.

XIII

Of great interest is the case of the so-called Einsteinian revolution—I mean Einstein's scientific revolution, which among intellectuals had an ideological influence comparable to that of the Copernican or Darwinian revolutions.

Of Einstein's many revolutionary discoveries in physics, there are two which are relevant here.

The first is special relativity, which overthrows Newtonian kinematics, replacing Galileo invariance by Lorentz invariance.[46] Of course, this revolution satisfies our criteria of rationality: The old theories are explained as approximately valid for velocities which are small compared with the velocity of light.

As to the ideological revolution linked with this scientific revolution, one element of it is due to Minkowski. We may state this element in Minkowski's own words. "The views of space and time I wish to lay before you," Minkowski wrote, ". . . are radical. Henceforth space by itself, and time by itself, are doomed to fade away into mere shadows, and only a kind of union of the two will preserve an independent reality."[47] This is an intellectually thrilling statement. But it is clearly not science; it is ideology. It became part of the ideology of the Einsteinian revolution. But Einstein himself was never quite happy about it. Two years before his death he wrote to Cornelius Lanczos: "One knows so much and comprehends so little. The four-dimensionality with the [Minkowski signature of] $+ + + -$ belongs to the latter category."

A more suspect element of the ideological Einsteinian revolution is the fashion of operationalism or positivism—a fashion which Einstein later rejected, although he himself was responsible for it, owing to what he had written about the operational definition of simultaneity. Although, as Einstein later realized,[48] operationalism is, logically, an untenable doctrine, it has been very influential ever since, in physics, and especially in behaviorist psychology.

With respect to the Lorentz transformations, it does not seem to have become part of the ideology that they limit the validity of the transitivity of simultaneity: The principle of transitivity remains valid within each inertial system while it becomes invalid for the transition from one system to another. Nor has it become part of the ideology that general relativity, or more especially Einstein's cosmology, allows the introduction of a preferred cosmic time and consequently of preferred local spatio-temporal frames.[49]

General relativity was in my opinion one of the greatest scientific revolutions ever, because it clashed with the greatest and best tested theory ever—Newton's theory of gravity and of the solar system. It contains, as it should, Newton's theory as an approximation; yet it contradicts it in several points. It yields different results for elliptic orbits of appreciable eccentricity; and it entails the astonishing result that any physical particle (photons included) which approaches the center of a gravitational field with a velocity exceeding six-tenths of the velocity of light is not accelerated by the gravitational field, as in Newton's theory, but decelerated: that is, not attracted by a heavy body, but repelled.[50]

This most surprising and exciting result has stood up to tests, but it does not seem to have become part of the ideology.

It is this overthrow and correction of Newton's theory which from a scientific (as opposed to an ideological) point of view is perhaps most significant in Einstein's general theory. This implies, of course, that Einstein's theory can be compared point by point with Newton's[51] and that it preserves Newton's theory as an approximation. Nevertheless, Einstein never believed that his theory was true. He shocked Cornelius Lanczos in 1922 by saying that his theory was merely a passing stage; he called it "ephemeral."[52] And he said to Leopold Infeld[53] that the left-hand side of his field equation[54] (the curvature tensor) was as solid as a rock, while the right-hand side (the momentum–energy tensor) was as weak as straw.

In the case of general relativity, an idea which had considerable ideological influence seems to have been that of a curved four-dimensional space. This idea certainly plays a role in both the scientific and the ideological revolution. But this makes it even more important to distinguish the scientific from the ideological revolution.

However, the ideological elements of the Einsteinian revolution influenced scientists, and thereby the history of science; and this influence was not all to the good.

First of all, the myth that Einstein had reached his result by an essential use of epistemological and especially operationalist methods had in my opinion a devastating effect upon science. (It is irrelevant whether you get your results—especially good results—by dreaming them, or by drinking black coffee, or even from a mistaken epistemology.)[55] Secondly, it led to the belief that quantum mechanics, the second great revolutionary theory of the century, must outdo the Einsteinian revolution, especially with respect to its epistemological depth. It seems to me that this belief affected some of the great founders of quantum mechanics,[56] and also some of the great founders of molecular biology.[57] It led to the dominance of a subjectivist interpretation of quantum mechanics; an interpretation which I have been combating for almost forty years. I cannot here describe the situation, but while I am aware of the dazzling achievement of quantum mechanics (which must not blind us to the fact that it is seriously incomplete[58]) I suggest that the orthodox interpretation of quantum mechanics is not part of physics, but an ideology. In fact, it is part of a modernistic ideology; and it has become a scientific fashion which is a serious obstacle to the progress of science.

XIV

I hope that I have made clear the distinction between a scientific revolution and the ideological revolution which may sometimes be linked with it. The ideological revolution may serve rationality or it may undermine it. But it is often nothing but an intellectual fashion. Even if it is linked to a scientific revolution it may be of a highly irrational character, and it may consciously break with tradition.

But a scientific revolution, however radical, cannot really break with tradition, since it must preserve the success of its predecessors. This is why scientific revolutions are rational. By this I do not mean, of course, that the great scientists who make the revolution are, or ought to be, wholly rational beings. On the contrary: Although I have been arguing here for the rationality of scientific revolutions, my guess is that should individual scientists ever become "objective and rational" in the sense of "impartial and detached," then we should indeed find the revolutionary progress of science barred by an impenetrable obstacle.

NOTES

[1] See, in the present series of Herbert Spencer Lectures, the concluding remark of the contribution by Professor W. F. Bodmer. My own misgivings concerning scientific advance and stagnation arise mainly from the changed spirit of science, and from the unchecked growth of Big Science which endangers great science. (See Section IX of this lecture.) Biology seems to have escaped this danger so far, but not, of course, the closely related dangers of large-scale application.

[2] The formation of membrane proteins, of the first viruses, and of cells, may perhaps have been among the earliest inventions of new environmental niches, though it is possible that other environmental niches (perhaps networks of enzymes invented by otherwise naked genes) may have been invented even earlier.

[3] It is an open problem whether one can speak in these terms ("in response") about the genetic level. . . . Yet if there were no variations, there could not be adaptation or evolution; and so we can say that the occurrence of mutations is either partly controlled by a need for them, or functions as if it was.

[4] When in this lecture I speak, for brevity's sake, of *mutation,* the possibility of recombination is of course always tacitly included.

[5] The realization of our ignorance has become pinpointed as a result, for example, of the astonishing revolution brought about by molecular biology.

[6] For the use of the term *blind* (especially in the second sense) see D. T. Campbell, "Methodological Suggestions from a Comparative Psychology of Knowledge Processes," *Inquiry* 2, 152–82 (1959); "Blind Variation and Selective Retention in Creative Thought as in Other Knowledge Processes," *Psychol. Rev.* 67, 380–400 (1960); and "Evolutionary Epistemology," in *The Philosophy of Karl Popper,* The Library of Living Philosophers (ed. P. A. Schilpp), pp. 413–63, The Open Court Publishing Co., La Salle, Illinois (1974).

[7] While the "blindness" of trials is relative to what we have found out in the past, randomness is relative to a set of elements (forming the "sample space"). On the genetic level these "elements" are the four nucleotide bases; on the behavioral level they are the constituents of the organism's repertoire of behavior. These constituents may assume different weights with respect to different needs or goals, and the weights may change through experience (lowering the degree of "blindness").

[8] On the importance of active participation, see R. Held and A. Hein, "Movement-produced Stimulation in the Development of Visually Guided Behavior," *J. Comp. Physiol. Psychol.* 56, 872–6 (1963); cf. J. C. Eccles, *Facing Reality,* pp. 66–7. The activity is, at least partly, one of producing hypotheses: see J. Krechevsky, "'Hypothesis' versus 'Chance' in the Pre-solution Period in Sensory Discrimination-learning," *Univ. Calif. Publ. Psychol.* 6, 27–44 (1932) (reprinted in *Animal Problem Solving* [ed. A. J. Riopelle], pp. 183–97, Penguin Books, Harmondsworth [1967]).

[9] I may perhaps mention here some of the differences between my views and the views of the Gestalt school. (Of course, I accept the fact of Gestalt perception; I am only dubious about what may be called Gestalt philosophy.)

I conjecture that the unity, or the articulation, of perception is more closely dependent on the motor control systems and the efferent neural systems of the brain than on afferent systems, that it is closely dependent on the behavioral repertoire of the organism. I conjecture that a spider or a mouse will never have insight (as had

Köhler's ape) into the possible unity of the two sticks which can be joined together, because handling sticks of that size does not belong to their behavioral repertoire. All this may be interpreted as a kind of generalization of the James-Lange theory of emotions (1884; see William James, *The Principles of Psychology,* Vol. II, pp. 449 ff. [1809] Macmillan and Co., London), extending the theory from our emotions to our perceptions (especially to Gestalt perceptions), which thus would not be "given" to us (as in Gestalt theory) but rather "made" by us, by decoding (comparatively "given") clues. The fact that the clues may mislead (optical illusions in man; dummy illusions in animals, etc.) can be explained by the biological need to impose our behavioral interpretations upon highly simplified clues. The conjecture that our decoding of what the senses tell us depends on our behavioral repertoire may explain part of the gulf that lies between animals and man, for through the evolution of the human language our repertoire has become unlimited.

[10] See W. H. Thorpe, *Learning and Instinct in Animals,* pp. 99 ff. Methuen, London (1956); 1963 edn, pp. 100-47; W. Köhler, *The Mentality of Apes* (1925); Penguin Books edn, (1957), pp. 166 ff.

[11] See I. P. Pavlov, *Conditioned Reflexes,* esp. pp. 11-12, Oxford University Press (1927). In view of what he calls "exploratory behavior" and the closely related "freedom behavior"—both obviously genetically based—and of the significance of these for scientific activity, it seems to me that the behavior of behaviorists who aim to supersede the value of freedom by what they call "positive reinforcement" may be a symptom of an unconscious hostility to science. Incidentally, what B. F. Skinner (cf. his *Beyond Freedom and Dignity* (1972) Cape, London) calls "the literature of freedom" did not arise as a result of negative reinforcement, as he suggests. It arose, rather, with Aeschylus and Pindar, as a result of the victories of Marathon and Salamis.

[12] Thus exploratory behavior and problem-solving create new conditions for the evolution of genetic systems, conditions which deeply affect the natural selection of these systems. One can say that once a certain latitude of behavior has been attained—as it has been attained even by unicellular organisms (see especially the classic work of H. S. Jennings, *The Behavior of the Lower Organisms,* Columbia University Press, New York [1906])—the initiative of the organism in selecting its ecology or habitat takes the lead, and natural selection within the new habitat follows the lead. In this way, Darwinism can simulate Lamarckism, and even Bergson's "creative evolution." This has been recognized by strict Darwinists. For a brilliant presentation and summary of the history, see Sir Alister Hardy, *The Living Stream,* Collins, London (1965), especially Lectures VI, VII, and VIII, where many references to earlier literature will be found, from James Hutton (who died in 1797) onwards (see pp. 178 ff.). See also Ernst Mayr, *Animal Species and Evolution,* The Belknap Press, Cambridge, Mass., and Oxford University Press, London (1963), pp. 604 ff. and 611; Erwin Schrödinger, *Mind and Matter,* Cambridge University Press (1958), Ch. 2; F. W. Braestrup, "The Evolutionary Significance of Learning," in *Vidensk. Meddr dansk naturh. Foren.* 134, 89-102 (1971) (with a bibliography); and also my first Herbert Spencer Lecture (1961) now in my *Objective Knowledge,* Clarendon Press, Oxford (1972, 1973).

[13] Quoted by Jacques Hadamard, *The Psychology of Invention in the Mathematical Field,* Princeton University Press (1945), and Dover edition (1954), p. 48.

[14] Behavioral psychologists who study "experimenter bias" have found that some albino rats perform decidedly better than others if the experimenter is led to believe (wrongly) that the former belong to a strain selected for high intelligence: see, "The Effect of Experimenter Bias on the Performance of the Albino Rat," *Behav. Sci.* 8, 183-9 (1963). The lesson drawn by the authors of this paper is that experiments should be made by "research assistants who do not know what outcome is desired" (p. 188). Like Bacon, these authors pin their hopes on the empty mind, forgetting that the expectations of the director of research may communicate themselves, without explicit disclosure, to his research assistants, just as they seem to have communicated themselves from each research assistant to his rats.

[15] Compare my *Logic of Scientific Discovery.* Section 8, and my *Objective Knowledge.*

. . .

[25] Thus Einstein's theory *contradicts* Newton's theory (although it contains Newton's theory as an approximation): In contradistinction to Newton's theory, Einstein's theory shows, for example, that in strong gravitational fields there cannot be a Keplerian elliptic orbit with appreciable eccentricity but without corresponding precession of the perihelion (as observed of Mercury).

[26] Even the collecting of butterflies is theory-impregnated (*butterfly* is a *theoretical* term, as is *water:* It involves a set of expectations). The recent accumulation of evidence concerning elementary particles can be interpreted as an accumulation of falsifications of the early electromagnetic theory of matter.

[27] An even more radical demand may be made; for we may demand that if the apparent laws of nature should change, then the new theory, invented to explain the new laws, should be able to explain the state of affairs both before and after the change, and also the change itself, from universal laws and (changing) initial conditions (cf. my *Logic of Scientific Discovery*, Section 79, esp. p. 253).

By stating these logical criteria for progress, I am implicitly rejecting the fashionable (anti-rationalistic) suggestion that two different theories such as Newton's and Einstein's are incommensurable. It may be true that two scientists with a verificationist attitude towards their favored theories (Newtonian and Einsteinian physics, say) may fail to understand each other. But if their attitude is critical (as was Newton's and Einstein's) they will understand both theories and see how they are related. See, for this problem, the excellent discussion of the comparability of Newton's and Einstein's theories by Troels Eggers Hansen in his paper, "Confrontation and Objectivity," *Danish Yb. Phil.* 7, 13 – 72 (1972).

[28] The logical demands discussed here (cf. Ch. 10 of my *Conjectures and Refutations* and Ch. 5 of *Objective Knowledge*), although they seem to me of fundamental importance, do not, of course, exhaust what can be said about the rational method of science. For example, in my *Postscript* (which has been in galley proofs since 1957, but which I hope will still be published one day) I have developed a theory of what I call metaphysical research programmes. This theory, it might be mentioned, in no way clashes with the theory of testing and of the revolutionary advance of science which I have outlined here. An example which I gave there of a metaphysical research programme is the use of the propensity theory of probability, which seems to have a wide range of applications.

What I say in the text should not be taken to mean that rationality depends on having a criterion of rationality. Compare my criticism of "criterion philosophies" in "Addendum I, Facts, Standards, and Truth," to Vol. ii of my *Open Society*.

[29] The story is reported by Paul A. M. Dirac, "The Evolution of the Physicist's Picture of Nature," *Scient. Am.* 208, No. 5, 45 – 53 (1963); see esp. p. 47.

[30] Cf. my criticism of the so-called "sociology of knowledge" in Ch. 23 of my *Open Society,* and pp. 155 f. of my *Poverty of Historicism.*

[31] Cf. Jacques Hadamard, *The Psychology of Invention in the Mathematical Field* (see note 13 above).

[32] A conversation with Eugene Wigner, *Science* 181, 527 – 33 (1973); see p. 533.

[33] For Aristarchus and Seleucus see Sir Thomas Heath, *Aristarchus of Samos,* Clarendon Press, Oxford (1966).

[34] See Max Jammer, *The Conceptual Development of Quantum Mechanics,* pp. 40 – 2, McGraw-Hill, New York (1966).

[35] See Heinrich Hertz, *Electric Waves,* Macmillan and Co., London (1894); Dover edn, New York (1962), pp. 12, 187 f., 273.

[36] See Jammer, op. cit., pp. 43 f., and Théo Kahan, "Un document historique de l'académie des sciences de Berlin sur l'activité scientific d'Albert Einstein" (1913), *Archs. Int. Hist. Sci.* 15, 337 – 42 (1962); see esp. p. 340.

[37] Compare Jammer's slightly different translation, loc. cit.

[38] Our Western societies do not, by their structure, satisfy the need for a father figure. I discussed the problems that arise from this fact briefly in my (unpublished) William James Lectures in Harvard (1950). My late friend, the psychoanalyst Paul Federn, showed me shortly afterwards an earlier paper of his devoted to this problem.

[39] An obvious example is the role of prophet played, in various movements, by Sigmund Freud, Arnold Schönberg, Karl Kraus, Ludwig Wittgenstein, and Herbert Marcuse.

[40] There are many kinds of "ideologies" in the wide and (deliberately) vague sense of the term I used in the text, and therefore many aspects to the distinction between science and ideology. Two may be mentioned here. One is that scientific theories can be distinguished or "demarcated" (see note 41) from non-scientific theories which, nevertheless, may strongly influence scientists and even inspire their work. (This influence, of course, may be good or bad or mixed.) A very different aspect is that of entrenchment: A scientific theory may function as an ideology if it becomes socially entrenched. This is why, when speaking of the distinction between scientific

revolutions and ideological revolutions, I include among ideological revolutions changes in non-scientific ideas which may inspire the work of scientists and also changes in the social entrenchment of what may otherwise be a scientific theory. (I owe the formulation of the points in this note to Jeremy Shearmur who has also contributed to other points dealt with in this lecture.)

[41] In order not to repeat myself too often, I did not mention in this lecture my suggestion for a criterion of the empirical character of a theory (falsifiability or refutability as the criterion of demarcation between empirical theories and non-empirical theories). Since in English "science" means "empirical science," and since the matter is sufficiently fully discussed in my books, I have written things like the following (for example, in *Conjectures and Refutations,* p. 39): ". . . in order to be ranked as scientific, [statements] must be capable of conflicting with possible, or conceivable, observations." Some people seized upon this like a shot (as early as 1932, I think). "What about your own gospel?" is the typical move. (I found this objection again in a book published in 1973.) My answer to the objection, however, was published in 1934 (see my *Logic of Scientific Discovery,* Ch. 2, Section 10 and elsewhere). I may restate my answer: My gospel is not "scientific," that is, it does not belong to empirical science, but it is, rather, a (normative) *proposal.* My gospel (and also my answer) is, incidentally, criticizable, though not just by observation, and it has been criticized.

[42] For a criticism of Social Darwinism see my *Open Society,* Ch. 10, note 71.

[43] Further to my use of the vague term "ideology" (which includes all kinds of theories, beliefs, and attitudes, including some that may influence scientists) it should be clear that I intend to cover by this term not only historicist fashions like "modernism," but also serious, and rationally discussable, metaphysical and ethical ideas. I may perhaps refer to Jim Erikson, a former student of mine in Christchurch, New Zealand, who once said in a discussion: "We do not suggest that science invented intellectual honesty, but we do suggest that intellectual honesty invented science." A very similar idea is to be found in Ch. ix ("The Kingdom and the Darkness") of Jacques Monod's book *Chance and Necessity,* Knopf, New York (1971). See also my *Open Society,* Vol. ii, Ch. 24 ("The Revolt against Reason"). We might say, of course, that an ideology which has learned from the critical approach of the sciences is likely to be more rational than one which clashes with science.

[44] Lord Rutherford, "The Development of the Theory of Atomic Structure," in J. Needham and W. Pagel (eds), *Background of Modern Science,* pp. 61-74, Cambridge University Press (1938); the quotation is from p. 68.

[45] See my "Quantum Mechanics without 'the Observer'," in *Quantum Theory and Reality* (ed. Mario Bunge), esp. pp. 8-9, Springer-Verlag, New York (1967). (It will form a chapter in my forthcoming volume *Philosophy and Physics.*)

The fundamental idea (that the inertial mass of the electron is in part explicable as the inertia of the moving electromagnetic field) that led to the electromagnetic theory of matter is due to J. J. Thomson, "On the Electric and Magnetic Effects Produced by the Motion of Electrified Bodies," *Phil. Mag.* (5th Ser.) 11, 229-49 (1881), and to O. Heaviside, "On the Electromagnetic Effects due to the Motion of Electrification through a Dielectric," *Phil Mag.* (5th Ser.) 27, 324-39 (1889). It was developed by W. Kaufmann ("Die magnetische und elektrische Ablenkbarkeit der Bequerelstrahlen und die scheinbare Masse der Elektronen," *Gött. Nachr.* 143-55 [1901], "Ueber die elektromagnetische Masse des Elektrons," 291-6 [1902], "Ueber die 'Elektromagnetische Masse' der Elektronen," 90-103 [1903]) and M. Abraham ("Dynamik des Elektrons," *Gött. Nachr.* 20-41 [1902], "Prinzipien der Dynamik des Elektrons," *Annln Phys.* [4th Ser.], 10, 105-79 [1903]) into the thesis that the mass of the electron is a purely electromagnetic effect. (See W. Kaufmann, "Die elektromagnetische Masse des Elektrons," *Phys. Z.* 4, 57-63 [1902-3] and M. Abraham, "Prinzipien der Dynamik des Elektrons," *Phys. Z.* 4, pp. 57-63 [1902-3] and M. Abraham, *Theorie der Elektrizität,* Vol. ii, pp. 136-249, Leipzig [1905].) The idea was strongly supported by H. A. Lorentz, "Elektromagnetische verschijnselen in een stelsel dat zich met willekeurige snelheid, kleiner dan die van het licht, beweegt," *Versl. gewone Vergad. wis- en natuurk. Afd. K. Akad. Wet. Amst.* 12, second part, 986-1009 (1903-4), and by Einstein's special relativity, leading to results deviating from those of Kaufmann and Abraham. The electromagnetic theory of matter had a great ideological influence on scientists because of the fascinating possibility of *explaining matter.* It was shaken and modified by Rutherford's discovery of the nucleus (and the proton) and by Chadwick's discovery of the neutron, which may help to explain why its final overthrow by the theory of nuclear forces was hardly taken notice of.

[46] The revolutionary power of special relativity lies in a new point of view which allows the derivation and interpretation of the Lorentz tranformations from two simple first principles. The greatness of this revolution

can be best gauged by reading Abraham's book (Vol. ii, referred to in note 45 above). This book, which is slightly earlier than Poincaré's and Einstein's papers on relativity, contains a full discussion of the problem situation, of Lorentz's theory of the Michelson experiment, and even of Lorentz's local time. Abraham comes, for example on pp. 143 f. and 370 f., quite close to Einsteinian ideas. It even seems as if Max Abraham was better informed about the problem situation than was Einstein. Yet there is no realization of the revolutionary potentialities of the problem situation; quite the contrary. For Abraham writes in his Preface, dated March 1905: "The theory of electricity now appears to have entered a state of quieter development." This shows how hopeless it is even for a great scientist like Abraham to foresee the future development of his science.

[47] See H. Minkowski, "Space and Time," in A. Einstein, H. A. Lorentz, H. Weyl, and H. Minkowski, *The Principle of Relativity*, Methuen, London (1923) and Dover edn, New York, p. 75. For the quotation from Einstein's letter to Cornelius Lanczos later in the same paragraph of my text, see C. Lanczos, "Rationalism and the Physical World," in R. S. Cohen and B. Wartofski (eds), *Boston Studies in the Philosophy of Science*, Vol. 3, pp. 181–98 (1967); see p. 198.

[48] See my *Conjectures and Refutations*, p. 114 (with footnote 30); also my *Open Society*, Vol. ii, p. 20, and the criticism in my *Logic of Scientific Discovery*, p. 440. I pointed out this criticism in 1950 to P. W. Bridgman, who received it most generously.

[49] See A. D. Eddington, *Space Time and Gravitation*, pp. 162 f., Cambridge University Press (1935). It is interesting in this context that Dirac (on p. 46 of the paper referred to in note 29 above) says that he now doubts whether four-dimensional thinking is a fundamental requirement of physics. (It is a fundamental requirement for driving a motor car.)

[50] More precisely, a body falling from infinity with a velocity $v > c/3^{1/2}$ toward the center of a gravitational field will be constantly decelerated in approaching this center.

[51] See the reference to Troels Eggers Hansen cited in note 27 above; and Peter Havas, "Four-dimensional Formulations of Newtonian Mechanics and Their Relation to the Special and the General Theory of Relativity," *Revs mod. Phys.* 36, 938–65 (1964), and "Foundation Problems in General Relativity," in *Delaware Seminar in the Foundations of Physics* (ed. M. Bunge), pp. 124–48 (1967). Of course, the comparison is not trivial: see, for example, pp. 52 f. of E. Wigner's book referred to in note 24 above.

[52] See C. Lanczos, op. cit., p. 196.

[53] See Leopold Infeld, *Quest*, p. 90. Victor Gollancz, London (1941).

[54] See A. Einstein, "Die Feldgleichungen der Gravitation," *Sber. Akad. Wiss. Berlin*, Part 2, 844–7 (1915); "Die Grundlage der allgemeinen Relativitätstheorie," *Annln Phys.*, (4th Ser.) 49, 769–822 (1916).

[55] I believe that §2 of Einstein's famous paper, "Die Grundlage der allgemeinen Relativitätstheorie" (see Note 54 above; English translation, "The Foundation of the General Theory of Relativity," *The Principle of Relativity*, pp. 111–64; see note 47 above) uses most questionable epistemological arguments *against* Newton's absolute space and *for* a very important theory.

[56] Especially Heisenberg and Bohr.

[57] Apparently it affected Max Delbrück; see *Perspectives in American History*, Vol. 2, Harvard University Press (1968), "Emigré Physicists and the Biological Revolution," by Donald Fleming, pp. 152–89, especially Sections iv and v. (I owe this reference to Professor Mogens Blegvad.)

[58] It is clear that a physical theory which does not explain such constants as the electric elementary quantum (or the fine structure constant) is incomplete, to say nothing of the mass spectra of the elementary particles. See my paper, "Quantum Mechanics without 'the Observer'," referred to in note 45 above.

STUDY   QUESTIONS   FOR   TOPIC   III

1. According to Kuhn's thesis of paradigm-driven science, a particular scientific term can be given different meanings in the context of different theories. For example, in the context of his theory of relativity Einstein gave a meaning to the term "mass" which differs from Newton's meaning of the same term. Based on Kuhn's ideas, is it possible to translate Newton's

meaning of "mass" into the language of Einstein's theory of relativity? A "yes" answer suggests that an accurate translation can be achieved without any loss of meaning; a "no" answer suggests that such a translation is not possible. Defend your answer.

2. Which one of Kuhn's stages of scientific development explicitly violates Popper's methodology of conjectures and refutations? Choose one stage and defend your answer.

3. Many people say that scientists seek true theories, which are roughly theories that correspond to real events in the universe. Would Kuhn agree that truth is always a goal of science?

4. What is the relationship between Kuhn's conception of science as paradigm-driven research and Hempel's covering law model of explanation? Select and defend one of the following claims: (a) one could consistently believe in both Kuhn's conception of science as paradigm-driven research and Hempel's model of explanation; or (b) one could not consistently believe in both Kuhn's conception of science and Hempel's model of explanation.

5. In his "Objectivity, Value Judgment, and Theory Choice" (selection #16), Kuhn tries to answer his critics against the charge that his conception of paradigm-driven science is irrational. But Laudan is unconvinced. What exactly are the reasons that Laudan gives to show that Kuhn does not adequately address this charge?

6. Kuhn advocates a discontinuous theory of scientific change, while Laudan advocates a gradualist theory. How would you describe Popper's theory? Discontinuous or gradualist, or perhaps neither?

7. What is the difference between Laudan's conception of scientific change and Popper's conception?

BIBLIOGRAPHY

Gould, S. J. *The Mismeasure of Man.* New York: W. W. Norton & Co., 1981, pp. 73–108.
Hacking, I., ed. *Scientific Revolutions.* Oxford: Oxford UP, 1981.
Hesse, M. *Revolutions and Reconstructions in the Philosophy of Science.* Brighton: Harvester P, 1980.
Hoyningen-Huene, P. *Reconstructing Scientific Revolutions: Thomas S. Kuhn's Philosophy of Science.* Trans. A. T. Levine. Chicago: U Chicago P, 1993.
Kuhn, T. "Afterwords." *World Changes.* Ed. P. Horwich. Cambridge: MIT, 1993, pp. 311–42.
———. "Commensurability, Comparability, Communicability." *PSA 1982.* Ed. P. Asquith and T. Nickles. East Lansing: Philosophy of Science Association, 1983, pp. 669–88.
———. *The Essential Tension.* Chicago: U Chicago P, 1979.
———. "Logic of Discovery or Psychology of Research?" *Criticisms and the Growth of Knowledge.* Ed. I. Lakatos and A. Musgrave. Cambridge: Cambridge UP, 1970, pp. 1–24.
———. "Rationality and Theory Choice." *Journal of Philosophy* 80 (1983): 563–70.
———. "Second Thoughts on Paradigms." *The Structure of Scientific Theories.* Ed. F. Suppe. Champaign: U Illinois P, 1974.
Lakatos, I. "Falsification and the Methodology of Scientific Research Programs." *Criticisms and the Growth of Knowledge.* Ed. I. Lakatos and A. Musgrave. Cambridge: Cambridge UP, 1970, pp. 91–196.
Laudan, L. *Science and Relativism.* Chicago: U Chicago P, 1990.
———. *Science and Values.* Berkeley: U California P, 1984.

McMullin, E. "Rationality and Paradigm Change in Science." *World Changes.* Ed. P. Horwich. Cambridge: MIT, 1993, pp. 55–80.

Newton-Smith, W. "T. S. Kuhn: From Revolutionary to Social Democrat," *The Rationality of Science.* London: Routledge & Kegan Paul Ltd., 1981, pp. 102–24.

Popper, K. *Objective Knowledge.* Oxford: Oxford UP, 1972.

———. "Normal Science and Its Dangers." *Criticisms and the Growth of Knowledge.* Ed. I. Lakatos and A. Musgrave. Cambridge: Cambridge UP, 1970, pp. 51–58.

Rothbart, D. "The Nature of a Scientific Prototype." *Explaining the Growth of Scientific Knowledge.* New York: Edwin Mellen, 1997, pp. 103–24.

Shapere, D. "The Structure of Scientific Revolutions." *Philosophical Review* 73 (1964): 383–94.

THE RELATIVISM
OF SCIENCE

INTRODUCTION

Do scientists act rationally during their professional work? Are their procedures and methods really objective? Many critics would say "No" to both questions. The idealized pictures of science portrayed by philosophers, such as Rudolf Carnap and Karl Popper (Topic I), grossly distort the actual patterns of scientific behavior. Philosophers of science romanticize scientific practice into a utopian dream of rationality, according to critics. These critics express disdain for the glorious words commonly attributed to scientific practice. We hear that scientists are *rational,* their methodology *objective,* and their conclusions *true.* But such honor functions in society as propaganda devices intended to deceive an unsuspecting public. From a candid examination of the social conditions driving scientific practice, many critics conclude that scientific disputes are not resolved rationally, the methodology driving their behavior is not objective, and their beliefs about the universe cannot be proven true.

According to these critics, the scientific investigation of phenomena must be relativized with respect to the social pressures, vested interests, and community norms which drive the profession. Inspired in part by Kuhn's sobering examination of scientific practice, many critics of science try to expose the arational forces at work—forces that do not always promote the acquisition of (genuine) knowledge. But social forces can have an enormous influence on scientists. Scientific institutions will typically tell researchers what to investigate, dictate certain normative procedures to be followed during laboratory research, and themselves determine the reliability of the results. In response to these critics, rationalists claim that the successes of science must be explained through idealized standards of scientific rationality, centering on the use of reliable evidence, reasoned argumentation, and sound guidelines of investigation. Rationalists of course are expected to define precisely these idealized standards. The relativist dismisses the entire enterprise of the rationalist, attempting instead to examine the various social, psychological, and anthropological influences. Again, scientific practice cannot be explained by the honorific concepts of rationality, objectivity, and truth. The stage is set for a heated debate between the rationalists and relativists.

SUMMARY OF READINGS

Barry Barnes and David Bloor advance a relativist conception of science (selection #19). Rational ideals advocated by many philosophers severely underestimate the importance of social pressures, conventions, and vested interest of participants. All scientific beliefs, whether true or false, are equally subject to a social examination of their origins. Even the rules for evaluating a scientific belief are themselves socially determined. For example, the principles of logic, which are designed to guide all rational argument, cannot be proven to be universally valid. On the contrary, such principles are *ad hoc* rules established by social convention and strictly enforced by educational institutions. So, such principles of reasoning are not universally valid, but are "locally" employed by a particular community.

Critics of Barnes and Bloor argue that the study of the social origins of scientific ideas does not imply a relativism of scientific knowledge. Surely Barnes and Bloor are confusing the socially determined causes of a belief with the reasons for the truth of the belief. Barnes and Bloor respond by rejecting the neutrality of all reasoning. All so-called objective standards for evaluating a theory, such as empirical evidence or logical principles, are socially determined.

Bruno Latour continues this attack on rational science with his anthropological study of the life of the experimental scientists (selection #20). He concludes that we can never separate physical reality from various ways in which we understand reality. We never hear the voice of Nature independently of our own voices, disputes, decisions, biases, and language. The evidence from the lab is inseparable from the procedures for acquiring evidence. After scientists announce their findings, they claim victory for having exposed Nature's secrets. However, "Nature is never used as the final arbiter since no one knows what she is and says. But once the *controversy is settled,* Nature is the ultimate referee" (Latour, B. *Science in Action.* Cambridge: Harvard U.P., 1987, p. 97). No impartial and rational referee can arbitrate laboratory disputes.

Can the rationalist program accommodate empirical studies from sociology and anthropology? According to Carl Hempel (selection #21), a notion of instrumental rationality combines the normative ideals of rational science with empirical studies of scientific practice. The rationalist program centers on the idealized standards for formulating, appraising, and changing scientific beliefs. To identify these standards, we must first discover the goals that practicing scientists actually share. Such a discovery requires descriptive studies from sociology, history, and anthropology. Once such goals are identified, philosophers can then articulate the most rational ways in which such goals can be attained. In this respect, descriptive studies from the empirical sciences provide important information for the philosophers' task of identifying the normative ideals.

However, relativism and rationality may be compatible with each other after all, according to Nelson Goodman (selection #22). He argues that the subject matter of science is not the singular "real world" of pure content, not a world undescribed, undepicted, and unperceived. The subject matter of science is inseparable from the categories, relations, and assumptions we use in our investigations of nature. A belief must be judged in relation to the reasoning standards appropriate to the investigation. A painting, a work of literature, and a scientific theory may each reveal reality, but any understanding of the world must be evaluated by the standards appropriate to the particular discipline. We cannot reduce all accounts—from physics, literature, and fine arts—to a representation of one single world. We cannot translate all information about the world into the language of physics. Thus, truth is not a severe master, but a docile and obedient servant, writes Goodman.

BARRY BARNES AND DAVID BLOOR
RELATIVISM, RATIONALISM AND THE SOCIOLOGY OF KNOWLEDGE

In the academic world relativism is everywhere abominated. Critics feel free to describe it by words such as "pernicious"[1] or portray it as a "threatening tide."[2] On the political Right relativism is held to destroy the defences against Marxism and Totalitarianism. If knowledge is said to be relative to persons and places, culture or history, then is it not but a small step to concepts like "Jewish physics"?[3] On the Left, relativism is held to sap commitment, and the strength needed to overthrow the defences of the established order. How can the distorted vision of bourgeois science be denounced without a standpoint which is itself special and secure?[4]

The majority of critics of relativism subscribe to some version of *rationalism* and portray relativism as a threat to rational, scientific standards. It is, however, a convention of academic discourse that might is not right. Numbers may favour the opposite position, but we shall show that the balance of argument favours a relativist theory of knowledge. Far from being a threat to the scientific understanding of forms of knowledge, relativism is required by it. Our claim is that relativism is essential to all those disciplines such as anthropology, sociology, the history of institutions and ideas, and even cognitive psychology, which account for the diversity of systems of knowledge, their distribution and the manner of their change. It is those who oppose relativism, and who grant certain forms of knowledge a privileged status, who pose the real threat to a scientific understanding of knowledge and cognition.[5]

I

There are many forms of relativism and it is essential to make clear the precise form in which we advocate it. The simple starting-point of relativist doctrines is (i) the observation that beliefs on a certain topic vary, and (ii) the conviction that which of these beliefs is found in a given context depends on, or is relative to, the circumstances of the users. But there is always a third feature of relativism. It requires what may be called a "symmetry" or an "equivalence" postulate. For instance, it may be claimed that general conceptions of the natural order, whether the Aristotelean world view, the cosmology of a primitive people, or the cosmology of an Einstein, are all alike in being false, or are all equally true. These alternative equivalence postulates lead to two varieties of relativism; and in general it is the nature of the equivalence postulate which defines a specific form of relativism.

The form of relativism that we shall defend employs neither of the equivalence postulates just mentioned, both of which run into technical difficulties. To say that all beliefs are equally true encounters the problem of how to handle beliefs which contradict one another. If one belief denies what the other asserts, how can they both be true? Similarly, to say that all beliefs are equally false poses the problem of the status of the relativist's own claims. He would seem to be pulling the rug from beneath his own feet.[6]

Our equivalence postulate is that all beliefs are on a par with one another with respect to the causes of their credibility. It is not that all beliefs are equally true or equally false, but that regardless of truth and falsity the fact of their credibility is to be seen as equally problematic. The position we shall defend is that the incidence of all beliefs without exception calls for empirical investigation and must be accounted for by finding the specific, local causes of this credibility. This means that regardless of whether the sociologist evaluates a belief as true or rational, or as false and irrational, he must search for the causes of its credibility. In all cases he will ask, for instance, if a belief is part of the routine cognitive and technical competences handed down from generation to generation. Is it enjoined by the authorities of the society? Is it transmitted by established institutions of socialization or supported by accepted agencies of social control? Is it bound up with patterns of vested interest? Does it have a role in furthering shared goals, whether political or technical, or both? What are the practical and immediate consequences of particular judgements that are made with respect to the belief? All of these questions can, and should, be answered without regard to the status of the belief as it is judged and evaluated by the sociologist's own standards.

A large number of examples could be provided from recent work by historians, sociologists and anthropologists which conform to the requirements of our equivalence postulate. For example, many excellent historical studies of scientific knowledge and evaluation now proceed without concern for the epistemological status of the cases being addressed. They simply investigate the contingent determinants of belief and reasoning without regard to whether the beliefs are true or the inferences rational. They exhibit the same degree and kind of curiosity in both cases.[7] Anthropologists too are increasingly accounting for systems of commonsense knowledge and pre-literate cosmologies in the same way.[8]

On the level of empirical investigation—and concentrating on the practice of investigators rather than the theoretical commentary they may provide—there is more evidence to be cited for relativism than against it. It is mainly on the programmatic level that the determined opposition to relativism is to be found. Since instances of the empirical material have been marshalled and discussed elsewhere[9] the issues that will be addressed here will be of a more methodological and philosophical character.

II

If the relativist places all beliefs on a par with one another for the purposes of explanation, then we can say that he is advocating a form of *monism*. He is stressing the essential identity of things that others would hold separate. Conversely, rationalists who reject relativism typically do so by insisting on a form of *dualism*. They hold on to the distinctions between true and false, rational and irrational belief and insist that these cases are vitally different from one another. They try to give the distinction a role in the conduct of the sociology of knowledge or anthropology or history, by saying that the explanations to be offered in the two cases are to be of a different kind. In particular, many of the critics of relativism implicitly reject our equivalence postulate by saying that rational beliefs must be explained wholly or partly by the fact that they *are* rational, whilst irrational beliefs call for no more than a causal, socio-psychological or "external" explanation. For example, Hollis has recently insisted that "true and rational beliefs need one sort of explanation, false and irrational beliefs another."[10] Imre Lakatos was one of the most strident advocates of a structurally similar view. He equated rational procedures in science with those that accord with some preferred philosophy of science. Exhibiting the cases which appear to conform to the preferred philosophy is called "internal history" or "rational reconstruction." He then asserts that "the rational aspect of scientific growth is fully accounted for by one's logic of scientific discovery." All the rest, which is not fully accounted for, is handed over to the sociologist for non-rational, causal explanation.[11] A version of this theory is endorsed by Laudan.[12] Even the sociologist Karl Mannheim adopted this dualist and rationalist view when he contrasted the "existential determination of thought" by "extra-theoretical factors" with development according to "immanent laws" derived from the "nature of things" of "pure logical possibilities." This is why he exempted the physical sciences and mathematics from his sociology of knowledge.[13]

As the first step in the examination of the rationalist case let us consider a charge that is sometimes made against the relativist. It is said, for example by Lukes, that the relativist has undermined his own right to use words like "true" or "false."[14] Answering this charge is not a difficult task, and it will help to bring the character of relativism, and the shortcomings of rationalism, into sharp focus.

Consider the members of two tribes, T1 and T2, whose cultures are both primitive but otherwise very different from one another. Within each tribe some beliefs will be preferred to others and some reasons accepted as more cogent than others. Each tribe will have a vocabulary for expressing these preferences. Faced with a choice between the beliefs of his own tribe and those of the other, each individual would typically prefer those of his own culture. He would have available to him a number of locally acceptable standards to use in order to assess beliefs and justify his preferences.

What a relativist says about himself is just what he would say about the tribesman. The relativist, like everyone else, is under the necessity to sort out beliefs, accepting some and rejecting others. He will naturally have preferences and these will typically coincide with those of others in his locality. The words "true" and "false" provide the idiom in which those evaluations are expressed, and the words "rational" and "irrational" will have a similar function. When confronted with an alien culture he, too, will probably prefer his own familiar and accepted beliefs and his local culture will furnish norms and standards which can be used to justify such preferences if it becomes necessary to do so.

The crucial point is that a relativist accepts that his preferences and evaluations are as context-bound as those of the tribes T1 and T2. Similarly he accepts that none of the justifications of his preferences can be formulated in absolute or context-independent terms. In the last analysis, he acknowledges that his justifications will stop at some principle or alleged matter of fact that only has local credibility. The only alternative is that justifications will begin to run in a circle and assume what they were meant to justify.[15]

For the relativist there is no sense attached to the idea that some standards or beliefs are really rational as distinct from merely locally accepted as such. Because he thinks that there are no context-free or super-cultural norms of rationality he does not see rationally and irrationally held beliefs as making up two distinct and qualitatively different classes of thing. They do not fall into two different natural kinds which make different sorts of appeal to the human mind, or stand in a different relationship to reality, or depend for their credibility on different patterns of social organization. Hence the relativist conclusion that they are to be explained in the same way.

III

A typical move at this point in the argument is to try to contain and limit the significance of the sociology of knowledge by declaring that because it is merely the study of *credibility* it can have no implications for *validity*. Validity, say the critics, is a question to be settled directly by appeal to evidence and reason and is quite separate from the contingencies of actual belief. As Professor Flew has put it, "an account of the sufficiently good reasons" for a belief must be distinguished from "an account of the psychological, physiological or sociological causes of inclinations to utter words expressing this belief when appropriately stimulated." [16] The question of the reasons for a belief and the question of its causes are quite separate sorts of issue. But having separated these two issues this critic then proceeds to shunt the sociologist and psychologist into the sidings where they can be forgotten. The rationalist is now free to operate in the realm of reason and make out its function and workings to be whatever he wishes. This is why we are told so emphatically that the sociologist of knowledge "must be concerned with causes of belief *rather than* with whatever evidencing reasons there may be for cherishing them." [17]

Unfortunately for the rationalist the freedom which this convenient division of labour would give him cannot be granted: the distinctions upon which it is based will not stand examination. The reason is that it would be difficult to find a commodity more contingent and more socially variable than Flew's "evidencing reasons." What counts as an "evidencing reason" for a belief in one context will be seen as evidence for quite a different conclusion in another context. For example, was the fact that living matter appeared in Pouchet's laboratory preparations evidence for the spontaneous generation of life, or evidence of the incompetence of the experimenter, as Pasteur maintained? As historians of science have shown, different scientists drew different conclusions and took the evidence to point in different directions. This was possible because something is only evidence for something else when set in the context of assumptions which give it meaning—assumptions, for instance, about what is *a priori* probable or improbable. If, on religious and political grounds, there is a desire to maintain a sharp and symbolically useful distinction between matter and life, then Pouchet must have blundered rather than have made a fascinating discovery. These were indeed the factors that conditioned the reception of his work in the conservative France of the Second Empire. [18] "Evidencing reasons," then, are a prime target for sociological enquiry and explanation. There is no question of the sociology of knowledge being confined to causes *rather than* "evidencing reasons." Its concern is precisely with causes *as* "evidencing reasons."

IV

Obviously, it would be possible for the rationalist to counterattack. He could say that the above argument only applies to what are *taken* to be reasons, rather than to what *really are* reasons.

Once again, the charge would be that the sociologists had conflated validity and credibility. But if a rationalist really were to insist on a total distinction between credibility and validity he would simply leave the field of discourse altogether. Validity totally detached from credibility is nothing. The sociologist of knowledge with his relativism and his monism would win by default: his theory would meet no opposition. It is because of the rationalist's desire to avoid this consequence that sooner or later, overtly or covertly, he will fuse validity and credibility. He too will treat validity and credibility as one thing by finding a certain class of reasons that are alleged to carry their own credibility with them: they will be visible because they glow by their own light.

To see how this comes about consider again the two tribes T1 and T2. For a member of T1 examining what is to him a peculiar belief from the culture of T2, there is a clear point to the distinction between the validity and the credibility of a belief. He will say that just because the misguided members of T2 believe something, that doesn't make it true. Its rightness and wrongness, he may add, must be established independently of belief. But, of course, what he will mean by "independently of belief" is independently of the belief of others, such as the members of T2. For his own part, he has no option but to use the accepted methods and assumptions of his own group. In practice this is what "directly" ascertaining truth or falsity comes down to.

The simple structure of the example makes it easy to see what is happening. The distinction between validity and credibility is sound enough in this case, but its real point, its scope and its focus, is entirely local. As the relativist would expect, it is not an absolute distinction, but one whose employment depends upon a taken-for-granted background. It is a move within a game, and it is with regard to the background knowledge, assumed by the move, that validity and credibility are tacitly brought together. Without this, the distinction itself could never be put to use, or its contrast be given an application.

If our imaginary tribesman was dialectically sophisticated he might realize that he is open to the charge of special pleading, and that he had, in his own case, collapsed the distinction upon which he had been insisting. How could he reply to the accusation that he had equated the validity and credibility of his own beliefs? As a more careful statement of his position he might claim that not even the fact that his own tribe believes something is, *in itself,* sufficient to make it true. But he would then have to mend the damage of this admission by adding that it just was a fact that what his tribe believed *was* true. A kindly providence, perhaps, had here united these two essentially different things.

For the sociologist of knowledge these refinements change nothing. They do not remove the special pleading, they simply elaborate upon it. But they remind us that we need to locate the point at which the rationalists of our culture make the same move. We must examine the rationalist case to find the point at which reasons are said to become visible by their own light and Reason in Action transcends the operation of causal processes and social conditions.

V

A familiar candidate to invoke for the role of Reason in Action is the class of beliefs which are supposed to be directly and immediately apprehended by experience. It may be said that some

knowledge claims can be sustained, and can attract credibility purely in virtue of their correspondence with reality—a correspondence which any reasonable agent can recognize. Some
things we just *know* by experience and no contingent factors, such as their support by authority or their coherence with the overall pattern of culture, are necessary for their maintenance.

Such a theory is easily recognized as a species of naïve empiricism and its weaknesses are
well known. Nevertheless similar assumptions can emerge in a disguised form. For example
Flew has argued that "when it is a question of accounting for beliefs about matters of everyday use and observation, then there is nothing like so much room for sophisticated social and
historical causes."[19] The polemical force of this appeal to everyday use and observation may
be gathered from the following claim which we shall assess in some detail:

> The cause of our belief that the ferry canoe is where it is on the Zaire River does not lie in the
> social structure of our tribe. It is to be found, instead, in certain intrusive non-social facts: that
> when we turn our eyes towards the right bit of the river the canoe causes appropriate sensory
> impressions; and that those heedlessly placing themselves in the water rather than the canoe
> are incontinently eaten by crocodiles.[20]

It would be possible to take exception to this passage by stressing how much more is involved
in the identification of an object as "the Zaire river ferry canoe" than turning our eyes in the
right direction. All the socially sustained classifications that are involved in the process have
been simply left out of account. But though such criticisms would be correct and well deserved, they would not fully meet the point being made. What is really at issue here is the status of certain skills such as our ability to navigate ourselves around our environment; avoiding
falling in rivers; and remembering the location of medium-scale physical objects. The question is: how do these skills relate to a relativist sociology of knowledge? Do they provide any
basis for criticism, and hence comfort for the rationalist?

The first point to notice is that the facts to be attended to are skills that individuals share
with non-linguistic animals. They are a real and important part of our mentality and, as Flew
has pointed out, they are not greatly illuminated by sociologists or historians. Indeed, they are
taken for granted by these disciplines. This is because they belong to the province of the biologist and the learning theorist. It is no surprise that different aspects of knowledge are divided
out amongst different scientific disciplines. But it is surely no skin off the sociologist's nose
that he cannot explain how a dog retrieves its buried bone.

The important point is that none of the work in cognitive psychology which might explain
this order of fact is going to be sufficient to account for the problems addressed by the sociologist. These concern variations in institutionalized patterns of knowledge. The difference
between knowledge as it concerns the sociologist and the kind of knowing used in the objection may be represented by an analogy: it is the difference between a *map* and an individual
organism's working knowledge of a terrain. There is a qualitative difference between these
two things: one is a collective, the other an individual, representation. A map is an impersonal
document, not a state of mind; it is a cultural product which requires conventions of representation. (And, of course, there are an indefinitely large number of different conventions which
may be agreed upon.) Information about the psychological capacities which permit individual

navigation won't add up to competent answers to questions, say, about the creation, mainte-nance, and change of cartographic norms.

That features of animal navigation should be seen as *criticism* of the sociology of knowl-edge simply reveals an individualistic bias in the way that the word "knowledge" is being con-strued. As an objection it trades on a muddle between social and individual accomplishments. Furthermore, the kinds of individual cognitive skills that are in question are increasingly com-ing under the scope of the *causal* theories produced by physiologists and psychologists. They are showing themselves to be amenable to precisely the type of explanation that, as a good ra-tionalist, Flew was at pains to *contrast* with the operation of reason. This hardly makes them fit candidates for the role of Reason in Action which was the use to which our rationalist critic was putting them. Some of the facts about everyday use and observation may indeed provide little room for sophisticated sociological or historical explanation, but that is because they provide room for sophisticated psychological explanations. While these can happily *co-exist* with the sociology of knowledge, they directly *contradict* the claims of the rationalist critics of that discipline.[21]

VI

There is no need for a relativist sociology of knowledge to take anything other than a com-pletely open and matter-of-fact stance towards the role of sensory simulation. The same ap-plies to any other of the physical, genetic or psychological and non-social causes that must eventually find a place in an overall account of knowledge. The stimulation caused by material objects when the eye is turned in a given direction is indeed a causal factor in knowledge and its role is to be understood by seeing how this cause interacts with other causes. There is no question of denying the effect on belief of the facts—that is, of the segment of *unverbalized reality* that is the focus of the beliefs in question. All that need be insisted upon is that when due allowance is made for the effect of "the facts" it is made in accordance with the equiva-lence postulate. This means that the effect of "the facts" on a believer plays the same general role whether the belief that results is a true one or a false one.

To show what is meant by this let us look at a simple, real-life case where, it may be con-sidered, reality impinges in the same causal way on those who held true and false beliefs about it. Consider the eighteenth-century chemists Priestley and Lavoisier who gave diverging ac-counts of what happens during combustion and calcination. For simplicity we may say that Priestley's phlogiston theory was false and Lavoisier's oxygen theory was true. Both Priestly and Lavoisier were looking at samples of (what we would call) lead oxide and mercuric oxide. They both arranged pieces of apparatus so that they could heat these substances. They then observed what happened, and recorded the behaviour of various volumes of gas given off and absorbed.

Nevertheless Priestley and Lavoisier believed totally different things: they gave sharply con-flicting accounts of the nature of the substances they observed and their properties and be-haviour. Indeed they asserted that quite different substances were present in the events they witnessed. Lavoisier denied that there was such a substance as phlogiston and postulated the existence of something called "oxygen." Priestley took exactly the opposite view. He insisted on the existence of phlogiston, identifying it with certain samples of gas agreed by both to be present in the experiment. Furthermore Priestley denied Lavoisier's "oxygen" and characterized the gas so labelled—which he had himself discovered—by means of his own theory.[22] Clearly the effect of "the facts" is neither simple nor sufficient to explain what needs explaining, viz. the theoretical divergence. It is because the effect of "the facts" is so different that the sociology of knowledge has a task.

There were, indeed, some occasions when for a while the experimenters observed different things from one another, e.g. when one came across a phenomenon that the other had not yet heard about. Furthermore, it is clear that when either of them observed something new in their apparatus it evoked a response. Thus Priestley spotted the appearance of water when, as we would say, he heated lead oxide in hydrogen. (For Priestley this was "minium" in "phlogiston.") But what the new observation did was to prompt the elaboration of his existing approach. Similarly, the *differential* exposure to facts merely resulted, for a while, in a slightly different degree of elaboration of their respective systems of thought.

The general conclusion is that reality is, after all, a common factor in all the vastly different cognitive responses that men produce to it. Being a common factor it is not a promising candidate to field as an explanation of that variation. Certainly any differences in the sampling of experience, and any differential exposure to reality must be allowed for. But that is in perfect accord with our equivalence postulate which enjoins the sociologist to investigate whatever local causes of credibility operate in each case. There is nothing in any of this to give comfort to the rationalist, or trouble to the relativist.

VII

Another important line of attack directed against relativism appears in a well-known sequence of papers by Martin Hollis and Steven Lukes.[23] They hold that all cultures share a common core of true beliefs and rationally-justified patterns of inference. This core is made up of statements which rational men "cannot fail to believe in simple perceptual situations" and "rules of coherent judgement, which rational men cannot fail to subscribe to."[24] Elsewhere these cultural universals are described as "material object perception beliefs" and "simple inferences, relying, say, on the law of non-contradiction."[25] According to Hollis and Lukes the truth of the statements in this core, and the validity of the inferences therein, are everywhere acknowledged because there are universal, context-independent criteria of truth and rationality, which all men recognize and are disposed to conform to. Without such universal criteria there would be no common core.

Clearly if there is indeed such a core, and it is sustained by context-independent criteria of truth and rationality, then relativism is confounded. But why must we accept that it exists? Interestingly, Lukes and Hollis make no serious attempt to describe the common core, or to mark its boundaries. Rather, they seek to show that it *must* exist, or at least that its existence must be assumed *a priori* if the possibility of communication and understanding between distinct cultures is admitted. We are asked to consider the problems facing say, an English-speaking anthropological field-worker, seeking to understand an alien culture. Such an individual must grasp the meaning of the alien concepts and beliefs, and this, we are told, requires him to *translate* them into English. This is where the common core comes in: it serves as the "rational bridgehead" which makes translation possible. It is the basis upon which simple equivalences between two languages can be initially established so that the enterprise of translation can get off the ground. By assuming that in "simple perceptual situations" the aliens perceive much as we do, infer much as we do, and say more or less what we would say, we can "define standard meanings for native terms." This then "makes it possible to identify utterances used in more ambiguous situations," lying outside the bridgehead, in which "supernatural" or "metaphysical" or "ritual" beliefs are expressed.[26] The basic point, however, is that without the rational bridgehead we would be caught in a circle. We need to translate "native" utterances in order to know what beliefs they express, while at the same time we need to know what is believed in order to know what is being said. Without an assumed bridgehead of shared beliefs there "would be no way into the circle," for there is, says Hollis, "no more direct attack on meaning available."[27]

Stated in abstract terms this argument has a certain plausibility. And if it were to prove correct it would certainly bolster the rationalist case and run counter to our equivalence postulate. The beliefs belonging to the rational bridgehead will be those whose enduring presence is explicable simply in virtue of the untrammelled operation of universal reason. Their credibility will be of a different sort from the diversity of beliefs that are peculiar to different cultures. The credibility of this latter class will have to be explained by special local causes, whilst the former "simply are rational."[28] The fact is, however, that the bridgehead argument fails as soon as it is measured against the realities of language learning and anthropological practice.

Notice how the whole argument hinges on the supposed role of translation: there is "no more direct attack on meaning available." But the fact is that translation is *not* the most direct attack on meaning that is available. It was not available, nor did it play any part at all, in the first and major attack that any of us made upon meaning when we acquired language in childhood. First language acquisition is not a translation process, and nothing that is absent here can be a necessary ingredient in subsequent learning. To understand an alien culture the anthropologist can proceed in the way that native speakers do. Any difficulties in achieving this stance will be pragmatic rather than *a priori*. There is, for instance, no necessity for the learner to assume shared concepts. Such an assumption would be false and would have nothing but nuisance value.

To see why this is so consider what is involved when a child learns an elementary concept like "bird". Such learning needs the continuing assistance of culturally competent adults. A teacher may gesture towards something in the sky and say "bird." Given the well-known indefiniteness of ostension a child would probably glean very little information from this: is it the object or the setting that is intended? But after a few acts of ostension, to different birds in different settings, he would begin to become competent in distinguishing "birds" from "nonbirds," and might perhaps himself tentatively point out and label putative birds.

Suppose now that the child labels a passing aeroplane a "bird." This would be a perfectly reasonable thing to do given the points of resemblance between aeroplanes and birds. Of course, there are noticeable differences too, but there are such differences between every successive instance of what are properly called "birds." All the instances of empirical concepts differ in detail from one another and we can never apply such concepts on the basis of perfect identity rather than resemblance. What the child is doing, in effect, is judging the resemblances between the aeroplane and the previous instances of "bird" to be more significant than the differences. The general form of his judgement, with its balancing of similarities and differences, is identical to those which lead to proper or accepted usage. It is only his knowledge of custom which is defective.

What happens in the case of the child is that he is overruled. "No, that is an aeroplane." This correction is at once an act of social control and of cultural transmission. It helps him to learn which of the possible judgements of sameness are accepted by his society as relevant to the use of "bird." In this way the particulars of experience are ordered into clusters and patterns *specific to a culture.*

The significance of this point becomes even more clear when we see how the things we call "birds" are dealt with in other cultures. When the anthropologist Bulmer visited the Karam of New Guinea he found that many of the instances of what we would call "bird" were referred to as "yakt." He also found that instances of bats were included amongst the "yakt," while instances of cassowaries were scrupulously denied admittance to the taxon. Objects were clustered in different ways, and the analogies that it is possible to discern amongst phenomena were channelled along different paths. Nevertheless, it was not too difficult to learn "yakt": the task simply involved noting what the Karam pointed out as "yakt" until it was possible to pick them out as well as the Karam did.[29]

What these examples show is that even empirical terms like "bird" do not constitute a special core of concepts whose application depends only upon an unconditioned reason. Learning even the most elementary of terms is a slow process that involves the acquisition from the culture of specific *conventions.* This makes apparently simple empirical words no different from others that are perhaps more obviously culturally influenced. There are no privileged occasions for the use of terms—no "simple perceptual situations"—which provide the researcher with "standard meanings" uncomplicated by cultural variables. In short, there is no bridgehead in Hollis' sense.[30]

Because there are no "standard meanings" there is no question of using them to provide a secure base from which to advance towards more ambiguous cases whose operation is to be understood in a qualitatively different and derivative way. All concepts and all usages stand on a par: none are intrinsically "unambiguous" or intrinsically "ambiguous" any more than some are intrinsically "literal" or intrinsically "metaphorical." Furthermore, there is no telling in advance which are the "problematic" cases where an alien culture will deviate from ours. For example, Bulmer could not have predicted in advance what the Karam would call bats or cassowaries, simply because of the initial identity of usage he discerned between the Karam "yakt" and our "bird." Similarly, no one could predict on the basis of past usage what the Karam would do with a hitherto unknown case such as, say, a barn-owl. Existing usage is only a precedent defined over a finite number of particular instances. It does not fix the proper handling of new cases in advance. Diverse developments are possible, and even where cultural diversity is not present it could emerge at any moment by a revision of the existing sequence of judgements of sameness and difference.

It might be objected, none the less, that the "rational bridgehead" was invoked to account for the possibility of translation, and translation is a *possible* mode of understanding alien culture, even if it is not a *necessary* mode. How is translation possible? Might not an anti-relativist argument be based simply upon the possibility of successful translation?

The way to proceed here is to assume nothing about translation in advance, least of all that it is successfully carried out. Instead we should ask what is implied for translation by the little empirical knowledge we possess of the simpler aspects of semantics and language learning. One clear implication arises from the character of concepts as arrays of judgements of sameness. Every such array, being the product of a unique sequence of judgements, is itself unique. No array in one culture can be unproblematically set into an identity with an array from another culture. Hence perfect translation cannot exist: there can only be translation acceptable for practical purposes, as judged by contingent, local standards. And this is a conclusion which fits well with what we know of the extremely complex procedures and activities which constitute translation as an empirical phenomenon.

Thus the rational bridgehead, the alleged common core of belief shared by all cultures, turns out to be a purely imaginary construct with no empirical basis at all. It is not difficult, however, to perceive its origins in the received culture of epistemologists. It is an old philosophical dualism dressed in a new garb. The distinction between the parts of a culture that belong to the rational core, and the parts that are specific and variable is just another version of the idea that observational predicates are qualitatively different from theoretical predicates. The bridgehead argument is a plea for a single pure observation language. Of all the dualisms of epistemology this must be the most discredited.[31] Surely, we now all recognize that although we may well all share the same unverbalized environment, there are any number of equally reasonable ways of speaking of it.

VIII

Hollis' and Lukes' argument includes the claim that there are simple forms of inference which all rational men find compelling. Among the instances offered here is "*p, p* implies *q*, therefore *q*." Hollis introduces this under the logicians' name of *modus ponens* and represents it by using the usual symbol for material implication, $(p. (p \rightarrow q)) \rightarrow q$.[32] It is noticeable, however, that Hollis and Lukes do not even begin to make their case. In particular they offer no relevant empirical evidence for their claim. None the less it is interesting to explore what follows if men do indeed evince some general disposition to conform to *modus ponens* and to other simple patterns of inference. It then becomes necessary to ask *why* men are disposed in favour of these forms of inference. What might account for the existence of such alleged universals of reason?

According to the rationalists there are two distinct issues here, and two ways of approaching the question. We can either search for the causes of the phenomenon, or we can seek to

furnish reasons for it. Naturally a rationalist will want to provide the sufficiently good reasons
that are at work, and hence show that deductive intuitions are explicable in rational terms. The
aim will be to show that deductive forms of inference can be shown to be rationally justified
in an absolute and context-free sense. Unfortunately for the rationalist there is little that he
can offer by way of reasoned argument in favour of adherence to deductive inference forms.
We have reached the end-point at which justification goes in a circle.

The predicament is neatly captured in Lewis Carroll's story of what the Tortoise said to
Achilles. Presented by Achilles with premises of the form "$p \rightarrow q$" and "p" the tortoise refuses
to draw the conclusion "q" until the step has been justified. Achilles obliges by formulating
the rule according to which the tortoise is to proceed. The rule makes clear the grounds upon
which the step to "q" may be taken. Given the rule "when you have '$p \rightarrow q$' and 'p' conclude
'q'" and given both "$p \rightarrow q$" and "p," will you *now* conclude "q"? he asks. Unfortunately the
tortoise is able to point out that when the justifying premise has been added the new inference
is again dependent on a step of the type that has been called into question: so he asks for yet
another premise to be formulated, and so on. The attempt at justification therefore fails, and
Achilles finds that he cannot use logic to force the tortoise to draw the desired conclusion.[33]

The basic point is that justifications of deduction themselves presuppose deduction. They
are circular because they appeal to the very principles of inference that are in question.[34] In
this respect the justification of deduction is in the same predicament as the justifications of induction which tacitly make inductive moves by appealing to the fact that induction "works."
Our two basic modes of reasoning are in an equally hopeless state with regard to their rational justification.[35]

As with induction a variety of attempts have been made to evade the circularity of justification.[36] Perhaps the most fully developed attempt at justification has been to say that the validity of inferences derives simply from the meaning of the formal signs or logical words used
in them. For instance, the meaning of "$\rightarrow$" is given by "truth table" definitions or the rules of
inference of the logical system of which it is a part, and the validity of the inferences in this
system derives from these meanings. This is the theory of "analytic validity." Unfortunately for
the rationalist this theory has been completely devastated by the logician A.N. Prior.[37]

Prior develops his argument by taking the case of the very simple logical connective "and."
Why is "p and q, therefore q" a valid inference? The theory of analytic validity says that it is
valid because of the meaning of "and." What is the meaning of "and"? This is given by stating
the role that the term has in forming compound propositions, or conjunctions, and drawing
inferences from them. "And" is defined by the rules that (i) from any pair of statements "p" and
"q," we can infer the statement "p and q," and (ii) from any conjunctive statement "p and q,"
we can infer either of the conjuncts. As an antidote to the seductive power of this circular
procedure Prior shows that a similar sequence of definitions would permit the introduction of
connectives that would justify the inference of any statement from any other. Consider, he
says, the new logical connective "tonk":

> Its meaning is completely given by the rules that (i) from any statement P we can infer any
> statement formed by joining P to any statement Q by "tonk" (which compound statement we

hereafter describe as "the statement P-tonk-Q"), and that (ii) from any "contonktive" statement P-tonk-Q we can infer the contained statement Q.[38]

Hence we can infer any *Q* from any *P.*

What Prior's paper shows is that appeal to rules and meanings cannot by itself justify our intuitions about validity, because these rules and meanings are themselves judged according to those intuitions, e.g. intuitions to the effect that "and" is defined by acceptable rules, whereas "tonk" is not. The theory of analytic validity invites us to run to meanings to justify our intuitions of validity, but then we have to run back again to our intuitions of validity to justify our selection of meanings. Our preference for the "right" rules which define "acceptable" connectives reveals the circularity of the intended justification. The intuitions are basic and the problem of justification set by the tortoise is the end-point after all. Like the good relativist that he is, the tortoise awaits a reasoned justification of deduction, confident that none will be forthcoming.[39]

IX

What else is there to do then but to turn to causes for an answer to the question of the widespread acceptance of deductive inference forms and the avoidance of inconsistency? A plausible strategy is to adopt a form of nativism: the disposition arises from our biological constitution and the way the brain is organized. Such a move, needless to say, gives no comfort to rationalism: epistemologically, to invoke neuronal structure is no better than to invoke social structure; both moves seek explanations rather than justifications. And for this very reason nativism is perfectly compatible with relativism. At whatever point it is found necessary, the explanation of credibility may swing from social to biological causes. Our empirical curiosity swings from asking how our society is organized to asking how the brain is organized. Our general cognitive proclivities become subject to empirical enquiry just as are the cognitive proclivities of other species. The empirical scientific investigation of human cognition, its manifest structure and its physiological basis, is, of course, a lengthy task. At any given time our overall understanding of the matter, and in particular our verbal accounts of it, will be provisional and liable to change. They are subject to the same fluctuations and redescriptions as are found in the study of any other empirical phenomenon.

This consideration reinforces an important point: no account of our biologically-based reasoning propensities will justify a unique system of logical conventions. Just as our experience of a shared material world does not itself guarantee shared verbal descriptions of it, so our shared natural rationality does not guarantee a unique logical system. Hollis and Lukes make the same mistake in dealing with logic as they do with descriptive predicates. They fail to keep what belongs to unverbalized reality separate from what belongs to language. Just as they conflated the two with their doctrine of a universal observation language; now they take the plausible belief that we possess deductive dispositions and render it, without a second thought, into the abstract and highly conventionalized notion of material implication. To combat this confusion we need to remember the gap between the varied systems of logic as they are developed by logicians and the primitive, biologically based, informal intuitions upon which they all depend for their operation. Hollis and Lukes' conflation soon takes its revenge on them: *modus ponens* for material implication, which they confidently take to be a rational universal, has been explicitly deemed to fail, and is rejected, in some interesting systems of logic.[40]

Logic, as it is systematized in textbooks, monographs or research papers, is a learned body of scholarly lore, growing and varying over time. It is a mass of conventional routines, decisions, expedient restrictions, dicta, maxims, and *ad hoc* rules. The sheer *lack* of necessity in granting its assumptions or adopting its strange and elaborate definitions is the point that should strike any candid observer. Why should anyone adopt a notion of "implication" whereby a contradiction "implies" any proposition? What is compelling about systems of logic which require massive and systematic deviation from our everyday use of crucial words like "if," "then," and "and"?[41] As a body of conventions and esoteric traditions the compelling character of logic, such as it is, derives from certain narrowly defined purposes and from custom and institutionalized usage. Its authority is moral and social, and as such it is admirable material for sociological investigation and explanation. In particular the credibility of logical conventions, just like the everyday practices which deviate from them, will be of an entirely local character. The utility of granting or modifying a definition for the sake of formal symmetry; the expediency of ignoring the complexity of everyday discourse and everyday standards of reasoning so that a certain abstract generality can be achieved: these will be the kinds of justification that will be offered and accepted or disputed by specialists in the field.

The point that emerges is that if any informal, intuitive reasoning dispositions are universally compelling, they are *ipso facto* without any reasoned justification. On the other hand, any parts of logic which can be justified will not be universal but purely local in their credibility. The rationalist goal of producing pieces of knowledge that are both universal in their credibility *and* justified in context-independent terms is unattainable.[42]

There is, of course, a final move that the rationalist can make. He can fall back into dogmatism, saying of some selected inference or conclusion or procedure: this just *is* what it is to be rational, or, this just *is* a valid inference.[43] It is at this point that the rationalist finally plucks victory out of defeat, for while the relativist can fight Reason, he is helpless against Faith. Just as Faith protects the Holy Trinity, or the Azande oracle, or the ancestral spirits of the Luba, so it can protect Reason. Faith has always been the traditional and most effective defence against relativism. But if at this point the relativist must retire defeated, to gaze from some far hilltop on the celebratory rites of the Cult of Rationalism, he can nevertheless quietly ask himself: what local, contingent causes might account for the remarkable intensity of the Faith in Reason peculiar to the Cult?[44]

NOTES

[1] E. Vivas, "Reiteration and second thoughts on cultural relativism" in H. Schoek and J. Wiggins (eds), *Relativism and the Study of Man* (Van Nostrand, Princeton, N.J., 1961).
[2] A. Musgrave, "The objectivism of Popper's epistemology" in P. A. Schilpp (ed.), *The Philosophy of Karl Popper* (Open Court, La Salle, Ill., 1974), ch. 15, p. 588.

[3] K. R. Popper, *The Open Society and its Enemies* (Routledge & Kegan Paul, London), vol. 2, 1966, p. 393; H. R. Post, *Against Ideologies* (Inaugural lecture, Chelsea College, University of London, 28 Nov 1974), p. 2, for Jewish physics. Vivas also invokes the image of Belsen.

[4] S. Rose and H. Rose (eds), *The Radicalisation of Science* (Macmillan, London, 1977).

[5] We refer to any collectively accepted system of belief as "knowledge." Philosophers usually adopt a different terminological convention confining "knowledge" to justified true belief. The reason for our preference should become clear in the course of the paper. For a full account of the ideas that form the background of this paper and a description of their implications for the sociology of knowledge, see B. Barnes, *Scientific Knowledge and Sociological Theory* (Routledge & Kegan Paul, London, 1974); B. Barnes, *Interests and the Growth of Knowledge* (Routledge & Kegan Paul, London, 1977); D. Bloor, *Knowledge and Social Imagery* (Routledge & Kegan Paul, London, 1976).

[6] These are the kinds of relativism that Popper identifies as his target on p. 387 and p. 388 of his *Open Society*, vol. 2. The claim that relativism is "self-refuting" is thoroughly discussed and thoroughly demolished in Mary Hesse, "The strong thesis of sociology of science," ch. 2 of her *Revolutions and Reconstructions in the Philosophy of Science* (Harvester Press, Brighton, 1980).

[7] As a selection of such work, see: A. Brannigan, "The reification of Mendel," *Social Studies of Science,* 9 (1979), pp. 423–54; T. M. Brown, "From mechanism to vitalism in eighteenth-century English physiology," *Journal of the History of Biology,* 7 (1974), pp. 179–216. K. L. Caneva, "From galvanism to electrodynamics: the transformation of German physics and its social context," *Historical Studies in the Physical Sciences,* 9 (1978), pp. 63–159; R. S. Cowan, "Francis Galton's statistical ideas: the influence of eugenics," *Isis,* 63 (1972), pp. 509–28; A. J. Desmond, "Designing the dinosaur: Richard Owen's response to Robert Edmond Grant," *Isis,* 70 (1979), pp. 224–34; J. Farley, *The Spontaneous Generation Controversy from Descartes to Oparin* (Baltimore, 1977); J. Farley and G. L. Geison, "Science, politics and spontaneous generation in nineteenth-century France: the Pasteur-Pouchet debate," *Bulletin of the History of Medicine,* 48 (1974), pp. 161–98; P. Forman, "Weimar culture, causality, and quantum theory, 1918–1927: adaptation by German physicists and mathematicians to a hostile intellectual environment," *Historical Studies in the Physical Sciences,* 3 (1971), pp. 1–115; E. Frankel, "Corpuscular optics and the wave theory of light: the science and politics of a revolution in physics," *Social Studies of Science,* 6 (1976), pp. 141–84; M. C. Jacob, *The Newtonians and the English Revolution, 1689–1720* (Ithaca, 1976); J. R. Jacob, "Boyle's atomism and the Restoration assault on pagan naturalism," *Social Studies of Science,* 8 (1978), pp. 211–33; J. R. Jacob, *Robert Boyle and the English Revolution. A Study in Social and Intellectual Change* (New York, 1977); J. R. Jacob, "The ideological origins of Robert Boyle's natural philosophy," *Journal of European Studies* 2 (1972), pp. 1–21; D. MacKenzie, "Statistical theory and social interests: a case study," *Social Studies of Science,* 8 (1978), pp. 35–83; D. MacKenzie, "Eugenics in Britain," *Social Studies of Science,* 6 (1976), pp. 499–532; D. MacKenzie, *Statistics in Britain 1865–1930: The Social Construction of Scientific Knowledge* (Edinburgh University Press, 1981); D. MacKenzie, S. B. Barnes, "Biometriker versus Mendelianer: Eine Kontroverse und ihre Erklärung," *Kölner Zeitschrift für Soziologie,* special edition 18 (1975), pp. 165–96; D. Ospovat, "Perfect adaptation and teleological explanation: approaches to the problem of the history of life in the mid-nineteenth century," *Studies in History of Biology,* 2 (1978), pp. 33–56; W. Provine, "Geneticists and the biology of race crossing," *Science,* 182 (1973), pp. 790–6; M.J.S. Rudwick, "The Devonian: a system born in conflict" in M. R. House *et al.* (eds), *The Devonian System* (London, 1979); S. Shapin, "The politics of observation: cerebral anatomy and social interests in the Edinburgh phrenology disputes" in R. Wallis (ed.), *On the Margins of Science: The Social Construction of Rejected Knowledge* (Sociological Review Monographs 27, Keele, 1979), pp. 139–78; R. S. Turner, "The growth of professorial research in Prussia, 1818–1848: causes and contexts," *Historical Studies in the Physical Sciences,* 3 (1971), pp. 137–82; R. S. Turner, "University reformers and professorial scholarship in Germany, 1760–1806" in L. Stone (ed.), *The University in Society* (Oxford, 1975), vol. II, pp. 495–531; Mary Winsor, *Starfish, Jellyfish and the Order of Life: Issues in Nineteenth-Century Science* (New Haven, 1976); B. Wynne, "C. G. Barkla and the J Phenomenon: a case study in the treatment of deviance in physics," *Social Studies of Science,* 6 (1976) pp. 304–47; B. Wynne, "Physics and psychics; science, symbolic action and social control in late Victorian England" in

B. Barnes and S. Shapin (eds), *Natural Order: Historical Studies of Scientific Culture* (Sage, London, 1979) ch. 7. A valuable review and discussion of this and other material is S. Shapin, "History of science and its sociological reconstruction," *History of Science,* 20, Sep 1982.

[8] M. Douglas, *Implicit Meanings* (Routledge, London, 1975); see also her "Cultural Bias," Occasional Paper 34, Royal Anthropological Institute (London, 1978); cf. also M. Cole, J. Gay, J. Glick, D. Sharp, *The Cultural Context of Learning and Thinking* (Basic Books, New York, 1969) and R. Horton, and R. Finnegan (eds), *Modes of Thought* (Faber, London, 1973).

[9] See B. Barnes, and S. Shapin, (eds), *Natural Order: Historical Studies of Scientific Culture* (Sage, London, 1979); D. Bloor, "The sociology of [scientific] knowledge" in W. Bynum, E. J. Browne and R. Porter (eds), *Dictionary of the History of Science* (Macmillan, London, 1981); S. Shapin, "Social uses of science" in G. S. Rousseau and R. S. Porter (eds), *The Ferment of Knowledge: Studies in the Historiography of Eighteenth-century Science* (Cambridge University Press, Cambridge, 1981) pp. 93–139.

[10] M. Hollis, "The social destruction of reality," (Ed. M. Hollis and S. Lukes *Rationality and Relativism,* Cambridge: MIT, 1982) p. 75.

[11] I. Lakatos, "History of science and its rational reconstructions" in R. Buck and R. Cohen (eds), *Boston Studies in the Philosophy of Science,* vol. 8 (Reidel, Dordrecht, 1971) p. 106.

[12] L. Laudan, *Progress and its Problems: Towards a Theory of Scientific Growth* (Routledge & Kegan Paul, London, 1977). For a critical review, see B. Barnes, "Vicissitudes of belief," *Social Studies of Science,* 9 (1979), p. 247–63.

[13] K. Mannheim, *Ideology and Utopia* (Routledge & Kegan Paul, London, 1936), p. 239. For a reply to Mannheim, see D. Bloor, "Wittgenstein and Mannheim on the sociology of mathematics," *Studies in History and Philosophy of Science,* 4 (1973), pp. 173–91.

[14] See, for instance, Lukes' critical reply to D. Bloor, "Durkheim and Mauss revisited: classification and the sociology of knowledge" in *Studies in History and Philosophy of Science* (forthcoming).

[15] It may be objected that the present argument would only apply in a world where people were divided into relatively isolated social groups and would fail in proportion to the degree that cosmopolitan uniformity prevailed—or when what Durkheim called an "international life" emerged. This is one of the objections E. Gellner presses against Winch in "The new idealism—cause and meaning in the social sciences" in I. Lakatos and A. Musgrave (eds), *Problems in the Philosophy of Science* (North Holland, Amsterdam, 1968), pp. 377–406, esp. p. 397. In fact in our argument the picture of the isolated tribes T1 and T2 is merely expository and not a necessary feature of the argument. The size of the context and the actual presence of alternatives is entirely contingent. The same point would apply even if there happened to be just one, homogeneous, international community.

[16] A.G.N. Flew, "Is the scientific enterprise self-refuting?," *Proceedings of the Eighth International Conference on the Unity of the Sciences, Los Angeles, 1979* (New York, 1980) vol. 1, pp. 34–60.

[17] Ibid.

[18] Farley and Geison, "Science, politics and spontaneous generation."

[19] Flew, "Is the scientific enterprise self-refuting?"

[20] Ibid.

[21] Of course it would be possible for the same argument, with the same monist and dualist alternatives, to be repeated on the level of psychological explanation. It has been known for philosophers to insist that, in psychology, causal accounts are only appropriate for pathological phenomena, e.g. saying that, while error and illusion might be causally explicable, normal or correct perception is not a fit subject for empirical investigation and causal explanation. See D. Hamlyn, *The Psychology of Perception* (Routledge & Kegan Paul, London, 1969), ch. 2, pp. 11–13; and G. Ryle *The Concept of Mind* (Hutchinson, London, 1949), p. 326.

In contrast, for fruitful and fascinating attempts to give good causal explanations of both successful and erroneous perception, see R. L. Gregory, *Eye and Brain* (Weidenfeld & Nicolson, London, 1966). Perhaps one day the dualist account of Ryle and Hamlyn will be developed into its ultimate form, and we will be told that the operations of adding machines are causally determined only when erroneous results are produced, and that at other times such machines operate rationally in ways which require no explanation.

[22] J. B. Conant, "The overthrow of phlogiston theory," in J. B. Conant and K. K. Nash (eds), *Harvard Case Histories in Experimental Science,* vol. I (Harvard University Press, Cambridge, Mass., 1966). Lavoisier's "oxygen" gas was conceived by him to be the principle of acidity plus caloric—the heat fluid. Caloric has now gone the same way as phlogiston and has been rejected as a theoretical entity, and it was later discovered that Lavoisier's "principle of acidity" was not present in hydrochloric acid.

[23] M. Hollis, "The limits of irrationality," *European Journal of Sociology,* 7 (1967), pp. 265–71; and "Reason and ritual," *Philosophy,* 43 (1967), pp. 231–47; and also this volume. See also S. Lukes, "Some problems about rationality," *European Journal of Sociology,* 7 (1967), pp. 247–64; "On the social determination of truth" in Horton and Finnegan, *Modes of Thought;* "Relativism, cognitive and moral," *Supplementary Proceedings of the Aristotelian Society,* 68 (1974), pp. 165–89; "Rationality and the explanation of belief," paper given at the Colloquium on "Irrationality: Explanation and Understanding," Maison des Sciences de l'Homme, Paris, 7–9 Jan 1980.

Note: Hollis' "The limits of rationality" and "Reason and ritual" and Lukes' "Some problems about rationality" have all been reprinted in B. R. Wilson (ed.), *Rationality* (Blackwell, 1970), chs. 9, 10 and 11. Page references will be to the Wilson volume, unless otherwise stated.

[24] Hollis, "The Social Destruction of Reality," *op. cit.,* p. 74.

[25] Lukes, "Rationality and the explanation of belief," p. 8.

[26] Hollis, "The limits of irrationality," pp. 215, 216, and "Reason and ritual," p. 221.

[27] Hollis, "The limits of irrationality," p. 208.

[28] Lukes, "Some problems about rationality," p. 208.

[29] R. Bulmer, "Why is the cassowary not a bird?," *Man,* n.s., 2 (1967), pp. 5–25.

[30] For a fuller development of these points, see M. Hesse, *The Structure of Scientific Inference* (Macmillan, London, 1974), chs 1 and 2. Their sociological significance is explored in B. Barnes, "On the conventional character of knowledge and cognition," *Philosophy of the Social Sciences,* 11 (1981), pp. 303–33. D. Bloor, "Durkheim and Mauss revisited: classification and the sociology of knowledge," *Studies in History and Philosophy of Science* (forthcoming)—a German version of this paper appeared in *Kölner Zeitschrift für Soziologie,* special issue, 23 (1980), pp. 20–51.

[31] Cf. Hesse, *The Structure of Scientific Inference.*

[32] Hollis, "Reason and ritual," p. 232.

[33] L. Carroll, "What the Tortoise said to Achilles," *Mind,* n.s., 4 (1895), pp. 278–80. Carroll, of course, does not use bare *p*s and *q*s but begins with a simple proposition from Euclid.

[34] It has been argued that there are technical defects in Carroll's paper and that the tortoise shifts his ground with regard to what has to be justified at different stages in the regress. See J. Thomson, "What Achilles should have said to the Tortoise," *Ratio,* 3 (1960), pp. 95–105. Nevertheless the basic thrust of Carroll's argument is correct. Circularity emerges whenever an attempt is made to ground our most general notions of validity. See W. Quine, "Truth by convention" in his *Ways of Paradox* (Random House, New York, 1966). See also J. McKinsey, *Journal of Symbolic Logic,* 13 (1948) pp. 114–15; and S. Kleene, ibid., pp. 173–4. These points are fully discussed in Susan Haack, "The justification of deduction," *Mind,* 85 (1976), pp. 112–19. In particular Haack shows that appeals to the truth table definition of material implication in order to justify *modus ponens* itself use that principle (p. 114).

[35] Haack, in "The justification of deduction" exhibits the similarity between the scandal of induction and the scandal of deduction. Needless to say, an *inductive* justification of deductive inference-forms and contradiction-avoiding rules is useless in the battle against relativism. If these rules and forms are favoured and institutionalized only where they prove profitable in discourse, then their incidence becomes intelligible in terms of contingent local determinants just as sociological relativism requires. And, conversely, all the deviations from the rules and forms are likely to become *equally* justified in the same way. This will show them to be just the same kinds of phenomena as the rules and forms themselves. Consider all the familiar locutions we find of pragmatic value in informal speech which appear to do violence to formal logical rules: "Yes and no," "It was, and yet it wasn't," "The whole was greater than its parts," "There is some truth in that statement," "That statement is nearer to the truth than this one," "*A* is a better proof than *B,*" and so on. All these locutions, indeed everything

in discourse which Lukes identifies as needing elucidation by "context-specific" rather than "universal" rules, become identical in character to "universally-rational" forms of discourse. The dualism essential to the anti-relativist position disappears.

36 For instance, it may be said that justifications of deduction are "superfluous" and that it is a mistake to concede that they are necessary. Critics of Lewis Carroll have taken this line, e.g. W. Rees, "What Achilles said to the Tortoise," *Mind,* n.s., 60 (1951), pp. 241–6. But judgements about what is, or is not, superfluous are highly subjective. In the present type of case we may suspect that they will derive their credibility entirely from their convenience for the purposes in hand, namely evading the problem that justifications are circular.

37 A. N. Prior, "The runabout inference ticket," *Analysis,* 21 (1960), pp. 38–9.

38 Ibid., p. 38.

39 Prior's paper has been discussed by N. Belnap, "Tonk, Plonk and Plink," *Analysis,* 22 (1962), pp. 130–4; J. T. Stevenson, "Roundabout the runabout inference ticket," *Analysis,* 21 (1962), pp. 124–8; and Susan Haack, *Philosophy of Logics* (Cambridge University Press, Cambridge, 1978), p. 31.

None of these commentators address the main point in Prior's argument. They all treat his paper as if it posed the question of how we should define logical connectives, rather than the question of the source of the validity of the inferences containing them. Thus their response takes the form of saying that *properly* chosen meanings accomplish valid inferences. The point, then, is to locate the source of propriety for these choices, and this reintroduces our intuitions of validity again. Belnap explicitly invokes these intuitions but, despite his appreciation of Prior's paper, appears not to see that he is supporting rather than correcting him.

Hollis' paper "A Retort to the Tortoise," *Mind,* 84 (1975), pp. 610–16, is simply another attempt to reify "meaning" and impute to it the power to solve basic problems of validity.

40 A. R. Anderson, and N. Belnap, "Tautological entailments," *Philosophical Studies,* 13 (1961), pp. 9–24. This paper develops some of the consequences of demanding that the entailment relation satisfy conditions of "relevance" between premise and conclusion. This is one of the plausible intuitive requirements that are violated by the "Lewis Principle," that a contradiction entails any statement: "P and not P entails Q," regardless of whether or not Q "has anything to do with" P or its negation. The Lewis Principle is a theorem of the axiom system sometimes called the system of tautological implication. To challenge the theorem means rejecting, for instance, the disjunctive syllogism which is equivalent to *modus ponens.* This is what Anderson and Belnap do on grounds of relevance. The result is a perfectly consistent axiom system: the four-valued logic of De Morgan implication. See Haack, *Philosophy of Logics,* pp. 200–1; D. Makinson, *Topics in Modern Logic* (Methuen, London, 1973), ch. 2.

It is ironic that logicians, who expose with admirable ruthlessness how problematic, variable and difficult to ground patterns of inference are, and who freely confess how very little is agreed upon by the totality of practitioners in their field, are turned to again and again to provide constraints upon the possibilities of rational thought. Just as there is always a certain demand for iron laws of economics, so there seems always to be a demand for iron laws of logic.

41 For a careful documentation of the relation between ordinary and technical usage, see P. Strawson, *Introduction to Logical Theory* (Methuen, London, 1952).

42 For an extension of this argument from logic to mathematics, see D. Bloor, *Knowledge and Social Imagery* (Routledge & Kegan Paul, 1966), chs. 5–7. Here a modified empiricist theory of mathematics is defended against Frege. See also Bloor, "Polyhedra and the abominations of Leviticus," *British Journal for the History of Science,* 11 (1478), pp. 245–72. This provides a sociological reading of I. Lakatos, *Proofs and Refutations* (Cambridge University Press, Cambridge, 1976).

43 Although dogmatic assertions are perhaps the most common ways in which philosophers indicate the end-points at which they revert to faith, there are other ways. Quine for example explicitly takes for granted currently accepted scientific knowledge. Similarly, logicians often set out the points where they allow "intuition" to decide for them which of different arguments they will accept.

Equally widespread, if less defensible, is the decision to reject an argument because of its consequences. If a series of inferences leads to solipsism, or scepticism, or relativism, it is assumed, simply by that very fact, that the series must contain an error. Thus, H. Putnam describes how one of his papers is designed to "block" a perfectly good, but inconvenient, inductive inference: "[There is] a serious worry . . . that eventually the following meta-induction becomes overwhelmingly compelling: *just as no term used in the science of more than 50 . . . years ago referred, so it will turn out that no term used now . . . refers.*"

It must obviously be a desideratum for the Theory of Reference that this meta-induction be blocked . . . ("What is realism?," *Philosophical Papers* (Cambridge University Press, Cambridge, 1975), vol. 2).

Finally, of course, there is the occasional quite straightforward profession of faith, which scorns any disguise. I. C. Jarvie, for example, is disarmingly frank when he opposes relativism by suggesting: "Perhaps, when we do science, and even more so mathematics, we participate in the divine . . . [It is] awe at the transcendental miracle of mathematics and science that has moved philosophers since Ancient Greece" ("Laudan's problematic progress and the social sciences," *Philosophy of the Social Sciences,* 9 [1979], p. 496).

[44] A plausible hypothesis is that relativism is disliked because so many academics see it as a dampener on their moralizing. A dualist idiom, with its demarcations, contrasts, rankings and evaluations is easily adapted to the tasks of political propaganda or self-congratulatory polemic. *This* is the enterprise that relativists threaten, not science. See notes 1 – 4 above. If relativism has any appeal at all, it will be to those who wish to engage in that eccentric activity called "disinterested research."

B R U N O   L A T O U R
SELECTIONS FROM *SCIENCE IN ACTION*

OPENING PANDORA'S BLACK BOX

Scene 1. On a cold and sunny morning in October 1985, John Whittaker entered his office in the molecular biology building of the Institut Pasteur in Paris and switched on his *Eclipse MV/8000* computer. A few seconds after loading the special programs he had written, a three-dimensional picture of the DNA double helix flashed onto the screen. John, a visiting computer scientist, had been invited by the Institute to write programs that could produce three-dimensional images of the coils of DNA and relate them to the thousands of new nucleic acid sequences pouring out every year into the journals and data banks. "Nice picture, eh?" said his boss, Pierre, who was just entering the office. "Yes, good machine too," answered John.

Scene 2: In 1951 in the Cavendish laboratory at Cambridge, England, the X-ray pictures of crystallised deoxyribonucleic acid were not "nice pictures" on a computer screen. The two young researchers, Jim Watson and Francis Crick,[1] had a hard time obtaining them from Maurice Wilkins and Rosalind Franklin in London. It was impossible yet to decide if the form of the acid was a triple or a double helix, if the phosphate bonds were at the inside or at the outside of the molecule, or indeed if it was an helix at all. It did not matter much to their boss, Sir Lawrence Bragg, since the two were not supposed to be working on DNA anyway, but it mattered a lot to them, especially since Linus Pauling, the famous chemist, was said to be about to uncover the structure of DNA in a few months.

Scene 3: In 1980 in a Data General building on Route 495 in Westborough, Massachusetts, Tom West[2] and his team were still trying to debug a makeshift prototype of a new machine nicknamed *Eagle* that the company had not planned to build at first, but that was beginning to rouse the marketing department's interest. However, the debugging program was a year behind schedule. Besides, the choice West had made of using the new PAL chips kept delaying the machine—renamed *Eclipse MV/8000,* since no one was sure at the time if the company manufacturing the chips could deliver them on demand. In the meantime, their main competitor, DEC, was selling many copies of its *VAX 11/780,* increasing the gap between the two companies.

(1) LOOKING FOR A WAY IN

Where can we start a study of science and technology? The choice of a way in crucially depends on good timing. In 1985, in Paris, John Whittaker obtains "nice pictures" of DNA on a "good machine." In 1951 in Cambridge Watson and Crick are struggling to define a shape for DNA that is compatible with the pictures they glimpsed in Wilkins's office. In 1980, in the basement of a building, another team of researchers is fighting to make a new computer work and to catch up with DEC. What is the meaning of these "flashbacks," to use the cinema term? They carry us back through space and time.

When we use this travel machine, DNA ceases to have a shape so well established that computer programs can be written to display it on a screen. As to the computers, they don't exist at all. Hundreds of nucleic acid sequences are not pouring in every year. Not a single one is known and even the notion of a sequence is doubtful since it is still unsure, for many people at the time, whether DNA plays any significant role in passing genetic material from one generation to the next. Twice already, Watson and Crick had proudly announced that they had solved the riddle and both times their model had been reduced to ashes. As to the "good machine" *Eagle,* the flashback takes us back to a moment when it cannot run any program at all. Instead of a routine piece of equipment John Whittaker can switch on, it is a disorderly array of cables and chips surveyed by two other computers and surrounded by dozens of engineers trying to make it work reliably for more than a few seconds. No one in the team knows yet if this project is not going to turn out to be another complete failure like the *EGO* computer on which they worked for years and which was killed, they say, by the management.

In Whittaker's research project many things are unsettled. He does not know how long he is going to stay, if his fellowship will be renewed, if any program of his own can handle millions of base pairs and compare them in a way that is biologically significant. But there are at least two elements that raise no problems for him: the double helix shape of DNA and his Data General computer. What was for Watson and Crick the problematic focus of a fierce challenge, what won them a Nobel Prize, is now the basic dogma of his program, embedded in thousand of lines of his listing. As for the machine that made West's team work day and night for years, it is now no more problematic than a piece of furniture as it hums quietly away in his office. To be sure, the maintenance man of Data General stops by every week to fix up some minor problems; but neither the man nor John have to overhaul the computer all over again and force the company to develop a new line of products. Whittaker is equally well aware of the many problems plaguing the Basic Dogma of biology—Crick, now an old gentleman, gave a lecture at the Institute on this a few weeks ago—but neither John nor his boss have to rethink entirely the shape of the double helix or to establish a new dogma.

The word *black box* is used by cyberneticians whenever a piece of machinery or a set of commands is too complex. In its place they draw a little box about which they need to know nothing but its input and output. As far as John Whittaker is concerned the double helix and the machine are two black boxes. That is, no matter how controversial their history, how complex their inner workings, how large the commercial or academic networks that hold them in place, only their input and output count. When you switch on the *Eclipse* it runs the programs you load; when you compare nucleic acid sequences you start from the double helix shape.

The flashback from October 1985 in Paris to Autumn 1951 in Cambridge or December 1980 in Westborough, Massachusetts, presents two completely different pictures of each of these two objects, a scientific fact—the double helix—and a technical artefact—the *Eagle,* minicomputer. In the first picture John Whittaker uses two black boxes because they are unproblematic and certain; during the flashback the boxes get reopened and a bright coloured light illuminates them. In the first picture, there is no longer any need to decide where to put the phosphate backbone of the double helix, it is just there at the outside; there is no longer any squabble to decide if the *Eclipse* should be a 32-bit fully compatible machine, as you just hook it up to the other NOVA computers. During the flashbacks, a lot of people are introduced back into the picture, many of them staking their career on the *decisions* they take: Rosalind Franklin decides to reject the model-building approach Jim and Francis have chosen and to concentrate instead on basic X-ray crystallography in order to obtain better photographs; West decides to make a 32-bit compatible machine even though this means building a tinkered "kludge," as they contemptuously say, and losing some of his best engineers, who want to design a neat new one.

In the Pasteur Institute John Whittaker is taking no big risk in believing the three-dimensional shape of the double helix or in running his program on the *Eclipse.* These are now routine choices. The risks he and his boss take lie elsewhere, in this gigantic program of comparing all the base pairs generated by molecular biologists all over the world. But if we go back to Cambridge, thirty years ago, who should we believe? Rosalind Franklin who says it might be a three-strand helix? Bragg who orders Watson and Crick to give up this hopeless work entirely and get back to serious business? Pauling, the best chemist in the world, who unveils a structure that breaks all the known laws of chemistry? The same uncertainty arises in the Westborough of a few years ago. Should West obey his boss, de Castro, when he is explicitly asked *not* to do a new research project there, since all the company research has now moved to North Carolina? How long should West pretend he is not working on a new computer? Should he believe the marketing experts when they say that all their customers want a fully compatible machine (on which they can reuse their old software) instead of doing as his competitor DEC does a "culturally compatible" one (on which they cannot reuse their software but only the most basic commands)? What confidence should he have in his old team burned out by the failure of the *EGO* project? Should he risk using the new PAL chips instead of the older but safer ones?

Uncertainty, people at work, decisions, competition, controversies are what one gets when making a flashback from certain, cold, unproblematic black boxes to their recent past. If you take two pictures, one of the black boxes and the other of the open controversies, they are utterly different. They are as different as the two sides, one lively, the other severe, of a

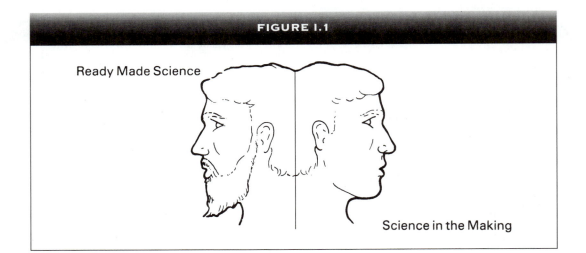

FIGURE I.1

Ready Made Science

Science in the Making

two-faced Janus. "Science in the making" on the right side, "all made science" or "ready made science" on the other; such is Janus *bifrons,* the first character that greets us at the beginning of our journey.

In John's office, the two black boxes cannot and should not be reopened. As to the two controversial pieces of work going on in the Cavendish and in Westborough, they are laid open for us by the scientists at work. The impossible task of opening the black box is made feasible (if not easy) by moving in time and space until one finds the controversial topic on which scientists and engineers are busy at work. This is the first decision we have to make: our entry into science and technology will be through the back door of science in the making, not through the more grandiose entrance of ready made science.

Now that the way in has been decided upon, with what sort of prior knowledge should one be equipped before entering science and technology? In John Whittaker's office the double helix model and the computer are clearly distinct from the rest of his worries. They do not interfere with his psychological mood, the financial problems of the Institute, the big grants for which his boss has applied, or with the political struggle they are all engaged in to create in France a big data bank for molecular biologists. They are just sitting there in the background, their scientific or technical contents neatly distinct from the mess that John is immersed in. If he wishes to know something about the DNA structure or about the *Eclipse,* John opens *Molecular Biology of the Gene* or the *User's Manual,* books that he can take off the shelf. However, if we go back to Westborough or to Cambridge this clean distinction between a context and a content disappears.

Scene 4: Tom West sneaks into the basement of a building where a friend lets him in at night to look at a VAX computer. West starts pulling out the printed circuits boards and analyses his competitor. Even his first analysis merges technical and quick economic calculations with the strategic decisions already taken. After a few hours, he is reassured.

> "I'd been living in fear of VAX for a year," West said afterward. (. . .) "I think I got a high when I looked at it and saw how complex and expensive it was. It made me feel good about some of the decisions we've made."

Then his evaluation becomes still more complex, including social, stylistic and organisational features:

> Looking into the VAX, West had imagined he saw a diagram of DEC's corporate organization. He felt that VAX was too complicated. He did not like, for instance, the system by which various parts of the machine communicated with each other, for his taste, there was too much protocol involved. He decided that VAX embodied flaws in DEC's corporate organization. The machine expressed that phenomenally successful company's cautious, bureaucratic style. Was this true? West said it did not matter, it was a useful theory. Then he rephrased his opinions. "With VAX, DEC was trying to minimize the risk," he said, as he swerved around another car. Grinning, he went on: "We're trying to maximize the win, and make Eagle go as fast as a raped ape."

> (Kidder: 1981, p. 36)

This heterogeneous evaluation of his competitor is not a marginal moment in the story; it is the crucial episode when West decides that in spite of a two-year delay, the opposition of the North Carolina group, the failure of the *EGO* project, they can still make the *Eagle* work. "Organisation," "taste," "protocol," "bureaucracy," "minimisation of risks," are not common technical words to describe a chip. This is true, however, only once the chip is a black box sold to consumers. When it is submitted to a competitor's trial, like the one West does, all these bizarre words become part and parcel of the technical evaluation. Context and contents merge.

Scene 5: Jim Watson and Francis Crick get a copy of the paper unveiling the structure of DNA written by Linus Pauling and brought to them by his son:

> Peter's face betrayed something important as he entered the door, and my stomach sank in apprehension at learning that all was lost. Seeing that neither Francis nor I could bear any further suspense, he quickly told us that the model was a three-chain helix with the sugar phosphate backbone in the center. This sounded so suspiciously like our aborted effort of last year that immediately I wondered whether we might already have had the credit and glory of a great discovery if Bragg had not held us back.
>
> (Watson: 1968, p. 102)

Was it Bragg who made them miss a major discovery, or was it Linus who missed a good opportunity for keeping his mouth shut? Francis and Jim hurriedly try out the paper and look to see if the sugar phosphate backbone is solid enough to hold the structure together. To their amazement, the three chains described by Pauling had no hydrogen atoms to tie the three strands together. Without them, if they knew their chemistry, the structure will immediately fly apart.

> Yet somehow Linus, unquestionably the world's most astute chemist, had come to the opposite conclusion. When Francis was amazed equally by Pauling's unorthodox chemistry, I began to breathe slower. By then I knew we were still in the game. Neither of us, however, had the slightest clue to the steps that had led Linus to his blunder. If a student had made a similar mistake, he would be thought unfit to benefit from Cal Tech's chemistry faculty. Thus, we could not but initially worry whether Linus's model followed from a revolutionary reevaluation of the acid-based properties of very large molecules. The tone of the manuscript, however, argued against any such advance in chemical theory.
>
> (idem: p. 103)

To decide whether they are still in the game Watson and Crick have to evaluate simultaneously Linus Pauling's reputation, common chemistry, the tone of the paper, the level of Cal Tech's students; they have to decide if a revolution is under way, in which case they have been beaten off, or if an enormous blunder has been committed, in which case they have to rush still faster because Pauling will not be long in picking it up:

> When his mistake became known, Linus would not stop until he had captured the right structure. Now our immediate hope was that his chemical colleagues would be more than ever awed by his intellect and not probe the details of his model. But since the manuscript had already been dispatched to the *Proceedings of the National Academy,* by mid-March at the latest Linus's

paper would be spread around the world. Then it would be only a matter of days before the error would be discovered. We had anywhere up to six weeks before Linus again was in full-time pursuit of DNA.

(idem: p. 104)

"Suspense," "game," "tone," "delay of publication," "awe," "six weeks delay" are not common words for describing a molecule structure. This is the case at least once the structure is known and learned by every student. However, as long as the structure is submitted to a competitor's probing, these queer words are part and parcel of the very chemical structure under investigation. Here again context and content fuse together.

The equipment necessary to travel through science and technology is at once light and multiple. Multiple because it means mixing hydrogen bonds with deadlines, the probing of one another's authority with money, debugging and bureaucratic style; but the equipment is also light because it means simply leaving aside all the prejudices about what distinguishes the context in which knowledge is embedded and this knowledge itself. At the entrance of Dante's Inferno is written:

ABANDON HOPE ALL YE WHO ENTER HERE

At the onset of this voyage should be written:

ABANDON KNOWLEDGE ABOUT KNOWLEDGE
ALL YE WHO ENTER HERE

Learning to use the double helix and *Eagle* in 1985 to write programs reveals none of the bizarre mixture they are composed of; studying these in 1952 or in 1980 reveals it all. On the two black boxes sitting in Whittaker's office it is inscribed, as on Pandora's box: DANGER: DO NOT OPEN. From the two tasks at hand in the Cavendish and in Data General Headquarters, passions, deadlines; decisions escape in all directions from a box that lies open. Pandora, the mythical android sent by Zeus to Prometheus, is the second character after Janus to greet us at the beginning of our trip. (We might need more than one blessing from more than one of the antique gods if we want to reach our destination safely.)

(2) WHEN ENOUGH IS NEVER ENOUGH

Science has two faces: one that knows, the other that does not know yet. We will choose the more ignorant. Insiders, and outsiders as well, have lots of ideas about the ingredients necessary for science in the making. We will have as few ideas as possible on what constitutes science. But how are we going to account for the closing of the boxes, because they do, after all, close up? The shape of the double helix is settled in John's office in 1985; so is that of the *Eclipse MV/8000* computer. How did they move from the Cavendish in 1952 or from Westborough, Massachusetts, to Paris 1985? It is all very well to choose controversies as a way in, but we need to follow also the closure of these controversies. Here we have to get used to a strange acoustic

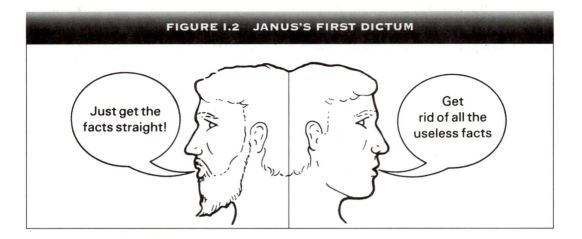

FIGURE I.2   JANUS'S FIRST DICTUM

phenomenon. The two faces of Janus talk at once and they say entirely different things that we should not confuse.

Scene 6: Jim copies from various textbooks the forms of the base pairs that make up DNA and plays with them trying to see if a symmetry can be seen when pairing them. To his amazement adenine coupled with adenine, cytosine with cytosine, guanine with guanine and thymine with thymine make very nice superimposable forms. To be sure this symmetry renders the sugar phosphate backbone strangely misshapen but this is not enough to stop Jim's pulse racing or to stop him writing a triumphant letter to his boss.

> I no sooner got to the office and began explaining my scheme than the American crystallographer Jerry Donohue protested that the idea would not work. The tautomeric forms I had copied out of Davidson's book were, in Jerry's opinion, incorrectly assigned. My immediate retort that several other texts also pictured guanine and thymine in the enol form cut no ice with Jerry. Happily he let out that for years organic chemists had been arbitrarily favoring particular tautomeric forms over their alternatives on only the flimsiest of grounds. (. . .) Though my immediate reaction was to hope that Jerry was blowing hot air, I did not dismiss his criticism. Next to Linus himself, Jerry knew more about hydrogen bonds than anyone in the world. Since for many years he had worked at Cal Tech on the crystal structures of small organic molecules, I couldn't kid myself that he did not grasp our problem. During the six months that he occupied a desk in our office, I had never heard him shooting off his mouth on subjects about which he knew nothing. Thoroughly worried, I went back to my desk hoping that some gimmick might emerge to salvage the like-with-like idea.

> (Watson: 1968, pp. 121–2)

Jim had got the facts straight out of textbooks which, unanimously, provided him with a nice black box: the enol form. In this case, however, this is the very fact that should be dismissed or put into question. Or at least this is what Donohue says. But whom should Jim believe? The unanimous opinion of organic chemists or *this* chemist's opinion? Jim, who tries to salvage his model, switches from one rule of method, "get the facts straight," to other more strategic ones, "look for a weak point," "choose who to believe." Donohue studied with Pauling, he worked on small molecules, in six months he never said absurd things. Discipline, affiliation, curriculum vitae, psychological appraisal are mixed together by Jim to reach a decision. Better sacrifice them and the nice like-with-like model, than Donohue's criticism. The fact, no matter how "straight," has to be dismissed.

> The unforeseen dividend of having Jerry share an office with Francis, Peter, and me, though obvious to all, was not spoken about. If he had not been with us in Cambridge, I might still have been pumping out for a like-with-like structure. Maurice, in a lab devoid of structural chemists, did not have anyone to tell him that all the textbook pictures were wrong. But for Jerry, only Pauling would have been likely to make the right choice and stick by its consequences.

> (idem: p. 132)

The advice of Janus' left side is easy to follow when things are settled, but not as long as things remain unsettled. What is on the left side, universal well-known facts of chemistry, becomes, from the right side point of view, scarce pronouncements uttered by two people in the whole world. They have a *quality* that crucially depends on localisation, on chance, on appraising simultaneously the worth of the people and of what they say.

Scene 7: West and his main collaborator, Alsing, are discussing how to tackle the debugging program:

> "I want to build a simulator, Tom."
> "It'll take too long, Alsing. The machine'll be debugged before you get your simulator debugged."
> This time, Alsing insisted. They could not build Eagle in anything like a year if they had to debug all the microcode on prototypes. If they went that way, moreover, they'd need to have at least one and probably two extra prototypes right from the start, and that would mean a

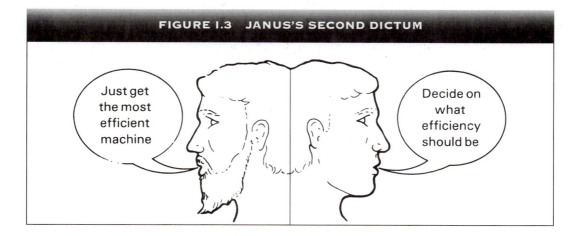

FIGURE I.3   JANUS'S SECOND DICTUM

Just get the most efficient machine

Decide on what efficiency should be

doubling of the boring, grueling work of updating boards. Alsing wanted a program that would behave like a perfected Eagle, so that they could debug their microcode separately from the hardware.

West said: "Go ahead. But I betchya it'll all be over by the time you get it done."

(Kidder: 1981, p. 146)

The right side's advice is strictly followed by the two men since they want to build the best possible computer. This however does not prevent a new controversy starting between the two men on how to mimic in advance an efficient machine. If Alsing cannot convince one of his team members, Peck, to finish in six weeks the simulator that should have taken a year and a half, then West will be right: the simulator is not an efficient way to proceed because it will come too late. But if Alsing and Peck succeed, then it is West's definition of efficiency which will turn out to be wrong. Efficiency will be the consequence of who succeeds; it does not help deciding, on the spot, who is right and wrong. The right side's advice is all very well once Eagle is sent to manufacturing; before that, it is the left side's confusing strategic advice that should be followed.

Scene 8: West has insulated his team for two years from the rest of the company. "Some of the kids," he says, "don't have a notion that there's a company behind all of this. It could be the CIA funding this. It could be a psychological test" (Kidder: 1982, p. 200). During this time, however, West has constantly lobbied the company on behalf of Eagle. Acting as a middle-man he has filtered the constraints imposed on the future machine by de Castro (the Big Boss), the marketing department, the other research group in North Carolina, the other machines presented in computer fairs, and so on. He was also the one who kept negotiating the deadlines that were never met. But there comes a point when all the other departments he has lobbied so intensely want to see something, and call his bluff. The situation becomes especially tricky when it is clear at last that the North Carolina group will not deliver a machine, that DEC is selling *VAX*

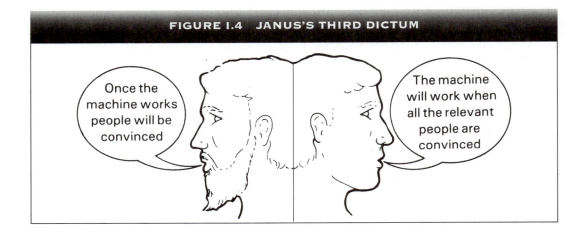

FIGURE I.4   JANUS'S THIRD DICTUM

Once the machine works people will be convinced

The machine will work when all the relevant people are convinced

like hot cakes and that all the customers want a supermini 32-bit fully compatible machine from Data General. At this point West has to break the protective shell he has built around his team. To be sure, he designed the machine so as to fit it in with the other departments' interests, but he is still uncertain of their reaction and of that of his team suddenly bereft of the machine.

> As the summer came on, increasing numbers of intruders were being led into the lab—diagnostic programmers and, particularly, those programmers from Software. Some Hardy Boys had grown fond of the prototypes of Eagle, as you might of a pet or a plant you've raised from a seedling. Now Rasala was telling them that they couldn't work on their machines at certain hours, because Software needed to use them. There was an explanation: the project was at a precarious stage; if Software didn't get to know and like the hardware and did not speak enthusiastically about it, the project might be ruined; the Hardy Boys were lucky that Software wanted to use the prototypes—and they had to keep Software happy.

> (idem: p. 201)

Not only the Software people have to be kept happy, but also the manufacturing people, those from marketing, those who write the technical documentation, the designers who have to place the whole machine in a nice looking box (not a black one this time!), not mentioning the stockholders and the customers. Although the machine has been conceived by West, through many compromises, to keep all these people happy and busy, he cannot be sure it is going to hold them together. Each of the interest groups has to try their own different sort of tests on the machine and see how it withstands them. The worst, for Tom West, is that the company manufacturing the new PAL chips is going bankrupt, that the team is suffering a *post partum* depression, and that the machine is not yet debugged. "Our credibility, I think, is running out, "West tells his assistants. Eagle still does not run more than a few seconds without flashing error messages on the screen. Every time they painstakingly pinpoint the bug, they fix it and then try a new and more difficult debugging program.

> Eagle was failing its Multiprogramming Reliability Test mysteriously. It was blowing away, crashing, going out to never-never land, and falling off the end of the world after every four hours or so of smooth running.
> "Machines somewhere in the agony of the last few bugs are very vulnerable," says Alsing. "The shouting starts about it. It'll never work, and so on. Managers and support groups start saying this. Hangers-on say, "Gee, I thought you'd get it done a lot sooner." That's when people start talking about redesigning the whole thing."
> Alsing added, "Watch out for Tom now."
> West sat in his office. "I'm thinking of throwing the kids out of the lab and going in there with Rasala and fix it. It's true. I don't understand all the details of that sucker, but I will, and I'll get it to work:
> "Gimme a few more days," said Rasala.

> (idem: p. 231)

A few weeks later, after Eagle has successfully run a computer game called Adventure, the whole team felt they had reached one approximate end: "It's a computer," Rasala said (idem: p. 233). On Monday 8 October, a maintenance crew comes to wheel down the hall what was quickly becoming a black box. Why has it become such? Because it is a good machine, says the left side of our Janus friend. But it was not a good machine before it worked. Thus while it is being made it cannot convince anyone *because* of its good working order. It is only after endless little bugs have been taken out, each bug being revealed by a new trial imposed by a new interested group, that the machine will *eventually* and *progressively* be made to work. All the reasons for why it will work once it is finished do not help the engineers while they are making it.

Scene 9. How does the double helix story end? In a series of trials imposed on the new model by each of the successive people Jim Watson and Francis Crick have worked with (or against). Jim is playing with cardboard models of the base pairs, now in the keto form suggested by Jerry Donohue. To his amazement he realises that the shape drawn by pairing adenine with thymine and guanine with cytosine are superimposable. The steps of the double helix have the same shape. Contrary to his earlier model, the structure might be complementary instead of being like-with-like. He hesitates a while, because he sees no reason at first for this complementarity. Then he remembers what was called "Chargaff laws," one of these many empirical facts they had kept in the background. These "laws" stated that there was always as much adenine as thymine and as much guanine as cytosine, no matter which DNA one chose to analyse. This isolated fact, devoid of any meaning in his earlier like-with-like model, suddenly brings a new strength to his emerging new model. Not only are the pairs superimposable, but Chargaff laws can be made a consequence of his model. Another feature came to strengthen the model: it suggests a way for a gene to split into two parts and then for each strand to create an exact complementary copy of itself. One helix could give birth to two identical helices. Thus biological meaning could support the model.

Still Jim's cardboard model could be destroyed in spite of these three advantages. Maybe Donohue will burn it to ashes as he did the attempt a few days earlier. So Jim called him to check if he had any objection. "When he said no, my morale skyrocketed" (Watson: 1968,

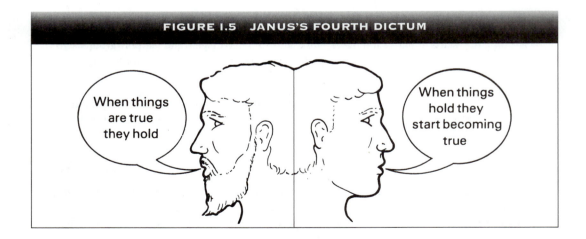

FIGURE I.5   JANUS'S FOURTH DICTUM

When things are true they hold

When things hold they start becoming true

p. 124). Then it is Francis who rushes into the lab and "pushes the bases together in a number of ways." The model, this time, *resists* Francis's scepticism. There are now many decisive elements tied together with and by the new structure.

Still, all the convinced people are in the same office and although they think they are right, they could still be deluding themselves. What will Bragg and all the other crystallographers say? What objections will Maurice Wilkins and Rosalind Franklin, the only ones with X-ray pictures of the DNA, have? Will they see the model as *the* only form able to give, by projection, the shape visible on Rosalind's photographs? They'd like to know fast but dread the danger of the final showdown with people who, several times already, have ruined their efforts. Besides, another ally is missing to set up the trial, a humble ally for sure but necessary all the same: "That night, however, we could not firmly establish the double helix. Until the metal bases were on hand, any model building would be too sloppy to be convincing" (idem: p. 127). Even with Chargaff laws, with biological significance, with Donohue's approval, with their excitement, with the base pairing all on their side, the helix is still sloppy. Metal is necessary to reinforce the structure long enough to withstand the trials that the competitors/colleagues are going to impose on it.

The remainder of the double helix story looks like the final rounds of a presidential nomination. Every one of the other contenders is introduced into the office where the model is now set up, fights with it for a while before being quickly overwhelmed and then pledging complete support to it. Bragg is convinced although still worried that no one more serious than Jim and Francis had checked the helix. Now for the big game, the encounter between the model and those who for years had captured its projected image. "Maurice needed but a minute's look at the model to like it." "He was back in London only two days before he rang up to say that both he and Rosy found that their X-ray data strongly supported the double helix" (p. 131). Soon Pauling rallies himself to the structure, then it is the turn of the referees of *Nature*.

"Of course," says the left side of Janus, "everyone is convinced because Jim and Francis stumbled on the right structure. The DNA shape itself is enough to rally everyone." "No," says the right side, "every time someone else is convinced it progressively becomes a more right structure." Enough is never enough: years later in India and New Zealand other researchers were working on a so-called "warped zipper"[3] model that did everything the double helix does—plus a bit more; Pauling strongly supported his own structure that had turned out to be entirely wrong; Jim found biological significance in a like-with-like structure that survived only a few hours; Rosalind Franklin had been stubbornly convinced earlier that it was a three-strand helix; Wilkins ignored the keto forms revealed by Jerry Donohue; Chargaff's laws were an insignificant fact they kept in the background for a long time; as to the metal atom toys, they have lent strong support to countless models that turned out to be wrong. All these allies appear strong once the structure is blackboxed. As long as it is not, Jim and Francis are still struggling to recruit them, modifying the DNA structure until everyone is satisfied. When they are through, they will follow the advice of Janus's right side. As long as they are still searching for the right DNA shape, they would be better off following the right side's confusing advices.

We could review all the opinions offered to explain why an open controversy closes, but we will always stumble on a new controversy dealing with how and why it closed. We will have to learn to live with two contradictory voices talking at once, one about science in the making, the other about ready made science. The latter produces sentences like "just do this . . . just do that . . ."; the former says "enough is never enough." The left side considers that facts and machines are well determined enough. The right side considers that facts and machines in the making are always *under-determined*.[4] Some little thing is always missing to close the black box once and for all. Until the last minute Eagle can fail if West is not careful enough to keep the Software people interested, to maintain the pressure on the debugging crew, to advertise the machine to the marketing department.

(3) THE FIRST RULE OF METHOD

We will enter facts and machines while they are in the making; we will carry with us no preconceptions of what constitutes knowledge; we will watch the closure of the black boxes and be careful to distinguish between two contradictory explanations of this closure, one uttered when it is finished, the other while it is being attempted. This will constitute our *first rule of method* and will make our voyage possible.

To sketch the general shape of this book, it is best to picture the following comic strip: we start with a textbook sentence which is devoid of any trace of fabrication, construction or ownership; we then put it in quotation marks, surround it with a bubble, place it in the mouth of someone who speaks; then we add to this speaking character another character *to whom* it is speaking; then we place all of them in a specific situation, somewhere in time and space, surrounded by equipment, machines, colleagues; then when the controversy heats up a bit we look at *where* the disputing people go and *what* sort of new elements they fetch, recruit or seduce in order to convince their colleagues; then, we see how the people being convinced stop discussing with one another; situations, localisations, even people start being slowly erased; on the last picture we see a new sentence, without any quotation marks, written in a text book similar to the one we started with in the first picture. This is the general movement of what we will study over and over again in the course of this book, penetrating science from the outside, following controversies and accompanying scientists up to the end, being slowly led out of science in the making.

In spite of the rich, confusing, ambiguous and fascinating picture that is thus revealed, surprisingly few people have penetrated from the outside the inner workings of science and technology, and then got out of it to explain to the outsider how it all works. For sure, many young people have entered science, but they have become scientists and engineers; what they have done is visible in the machines we use, the textbooks we learn, the pills we take, the landscape we look at, the blinking satellites in the night sky above our head. How they did it, we don't know. Some scientists talk about science, its ways and means, but few of them accept the discipline of becoming also an outsider; what they say about their trade is hard to double check in the absence of independent scrutiny. Other people talk about science, its solidity, its foundation, its development or its dangers; unfortunately, almost none of them are interested in science in the making. They shy away from the disorderly mixture revealed by science in action and prefer the orderly pattern of scientific method and rationality. Defending science and

FIGURE I.6

The DNA molecule has the shape of a double helix

"The DNA molecule has the shape of a double helix"

The DNA molecule has the shape of a double helix

Why don't you guys do something serious?

Maybe it is a triple helix

It is not a helix at all

If it had the shape of a double helix

This would explain Chargaff

and it would be pretty

They say that Watson and Crick have shown that DNA is a double helix

"Watson and Crick have shown that the DNA molecule has the shape of a double helix"

Since the molecule of DNA has the shape of a double helix the replication of genes is made understandable reason against pseudo-sciences, against fraud, against irrationality, keeps most of these people too busy to study it. As to the millions, or billions, of outsiders, they know about science and technology through popularisation only. The facts and the artefacts they produce fall on their head like an external fate as foreign, as inhuman, as unpredictable as the olden *Fatum* of the Romans.

Apart from those who make science, who study it, who defend it or who submit to it, there exist, fortunately, a few people, either trained as scientists or not, who open the black boxes so that outsiders may have a glimpse at it. They go by many different names (historians of science and technology, economists, sociologists, science teachers, science policy analysts, journalists, philosophers, concerned scientists and citizens, cognitive anthropologists or cognitive psychologists), and are most often filed under the general label of "science, technology and society." It is on their work that this book is built. A summary of their many *results* and achievements would be worth doing but is beyond the scope of my knowledge. I simply wish to summarise their *method* and to sketch the ground that, sometimes unwittingly, they all have in common. In doing so I wish to help overcome two of the limitations of "science, technology and society" studies that appear to me to thwart their impact, that is their organisation *by discipline* and *by object.*

Economists of innovation ignore sociologists of technology; cognitive scientists never use social studies of science; ethnoscience is far remote from pedagogy; historians of science pay little attention to literary studies or to rhetoric; sociologists of science often see no relation between their academic work and the *in vivo* experiments performed by concerned scientists or citizens; journalists rarely quote scholarly work on social studies of science; and so on.

This Babel of disciplines would not matter much if it was not worsened by another division made according to the objects each of them study. There exist historians of eighteenth-century chemistry or of German turn-of-the-century physics; even citizens' associations are specialised, some in fighting atomic energy, others in struggling against drug companies, still others against new math teaching; some cognitive scientists study young children in experimental settings while others are interested in adult daily reasoning; even among sociologists of science, some focus on micro-studies of science while others tackle large-scale engineering projects; historians of technology are often aligned along the technical specialities of the engineers, some studying aircraft industries while others prefer telecommunications or the development of steam engines; as to the anthropologists studying "savage" reasoning, very few get to deal with modern knowledge. This scattering of disciplines and objects would not be a problem if it was the hallmark of a necessary and fecund *specialisation,* growing from a core of common problems and methods. This is however far from the case. The sciences and the technologies to be studied are the main factors in determining this haphazard growth of interests and methods. I have never met two people who could agree on what the domain called "science, technology and society" meant—in fact, I have rarely seen anyone agree on the name or indeed that the domain exists!

I claim that the domain exists, that there is a core of common problems and methods, that it is important and that all the disciplines and objects of "science, technology and society" studies can be employed as so much specialised material with which to study it. To define what is at stake in this domain, the only thing we need is a few sets of concepts sturdy enough to stand the trip through all these many disciplines, periods and objects.

I am well aware that there exist many more sophisticated, subtle, fast or powerful notions than the ones I have chosen. Are they not going to break down? Are they going to last the distance? Will they be able to tie together enough empirical facts? Are they handy enough for doing practical exercises? These are the questions that guided me in selecting from the literature *rules of method* and *principles* and to dedicate one chapter to each pair. The status of these rules and that of the principles is rather distinct and I do not expect them to be evaluated in the same way. By "rules of method" I mean what a priori decisions should be made in order to consider all of the empirical facts provided by the specialised disciplines as being part of the domain of "science, technology and society." By "principles" I mean what is *my* personal summary of the empirical facts at hand after a decade of work in this area. Thus, I expect these principles to be debated, falsified, replaced by other summaries. On the other hand, the rules of method are a package that do not seem to be easily negotiable without losing sight of the common ground I want to sketch. With them it is more a question of all or nothing, and I think they should be judged only on this ground: do they link more elements than others? Do they allow outsiders to follow science and technology further, longer and more independently? This will be the only rule of the game, that is, the only "meta" rule that we will need to get on with our work.

APPEALING (TO) NATURE

Some readers will think that it is about time I talked of Nature and the real objects *behind* the texts and behind the labs. But it is not I who am late in finally talking about reality. Rather, it is Nature who always arrives late, too late to explain the rhetoric of scientific texts and the building of laboratories. This belated, sometimes faithful and sometimes fickle ally has complicated the study of technoscience until now so much that we need to understand it if we wish to continue our travel through the construction of facts and artefacts.

(1) "NATUR MIT UNS"

"Belated?" "Fickle?" I can hear the scientists I have shadowed so far becoming incensed by what I have just written. "All this is ludicrous because the reading and the writing, the style and the black boxes, the laboratory set-ups—indeed all existing phenomena—are simply *means* to express something, vehicles for conveying this formidable ally. We might accept these ideas of 'inscriptions,' your emphasis on controversies, and also perhaps the notions of 'ally,' 'new object,' 'actant,' end 'supporter,' but you have omitted the only important one, the only supporter who really counts, Nature herself. Her presence or absence explains it all. Whoever has Nature in their camp wins, no matter what the odds against them are. Remember Galileo's sentence, '1000 Demosthenes and 1000 Aristotles may be routed by any average man who brings

Nature in.' All the flowers of rhetoric, all the clever contraptions set up in the laboratories you describe, all will be dismantled once we go from controversies about Nature to what Nature is. The Goliath of rhetoric with his laboratory set-up and all his attendant Philistines will be put to flight by one David alone using simple truths about Nature in his slingshot! So let us forget all about what you have been writing for a hundred pages—even if you claim to have been simply following us—and let us see Nature face to face!"

Is this not a refreshing objection? It means that Galileo was right after all. The dreadnoughts I studied . . . may be easily defeated in spite of the many associations they knit, weave and knot. Any dissenter has got a chance. When faced with so much scientific literature and such huge laboratories, he or she has just to look at Nature in order to win. It means that there is a *supplement,* something more which is nowhere in the scientific papers and nowhere in the labs which is able to settle all matters of dispute. This objection is all the more refreshing since it is made by the scientists themselves, although it is clear that this rehabilitation of the average woman or man, of Ms or Mr Anybody, is also an indictment of these crowds of allies mustered by the same scientists.

Let us accept this pleasant objection and see how the appeal to Nature helps us to distinguish between, for instance, Schally's claim about GHRH and Guillemin's claim about GRF. They both wrote convincing papers, arraying many resources with talent. One is supported by Nature—so his claim will be made a fact—and the other is not—it ensues that his claim will be turned into an artefact by the others. According to the above objections, readers will find it easy to give the casting vote. They simply have to see who has got Nature on his side.

It is just as easy to separate the future of fuel cells from that of batteries. They both contend for a slice of the market; they both claim to be the best and most efficient. The potential buyer, the investor, the analyst are lost in the mist of a controversy, reading stacks of specialised literature. According to the above objection, their life will now be easier. Just watch to see on whose behalf Nature will talk. It is as simple as in the struggles sung in the Iliad: wait for the goddess to tip the balance in favour of one camp or the other.

A fierce controversy divides the astrophysicists who calculate the number of neutrinos coming out of the sun and Davis, the experimentalist who obtains a much smaller figure. It is easy to distinguish them and put the controversy to rest. Just let us see for ourselves in which camp the sun is really to be found. Somewhere the natural sun with its true number of neutrinos will close the mouths of dissenters and force them to accept the facts no matter how well written these papers were.

Another violent dispute divides those who believe dinosaurs to have been cold-blooded (lazy, heavy, stupid and sprawling creatures) and those who think that dinosaurs were warm-blooded (swift, light, cunning and running animals).[16] If we support the objection, there would be no need for the "average man" to read the piles of specialised articles that make up this debate. It is enough to wait for Nature to sort them out. Nature would be like God, who in medieval times judged between two disputants by letting the innocent win.

In these four cases of controversy generating more and more technical papers and bigger and bigger laboratories or collections, Nature's voice is enough to stop the noise. Then the obvious question to ask, if I want to do justice to the objection above, is "what does Nature say?"

Schally knows the answer pretty well. He told us in his paper, GHRH *is* this amino-acid sequence, not because he imagined it, or made it up, or confused a piece of haemoglobin for this long-sought-after hormone, but because this is what the molecule is in Nature, independently of his wishes. This is also what Guillemin says, not of Schally's sequence, which is a mere artefact, but of his substance, GRF. There is still doubt as to the exact nature of the real hypothalamic GRF compared with that of the pancreas, but on the whole it is certain that GRF is indeed the amino-acid sequence. . . . Now, we have got a problem. Both contenders have Nature in their camp and say what it says. Hold it! The challengers are supposed to be refereed by Nature, and not to start another dispute about what Nature's voice really said.

We are not going to be able to stop this new dispute about the referee, however, since the same confusion arises when fuel cells and batteries are opposed. "The technical difficulties are not insurmountable," say the fuel cell's supporters. "It's just that an infinitesimal amount has been spent on their resolution compared to the internal combustion engine's. Fuel cells are Nature's way of storing energy; give us more money and you'll see." Wait, wait! We were supposed to judge the technical literature by taking another outsider's point of view, not to be driven back *inside* the literature and *deeper* into laboratories.

Yet it is not possible to wait outside, because in the third example also, more and more papers are pouring in, disputing the model of the sun and modifying the number of neutrinos emitted. The real sun is alternately on the side of the theoreticians when they accuse the experimentalists of being mistaken and on the side of the latter when they accuse the former of having set up a fictional model of the sun's behaviour. This is too unfair. The real sun was asked to tell the two contenders apart, not to become yet another bone of contention.

More bones are to be found in the paleontologists' dispute where the real dinosaur has problems about giving the casting vote. No one knows for sure what it was. The ordeal might end, but is the winner really innocent or simply stronger or luckier? Is the warm-blooded dinosaur more like the real dinosaur, or is it just that its proponents are stronger than those of the cold-blooded one? We expected a final answer by using Nature's voice. What we got was a new fight over the composition, content, expression and meaning of that voice. That is, we get *more* technical literature and *larger* collections in bigger Natural History Museums, not less; *more* debates and not less.

I interrupt the exercise here. It is clear by now that applying the scientists' objection to any controversy is like pouring oil on a fire, it makes it flare anew. Nature is not outside the fighting camps. She is much like God in not-so-ancient wars, asked to support all the enemies at once. "Natur mit uns" is embroidered on all the banners and is not sufficient to provide one camp with the winning edge. So what is sufficient?

(2) THE DOUBLE-TALK OF THE TWO-FACED JANUS

I could be accused of having been a bit disingenuous when applying scientists' objections. When they said that something more than association and numbers is needed to settle a debate, something outside all our human conflicts and interpretations, something they call "Nature" for want of a better term, something that eventually will distinguish the winners and the losers, they did not mean to say that we know what it is. This supplement beyond the literature and laboratory trials is unknown and this is why they look for it, call themselves "researchers," write so many papers and mobilise so many instruments.

"It is ludicrous," I hear them arguing, "to imagine that Nature's voice could stop Guillemin and Schally from fighting, could reveal whether fuel cells are superior to batteries or whether Watson and Crick's model is better than that of Pauling. It is absurd to imagine that Nature, like a goddess, will visibly tip the scale in favour of one camp or that the Sun God will barge into an astrophysics meeting to drive a wedge between theoreticians and experimentalists; and still more ridiculous to imagine real dinosaurs invading a Natural History Museum in order to be compared with their plaster models! What we meant, when contesting your obsession with rhetoric and mobilisation of black boxes, was that *once the controversy is settled, it is Nature the final ally that has settled it* and not any rhetorical tricks and tools or any laboratory contraptions."

If we still wish to follow scientists and engineers in their construction of technoscience, we have got a major problem here. On the one hand scientists herald Nature as the only possible adjudicator of a dispute, on the other they recruit countless allies while waiting for Nature to declare herself. Sometimes David is able to defeat all the Philistines with only one slingshot; at other times, it is better to have swords, chariots and many more, better-drilled soldiers than the Philistines!

It is crucial for us, laypeople who want to understand technoscience, to decide which version is right, because in the first version, as Nature is enough to settle all disputes, we have nothing to do since no matter how large the resources of the scientists are, they do not matter in the end—only Nature matters. Our chapters may not be all wrong, but they become useless since they merely look at trifles and addenda and it is certainly no use going on for four other chapters to find still more trivia. In the second version, however, we have a lot of work to do since, by analysing the allies and resources that settle a controversy we understand *everything* that there is to understand in technoscience. If the first version is a correct, there is nothing for us to do apart from catching the most superficial aspects of science; if the second version is maintained, there is everything to understand except perhaps the most superfluous and flashy aspects of science. Given the stakes, the reader will realise why this problem should be tackled with caution. The whole book is in jeopardy here. The problem is made all the more tricky since scientists *simultaneously* assert the two contradictory versions, displaying an ambivalence which could paralyse all our efforts to follow them.

We would indeed be paralysed, like most of our predecessors, if we were not used to this double-talk or the two-faced Janus (see introduction). The two versions are contradictory but they are not uttered by the same face of Janus. There is again a clear-cut distinction between what scientists say about the cold settled part and about the warm unsettled part of the research front. As long as controversies are rife, Nature is never used as the final arbiter since no one knows what she is and says. But *once the controversy is settled,* Nature is the ultimate referee.

This sudden inversion of what counts as referee and what counts as being refereed, although counter-intuitive at first, is as easy to grasp as the rapid passage from the "name of action" given to a new object to when it is given its name as a thing (see above). As long as there is a debate among endocrinologists about GRF or GHRH, no one can intervene in the debates by saying, "I know what it is, Nature told me so. It is that amino-acid sequence." Such a claim would be greeted with derisive shouts, unless the proponent of such a sequence is able to show his figures, cite his references, and quote his sources of support, in brief, write another scientific paper and equip a new laboratory, as in the case we have studied. However, once the collective decision is taken to turn Schally's GHRH into an artefact and Guillemin's GRF into an incontrovertible fact, the reason for this decision is not imputed to Guillemin, but is immediately attributed to the independent existence of GRF in Nature. As long as the controversy lasted, no appeal to Nature could bring any extra strength to one side in the debate (it was at best an invocation, at worst a bluff). As soon as the debate is stopped, the supplement of force offered by Nature is made the explanation as to why the debate did stop (and why the bluffs, the frauds and the mistakes were at last unmasked).

So we are confronted with two almost simultaneous suppositions:

Nature is the final cause of the settlement of all controversies, *once controversies are settled.*

As long as they last *Nature will appear simply as the final consequence of the controversies.*

When you wish to attack a colleague's claim, criticise a world-view, modalise a statement you cannot *just* say that Nature is with you; "just" will never be enough. You are bound to use other allies besides Nature. If you succeed, then Nature will be enough and all the other allies and resources will be made redundant. A political analogy may be of some help at this point. Nature, in scientists' hands, is a constitutional monarch, much like Queen Elizabeth the Second. From the throne she reads with the same tone, majesty and conviction a speech written by Conservative or Labour prime ministers depending on the election outcome. Indeed she *adds* something to the dispute, but only after the dispute has ended; as long as the election is going on she does nothing but wait.

This sudden reversal of scientists' relations to Nature and to one another is one of the most puzzling phenomena we encounter when following their trails. I believe that it is the difficulty of grasping this simple reversal that has made technoscience so hard to probe until now.

The two faces of Janus talking together make, we must admit, a startling spectacle. On the left side Nature is cause, on the right side consequence of the end of controversy. On the left side scientists are *realists,* that is they believe that representations are sorted out by what really is outside, by the only independent referee there is, Nature. On the right side, the same scientists are *relativists,* that is, they believe representations to be sorted out among themselves and the actants they represent, without independent and impartial referees lending their weight to any one of them. We know why they talk two languages at once: the left mouth speaks about settled parts of science, whereas the right mouth talks about unsettled parts. On the left side polonium was discovered long ago by the Curies; on the right side there is a long list of actions effected by an unknown actant in Paris at the Ecole de Chimie which the Curies propose to call "polonium." On the left side all scientists agree, and we hear only Nature's voice, plain and clear; on the right side scientists disagree and no voice can be heard over theirs.

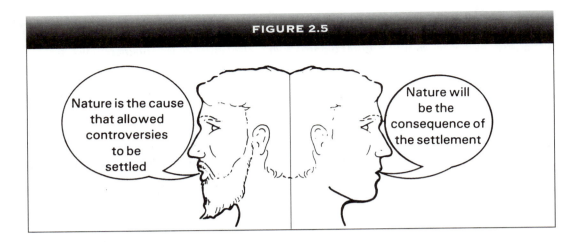

FIGURE 2.5

(3) THE THIRD RULE OF METHOD

If we wish to continue our journey through the construction of facts, we have to adapt our method to scientists' double-talk. If not, we will always be caught on the wrong foot: unable to withstand either their first (realist) or their second (relativist) objection. We will then need to have two different discourses depending on whether we consider a settled or an unsettled part of technoscience. We too will be relativists in the latter case and realists in the former. When studying controversy—as we have so far—we cannot be *less* relativist than the very scientists and engineers we accompany; they do not *use* Nature as the external referee, and we have no reason to imagine that we are more clever than they are. For these parts of science our *third rule of method* will read: since the settlement of a controversy is *the cause* of Nature's representation not the consequence, *we can never use the outcome—Nature—to explain how and why a controversy has been settled.*

This principle is easy to apply as long as the dispute lasts, but is difficult to bear in mind once it has ended, since the other face of Janus takes over and does the talking. This is what makes the study of the past of technoscience so difficult and unrewarding. You have to hang onto the words of the right face of Janus—now barely audible—and ignore the clamours of the left side. It turned out for instance that the N-rays were slowly transformed into artefacts much like Schally's GHRH. How are we going to study this innocent expression "it turned out"? Using the physics of the present day there is unanimity that Blondlot was badly mistaken. It would be easy enough for historians to say that Blondlot failed because there was "nothing really behind his N-rays" to support his claims. This way of analysing the past is called Whig history, that is, a history that crowns the winners, calling them the best and the brightest and which says the losers like Blondlot lost simply *because* they were wrong. We recognise here the left side of Janus' way of talking where Nature herself discriminates between the bad guys and the good guys. But, is it possible to use this as the reason why in Paris, in London, in the United States, people slowly turned N-rays into an artefact? Of course not, since at that time today's physics obviously could not be used as the touchstone, or more exactly since today's state is, in part, the *consequence* of settling many controversies such as the N-rays!

Whig historians had an easy life. They came after the battle and needed only one reason to explain Blondlot's demise. He was wrong all along. This reason is precisely what does not make the slightest difference while you are searching for truth in the midst of a polemic. We need, not one, but *many* reasons to explain how a dispute stopped and a black box was closed.[17]

However, when talking about a cold part of technoscience we should shift our method like the scientists themselves who, from hard-core relativists, have turned into dyed-in-the-wool realists. Nature is now taken as the cause of accurate descriptions of herself. We cannot be more relativist than scientists about these parts and keep on denying evidence where no one else does. Why? Because the cost of dispute is too high for an average citizen, even if he or she is a historian and sociologist of science. If there is no controversy among scientists as to the status of facts, then it is useless to go on talking about interpretation, representation, a biased or distorted world-view, weak and fragile pictures of the world, unfaithful spokesmen. Nature talks straight, facts are facts. Full stop. There is nothing to add and nothing to subtract.

This division between relativists and realist interpretation of science has caused analysts of science to be put off balance. Either they went on being relativists even about the settled parts of science—which made them look ludicrous; or they continued being realists even about the warm uncertain parts—and they made fools of themselves. The third rule of method stated above should help us in our study because it offers us a good balance. We do not try to undermine the solidity of the accepted parts of science. We are realists as much as the people we travel with and as much as the left side of Janus. But as soon as a controversy starts we become as relativist as our informants. However we do not follow them passively because our method allows us to document both the construction of fact and of artefact, the cold and the warm, the demodalised and the modalised statements, and, in particular, it allows us to trace with accuracy the sudden shifts from one face of Janus to the other. This method offers us, so to speak, a stereophonic rendering of fact-making instead of its monophonic predecessors!

NOTES

[1] I am following here James Watson's account (1968).

[2] I am following here Tracy Kidder's book (1981). This book, like Watson's, is compulsory reading for all of those interested in science in the making.

[3] On this episode see T. D. Stokes (1982).

[4] This notion of under-determination is also called the Duhem-Quine principle. It asserts that no one single factor is enough to explain the closure of a controversy or the certainty acquired by scientists. This principle forms the philosophical basis of most social history of sociology of science.

. . .

[16] I am alluding here to the remarkable work by A. Desmond (1975).

[17] This basic question of relativism has been nicely summed up in many articles by Harry Collins. See in particular his latest book (1985).

REFERENCES

Collins, Harry (1985). *Changing Order: Replication and Induction in Scientific Practice.* London and Los Angeles, Sage.

Desmond, Adrian (1975). *The Hot-Blooded Dinosaurs: A Revolution in Paleontology.* London, Blond & Briggs.

Kidder, Tracy (1981). *The Soul of a New Machine.* London, Allen Lane.

Stokes, T. D. (1982). "The double-helix and the warped zipper: an exemplary tale." *Social Studies of Science,* vol. 12, no. 3, pp. 207–40.

Watson, James (1968). *The Double Helix.* New York, Mentor Books.

CARL G. HEMPEL
SCIENTIFIC RATIONALITY:
ANALYTIC VS. PRAGMATIC PERSPECTIVES

I. INTRODUCTION

Of all the current topics of inquiry in the philosophy of science, none has provoked a more intensive and fruitful discussion than the conflicting conceptions of science and its methodology that have been developed by analytic empiricists on one hand and by historically and sociologically oriented thinkers on the other.

By analytic empiricism, I understand here a body of ideas that has its roots in the logical empiricism of the Vienna Circle and the Berlin group, as well as in the work of kindred thinkers, such as Popper, Braithwaite, and Nagel. Among the protagonists of the more recent historic-sociological approach, I have in mind particularly Thomas Kuhn, Paul Feyerabend, and the late R. N. Hanson.

The considerations I propose to put before you concern two fundamental problems that have been at the center of the controversy between the two schools: namely

(1) *The problem of the rationality of science:* in what sense, on what grounds, and to what extent can scientific inquiry be qualified as a rational enterprise? and
(2) *The problem of cognitive status of the methodology and philosophy of science:* are the principles set forth by these disciplines intended to provide norms for rational scientific inquiry, or are they meant to give an explanatory account of scientific research as a human activity?

Let me broadly and somewhat schematically, sketch the background for this discussion. Analytic empiricism views the philosophy of science as a discipline which by "logical analysis" and "rational reconstruction" seeks to "explicate" the meanings of scientific terms and sentences and to exhibit the logical structure and the rationale of scientific theorizing. The philosophy of science is regarded as concerned exclusively with the logical and systematic aspects of sound scientific theorizing and of the knowledge claims it yields. On this view, the psychological, sociological, and historical facets of science as a human enterprise are irrelevant to the philosophy of science, much as the genetic and psychological aspects of human reasoning are held to be irrelevant for pure logic, which is concerned only with questions of the deductive validity of inferences, logical truth and falsity, consistency, provability, definability, and the like. The principles of logical theory clearly do not, and are not meant to, give a descriptive account of "how we think," of how human beings actually reason; but in so far as they provide criteria of logical validity and truth, they can be employed normatively, as standards for the critical appraisal of particular inferences and logical claims.

In view of analytic empiricism, the methodology of science similarly has the task of explicating standards for rational modes of formulating, appraising, and changing scientific knowledge claims; such explications may then serve as norms for the guidance of inquiry and for the

critical appraisal of particular research procedures and theoretical claims: the logical empiricists' rejection of neo-vitalism as a pseudo-theory and Popper's exclusion of psychoanalysis
from the realm of scientific theories illustrate this point.

The historic-sociological school, on the other hand, rejects the idea of methodological
principles arrived at, as it seems, by purely philosophical analysis; it insists that an adequate
methodology must be based on a close study of the practice of scientific inquiry and must be
capable of explaining certain characteristics of past and present research and theory change
in science.

The contrasting views of the two schools have been thrown into sharp relief in their debate over the extent to which and the grounds on which it is possible to formulate and justify
methodological principles for a rational choice between competing scientific theories.

According to analytic empiricism, such methodological principles have the character to
generate criteria for rational theory choice; they might determine, for example, which of two
competing theories possesses the higher rational credibility or acceptability in consideration
of all the pertinent information available at the time. In fact, analytic attempts at explicating
the notions of confirmation and of inductive probability and at formulating "rules of acceptance" for scientific hypotheses were efforts in just that direction.

Kuhn, in whose account of scientific revolutions the problem of choice between conflicting paradigmatic theories plays a central role, regards the search for such analytic criteria as
basically misguided and as doomed to failure. He does acknowledge that there are certain
considerations, noted also in the earlier philosophy of science, which influence the decisions
scientists make in the context of theory choice; he speaks of them as professionally shared
preferences or values. Among them are a preference for theories of quantitative form whose
predictions show a close fit with experimental or observational findings; for theories of wide
scope; for theories that correctly predict novel phenomena; and some others. All these characteristics, he says, provide "good reasons for theory choice."[1]

But Kuhn rightly notes that those desiderata do not remotely suffice to determine a unique
choice between competing theories, and he further insists that there are no methodological
criteria which have that power and which would command the assent of the scientific community: there are no generally binding rules that compel the choice between theories on the
basis of logic and experiment alone.[2] Theory choice is emphatically presented as the result of
group decisions which are not determined by rules of rational procedure of the sort analytic
empiricism would envision.

Yet despite this naturalistic emphasis, Kuhn views science as a rational enterprise. Thus,
he says: "scientific behavior, taken as a whole, is the best example we have of rationality" and
"if history or any other empirical discipline leads us to believe that the development of science
depends essentially on behavior that we have previously thought to be irrational, then we
should conclude not that science is irrational, but that our notion of rationality needs adjustment here and there."[3] Thus, Kuhn regards his account of science as both empirical and normative. In response to the question, raised by Feyerabend, whether his pronouncements are to
be read as descriptive or as prescriptive, he has said quite explicitly: "they should be read in
both ways at once."[4]

II. THE JANUS-HEAD OF RATIONAL EXPLANATION
AND THE IDEA OF AN E-N METHODOLOGY

But surely, the principles of a given methodology cannot literally be both explanatory and normative. For in the former case, they would form an empirical theory, supported by pertinent evidence, which would serve to explain certain significant aspects of the research behavior of scientists; whereas in the latter case, they would express conditions of rationality for scientific inquiry.

Yet the conception of a methodology, or some methodological principles, having this double aspect can be given a plausible construal, as is suggested by the following consideration: An explanation of a particular case of theory-choice or paradigm-change is clearly an explanation of a human decision. Now, human decisions and actions are typically explained by reference to the agent's motivating reasons; and in the formulation and even in the philosophical analysis of such accounts two distinct senses of accounting are not infrequently confounded or fused, namely, accounting for a decision in the sense of explaining it and accounting for a decision in the sense of justifying it. This is illustrated by formulations of the following type:

> Agent A intended to attain goal G and had a set B of beliefs about the circumstances in which he had to act—particularly about alternative means available to him for attaining his goal. But given A's goal and his beliefs, the appropriate or rational thing for him to do was X. That is why A decided on course of action X.

But surely, an account of this kind cannot explain why A did in fact choose X. For the norm it invokes about the proper thing to do under the specified circumstances has no explanatory force at all. Even if the norm be granted, it is entirely possible that A may have been aware of, or not committed to, the standard of appropriateness or rationality it expresses, and that he might, therefore, in fact not have chosen X. The argument invoking the normative principle offers no explanation of A's choice; but it does offer a *justification* for it by showing that what A chose to do was appropriate in the sense of the cited norm.

A corresponding *explanation* requires, instead of that norm, a psychological hypothesis to the effect that A had adopted the norm and thus had acquired a disposition to act in accordance with it. Let us note in passing that whereas a justificatory account will be acceptable only if the norm in question is acknowledged as sound, the acceptability of the corresponding explanatory account is subject to no such condition. If indeed A was disposed to act in accordance with the cited norm, then this fact can be invoked to explain A's decision, no matter whether the norm is deemed to be sound.

The tendency to fuse explanation with justification in accounting for human decisions is thus closely linked to the fact that when a decision is explained by attributing to the agent certain motivating considerations, then these considerations, if suitably spelled out, can be evaluated in their own right as to their "rationality"; and such evaluation may indeed afford a justification of the given decision. An account which does possess this double aspect of explanation and justification might be called an *ideal rational account*.

There are some kinds of human decision which seem, in fairly close approximation, to admit of such a two-faced account. Consider, for example, the case of an engineer in charge of quality control who has to decide, on the basis of sample tests, whether a given batch of hormone tablets or of ball bearings manufactured by his firm is to be released for sale or rather to be reprocessed or destroyed because of excessive flaws. His decisions may well be explainable, and indeed predictable, on the basis of the sample findings, by the assumption that he has acquired the disposition to follow such and such specific decision criteria; while on the other hand, the criteria—or some more general decision-theoretical principles from which they can be derived—provide a justification for his particular decisions.

These considerations suggest a plausible construal (I am inclined to think: the only plausible construal) of the idea that certain principles in the methodology of science can play both an explanatory and a normative role. Such a two-faced, Janus-head methodological theory would have to present certain aspects of scientific research, such as theory testing and theory choice, as activities aimed at certain scientific goals, and carried out in accordance with specified rules which can be justified by showing that the modes of procedure they prescribe are rational means of pursuing the given goals.

In order to fulfill both its explanatory and its justificatory function, such a methodological theory for science or for some segment of it would have to specify certain goals of inquiry for the given field and certain procedural norms or rules for the pursuit of those goals; and it would then have to make two quite different claims:

(ı) an explanatory claim, briefly to the effect that the practitioners of the science in question share a commitment, and thus a general disposition, to pursue the specified goals in accordance with the specified rules; and that, as a consequence, certain professional decisions made by the scientists can be explained by reference to those commitments;

(ıı) a justificatory claim to the effect that the specified procedural rules determine appropriate, or "rational," ways of pursuing the given goals. (How the notion of rationality might be construed here is a question that will be considered shortly.)

I shall refer to a methodological theory of the kind here adumbrated as an explanatory-normative methodology, or as an *E-N methodology* for short. This is clearly an idealized notion: it is not to be expected that an *E-N methodology* can be formulated which would afford a satisfactory explanation even for the major turns in the development of science. Thus, for example, Lakatos, whose conception of a methodological theory has a certain affinity to that of an *E-N methodology,* emphasizes that for an explanation of actual occurrences in the history of science, "external" factors must often be invoked in addition to "internal," methodological, considerations.[5]

III. ON THE NOTION OF SCIENTIFIC RATIONALITY

Let me now turn to the idea of rationality of scientific inquiry, which has been the subject of extensive controversy in the recent philosophy of science.

I think it interesting, but also somewhat disturbing, that Popper, Lakatos, Kuhn, Feyerabend, and others have made diverse pronouncements concerning the rationality or irrationality of science or of certain modes of inquiry without, however, as far as I am aware, giving a reasonably explicit characterization of the concept of rationality which they have in mind and which they seek to illuminate or to disparage in their methodological investigations. Thus we find Lakatos bringing the charge of irrationalism against Kuhn's account of scientific theorizing, whereas Kuhn, as noted earlier, claims that his account takes scientific research behavior, as a whole, to be the best example we have of rationality.

What is to be understood here by "rationality," and what kinds of consideration could be properly adduced in a critical appraisal of attributions of rationality to science as a whole or to certain modes of inquiry? I have no satisfactory general answers to these questions, but I would like to put before you some tentative reflections on the subject.

First, a mode of procedure or a rule calling for that procedure surely can be called rational or irrational only relative to the goals the procedure is meant to attain. In so far as a methodological theory does propose rules or norms, these norms have to be regarded as instrumental norms: their appropriateness must be judged by reference to the objectives of the inquiry to which they pertain or, more ambitiously, by reference to the goals of pure scientific research in general.

Any attempt to give a characterization of "the goals of science" faces serious difficulties. But I hope you will permit me to begin with an avowedly oversimplified construal of those objectives; for even this schematic conception can serve quite well as a background against which to formulate some reflections concerning rationality which should be relevant also to more complex construals of the goals of scientific inquiry.

Let us assume, then, that science aims at establishing a sequence of increasingly comprehensive and accurate systems of empirical knowledge. Each such system might be thought of as represented by a set K of sentences which has been adopted, and is bound to be modified, in accordance with certain procedural rules.

Given this goal, there are certain methodological norms which can be qualified as requirements of rational procedure on the ground that—speaking somewhat charitably—they are necessary conditions for anyone of the changing systems K which science might accept at some time or another.

Among these necessary conditions are the requirement of intersubjective testability and the requirement of actual test with satisfactory outcome. Another such condition would require that any of the classes K be deductively closed, since the logical consequences of sentences accepted as presumably true must be presumed to be true as well. Another necessary condition would be that of logical consistency; and there may well be some others.

The goal-dependence of these conditions of rationality is clear. If, for example, it should be our goal to form a set of beliefs about the world that is emotionally reassuring or esthetically satisfying, then different procedural principles would qualify as rational. To further the attainment of our objectives, we might do well not to acknowledge all the logical consequences of accepted sentences and not to judge proposed beliefs in the light of all the relevant evidence obtainable—or better yet, perhaps, simply to forego empirical testing altogether.

In his plea for methodological anarchy, Feyerabend raises the question whether instead of "science as we know it today (the science of critical rationalism that has been freed from all inductive elements)," we would not prefer a science that is "more anarchistic and more subjective." [6] One might surely prefer the pursuit of the goals suggested by Feyerabend, and one might be convinced, as he seems to be, that it would be better for humanity to abandon "science as we know it"; but this does not change the fact that the modes of procedure appropriate for the pursuit of Feyerabend's objectives are not rational for science as it is commonly understood, and certainly not for the pursuit of the goals of science envisaged in our simple construal.

The modest norms of scientific rationality we have noted so far reflect necessary conditions for the attainment of the objectives of science. Could there be procedural norms reflecting sufficient conditions? Surely not; for such norms would, in effect, afford a solution to the problem of induction.

Let us look next at the familiar features—also mentioned by Kuhn—which scientists agree in regarding as desirable characteristics of scientific theories, and which therefore provide some basis for choosing between competing theories: closeness of quantitative fit between theoretical predictions and scientific data, large scope, prediction of novel effects, and some others. It seems to me that most of these desiderata are best regarded as providing a fuller characterization of the goals of scientific theorizing rather than as instrumental norms aimed at enhancing the prospects of achieving those goals. (Simplicity might similarly be regarded as a feature characterizing the goals of scientific theorizing; but alternatively, it might be viewed as an instrumental norm on the ground of the belief that the simpler theory is more likely to be true.)

But regardless of what role is assigned to the desiderata, it is clear, as Kuhn has stressed, that even if they are generally acknowledged by (belong to the "shared values" of) a scientific community, different scientists may, and do, understand them in somewhat different ways and may therefore differ in their judgments as to which of two theories satisfies a particular desideratum more fully. Moreover, scientists may differ in the priorities or relative weights they assign to the various desiderata. In sum, commitment to those norms does not ensure a uniform decision as to which of two theories outranks the other, by way of satisfying the entire set of desiderata.

Now, these last considerations are psychological and sociological and cannot, of course, prove it impossible to formulate precise general criteria of theory choice embodying those desiderata; but the difficulties encountered by analytic efforts to explicate such notions as the simplicity of theories or the degree of variety of the empirical phenomena covered by a theory (and thus, perhaps, its scope) do not augur well for the attainability of those analytic objectives. Indeed, Ernest Nagel argued long ago, on essentially the grounds just surveyed, that efforts to construct a general criterion of this kind were futile.[7]

IV. ON THE RELEVANCE OF DECISION THEORY TO PROBLEMS OF THEORY CHOICE

The preceding considerations also cast serious doubt on the promise of another idea that might suggest itself here, namely, an appeal to mathematical decision theory as a possible source of rational standards for a choice between competing theories, or knowledge systems, or paradigms.

Decision theory does provide objective criteria for choosing between alternative hypotheses; but these criteria presuppose that in addition to the hypotheses in question, a precise comparative or quantitative specification is given of the advantages that would result from adopting a given hypothesis if it is true, and the disadvantages that would result from adopting it if it should be false; and similarly, a specification of advantages or disadvantages connected with the rejection of a hypothesis which may in fact be true or false. "Utilities" and "disutilities" of the requisite kind can plausibly be specified in certain cases where the adoption of a hypothesis amounts to its application for some particular practical purpose, as in the case of industrial quality control. For theory choice is pure science, the requisite utilities or disutilities would have to express the gain or loss that would come from the adoption or the rejection of a true theory or a false one, in the light of the objectives of scientific research. But among those objectives are the desiderata considered a moment ago; and as far as these defy precise explication, decision theory is inapplicable.

Considerations of the kind outlined in the preceding section concerning the widely acknowledged desiderata for scientific theories led Kuhn to the claim that there are no generally binding rules of scientific procedure which unambiguously determine theory choice in the light of logic and experience alone. Kuhn therefore presented theory choice as the result of group decisions made by the scientists in the field, which are not fully governed by general rules, and which have to be accounted for in terms of the common training of the members of the group. This characterization was received by some critics with the charge of irrationalism and of appeal to mob psychology—a charge that may have seemed to be substantiated by Kuhn's comparison of theory change in science to a religious conversion experience involving a leap of faith. This may have seemed to license the adoption of any theory one might have faith in. But the requirements of testability, predictivity, evidential fit, and large scope, which Kuhn acknowledges, would suffice, despite their vagueness, to rule out, say, astrology or chiromancy, and in a competition with currently accepted theories.

And as for Kuhn's invocation, in the context of theory choice, of group decisions not governed by general rules of procedure, it may be of interest to note that in the first decade of this century, Pierre Duhem expressed quite a similar view. He argued, on purely logical grounds, that the outcome of a scientific experiment cannot refute a theoretical assumption in isolation, but only a comprehensive set of assumptions. If the experimental findings conflict with predictions deducible from the set, then some change has to be made in the total theory; but no objective logical criteria determine uniquely what changes should be made. That decision, Duhem says, must be left to "the good sense" of the scientists in the field.[8] Here, then, normative methodology leaves off, and only socio-psychological considerations are invoked, with perhaps a vaguely explanatory intent.

As for the charge of irrationalism that has been brought against Kuhn's account, I have to say that I cannot point to any justifiable canons of rational inquiry that Kuhn could be accused of having denied or slighted.

V. RATIONALITY AND INCOMMENSURABILITY

I want to take issue, however, with one argument, offered especially by Feyerabend, for the thesis that there can be no general criteria of choice between competing comprehensive theories. The argument is based on the idea that such theories do not share a single statement, that they are "completely disjointed, or incommensurable"; he cites classical and relativistic physics as an example.[9] I have strong doubts about this idea, largely because the notion of incommensurability is not made sufficiently clear. Feyerabend seems to hold that in the transition from one paradigm to another, all the terms taken over from the old theory into the new one come to function in a new set of theoretical principles and therefore change their meanings,—that this is the case even for the terms used to describe instrument readings and observational findings, and that therefore there is no possibility at all of comparing the two theories or the bodies of evidence relevant to them. In fact, Feyerabend concludes, concerning the possible bases of theory choice: "What remains are esthetic judgments, judgments of taste, and our subjective wishes."[10] Kuhn, too, has placed considerable emphasis on the incommensurability of paradigms, but he has not drawn quite such extreme and subjective conclusions.

Now, the transition from one paradigm to another clearly does bring with it considerable changes in the *use* of the terms taken over into the new theory: the paradigms differ in many of the sentences containing those terms. But why should a change of this kind be taken to signal a change in the meanings of the terms concerned rather than a change in the claims made about the entities they refer to? To illustrate: In *The Structure of Scientific Revolutions,* Kuhn remarks that the transition from the Ptolemaic to the Copernican System effected a change in the meanings of such terms as 'planet', 'earth', and 'motion'.[11] But on what grounds can it be claimed that the change in the statements containing those terms reflects a change in the meanings of the words rather than a change in what is assumed or asserted about the earth, the planets, and their motions?

In the absence of a more explicit account of meaning change for theoretical terms, claims of incommensurability cannot, I think, establish the impossibility of formulating criteria for a comparative evaluation of competing paradigms. It seems clear, for example, that the results of parallax measurements constitute evidence that is relevant to the Copernican as well as to the Ptolemaic theory, and that they thus form some basis for a comparison between the two.

VI. ON THE "TIMELESSNESS" OF METHODOLOGICAL NORMS

The methodological efforts of logical empiricism were not very much concerned with problems of theory change in science; but they did yield theories of confirmation and of probability for scientific hypotheses, which propounded explicit and precise standards for the comparison or appraisal of hypotheses in regard to the evidential support conferred upon them by the available empirical data. Carnap referred to his quantitative theory of confirmation as "inductive logic"; as the term suggests, the principles aimed at by theories of inductive support were thought of as being analogous to the principles of valid deductive inference formulated by deductive logic. At least implicitly, I think, it was assumed that methodological principles for appraising the rational credibility of hypotheses would have to hold *a priori* as it were, independently of any empirical matters, and immutably at all times—all this in analogy to the standard conception of the timelessness and immutable validity of the principles of deductive logic.

But it seems to me open to question whether this conception can be reasonably applied to all methodological principles of rational theory choice. For what kinds of theory can be reasonably entertained, or be regarded as worth serious consideration, will depend on the general view of the world—especially of its deep and pervasive features—that prevails at the time.

Thus, for example, Maxwell held that space and time coordinates should enter into scientific laws and theories, not absolutely or explicitly, but only in the form of differences; his reason being that the mere spatio-temporal location of an event could exert no causal influence on the course taken by that event: what occurs, under given physical conditions, at one spatio-temporal location will under the same physical conditions, equally happen at any other spatio-temporal location. Maxwell regarded this principle as providing a more precise expression of the idea that "the same causes will always produce the same effects." [12] Actually, we might note, his condition is satisfied not only by strictly causal or deterministic laws, but also by the probabilistic laws of contemporary science. It may be said to impose a constraint on rational theory choice, reflecting the assumption that in our world spatio-temporal locations have no "nomic efficacy," whether of a causal or of a probabilistic kind. But it is conceivable that that assumption may eventually come to be abandoned in the light of new scientific findings: and in this case, the methodological norm would have to be abandoned as well.

Similarly, 150 years ago, a theory propounding quantization of energy or perhaps even of space and time, or postulating the creation of electrons from empty space, would presumably not have been regarded as a rationally open theoretical option.

And Carnap himself, the leading figure among logical analysts, provided in his theory of inductive probability for a "continuum of inductive methods," each characterized by a real-number value of a parameter lambda, with the explicit understanding that the value of that parameter, and thereby the principles of the inductive methodology, could be changed in consideration of certain very general features of the empirical knowledge available at a given time.

That the standards of choice among the hypotheses or theories should depend on such general assumptions about the causal structure or about the basic articulation and the degree of orderliness of the world seems quite plausible and reasonable: but then, the conception of timelessness for all standards of rational theory choice must be abandoned. On this point, I find myself in agreement even with Feyerabend, though, as indicated earlier, I cannot follow him the rest of the way to anarchy.

VII. THE CONCEPTION OF RATIONALITY IN KUHN'S PERSPECTIVE ON SCIENCE

I have argued that to the extent that a methodological theory of science is to provide standards of rationality for scientific inquiry as well as a basis for explaining certain aspects of the actual research behavior of scientists, the theory must have the character of an *E-N* methodology: its norms must express goal-dependent, instrumental, conditions of rationality; and its explanatory potential must lie in its ability to "rationalize" significant aspects of scientific research, i.e., to explain them by the assumption that the scientists in question are disposed to act in accordance with the specified norms.

Consider from this point of view Kuhn's remark, cited earlier, that his methodological pronouncements should be read as prescriptive and as descriptive at once.

Let us look first at their prescriptive import, which Kuhn characterizes schematically as follows: "The structure of my argument is simple and, I think, unexceptionable: scientists behave in the following ways; those modes of behavior have (here theory enters) the following essential functions; in the absence of an alternate mode *that would serve similar functions,* scientists should behave essentially as they do if their concern is to improve scientific knowledge." [13] This statement does seem to reflect an instrumental conception of the rationality of scientific behavior, the "essential function" of such behavior being the improvement of scientific knowledge. But surely, a methodological theory can yield prescriptions for scientific inquiry only in so far as it formulates explicit rules or norms for the conduct of inquiry: and it seems very questionable to me whether a theory in Kuhn's style and spirit can provide the requisite rules or norms.

I referred earlier to Kuhn's remark that scientific behavior is the best example we have of rationality, and that we had better change our standards of rationality if science seems to violate them. But any given piece of behavior can be described in many different ways; yet it can be qualified as rational or as irrational, if at all, then only under certain particular kinds of description, which represent it as a rule—following activity conforming to certain explicitly specified rules, in the pursuit of specified goals.

To put the point somewhat differently: Kuhn's remark that "scientists should behave essentially as they do if their concern is to improve scientific knowledge" leaves open the question: in what respects? What aspects, what characteristics of the actual behavior of scientists are the ones that matter, the ones to be emulated in a rational pursuit of the improvement of scientific knowledge? And in what sense, and on what grounds, can those characteristics be held to serve the function of improving scientific knowledge?

Kuhn's construal of the explanatory import of his ideas for actual cases of theory choice seems to me open to similar questions. Kuhn describes that import as follows: "take a *group* of the ablest available people with the most appropriate motivation; train them in some science and in the special ties relevant to the choice at hand; imbue them with the value system, the ideology, current in their discipline (and to a great extent in other scientific fields as well); and, finally, *let them make their choice.* If that technique does not account for scientific development as we know it, then no other will." [14]

But, literally speaking, a technique for training or programming people does not constitute an explanation of any part of their subsequent behavior. For that, we need an empirical theory which yields explicit specifications of those beliefs, values, ideological principles, etc. whose acceptance will account for the theory choices in question. The claim that persons who are motivated and trained in the ways in which scientists are will make the choices actually encountered in science fails to specify just what aspects of the behavior of scientists are relevant to the explanation of theory choice; and in so far as those aspects are not made explicit, no explanatory claim can be made for the methodological theory.

VIII. CONCLUSION

The conception of science as the exemplar of the rational pursuit of knowledge was emphatically held also by logical empiricism, which frequently supported and revised its explications of scientific concepts and procedures by appeal to scientific usage. One familiar example of this process is the gradual expansion of the ways in which Carnap explicated scientific modes of introducing new terms: from explicit definition to the use of reduction sentences and chains of such sentences on to the global specification of a set of theoretical concepts by means of theoretical postulates and correspondence rules: ever closer attention to the modes and needs of scientific theorizing led here to a far-reaching liberalization of what were regarded as essential conditions for the introduction of "meaningful" new terms. In this sense, the rational reconstructions formulated by logical empiricists did have a descriptive facet. But it must be acknowledged that the analytic empiricist concern with clarity and rigor and with systematic comprehensiveness and formal simplicity encouraged the formulation of some technically very impressive explicatory systems which are rather far removed from the objectives and modes of thinking that prompt scientific investigations; those systems, accordingly, possess only very limited explanatory potential.

Reconsideration and reorientation are thus clearly needed, and the critical and constructive ideas of the historic-pragmatic school have opened highly illuminating and promising new perspectives on issues of central concern to the methodology of science. But in so far as a proposed methodological theory of science is to afford an account of scientific inquiry as a rational pursuit, it will have to specify certain goals of scientific inquiry as well as some methodological principles observed in their pursuit; finally, it will have to exhibit the instrumental rationality of the principles in relation to the goals. Only to the extent that this can be done does the conception of science as the exemplar of rationality appear to be viable.

NOTES

[1] See Kuhn (1970a), pp. 155ff.: (1970b), pp. 261f.
[2] Kuhn (1971), pp. 144–145.
[3] Kuhn (1971), p. 144.
[4] Kuhn (1970b), p. 237.
[5] See, for example, Lakatos (1971), pp. 105–108.
[6] Feyerabend (1970), p. 76.
[7] Nagel (1939), Chapter 11, sec. 8.
[8] Cf. Duhem (1962), Part II, chapter VI, section 10.
[9] Feyerabend (1970), p. 280.
[10] Feyerabend (1970), p. 90.
[11] Kuhn (1970a), pp. 128, 149–150.
[12] Maxwell (1887), pp. 31–32.
[13] Kuhn (1970b), p. 237 (italics in original).
[14] Kuhn (1970b), pp. 237–238 (italics in original).

REFERENCES

Duhem, P. (1962). *The Aim and Structure of Physical Theory* (New York: Atheneum). (French original first published in 1906).

Feyerabend P. (1970). "Against Method: Outline of an Anarchistic Theory of Knowledge," in Radner, M. and Winokur, S., eds., *Minnesota Studies in the Philosophy of Science,* vol. IV, pp. 17–130.

Kuhn, T. S. (1970a). *The Structure of Scientific Revolutions,* Second edition, (Chicago University Press).

——. (1970b). "Reflections on My Critics," in Lakatos, I. and Musgrave, A., ed., *Criticism and the Growth of Knowledge* (Cambridge University Press), pp. 231–278.

——. (1971). "Notes on Lakatos," in Cohen, R. S. and Buck, R. C., eds., *P.S.A. 1970, Boston Studies in the Philosophy of Science,* vol. VIII, pp. 137–146.

Lakatos, I. (1971), "History of Science and Its Rational Reconstruction," in Cohen, R. S. and Buck, R. C., eds., *P.S.A. 1970, Boston Studies in the Philosophy of Science,* vol. VIII, pp. 91–136.

Maxwell, J. C. (1878). *Matter and Motion* (New York: D. Van Nostrand).

Nagel, E. (1939). *Principles of the Theory of Probability* (University of Chicago Press).

Popper, K. R. (1959). *The Logic of Scientific Discovery* (London: Hutchinson).

NELSON GOODMAN
WORDS, WORKS, WORLDS

1. QUESTIONS

Countless worlds made from nothing by use of symbols—so might a satirist summarize some major themes in the work of Ernst Cassirer. These themes—the multiplicity of worlds, the speciousness of "the given," the creative power of the understanding, the variety and formative function of symbols—are also integral to my own thinking. Sometimes, though, I forget how eloquently they have been set forth by Cassirer,[1] partly perhaps because his emphasis on myth, his concern with the comparative study of cultures, and his talk of the human spirit have been mistakenly associated with current trends toward mystical obscurantism, anti-intellectual intuitionism, or anti-scientific humanism. Actually these attitudes are as alien to Cassirer as to my own skeptical, analytic, constructionalist orientation.

My aim in what follows is less to defend certain theses that Cassirer and I share than to take a hard look at some crucial questions they raise. In just what sense are there many worlds? What distinguishes genuine from spurious worlds? What are worlds made of? How are they made? What role do symbols play in the making? And how is worldmaking related to knowing? These questions must be faced even if full and final answers are far off.

2. VERSIONS AND VISIONS

As intimated by William James's equivocal title *A Pluralistic Universe,* the issue between monism and pluralism tends to evaporate under analysis. If there is but one world, it embraces a multiplicity of contrasting aspects; if there are many worlds, the collection of them all is one. The one world may be taken as many, or the many worlds taken as one; whether one or many depends on the way of taking.[2]

Why, then, does Cassirer stress the multiplicity of worlds? In what important and often neglected sense are there many worlds? Let it be clear that the question here is not of the possible worlds that many of my contemporaries, especially those near Disneyland, are busy making and manipulating. We are not speaking in terms of multiple possible alternatives to a single actual world but of multiple actual worlds. How to interpret such terms as "real," "unreal," "fictive," and "possible" is a subsequent question.

Consider, to begin with, the statements "The sun always moves" and "The sun never moves" which, though equally true, are at odds with each other. Shall we say, then, that they describe different worlds, and indeed that there are as many different worlds as there are such mutually exclusive truths? Rather, we are inclined to regard the two strings of words not as complete statements with truth-values of their own but as elliptical for some such statements as "Under frame of reference *A,* the sun always moves" and "Under frame of reference *B,* the sun never moves"—statements that may both be true of the same world.

Frames of reference, though, seem to belong less to what is described than to systems of description: and each of the two statements relates what is described to such a system. If I ask about the world, you can offer to tell me how it is under one or more frames of reference; but if I insist that you tell me how it is apart from all frames, what can you say? We are confined to ways of describing whatever is described. Our universe, so to speak, consists of these ways rather than of a world or of worlds.

The alternative descriptions of motion, all of them in much the same terms and routinely transformable into one another, provide only a minor and rather pallid example of diversity in accounts of the world. Much more striking is the vast variety of versions and visions in the several sciences, in the works of different painters and writers, and in our perceptions as informed by these, by circumstances, and by our own insights, interests, and past experiences. Even with all illusory or wrong or dubious versions dropped, the rest exhibit new dimensions of disparity. Here we have no neat set of frames of reference, no ready rules for transforming physics, biology, and psychology into one another, and no way at all of transforming any of these into Van Gogh's vision, or Van Gogh's into Canaletto's. Such of these versions as are depictions rather than descriptions have no truth-value in the literal sense, and cannot be combined by conjunction. The difference between juxtaposing and conjoining two statements has no evident analogue for two pictures or for a picture and a statement. The dramatically contrasting versions of the world can of course be relativized: each is right under a given system— for a given science, a given artist, or a given perceiver and situation. Here again we turn from describing or depicting "the world" to talking of descriptions and depictions, but now without even the consolation of intertranslatability among or any evident organization of the several systems in question.

Yet doesn't a right version differ from a wrong one just in applying to the world, so that rightness itself depends upon and implies a world? We might better say that "the world" depends upon rightness. We cannot test a version by comparing it with a world undescribed, undepicted, unperceived, but only by other means that I shall discuss later. While we may speak of determining what versions are right as "learning about the world," "the world" supposedly being that which all right versions describe, all we learn about the world is contained in right versions of it; and while the underlying world, bereft of these, need not be denied to those who love it, it is perhaps on the whole a world well lost. For some purposes, we may want to define a relation that will so sort versions into clusters that each cluster constitutes a world, and the members of the cluster are versions of that world; but for many purposes, right world-descriptions and world-depictions and world-perceptions, the ways-the-world-is, or just versions, can be treated as our worlds.[3]

Since the fact that there are many different world-versions is hardly debatable, and the question how many if any worlds-in-themselves there are is virtually empty, in what non-trivial sense are there, as Cassirer and like-minded pluralists insist, many worlds? Just this, I think: that many different world-versions are of independent interest and importance, without any requirement or presumption of reducibility to a single base. The pluralist, far from being anti-scientific, accepts the sciences at full value. His typical adversary is the monopolistic materialist or physicalist who maintains that one system, physics, is preeminent and all-inclusive, such that every other version must eventually be reduced to it or rejected as false or meaningless. If all right versions could somehow be reduced to one and only one, that one might with some semblance of plausibility[4] be regarded as the only truth about the only world. But the evidence for such reducibility is negligible, and even the claim is nebulous since physics itself is fragmentary and unstable and the kind and consequences of reduction envisaged are vague. (How do you go about reducing Constable's or James Joyce's world-view to physics?) I am the last person likely to underrate construction and reduction.[5] A reduction from one system to another can make a genuine contribution to understanding the interrelationships among world-versions; but reduction in any reasonably strict sense is rare, almost always partial, and seldom if ever unique. To demand full and sole reducibility to physics or any other one version is to forego nearly all other versions. The pluralists' acceptance of versions other than physics implies no relaxation of rigor but a recognition that standards different from yet no less exacting than those applied in science are appropriate for appraising what is conveyed in perceptual or pictorial or literary versions.

So long as contrasting right versions not all reducible to one are countenanced, unity is to be sought not in an ambivalent or neutral *something* beneath these versions but in an overall organization embracing them. Cassirer undertakes the search through a cross-cultural study of the development of myth, religion, language, art, and science. My approach is rather through an analytic study of types and functions of symbols and symbol systems. In neither case should a unique result be anticipated; universes of worlds as well as worlds themselves may be built in many ways.

3. HOW FIRM A FOUNDATION?

The non-Kantian theme of multiplicity of worlds is closely akin to the Kantian theme of the vacuity of the notion of pure content. The one denies us a unique world, the other the common stuff of which worlds are made. Together these theses defy our intuitive demand for something stolid underneath, and threaten to leave us uncontrolled, spinning out our own inconsequent fantasies.

The overwhelming case against perception without conception, the pure given, absolute immediacy, the innocent eye, substance as substratum, has been so fully and frequently set forth—by Berkeley, Kant, Cassirer, Gombrich,[6] Bruner,[7] and many others—as to need no restatement here. Talk of unstructured content or an unconceptualized given or a substratum without properties is self-defeating; for the talk imposes structure, conceptualizes, ascribes properties. Although conception without perception is merely *empty,* perception without conception is *blind* (totally inoperative). Predicates, pictures, other labels, schemata, survive want of application, but content vanishes without form. We can have words without a world but no world without words or other symbols.

The many stuffs—matter, energy, waves, phenomena—that worlds are made of are made along with the worlds. But made from what? Not from nothing, after all, but *from other worlds.* Worldmaking as we know it always starts from worlds already on hand; the making is a remaking. Anthropology and developmental psychology may study social and individual histories of such world-building, but the search for a universal or necessary beginning is best left to theology.[8] My interest here is rather with the processes involved in building a world out of others.

With false hope of a firm foundation gone, with the world displaced by worlds that are but versions, with substance dissolved into function, and with the given acknowledged as taken, we face the questions how worlds are made, tested, and known.

4. WAYS OF WORLDMAKING

Without presuming to instruct the gods or other worldmakers, or attempting any comprehensive or systematic survey, I want to illustrate and comment on some of the processes that go into worldmaking. Actually, I am concerned more with certain relationships among worlds than with how or whether particular worlds are made from others.

(A) COMPOSITION AND DECOMPOSITION

Much but by no means all worldmaking consists of taking apart and putting together, often conjointly: on the one hand, of dividing wholes into parts and partitioning kinds into subspecies, analyzing complexes into component features, drawing distinctions; on the other hand, of composing wholes and kinds out of parts and members and subclasses, combining features into complexes, and making connections. Such composition or decomposition is normally effected or assisted or consolidated by the application of labels: names, predicates, gestures, pictures, etc. Thus, for example, temporally diverse events are brought together under a proper name or identified as making up "an object" or "a person"; or snow is sundered into several materials under terms of the Eskimo vocabulary. Metaphorical transfer—for example, where taste predicates are applied to sounds—may effect a double reorganization, both re-sorting the new realm of application and relating it to the old one (*LA:* II).

Identification rests upon organization into entities and kinds. The response to the question "Same or not the same?" must always be "Same what?"[9] Different soandsos may be the same such-and-such: what we point to or indicate, verbally or otherwise, may be different events but the same object, different towns but the same state, different members but the same club or different clubs but the same members, different innings but the same ball game. "The ball-in-play" of a single game may be comprised of temporal segments of a dozen or more baseballs. The psychologist asking the child to judge constancy when one vessel is emptied into another must be careful to consider *what* constancy is in question—constance of volume or depth or shape or kind of material, etc.[10] Identity or constancy in a world is identity with respect to what is within that world as organized.

Motley entities cutting across each other in complicated patterns may belong to the same world. We do not make a new world every time we take things apart or put them together in another way; but worlds may *differ* in that not everything belonging to one belongs to the other. The world of the Eskimo who has not grasped the comprehensive concept of snow differs not only from the world of the Samoan but also from the world of the New Englander who has not grasped the Eskimo's distinctions. In other cases, worlds differ in response to theoretical rather than practical needs. A world with points as elements cannot be the Whiteheadian world having points as certain classes of nesting volumes or having points as certain pairs of intersecting lines or as certain triples of intersecting planes. That the points of our everyday world can be equally well defined in any of these ways does not mean that a point can be identified in any one world with a nest of volumes and a pair of lines and a triple of planes; for all these are different from each other. Again the world of a system taking minimal concrete phenomena as atomic cannot admit qualities as atomic parts of these concreta.[11]

Repetition as well as identification is relative to organization. A world may be unmanageably heterogeneous or unbearably monotonous according to how events are sorted into kinds. Whether or not today's experiment repeats yesterday's, however much the two events may differ, depends upon whether they test a common hypothesis; as Sir George Thomson puts it:

> There will always be something different. . . . What it comes to when you say you repeat an experiment is that you repeat all the features of an experiment which a theory determines are relevant. In other words you repeat the experiment as an example of the theory.[12]

Likewise, two musical performances that differ drastically are nevertheless performances of the same work if they conform to the same score. The notational system distinguishes constitutive from contingent features, thus picking out the performance-kinds that count as works (*LA*, pp. 115–130). And things "go on in the same way" or not according to what is regarded as the same way; "now I can go on,"[13] in Wittgenstein's sense, when I have found a familiar pattern, or a tolerable variation of one, that fits and goes beyond the cases given. Induction requires taking some classes to the exclusion of others as relevant kinds. Only so, for example, do our observations of emeralds exhibit any regularity and confirm that all emeralds are green rather than that all are grue (i.e. examined before a given date and green, or not so examined and blue—*FFF*, pp. 72–80). The uniformity of nature we marvel at or the unreliability we protest belongs to a world of our own making.

In these latter cases, worlds differ in the relevant kinds they comprise. I say "relevant" rather than "natural" for two reasons: first, "natural" is an inapt term to cover not only biological species but such artificial kinds as musical works, psychological experiments, and types of machinery; and second, "natural" suggests some absolute categorical or psychological priority, while the kinds in question are rather habitual or traditional or devised for a new purpose.

(B) WEIGHTING

While we may say that in the cases discussed some relevant kinds[14] of one world are missing from another, we might perhaps better say that the two worlds contain just the same classes sorted differently into relevant and irrelevant kinds. Some relevant kinds of the one world, rather than being absent from the other, are present as irrelevant kinds; some differences among worlds are not so much in entities comprised as in emphasis or accent, and these differences are no less consequential. Just as to stress all syllables is to stress none, so to take all classes as relevant kinds is to take none as such. In one world there may be many kinds serving different purposes; but conflicting purposes may make for irreconcilable accents and contrasting worlds, as may conflicting conceptions of what kinds serve a given purpose. Grue cannot be a relevant kind for induction in the same world as green, for that would preclude some of the decisions, right or wrong, that constitute inductive inference.

Some of the most striking contrasts of emphasis appear in the arts. Many of the differences among portrayals by Daumier, Ingres, Michelangelo, and Rouault are differences in aspects accentuated. What counts as emphasis, of course, is departure from the relative prominence accorded the several features in the current world of our everyday seeing. With changing interests and new insights, the visual weighting of features of bulk or line or stance or light alters, and yesterday's level world seems strangely perverted—yesterday's realistic calendar landscape becomes a repulsive caricature.

These differences in emphasis, too, amount to a difference in relevant kinds recognized. Several portrayals of the same subject may thus place it according to different categorial schemata. Like a green emerald and a grue one, even if the same emerald, a Piero della Francesca *Christ* and a Rembrandt one belong to worlds organized into different kinds.

Works of art, though, characteristically illustrate rather than name or describe relevant kinds. Even where the ranges of application—the things described or depicted—coincide, the features or kinds exemplified or expressed may be very different. A line drawing of softly draped cloth may exemplify rhythmic linear patterns; and a poem with no words for sadness and no mention of a sad person may in the quality of its language be sad and poignantly express sadness. The distinction between saying or representing on the one hand and showing or exemplifying on the other becomes even more evident in the case of abstract painting and music and dance that have no subject-matter but nevertheless manifest—exemplify or express—forms and feelings. Exemplification and expression, though running in the opposite direction from denotation—that is, from the symbol to a literal or metaphorical feature of it instead of to something the symbol applies to—are no less symbolic referential functions and instruments of worldmaking.[15]

Emphasis or weighting is not always binary as is a sorting into relevant and irrelevant kinds or into important and unimportant features. Ratings of relevance, importance, utility, value often yield hierarchies rather than dichotomies. Such weightings are also instances of a particular type of ordering.

(C) ORDERING

Worlds not differing in entities or emphasis may differ in ordering; for example, the worlds of different constructional systems differ in order of derivation. As nothing is at rest or is in motion apart from a frame of reference, so nothing is primitive or is derivationally prior to anything apart from a constructional system. However, derivation unlike motion is of little immediate practical interest; and thus in our everyday world, although we must always adopt a frame of reference at least temporarily, we seldom adopt a derivational basis. Earlier I said that the difference between a world having points as pairs of lines and a world having lines as composed of points is that the latter but not the former admits as entities nonlinear elements comprised within lines. But alternatively we may say that these worlds differ in their derivational ordering of lines and points of the not-derivationally-ordered world of daily discourse.

Orderings of a different sort pervade perception and practical cognition. The standard ordering of brightness in color follows the linear increase in physical intensity of light, but the standard ordering of hues curls the straight line of increasing wavelength into a circle. Order includes periodicity as well as proximity; and the standard ordering of tones is by pitch and octave. Orderings alter with circumstances and objectives. Much as the nature of shapes changes under different geometries, so do perceived patterns change under different orderings; the patterns perceived under a twelve-tone scale are quite different from those perceived under the traditional eight-tone scale, and rhythms depend upon the marking off into measures.

Radical reordering of another sort occurs in constructing a static image from the input on scanning a picture, or in building a unified and comprehensive image of an object or a city from temporally and spatially and qualitatively heterogeneous observations and other items of information.[16] Some very fast readers recreate normal word-ordering from a series of fixations that proceed down the left-hand page and then up the right-hand page of a book.[17] And spatial order in a map or a score is translated into the temporal sequence of a trip or a performance.

All measurement, furthermore, is based upon order. Indeed, only through suitable arrangements and groupings can we handle vast quantities of material perceptually or cognitively. Gombrich discusses the decimal periodization of historical time into decades, centuries, and millennia.[18] Daily time is marked off into twenty-four hours, and each of these into sixty minutes of sixty seconds each. Whatever else may be said of these modes of organization, they are not "found in the world" but *built into a world.* Ordering, as well as composition and decomposition and weighting of wholes and kinds, participates in worldmaking.

(D) DELETION AND SUPPLEMENTATION

Also, the making of one world out of another usually involves some extensive weeding out and filling—actual excision of some old and supply of some new material. Our capacity for overlooking is virtually unlimited, and what we do take in usually consists of significant fragments and clues that need massive supplementation. Artists often make skillful use of this: a lithograph by Giacometti fully presents a walking man by sketches of nothing but the head, hands, and feet in just the right postures and positions against an expanse of blank paper; and a drawing by Katharine Sturgis conveys a hockey player in action by a single charged line.

That we find what we are prepared to find (what we look for or what forcefully affronts out expectations), and that we are likely to be blind to what neither helps nor hinders our pursuits, are commonplaces of everyday life and amply attested in the psychological laboratory.[19] In the painful experience of proofreading and the more pleasurable one of watching a skilled magician, we incurably miss something that is there and see something that is not there. Memory edits more ruthlessly; a person with equal command of two languages may remember a learned list of items while forgetting in which language they were listed.[20] And even within what we do perceive and remember, we dismiss as illusory or negligible what cannot be fitted into the architecture of the world we are building.

The scientist is no less drastic, rejecting or purifying most of the entities and events of the world of ordinary things while generating quantities of filling for curves suggested by sparse data, and erecting elaborate structures on the basis of meagre observations. Thus does he strive to build a world conforming to his chosen concepts and obeying his universal laws.

Replacement of a so-called analog by a so-called digital system through the articulation of separate steps involves deletion; for example, to use a digital thermometer with readings in tenths of a degree is to recognize no temperature as lying between 90 and 90.1 degrees. Similar deletion occurs under standard musical notation, which recognizes no pitch between *c* and *c#* and no duration between a sixty-fourth and a one hundred-and-twenty-eighth note. On the other hand, supplementation occurs when, say, an analog replaces a digital instrument for registering attendance, or reporting money raised, or when a violinist performs from a score.

Perhaps the most spectacular cases of supplementation, though, are found in the perception of motion. Sometimes motion in the perceptual world results from intricate and abundant fleshing out of the physical stimuli. Psychologists have long known of what is called the "phi phenomenon": under carefully controlled conditions, if two spots of light are flashed a short distance apart and in quick succession, the viewer normally sees a spot of light moving continuously along a path from the first position to the second. That is remarkable enough in itself since of course the direction of motion cannot have been determined prior to the second flash; but perception has even greater creative power. Paul Kolers has recently shown[21] that if the first stimulus spot is circular and the second square, the seen moving spot transforms smoothly from circle to square; and transformations between two-dimensional and three-dimensional shapes are often effected without trouble. Moreover, if a barrier of light is interposed between the two stimulus spots, the moving spot detours around the barrier. Just why these supplementations occur as they do is a fascinating subject for speculation. . . .

(E) DEFORMATION

Finally, some changes are reshapings or deformations that may according to point of view be considered either corrections or distortions. The physicist smooths out the simplest rough curve that fits all his data. Vision stretches a line ending with arrowheads pointing *in* while shrinking a physically equal line ending with arrowheads pointing *out,* and tends to expand the size of a smaller more valuable coin in relation to that of a larger less valuable one.[22] Caricaturists often go beyond overemphasis to actual distortion. Picasso starting from Velasquez's *Las Meninas,* and Brahms starting from a theme of Haydn's, work magical variations that amount to revelations.

These then are ways that worlds are made. I do not say *the* ways. My classification is not offered as comprehensive or clearcut or mandatory. Not only do the processes illustrated often occur in combination but the examples chosen sometimes fit equally well under more than one heading; for example, some changes may be considered alternatively as reweightings or reorderings or reshapings or as all of these, and some deletions are also matters of differences in composition. All I have tried to do is to suggest something of the variety of processes in constant use. While a tighter systematization could surely be developed, none can be ultimate; for as remarked earlier, there is no more a unique world of worlds than there is a unique world.

5. TROUBLE WITH TRUTH

With all this freedom to divide and combine, emphasize, order, delete, fill in and fill out, and even distort, what are the objectives and the constraints? What are the criteria for success in making a world?

Insofar as a version is verbal and consists of statements, truth may be relevant. But truth cannot be defined or tested by agreement with "the world"; for not only do truths differ for different worlds but the nature of agreement between a version and a world apart from it is notoriously nebulous. Rather—speaking loosely and without trying to answer either Pilate's question or Tarski's—a version is taken to be true when it offends no unyielding beliefs and none of its own precepts. Among beliefs unyielding at a given time may be long-lived reflections of laws of logic, short-lived reflections of recent observations, and other convictions and prejudices ingrained with varying degrees of firmness. Among precepts, for example, may be choices among alternative frames of reference, weightings, and derivational bases. But the line between beliefs and precepts is neither sharp nor stable. Beliefs are framed in concepts informed by precepts; and if a Boyle ditches his data for a smooth curve just missing them all, we may say either that observational volume and pressure are different properties from theoretical volume and pressure or that the truths about volume and pressure differ in the two worlds of observation and theory. Even the staunchest belief may in time admit alternatives; "The earth is at rest" passed from dogma to dependence upon precept.

Truth, far from being a solemn and severe master, is a docile and obedient servant. The scientist who supposes that he is single-mindedly dedicated to the search for truth deceives himself. He is unconcerned with the trivial truths he could grind out endlessly; and he looks to the multifaceted and irregular results of observations for little more than suggestions of overall structures and significant generalizations. He seeks system, simplicity, scope; and when satisfied on these scores he tailors truth to fit (*PP:* VII, 6–8). He as much decrees as discovers the laws he sets forth, as much designs as discerns the patterns he delineates.

Truth, moreover, pertains solely to what is said, and literal truth solely to what is said literally. We have seen, though, that worlds are made not only by what is said literally but also by what is said metaphorically, and not only by what is said either literally or metaphorically but also by what is exemplified and expressed—by what is shown as well as by what is said. In a scientific treatise, literal truth counts most; but in a poem or novel, metaphorical or allegorical truth may matter more, for even a literally false statement may be metaphorically true (*LA,* pp. 51, 68–70) and may mark or make new assertions and discriminations, change emphases, effect exclusions and additions. And statements whether literally or metaphorically true or false may show what they do not say, may work as trenchant literal or metaphorical examples of unmentioned features and feelings. In Vachel Lindsay's *The Congo,* for example, the pulsating pattern of drumbeats is insistently exhibited rather than described.

Finally, for nonverbal versions and even for verbal versions without statements, truth is irrelevant. We risk confusion when we speak of pictures or predicates as "true of" what they depict or apply to; they have no truth-value and may represent or denote some things and not others, while a statement does have truth-value and is true of everything if of anything.[23] A nonrepresentational picture such as a Mondrian says nothing, denotes nothing, pictures nothing, and is neither true nor false, but shows much. Nevertheless, showing or exemplifying, like denoting, is a referential function; and much the same considerations count for pictures as for the concepts of predicates of a theory: their relevance and their revelations, their force and their fit—in sum their *rightness.* Rather than speak of pictures as true or false we might better speak of theories as right or wrong; for the truth of the laws of a theory is but one special feature and is often, as we have seen, overridden in importance by the cogency and compactness and comprehensiveness, the informativeness and organizing power of the whole system.

"The truth, the whole truth, and nothing but the truth" would thus be a perverse and paralyzing policy for any worldmaker. The whole truth would be too much; it is too vast, variable, and clogged with trivia. The truth alone would be too little, for some right versions are not true—being either false or neither true nor false—and even for true versions rightness may matter more.

6. RELATIVE REALITY

Shouldn't we now return to sanity from all this mad proliferation of worlds? Shouldn't we stop speaking of right versions as if each were, or had, its own world, and recognize all as versions of one and the same neutral and underlying world? The world thus regained, as remarked earlier, is a world without kinds or order or motion or rest or pattern—a world not worth fighting for or against.

We might, though, take the real world to be that of some one of the alternative right versions (or groups of them bound together by some principle of reducibility or translatability) and regard all other versions as versions of that same world differing from the standard version in accountable ways. The physicist takes his world as the real one, attributing the deletions, additions, irregularities, emphases of other versions to the imperfections of perception, to the urgencies of practice, or to poetic license. The phenomenalist regards the perceptual world as fundamental, and the excisions, abstractions, simplifications, and distortions of other versions as resulting from scientific or practical or artistic concerns. For the man-in-the-street, most versions from science, art, and perception depart in some ways from the familiar serviceable world he has jerry-built from fragments of scientific and artistic tradition and from his own struggle for survival. This world, indeed, is the one most often taken as real; for reality in a world, like realism in a picture, is largely a matter of habit.

Ironically, then, our passion for *one* world is satisfied, at different times and for different purposes, in *many* different ways. Not only motion, derivation, weighting, order, but even reality is relative. That right versions and actual worlds are many does not obliterate the distinction between right and wrong versions, does not recognize merely possible worlds answering to wrong versions, and does not imply that all right alternatives are equally good for every or indeed for any purpose. Not even a fly is likely to take one of its wing-tips as a fixed point; we do not welcome molecules or concreta as elements of our everyday world, or combine tomatoes and triangles and typewriters and tyrants and tornadoes into a single kind; the physicist will count none of these among his fundamental particles; the painter who sees the way the man-in-the-street does will have more popular than artistic success. And the same philosopher who here metaphilosophically contemplates a vast variety of worlds finds that only versions meeting the demands of a dogged and deflationary nominalism suit his purposes in constructing philosophical systems.

Moreover, while readiness to recognize alternative worlds may be liberating, and suggestive of new avenues of exploration, a willingness to welcome all worlds builds none. Mere acknowledgement of the many available frames of reference provides us with no map of the motions of heavenly bodies; acceptance of the eligibility of alternative bases produces no scientific theory or philosophical system; awareness of varied ways of seeing paints no pictures. A broad mind is no substitute for hard work.

7. NOTES ON KNOWING

What I have been saying bears on the nature of knowledge. On these terms, knowing cannot be exclusively or even primarily a matter of determining what is true. Discovery often amounts, as when I place a piece in a jigsaw puzzle, not to arrival at a proposition for declaration or defense, but to finding a fit. Much of knowing aims at something other than true, or any, belief. An increase in acuity of insight or in range of comprehension, rather than a change in belief, occurs when we find in a pictured forest a face we already knew was there, or learn to distinguish stylistic differences among works already classified by artist or composer or writer, or study a picture or a concerto or a treatise until we see or hear or grasp features and structures we could not discern before. Such growth in knowledge is not by formation or fixation of belief[24] but by the advancement of understanding.[25]

Furthermore, if worlds are as much made as found, so also knowing is as much remaking as reporting. All the processes of worldmaking I have discussed enter into knowing. Perceiving motion, we have seen, often consists in producing it. Discovering laws involves drafting them. Recognizing patterns is very much a matter of inventing and imposing them. Comprehension and creation go on together.

I shall return in Chapters VI and VII to many of the questions surveyed here. Now I want to consider two much more specific topics: in Chapter II, a subtle categorization peculiarly significant for the arts; and in Chapter III, a sample tracing of a notion across versions in various systems and media.

NOTES

[1] E.g. in *Language and Myth,* translated by Susanne Langer (Harper, 1946).

[2] But see (N. Goodman, *Ways of Worldmaking,* Indianapolis, Indiana: Hackett Publishing Co., 1978), VII: 1.

[3] Cf. "The Way the World Is" (1960), *PP,* pp. 24–32, and Richard Rorty, "The World Well Lost," *Journal of Philosophy,* Vol. 69 (1972), pp. 649–665.

[4] But not much, for no one type of reducibility serves all purposes.

[5] Cf. "The Revision of Philosophy" (1956), *PP,* pp. 5–23; and also *SA.*

6. In *Art and Illusion* (Pantheon Books, 1960), E. H. Gombrich argues in many passages against the notion of "the innocent eye."

7 See the essays in Jerome S. Bruner's *Beyond the Information Given* [hereinafter *BI*], Jeremy M. Anglin, ed. (W. W. Norton, 1973). Chap. 1.

8 Cf. *SA,* pp. 127–145; and "Sense and Certainty" (1952) and "The Epistemological Argument" (1967), *PP,* pp. 60–75. We might take construction of a history of successive development of worlds to involve application of something like a Kantian regulative principle, and the search for a first world thus to be as misguided as the search for a first moment of time.

9 This does not, as sometimes is supposed, require any modification of the Leibniz formula for identity, but merely reminds us that the answer to a question "Is this the same as that?" may depend upon whether the "this" and the "that" in the question refer to thing or event or color or species, etc.

10 See *BI,* pp. 331–340.

11 See further *SA,* pp. 3–22, 132–135, 142–145.

12 In "Some Thoughts on Scientific Method" (1963), in *Boston Studies in the Philosophy of Science,* Vol. 2 (Humanities Press, 1965), p. 85.

13 Discussion of what this means occupies many sections, from about Sec. 142 on, of Ludwig Wittgenstein's *Philosophical Investigations,* translated by G. E. M. Anscombe (Blackwell, 1953). I am not suggesting that the answer I give here is Wittgenstein's.

14 I speak freely of kinds here. Concerning ways of nominalizing such talk, see *SA* : II and *PP* : IV.

15 On exemplification and expression as referential relations see *LA,* pp. 50–57, 87–95.

16 See *The Image of the City* by Kevin Lynch (Cambridge, Technology Press, 1960).

17 See E. Llewellyn Thomas, "Eye Movements in Speed Reading," in *Speed Reading: Practices and Procedures* (University of Delaware Press, 1962), pp. 104–114.

18 In "Zeit, Zahl, und Zeichen," delivered at the Cassirer celebration in Hamburg, 1974.

19 See "On Perceptual Readiness" (1957) in *BI,* pp. 7–42.

20 See Paul Kolers, "Bilinguals and Information Processing," *Scientific American* 218 (1968), 78–86.

21 *Aspects of Motion Perception* (Pergamon Press, 1972), pp. 47ff.

22 See "Value and Need as Organizing Factors in Perception" (1947), in *BI,* pp. 43–56.

23 E.g., "2 + 2 = 4" is true of everything in that for every x, x is such that $2 + 2 = 4$. A statement S will normally not be *true about* x unless S is about x in one of the senses of "about" defined in "About" (*PP,* pp. 246–272); but definition of "about" depends essentially on features of statements that have no reasonable analogues for pictures. See further: Joseph Ullian and Nelson Goodman, "Truth about Jones," *Journal of Philosophy,* Vol. 74 (1977), pp. 317–338; also VII:5 below.

24 I allude here to Charles S. Peirce's paper, "The Fixation of Belief" (1877), in *Collected Papers of Charles Sanders Peirce,* Vol. 5 (Harvard University Press, 1934), pp. 223–247.

25 On the nature and importance of understanding in the broader sense, see M. Polanyi, *Personal Knowledge* (University of Chicago Press, 1960).

STUDY QUESTIONS FOR TOPIC IV

1. What is your opinion concerning the following dispute? Barnes and Bloor claim that all expressions of science, such as descriptive statements, laws of nature, and scientific theories, must be relativized to the social community from which such expressions are voiced. But, rationalists respond that the relativistic approach cannot account for the obvious cases of genuine understanding of nature. If all scientific beliefs merely convey the practices and social norms of the scientific community, then any declaration of access to Nature is illusory.

Thus, the relativistic cannot explain the success of science. Defend your own position on this controversy.

2. Consider the following "fact": the table on which you are reading this book is less than ten feet long. Do you believe that this "fact" is relativized to the social convention, rules of language, and norms of behavior, without any contact to the physical world?

3. Based on Latour's examination of laboratory life, is it possible for experimenters to observe Nature independently of all assumptions, biases, and language?

4. Examine carefully the meanings of the following questions: (a) What was the warranting evidence used by ancient people on behalf of their belief that the earth is flat? (b) What were the social and historical factors which motivated ancient people into believing that the earth is flat?

   Do questions (a) and (b) have the same or different meanings? To answer this issue, imagine some possible answers to (a) and to (b). Would the possible answers to (a) be identical to the possible answers to (b)?

5. According to many rationalists, the descriptive studies of the actual practice of scientists are irrelevant to the philosophy of science, since philosophy centers on the purely idealized standards that guide scientific inquiry. Would Hempel agree with this separation between descriptive studies and (prescriptive) philosophy? That is, what exactly did Hempel say about the apparent irrelevance of descriptive studies of scientists to philosophy of science?

6. What are the similarities and differences between the relativism of Nelson Goodman and the relativism of Barnes and Bloor?

7. Based on Goodman's relativism, is it the case that all possible belief systems about the world are equally valid? Answer "yes" or "no," and provide a detailed defense.

BIBLIOGRAPHY

Barnes, B. *Interests and the Growth of Knowledge.* London: Routledge & Kegan Paul, 1977.
————. *Scientific Knowledge and Sociological Theory.* London: Routledge and Kegan Paul, 1974.
Bloor, D. *Knowledge and Social Imagery.* London: Routledge and Kegan Paul, 1976.
————. "The Strengths of the Strong Programme," *The Philosophy of the Social Science* 11: 1981, 199–213.
————. *Wittgenstein: A Social Theory of Knowledge.* New York: Columbia UP, 1983.
Brown, J. R., ed., *Scientific Rationality: The Sociological Turn.* Dordrecht-Holland: D. Reidel, 1984.
Collins, H. M. *Changing Order: Replication and Induction in Scientific Practice.* London: Sage, 1985.
Fuller, S. *Social Epistemology.* Bloomington: Indiana UP, 1988.
Hollis, M. "The Social Destruction of Reality," *Rationality and Relativism.* Ed. M. Hollis and S. Lukes. Cambridge: MIT, 1982, pp. 67–86.
Latour, B. "Postmodern? No, Simply Amodern! Steps towards an Anthropology of Science." *Studies in History and Philosophy of Science* 21: 145–171.
Latour, B. and S. Woolgar. *Laboratory Life: The Construction of Scientific Facts.* Princeton: Princeton UP, 1986.
Rorty, R. *Philosophy and the Mirror of Nature.* Oxford: Basil Blackwell, 1980.

THE
REALIST/ANTIREALIST
DEBATES

INTRODUCTION

How would you convince a very skeptical person that some ordinary objects, such as cars or hamburgers, really exist? How would you demonstrate that forest fires or thunderstorms actually occur in nature? Most people would appeal to eyewitness testimony. For example, we can demonstrate that a thunderstorm struck a certain area by speaking to witnesses. Such conversations may constitute evidence for the occurrence of the thunderstorm. Based on such conversations, we would probably rule out the thought that the event was fabricated by weather forecasters and magnified by a media frenzy. We would describe the event as a real natural phenomenon.

But, such commonsense experience cannot be used to determine the existence of a wide range of so-called theoretical entities. Although these entities are not empirically observable, scientists freely talk about them in the context of a scientific theory. For example, astrophysicists talk about black holes in which presumably light rays can enter but cannot escape; physicists talk about the curvature of the universe in terms of four or more dimensions; chemists claim that the atoms of a water molecule are bound together by unobservable forces of attraction called electrostatic forces. Should we accept the existence of black holes, space-time curvature, and electrostatic forces, in spite of the fact that they are immune to direct observable detection?

This question has generated heated debates among philosophers of science. Two rival positions are frequently expressed. One position is called *scientific realism.* In this view, any so-called theoretical entity is real as long as scientists claim that such entities must exist in order to explain certain observed events. For example, the electrostatic force of attraction between molecules is real because the explanation of freezing water must include a belief in the existence of such a force. Even though such a force cannot be observed, its existence is an inescapable conclusion from modern chemistry. So, according to most scientific realists, *if* we endorse a particular scientific theory which includes claims about the existence of certain theoretical entities, *then* we are committed to the existence of such entities.

A competing philosophical position is called *scientific antirealism.* Many, but not all, antirealists argue that our acceptance of a particular scientific theory does not require that we believe in the existence of the so-called theoretical entities. A theory's value centers on the ways in which scientists use the theory to summarize all the data, in order to explain past events, and to predict the future. For example, theories of physical chemistry are extremely useful for explaining how a liquid can be converted to a gas. But these explanations do not require commitment to the existence of the unobservable forces of attraction and repulsion, even though chemists talk about such forces. Moreover, the antirealist insists on reasonable caution when discussing unobservable processes. If a certain belief cannot be tested experimentally, then the belief must fall outside of the realm of scientific knowledge. Although the term "electrostatic force" appears frequently in the literature of chemistry, this term does not refer to anything that can be detected experimentally. We must avoid unwarranted leaps of faith concerning the existence of so-called unobservable entities, according to the antirealist.

The realist/antirealist controversy reflects the culmination of many issues in philosophy of science. In relation to Topic II we see that the realist typically has a different conception of a scientific explanation from that of the antirealist. According to the realist, an event is explained by appeal to the unseen causal processes that generated the event in question. The antirealist objects that such an appeal is highly speculative, and not even necessary to explain the event. Furthermore, concerning Topic IV, many antirealists would agree with realists that the successes of science can be understood by "rational" standards of evaluation. Other antirealists, motivated by the writings from the sociology of science, argue that any standard for evaluating a theory must be relativized to the social values and interests of a particular scientific community.

S U M M A R Y   O F   R E A D I N G S

In the tradition of David Hume, W. T. Stace argues for a strict antirealism (selection #23). All claims about the existence of real-world processes are at best misleading, and at worst, fantasies.

When I say that water exists, I mean that I can experience certain visual and tactile sensations which I customarily associate with the idea of water. Our belief that water exists actually reduces to a collection of possible sensations which we typically associate with the notion of water. The so-called entities that are presumably immune from direct empirical inspection, such as unseen forces of attraction, are pure fictions. Any talk of unobservable entities must be abandoned altogether, according to Stace.

Not all antirealists are as skeptical as Stace. According to Bas van Fraassen, we should believe in the existence of a theory's observable entities, such as water, because these entities are subject to strong empirical support (selection #24). But the unobservable entities from our best theories are never empirically detectable. Van Fraassen's antirealism rests on a principled distinction between a theory's observable and unobservable entities, a distinction that can be applied to any scientific theory. We can believe in the existence of observable entities but not unobservable ones. A theoretical concept such as the notion of electromagnetic force may be useful for making predictions about future events, but this concept does not refer to any real-world process, according to van Fraassen.

Van Fraassen's observable/unobservable distinction has no philosophical value, writes Paul Churchland (selection #25). Van Fraassen is wrong to give a privileged status to claims about observable entities, because many of these claims are grounded on highly abstract theoretical assumptions. Consider the belief in the existence of an observable entity which is far removed from our immediate experience, such as a distant star. Such a belief relies on a vast reservoir of theoretical abstraction, comparable to beliefs in the existence of unobservable entities, according to Churchland. We have no reason to prefer *in advance* existence claims about observable entities over those about unobservables. Churchland rejects the antirealism of both van Fraassen and Stace.

Most advocates of scientific realism argue that the abstract terms of our best theories do refer to real properties of the universe. But Ronald Giere presents a completely different argument for realism, based on his ideas about the character of scientific knowledge (selection #26). He believes that scientific knowledge does not always come to us through the use of language, such as sentences or terms. The primary unit of scientific knowledge is, rather, the theoretical model. The model is a set of concepts designed to approximate a few properties of the material universe. Scientists construct a model to represent conceptually some segment of nature. For example, the meteorite falling to earth can be represented conceptually by a Newtonian model of a freely falling projectile in a uniform gravitational field. This model selectively highlights the properties of initial velocity, acceleration, gravitational attraction, and so on. We can say that our best scientific models simulate nature and the concepts of the models refer to real properties.

Advocating a different conception of realism, Ernan McMullin argues that our belief in the existence of real properties is the only way to explain scientific progress (selection #27). For example, progress in chemistry over the past century can be seen from the development of theoretical models of molecular structures. An indication of such progress is the fertility of these models to yield novel predictions, beyond what was known to scientists at a given time.

Van Fraassen would agree with Giere and McMullin that the primary unit of scientific knowledge is a theoretical model. But their disagreement centers on the capacity of such models to expose nature's secrets. According to Giere and McMullin, theoretical models have the capacity to reveal the real-world processes which are causally responsible for generating observable phenomena. Van Fraassen rejects this function of models.

Ian Hacking develops another argument for scientific realism, one that directly contradicts the positions of Giere and McMullin. According to Hacking, we can never be sure that an abstract theoretical model simulates real-world processes (selection #28). But we can accept the existence of so-called unobservable entities when such entities become central to the use of modern instrumental apparatus. When the electron microscope is used properly, for example, scientists exploit the properties of electrons. So, we know that electrons are real because electrons function as tools during the experimental study of some other segment of nature.

W. T. STACE
SCIENCE AND THE PHYSICAL WORLD

So far as I know scientists still talk about electrons, protons, neutrons, and so on. We never directly perceive these, hence if we ask how we know of their existence the only possible answer seems to be that they are an inference from what we do directly perceive. What sort of an inference? Apparently a causal inference. The atomic entities in some way impinge upon the sense of the animal organism and cause that organism to perceive the familiar world of tables, chairs, and the rest.

But is it not clear that such a concept of causation, however interpreted, is invalid? The only reason we have for believing in the law of causation is that we *observe* certain regularities or sequences. We observe that, in certain conditions, A is always followed by B. We call A the cause, B the effect. And the sequence A-B becomes a causal law. It follows that all *observed* causal sequences are between sensed objects in the familiar world of perception, and that all known causal laws apply solely to the world of sense and not to anything beyond or behind it. And this in turn means that we have not got, and never could have, one jot of evidence for believing that the law of causation can be applied *outside* the realm of perception, or that that realm can have any causes (such as the supposed physical objects) which are not themselves perceived.

Put the same thing in another way. Suppose there is an observed sequence *A-B-C,* represented by the vertical lines in the diagram below.

The observer X sees, and can see, nothing except things in the familiar world of perception. What *right* has he, and what *reason* has he, to assert causes of A, B, and C, such as a′, b′, c′, which he can never observe, behind the perceived world? He has no *right,* because the law

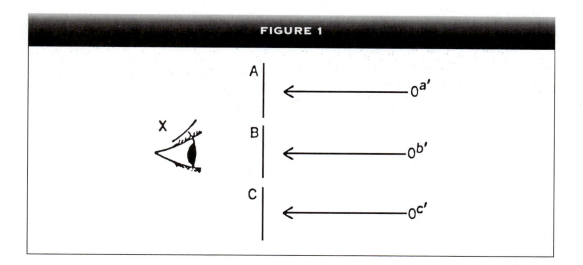

FIGURE 1

of causation on which he is relying has never been observed to operate outside the series of perceptions, and he can have, therefore, no evidence that it does so. And he has no *reason* because the phenomenon C is *sufficiently* accounted for by the cause B, B by A, and so on. It is unnecessary and superfluous to introduce a *second* cause b′ for B, c′ for C, and so forth. To give two causes for each phenomenon, one in one world and one in another, is unnecessary, and perhaps even self-contradictory.

Is it denied, then, it will be asked, that the star causes light waves, that the waves cause retinal changes, that these cause changes in the optic nerve, which in turn causes movement in the brain cells, and so on? No, it is not denied. But the observed causes and effects are all in the world of perception. And no sequences of sense-data can possibly justify going outside that world. If you admit that we never observe anything except sensed objects and their relations, regularities, and sequences, then it is obvious that we are completely shut in by our sensations and can never get outside them. Not only causal relations, but all other observed relations, upon which *any* kind of inferences might be founded, will lead only to further sensible objects and their relations. No inference, therefore, can pass from what is sensible to what is not sensible.

The fact is that atoms are *not* inferences from sensations. No one denies, of course, that a vast amount of perfectly valid inferential reasoning takes place in the physical theory of the atom. But it will not be found to be in any strict logical sense inference from *sense-data to atoms.* An *hypothesis* is set up, and the inferential processes are concerned with the application of the hypothesis, that is, with the prediction by its aid of further possible sensations and with its own internal consistency.

That atoms are not inferences from sensations means, of course, that from the existence of sensations we cannot validly infer the existence of atoms. And this means that we cannot have any reason at all to believe that they exist. And that is why I propose to argue that they do not exist—or at any rate that no one could know it if they did, and that we have absolutely no evidence of their existence.

What status have they, then? Is it meant that they are false and worthless, merely untrue? Certainly not. No one supposes that the entries in the nautical almanac "exist" anywhere except on the pages of that book and in the brains of its compilers and readers. Yet they are "true," inasmuch as they enable us to predict certain sensations, namely, the positions and times of certain perceived objects which we call the stars. And so the formulae of the atomic theory are true in the same sense, and perform a similar function.

I suggest that they are nothing but shorthand formulae, ingeniously worked out by the human mind, to enable it to predict its experience, i.e. to predict what sensations will be given to it. By "predict" here I do not mean to refer solely to the future. To calculate that there was an eclipse of the sun visible in Asia Minor in the year 585 B.C. is, in the sense in which I am using the term, to predict.

In order to see more clearly what is meant, let us apply the same idea to another case, that of gravitation. Newton formulated a law of gravitation in terms of "forces." It was supposed that this law—which was nothing but a mathematical formula—governed the operation of these existent forces. Nowadays it is no longer believed that these forces exist at all. And yet the law can be applied just as well without them to the prediction of astronomical phenomena. It is a matter of no importance to the scientific man whether the forces exist or not. That may be said to be a purely philosophical question. And I think the philosopher should pronounce them fictions. But that would not make the law useless or untrue. If it could still be used to predict phenomena, it would be just as true as it was.

It is true that fault is now found with Newton's law, and that another law, that of Einstein, has been substituted for it. And it is sometimes supposed that the reason for this is that forces are no longer believed in. But this is not the case. Whether forces exist or not simply does not matter. What matters is the discovery that Newton's law does *not* enable us accurately to predict certain astronomical facts such as the exact position of the planet Mercury. Therefore another formula, that of Einstein, has been substituted for it which permits correct predictions. This new law, as it happens, is a formula in terms of geometry. It is pure mathematics and nothing else. It does not contain anything about forces. In its pure form it does not even contain, so I am informed, anything about "humps and hills in space-time." And it does not matter whether any such humps and hills exist. It is truer than Newton's law, not because it substitutes humps and hills for forces, but solely because it is a more accurate formula of prediction.

Not only may it be said that forces do not exist. It may with equal truth be said that "gravitation" does not exist. Gravitation is not a "thing," but a mathematical formula, which exists only in the heads of mathematicians. And as a mathematical formula cannot cause a body to fall, so gravitation cannot cause a body to fall. Ordinary language misleads us here. We speak of the law "of" gravitation, and suppose that this law "applies to" the heavenly bodies. We are thereby misled into supposing that there are *two* things, namely, the gravitation and the heavenly bodies, and that one of these things, the gravitation, causes changes in the other. In reality nothing exists except the moving bodies. And neither Newton's law nor Einstein's law is, strictly speaking, a law of gravitation. They are both laws of moving bodies, that is to say, formulae which tell us how these bodies will move.

Now, just as in the past "forces" were foisted into Newton's law (by himself, be it said), so now certain popularizers of relativity foisted "humps and hills in space-time" into Einstein's law. We hear that the reason why the planets move in curved courses is that they cannot go through these humps and hills, but have to go round them! The planets just get "shoved about," not by forces, but by the humps and hills! But these humps and hills are pure metaphors. And anyone who takes them for "existences" gets asked awkward questions as to what "curved space" is curved "in."

It is not irrelevant to our topic to consider *why* human beings invent these metaphysical monsters of forces and bumps in space-time. The reason is that they have never emancipated themselves from the absurd idea that science "explains" things. They were not content to have laws which merely told them *that* the planets will, as a matter of fact, move in such and such ways. They wanted to know "why" the planets move in those ways. So Newton replied, "Forces." "Oh," said humanity, "that explains it. We understand forces. We feel them every time someone pushes or pulls us." Thus the movements were supposed to be "explained" by entities familiar because analogous to the muscular sensations which human beings feel. The humps and hills were introduced for exactly the same reason. They seem so familiar. If there is a bump in the billiard table, the rolling billiard ball is diverted from a straight to a curved course. Just the same with the planets. "Oh, I see!" says humanity, "that's quite simple. That *explains* everything."

But scientific laws, properly formulated, never "explain" anything. They simply state, in an abbreviated and generalized form, *what happens.* No scientist, and in my opinion no philosopher, knows *why* anything happens, or can "explain" anything. Scientific laws do nothing except state the brute fact that "when *A* happens, *B* always happens too." And laws of this kind obviously enable us to predict. If certain scientists substituted humps and hills for forces, then they have just substituted one superstition for another. For my part I do not believe that *science* has done this, though some *scientists* may have. For scientists, after all, are human beings with the same craving for "explanations" as other people.

I think that atoms are in exactly the same position as forces and the humps and hills of space-time. In reality the mathematical formulae which are the scientific ways of stating the atomic theory are simply formulae for calculating what sensations will appear in given conditions. But just as the weakness of the human mind demanded that there should correspond to the formula of gravitation a real "thing" which could be called "gravitation itself" or "force," so the same weakness demands that there should be a real thing corresponding to the atomic formulae, and this real thing is called the atom. In reality the atoms no more cause sensations than gravitation causes apples to fall. The only causes of sensations are other sensations. And the relation of atoms to sensations to be felt is not the relation of cause to effect, but the relation of a mathematical formula to the facts and happenings which it enables the mathematician to calculate.

Some writers have said that the physical world has no color, no sound, no taste, no smell. It has no spatiality. Probably it has not even number. We must not suppose that it is in any way like our world, or that we can understand it by attributing to it the characters of our world. Why not carry this progress to its logical conclusion? Why not give up the idea that it has even the character of "existence" which our familiar world has? We have given up smell, color, taste. We have given up even space and shape. We have given up number. Surely, after all that, mere existence is but a little thing to give up. No? Then is it that the idea of existence conveys "a sort of halo"? I suspect so. The "existence" of atoms is but the expiring ghost of the pellet and billiard-ball atoms of our forefathers. They, of course, had size, shape, weight, hardness. These have gone. But thinkers still cling to their existence, just as their fathers clung to the existence of forces, and for the same reason. Their reason is not in the slightest that science has any use for the existent atom. But the *imagination* has. It seems somehow to explain things, to make them homely and familiar.

It will not be out of place to give one more example to show how common fictitious existences are in science, and how little it matters whether they really exist or not. This example has no strange and annoying talk of "bent spaces" about it. One of the foundations of physics is, or used to be, the law of the conservation of energy. I do not know how far, if at all, this has been affected by the theory that matter sometimes turns into energy. But that does not affect the lesson it has for us. The law states, or used to state, that the amount of energy in the universe is always constant, that energy is never either created or destroyed. This was highly convenient, but it seemed to have obvious exceptions. If you throw a stone up into the air, you are told that it exerts in its fall the same amount of energy which it took to throw it up. But suppose it does not fall. Suppose it lodges on the roof of your house and stays there. What has happened to the energy which you can nowhere perceive as being exerted? It seems to have disappeared out of the universe. No, says the scientist, it still exists as *potential* energy. Now what does this blessed word "potential"—which is thus brought in to save the situation—mean as applied to energy? It means, of course, that the energy does not exist in any of its regular "forms," heat, light, electricity, etc. But this is merely negative. What positive meaning has the term? Strictly speaking, none whatever. Either the energy exists or it does not exist. There is no realm of the "potential" half-way between existence and non-existence. And the existence of energy can only consist in its being exerted. If the energy is not being exerted, then it is not energy and does not exist. Energy can no more exist without energizing than heat can exist without being hot. The "potential" existence of the energy is, then, a fiction. The actual empirically verifiable facts are that if a certain quantity of energy *e* exists in the universe and then disappears out of the universe (as happens when the stone lodges on the roof), the same amount of energy *e* will always reappear, begin to exist again, in certain known conditions. That is the fact which the law of the conservation of energy actually expresses. And the fiction of potential energy is introduced simply because it is convenient and makes the equations easier to work. They could be worked quite well without it, but would be slightly more complicated. In either case the function of the law is the same. Its object is to apprise us that if in certain conditions we have certain perceptions (throwing up the stone), then in certain other conditions we shall get certain other perceptions (heat, light, stone hitting skull, or other such). But there will always be a temptation to hypostatize the potential energy as an "existence," and to believe that it is a "cause" which "explains" the phenomena.

If the views which I have been expressing are followed out, they will lead to the conclusion that, strictly speaking, *nothing exists except sensations* (and the minds which perceive them). The rest is mental construction or fiction. But this does not mean that the conception of a star or the conception of an electron are worthless or untrue. Their truth and value consist in their capacity for helping us to organize our experience and predict our sensations.

BAS C. VAN FRAASSEN
ARGUMENTS CONCERNING SCIENTIFIC REALISM

The rigour of science requires that we distinguish well the undraped figure of nature itself from the gay-coloured vesture with which we clothe it at our pleasure.

Heinrich Hertz, quoted by Ludwig Boltzmann, letter to Nature, *28 February 1895*

In our century, the first dominant philosophy of science was developed as part of logical positivism. Even today, such an expression as "the received view of theories" refers to the views developed by the logical positivists, although their heyday preceded the Second World War.

In this [reading] I shall examine, and criticize, the main arguments that have been offered for scientific realism. These arguments occurred frequently as part of a critique of logical positivism. But it is surely fair to discuss them in isolation, for even if scientific realism is most easily understood as a reaction against positivism, it should be able to stand alone. The alternative view which I advocate—for lack of a traditional name I shall call it *constructive empiricism*—is equally at odds with positivist doctrine.

§1. SCIENTIFIC REALISM AND CONSTRUCTIVE EMPIRICISM

In philosophy of science, the term "scientific realism" denotes a precise position on the question of how a scientific theory is to be understood, and what scientific activity really is. I shall attempt to define this position, and to canvass its possible alternatives. Then I shall indicate, roughly and briefly, the specific alternative which I shall advocate and develop in later chapters.

§1.1 STATEMENT OF SCIENTIFIC REALISM

What exactly is scientific realism? A naïve statement of the position would be this: the picture which science gives us of the world is a true one, faithful in its details, and the entities postulated in science really exist: the advances of science are discoveries, not inventions. That statement is too naïve; it attributes to the scientific realist the belief that today's theories are correct. It would mean that the philosophical position of an earlier scientific realist such as C. S. Peirce had been refuted by empirical findings. I do not suppose that scientific realists wish to be committed, as such, even to the claim that science will arrive in due time at theories true in all respects—for the growth of science might be an endless self-correction; or worse, Armageddon might occur too soon.

But the naïve statement has the right flavour. It answers two main questions: it characterizes a scientific theory as a story about what there really is, and scientific activity as an enterprise of discovery, as opposed to invention. The two questions of what a scientific theory is, and what a scientific theory does, must be answered by any philosophy of science. The task we have at this point is to find a statement of scientific realism that shares these features with the naïve statement, but does not saddle the realists with unacceptably strong consequences. It is especially important to make the statement as weak as possible if we wish to argue against it, so as not to charge at windmills.

As clues I shall cite some passages most of which will also be examined below in the contexts of the authors' arguments. A statement of Wilfrid Sellars is this:

> to have good reason for holding a theory is *ipso facto* to have good reason for holding that the entities postulated by the theory exist.[1]

This addresses a question of epistemology, but also throws some indirect light on what it is, in Sellars's opinion, to hold a theory. Brian Ellis, who calls himself a scientific entity realist rather than a scientific realist, appears to agree with that statement of Sellars, but gives the following formulation of a stronger view:

> I understand scientific realism to be the view that the theoretical statements of science are, or purport to be, true generalized descriptions of reality.[2]

This formulation has two advantages: It focuses on the understanding of the theories without reference to reasons for belief, and it avoids the suggestion that to be a realist you must believe current scientific theories to be true. But it gains the latter advantage by use of the word "purport," which may generate its own puzzles.

Hilary Putnam . . . gives a formulation which he says he learned from Michael Dummett:

> A realist (with respect to a given theory or discourse) holds that (1) the sentences of that theory are true or false; and (2) that what makes them true or false is something external—that is to say, it is not (in general) our sense data, actual or potential, or the structure of our minds, or our language, etc.[3]

He follows this soon afterwards with a further formulation which he credits to Richard Boyd:

> That terms in mature scientific theories typically refer (this formulation is due to Richard Boyd), that the theories accepted in a mature science are typically approximately true, that the same term can refer to the same thing even when it occurs in different theories—these statements are viewed by the scientific realist . . . as part of any adequate scientific description of science and its relations to its objects.[4]

None of these were intended as definitions. But they show I think that truth must play an important role in the formulation of the basic realist position. They also show that the formulation must incorporate an answer to the question what it is to *accept* or *hold* a theory. I shall now propose such a formulation, which seems to me to make sense of the above remarks, and also renders intelligible the reasoning by realists which I shall examine below—without burdening them with more than the minimum required for this.

Science aims to give us, in its theories, a literally true story of what the world is like; and acceptance of a scientific theory involves the belief that it is true. This is the correct statement of scientific realism.

Let me defend this formulation by showing that it is quite minimal, and can be agreed to by anyone who considers himself a scientific realist. The naïve statement said that science tells a true story; the correct statement says only that it is the aim of science to do so. The aim of science is of course not to be identified with individual scientists' motives. The aim of the game of chess is to checkmate your opponent; but the motive for playing may be fame, gold, and glory. What the aim is determines what counts as success in the enterprise as such; and this aim may be pursued for any number of reasons. Also, in calling something *the* aim, I do not deny that there are other subsidiary aims which may or may not be means to that end: everyone will readily agree that simplicity, informativeness, predictive power, explanation are (also) virtues. Perhaps my formulation can even be accepted by any philosopher who considers the most important aim of science to be something which only *requires* the finding of true theories—given that I wish to give the weakest formulation of the doctrine that is generally acceptable.

I have added "literally" to rule out as realist such positions as imply that science is true if "properly understood" but literally false or meaningless. For that would be consistent with conventionalism, logical positivism, and instrumentalism. I will say more about this below. . . .

The second part of the statement touches on epistemology. But it only equates acceptance of a theory with belief in its truth.[5] It does not imply that anyone is ever rationally warranted in forming such a belief. We have to make room for the epistemological position, today the subject of considerable debate, that a rational person never assigns personal probability 1 to any proposition except a tautology. It would, I think, be rare for a scientific realist to take this stand in epistemology, but it is certainly possible.[6]

To understand qualified acceptance we must first understand acceptance *tout court*. If acceptance of a theory involves the belief that it is true, then tentative acceptance involves the tentative adoption of the belief that it is true. If belief comes in degrees, so does acceptance, and we may then speak of a degree of acceptance involving a certain degree of belief that the theory is true. This must of course be distinguished from belief that the theory is approximately true, which seems to mean belief that some member of a class centring on the mentioned theory is (exactly) true. In this way the proposed formulation of realism can be used regardless of one's epistemological persuasion.

§1.2 ALTERNATIVES TO REALISM

Scientific realism is the position that scientific theory construction aims to give us a literally true story of what the world is like, and that acceptance of a scientific theory involves the belief that it is true. Accordingly, anti-realism is a position according to which the aim of science can well be served without giving such a literally true story, and acceptance of a theory may properly involve something less (or other) than belief that it is true.

What does a scientist do then, according to these different positions? According to the realist, when someone proposes a theory, he is asserting it to be true. But according to the anti-realist, the proposer does not assert the theory; *he displays it,* and claims certain virtues for it. These virtues may fall short of truth: empirical adequacy, perhaps; comprehensiveness, acceptability for various purposes. This will have to be spelt out, for the details here are not determined by the denial of realism. For now we must concentrate on the key notions that allow the generic division.

The idea of a literally true account has two aspects: the language is to be literally construed; and so construed, the account is true. This divides the anti-realists into two sorts. The first sort holds that science is or aims to be true, properly (but not literally) construed. The second holds that the language of science should be literally construed, but its theories need not be true to be good. The anti-realism I shall advocate belongs to the second sort.

It is not so easy to say what is meant by a literal construal. The idea comes perhaps from theology, where fundamentalists construe the Bible literally, and liberals have a variety of allegorical, metaphorical, and analogical interpretations, which "demythologize." The problem of explicating "literal construal" belongs to the philosophy of language. . . . The term "literal" is well enough understood for general philosophical use, but if we try to explicate it we find ourselves in the midst of the problem of giving an adequate account of natural language. It would be bad tactics to link an inquiry into science to a commitment to some solution to that problem. The following remarks . . . should fix the usage of "literal" sufficiently for present purposes.

The decision to rule out all but literal construals of the language of science, rules out those forms of anti-realism known as *positivism* and *instrumentalism*. First, on a literal construal, the apparent statements of science really are statements, *capable of* being true or false. Secondly, although a literal construal can elaborate, it cannot change logical relationships. (It is possible to elaborate, for instance, by identifying what the terms designate. The "reduction" of the language of phenomenological thermodynamics to that of statistical mechanics is like that: bodies of gas are identified as aggregates of molecules, temperature as mean kinetic energy, and so on.) On the positivists' interpretation of science, theoretical terms have meaning only through their connection with the observable. Hence they hold that two theories may in fact *say the same thing* although in form they contradict each other. (Perhaps the one says that all matter consists of atoms, while the other postulates instead a universal continous medium; they will say the same thing nevertheless if they agree in their observable consequences, according to the positivists.) But two theories which contradict each other in such a way can "really" be saying the same thing only if they are not literally construed. Most specifically, if a theory says that something exists, then a literal construal may elaborate on what that something is, but will not remove the implication of existence.

There have been many critiques of positivist interpretations of science, and there is no need to repeat them. I shall add some specific criticisms of the positivist approach in the next chapter.

§1.3 CONSTRUCTIVE EMPIRICISM

To insist on a literal construal of the language of science is to rule out the construal of a theory as a metaphor or simile, or as intelligible only after it is "demythologized" or subjected to some other sort of "translation" that does not preserve logical form. If the theory's statements include "There are electrons," then the theory says that there are electrons. If in addition they include "Electrons are not planets," then the theory says, in part, that there are entities other than planets.

But this does not settle very much. It is often not at all obvious whether a theoretical term refers to a concrete entity or a mathematical entity. Perhaps one tenable interpretation of classical physics is that there are no concrete entities which are forces—that "there are forces such that . . ." can always be understood as a mathematical statement asserting the existence of certain functions. That is debatable.

Not every philosophical position concerning science which insists on a literal construal of the language of science is a realist position. For this insistence relates not at all to our epistemic attitudes toward theories, nor to the aim we pursue in constructing theories, but only to the correct understanding of *what a theory says*. (The fundamentalist theist, the agnostic, and the atheist presumably agree with each other [though not with liberal theologians] in their understanding of the statement that God, or gods, or angels exist). After deciding that the language of science must be literally understood, we can still say that there is no need to believe good theories to be true, nor to believe *ipso facto* that entities they postulate are real.

Science aims to give us theories which are empirically adequate; and acceptance of a theory involves as belief only that it is empirically adequate. This is the statement of the antirealist position I advocate; I shall call it *constructive empiricism*.

This formulation is subject to the same qualifying remarks as that of scientific realism in Section 1.1 above. In addition it requires an explication of "empirically adequate." For now, I shall leave that with the preliminary explication that a theory is empirically adequate exactly if what it says about the observable things and events in this world, is true — exactly if it "saves the phenomena." A little more precisely: such a theory has at least one model that all the actual phenomena fit inside. I must emphasize that this refers to *all* the phenomena; these are not exhausted by those actually observed, nor even by those observed at some time, whether past, present, or future. . . .

The distinction I have drawn between realism and anti-realism, in so far as it pertains to acceptance, concerns only how much belief is involved therein. Acceptance of theories (whether full, tentative, to a degree, etc.) is a phenomenon of scientific activity which clearly involves more than belief. One main reason for this is that we are never confronted with a complete theory. So if a scientist accepts a theory, he thereby involves himself in a certain sort of research programme. That programme could well be different from the one acceptance of another theory would have given him, even if those two (very incomplete) theories are equivalent to each other with respect to everything that is observable — in so far as they go.

Thus acceptance involves not only belief but a certain commitment. Even for those of us who are not working scientists, the acceptance involves a commitment to confront any future phenomena by means of the conceptual resources of this theory. It determines the terms in which we shall seek explanations. If the acceptance is at all strong, it is exhibited in the person's assumption of the role of explainer, in his willingness to answer questions *ex cathedra*. Even if you do not accept a theory, you can engage in discourse in a context in which language use is guided by that theory — but acceptance produces such contexts. There are similarities in all of this to ideological commitment. A commitment is of course not true or false: The confidence exhibited is that it will be *vindicated*.

This is a preliminary sketch of the *pragmatic* dimension of theory acceptance. Unlike the epistemic dimension, it does not figure overtly in the disagreement between realist and antirealist. But because the amount of belief involved in acceptance is typically less according to anti-realists, they will tend to make more of the pragmatic aspects. It is as well to note here the important difference. Belief that a theory is true, or that it is empirically adequate, does not imply, and is not implied by, belief that full acceptance of the theory will be vindicated. To see this, you need only consider here a person who has quite definite beliefs about the future of the human race, or about the scientific community and the influences thereon and practical limitations we have. It might well be, for instance, that a theory which is empirically adequate will not combine easily with some other theories which we have accepted in fact, or that Armageddon will occur before we succeed. Whether belief that a theory is true, or that it is empirically adequate, can be equated with belief that acceptance of it would, under ideal research conditions, be vindicated in the long run, is another question. It seems to me an irrelevant question within philosophy of science, because an affirmative answer would not obliterate the distinction we have already established by the preceding remarks. (The question may also assume that counterfactual statements are objectively true or false, which I would deny.)

Although it seems to me that realists and anti-realists need not disagree about the pragmatic aspects of theory acceptance, I have mentioned it here because I think that typically they do. We shall find ourselves returning time and again, for example, to requests for explanation to which realists typically attach an objective validity which anti-realists cannot grant.

§2. THE THEORY/OBSERVATION "DICHOTOMY"

For good reasons, logical positivism dominated the philosophy of science for thirty years. In 1960, the first volume of *Minnesota Studies in the Philosophy of Science* published Rudolf Carnap's "The Methodological Status of Theoretical Concepts," which is, in many ways, the culmination of the positivist programme. It interprets science by relating it to an observation language (a postulated part of natural language which is devoid of theoretical terms). Two years later this article was followed in the same series by Grover Maxwell's "The Ontological Status of Theoretical Entities," in title and theme a direct counter to Carnap's. This is the *locus classicus* for the new realists' contention that the theory/observation distinction cannot be drawn.

I shall examine some of Maxwell's points directly, but first a general remark about the issue. Such expressions as "theoretical entity" and "observable–theoretical dichotomy" are, on the face of it, examples of category mistakes. Terms or concepts are theoretical (introduced or adapted for the purposes of theory construction); entities are observable or unobservable. This may seem a little point, but it separates the discussion into two issues. Can we divide our language into a theoretical and non-theoretical part? On the other hand, can we classify objects and events into observable and unobservable ones?

Maxwell answers both questions in the negative, while not distinguishing them too carefully. On the first, where he can draw on well-known supportive essays by Wilfrid Sellars and Paul Feyerabend, I am in total agreement. All our language is thoroughly theory-infected. If we could cleanse our language of theory-laden terms, beginning with the recently introduced ones like "VHF receiver," continuing through "mass" and "impulse" to "element" and so on into the prehistory of language formation, we would end up with nothing useful. The way we talk, and scientists talk, is guided by the pictures provided by previously accepted theories. This is true also, as Duhem already emphasized, of experimental reports. Hygienic reconstructions of language such as the positivists envisaged are simply not on. I shall return to this criticism of positivism in the next chapter.

But does this mean that we must be scientific realists? We surely have more tolerance of ambiguity than that. The fact that we let our language be guided by a given picture, at some point, does not show how much we believe about that picture. When we speak of the sun coming up in the morning and setting at night, we are guided by a picture now explicitly disavowed. When Milton wrote *Paradise Lost* he deliberately let the old geocentric astronomy guide his poem, although various remarks in passing clearly reveal his interest in the new astronomical discoveries and speculations of his time. These are extreme examples, but show that no immediate conclusions can be drawn from the theory-ladenness of our language.

However, Maxwell's arguments are directed against the observable–unobservable distinction. Let us first be clear on what this distinction was supposed to be. The term "observable" classifies putative entities (entities which may or may not exist). A flying horse is observable — that is why we are so sure that there aren't any — and the number seventeen is not. There is supposed to be a correlate classification of human acts: an unaided act of perception, for instance, is an observation. A calculation of the mass of a particle from the deflection of its trajectory in a known force field, is not an observation of that mass.

It is also important here not to confuse *observing* (an entity, such as a thing, event, or process) and *observing that* (something or other is the case). Suppose one of the Stone Age people recently found in the Philippines is shown a tennis ball or a car crash. From his behaviour, we see that he has noticed them; for example, he picks up the ball and throws it. But he has not seen *that* it is a tennis ball, or *that* some event is a car crash, for he does not even have those concepts. He cannot get that information through perception; he would first have to learn a great deal. To say that he does not see the same things and events as we do, however, is just silly; it is a pun which trades on the ambiguity between seeing and seeing that. (The truth-conditions for our statement "x observes *that A*" must be such that what concepts x has, presumably related to the language x speaks if he is human, enter as a variable into the correct truth definition, in some way. To say that x observed the tennis ball, therefore, does not imply at all that x observed that it was a tennis ball; that would require some conceptual awareness of the game of tennis.)

The arguments Maxwell gives about observability are of two sorts: one directed against the possibility of drawing such distinctions, the other against the importance that could attach to distinctions that can be drawn.

The first argument is from the continuum of cases that lie between direct observation and inference:

> there is, in principle, a continuous series beginning with looking through a vacuum and containing these as members: looking through a windowpane, looking through glasses, looking through binoculars, looking through a low-power microscope, looking through a high-power microscope, etc., in the order given. The important consequence is that, so far, we are left without criteria which would enable us to draw a non-arbitrary line between "observation" and "theory."[7]

This continuous series of supposed acts of observation does not correspond directly to a continuum in what is supposed observable. For if something can be seen through a window, it can also be seen with the window raised. Similarly, the moons of Jupiter can be seen through a telescope; but they can also be seen without a telescope if you are close enough. That something is observable does not automatically imply that the conditions are right for observing it now. The principle is:

> X is observable if there are circumstances which are such that, if X is present to us under those circumstances, then we observe it.

This is not meant as a definition, but only as a rough guide to the avoidance of fallacies.

We may still be able to find a continuum in what is supposed detectable: perhaps some things can only be detected with the aid of an optical microscope, at least; perhaps some require an electron microscope, and so on. Maxwell's problem is: where shall we draw the line between what is observable and what is only detectable in some more roundabout way?

Granted that we cannot answer this question without arbitrariness, what follows? That "observable" is a *vague predicate.* There are many puzzles about vague predicates, and many sophisms designed to show that, in the presence of vagueness, no distinction can be drawn at all. In Sextus Empiricus, we find the argument that incest is not immoral, for touching your mother's big toe with your little finger is not immoral, and all the rest differs only by degree. But predicates in natural language are almost all vague, and there is no problem in their use; only in formulating the logic that governs them.[8] A vague predicate is usable provided it has clear cases and clear counter-cases. Seeing with the unaided eye is a clear case of observation. Is Maxwell then perhaps challenging us to present a clear counter-case? Perhaps so, for he says "I have been trying to support the thesis that any (non-logical) term is a *possible* candidate for an observation term."

A look through a telescope at the moons of Jupiter seems to me a clear case of observation, since astronauts will no doubt be able to see them as well from close up. But the purported observation of micro-particles in a cloud chamber seems to me a clearly different case—if our theory about what happens there is right. The theory says that if a charged particle traverses a chamber filled with saturated vapour, some atoms in the neighbourhood of its path are ionized. If this vapour is decompressed, and hence becomes supersaturated, it condenses in droplets on the ions, thus marking the path of the particle. The resulting silver-grey line is similar (physically as well as in appearance) to the vapour trail left in the sky when a jet passes. Suppose I point to such a trail and say: "Look, there is a jet!"; might you not say: "I see the vapour trail, but where is the jet?" Then I would answer: "Look just a bit ahead of the trail . . . there! Do you see it?" Now, in the case of the cloud chamber this response is not possible. So while the particle is detected by means of the cloud chamber, and the detection is based on observation, it is clearly not a case of the article's being observed.

As second argument, Maxwell directs our attention to the "can" in "what is observable is what can be observed." An object might of course be temporarily unobservable—in a rather different sense: it cannot be observed in the circumstances in which it actually is at the moment, but could be observed if the circumstances were more favourable. In just the same way,

I might be temporarily invulnerable or invisible. So we should concentrate on "observable" *tout court,* or on (as he prefers to say) "unobservable in principle." This Maxwell explains as meaning that the relevant scientific theory *entails* that the entities cannot be observed in any circumstances. But this never happens, he says, because the different circumstances could be ones in which we have different sense organs—electron-microscope eyes, for instance.

This strikes me as a trick, a change in the subject of discussion. I have a mortar and pestle made of copper and weighing about a kilo. Should I call it breakable because a giant could break it? Should I call the Empire State Building portable? Is there no distinction between a portable and a console record player? The human organism is, from the point of view of physics, a certain kind of measuring apparatus. As such it has certain inherent limitations—which will be described in detail in the final physics and biology. It is these limitations to which the "able" in "observable" refers—our limitations, *qua* human beings.

As I mentioned, however, Maxwell's article also contains a different sort of argument: even if there is a feasible observable/unobservable distinction, this distinction has no importance. The point at issue for the realist is, after all, the reality of the entities postulated in science. Suppose that these entities could be classified into observables and others; what relevance should that have to the question of their existence?

Logically, none. For the term "observable" classifies putative entities, and has logically nothing to do with existence. But Maxwell must have more in mind when he says: "I conclude that the drawing of the observational-theoretical line at any given point is an accident and a function of our physiological make-up, . . . and, therefore, that it has no ontological significance whatever.[9] No ontological significance if the question is only whether "observable" and "exists" imply each other—for they do not; but significance for the question of scientific realism?

Recall that I defined scientific realism in terms of the aim of science, and epistemic attitudes. The question is what aim scientific activity has, and how much we shall believe when we accept a scientific theory. What is the proper form of acceptance: belief that the theory, as a whole, is true; or something else? To this question, what is observable by us seems eminently relevant. Indeed, we may attempt an answer at this point: to accept a theory is (for us) to believe that it is empirically adequate—that what the theory says *about what is observable* (by us) is true.

It will be objected at once that, on this proposal, what the anti-realist decides to believe about the world will depend in part on what he believes to be his, or rather the epistemic community's, accessible range of evidence. At present, we count the human race as the epistemic community to which we belong; but this race may mutate, or that community may be increased by adding other animals (terrestrial or extra-terrestrial) through relevant ideological or moral decisions ("to count them as persons"). Hence the anti-realist would, on my proposal, have to accept conditions of the form

If the epistemic community changes in fashion *Y,* then my beliefs about the world will change in manner *Z.*

To see this as an objection to anti-realism is to voice the requirement that our epistemic policies should give the same results independent of our beliefs about the range of evidence accessible to us. That requirement seems to me in no way rationally compelling; it could be honoured, I should think, only through a thoroughgoing scepticism or through a commitment to wholesale leaps of faith. But we cannot settle the major questions of epistemology *en passant* in philosophy of science; so I shall just conclude that it is, on the face of it, not irrational to commit oneself only to a search for theories that are empirically adequate, ones whose models fit the observable phenomena, while recognizing that what counts as an observable phenomenon is a function of what the epistemic community is (that *observable* is *observable-to-us*).

The notion of empirical adequacy in this answer will have to be spelt out very carefully if it is not to bite the dust among hackneyed objections. . . . But the point stands: even if observability has nothing to do with existence (is, indeed, too anthropocentric for that), it may still have much to do with the proper epistemic attitude to science.

NOTES

[1] *Science, Perception and Reality* (New York: Humanities Press, 1962). See my review of his *Studies in Philosophy and Its History,* in *Annals of Science,* January 1977.

[2] Brian Ellis, *Rational Belief Systems* (Oxford: Blackwell, 1979), p. 28.

[3] Hilary Putnam, *Mathematics, Matter and Method* (Cambridge: Cambridge University Press, 1975), vol. I, pp. 69f.

[4] Putnam, op cit., p. 73, n. 29. The argument is reportedly developed at greater length in Boyd's forthcoming book *Realism and Scientific Epistemology* (Cambridge University Press).

[5] Hartry Field has suggested that "acceptance of a scientific theory involves the belief that it is true" be replaced by "any reason to think that any part of a theory is not, or might not be, true, is reason not to accept it." The drawback of this alternative is that it leaves open what epistemic attitude acceptance of a theory does involve. This question must also be answered, and as long as we are talking about full acceptance—as opposed to tentative or partial or otherwise qualified acceptance—I cannot see how a realist could do other than equate that attitude with full belief. (That theories believed to be false are used for practical problems, for example, classical mechanics for orbiting satellites, is of course a commonplace.) For if the aim is truth, and acceptance requires belief that the aim is served . . . I should also mention the statement of realism at the beginning of Richard Boyd, "Realism, Underdetermination, and a Causal Theory of Evidence," *Noûs,* 7 (1973), 1–12. Except for some doubts about his use of the terms "explanation" and "causal relation" I intend my statement of realism to be entirely in accordance with his. Finally, see C. A. Hooker, "Systematic Realism," *Synthese,* 26 (1974), 409–97, esp. pp. 409 and 426.

[6] More typical of realism, it seems to me, is the sort of epistemology found in Clark Glymour's forthcoming book, *Theory and Evidence* (Princeton: Princeton University Press, 1980), except of course that there it is fully and carefully developed in one specific fashion. (See esp. his chapter "Why I am not a Bayesian" for the present issue.) But I see no reason why a realist, as such, could not be a Bayesian of the type of Richard Jeffrey, even if the Bayesian position has in the past been linked with anti-realist and even instrumentalist views in philosophy of science.

[7] G. Maxwell, "The Ontological Status of Theoretical Entities," *Minnesota Studies in Philosophy of Science,* III (1962), p. 7.

[8] There is a great deal of recent work on the logic of vague predicates; especially important, to my mind, is that of Kit Fine ("Vagueness, Truth, and Logic," *Synthese,* 30 (1975), 265–300) and Hans Kamp. The latter is currently working on a new theory of vagueness that does justice to the "vagueness of vagueness" and the context-dependence of standards of applicability for predicates.

[9] Op. cit., p. 15. [. . .] At this point I may be suspected of relying on modal distinctions which I criticize elsewhere. After all, I am making a distinction between human limitations, and accidental factors. A certain apple was dropped into the sea in a bag of refuse, which sank; relative to that information it is necessary that no one

ever observed the apple's core. That information, however, concerns an accident of history, and so it is not human limitations that rule out observation of the apple core. But unless I assert that some facts about humans are essential, or physically necessary, and others accidental, how can I make sense of this distinction? This question raises the difficulty of a philosophical retrenchment for modal language. This I believe to be possible through an ascent to pragmatics. In the present case, the answer would be, to speak very roughly, that the scientific theories we accept are a determining factor for the set of features of the human organism counted among the limitations to which we refer in using the term "observable." The issue of modality will occur explicitly again in the chapter on probability.

PAUL M. CHURCHLAND
THE ONTOLOGICAL STATUS OF OBSERVABLES: IN PRAISE OF THE SUPEREMPIRICAL VIRTUES

At several points in the reading of van Fraassen's book, I feared I would no longer be a realist by the time I completed it. Fortunately, sheer doxastic inertia has allowed my convictions to survive its searching critique, at least temporarily, and, as we address you today, van Fraassen and I still hold different views. I am a scientific realist, of unorthodox persuasion, and van Fraassen is a constructive empiricist, whose persuasions currently define the doctrine. I assert that global excellence of theory is the ultimate measure of truth and ontology at all levels of cognition, even at the observational level. Van Fraassen asserts that descriptive excellence at the observational level is the only genuine measure of any theory's truth and that one's acceptance of a theory should create no ontological commitments whatever beyond the observational level.

Against his first claim I will maintain that observational excellence or "empirical adequacy" is only one epistemic virtue among others of equal or comparable importance. And against his second claim I will maintain that the ontological commitments of any theory are wholly blind to the idiosyncratic distinction between what is and what is not humanly observable, and so should be our own ontological commitments. Criticism will be directed primarily at van Fraassen's *selective* skepticism in favor of observable ontologies over unobservable ontologies and against his view that the "superempirical" theoretical virtues (simplicity, coherence, explanatory power) are merely pragmatic virtues, irrelevant to the estimate of a theory's truth. My aims are not merely critical, however. Scientific realism does need reworking, and there are good reasons for moving it in the direction of van Fraassen's constructive empiricism, as will be discussed in the closing section of this paper. But those reasons do not support the skeptical theses at issue.

I. OBSERVATION AND ONTOLOGICAL COMMITMENT

Before pursuing our differences, it will prove useful to emphasize certain convictions we share. Van Fraassen is already a scientific realist in the minimal sense that he interprets theories literally and he concedes them a truth value. Further, we agree that the observable/unobservable distinction is entirely distinct from the nontheoretical/theoretical distinction, and we agree as well that all observation sentences are irredeemably laden with theory.

Additionally, I absolutely reject many sanguine assumptions common among realists. I do not believe that on the whole our beliefs must be at least roughly true; I do not believe that the

Previously published in a shorter form as "The Anti-Realist Epistemology of van Fraassen's *The Scientific Image*," *Pacific Philosophical Quarterly* 63 (July 1982): 226–36. Reproduced by permission. I thank Hartry Field, Michael Stack, Bas van Fraassen, Clark Glymour, Barney Keaney, Stephen Stich, and Patricia Churchland for helpful discussion of the issues here addressed.

terms of "mature" sciences must typically refer to real things; and I very much doubt that the reason of *homo sapiens,* even at its best and even if allowed infinite time, would eventually encompass all and/or only true statements.

This skepticism is born partly from a historical induction: so many past theories, rightly judged excellent at the time, have since proved to be false. And their current successors, though even better founded, seem but the next step in a probably endless and not obviously convergent journey. (For a most thorough and insightful critique of typical realist theses, see the recent paper by Laudan [1981].)

Evolutionary considerations also counsel a healthy skepticism. Human reason is a hierarchy of heuristics for seeking, recognizing, storing, and exploiting information. But those heuristics were invented at random, and they were selected for within a very narrow evolutionary environment, cosmologically speaking. It would be *miraculous* if human reason were completely free of false strategies and fundamental cognitive limitations, and doubly miraculous if the theories we accept failed to reflect those defects.

Thus some very realistic reasons for skepticism with respect to any theory. Why, then, am I still a scientific realist? Because these reasons fail to discriminate between the integrity of observables and the integrity of unobservables. If anything is compromised by these considerations, it is the integrity of theories generally. That is, of *cognition* generally. Since our observational concepts are just as theory-laden as any others, and since the integrity of those concepts is just as contingent on the integrity of the theories that embed them, our observational ontology is rendered *exactly as dubious* as our nonobservational ontology.

This parity should not seem surprising. Our history contains real examples of mistaken ontological commitments in both domains. For example, we have had occasion to banish phlogiston, caloric, and the luminiferous ether from our ontology—but we have also had occasion to banish witches and the starry sphere that turns about us daily. These latter items were as "observable" as you please and were widely "observed" on a daily basis. We are too often misled, I think, by our casual use of *observes* as a success verb; we tend to forget that, at any stage of our history, the ontology presupposed by our observational judgments remains essentially speculative and wholly revisable, however entrenched and familiar it may have become.

Accordingly, since the skeptical considerations adduced above are indifferent to the distinction between what is and what is not observable, they provide no reason for resisting a commitment to unobservable ontologies *while allowing* a commitment to what we take to be observable ontologies. The latter appear as no better off than the former. For me, then, the "empirical success" of a theory remains a reason for thinking the theory to be true and for accepting its overall ontology. The inference from success to truth should no doubt be severely tempered by the skeptical considerations adduced, but the inference to *un*observable ontologies is not rendered *selectively* dubious. Thus, I remain a scientific realist. My realism is highly circumspect, but the circumspection is uniform for unobservables and observables alike.

Perhaps I am wrong in this. Perhaps we should be selectively skeptical in the fashion van Fraassen recommends. Does he have other arguments for refusing factual belief and ontological commitment beyond the observational domain? Indeed he does. In fact, he does not appeal to historical induction or evolutionary humility at all. These are *my* reasons for skepticism (and they will remain, even if we manage to undermine van Fraassen's). They have been introduced here to show that, while there are some powerful reasons for skepticism, those reasons do not place unobservables at a selective disadvantage.

Very well, what are van Fraassen's reasons for skepticism? They are very interesting. To summarize quickly, he does a compelling job of deflating certain standard realist arguments (from Smart, Sellars, Salmon, Boyd, and others) to the effect that, given the aims of science, we have no alternative but to bring unobservables (not just into our calculations, but) into our literal ontology. He also argues rather compellingly that the superempirical virtues, such as simplicity and comprehensive explanatory power, are at bottom merely pragmatic virtues, having nothing essential to do with any theory's truth. This leaves only empirical adequacy as a genuine measure of any theory's truth. Roughly, a theory is empirically adequate if and only if everything it says about *observable* things is true. Empirical adequacy is thus a necessary condition of a theory's truth.

However, claims van Fraassen, the truth of any theory whose ontology includes unobservables is always radically underdetermined by its empirical adequacy, since a great many logically incompatible theories can all be empirically equivalent. Accordingly, the inference from empirical adequacy to truth now appears presumptuous in the extreme, especially since it has just been disconnected from additional selective criteria such as simplicity and explanatory power, criteria which might have reduced the arbitrariness of the particular inference drawn. Fortunately, says van Fraassen, we do not need to make such wanton inferences, since we can perfectly well understand science as an enterprise that never really draws them. Here we arrive at his positive conception of science as an enterprise whose sole intellectual aims are empirical adequacy and the satisfaction of certain human intellectual needs.

The central element in this argument is the claim that, in the case of a theory whose ontology includes unobservables, its empirical adequacy underdetermines its truth. (We should notice that, in the case of a theory whose ontology is completely free of unobservables, its empirical adequacy does not underdetermine its truth: in that case, truth and empirical adequacy are obviously identical. Thus van Fraassen's *selective* skepticism with respect to unobservables.) That is, for any theory T inflated with unobservables, there will always be many other such theories incompatible with T but empirically equivalent to it.

In my view, the notions of "empirical adequacy" and its cognate relative term "empirically equivalent" are extremely thorny notions of doubtful integrity. If we attempt to explicate a theory's "empirical content" in terms of the observation sentences it entails (or entails if conjoined with available background information or with possible future background information or with possible future theories), we generate a variety of notions which are variously empty, context-relative, ill defined, or flatly incompatible with the claim of underdetermination. Van Fraassen expresses awareness of these difficulties and proposes to avoid them by giving the notions at issue a model-theoretic rather than a syntactic explication. I am unconvinced that this improves matters decisively (on this issue, see Wilson 1980 . . .). In particular, I think van Fraassen has not dealt adequately with the problem of how the so-called "empirical equivalence" of two incompatible theories remains relative to *which* background theories are added to the evaluative context, especially background theories that in some way revise our conception of what humans can observe. I intend to sidestep this issue for now, however, since the matter is complex and there is a much simpler objection to be voiced.

Let me approach my objection by first pointing out that the empirical adequacy of any theory is itself something that is radically underdetermined by any evidence conceivably available to us. Recall that, for a theory to be empirically adequate, what it says about observable things must be true—*all* observable things, in the past, in the indefinite future, and in the most distant corners of the cosmos. But, since any actual data possessed by us must be finite in its scope, its is plain that we here suffer an underdetermination problem no less serious than that claimed above. This is Hume's problem, and the lesson is that even observation-level theories must suffer radical underdetermination by the evidence. Accordingly, theories about observables and theories about unobservables appear on a par again, so far as skepticism is concerned.

Van Fraassen thinks there is an important difference between the two cases, and one's first impulse is to agree with him. We are all willing to concede the existence of Hume's problem—the problem of justifying the inference to unobserv*ed* entities. But the inference to entities that are downright unobserv*able* appears as a different and *additional* problem.

The appearance is an illusion, as the following considerations will show. Consider some of the different reasons why entities or processes may go unobserved by us. First, they may go unobserved because, relative to our natural sensory apparatus, they fail to enjoy an appropriate spatial or temporal *position.* They may exist in the Upper Jurassic period, for example, or they may reside in the Andromeda galaxy. Second, they may go unobserved because, relative to our natural sensory apparatus, they fail to enjoy the appropriate spatial or temporal *dimensions.* They may be too small or too brief or too large or too protracted. Third, they may fail to enjoy the appropriate *energy,* being too feeble or too powerful to permit useful discrimination. Fourth and fifth, they may fail to have an appropriate *wavelength* or an appropriate *mass.* Sixth, they may fail to "feel" the relevant fundamental forces our sensory apparatus exploits, as with our inability to observe the background neutrino flux, despite the fact that its energy density exceeds that of light itself.

This list could be lengthened, but it is long enough to suggest that being spatially or temporally distant from our sensory apparatus is only one among many ways in which an entity or process can fall outside the compass of human observation, a way distinguished by no relevant epistemological or ontological features.

There is clearly some *practical* point in our calling a thing "observ*able*" if it fails *only* the first test (spatiotemporal proximity) and "*un*observable" if it fails any of the others. But this is only because of the contingent practical fact that humans generally have somewhat more *control* over the spatiotemporal perspective of their sensory systems than they have over their size or reaction time or mass or wavelength sensitivity or chemical constitution. Had we been less mobile than we are—rooted to the earth like Douglas firs, say—yet been more voluntarily plastic in our sensory constitution, the distinction between the "merely unobserved" and the "downright unobservable" would have been very differently drawn. It may help to imagine here a suitably rooted arboreal philosopher named (what else?) Douglas van Fiirrsen, who, in his sedentary wisdom, urges an antirealist skepticism concerning the spatially very *distant* entities postulated by his fellow trees.

Admittedly, for any distant entity, one can in principle always change the relative spatial position of one's sensory apparatus so that the entity is observed: one can go to it. But equally, for any microscopic entity, one can in principle always change the relative spatial *size* or *configuration* of one's sensory apparatus so that the entity is observed. Physical law imposes certain limitations on such plasticity, but so also does physical law limit how far one can travel in a lifetime.

To emphasize the importance of these considerations, let me underscore the structure of my objection here. Consider the distinction between

(1) things observed by some human (with unaided senses),
(2) things thus observable by humans, but not in fact observed, and
(3) things not observable by humans at all.

Van Fraassen's position would exclude (3) from our rational ontology. This has at least some initial plausibility. But his position would not be at all plausible if it were committed to excluding both (3) *and* (2) from our rational ontology. No party to the present discussion is willing to restrict rational ontology to (1) alone. Van Fraassen's position thus requires a *principled* distinction between (2) and (3), a distinction *adequate* to the radical difference in epistemic attitude he would have us adopt toward them. The burden of my argument is that the distinction between (2) and (3), once it is unearthed, is only very feebly principled and is wholly inadequate to bear the great weight that van Fraassen puts on it.

The point of all this is that there is no special or novel problem about inferences to the existence of entities commonly called "unobserv*ables.*" Such entities are merely those that go unobserved by us for reasons *other* than their spatial or temporal distance from us. But whether the "gap" to be bridged is spatiotemporal or one of the many other gaps, the logical/epistemological problem is the same in all cases: ampliative inference and underdetermined hypotheses. I therefore fail to see how van Fraassen can justify tolerating an ampliative inference when it bridges a gap of spatial distance, while refusing to tolerate an ampliative inference when it bridges a gap of, for example, spatial size. Hume's problem and van Fraassen's problem collapse into one.

Van Fraassen attempts to meet such worries about the inescapable ubiquity of speculative activity by observing that "it is not an epistemological principle that one may as well hang for a sheep as for a lamb" (1980, 72). Agreed. But it is a principle of *logic* that one may as well hang for a sheep as for a sheep, and van Fraassen's lamb (empirical adequacy) is just another sheep.

Simply to hold *fewer* beliefs from a given set is of course to be less adventurous, but it is not necessarily to be applauded. One might decide to relinquish all one's beliefs save those about objects weighing less than five hundred kilograms, and perhaps, one would then be logically safer. But, in the absence of some relevant epistemic difference between one's beliefs about such objects and one's beliefs about other objects, that is perversity, not parsimony.

Let me summarize. As van Fraassen sets it up, and as the instrumentalists set it up before him, the realist looks more gullible than the nonrealist, since the realist is willing to extend belief beyond the observable, while the nonrealist insists on confining belief within that domain. I suggest, however, that it is really the nonrealists who are being the more gullible in this matter, since they suppose that the epistemic situation of our beliefs about observables is in some way superior to that of our beliefs about unobservables. But in fact their epistemic situation is not superior. They are exactly as dubious as their nonobservational cousins. Their *causal history* is different (they are occasioned by activity in the sensory pathways), but the ontology they presuppose enjoys no privilege or special credibility.

II. BELIEFWORTHINESS AND THE SUPEREMPIRICAL VIRTUES

Let me now try to address the question of whether the theoretical virtues such as simplicity, coherence, and explanatory power are *epistemic* virtues genuinely relevant to the estimate of a theory's truth, as tradition says, or merely *pragmatic* virtues, as van Fraassen urges. His view promotes empirical adequacy, or evidence of empirical adequacy, as the only genuine measure of a theory's truth, the other virtues (insofar as they are distinct from these) being cast as purely pragmatic virtues, to be valued only for the human needs they satisfy. Despite certain compelling features of the account of explanation that van Fraassen provides, I remain inclined toward the traditional view.

My reason is simplicity itself. Since there is no way of conceiving or representing "the empirical facts" that is completely independent of speculative assumptions, and since we will occasionally confront theoretical alternatives on a scale so comprehensive that we must also choose between competing modes of conceiving what the empirical facts before us *are,* then the epistemic choice between these global alternatives cannot be made by comparing the extent to which they are adequate to some common touchstone, "the empirical facts." In such a case, the choice must be made on the comparative global virtues of the two global alternatives, T_1-plus-the-observational-evidence-therein-construed, versus T_2-plus-the-observational-evidence-therein-(differently)-construed. That is, it must be made on *superempirical* grounds such as relative coherence, simplicity, and explanatory unity.

Van Fraassen has said that to "save the appearances" is to exhibit them as a fragment of a larger unity. With this I wholly agree. But I am here pointing out that it is a decision between competing "larger unities" that determines what we count as "the true appearances" in the first place. There is no independent way to settle that question. And, if such global decisions can only be made on what van Fraassen calls "pragmatic" grounds, then it would seem to follow that any decision concerning what the *observable* world contains must be essentially "pragmatic" also! Inflationary metaphysics and "pragmatic" decisions begin, it seems, as soon as we open our eyes.

Global issues such as these are reminiscent of Carnap's "external" questions, and I think it likely that van Fraassen, like Carnap, does not regard them as decidable in any but a second-rate sense, since they can be decided only by second-rate (i.e., by "pragmatic") considerations. If so, however, it is difficult to see how van Fraassen can justify a selectively realist attitude toward "observables," since, as we have seen, pragmatic considerations must attend their selection, also. (These issues receive extended treatment in Churchland 1979, sec. 2, 3, 7, and 10.) What all of this illustrates, I think, is the poverty of van Fraassen's crucial distinction between factors that are "empirical, and therefore truth-relevant," and factors that are "superempirical, and therefore *not* truth-relevant."

As I see it, then, values such as ontological simplicity, coherence, and explanatory power are some of the brain's most basic criteria for recognizing information, for distinguishing information from noise. And I think they are even more fundamental values than is "empirical adequacy," since collectively they can overthrow an entire conceptual framework for representing the empirical facts. Indeed, they even dictate how such a framework is constructed by the questing infant in the first place. One's observational taxonomy is not "read off" the world directly; rather, one comes to it piecemeal and by stages, and one settles on that taxonomy which finds the greatest coherence and simplicity in the world and the most and the simplest lawful connections.

I can bring together my protective concerns for unobservables and for the superempirical virtues by way of the following thought experiment. Consider a man for whom absolutely *nothing* is observable. All of his sensory modalities have been surgically destroyed, and he has no visual, tactile, or other sensory experience of any kind. Fortunately, he has mounted on top of his skull a microcomputer fitted out with a variety of environmentally sensitive transducers. The computer is connected to his association cortex (or perhaps the frontal lobe or Wernicke's area) in such a way as to cause in him a continuous string of singular beliefs about his local environment. These "intellectual intuitions" are not infallible, but let us suppose that they provide him with much the same information that our perceptual judgments provide us.

For such a person, or for a society of such persons, the *observable* world is an empty set. There is no question, therefore, of their evaluating any theory by reference to its "empirical adequacy," as characterized by van Fraassen (i.e., isomorphism between some observable features of the world and some "empirical substructure" of one of the theory's models). But such a society is still capable of science, I assert. They can invent theories, construct explanations of the facts-as-represented-in-past-spontaneous-beliefs, hazard predictions of the facts-as-represented-in-future-spontaneous-beliefs, and so forth. In principle, there is no reason they could not learn as much as we have (cf. Feyerabend 1969).

But it is plain in this case that the global virtues of simplicity, coherence, and explanatory unification are what *must* guide the continuing evolution of their collected beliefs. And it is plain as well that their ontology, whatever it is, must consist entirely of *un*observable entities. To invite a van Fraassenean disbelief in unobservable entities is in this case to invite the suspension of all beliefs beyond tautologies! Surely reason does not require them to be so abstemious.

It is time to consider the objection that those aspects of the world which are successfully monitored by the transducing microcomputer should count as "observables" for the folk described, despite the lack of any appropriate field of internal sensory qualia to mediate the external circumstance and the internal judgment it causes. Their tables-and-chairs ontology, as expressed in their spontaneous judgments, could then be conceded legitimacy.

I will be the first to accept such an objection. But, if we do accept it, then I do not see how we can justify van Fraassen's selective skepticism with respect to the wealth of "unobservable" entities and properties reliably monitored by *our* transducing measuring instruments (electron microscopes, cloud chambers, chromatographs, etc.). The spontaneous singular judgments of the working scientist, at home in his theoretical vocabulary and deeply familiar with the measuring instruments to which his conceptual system is responding, are not worse off, causally or epistemologically, than the spontaneous singular judgments of our transducer-laden friends. If skepticism is to be put aside above, it must be put aside here, as well.

My concluding thought experiment is a complement to the one just outlined. Consider some folk who observe, not less of the world than we do, but more of it. Suppose them able to observe a domain normally closed to us: the microworld of virus particles, DNA strands, and large protein molecules. Specifically, suppose a race of humanoid creatures each of whom is born with an electron microscope permanently in place over his left "eye." The scope is biologically constituted, let us suppose, and it projects its image onto a human-style retina, with the rest of their neurophysiology paralleling our own.

Science tells us, and I take it that van Fraassen would agree, that virus particles, DNA strands, and most other objects of comparable dimensions count as observable entities for the humanoids described. The humanoids, at least, would be justified in so regarding them and in including them in their ontology.

But we humans may not include such entities in our ontology, according to van Fraassen's position, since they are not observable with our unaided perceptual apparatus. We may not include such entities in our ontology *even though we can construct and even if we do construct electron microscopes of identical function, place them over our left eyes, and enjoy exactly the same microexperience as the humanoids.*

The difficulty for van Fraassen's position, if I understand it correctly, is that his position requires that a humanoid and a scope-equipped human must embrace *different* epistemic attitudes toward the microworld, even though their causal connections to the world and their continuing experience of it be identical: the humanoid is required to be a realist with respect to the microworld, and the human is required to be an antirealist (i.e., an agnostic) with respect to the microworld. But this distinction between what we and they may properly embrace as real seems to me to be highly arbitrary and radically undermotivated. For the only difference between the humanoid and a scope-equipped human lies in the *causal origins* of the transducing instruments feeding information into their respective brains. The humanoid's scope owes its existence to information coded in his genetic material. The human's scope owes its existence to information coded in his cortical material or in technical libraries. I do not see why this should make any difference in their respective ontological commitments, whatever they are, and I must decline to embrace any philosophy of science which says that it must.

III. TOWARD A MORE RATIONAL REALISM

I now turn from critic of van Fraassen's position to advocate. One of the most central elements in his view seems to me to be well motivated and urgently deserving of further development. As he explains in his introductory chapter, his aim is to reconceive the relation of theory to world, and the units of scientific cognition, and the virtue of those units when successful. He says, "I use the adjective 'constructive' to indicate my view that scientific activity is one of construction rather than discovery: construction of models that must be adequate to the phenomena, and not discovery of truth concerning the unobservable" (1980, 5).

The traditional view of human knowledge is that the unit of cognition is the sentence or proposition and the cognitive virtue of such units is truth. Van Fraassen rejects this overtly linguistic guise for his empiricism. He invites us to reconceive a theory as a set of models (rather than as a set of sentences), and he sees empirical adequacy (rather than truth) as the principal virtue of such units.

Though I reject his particular reconception and the selective skepticism he draws from it, I think the move away from the traditional conception is entirely correct. The criticism to which I am inclined is that van Fraassen has not moved quite far enough. Specifically, if we are to reconsider truth as the aim or product of cognitive activity, I think we must reconsider its applicability right across the board and not just in some arbitrarily or idiosyncratically segregated domain of "unobservables." That is, if we are to move away from the more naive formulations of scientific realism, we should move in the direction of *pragmatism* rather than in the direction of a positivistic instrumentalism. Let me elaborate.

When we consider the great variety of cognitively active creatures on this planet—sea slugs and octopi, bats, dolphins, and humans; and when we consider the ceaseless reconfiguration in which their brains or central ganglia engage—adjustments in the response potentials of single neurons made in the microsecond range, changes in the response characteristics of large systems of neurons made in the seconds-to-hours range, dendritic growth and new synaptic connections and the selective atrophy of old connections effected in the day-upwards range—then van Fraassen's term "construction" begins to seem highly appropriate. There is endless construction and reconstruction, both functional and structural. Further, it is far from obvious that truth is either the primary aim or the principal product of this activity. Rather, its function would appear to be the ever more finely tuned administration of the organism's *behavior*. Natural selection does not care whether a brain has or tends toward true beliefs, so long as the organism reliably exhibits reproductively advantageous behavior. Plainly, there is going to be *some* connection between the faithfulness of the brain's "world-model" and the propriety of the organism's behavior. But just as plainly the connection is not going to be direct.

While we are considering cognitive activity in biological terms and in all branches of the phylogenetic tree, we should note that it is far from obvious that sentences or propositions or anything remotely like them constitute the basic elements of cognition in creatures generally. Indeed, as I have argued at length elsewhere (1979, chap. 5; 1981), it is highly unlikely that the sentential kinematics embraced by folk psychology and orthodox epistemology represents or captures the basic parameters of cognition and learning even in humans. That framework is part of a commonsense theory that threatens to be either superficial or false. If we are ever to understand the *dynamics* of cognitive activity, therefore, we may have to reconceive our basic unit of cognition as something other than the sentence or proposition, and reconceive its virtue as something other than truth.

Success of this sort on the descriptive/explanatory front would likely have normative consequences. Truth, as currently conceived, might cease to be an aim of science. Not because we had lowered our sights and reduced our epistemic standards, as van Fraassen's constructive empiricism would suggest, but because we had *raised* our sights, in pursuit of some epistemic goal even *more* worthy than truth. I cannot now elucidate such goals, but we should be sensible of their possible existence. The notion of "truth," after all, is but the central element in a clutch of descriptive and normative *theories* (folk psychology, folk epistemology, folk semantics, classical logic), and we can expect conceptual progress here as appropriately as anywhere else.

The notion of truth is suspect on purely metaphysical grounds, anyway. It suggests straightaway the notion of The Complete and Final True Theory: at a minimum, the infinite set of all true sentences. Such a theory would be, by epistemic criteria, the best theory possible. But nothing whatever guarantees the existence of such a unique theory. Just as there is no largest positive integer, it may be that there is no best theory. It may be that, for any theory whatsoever, there is always an even better theory, and so *ad infinitum.* If we were thus unable to speak of *the* set of all true sentences, what sense could we make of truth sentence by sentence?

These considerations do invite a "constructive" conception of cognitive activity, one in which the notion of truth plays at best a highly derivative role. The formulation of such a conception, adequate to all of our epistemic criteria, is the outstanding task of epistemology. I do not think we will find that conception in van Fraassen's model-theoretic version of "positivistic instrumentalism," nor do I think we will find it quickly. But the empirical brain begs unraveling, and we have plenty of time.

Finally, there is a question put to me by Stephen Stich. If ultimately my view is even more skeptical than van Fraassen's concerning the relevance or applicability of the notion of truth, why call it scientific *realism* at all? For at least two reasons. The term *realism* still marks the principal contrast with its traditional adversary, positivistic instrumentalism. Whatever the integrity of the notion of truth, theories about unobservables have just *as much* a claim to truth, epistemologically and metaphysically, as theories about observables. Second, I remain committed to the idea that there exists a world, independent of our cognition, with which we interact and of which we construct representations: for varying purposes, with varying penetration, and with varying success. Lastly, our best and most penetrating grasp of the real is still held to reside in the representations provided by our best theories. Global excellence of theory remains the fundamental measure of rational ontology. And that has always been the central claim of scientific realism.

REFERENCES

Churchland, Paul M. 1979. *Scientific Realism and the Plasticity of Mind.* Cambridge: Cambridge University Press.
———. 1981. "Eliminative Materialism and the Propositional Attitudes." *Journal of Philosophy* 78, no. 2.
———. 1982. "The Anti-Realist Epistemology of van Fraassen's *The Scientific Image.*" *Pacific Philosophical Quarterly* 63, no. 2.
Feyerabend, Paul K. 1969. "Science without Experience." *Journal of Philosophy* 66, no. 22.
Laudan, Larry. 1981. "A Confutation of Convergent Realism." *Philosophy of Science* 48, no. 1.
Van Fraassen, Bas C. 1980. *The Scientific Image.* Oxford: Clarendon Press.
———. 1981. Critical notice of *Scientific Realism and the Plasticity of Mind,* by Paul Churchland. *Canadian Journal of Philosophy* 11, no. 3.
Wilson, Mark. 1980. "The Observational Uniqueness of Some Theories." *Journal of Philosophy* 77, no. 4.

R O N A L D   N .   G I E R E
CONSTRUCTIVE REALISM

Everyone who has puzzled over the nature of scientific theories has struggled to understand how theories relate to the world. This statement includes both philosophers and sociologists. In this [reading] the emphasis is on philosophical concerns. . . .

Most philosophical objections to realism can be put into one of two general categories: conceptual and epistemological. The *conceptual* objections question whether realism can be formulated as a coherent thesis that is neither vacuous nor obviously false. Many of those objections could also be called semantic because they focus on the meaning of "truth" for theoretical claims. In particular, does a correspondence theory of truth make sense for theoretical claims?

The *epistemological* objections, by contrast, typically grant that realist claims make sense. They do question, however, whether there could, in general, be adequate justification for realist claims. In particular, can one justify any inference from experimental success to the truth of a theoretical hypothesis?[1]

In this [reading] I shall be concerned mainly with the conceptual sorts of objections. My aim will be to formulate a version of realism that is conceptually coherent and neither trivially true nor obviously false. The same process also promotes the formulation of various alternative views falling in the anti-realist camp. In the final section of the [reading] I will offer replies to several specific conceptual objections. . . .

RESPECTS OF SIMILARITY

Scientists construct theoretical models that they intend to be at least partial representations of systems in the real world. . . . The primary relationship between models and the world is not truth, or correspondence, or even isomorphism, but *similarity*. A theoretical hypothesis asserts the existence of a similarity between a specified theoretical model and a designated real system. But since anything is similar to anything else in some way or other, the claim of similarity must be limited (at least implicitly) to a specified set of respects and degrees.

In recent years many philosophical differences between realist and antirealist interpretations of science have been formulated in semantical terms like "truth" and "reference." In what sense, if any, can a scientific hypothesis be said to be "true"? Do theoretical terms genuinely "refer"? My interpretation bypasses these semantical questions and focuses directly on the respects and degrees of claimed similarity between model and real system.

The respects in which similarity may be claimed can only be those represented in the model. One cannot claim, for example, that a mechanical system is similar to a classical model with respect to color simply because there is nothing which represents color in any classical model. The models themselves provide an upper limit on the respects in which similarity can be claimed.

Not so with degrees of similarity. The models themselves put no restrictions on the degree to which similarity might be claimed. One might claim, for example, that the successive positions of a pendulum bob are *exactly* as represented in a specified model. Any asserted degree of similarity less than perfection must, therefore, be determined by something other than the model itself. I will consider what this additional something might be a little later. For the moment I shall focus on *respects* of similarity. It is respects of similarity, not degrees, that primarily separate realists from anti-realists.

Although models themselves provide an upper limit on claimed respects of similarity, one may consistently limit claims of similarity between a model and reality to as few aspects of the model as one desires. In general, realists are relatively liberal in the range of respects in which they will attribute similarity between a model and a real system. Empiricists are rather more restrictive. Some constructivist sociologists seem prepared to deny claims of similarity in any respects whatsoever. Models, in this view, are not representations at all.

Mention of constructivism raises a question about my use of the term "constructive realism." To many ears it may sound like a contradiction. In fact it originated as a realistic alternative to van Fraassen's "constructive empiricism" (Giere 1985). The term emphasizes the fact that models are deliberately created, "socially constructed" if one wishes, by scientists. Nature does not reveal to us directly how best to represent her. I see no reason why realists should not also enjoy this insight.

One must remember, however, that constructive realism is a doctrine only about the nature of scientific models and hypotheses, that is, only about scientific representations. It is not a doctrine about scientific judgment, that is, about how scientists judge which models best represent the world. Constructive realism is compatible with these judgments being made in accord with a priori rules of rational choice or by means of purely social negotiations. My claim will be that scientific judgment is a natural, cognitive process. The resulting view is a naturalistic, constructive realism.

VARIETIES OF EMPIRICISM

The general strategy of all forms of empiricism is to restrict claims of similarity to just those respects in which our models correspond to empirical aspects of the world. In van Fraassen's terms hypotheses are restricted to claims about the "empirical substructure" of models. That is all "empirical adequacy" requires. The rest, the theoretical superstructure, may be in some sense "accepted," but not genuinely believed to correspond to anything in the world.

What distinguishes the empirical from the nonempirical? The almost universal answer is observability. Thus, for example, most present-day empiricists, such as van Fraassen, would allow that the positions of a normal pendulum bob are observable. They would therefore be willing to assert that the real pendulum is similar to a theoretical model with respect to claims about successive positions of the bob. But they would not assert similarity for other aspects of the model, for example, the uniform downward gravitational force, which in the model has magnitude—*mg.* Forces have always been a prime candidate for something that is not observable.

Given a distinction between what is observable and what is not, we can distinguish several varieties of empiricism: (1) empiricism that limits claims of similarity to just those aspects of real systems that have in fact already been observed; (2) empiricism that limits claims of similarity to all aspects of real systems that have been, are now, and ever will be observed; (3) empiricism that limits claims of similarity to those aspects of real systems that are *observable,* whether or not they ever are in fact observed. One can find plausible candidates for each of these positions among past and present philosophers. Van Fraassen, for example, favors the more liberal, third variety of empiricism based on observables.[2]

IS THE OBSERVABLE A USEFUL CATEGORY?

One of the major philosophical objections to empiricism has been the viability of the required distinction between observational and nonobservational aspects of the world. The distinction was in fact much more secure when the word "observational" was identified with what could be subjectively experienced. Sense data at least provided a homogeneous class of things that are uniquely observable. Hardly anyone today, however, is willing to defend so radical an empiricism. This forces the modern empiricist to draw the limits on what is observable somewhere between pendulum bobs and electrons.

The logical empiricists, of course, attempted to draw the distinction linguistically. Some terms, they said, are "observation terms." Thus was born "the problem of theoretical terms." This strategy has many undesirable consequences, and modern empiricists like van Fraassen therefore avoid it. "Black," for example, turns out to be an observation term applied to an eight ball but not to a mite (Suppe 1974).

Van Fraassen suggested we take it as an empirical problem to determine what average humans can in fact observe with their unaided senses. But even this ploy has strange consequences. Imagine a small but clearly visible mass suspended in equilibrium position between two relatively stiff springs. Once set in motion, however, the mass becomes a complete blur. No one with normal vision can observe when it passes through its original equilibrium position or, indeed, which way it is moving at any instant. Are we to say the position of the mass is observable when it is at rest, but not when in motion?

More important than these philosophical arguments is the fact that the required distinction is simply not found in the practice of science. Textbooks on mechanics, for example, do not distinguish the observability of forces as opposed to positions. Nor are any difficulties of principle raised about measuring forces as opposed to positions. Occasionally, one finds discussion of the typically philosophical issue whether forces can be defined in terms of other quantities, like mass and acceleration. But this is an entirely different issue from the question of observability.

Scientists do, of course, raise questions about what *is* observable. Astrophysicists, for example, have discussed the fact that high-energy solar neutrinos can now be observed, but lower energy neutrinos, which, according to standard models, make up the bulk of the solar neutrino flux, are not observable with existing instruments. This is obviously not the kind of distinction empiricist philosophers have had in mind. In astrophysics "observable" means something like "reliably detectable with existing instrumentation." By any empiricist standards high-energy neutrinos are as unobservable as their low-energy cousins.[3]

I shall not pursue such arguments further here. My objective at the moment is not so much to refute empiricism as to make sense of realism.

UNRESTRICTED REALISM

Having outlined various versions of empiricism, I shall now survey several possible versions of realism. In the framework developed so far, the most straightforward realistic interpretation of any theoretical hypothesis would be as an assertion of similarity between the real system and *every* aspect of the model. Let us call this view "unrestricted realism." It is easy to see, however, that unrestricted realism is too strong a view.

Returning to mechanics, consider a representation of an apple falling from a tree by a simple model of free fall in a uniform gravitational field. Let the height from the ground be represented by the variable y. The relationship between the height, h, from which the apple falls with zero initial velocity and the time taken to reach the ground is given by the familiar formula $h = 1/2 \, gt^2$. If h is given, we can solve for the time to reach "ground zero," which is $t = \pm\sqrt{2h/g}$.

We of course disregard the solution in which time has a negative value. If we regard negative values of time as aspects of the model, we are not practicing unrestricted realism. We restrict claims about the apple to positive values of time. But it may reasonably be claimed that the negative solutions are not to be regarded as "in the model" in the first place. After all, we have an *interpreted* model, and t is interpreted as "time," which, we normally say, has only positive values.

The same, however, cannot be said for positive values of t *greater than* $\sqrt{2h/g}$. These values correspond to negative values of y, the position of the apple. In general, there is nothing wrong with negative values of position in models of free fall. They are merely an artifact of where one chooses to put the origin of the coordinate system. Thus, the general interpretation of the variable y as position does not require that it take only positive values. But in this particular application the origin corresponds to the place where the apple hits the ground. It cannot go any further. Time may go on, but the apple cannot. We use this extra knowledge to limit application of the model in this particular problem.

Anyone familiar with other branches of physics can think of many similar examples in which features of the model are not thought to have any counterpart in the world. I doubt there is any general rule about this. And I am almost certain there is no purely formal rule. That is, nothing in the formal, mathematical structure of the models distinguishes between features we will assume to have a real counterpart and those we will not. And even if we add standard "interpretations" of the variables, often we still have to ignore some features of any model for specific applications.

On the other hand, sometimes taking seriously formal aspects of a model ordinarily thought to have no real counterparts can lead to important discoveries. This was apparently the case with Dirac's discovery of the positron, which appeared first as the representation of an electron with a negated negative charge.

The view I call constructive realism, then, is intended to be a *restricted* form of realism in the sense that theoretical hypotheses are interpreted as asserting a similarity between a real system and some, but not necessarily all, aspects of a model. The question of which aspects, and why not others, is left to be resolved on a case-by-case basis by scientists themselves.

THE CHARYBDIS OF REALISM

Since its inception quantum theory has provided a focus for discussions of realism by both philosophers and physicists. In general, its influence has been at least to soften realist pretensions if not to foster various forms of anti-realism, including positivism. This tradition of employing quantum theory in the service of empiricism is exemplified in a recent article by van Fraassen (1982) bearing the above title.

The target of van Fraassen's attack is the principle of common cause espoused by many realists such as Salmon (1975). Briefly, the principle is this: If two types of events are correlated, either one is the cause of the other, or they are both the effect of a common cause. Van Fraassen argues quite convincingly that the recent experimental verification of Bell's inequality shows the principle of a common cause is violated in some quantum processes. As van Fraassen (1982, 35) put it: "There are well-attested phenomena which cannot be embedded in any common-cause model." The realist is thus left with the choice between rejecting a well-attested physical theory and rejecting the principle of common cause.

As I wish to understand it, constructive realism incorporates no general principles, like that of common cause, that any adequate scientific theory must follow. It is not the job of a theory of science to legislate, a priori, the form scientific theories must take. Nor, I would add, can anyone outside of science hold such authority. I am therefore quite willing to agree with the judgment of physicists that there seem to be some correlations without any physically possible common cause. The most one can say is that this judgment is unprecedented in the history of science. The search for common causes has very often been strikingly successful. But if good evidence shows that quantum processes are an exception, so be it. That may be the way the world is.

The thrust of constructive realism is in the other direction. It rejects all attempts to place general, a priori restrictions on which aspects of scientific models may or may not be asserted to resemble features of real systems—the empiricists' restriction to observable aspects of reality being a prime example.

METAPHYSICAL REALISM

Hilary Putnam has accused scientific realists of holding to a "metaphysical realism," which asserts that "there is exactly one true and complete description of 'the way the world is'" (1981,

49). His rejection of realism consists of arguing that metaphysical realism is incoherent. Putnam's formulation of metaphysical realism is in a linguistic rather than a model-theoretic framework. Let us see what sense we can make of such a view in my suggested framework.

Note, first of all, that metaphysical realism is not a thesis about any theory now known. It is about some possible theory. Unlike classical mechanics, this possible theory could not consist of a family of related models. It would have to be just one big model. Every aspect of this model would have to correspond to a feature of the world, and there could be no feature of the world left out. Moreover, the similarity relationship would have to be unique. No other model could do an equally good job. Thus, metaphysical realism is not only "unrestricted," but also "complete," "perfect," and "unique."

As I understand it, Putnam's main argument against metaphysical realism is that the uniqueness requirement is impossible to satisfy. And the impossibility must be a logical, or conceptual, impossibility because Putnam's argument is purely logical, or conceptual. Now, one can question whether Putnam's argument is valid, but in the present context the point is moot.

Perhaps Laplace was a metaphysical realist. Perhaps some recent philosophers, including Putnam himself a decade ago, have been metaphysical realists. But metaphysical realism plays no role in modern science. On my analysis a major exemplar of a scientific theory, classical mechanics, is not even regarded as being fully realistic, let alone complete, perfect, and unique. And then there is quantum theory. The rejection of metaphysical realism therefore eliminates nothing that an adequate theory of science might require.

MODAL REALISM

Most recent debates between empiricists and realists have focused on the distinction between empirical and theoretical aspects of reality. It seems to me, however, that *modal* claims, claims of possibility and necessity, provide an even more critical dividing line. Van Fraassen provided a good index of the relative importance of these two issues. He was willing to grant that real systems may, in fact, possess the theoretical structure of scientific models. He merely insisted that no one could ever justifiably assert that resemblance. Regarding modality, however, he was not merely agnostic but atheistic. "The locus of possibility," he insisted (1980, 202) "is the model, not a reality behind the phenomena." In short, possibilities and necessities are only figments of our models — useful, perhaps, but not even candidates for reality.

Modality is important because of its close connection with *causality*. One way of understanding at least some aspects of causality is to regard the modal structure of scientific models as representing a causal structure in real systems. Modal realism is the view that, in some cases at least, a causal counterpart of the modal structure of a scientific model may exist in nature.

CAUSALITY IN MECHANICAL SYSTEMS

Mechanical systems have long been exemplars of causal systems — at least in Western culture. Let us therefore focus once again on the Hooke's law model of a simple harmonic oscillator, this time in its Hamiltonian formulation. While the Hamiltonian version of Newton's laws in fact fits van Fraassen's own preferred form for presenting theories, it nevertheless also provides an excellent framework for expressing the claims of modal realism. To eliminate controversy over theoretical aspects of the system, let us concentrate on position as the variable of interest.

Everyone agrees that the *model* exhibits a modal structure. For example, the model allows a wide range of different *possible* initial conditions, only one of which can be exhibited at any given time. For each of these (continuously many) different possible sets of initial conditions, one can calculate, using the equations defining the model, a trajectory for the system in the state space. . . .

Now let us shift our focus from the model to a real mass-spring system. Suppose that the real mass had in fact been started in motion with zero initial velocity. Van Fraassen's constructive empiricist and my constructive realist would agree that this real mass should resemble the model with respect to its actual positions in time. But what about the possible positions that would result from different initial conditions, such as some nonzero initial velocity. Does our claim of similarity between model and real system extend to the modal aspects of the model? Do we claim that the real system possesses these possibilities as well? Or, to use a more traditional philosophical formulation, is it true of the real system, as well as of the model, that its positions would follow some definite other pattern if its initial conditions were different?

Modal realism embraces the affirmative answer to these questions. Modal anti-realists, like van Fraassen, could also be called *actualists.* They claim that science aims only at discovering similarities between our models and the actual histories of real systems. The other possibilities are not inherent in real systems, but exist merely in our models.

EMPIRICIST OBJECTIONS

Empiricist arguments against modal realism are apparently stronger than those against theoretical realism. There is no possibility that one could observe states of a real system that might have been, but were not in fact, realized. It is not as if someone might invent a new type of microscope that would expose these possibilities to direct observation.

But this argument is conclusive only if one accepts the empiricist doctrine that ultimately all evidence rests on direct observation. If we allow that there might be other bases for making modal claims, the argument ceases to be conclusive. . . .

Another argument against modal realism, as Quine (1953) has long delighted in pointing out, is that it is often difficult to individuate possibilities. Often, yes, but not always. Many models in which the laws are expressed as differential equations provide an unambiguous criterion for individuating the possible histories of the model. These histories are the trajectories in state-space corresponding to all possible initial conditions. Threatened ambiguities in the set of possible initial conditions can be eliminated by explicitly restricting this set in the definition of the theoretical model. Nor is this criterion limited to models defined in terms of differential equations. A clear distinction between system laws and parameters or initial conditions is generally sufficient. Of course, even classical physics presents cases in which the specification of boundary conditions is ambiguous. But the ambiguity is not nearly so great as a Quine, or a van Fraassen, would suggest.

One could, of course, defend an actualist version of constructive realism. This would be the view that scientific models represent only the actual behavior of both empirical and theoretical aspects of real systems. I will, however, adopt a modal realist interpretation. In spite of philosophical arguments to the contrary, this seems to me the empirically best supported account of theoretical hypotheses.

MODALITY AND CAUSALITY

The oscillating spring is a causal system if anything is. The theoretical model shows us that the frequency of oscillation, f, is functionally related to the ratio, k/m, and functionally independent of the amplitude, A. If the functional relationship obtains merely between the *actual* values of these quantities, it is difficult to see what more there could be to *causality* than merely this functional relationship—as Russell (1912–13) long ago pointed out.

Empiricists have traditionally sought to ground the causal claim in universal generalizations, for example, the claim that *all* oscillating springs exhibit these relationships. On examination such generalizations turn out to be either false or vacuous. For the modal realist the *modal* structure of the model represents, to some degree of approximation, the *causal* structure of the real system. For any real system of the relevant type, then, the functional relationships among the actual values of f, m, k, and A represent causal relationships not because they hold among the actual values in all such real systems, but because they hold among all the possible values in this particular system.

NECESSITY AND PROPENSITY

I have introduced the modal version of constructive realism in the context of deterministic systems of the kind described by classical mechanics. This understanding of how theoretical hypotheses are used is, however, in no way tied to classical mechanics or even to deterministic theories. If one wishes to allow the possibility of genuinely stochastic systems, as quantum systems are widely believed to be, there is a natural extension of strict causal necessity that generally goes by the name "propensity." [4]

Probability models are used in nearly all the sciences, ranging from quantum physics through anthropology. No doubt their wide range of applicability is partly due to their exceedingly simple structure. But what do probability models represent?

The simplest empiricist answer is that they represent actual relative frequencies of kinds of individuals in finite populations. This is the probabilistic analogue of saying that strict causal necessity consists of universal occurrence in all cases. In fact, because of the mistaken (I think) belief that there should be a strict isomorphism between a model and what it represents, most empiricist philosophers postulate hypothetical limiting relative frequencies in infinite sequences to be the real world counterparts of probability models. We need not, however, pursue this internal contradiction in empiricist philosophies of science. It is clear that their aim has been to be as "actualist" as possible. [5]

For the modal realist the analogue of strict causal necessity is a "propensity" existing within the individual system. The exemplar is a single radioactive nucleus. Its probability of one half to decay in a time defined as its "half life" is taken to be a measure of its "causal tendency" to decay in that length of time. Causal tendencies are, for the modal realist, taken to be features of the real world.

Whether macroscopic objects, like human bodies, have propensities, for example, to develop lung cancer, is an open, scientific question. But even if objects like human bodies are strictly deterministic, the number of contributing variables is so large, and the variation among individuals so great, that the similarity between a probability model with probabilities interpreted as propensities and, for example, individual human smokers, is quite strong.

We need not pursue these technicalities any further. My main point is that a modal realist understanding of causality is not tied to nineteenth century conceptions of science.

LAWS AS UNIVERSAL GENERALIZATIONS

The related notions of "law" and "universal generalization" play a major role in logical empiricist and in other accounts of science. In the logical empiricist account of theories, for example, the axioms of a scientific theory were taken to be laws, which were understood as universal generalizations. These notions have a far diminished role in the theory of science unfolding in these pages. [Elsewhere] I challenged the view that the laws of motion of classical mechanics function as true, or even well-confirmed, empirical statements. Here I wish to challenge the view that science requires laws that have the form of universal generalizations.

The idea that statements of universal form (All *F*'s are *G*) play a major role in science goes back to Aristotle. Such statements are well suited to codification in a syllogistic system. Biological classification (species, genus, and so on) still exhibits its debt to the Aristotelian world view.

Although the scientific revolution of the seventeenth century was part of the rejection of an Aristotelian point of view, the goal of discovering universal truths survived. Indeed, that goal was reinforced by the success of Newton's law of universal gravitation. Hume based his analysis of causality on universal laws of association. Kant took universality to be the mark of necessity. And Popper's whole philosophy of science rests on the deductive falsifiability of universal statements by singular statements (This *F* is not *G*). Nevertheless, the importance of universal generalizations is not supported by an examination of contemporary scientific practice.

Let us look at how the venerated law of universal gravitation is treated in standard textbook presentations. Surprisingly, some textbooks of classical mechanics (generally the more advanced) never explicitly state the law of universal gravitation. Nothing of the form "For all bodies . . ." ever appears. Instead, one finds a treatment of models with two bodies moving in two dimensions subject only to a central force. The inverse square law is introduced as the most important form of a central force. Then one typically finds a derivation of Kepler's laws! These are often mentioned by name. Additional applications include the motion of the planets, the moon, and, recently, artificial satellites. These are cases in which the inverse square force model has been found to fit fairly well. In short, classical mechanics can be presented, and sometimes is presented, without ever invoking gravitation in the form of a universal law.

What, then, is the role of the law in those texts that do explicitly state it? At first sight it seems to be invoked to *justify* the choice of an inverse square force function in constructing theoretical models to solve various problems. A standard problem, for example, is to determine the velocity at which a satellite escapes from its orbit. The solution is derived from a model that incorporates an inverse square force. But one wonders whether the reference to the law of universal gravitation is in fact playing any justificatory role. After the solution of the problem has been derived from the model, it is often pointed out that the value obtained does in fact agree quite well with actual observations. The choice of an inverse square force therefore seems to be justified not by appeal to the law of universal gravitation, but by the fact that the resulting model agrees with observations.

This is not to argue that generalizations play no role in mechanics. I claim only that *universal* generalizations play no role. What one does find is catalogs of cases in which various force functions yield models that fit tolerably well. Putting all those catalogs together yields a truly impressive range of cases. This finite, and not well defined, range of cases constitutes the empirical content of classical mechanics. Nevertheless, the range is surely of sufficient scope to account for the importance of mechanics over the past 300 years. The stature of mechanics is not diminished by eliminating the grand generalizations, which, however important they may have seemed in centuries past, are not essential to the science as it is now conceived.

The idea that the content of a science must include universal generalizations is part of the view that the real content is contained in a set of axioms from which applications are deduced. However much their practice may have deviated from the ideal, Newton and his successors seem to have held this view. So have many philosophers down to the present day. But this ideal does not fit mechanics as it is now taught and understood. The relationship between the basic principles and applications is very different in ways I have tried to describe.

CAUSAL MODELS AND CAUSAL EXPLANATIONS

Forty years after Hempel's famous paper (Hempel and Oppenheim 1948), explanation continues to be a major topic within the philosophy of science—as evidenced by the recent appearance of two major books (Achinstein 1983; Salmon 1984) and other important works on the topic (van Fraassen 1980, chap. 5; Kitcher 1981). What has changed, however, is the emphasis, particularly in Salmon, on the role of causality in explanation. In this context one might well wonder whether a constructive, causal realism, as part of a cognitive theory of science, has any relevance to recent theories of explanation. The answer is yes, but not in the way one might think.

Although differing with Hempel in major respects, most philosophical writers on explanation agree with his assumption that there exists a distinct category of things properly called "scientific explanations" and that by studying the distinctive features of these explanations one can learn something important about science. As Salmon (1984, ix) put it:

> Our aim is to understand scientific understanding. We secure scientific understanding by providing scientific explanations; thus our main concern will be with the nature of scientific explanation.

Scientific explanation, then, is taken as providing a window on science.

Although everyone from Hempel on has acknowledged the possibility of explaining "laws," by far the major emphasis in philosophical studies has been on explaining *particular events*. This is curious. If there is anywhere one would expect to find scientific explanations, it is in standard textbooks. Yet explanations of particular events are almost nonexistent in textbooks. What one finds, as I have emphasized, is the development of families of models together with exemplary applications to the behavior of particular kinds of systems.

Why, then, do philosophical writers on explanation emphasize the explanation of particular events? Because that is the kind of explanation one finds most often in everyday life. Why did the Chernobyl nuclear reactor break down? What caused the Challenger rocket to explode? And so on. It turns out, therefore, that most philosophical writing on "scientific explanation" is not really about explanations *within* science, but about the use of scientific knowledge in the explanation of events in everyday life. This reflection suggests a very different picture of the relationship between the study of science and the study of explanation than that generally held.

Explaining is a human activity whose practice long antedated the rise of modern science. Indeed, it seems just the kind of activity whose study the cognitive sciences are now poised to undertake. It is already clear that a large part of any cognitive theory of explanation would be an account of how people deploy various sorts of schemata in giving explanations—and in understanding them. And much of this account could be relatively independent of the content of the schemata employed.[6]

From this point of view, all that is distinctive about "scientific" explanations, whether in science or everyday life, is that they deploy models developed in the sciences. Thus, studying scientific explanations is at best a very indirect way of studying science. Little can be learned in this way about science that could not be learned more directly by examining the nature of scientific models and how they are developed.[7]

What science provides for "scientific explanations" is a resource consisting of sets of well-authenticated models. How people deploy those models in the process of constructing or understanding explanations depends on the *extrascientific* context. To take a standard example, it is not part of the science of mechanics to say whether the length of a pendulum explains its period or the period explains its length. What the science of mechanics provides is a model that exhibits the causal structure in which both the length and period are a part. Moreover, the model may even exhibit asymmetries among elements of the causal structure. In the pendulum example length is a free parameter in the original equations of motion—the period is not. The period is derived in the process of obtaining a solution to the equations of motion. But this fact tells us nothing in general about explanatory priority. As van Fraassen eloquently demonstrated with the story of the tower and the shadow (1980, 132–34), one might well explain why a particular pendulum has the length it does by reference to someone's desire to have a pendulum with a predetermined period.

Am I, then, like van Fraassen, advocating a "pragmatic" theory of scientific explanation? Not quite. My position is even more radical. A theory of explanation, for me, is not to be judged by philosophical standards, but by the standards of the cognitive sciences. That is, an empirical theory of explaining would be judged by the sorts of evidence relevant to theories of other higher level cognitive activities such as language comprehension and problem solving. How well van Fraassen's account would fare by these standards is an open question.

REALISTIC REJOINDERS

I will conclude this [reading] by replying to four types of arguments against any realistic in-terpretation of scientific hypotheses. In keeping with the general strategy of this chapter, these arguments are all designed to show that a realistic interpretation is in general incoherent or obviously false. Epistemological arguments against realism will be addressed later.

THE APPROXIMATION PUZZLE

With very little prodding, most scientific realists will admit that, strictly speaking, many, and perhaps even all, realistically interpreted hypotheses are not literally true. But realists will quickly add that most such hypotheses are *approximately* true. At this point the anti-realists, such as Laudan (1981), will reply that what might be meant by "approximately true" is by no means clear. And they have a point—up to a point.

Approximate truth is not a kind of truth. Indeed, it is a kind of falsehood! Approximately true implies "not exactly true," which means false. Moreover, recent attempts to explicate the notion of approximate truth, such as Popper's notion of verisimilitude (1972, 47–60; Newton-Smith 1981, 52–59), have met with little success. Yet the failure of philosophers to ex-plicate a viable notion of approximate truth must not be taken as grounds for concluding that approximation is not central to the practice of science. Perhaps the source of the difficulty is the philosophers' insistence on understanding approximation in terms of a notion of approx-imate truth.

Van Fraassen was closer to the mark. He suggested (1980, 9) that for a hypothesis to be ap-proximately correct it must encompass a family of models, one of which is exactly correct, that is, isomorphic with the intended real system. But even this definition is too restrictive. What-ever approximation means in science, it must be true that the dynamical models of classical me-chanics are approximately correct for many real systems. Yet if it is agreed that the world is really Einsteinian rather than Newtonian, no dynamical Newtonian model is exactly correct for any real system.

My suggestion, of course, is that the notion of *similarity* between models and real systems provides a much needed resource for understanding approximation in science. For one thing, it eliminates the need for a bastard semantical relationship—approximate truth. For another, it immediately reveals—what talk about approximate truth conceals—that approximation has at least *two* dimensions: approximation in *respects,* and approximation in *degrees.* Armed with just these distinctions, we can begin to attack other recent objections to realism.

THE HISTORICAL ARGUMENT AGAINST REALISM

The historical argument against realism, as popularized, for example, by Laudan (1981, 1984), is basically this: The history of science provides many instances of discarded theories whose central terms did not refer to anything—the phlogiston theory and the ether theory being prime examples. Those theories could not, therefore, be regarded as having been even ap-proximately true. Moreover, the evidence on which those theories were originally accepted was no different in kind from that on which our current theories have been accepted. Thus, there is no reason to think that the same fate could not befall our current theories. Indeed, the historical evidence is that many of our current theories will meet similar ends. The historical evidence is strong that realistically interpreted hypotheses often turn out to be false even when claimed to be only "approximately" true.

This argument rests on the unstated intuition that approximation is always a matter of *degrees*. If the ether does not exist, claims involving the ether cannot be just a little bit off. They must be mistaken in some more radical sense. The argument collapses, however, if we abandon talk of approximate truth in favor of similarity between the model and the world, which allows approximation to include respects as well as degrees of similarity.

Whether the ether exists or not, there are many respects in which electromagnetic radiation is like a disturbance in an ether. Ether theories are thus, in this sense, approximations. The fact that there is no ether is one very important respect in which there fails to be a strong similarity between ether models and the world. That failure is a good basis for rejecting ether models, but not for denying *all* realistically understood claims about similarities between ether models and the world.

One way science advances is by discovering new aspects of the world, that is, new respects in which our models might resemble the world. Science also advances by discovering some respects in which similarities between model and world are *not* as commonly thought. Neither sort of advance, however, is inconsistent with constructive realism.

THE SIMILARITY ARGUMENT

At first sight it seems that even a modest constructive realism is incompatible with relativism. Yet both Barnes (1982, chap. 2) and Bloor (1982) have recently presented an argument that, if correct, would place constructive realism snugly in the relativist household. The argument in question is purely theoretical (it makes no appeal to sociological data) and is attributed both to Mary Hesse (1974, chap. 3) and to Kuhn (1961, 1974). Applied to my account of theoretical hypotheses, the argument proceeds as follows.

The relationship between a theoretical model and the world has been presented as one of similarity. Now, as a matter of logic anything is similar to anything else in some respects and to some degrees. To keep theoretical hypotheses from being merely vacuously true, one must specify respects and degrees. But then the truth or falsity of the hypothesis depends entirely upon that specification. And agreement on its truth or falsity depends on a prior agreement regarding specifications of respects and degrees. But these specifications are determined neither by the character of our theoretical models nor by the nature of any real system. If there is agreement, therefore, it can only be because there was a prior agreement on respects and degrees that is socially sanctioned and enforced. Thus, which hypotheses are called true and which false depends entirely on social agreements, which are totally independent of our models and of how the world really is.

I agree with the premises of this argument. A theoretical hypothesis is like a formula with several free parameters. Until the parameters are filled in, the truth or falsity of the hypothesis is indeterminate. Moreover, neither the indeterminate hypothesis itself nor the world determine the respects or the degrees to be included in the claim of similarity. The conclusion of complete social determination, however, does not follow.

The argument assumes that specification of the relevant respects and degrees remains in the background and is not part of the hypothesis itself. The claims whose truth or falsity is at issue therefore merely assert a similarity, with respects and degrees left tacit. In this case the truth or falsity of the explicit assertion of similarity clearly does depend on tacit specifications of respects and degrees. But these specifications need not be tacit, and in science they often are not.

To take a simple sort of case, imagine a model that predicts the values of a specified parameter. A set of measurements are made, all of which are within 10 percent of the predicted values but none of which are within 2 percent. A claim of agreement to within 10 percent would be true, while a claim of agreement to within 2 percent would be false. The relativity to prior agreement has been eliminated by bringing the object of prior agreement within the hypothesis itself. This simple example shows that claims of the kind required by constructive realism can legitimately be made.

The example does not, however, eliminate the problem of deciding whether, in the context, accuracy just within 10 percent is acceptable. That is a separate decision. But the fact that such a decision must be made does not restore the conclusion of complete social determination. Indeed, a judgment on the accuracy of the data must precede the judgment whether that degree of accuracy is acceptable.

We can, however, go beyond this technical refutation of the similarity argument. As is suggested by its more usual formulation in terms of perceptual judgments, the similarity argument is rooted in traditional empiricist epistemology. It assumes a version of the Humean view that there is no natural connection between any two impressions. The only connections are those we impose.

As was pointed out earlier, traditional empiricism is particularly vulnerable to an attack based on post-Darwinian biology. The effect of evolution on our sensory apparatus is known to have been particularly strong. Animals are capable of incredibly fine discriminations among objects in their environment without benefit of social conventions. And so—being fairly intelligent, talking primates—are we. As Bloor (1982) himself acknowledged, no human group among the many that have been studied fails to distinguish red from green, though many do not distinguish pink from red (Berlin and Kay 1969). This fact has a ready explanation in the evolved physiology of our color-sensing mechanisms. Our ability to distinguish colors derives from three pigments sensitive to the whole visible spectrum but which have their peak sensitivities roughly in the blue, green, and yellow regions, respectively. We perceive other colors by adding and subtracting signals from these three types of receptors (P. S. Churchland 1986, 454–55). For at least some perceptual judgments, therefore, the fact of widespread agreement does not require a social explanation. The explanations of evolutionary biology and physiology are sufficient.

Obviously, the acquisition of scientific knowledge, like all human activities, takes place in a social environment. That is not at issue. But humans are also biological creatures with complex, evolved cognitive capacities for interacting with their environment. The task of a theory of science is to discover empirically how all these elements fit together. In this task general sociological arguments that scientific knowledge is completely relative to social agreements are no more helpful than philosophical arguments that scientific knowledge necessarily requires the application of some a priori rules of rationality.

THE PROBLEM OF INDEPENDENT ACCESS

Attempts to describe a realist position within the confines of traditional empiricism have always faced the problem of independent access. Suppose, with Hume or Mill or Russell, that all one "directly" experiences are one's own sensations. How, then, could one compare one's sensations with the world to determine whether they correspond to it? Since all one could experience is another sensation, one could at best compare two different sensations. In short, there is no "independent access" to the world.

Since radical empiricism is now out of fashion, we no longer find that argument stated so baldly. Yet it is still influential. A patient reading of Putnam's recent work (1981, 1983), for example, reveals a more Kantian version of the argument.

Approaching the problem from the perspective of the cognitive sciences and evolutionary naturalism allows one to bypass several centuries of fruitless philosophical debate. Rats (Tolman 1948; O'Keefe and Nadel 1978), and even wasps (Gallistel 1980, 345–49), have the capacity to construct internal "maps" of their environment. They produce those maps through causal interaction with the world in a way that yields useful similarities with that world. Of course, evolution produced the neural capacity for generating such maps—again as a result of long-term causal interactions with the world. And versions of those same mechanisms exist as well in the human brain (P. S. Churchland 1986).

It would be strange to think that as a result of acquiring greatly enhanced cognitive capacities, including those for language and self-conscious reflection, humans somehow lost the ability to interact cognitively with the world in the simpler ways available to lower animals. That is scarcely possible. The problem lies, rather, with the way humans in various intellectual traditions have represented their own capacities for representing and interacting with the world. Once the inadequacies of those traditions are recognized, the way is clear to begin the more fruitful scientific task of explaining how, beginning with the biological and cultural resources of our ancestors, we humans have managed to construct modern science.

NOTES

[1] For a good introduction to the latest philosophical thinking on realism see the essays in Leplin (1984) or Churchland and Hooker (1985). For extended developments of individual viewpoints see Blackburn (1984), Devitt (1984), and Hooker (1987).

[2] As a philosophical exercise one might consider whether the arguments van Fraassen uses against realism, and in favor of empiricism, might not also be used against his liberal empiricism (3) in favor of the more restricted versions (1) or (2). He would surely be uncomfortable with the more restrictive versions, but he perhaps cannot avoid them. This sort of argument has not been pushed against van Fraassen, perhaps simply because everyone is busy defending realism and no one wishes to defend more restrictive forms of empiricism.

[3] The example of solar neutrinos, and its implications for philosophical discussions of observation, is nicely exploited by Shapere (1982).

[4] Propensity interpretations of probability go back to Peirce, but their modern popularity began with Popper (1959). I myself have developed propensity ideas in a number of papers (1973, 1976a, 1976b, 1979, 1980). For a review from another perspective see Salmon (1979).

[5] In standard probability models the probability function takes real numbers as values. Ratios in finite populations are restricted to rational numbers. It is because of this discrepancy that most empiricist philosophers postulate limiting relative frequencies in infinite sequences to be the real world counterparts of probability models. The trouble, of course, is that the real world contains no infinite sequences. And so one invents hypothetical infinite sequences. Salmon (1967) provided a readable account of frequency interpretations of probability. Van Fraassen (1980, chap. 6) developed a more adequate, but less accessible, empiricist account.

[6] Roger Shank, a specialist in artificial intelligence, has recently been giving lectures on "explanation." This is a natural extension of his earlier well-known work (Shank and Abelson 1977).

[7] Salmon (1984, 119) considered the possibility that science might be primarily concerned with causal structure and not with individual events, and he therefore appealed to the existence of "applied science" to justify a concern with explaining individual events. But this put him in the awkward position of seeking to "understand scientific understanding" largely through the study of explanations in applied science. My hypothesis as to why Salmon has not been more bothered by this discrepancy is that his real concern is less with *understanding* scientific explanations than with *justifying* them. His main concern throughout is with the characteristics that distinguish a legitimate scientific explanation from nonscientific, or pseudoscientific, explanations. Thus, for Salmon, as for logical empiricists generally, the study of explanation is another means toward the overall goal of providing a philosophical justification for science. Recall that Salmon's earlier work (1967) focused on the traditional problem of justifying induction.

REFERENCES

Achinstein, P. 1983. *The Nature of Explanation.* New York: Oxford University Press.

Barnes, B. 1982. *T. S. Kuhn and Social Science.* New York: Columbia University Press.

Berlin, B. and P. Kay. 1969. *Basic Color Terms: Their Universality and Evolution.* Berkeley: University of California Press.

Blackburn, S. 1984. *Spreading the Word.* Oxford: Clarendon Press.

Bloor, D. 1982. "Durkheim and Mauss Revisited: Classification and the Sociology of Knowledge." *Studies in the History and Philosophy of Science* 13: 267–97.

Churchland, P. M. and C. A. Hooker, eds. 1985. *Images of Science.* Chicago: University of Chicago Press.

Churchland, P. S. 1986. *Neurophilosophy.* Cambridge: MIT Press.

Devitt, M. 1984. *Realism and Truth.* Princeton: Princeton University Press.

Gallistel, C. R. 1980. *The Organization of Action: A New Synthesis.* Hillsdale, N.J.: Erlbaum.

Giere, R. N. 1973. "Objective Single Case Probabilities and the Foundations of Statistics." In *Logic, Methodology, and Philosophy of Science,* vol. 4, ed. P. Suppes et al., 467–83. Amsterdam: North-Holland.

———. 1976a. "A Laplacean Formal Semantics for Single-Case Propensities." *Journal of Philosophical Logic* 5: 321–53.

———. 1976b. "Empirical Probability, Objective Statistical Methods, and Scientific Inquiry." In *Foundations of Probability Theory, Statistical Inference, and Statistical Theories of Science,* vol. 2, ed. C. A. Hooker and W. Harper, 63–101. Dordrecht: Reidel.

———. 1979. "Propensity and Necessity." *Synthese* 40: 439–51.

———. 1980. "Causal Systems and Statistical Hypotheses." In *Applications of Inductive Logic,* ed. L. J. Cohen and M. B. Hesse, 251–70. Oxford: Oxford University Press.

———. 1985. "Constructive Realism." In *Images of Science,* ed. P. M. Churchland and C. A. Hooker. Chicago: University of Chicago Press.

Hempel, C. G. and P. Oppenheim. 1948. "Studies in the Logic of Explanation," *Philosophy of Science* 15: 135–175.

Hesse, M. 1974. *The Structure of Scientific Inference.* Berkeley, California: University of California Press.

Hooker, C. A. 1987. *A Realistic Theory of Science.* Albany, New York: SUNY Press.

Kitcher. 1981. "Explanatory Unification." *Philosophy of Science* 48: 507–31.

Kuhn, T. S. 1961. "The Function of Measurement in Modern Physical Science." *Isis* 52: 161–90. Reprinted in Kuhn (1977).

———. 1974. "Second Thoughts on Paradigms." In *The Structure of Scientific Theories,* ed. F. Suppe. Urbana: University of Illinois Press. Reprinted in Kuhn (1977).

———. 1977. *The Essential Tension.* Chicago: University of Chicago Press.

Laudan, L. 1981. "A Confutation of Convergent Realism." *Philosophy of Science* 48: 19–48.

———. 1984. *Science and Values.* Berkeley: University of California Press.

Leplin, J., ed. 1984. *Scientific Realism.* Berkeley: University of California Press.

Newton-Smith, W. H. 1981. *The Rationality of Science.* London: Routledge & Kegan Paul.

O'Keefe, J., and L. Nadel. 1978. *The Hippocampus as a Cognitive Map.* Oxford: Clarendon Press.

Popper, K. R. 1959. "The Propensity Interpretation of Probability." *British Journal for the Philosophy of Science* 10: 25–42.

———. 1972. *Objective Knowledge.* Oxford: Oxford University Press (2d ed., 1979).

Putnam, H. 1981. *Reason, Truth, and History.* Cambridge: Cambridge University Press.

———. 1983. *Realism and Reason,* vol. 3 of *Philosophical Papers.* Cambridge: Cambridge University Press.

Quine, W. V. O. 1953. *From a Logical Point of View.* Cambridge: Harvard University Press.

Russell, B. 1912–13. "On the Notion of Cause." *Proceedings of the Aristotelian Society.* Reprinted in Russell (1918).

———. 1918. *Mysticism and Logic.* New York: Longman.

Salmon, W. C. 1967. *The Foundations of Scientific Inference.* Pittsburgh: University of Pittsburgh Press.

———. 1975. "Theoretical Explanation." In *Explanation,* ed. S. Körner, 118–45. Oxford: Basil Blackwell.

———. 1979. "Propensities: A Discussion Review." *Erkenntnis* 14: 183–216.

———. 1984. *Scientific Explanation and the Causal Structure of the World.* Princeton: Princeton University Press.

Shank, R. C. and R. P. Abelson. 1977. *Scripts, Plans, Goals, and Understanding.* Hillsdale, N.J.: Erlbaum.

Shapere, D. 1982. "The Concept of Observation in Science and Philosophy." *Philosophy of Science* 49: 485–525.

Suppe, F., ed. 1974. *The Structure of Scientific Theories.* Urbana: University of Illinois Press (2d ed., 1977).

Tolman, E. C. 1948. "Cognitive Maps in Rats and Men." *Psychological Review* 55: 189–208.

van Fraassen, B. C. 1980. *The Scientific Image.* Oxford: Clarendon Press.

———. 1982. "The Charybdis of Realism: Epistemological Implications of Bell's Inequality." *Synthese* 52: 25–38.

ERNAN MCMULLIN
A CASE FOR SCIENTIFIC REALISM

When Galileo argued that the familiar patterns of light and shade on the face of the full moon could best be accounted for by supposing the moon to possess mountains and seas like those of earth, he was employing a joint mode of inference and explanation that was by no means new to natural science but which since then has come to be recognized as central to scientific explanation. In a retroduction, the scientist proposes a model whose properties allow it to account for the phenomena singled out for explanation. Appraisal of the model is a complex affair, involving criteria such as coherence and fertility, as well as adequacy in accounting for the data. The theoretical constructs employed in the model may be of a kind already familiar (such as "mountain" and "sea" in Galileo's moon model) or they may be created by the scientist specifically for the case at hand (such as "galaxy," "gene," or "molecule").

Does a successful retroduction permit an inference to the existence of the entities postulated in the model? The instincts of the working scientist are to respond with a strong affirmative. Galaxies, genes, and molecules exist (he would say) in the straightforward sense in which the mountains and seas of the earth exist. The immense and continuing success of the retroductions employing these constructs is (in the scientist's eyes) a sufficient testimony to this. Scientists are likely to treat with incredulity the suggestion that constructs such as these are no more than convenient ways of organizing the data obtained from sophisticated instruments, or that their enduring success ought not lead us to believe that the world actually contains entities corresponding to them. The near-invincible belief of scientists is that we come to discover more and more of the entities of which the world is composed through the constructs around which scientific theory is built.[1]

But how reliable *is* this belief? And how is it to be formulated? This is the issue of scientific realism that has once again come to be vigorously debated among philosophers, after a period of relative neglect. The "Kuhnian revolution" in the philosophy of science has had two quite opposite effects in this regard. On the one hand, the new emphasis on the *practice* of science as the proper basis for the philosophy of science led to a more sensitive appreciation of the role played by theoretical constructs in guiding and defining the work of science. The restrictive empiricism of the logical positivists had earlier shown itself in their repeated attempts to "reduce" theoretical terms to the safer language of observation. The abandonment of this program was due not so much to the failure of the reduction techniques as to a growing realization that theoretical terms have a distinctive and indispensable part to play in science.[2] It was only a step from this realization to an acknowledgment that these terms carry with them an ontology, though admittedly an incomplete and tentative one. For a time, it seemed as though realism was coming into its own again.

But there were also new influences in the opposite direction. The focus of attention in the philosophy of science was now on scientific change rather than on the traditional topic of justification, and so the instability of scientific concepts became a problem with which the realist had to wrestle. For the first time, philosophers of language were joining the fray, and puzzles about truth and reference began to build into another challenge for realism. And so antirealism has reemerged, this time, however, much more sophisticated than it was in its earlier positivist dress.

When I say "antirealism," I make it sound like a single coherent position. But of course, antirealism is at least as far from a single coherent position as realism itself is. Though my concern is to construct a case for realism, it will be helpful first to survey the sources and varieties of antirealism. I will comment on these as I go, noting ambiguities and occasional misunderstandings. This will help to clarify the sort of scientific realism that in the end can be defended.

SOURCES OF ANTIREALISM: SCIENCE

CLASSICAL MECHANICS

It is important to recall that scientists themselves have often been dubious about some of their own theoretical constructs, not because of some general antirealist sentiment, but because of some special features of the particular constructs themselves. Such constructs may seem like extra baggage—additional interpretations imposed on the theories themselves—much as the crystalline spheres seemed to many of the astronomers of the period between Ptolemy and Copernicus. Or it may be very difficult to characterize them in a consistent way, a problem that frequently bedeviled the proponents of ethers and fluids in nineteenth-century mechanics.

The most striking example of this sort of hesitation is surely that of Newton in regard to his primary explanatory construct, *attraction.* Despite the success of the mechanics of the *Principia,* Newton was never comfortable with the implications of the notion of attraction and the more general notion of force. Part of his uneasiness stemmed from his theology; he could not conceive that matter might of itself be active and thus in some sense independent of God's directing power. The apparent implication of action at a distance also distressed him. But then, how were these forces to be understood ontologically? *Where* are they, in what do they reside, and does the postulating of an inverse-square law of force between sun and planet say anything more than that each tends to move in a certain way in the proximity of the other?

The Cartesians, Leibniz, and later Berkeley, charged that the new mechanics did not really *explain* motion, since its central notion, *force,* could not be given an acceptable interpretation. Newton was sensitive to this charge and, in the decades following the publication of *Principia,* kept trying to find an ontology that might satisfy his critics.[3] He tried "active principles" that would somehow operate outside bodies. He even tried to reintroduce an ether with an extraordinary combination of properties—this despite his convincing refutation of mechanical ethers in *Principia.*[4] None of these ideas, however, were satisfactory. There were either problems of coherence and fit (the ether) or of specification (the active principles). After Newton's death, the predictive successes of his mechanics gradually stilled the doubts about the explanatory credentials of its central concept. But these doubts did not entirely vanish; Mach's *Science of Mechanics* (1881) would give them enduring form.

What are the implications of this often-told story for the realist thesis? It might seem that the failure of the attempts to interpret the concept of force in terms of previously familiar causal categories was a failure for realism also, and that the gradual laying aside in mechanics of questions about the underlying ontology was, in effect, an endorsement of antirealism. This would be so, however, only if one were to suppose the realist to be committed to theories that permit interpretation in familiar categories or, at the very least, in categories that are immediately interpretable. Naive realism of *this* sort is, indeed, easily undermined. But this is not the view that scientific realists ordinarily defend, as will be seen.

How should Newton's attempts at "interpretation" be regarded, after the fact? Were they an improper intrusion of "metaphysics," the sort of thing that science today would bar? The term "underlying ontology" that I have used might mislead here. A scientist *can* properly attempt to specify the mechanisms that underlie his equations. Newton's ether *might* have worked out; it was a potentially testable hypothesis, prompted by analogies with the basic explanatory paradigm of an earlier mechanical tradition. The metaphor of "active principle" proved a fruitful one; it was the ancestor of the notion of field, which would much later show its worth.[5]

In one of his critiques of "metaphysical realism," Putnam argues that "the whole history of science has been antimetaphysical from the seventeenth century on."[6] Where different "metaphysical" interpretations can be given of the same set of equations (e.g., the action-at-a-distance and the field interpretations of Newtonian gravitation theory), Putnam claims that competent physicists have focused on the equations and have left to philosophers the discussion of which of the empirically equivalent interpretations is "right." But this is not a good reading of the complicated history of Newtonian physics. First and foremost, it does not apply to Newton himself nor to many of his most illustrious successors, such as Faraday and Maxwell.[7]

Scientists have never thought themselves disqualified from pursuing one of a number of physical models that, for the moment, appear empirically equivalent. As metaphors, these models may give rise to quite different lines of inquiry, leading eventually to their empirical separation. Or it may be that one of the alternative models appears undesirable on other grounds than immediate empirical adequacy (as action at a distance did to Newton). If prolonged efforts to separate the models empirically are unsuccessful, or if it comes to be shown that the models are in principle empirically equivalent, scientists will, of course, turn to other matters. But this is not a rejection of realism. It is, rather, an admission that no decision can be made in this case as to what the theory, on a realist reading, commits us to.

What makes mechanics unique (and therefore an improper paradigm for the discussion of realism with regard to the theoretical entities of science generally) is that this kind of barrier occurs so frequently there. This would seem to derive from its status as the "ultimate" natural science, the basic mode of explanation of motions. The realist can afford to be insouciant about his inability to construe, for example, "a force of attraction between sun and earth . . . [as] responsible for the elliptical shape of the earth's orbit" in ontological terms, as long as he *can* construe astrophysics to give at least tentative warrant to his claim that the sun is a sphere of gas emitting light through a process of nuclear fusion. There was no way for Newton to know that attempts to interpret force in terms of the simple ontological alternatives he posed would ultimately fail, whereas the ontology of "insensible corpuscles," which he proposes in *Opticks,* would prosper. Each of these ventures was "metaphysical" in the sense that no evidence then available could determine the likelihood of its ever becoming an empirically decidable issue. But it is of such ventures that science is made.

QUANTUM MECHANICS

In the debates between realists and antirealists, one claim that antirealists constantly make is that quantum mechanics has decided matters in their favor. In particular, the outcome of the famous controversy involving Bohr and Einstein, leading to the defeat (in most physicists' eyes) of Einstein, is taken to be a defeat for realism also. Once again, I want to show that this inference cannot be directed against the realist position proper.

Was the Copenhagen interpretation of quantum mechanics antirealist in its thrust?[8] Did Bohr's "complementary principle" imply that the theoretical entities of the new mechanics do not license any sort of existence claims about the structures of the world? It would seem not, for Bohr argues that the world is much more complex than classical physics supposed, and that the debate as to whether the basic entities of optics and mechanics are waves or particles cannot be resolved because its terms are inadequate. Bohr believes that the wave picture and the particle picture are *both* applicable, that *both* are needed, each in its own proper context. He is not holding that from his interpretation of quantum mechanics nothing can be inferred about the entities of which the world is composed; quite the reverse. He is arguing that what can be inferred is entirely at odds with what the classical world view would have led one to expect.

Of course, Einstein was a realist in regard to science. But he was also much more than a realist. He maintained a quite specific view about the nature of the world and about its relationship to observation; namely, that dynamic variables have unique real values at all times, that measurement reveals (or should reveal) these values as they exist prior to the measurement, and that there is a deterministic relationship between successive sets of these values. It was thus further specification of realism that Bohr disputed.[9]

It is important to note that Einstein *might* have been right here. There is nothing about the nature of science per se that, in retrospect, allows us to say that Bohr *had* to be right. There could well be a world of which Einstein's version of realism would hold true. And in the 1930s, it was not yet clear that it might not just be our world. We now know that it is not and, furthermore, that this was implicit from the beginning in certain features of the quantum formalism itself, once this formalism was shown to predict correctly. (J. S. Bell's theorem could, in principle, have been proved as easily in 1934 as in 1964; no new empirical results were needed for it.)

What we have discovered as a result of this controversy is, in the first instance, something about the kind of world we live in.[10] The dynamical variables associated with its macro- and microconstituents are measurement-dependent in an unexpected way. (E. Wigner tried to show more specifically that they are *observer*-dependent, in the sense of being affected by the consciousness of the observer, but few have followed him in this direction.) Does the fact that quantum systems are partially indeterminate in this way affect the realist thesis? Not as far as I can see, unless a confusion is first made between scientific realism and the "realism" that is opposed to idealism, and then the measurement-dependence is somehow read as idealist in its implications. It *does* mean, of course, that the quantum formalism is incomplete by the standards of classical mechanics and that a quantum system lacks some kinds of ontological determinacy that classical systems possessed.

This was what Einstein objected to. This was why he sought an "underlying reality" (specifiable ultimately in terms of "hidden parameters" or the like) which would restore determinism of the classical sort. But to search for a completeness of the classical sort was no more "realist" than to maintain (as Bohr did) that the old completeness could never be regained. Recall that realism has to do with the existence-implications of the theoretical entities of successful theories. Einstein's ideal of physics would have the world entirely determinate against the mapping of variables of a broadly Newtonian type; Bohr's would not. The implications for the realist of Bohr's science are, it is true, more difficult to grasp. But why should we have expected the ontology of the microworld to be like that of the macroworld? Newton's third rule of philosophizing (which decreed that the macroworld should resemble the microworld in all essential details) was never more than a pious hope.

ELEMENTARY-PARTICLE PHYSICS

And this dissimilarity of the macrolevel and microlevel is even plainer when one turns from dynamic variables to the entities which these variables characterize. In the plate tectonic model that has had such striking success in recent geology, the continents are postulated to be carried on large plates of rocky material which underlie the continents as well as the oceans and which move very slowly relative to one another. There is no problem as to what an existence-claim means in this case. But problems do arise when we consider such microentities as electrons. For one thing, these are not particles strictly speaking, though custom dies hard and the label "elementary-particle physics" is still widely used. Electrons do not obey classical (Boltzman) statistics, as the familiar enduring individuals of our middle-sized world do.

The use of namelike terms, such as "electron," and the apparent causal simplicity of oil-drop or cloud-track experiments, could easily mislead one into supposing that electrons are very small localized individual entities with the standard mechanical properties of mass and momentum. Yet a bound electron might more accurately be thought of as a state of the system in which it is bound than as a separate discriminable entity. It is only because the charge it carries (which is a measure of the proton coupling to the electron) happens to be small that the free electron can be represented as an independent entity. When the coupling strength is greater, as it is between such nuclear entities as protons and neutrons, the matter becomes even more problematic. According to relativistic quantum theory, the forces between these entities are produced by the exchange of mesons. What is meant by "particle" in this instance reduces to the expression of a force characteristic of a particular field, a far cry from the hard massy points of classical mechanics. And the situation is still more complicated if one turns to the quark hypothesis in quantum field theory. Though quarks are supposed to "constitute" such entities as protons, they cannot be regarded as "constituents" in the ordinary physical sense; that is, they cannot be dissociated nor can they exist in the free state.

The moral is not that elementary-particle physics makes no sort of realist claim, but that the claim it makes must be construed with caution. The denizens of the microworld with their "strangeness" and "charm" can hardly be said to be imaginable in the ordinary sense. At that level, we have lost many of the familiar bearings (such as individuality, sharp location, and measurement-independent properties) that allow us to anchor the reference of existence-claims in such macrotheories as geology or astrophysics. But imaginability must not be made the test for ontology. The realist claim is that the scientist is discovering the structures of the world; it is not required in addition that these structures be imaginable in the categories of the macroworld.

The form of the successful retroductive argument is the same at the micro- as at the macrolevel. If the success of the argument at the macrolevel is to be explained by postulating that something like the entities of the theory exist, the same ought to be true of arguments at the microlevel. Are there electrons? Yes, there are, just as there are stars and slowly moving geological plates bearing the continents of earth. What are electrons? Just what the theory of electrons says they are, no more, no less, always allowing for the likelihood that the theory is open to further refinement. If we cannot quite imagine what they are, this is due to the distance of the microworld from the world in which our imaginations were formed, not to the existential shortcomings of electrons (if I may so express the doubts of the antirealist).

A STRATEGY FOR SCIENTISTS?

Some of the critics of realism assume that defenders of realism are prescribing a strategy for scientists, a kind of regulative principle that will separate the good from the bad among proposed explanatory models. Since the critics believe this strategy to be defective, they have an additional argument against realism. In their view, nonrealist strategies as often as not work out. Indeed, two such episodes might be said to be foundational for modern science: Einstein's laying aside of ontological scruples in his rejection of classical space and time when formulating his general theory of relativity, and Heisenberg's restriction of matrix mechanics to observable quantities only.[11]

A contemporary example of a similarly non-realist strategy can be found among the proponents of S-matrix theory. Geoffrey Chew defends this approach against its rival, quantum field theory with its horde of theoretical entities, by claiming as an advantage that it has no "implication of physical meaning" and that its ability to dispense with an equation of motion allows it also to dispense with any sort of fundamental entities, such as particles or fields.[12] In some of his later essays, Heisenberg (the original proponent of the S-matrix formalism) dwelt on the choice facing quantum physicists of whether to opt for the Democritean approach, utilizing constituent entities, which has been canonical since the seventeenth century, or the Pythagorean approach, which relies on the resources of pure mathematics alone.[13] Heisenberg argued that the Pythagorean approach is now coming into its own, as the resources of the Democritean physical models are close to exhaustion at the quantum level.[14]

It is important to see why a realist could have supported Chew's effort and why the success of Heisenberg's early matrix mechanics must not be credited to antirealism. The realism/antirealism debate has to do with the assessment of the existential implications of successful theories *already in place*. It is not directed to strategies for *further* development, for deciding among alternative formalisms with respect to their likely future potential. A scientist who is persuaded of the truth of realism *might* very well decide that a fresh start is needed when he cannot find a coherent physical model around which to build a new theory. Positivism of this sort may well be called for in some situations, and the realist need not oppose it.

A realist might even decide that at some point the program of Heisenberg and Chew offers more promise, without repudiating his confidence in constructs that have been validated by earlier work. It is true, of course, that a realist will be less likely to turn in this direction than a nonrealist would; the extended successes of the Democritean approach and the knowledge of physical structure it has made possible might weigh more heavily, as a sort of inductive argument, with the realist.

Nevertheless, there is no necessary connection; the defender of realism must not be saddled with a normative doctrine of the kind attributed here. One reason, perhaps, why this sort of confusion occurs is that Einstein's stand against Bohr is so often taken to be the paradigm of realism. And it did, indeed, involve a strongly normative doctrine in regard to the proper strategy for quantum physics. But Einstein's world view included, as I have shown, much more than realism; where it failed was not in its realistic component, but in the conservative constraints on future inquiry that Einstein felt the success of classical physics warranted.

As a footnote to this discussion, it may be worth emphasizing that the realist of whom I speak here is, in the first instance, a philosopher. The qualifier "scientific" in front of "realist" should not be allowed to mislead. It is used to distinguish the realism I am discussing from the many others that dot the history of philosophy. The realisms that philosophers in the past opposed to nominalism and to idealism are very different doctrines, and neither is connected, in any straightforward way at least, with the realism being referred to here. In the past, the realism I am speaking of has been most often contrasted with fictionalism or with "instrumentalism"; but at this point the term is almost hopelessly equivocal.

"Scientific realism" is scientific because it proposes a thesis *in regard to* science. Though the case to be made for it may employ the inference-to-best-explanation technique also used in science, the doctrine itself is still a philosophic one. The scientist qua scientist is not called on to take a stand on it one way or another. Most scientists *do* have views on the issue, sometimes on the basis of much reflection but more often of a spontaneous kind. Indeed, it could be argued that worrying about whether or not their constructs approximate the real is more apt to hinder than to help their work as scientists!

SOURCES OF ANTIREALISM: HISTORY OF SCIENCE

The most obvious source of antirealism in recent decades is the new concern for the history of science on the part of philosophers of science. Thomas Kuhn's emphasis on the discontinuity that, according to him, characterizes the "revolutionary" transitions in the history of science also led him to a rejection of realism: "I can see [in the systems of Aristotle, Newton, and Einstein] no coherent direction of ontological development." [15] Kuhn is willing to attribute a cumulative character to the low-level empirical laws of science. But he denies any cumulative character to theory: theories come and go, and many leave little of themselves behind.

Among the critics of realism, Larry Laudan is perhaps the one who sets most store in considerations drawn from the history of science. He displays an impressive list of once-respected theories that now have been discarded, and guesses that "for every highly successful theory in the past of science which we now believe to be a genuinely referring theory, one could find half a dozen once successful theories which we now regard as substantially non-referring."[16]

To meet this challenge adequately, it would be necessary to look closely at Laudan's list of discarded theories, and that would require an essay in its own right. But a few remarks are in order. The sort of theory on which the realist grounds his argument is one in which an increasingly finer specification of internal structure has been obtained over a long period, in which the theoretical entities function *essentially* in the argument and are not simply intuitive postulations of an "underlying reality," and in which the original metaphor has proved continuously fertile and capable of increasingly further extension. (More on this will follow.)

This excludes most of Laudan's examples right away. The crystalline spheres of ancient astronomy, the universal Deluge of catastrophist geology, theories of spontaneous generation—none of these would qualify. That is not to say that the entities or events they postulated were not firmly believed in by their proponents. But realism is not a blanket approval for all the entities postulated by long-supported theories of the past. Ethers and fluids are a special category, and one which Laudan stresses. I would argue that these were often, though not always, interpretive additions, that is, attempts to specify what "underlay" the equations of the scientist in a way which the equations (as we now see) did not really sanction. The optical ether, for example, in whose existence Maxwell had such confidence, was no more than a carrier for variations in the electromagnetic potentials. It seemed obvious that a vehicle of some sort *was* necessary; undulations cannot occur (as it was often pointed out) unless there is something to undulate! Yet nothing could be inferred about the carrier itself; it was an "I-know-not-what," precisely the sort of unknowable "underlying reality" that the antirealist so rightly distrusts.

The theory of circular inertia and the effluvial theory of static electricity were first approximations, crude it is true, but effective in that the metaphors they suggested gradually were winnowed through, and something of the original was retained. Phlogiston left its antiself, oxygen, behind. The view that the continents were static, which preceded the plate-tectonic model of contemporary geology, was not a theory; it was simply an assumption, one that is correct to a fairly high approximation. The early theories of the nucleus, which assumed it to be homogeneous, were simply idealizations; it was not known whether the nucleus was homogeneous or not, but a decision on that could be put off until first the notion of the nuclear atom itself could be fully explored. These are all examples given by Laudan. Clearly, they need more scrutiny than I have given them. But equally clearly, Laudan's examples may not be taken without further examination to count on the antirealist side. The value of this sort of reminder, however, is that it warns the realist that the ontological claim he makes is at best tentative, for surprising reversals *have* happened in the history of science. But the nonreversals (and a long list is easy to construct here also) still require some form of (philosophic) explanation, or so I shall argue.

SOURCES OF ANTIREALISM: PHILOSOPHY

According to the classic ideal of science as demonstration which dominated Western thought from Aristotle down to Descartes, hypothesis can be no more than a temporary device in science. Of course, one can find an abundance of retroductive reasoning in Aristotle's science as in Descartes', a tentative working back from observed effect to unobserved cause. But there was an elaborate attempt to ensure that *real* science, *scientia propter quid,* would not contain theoretical constructs of a hypothetical kind. And there was a tendency to treat these latter constructs as fictions, in particular the constructs of mathematical astronomy. Duhem has left us a chronicle of the antirealism with which the medieval philosophers regarded the epicycles and eccentrics of the Ptolemaic astronomer.

EMPIRICISM

As the bar to hypothesis gradually came to be dropped in the seventeenth century, another source of opposition to theoretical constructs began to appear. The new empiricism was distrustful of unobserved entities, particularly those that were unobservable in principle. One finds this sort of skepticism already foreshadowed in some well-known chapters of Locke's *Essay Concerning Human Understanding.* Locke concluded there (Book IV) that a "science of bodies" may well be forever out of reach because there is no way to reason securely from the observed secondary qualities of things to the primary qualities of the minute parts on which those secondary qualities are supposed to depend. Hume went much further and restricted science to the patterning of sense impressions. He simply rejects the notion of cause according to which one could try to infer from these impressions to the unobserved entities causing them.

Kant tried to counter this challenge to the realistic understanding of Newtonian physics. He argued that entities such as the "magnetic matter pervading all bodies" need not be perceivable by the unaided senses in order to qualify as real.[17] He established a notion of cause sufficiently large to warrant causal inference from sense-knowledge to such unobservables as the "magnetic matter." Even though the transcendental deductions of the first *Critique* bear on the prerequisites of possible experience, "experience" must be interpreted here as extending to all spatio-temporal entities that can be causally connected with the deliverances of our senses.[18]

Despite Kant's efforts, the skeptical empiricism of Hume has continued to find admirers. The logical positivists were attracted by it but were sufficiently impressed by the central role of theoretical constructs in science not to be quite so emphatic in their rejection of the reality of unobservable theoretical entities. The issue itself tended to be pushed aside and to be treated by them as undecidable; E. Nagel's *The Structure of Science* gives classical expression to this view. This sort of agnosticism alternated with a more definitely skeptical view in logical positivist writings. If one takes empiricism as a starting point, it is tempting to push it (as Hume did) to yield the demand not just that every claim about the world must ultimately rest on sense experience but that every admissible entity must be directly certifiable by sense experience.

This is the position taken by Bas van Fraassen. His antirealism is restricted to those theoretical entities that are in principle unobservable. He has no objection to allowing the reality of such theoretical entities as stars (interpreted as large glowing masses of gas) because these are, in his view, observable in principle since we could approach them by spaceship, for example. It is part of what he calls the "empirical adequacy" of a stellar theory that it should predict what we would observe should we come to a star. This criterion, which he makes the single aim of science, is sufficiently broad, therefore, to allow reality-claims for any theoretical entity that, though at present unobserved, is at least in principle directly observable by us. His antirealism has more than a tinge of old-fashioned nominalism about it, the rejection of what he calls an "inflationary metaphysics" of redundant entities.[19] Since neither of the two main arguments he lists for realism, inference to the best explanation and the common cause argument, are (in his view) logically compelling, this is taken to justify his application of Occam's razor.

One immediate difficulty with this position is, of course, the distinction drawn between the observable and the unobservable. Since entities on one side of the line are ontologically respectable and those on the other are not, it is altogether crucial that there be some way not only to draw the distinction but also to confer on it the significance that van Fraassen attributes to it. In one of the classic papers in defense of scientific realism, Grover Maxwell argued in 1962 that there is a continuum in the spectrum of observation from ordinary unaided seeing down to the operation of a high-power microscope.[20] Van Fraassen concedes that the distinction is not a sharp one, that "observe" is a vague predicate, but insists that it is sufficient if the ends of the spectrum be clearly distinct, that is, that there be at least some clear cases of supposed interaction with theoretical entities which would not count as "observing."[21] He takes the operation of a cloud chamber, with its ionized tracks allegedly indicating the presence of charged entities such as electrons, to be a case where "observe" clearly ought not be used. One must not say, on noting such a track: I observed an electron.

To lay as much weight as this on the contingencies of the human sense organs is obviously problematic, as van Fraassen recognizes. There are organisms with sense-organs very different from ours that can perceive phenomena such as ultraviolet light or the direction of optical polarization. Why could there not, in principle, be organisms much smaller than we, able to perceive microentities that for us are theoretical and able also to communicate with us? Is not the notion of "observable in principle" hopelessly vague in the face of this sort of objection? How can it be used to draw a usable distinction between theoretical entities that do have ontological status and those that do not? Van Fraassen's response is cautious:

> It is, on the face of it, not irrational to commit oneself only to a search for theories that are empirically adequate, ones whose models fit the observable phenomena, while recognizing that what counts as an observable phenomenon is a function of what the epistemic community is (that *observable* is *observable-to-us*).[22]

So "observable" means here "observable in principle by us with the sense organs we presently have." But once again, why would "unobservable" in this sense be allowed the implications for epistemology and ontology that van Fraassen wants to attach to it?[23] The question is not whether the aim of science ought to be broadened to include the search for unobservable but real entities, though something could be said in favor of such a proposal. It is sufficient for the purposes of the realist to ask whether theories that are in van Fraassen's sense empirically adequate can also be shown under certain circumstances to have likely ontological implications.

Van Fraassen allows that the moons of Jupiter can be observed through a telescope; this counts as observation proper "since astronauts will no doubt be able to see them as well from close up."[24] But one cannot be said to "observe" by means of a high-power microscope (he alleges) because no such direct alternative is available to us in this case. What matters here is not so much the way the instrument works, the precise physical or theoretical principles involved. It is whether there is also, in principle, a direct unmediated alternative mode of observation available to us. The entity need not be observable *in practice*. The iron core that geologists tell us lies at the center of the earth is certainly not observable in practice; it is a theoretical entity since its existence is known only through a successful theory, but it may nonetheless be regarded as real, van Fraassen would say, because *in principle* we could go down there and check it out.

The quality of the evidence for this geological entity might, however, seem no better than that available for the chromosome viewed by microscope. Van Fraassen rests his case on an analysis of the aims of science, in an abstract sense of the term "aim," on the "epistemic attitude" (as he calls it) proper to science as an activity. And he thinks that reality-claims in the case of the chromosomes, but not the iron core, lie outside the permissible aims of science. Is there any way to make this distinction more plausible?

REFERENCE

Some theoretical entities (such as the iron core or the star) are of a kind that is relatively familiar from other contexts. We do not need a theory to tell us that iron exists or how it may be distinguished. But electrons are what quantum theory says they are, and our only warrant for knowing that they exist is the success of that theory. So there is a special class of theoretical entities whose *entire* warrant lies in the theory built around them. They correspond more or less to the unobservables of van Fraassen.

What makes them vulnerable is that the theory postulating them may itself change or even be dropped. This is where the problems of meaning change and of theory replacement so much discussed in recent philosophy of science become relevant. The antirealist might object to a reality-claim for electrons or genes not so much because they are unobservable but because the reference of the term "electron" may shift as theory changes. To counter this objection, it sounds as though the realist will have to provide a theory of reference that is able to secure a constancy of reference in regard to such theoretical terms. R. Rorty puts it this way:

> The need to pick out objects without the help of definitions, essences, and meanings of terms, produced (philosophers thought) a need for a "theory of reference" which would not employ the Fregean machinery which Quine had rendered dubious. This call for a theory of reference became assimilated to the demand for a "realistic" philosophy of science which would reinstate the pre-Kuhnian and pre-Feyerabendian notion that scientific inquiry made progress by finding out more and more about the same objects.[25]

Rorty is, of course, skeptical of theories of reference generally, and derides the idea that the problems of realism could be handled by such a theory. He chides Putnam, in particular, for leading philosophers to believe that they could be. Recall the celebrated realist's nightmare conjured up by Putnam:

> What if all the theoretical entities postulated by one generation (molecules, genes, etc. as well as electrons) invariably "don't exist" from the standpoint of later science? . . . One reason this

is a serious worry is that eventually the following meta-induction becomes compelling: just as no term used in the science of more than 50 (or whatever) years ago referred, so it will turn out that no term used now (except maybe observation-terms if there are such) refers.[26]

This is the "disastrous meta-induction" which at that time Putnam felt had to be blocked at all costs. But, of course, if the theoretical entities of one generation really did *not* have any existential claim on the next, realism simply would be false. It is, in part at least, because the history of science testifies to a substantial continuity in theoretical structures that we are led to the doctrine of scientific realism at all. Were the history of science *not* to do so, then we would have no logical or metaphysical grounds for believing in scientific realism in the first place. But this is to get ahead of the story. I introduced the issue of reference here not to argue its relevance one way or the other, but to note that one form of antirealism can be directed against the subset of theoretical entities which derive their definition entirely from a particular theory.

One way for a realist to evade objections of this kind is to focus on the manner in which theoretical entities can be causally connected with our measurement apparatus. An electron may be defined as the entity that is causally responsible for, among other things, certain kinds of cloud tracks. A small number of parameters, such as mass and charge, can be associated with it. Such an entity will be said to exist, that is, not to be an artifact of the apparatus, if a number of convergent sorts of causal lines lead to it. There would still have to be a theory of some sort to enable the causal tracking to be carried out. But the reason to affirm the entity's existence lies not in the success of the theory in which it plays an explanatory role, but in the operation of traceable causal lines. Ian Hacking urges that this defense of realism, which relies on experiential interactions, avoids the problems of meaning-change that beset arguments based on inference to the best explanation.[27]

TRUTH AS CORRESPONDENCE

The most energetic criticisms of realism, of late, have been coming from those who see it as the embodiment of an old-fashioned, and now (in their view) thoroughly discredited, attachment to the notion of truth as some sort of "correspondence" with an "external world." These criticisms take quite different forms, and it is impossible to do them justice in a short space. The rejected doctrine is one that would hold that even in the ideal limit, the best scientific theory, one that has all the proper methodological virtues, could be false. This embodies what the critics have come to call the "God's eye view," the view that there may be more to the world than our language and our sciences can, even in principle, express. They concede that the doctrine has been a persuasive one ("it is impossible to find a philosopher before Kant who was *not* a metaphysical realist");[28] its denial seems, indeed, shockingly anthropomorphic. But they are in agreement that no philosophic sense can be made of the central metaphor of correspondence: "To single out a correspondence between two domains, one needs some independent access to both domains."[29] And, of course, an independent "access to the noumenal objects" is impossible.

The two main protagonists of this view are, perhaps, Rorty and Putnam. Rorty is the more emphatic of the two. He defends a form of pragmatism that discounts the traditional preoccupations of the philosopher with such Platonic notions as truth and goodness. He sees the Greek attempt to separate *doxa* and *epistēmē* as misguided; he equally refuses the modern trap of trying to analyze the meaning of "true," because it would involve an "impossible attempt to step outside our skins." [30] The pragmatist

> drops the notion of truth as correspondence with reality altogether, and says that modern science does not enable us to cope because it corresponds, it just plain enables us to cope. His argument for the view is that several hundred years of effort have failed to make interesting sense of the notion of "correspondence," either of thoughts to things or of words to things. [31]

Does Rorty deny scientific realism, that is, the view that the long-term success of a scientific theory gives us a warrant to believe that the entities it postulates do exist? It is not clear. What is clear, first, is that he rejects any kind of argument for scientific realism that would explain the success of a theory in terms of a correspondence with the real. And second, he denies that scientific claims have a privileged status, that the scientists' table (in Eddington's famous story) is the only real table. Science, he retorts, is just "one genre of literature," a way "to cope with various bits of the universe," just as ethics helps us cope with other bits. [32]

Putnam, in contrast, is willing to ask the traditional philosophic questions. His patron is Kant rather than James. [33] "Truth" he defines as "an idealization of rational acceptability." [34] He has more specific objections to urge against the offending metaphysical version of realism than does Rorty, whose argument amounts to claiming that it has failed to make "interesting sense." [35] Does he link this rejection with a rejection of scientific realism? Certainly not in his *Meaning and the Moral Sciences* (1978), where he defends scientific realism by urging that it permits the best explanation of the success of science. It is somewhat more difficult to be sure where his allegiance lies in his more recent pieces; his earlier enthusiasm for scientific realism seems, at the least, to be waning. [36] He attacks materialism with its assumption of mind-independent things, [37] as well as reductionism.

> We are too realistic about physics . . . [because] we see physics (or some hypothetical future physics) as the One True Theory, and not simply as a rationally acceptable description suited for certain problems and purposes. [38]

This does not sound like scientific realism. Be this as it may, however, it seems clear that scientific realism is not the main target in this debate. The target is a set of metaphysical views, views (it is true) that scientific realists have in the past usually taken for granted. I suspect that Rorty would allow that genes exist and that dinosaurs once roamed the earth, as long as these claims are not given a status that is denied to more mundane statements about chairs and goldfish. But can we allow him this position so easily?

Recall that the original motivation for the doctrine of scientific realism was not a perverse philosopher's desire to inquire into the unknowable or to show that only the scientist's entities are "really real." It was a response to the challenges of fictionalism and instrumentalism, which over and over again in the history of science asserted that the entities of the scientist are fictional, that they do not exist in the everyday sense in which chairs and goldfish do. Now, how does Rorty respond to this? Has he an argument to offer? If he has, it would be an argument for scientific realism. It would also (as far as I can see) be a return to philosophy in the "old style" that he thinks we ought to have outgrown.

My own inclinations are to defend a form of metaphysical realism, though not necessarily under all the diverse specifications Putnam offers of it.[39] But that is not to the point here. What is to the point is that scientific realism is not immediately undermined by the rejection of metaphysical realism, though the character of the claim scientific realism makes obviously depends on whether or not it is joined to a concept of truth in which the embattled notion of "correspondence" plays a part. Further, the type of argument most often alleged in its support *does* use the language of correspondence: it is the approximate correspondence between the physical structure of the world and postulated theoretical entities that is held to explain why a theory succeeds as well as it does.[40] Readers will have to decide for themselves whether my argument below does "make interesting sense" or not.

VARIETIES OF ANTIREALISM

It may be worthwhile at this point, looking back at the territory we have traversed, to draw two rough distinctions between types of antirealism. *General antirealism* denies ontological status to theoretical entities of science generally, while *limited antirealism* denies it only to certain classes of theoretical entities, such as those that are said to be unobservable in principle. Thus, the arguments of Laudan, based as they are on a supposedly general review of the history of scientific theories, would lead him to a *general* form of antirealism, one that would exclude existence status to *any* theoretical entity whose existence is warranted only by the success of the theory in which it occurs. In contrast, van Fraassen is claiming, as I have shown, only a *limited* form of antirealism.

Second, we might distinguish between *strong antirealism,* which denies any kind of ontological status to all (or part) of the theoretical entities of science, and *weak antirealism* which allows theoretical entities existence of an everyday "chairs and goldfish" kind,[41] but insists that there is some further sense of "really really there," which realists purportedly have in mind, that is to be rejected. Classical instrumentalism would be of the former kind (strong antirealists), whereas many of the more recent critics of scientific realism appear to fall in the latter category (weak antirealists). These (weak antirealist) critics are often, as I have shown, hard to place. They reject any attempt to justify scientific realism as involving dubious metaphysics, but appear to accept a weak (realist) claim of the "everyday" kind without any form of supporting argument.[42] Their rhetoric is antirealist in tone, but their position often seems compatible with the most basic claim of scientific realism, namely that there is reason to believe that the theoretical terms of successful theories refer. This gives the weak antirealists' position a puzzling sort of undeclared status where they appear to have the best of both worlds. I am inclined to think that their effort to have it both ways must in the end fail.

THE CONVERGENCES OF STRUCTURAL EXPLANATION

The basic claim made by scientific realism, once again, is that the long-term success of a scientific theory gives reason to believe that something like the entities and structure postulated by the theory actually exists. There are four important qualifications built into this: (1) the theory must be successful over a significant period of time; (2) the explanatory success of the theory gives some reason, though not a conclusive warrant, to believe it; (3) what is believed is that the theoretical structures are *something like* the structure of the real world; (4) no claim is made for a special, more basic, privileged, form of existence for the postulated entities.[43] These qualifications: "significant period," "some reason," "something like," sound very vague, of course, and vagueness is a challenge to the philosopher. Can they not be made more precise? I am not sure that they can; efforts to strengthen the thesis of scientific realism have, as I have shown, left it open to easy refutation.

The case for scientific realism can be made in a variety of ways. Maxwell, Salmon, Newton-Smith, Boyd, Putnam, and others have argued it in well-known essays. I am not going to comment on their arguments here since my aim is to outline what I think to be the best case for scientific realism. My argument will, of course, bear many resemblances to theirs. What may be the most distinctive feature of my argument is my stress on structural types of explanation, and on the role played by the criterion of fertility in such explanations.

Stage one of the argument will be directed especially against general antirealism. I want to argue that in many parts of natural science there has been, over the last two centuries, a progressive discovery of *structure*. Scientists construct theories which explain the observed features of the physical world by postulating models of the hidden structure of the entities being studied. This structure is taken to account causally for the observable phenomena, and the theoretical model provides an approximation of the phenomena from which the explanatory power of the model derives. This is the standard account of structural explanation, the type of explanation that first began to show its promise in the eighteenth and early nineteenth centuries in such sciences as geology and chemistry.[44]

I want to consider some of the areas where the growth in our knowledge of structure has been relatively steady. Let me begin with geology, a good place for a realist to begin. The visible strata and their fossil contents came to be interpreted as the evidence for an immense stretch of time past in which various processes such as sedimentation and volcanic activity occurred. There was a lively debate about the mechanisms of mountain building and the like, but gradually a more secure knowledge of the past aeons built up. The Carboniferous period succeeded the Devonian and was, in turn, succeeded by the Permian. The length of the periods, the climatic changes, and the dominant life forms were gradually established with increasing accuracy. It should be stressed that a geological period, such as the Devonian, is a theoretical entity. Further, it is, in principle, inaccessible to our direct observation. Yet our theories have allowed us to set up certain temporal boundaries, in this case (the Devonian period) roughly 400 to 350 million years ago, when the dominant life form on earth was fish and a number of important developments in the vertebrate line occurred.

The long-vanished species of the Devonian are theoretical entities about which we have come to know more and more in a relatively steady way. Of course, there have been controversies, particularly over the sudden extinction of life forms such as occurred at the end of the Cretaceous period and over the precise evolutionary relationships among given species. But the very considerable theory changes that have occurred since Hutton's day do not alter the fact that the growth in our knowledge of the sorts of life forms that inhabited the earth aeons ago has been pretty cumulative. The realist would say that the success of this synthesis of geological, physical, and biological theories gives us good reason to believe that species of these kinds did exist at the times and in the conditions proposed. Most antirealists (I suspect) would agree. But if they do, they must concede that this mode of retroductive argument can warrant, at least in some circumstances, a realist implication.

Geologists have also come to know (in the scientists' sense of the term "know") a good deal about the interior of the earth. There is a discontinuity between the material of the crust and the much denser mantle, the "Moho" as it is called after its Yugoslavian discoverer, about 5 kilometers under the ocean bed and much deeper, around 30 or 40 kilometers, under the continents. There is a further discontinuity between the solid mantle and the molten core at a depth of 2,900 kilometers. All this is inferred from the characteristics of seismic waves at the surface. Does this structural model of the earth simply serve as a device to enable the scientist to predict the seismic findings more accurately, or does it enable an additional ontological claim to be made about the actual hidden structures of earth? The realist would argue that the explanatory power of the geologist's hypothesis, its steadily improving accuracy, gives good ground to suppose that something can be inferred about real structures that lie far beneath us.

An elegant example of a quite different sort would come from cell biology. Here, the techniques of microscopy have interwoven with the theories of genetics to produce an ever more detailed picture of what goes on inside the cell. The chromosome first appeared under a microscope; only gradually was the gene, the theoretical unit of hereditary transmission, linked to it. Later the gene came to be associated with a particular locus on the chromosome. The unraveling by Crick and Watson of the biochemical structure of the chromosome made it possible to define the structure of the gene in a relatively simple way and has allowed at least the beginnings of an understanding of how the gene operates to direct the growth of the organism. In his book, *The Matter of Life,* Michael Simon has traced this story in some detail, and has argued that its progressive character can best be understood in terms of a realist philosophy of science.[45]

One further example of this sort of progression can be found in chemistry. The complex molecules of both inorganic and organic chemistry have been more accurately charted over the past century. The atomic constituents and the spatial relations among them can be specified on the basis both of measurement, using X-ray diffraction patterns, for example, and on the basis of a theory that specifies where each kind of atom *ought* to fit. Indeed, this knowledge has enabled a computer program to be designed that can "invent" molecules, can suggest that certain configurations would yield a new type of complex molecule and can even predict what some of the molecule's properties are likely to be.

To give a realist construal to the molecular models of the chemist is not to imply that the nature of the constituent atoms and of the bonding between them is exhaustively known. It is only to suppose that the elements and spatial relationships of the model disclose, in a partial and tentative way, real structures within complex molecules. These structures are coming to be more exactly charted, using a variety of techniques both experimental and theoretical. The coherence of the outcome of these widely different techniques, and the reliability of the chemist's intuitions as he decides which atom must fit a particular spot in the lattice, are most easily understood in terms of the realist thesis.

These examples may serve to make two points. The first is that the discontinuous replace-ment account of the history of theories favored by antirealists is seen to be one-sided. If one focuses on global explanatory theories, particularly in mechanics, it can come to seem that theoretical entities are modified beyond recognition as theories change. Dirac's electron has little in common with the original Thomson electron; Einstein's concept of time is a long way from Newton's, and so on. These conventional examples of conceptual change could them-selves be scrutinized to see whether they will bear the weight the antirealist gives them. But it may be more effective to turn from explanatory elements such as electrons to explanatory structures such as those of the organic chemist, and note, as a historical fact, the high degree of continuity in the relevant history.

Second, one could note the sort of confidence that scientists have in structural explana-tions of this sort. It is not merely a confidence in the empirical adequacy of the predictions these models enable them to make. It is a confidence in the model itself as an analysis of com-plex real structure. Look at any textbook of polymer chemistry to verify this. Of course, the chemists could be wrong to build this sort of realist expectation into their work, but the ar-guments of philosophers are not likely to convince them of it.

A third consequence one might draw from the history of the structural sciences is that there is a single form of retroductive inference involved throughout. As C. S. Peirce stressed in his discussion of retroduction, it is the degree of success of the retroductive hypothesis that warrants the degree of its acceptance as truth. The point is a simple one, and indeed is already implicit in Aristotle's *Posterior Analytics.* Aristotle indicates that what certifies as *demonstra-tive* a piece of reasoning about the relation between the nearness of planets and the fact that they do not twinkle, is the degree to which the reasoning *explains.* This connection between the explanatory and the epistemic character of scientific reasoning is constantly stressed in Renaissance and early modern discussions of hypothetical reasoning.[46]

What the history of recent science has taught us is not that retroductive inference yields a plausible knowledge of causes. We already knew this on *logical* grounds. What we have learned is that retroductive inference *works* in the world we have and with the senses we have for investigating that world. This is a contingent fact, as far as I can see. This is why realism as I have defined it is in part an empirical thesis. There could well be a universe in which ob-servable regularities would *not* be explainable in terms of hidden structures, that is, a world in which retroduction would not work. Indeed, until the eighteenth century, there was no strong empirical case to be made against that being *our* universe. Scientific realism is not a logical doctrine about the implications of successful retroductive inference. Nor is it a metaphysical claim about how any world *must* be. It has both logical and metaphysical components. It is a quite limited claim that purports to explain why certain ways of proceeding in science have worked out as well as they (contingently) have.

That they have worked out well in such structural sciences as geology, astrophysics, and molecular biology, is apparent. And the presumption in these sciences is that the model-structures provide an increasingly accurate insight into the real structures that are causally responsible for the phenomena being explained. This may be thought to give a reliable pre-sumption in favor of the realist implications of retroductive inference in natural science generally. But one has to be wary here. Much depends on the sort of theoretical entity one is dealing with; I have already noted, for instance, some of the perplexities posed by quantum-mechanical entities. Much depends too on how *well* the theoretical entity has served to explain: How important a part of the theory has it been? Has it been a sort of optional extra feature like the solid spheres of Ptolemaic astronomy? Or has it guided research in the way the Bohr model of the hydrogen atom did? What kind of fertility has the theoretical entity shown?

FERTILITY AND METAPHOR

Kuhn lists five values that scientists look for when evaluating a scientific theory: predictive accuracy, consistency, breadth of scope, simplicity, fertility.[47] It is the last of these that bears most directly on the problem of realism. Fertility is usually equated with the ability to make novel predictions. A good theory is expected to predict novel phenomena, that is, phenomena that were not part of the set to be explained. The further in kind these novel phenomena are from the original set, and thus the more unexpected they are, the better the model is said to be. The display of this sort of fertility reduces the likelihood of the theory's being an ad hoc one, one invented just for the original occasion but with no further scope to it.

There has been much debate about the significance of his notion of ad hoc. Clearly, it will appeal to the realist and will seem arbitrary to the antirealist. The realist takes an ad hoc hypothesis not to be a genuine theory, that is, not to give any insight into real structure and therefore to have no ground for further extension. The fact that it accounts for the original data is accidental and testifies to the ingenuity of the inventor rather than to any deeper fit. When the theory is first proposed, it is often difficult to tell whether or not it is ad hoc on the basis of the other criteria of theory appraisal. This is why fertility is so important a criterion from the realist standpoint.

The antirealist will insist that the novel facts predicted by the theory simply increases its scope and thus makes it more acceptable. They will say that there is no significance to the time order in which predictions are made; if they are successful, they count as evidence whether or not they pertain to the data originally to be explained. A straightforward application of Bayes's theorem shows this, assuming of course the antirealist standpoint. Yet scientists seem to set a lot of store in the notion of ad hoc. Are scientific intuitions sufficiently captured by a translation into antirealist language? Is an ad hoc hypothesis one that just happens not to be further generalizable, or is it one that does not give sufficient insight into real structure to permit any further extension?

Rather than debate this already much-debated issue further, let me turn to a second aspect of fertility which is less often noted but which may be more significant for our problem.[48] The first aspect of fertility, novelty, had to do with what could logically be inferred from the theory, its logical resources, one might put it. But a good model has more resources than these. If an anomaly is encountered or if the theory is unable to predict one way or the other in a domain where it seems it *should* be able to do so, the model itself may serve to suggest possible modifications or extensions. These are *suggested,* not implied. Therefore, a creative move on the part of the scientist is required.

In this case, the model functions somewhat as a metaphor does in language. The poet uses a metaphor not just as decoration but as a means of expressing a complex thought. A good metaphor has its own sort of precision, as any poet will tell you. It can lead the mind in ways that literal language cannot. The poet who is developing a metaphor is led by suggestion, not by implication; the reader of the poem queries the metaphor and searches among its many resonances for the ones that seem best to bear insight. The simplistic "man is a wolf" examples of metaphors have misled philosophers into supposing that what is going on in metaphor is a comparison between two already partly understood things. The only challenge then would be to decide in what respects the analogy holds. In the more complex metaphors of modern poetry, something much more interesting is happening. The metaphor is helping to illuminate something that is not well understood in advance, perhaps, some aspect of human life that we find genuinely puzzling or frightening or mysterious. The manner in which such metaphors work is by tentative suggestion. The minds of poet and reader alike are actively engaged in creating. Obviously, much more would need to be said about this, but it would lead me too far afield at this point.[49]

The good model has something of this metaphoric power.[50] Let me recall another one here, from geology once again. It had long been known that the west coast of Africa and the east coast of South America show striking similarities in terms of strata and their fossil contents. In 1915, Alfred Wegener put forward a hypothesis to explain these and other similarities, such as those between the major systems of folds in Europe and North America. The continental drift notion that he developed in *The Origins of Continents and Oceans* was not at first accepted, although it admittedly did explain a great deal. There were too many anomalies: How could the continents cut through the ocean floor, for example, since the material of the ocean floor is considerably harder than that of the continents? In the 1960s, new evidence of seafloor spreading led H. Hess and others to a modification of the original model. The moving elements are not the continents but rather vast plates on which the continents as well as the seafloor are carried. And so the continental drift hypothesis developed into the plate tectonic model.

The story has been developed so ably from the methodological standpoint by Rachel Laudan[51] and Henry Frankel[52] that I can be very brief, and simply refer you to their writings. The original theoretical entity, a floating continent, did not logically entail the plates of the new model. But in the context of anomalies and new evidence it did *suggest* them. And these plates in turn suggested new modifications. What happens when the plates pull apart are seafloor rifts, with quite specific properties. The upwelling lava will have magnetic directional properties that will depend on its orientation relative to the earth's magnetic field at the time. This allows the lava to be dated, and the gradual pulling apart of the plates to be charted. It was the discovery of such dated strips paralleling the midocean rifts that proved decisive in swinging geologists over to the new model in the mid-1960s. What happens when the plates collide? One is carried down under (subduction); the other may be upthrust to form a mountain ridge. One can see here how the original metaphor is gradually extended and made more specific.

In a recent critical discussion of my views on fertility and metaphor,[53] Michael Bradie has urged as a weakness of my argument that one needs to give a sufficiently precise account of metaphor to allow one to understand what would count as a metaphorical extension, so as to know when two theory stages can be identified as different stages of the same theory. My response is simple and, perhaps, simplistic. If the original model (say, continental drift) suggested the later modification as a plausible way of meeting the known anomalies and of incorporating the new evidence, then I would call this a metaphorical extension. Are continental drift and the plate tectonic model two stages of the same theory or two different theories? It all depends on how "theory" is defined and how sharply theories are individuated. I do not see that very much hangs on this decision, one way or the other.

The important thing to note is that there *are* structural continuities from one stage to the next, even though there are also important structural modifications. What provides the continuity is the underlying metaphor of moving continents that had been in contact a long time ago and had very gradually developed over the course of time. One feature of the original theory, that the continents are the units, is eventually dropped; other features, such as what happens when the floating plates collide, are thought through and made specific in ways that allow a whole mass of new data to fall into place.

How does all this bear on the argument for realism? The answer should be obvious. This kind of fertility is a persistent feature of structural explanations in the natural sciences over the last three centuries and especially during the last century. How can it best be understood? It appears to be a contingent feature of the history of science. There seems to be no a priori reason why it *had* to work out that way, as I have already shown. What best explains it is the supposition that the model approximates sufficiently well the structures of the world that are causally responsible for the phenomena to be explained to make it profitable for the scientist to take the model's metaphoric extensions seriously. It is because there is something like a floating plate under our feet that it is proper to ask: What happens when plates collide, and what mechanisms would suffice to keep them in motion? These questions do not arise from the original theory if it is taken as no more than a formalism able to give a reasonably accurate predictive account of the data then at hand. If the continental drift hypothesis had no implications for what is really going on beneath us, for the hidden structures responsible for the phenomena of the earth's surface, then the subsequent history of that hypothesis would be unintelligible. The antirealist cannot, it seems to me, make sense of such sequences, which are pretty numerous in the recent history of all the natural sciences, basic mechanics, as always, constituting a special case.

One further point is worth stressing in regard to our geological story. Some theoretical features of the model, such as the midocean rifts, could be checked directly and their existence observationally shown. Here, as so often in science, theoretical entities previously unobserved, or in some cases even thought to be unobservable, are in fact observed and the expectations of theory are borne out, to no one's surprise. The separation between observable and unobservable postulated by many antirealists in regard to ontological status does not seem to stand up. The same mode of argument is used in each case; it is not clear why in one case expectations of real existence are accorded to the theoretical entity whereas in other cases, logically similar in explanatory character, these expectations are denied. The ontological inference, let me insist again, must be far more hesitant in some cases than in others. There is no question of according the same ontological status to *all* theoretical entities by virtue of a similar degree of fertility evinced over a significant period of time. Nonetheless, such fertility finds its best explanation in a broadly realist account of science.

Does this form of argument commit the realist to holding that every regularity in the world must be explained in terms of ontological structure? This turns out to be van Fraassen's main line of attack against realism. He takes it that the realist is committed to finding hidden variables in quantum mechanics. Since the odds against this are now quite high, and since, in any event, this would commit the realist to one possible world where the other looks just as possible, van Fraassen takes this to refute realism. But as I have shown, realism is not a regulative principle, and it does not lay down a strategy for scientists. Realism would not be refuted if the decay of individual radioactive atoms turns out to be genuinely undetermined. It does not look to the future; much more modestly, realism looks to quite specific past historical sequences and asks what best explains them. Realism does not look at *all* science, nor at all future science, just at a good deal of past science which (let me say it again) might not have worked out to support realism the way it did. The realist seeks an explanation for the regularities he finds in science, just as the scientist seeks an explanation for regularities he finds in the world. But if in particular cases he cannot find an explanation or cannot even show that there is no explanation, this in no sense shows that his original aim has somehow been discredited.

Thus, what van Fraassen describes as the "nominalist response" of the antirealist must in the end be rejected. He characterizes it in this way:

> That the observable phenomena exhibit these regularities, because of which they fit the theory, is merely a brute fact, and may or may not have an explanation in terms of unobservable facts "behind the phenomena"—it really does not matter to the goodness of the theory, nor to our understanding of the world.[54]

I hope I have shown that the nominalist resolve to leave such regularities as the extraordinary fertility of our scientific theories at the level of brute fact is unphilosophical. Furthermore, I hope I have shown that it makes a very great deal of difference to the explanatory power or goodness of a theory whether it can call on effective metaphors of hidden structure. And I doubt whether it is really necessary to prove that such metaphors are important to our understanding of the world and of the role of science in achieving such understanding.

EPILOGUE

Finally, I return to the weighty issues of reference and truth which are so dear to the heart of the philosopher. Clearly, my views on metaphor would lead me to reject the premise on which so much of the recent debate on realism has been based. Van Fraassen puts it thus:

> Science aims to give us, in its theories, a literally true story of what the world is like; and acceptance of a scientific theory involves the belief that it is true. This is the correct statement of scientific realism.[55]

I do not think that acceptance of a scientific theory involves the belief that it is true. Science aims at fruitful metaphor and at ever more detailed structure. To suppose that a theory is literally true would imply, among other things, that no further anomaly could, in principle, arise from any quarter in regard to it. At best, it is hard to see this as anything more than an idealized "horizon-claim," which would be quite misleading if applied to the actual work of the scientist.

The point is that the resources of metaphor are essential to the work of science and that the construction and retention of metaphor must be seen as part of the aim of science.

Scientists in general accept the quantum theory of radiation. Do they believe it to be true? Scientists are very uncomfortable at this use of the word "true," because it suggests that the theory is definitive in its formulation. As has often been pointed out, the notion of *acceptance* is very complex, indeed ambiguous. It is basically a pragmatic notion: one accepts an explanation as the best one available; one accepts a theory as a good basis for further research, and so forth. In no case would it be correct to say that acceptance of a theory entails belief in its truth.

The realist would not use the term "true" to describe a good theory. He would suppose that the structures of the theory give some insight into the structures of the world. But he could not, in general, say how good the insight is. He has no independent access to the world, as the antirealist constantly reminds him. His assurance that there is a fit, however rough, between the structures of the theory and the structures of the world comes not from a comparison between them but from the sort of argument I sketched above, which concludes that only this sort of reasoning would explain certain contingent features of the history of recent science. The term "approximate truth," which has sometimes been used in this debate, is risky because it immediately invites questions such as: *how* approximate?, and how is the degree of approximation to be measured? If I am right in my presentation of realism, these questions are unanswerable because they are inappropriate.

The language of theoretical explanation is of a quite special sort. It is open-ended and ever capable of further development. It is metaphoric in the sense in which the poetry of the symbolists is metaphoric, not because it uses explicit analogy or because it is imprecise, but because it has resources of suggestion that are the most immediate testimony of its ontological worth. Thus, the M. Dummett-Putnam claim that a realist is committed to holding with respect to any given theory, that the sentences of the theory are either true or false,[56] quite misses the mark where scientific realism is concerned. Indeed, I am tempted to say (though this would be a bit too strong) that if they are literally true or false, they are not of much use as the basis for a research program.

Ought the realist be apologetic, as his pragmatist critic thinks he should be, about such vague-sounding formulations as these: that a good model gives an insight into real structure and that the long-term success of a theory, in most cases, gives reason to believe that something like the theoretical entities of that theory actually exist? I do not think so. The temptation to try for a sharper formulation must be resisted by the realist, since it would almost certainly compromise the sources from which his case derives its basic strength. And the antirealist must beware of the opposite temptation to suppose that whatever cannot be said in a semantically definitive way is not worth saying.

NOTES

The first version of this essay was delivered as an invited paper at the Western Division meeting of the American Philosophical Association in April 1981. I am indebted to Larry Laudan for his incisive commentary on that occasion, and to the numerous discussions we have had on this topic.

[1] It was the confidence that, as a student of physics, I had developed in this belief that led me, in my first published paper in philosophy, to formulate a defense of scientific realism against the instrumentalism prevalent at the time among philosophers of science. (See "Realism in Modern Cosmology," *Proceedings American Catholic Philosophical Association* 29 [1955]: 137–150.) Much has changed in philosophy of science since that time; a different sort of defense is (as we shall see) now called for.

[2] This is the theme of C. G. Hempel's classic essay, "The Theoretician's Dilemma," *Minnesota Studies in the Philosophy of Science* 3 (1958): 37–98.

[3] For the details of this story, see E. McMullin, *Newton on Matter and Activity* (Notre Dame: University of Notre Dame Press, 1978), especially chap. 4: "How is Matter Moved?"

[4] In a recent critique of "metaphysical realism," Hilary Putnam has Newton defending the view that particles act at a distance across empty space. *Reason, Truth and History* (Cambridge: Cambridge University Press, 1981), 73. Though the *Principia* has often been made to yield that claim, this view is, in fact, the one alternative that Newton at all times steadfastly rejected.

[5] Newton's other suggestion, briefly explored in the 1690s, that forces might be nothing other than the manifestations of God's direct involvement in the governance of the universe, *could,* however, be properly described as "metaphysical"; this is not, of course, to say that it was illegitimate.

[6] H. Putnam, "Why There Isn't a Ready-Made World," *Synthese* 51 (1982): 141–168; see 163. Also available in volume 3 of Putnam's Philosophical Papers Series, *Realism and Reason* (Cambridge: Cambridge University Press, 1983).

[7] According to Putnam, Newton, though no positivist, "strongly rejected the idea that his theory of universal gravitation could or should be read as a description of metaphysically ultimate fact. 'Hypotheses non fingo' was a rejection of metaphysical hypotheses, not of scientific ones" (*Reason, Truth and History,* 163). This supposed rejection of metaphysics would, however, place Newton much closer to positivism than he really was. In the *Principia,* Newton shows himself well aware that different interpretations (he calls them "physical," not "metaphysical") can be given of attraction, and he tries to deflect anticipated criticism of this ambiguity by intimating that one can prescind such interpretation by remaining at the "mathematical" level. But he knew perfectly well that he could not *remain* at this level and still claim to have "explained" the planetary motions. In his own later writing, much of it unpublished in his lifetime, he constantly tried out different hypotheses, as I have already noted. He knew, of course, that these were speculative, that none of them was "metaphysically ultimate fact." But I can find nothing in his writing to suggest that he believed that in principle a decision between these alternatives could not be reached. The task of the natural philosopher (he would have said) was to try to adjudicate between them.

[8] As Fine argues in "The Natural Ontological Attitude," (in J. Leplin [ed.], *Scientific Realism.* Berkeley, California: University of California Press, pp. 83–107).

[9] Richard Healey calls it "naive realism"; "naive" not in a deprecatory sense, but as connoting the "natural attitude." See "Quantum Realism: Naiveté Is No Excuse," *Synthese* 42 (1979): 121–144.

[10] Especially owing to the developments in recent years of the original quantum formalism, associated not only with physicists (Bell, Kochen, Specker, Wigner) but also with philosophers of science (Cartwright, Fine, Gibbins, Glymour, Putnam, Redhead, Shimony, van Fraassen, and others).

[11] This argument may be found, for example, in Fine, "Natural Ontological Attitude," sec. II.

[12] G. Chew, "Impasse for the Elementary-Particle Concept," *Great Ideas Today* (Chicago: Encyclopedia Britannica, 1973), 367–389; see 387–389. In his more recent, and very speculative combinatorial topology, Chew has managed to construct a formalism in which the various elementary "particles" are replaced by combinations of triangles (shades of the *Timaeus*!). Though quarks do not appear in his formalism, Chew has hopes of obtaining all the results that quantum field theory does and perhaps even more.

[13] See, for example, W. Heisenberg, "Tradition in Science," in *The Nature of Scientific Discovery,* ed. O. Gingerich (Washington: Smithsonian, 1975), 219–236.

[14] In the last few years, this claim has come to seem a lot less plausible, in the short run at least, since quantum field theory has been scoring notable successes, while work on the S-matrix formalism has been all but abandoned.

[15] T. Kuhn, *The Structure of Scientific Revolutions,* 2d ed. (Chicago: University of Chicago Press, 1970), 206.

[16] See, in particular, L. Laudan, "A Confutation of Convergent Realism," (Leplin [ed.], *Scientific Realism, op. cit.,* pp. 140–153).

[17] E. Kant, *Critique of Pure Reason,* A226/B273.

[18] See G. G. Brittan, *Kant's Theory of Science* (Princeton: Princeton University Press, 1978), chap. 5.

[19] B. C. van Fraassen, *The Scientific Image* (Oxford: Clarendon Press, 1980), 73.

[20] G. Maxwell, "The Ontological Status of Theoretical Entities," *Minnesota Studies in Philosophy of Science* 3 (1962): 3–27.

[21] Van Fraassen, *The Scientific Image,* 16.

[22] Ibid., 19.

[23] Van Fraassen complicates the picture further by also allowing the sense of "observable" to depend on the theory being tested. "To find the limits of what is observable in the world described by theory T, we must inquire into T itself, and the theories used as auxiliaries in the testing and application of T." Ibid., 57.

[24] Ibid., 16.

[25] R. Rorty, *Philosophy and the Mirror of Nature* (Princeton: Princeton University Press, 1979), 274–275.

[26] H. Putnam, "What is Realism?" (Leplin [ed.], *Scientific Realism, op. cit.,* pp. 140–153).

[27] See I. Hacking, "Experimentation and Scientific Realism," (Leplin [ed.], *Scientific Realism, op. cit.,* pp. 154–172). It is not clear to me whether one comes up with the same list of entities using Hacking's way as one does with the more usual form of argument relying on explanatory efficacy.

[28] Putnam, *Reason, Truth and History,* 57.

[29] Ibid., 74.

[30] R. Rorty, *Consequences of Pragmatism* (Minneapolis: University of Minnesota Press, 1982), xix.

[31] Ibid., xvii.

[32] Ibid., xliii.

[33] I must say that I have difficulties in seeing that Kant "all but says that he is giving up the correspondence theory of truth" (Putnam, *Reason, Truth and History,* 63), and that he "is best read as proposing for the first time what I have called the 'internalist' or 'internal realist' view of truth" (ibid., 60).

[34] Ibid., 55. This puts him close to Dummett's camp in a different philosophical battle.

[35] These are briefly sketched in "Realism and Reason," final chapter of H. Putnam's *Meaning and the Moral Sciences* (London: Routledge, 1978). See also Putnam, "Why There Isn't a Ready-Made World." His main argument is that even if the world did have a "built-in structure" (which he denies), this could not single out *one* correspondence between signs and objects.

[36] "Scientific realism" does not occur in the topic index of Putnam's, *Reason, Truth and History,* even though other "realisms" are discussed extensively.

[37] See Putnam, "Why There Isn't a Ready-Made World."

[38] Putnam, *Reason, Truth and History,* 143. It is curious that both he and Rorty (*Consequences of Pragmatism,* xxvi) criticize the realistic tendency to suppose that physics can reach the "one true theory." But they both define the offending sort of realism precisely as the view that supposes that even in the ideal limit such a theory may not be reached. In fact, according to Putnam's own definition, the "one true theory" is, by definition, what physics *does* reach!

[39] These become less and less sympathetic as time goes on. I do not see, for example, why a metaphysical realist should defend the claim that "the world consists of some fixed totality of mind-independent objects," or that "there is exactly one true and complete description of the way 'the world is'" (Putnam, *Reason, Truth and History,* 49). Paul Horwich, in an attempt to pin down Putnam's notion, makes it follow from "a more general and fundamental aspect of metaphysical realism," namely, "the view according to which truth is so inexorably separated from our practice of confirmation that we can have no reasonable expectation that our methods of justification are even remotely correct." Horwich claims that Putnam's notion is "committed to an uncomfortable extent to the possibility of unverifiable truth: no truths are verifiable or even inconclusively confirmable" (P. Horwich, "Three Forms of Realism," *Synthese* 51 [1982]: 181–201; see 188, 189). Not only does this go a long way, in my opinion, beyond what Putnam believes metaphysical realism amounts to, but it also makes a

straw man of the position. In fact, I know of no philosopher who would defend it in the form in which Horwich states it.

[40] Since this was the type of argument that Putnam endorsed in his earlier work, citing Boyd, one can see why he might now have backed away not only from the supporting argument but also from the thesis itself.

[41] This is what Horwich calls "epistemological realism." P. Horwich, "Three Forms of Realism," 181. I am not as convinced as he is that this position is "opposed only by the rare skeptic."

[42] Fine's essay . . . appears to fall into this category. The first section of it is devoted to a critique of all the arguments normally brought in support of scientific realism; the second section argues that instrumentalism had a much more salutary influence than realism did on the growth of modern science. But the final section proposes, as the consequence of a "natural ontological attitude," that "there really are molecules and atoms" and rejects the instrumentalist assertion that they are just fictions. But some argument is needed for this, beyond calling this attitude "natural." And to say that the realist adds to this acceptable "core position" an unacceptable "foot-stamping shout of 'Really,'" an "emphasis that all this is really so," leaves me puzzled as to what this difference is supposed to amount to.

[43] The issues as to whether these entities *ought* to be attributed privileged status (as materialism and various forms of reductionism maintain) will not be discussed here.

[44] I traced the history and main features of this form of explanation in "Structural Explanation," *American Philosophical Quarterly* 15 (1978): 139–147.

[45] M. Simon, *The Matter of Life* (New Haven: Yale University Press, 1971).

[46] See the discussion of this in E. McMullin, "The Conception of Science in Galileo's Work," *New Perspectives on Galileo,* ed. R. Butts and J. Pitt (Dordrecht: Reidel, 1978), 209–257.

[47] T. Kuhn, *The Essential Tension* (Chicago: University of Chicago Press, 1977), 321–322. See also E. McMullin, "Values in Science," PSA Presidential Address 1982, in *PSA* 1982, vol. 2.

[48] For a fuller discussion of the criterion of fertility, see E. McMullin, "The Fertility of Theory and the Unit for Appraisal in Science," *Boston Studies in the Philosophy of Science,* ed. R. S. Cohen et al., 39 (1976): 395–432.

[49] See, for instance, P. Wheelwright, *Metaphor and Reality* (Bloomington: Indiana University Press, 1962), esp. chap. 4, "Two Ways of Metaphor"; and E. McMullin, "The Motive for Metaphor," *Proceedings American Catholic Philosophical Association* 55 (1982): 27–39.

[50] I have elsewhere developed one instance of this in some detail, the Bohr model of the H-atom as it guided research from 1911 to 1926. See E. McMullin, "What Do Physical Models Tell Us?" in *Logic, Methodology and Philosophy of Science,* Proceedings Third International Congress, ed. B. van Rootselaar (Amsterdam, 1968), 3: 389–396.

[51] See, for example, R. Laudan, "The Recent Revolution in Geology and Kuhn's Theory of Scientific Change," in *Paradigms and Revolutions,* ed. G. Gutting (Notre Dame, Indiana: University of Notre Dame Press, 1980), 284–296; R. Laudan, "The Method of Multiple Working Hypotheses and the Development of Plate-Tectonic Theory," in press.

[52] H. Frankel, "The Reception and Acceptance of Continental Drift Theory as a Rational Episode in the History of Science," in *The Reception of Unconventional Science,* ed. S. Mauskopf (Boulder: Westview Press, 1978), 51–89; H. Frankel, "The Career of Continental Drift Theory," *Studies in the History and Philosophy of Science* 10 (1979): 21–66.

[53] M. Bradie, "Models, Metaphors and Scientific Realism," *Nature and System* 2 (1980): 3–20.

[54] Van Fraassen, *The Scientific Image,* 24.

[55] Ibid., 8.

[56] H. Putnam, "What Is Mathematic Truth?", *Mathematics, Matter and Method* (Cambridge: Cambridge University Press), 69–70.

IAN HACKING
EXPERIMENTATION AND SCIENTIFIC REALISM

Experimental work provides the strongest evidence for scientific realism. This is not because we test hypotheses about entities. It is because entities that in principle cannot be "observed" are regularly manipulated to produce a new phenomena [sic] and to investigate other aspects of nature. They are tools, instruments not for thinking but for doing. The philosopher's favourite theoretical entity is the electron. I shall illustrate how electrons have become experimental entities, or experimenter's entities. In the early stages of our discovery of an entity, we may test the hypothesis that it exists. Even that is not routine. When J. J. Thomson realized in 1897 that what he called "corpuscles" were boiling off hot cathodes, almost the first thing he did was to measure the mass of these negatively charged particles. He made a crude estimate of e, the charge, and measured e/m. He got m about right, too. Millikan followed up some ideas already under discussion at Thomson's Cavendish Laboratory, and by 1908 had determined the charge of the electron, that is, the probable minimum unit of electric charge. Hence from the very beginning people were less testing the existence of electrons than interacting with them. The more we come to understand some of the causal powers of electrons, the more we can build devices that achieve well-understood effects in other parts of nature. By the time that we can use the electron to manipulate other parts of nature in a systematic way, the electron has ceased to be something hypothetical, something inferred. It has ceased to be theoretical and has become experimental.

EXPERIMENTERS AND ENTITIES

The vast majority of experimental physicists are realists about some theoretical entities, namely the ones they *use.* I claim that they cannot help being so. Many are also, no doubt, realists about theories too, but that is less central to their concerns.

Experimenters are often realists about the entities that they *investigate,* but they do not have to be so. Millikan probably had few qualms about the reality of electrons when he set out to measure their charge. But he could have been skeptical about what he would find until he found it. He could even have remained skeptical. Perhaps there is a least unit of electric charge, but there is no particle or object with exactly that unit of charge. Experimenting on an entity does not commit you to believing that it exists. Only *manipulating* an entity, in order to experiment on something else, need do that.

Moreover it is not even that you use electrons to experiment on something else that makes it impossible to doubt electrons. Understanding some causal properties of electrons, you guess how to build a very ingenious complex device that enables you to line up the electrons the way you want, in order to see what will happen to something else. Once you have the right experimental idea you know in advance roughly how to build the device, because you know that this is the way to get the electrons to behave in such and such a way. Electrons are no longer ways of organizing our thoughts or saving the phenomena that have been observed. They are ways of creating phenomena in some other domain of nature. Electrons are tools.

There is an important experimental contrast between realism about entities and realism about theories. Suppose we say that the latter is belief that science aims at true theories. Few experimenters will deny that. Only philosophers doubt it. Aiming at the truth is, however, something about the indefinite future. Aiming a beam of electrons is using present electrons. Aiming a finely tuned laser at a particular atom in order to knock off a certain electron to produce an ion is aiming at present electrons. There is in contrast no present set of theories that one has to believe in. If realism about theories is a doctrine about the aims of science, it is a doctrine laden with certain kinds of values. If realism about entities is a matter of aiming electrons next week, or aiming at other electrons the week after, it is a doctrine much more neutral between values. The way in which experimenters are scientific realists about entities is entirely different from ways in which they might be realists about theories.

This shows up when we turn from ideal theories to present ones. Various properties are confidently ascribed to electrons, but most of the confident properties are expressed in numerous different theories or models about which an experimenter can be rather agnostic. Even people in a team, who work on different parts of the same large experiment, may hold different and mutually incompatible accounts of electrons. That is because different parts of the experiment will make different uses of electrons. Models good for calculations on one aspect of electrons will be poor for others. Occasionally a team actually has to select a member with a quite different theoretical perspective simply in order to get someone who can solve those experimental problems. You may choose someone with a foreign training, and whose talk is well nigh incommensurable with yours, just to get people who can produce the effects you want.

But might there not be a common core of theory, the intersection of everybody in the group, which is the theory of the electron to which all the experimenters are realistically committed? I would say common lore, not common core. There are a lot of theories, models, approximations, pictures, formalisms, methods and so forth involving electrons, but there is no reason to suppose that the intersection of these is a theory at all. Nor is there any reason to think that there is such a thing as "the most powerful non-trivial *theory* contained in the intersection of all the theories in which this or that member of a team has been trained to believe." Even if there are a lot of shared beliefs, there is no reason to suppose they form anything worth calling a theory. Naturally teams tend to be formed from like-minded people at the same institute, so there is usually some real shared theoretical basis to their work. That is a sociological fact, not a foundation for scientific realism.

I recognize that many a scientific realism concerning theories is a doctrine not about the present but about what we might achieve, or possibly an ideal at which we aim. So to say that there is no present theory does not count against the optimistic aim. The point is that such scientific realism about theories has to adopt the Peircian principles of faith, hope and charity.[1] Scientific realism about entities needs no such virtues. It arises from what we can do at present. To understand this, we must look in some detail at what it is like to build a device that makes the electrons sit up and behave.

MAKING

Even if experimenters are realists about entities, it does not follow that they are right. Perhaps it is a matter of psychology: maybe the very skills that make for a great experimenter go with a certain cast of mind that objectifies whatever it thinks about. Yet this won't do. The experimenter cheerfully regards neutral bosons as merely hypothetical entities, while electrons are real. What is the difference?

There are an enormous number of ways in which to make instruments that rely on the causal properties of electrons in order to produce desired effects of unsurpassed precision. I shall illustrate this. The argument—it could be called the experimental argument for realism— is not that we infer the reality of electrons from our success. We do not make the instruments and then infer the reality of the electrons, as when we test an hypothesis, and then believe it because it passed the test. That gets the time-order wrong. By now we design apparatus relying on a modest number of home truths about electrons, in order to produce some other phenomenon that we wish to investigate.

That may sound as if we believe in the electrons because we predict how our apparatus will behave. That too is misleading. We have a number of general ideas about how to prepare polarized electrons, say. We spend a lot of time building prototypes that don't work. We get rid of innumerable bugs. Often we have to give up and try another approach. Debugging is not a matter of theoretically explaining or predicting what is going wrong. It is partly a matter of getting rid of "noise" in the apparatus. Although it also has a precise meaning, "noise" often means all the events that are not understood by any theory. The instrument must be able to isolate, physically, the properties of the entities that we wish to use, and damp down all the other effects that might get in our way. *We are completely convinced of the reality of electrons when we regularly set out to build—and often enough succeed in building—new kinds of device[s] that use various well-understood causal properties of electrons to interfere in other more hypothetical parts of nature.*

It is not possible to grasp this without an example. Familiar historical examples have usually become encrusted by false theory-oriented philosophy or history. So I shall take something new. This is a polarizing electron gun whose acronym is PEGGY II. In 1978 it was used in a fundamental experiment that attracted attention even in *The New York Times.* In the next section I describe the point of making PEGGY II. So I have to tell some new physics. You can omit this and read only the engineering section that follows. Yet it must be of interest to know the rather easy-to-understand significance of the main experimental results, namely (1) parity is not conserved in scattering of polarized electrons from deuterium, and (2) more generally, parity is violated in weak neutral current interactions.[2]

PARITY AND WEAK NEUTRAL CURRENTS

There are four fundamental forces in nature, not necessarily distinct. Gravity and electromagnetism are familiar. Then there are the strong and weak forces, the fulfilment of Newton's programme, in the *Optics,* which taught that all nature would be understood by the interaction of particles with various forces that were effective in attraction or repulsion over various different distances (i.e. with different rates of extinction).

Strong forces are 100 times stronger than electromagnetism but act only for a minuscule distance, at most the diameter of a proton. Strong forces act on "hadrons," which include protons, neutrons, and more recent particles, but not electrons or any other members of the class of particles called "leptons."

The weak forces are only 1/10000 times as strong as electromagnetism, and act over a distance 1/100 times smaller than strong forces. But they act on both hadrons and leptons, including electrons. The most familiar example of a weak force may be radioactivity.

The theory that motivates such speculation is quantum electrodynamics. It is incredibly successful, yielding many predictions better than one part in a million, a miracle in experimental physics. It applies over distances ranging from the diameter of the earth to 1/100 the diameter of the proton. This theory supposes that all the forces are "carried" by some sort of particle. Photons do the job in electromagnetism. We hypothesize "gravitons" for gravity.

In the case of interactions involving weak forces, there are charged currents. We postulate that particles called bosons carry these weak forces. For charged currents, the bosons may be positive or negative. In the 1970s there arose the possibility that there could be weak "neutral" currents in which no charge is carried or exchanged. By sheer analogy with the vindicated parts of quantum electrodynamics, neutral bosons were postulated as the carriers in weak interactions.

The most famous discovery of recent high energy physics is the failure of the conservation of parity. Contrary to the expectations of many physicists and philosophers, including Kant, nature makes an absolute distinction between right-handedness and left-handedness. Apparently this happens only in weak interactions.

What we mean by right- or left-handed in nature has an element of convention. I remarked that electrons have spin. Imagine your right hand wrapped around a spinning particle with the fingers pointing in the direction of spin. Then your thumb is said to point in the direction of the spin vector. If such particles are travelling in a beam, consider the relation between the spin vector and the beam. If all the particles have their spin vector in the same direction as the beam, they have right-handed linear polarization, while, if the spin vector is opposite to the beam direction, they have left-handed linear polarization.

The original discovery of parity violation showed that one kind of product of a particle decay, a so-called muon neutrino, exists only in left-handed polarization and never in right-handed polarization.

Parity violations have been found for weak *charged* interactions. What about weak *neutral* currents? The remarkable Weinberg–Salam model for the four kinds of force was proposed independently by Stephen Weinberg in 1967 and A. Salam in 1968. It implies a minute violation of parity in weak neutral interactions. Given that the model is sheer speculation, its success has been amazing, even awe-inspiring. So it seemed worthwhile to try out the predicted failure of parity for weak neutral interactions. That would teach us more about those weak forces that act over so minute a distance.

The prediction is: Slightly more left-handed polarized electrons hitting certain targets will scatter, than right-handed electrons. Slightly more! The difference in relative frequency of the two kinds of scattering is one part in 10000, comparable to a difference in probability between 0.50005 and 0.49995. Suppose one used the standard equipment available at the Stanford Linear Accelerator in the early 1970s, generating 120 pulses per second, each pulse providing one electron event. Then you would have to run the entire SLAC beam for 27 years in order to detect so small a difference in relative frequency. Considering that one uses the same beam for lots of experiments simultaneously, by letting different experiments use different pulses, and considering that no equipment remains stable for even a month, let alone 27 years, such an experiment is impossible. You need enormously more electrons coming off in each pulse. We need between 1000 and 10000 more electrons per pulse than was once possible. The first attempt used an instrument now called PEGGY I. It had, in essence, a high-class version of J. J. Thomson's hot cathode. Some lithium was heated and electrons were boiled off. PEGGY II uses quite different principles.

PEGGY II

The basic idea began when C. Y. Prescott noticed (by "chance"!) an article in an optics magazine about a crystalline substance called gallium arsenide. GaAs has a curious property. When it is struck by circularly polarized light of the right frequencies, it emits lots of linearly polarized electrons. There is a good rough and ready quantum understanding of why this happens, and why half the emitted electrons will be polarized, $\frac{3}{4}$ polarized in one direction and $\frac{1}{4}$ polarized in the other.

PEGGY II uses this fact, plus the fact that GaAs emits lots of electrons due to features of its crystal structure. Then comes some engineering. It takes work to liberate an electron from a surface. We know that painting a surface with the right stuff helps. In this case, a thin layer of cesium and oxygen is applied to the crystal. Moreover the less air pressure around the crystal, the more electrons will escape for a given amount of work. So the bombardment takes place in a good vacuum at the temperature of liquid nitrogen.

We need the right source of light. A laser with bursts of red light (7100 Ångstroms) is trained on the crystal. The light first goes through an ordinary polarizer, a very old-fashioned prism of calcite, or Iceland spar. This gives linearly polarized light. We want circularly polarized light to hit the crystal. The polarized laser beam now goes through a cunning device called a Pockel's cell. It electrically turns linearly polarized photons into circularly polarized ones. Being electric, it acts as a very fast switch. The direction of circular polarization depends on the direction of current in the cell. Hence the direction of polarization can be varied randomly. This is important, for we are trying to detect a minute asymmetry between right- and left-handed polarization. Randomizing helps us guard against any systematic "drift" in the equipment. The randomization is generated by a radioactive decay device, and a computer records the direction of polarization for each pulse.

A circularly polarized pulse hits the GaAs crystal, resulting in a pulse of linearly polarized electrons. A beam of such pulses is manoeuvred by magnets into the accelerator for the next bit of the experiment. It passes through a device that checks on a proportion of polarization along the way. The remainder of the experiment requires other devices and detectors of comparable ingenuity, but let us stop at PEGGY II.

BUGS

Short descriptions make it all sound too easy, so let us pause to reflect on debugging. Many of the bugs are never understood. They are eliminated by trial and error. Let us illustrate three different kinds: (1) the essential technical limitations that in the end have to be factored into the analysis of error; (2) simpler mechanical defects you never think of until they are forced on you; (3) hunches about what might go wrong.

(1) Laser beams are not as constant as science fiction teaches, and there is always an irremediable amount of "jitter" in the beam over any stretch of time.

(2) At a more humdrum level the electrons from the GaAs crystal are back-scattered and go back along the same channel as the laser beam used to hit the crystal. Most of them are then deflected magnetically. But some get reflected from the laser apparatus and get back into the system. So you have to eliminate these new ambient electrons. This is done by crude mechanical means, making them focus just off the crystal and so wander away.

(3) Good experimenters guard against the absurd. Suppose that dust particles on an experimental surface lie down flat when a polarized pulse hits them, and then stand on their heads when hit by a pulse polarized in the opposite direction? Might that have a systematic effect, given that we are detecting a minute asymmetry? One of the team thought of this in the middle of the night, and came down next morning frantically using antidust spray. They kept that up for a month, just in case.

RESULTS

Some 10^{11} events were needed to obtain a result that could be recognized above systematic and statistical error. Although the idea of systematic error presents interesting conceptual problems, it seems to be unknown to philosophers. There were systematic uncertainties in the detection of right- and left-handed polarization, there was some jitter, and there were other problems about the parameters of the two kinds of beam. These errors were analysed and linearly added to the statistical error. To a student of statistical inference this is real seat-of-the-pants analysis with no rationale whatsoever. Be that as it may, thanks to PEGGY II the number of events was big enough to give a result that convinced the entire physics community. Left-handed polarized electrons were scattered from deuterium slightly more frequently than right-handed electrons. This was their first convincing example of parity violation in a weak neutral current interaction.

COMMENT

The making of PEGGY II was fairly non-theoretical. Nobody worked out in advance the polarizing properties of GaAs—that was found by chance encounter with an unrelated experimental investigation. Although elementary quantum theory of crystals explains the polarization effect, it does not explain the properties of the actual crystal used. No one has got a real crystal to polarize more than 37% of the electrons, although in principle 50% should be polarized.

Likewise although we have a general picture of why layers of cesium and oxygen will "produce negative electron affinity," that is, make it easier for electrons to escape, we have no quantitative understanding of why this increases efficiency to a score of 37%.

Nor was there any guarantee that the bits and pieces would fit together. To give an even more current illustration, future experimental work, briefly described below, makes us want even more electrons per pulse than PEGGY II could give. When the parity experiment was reported in *The New York Times,* a group at Bell Laboratories read the newspaper and saw what was going on. They had been constructing a crystal lattice for totally unrelated purposes. It uses layers of GaAs and a related aluminum compound. The structure of this lattice leads one to expect that virtually all the electrons emitted would be polarized. So we might be able to double the efficiency of PEGGY II. But at present that nice idea has problems. The new lattice should also be coated in work-reducing paint. The cesium–oxygen compound is applied at high temperature. Hence the aluminum tends to ooze into the neighbouring layer of GaAs, and the pretty artificial lattice becomes a bit uneven, limiting its fine polarized-electron-emitting properties. So perhaps this will never work. Prescott is simultaneously reviving a souped-up new thermionic cathode to try to get more electrons. "Theory" would not have told us that PEGGY II would beat out thermionic PEGGY I. Nor can it tell if some thermionic PEGGY III will beat out PEGGY II.

Note also that the Bell people did not need to know a lot of weak neutral current theory to send along their sample lattice. They just read *The New York Times.*

MORAL

Once upon a time it made good sense to doubt that there are electrons. Even after Thomson had measured the mass of his corpuscles, and Millikan their charge, doubt could have made sense. We needed to be sure that Millikan was measuring the same entity as Thomson. More theoretical elaboration was needed. The idea needed to be fed into many other phenomena. Solid state physics, the atom, superconductivity: all had to play their part.

Once upon a time the best reason for thinking that there are electrons might have been success in explanation. . . . Lorentz explained the Faraday effect with his electron theory. I have said that ability to explain carries little warrant of truth. Even from the time of J. J. Thomson it was the measurements that weighed in, more than the explanations. Explanations did help. Some people might have had to believe in electrons because the postulation of their existence could explain a wide variety of phenomena. Luckily we no longer have to pretend to infer from explanatory success (i.e. from what makes our minds feel good). Prescott *et al.* don't explain phenomena with electrons. They know how to use them. Nobody in their right mind thinks that electrons "really" are just little spinning orbs around which you could, with a small enough hand, wrap the fingers and find the direction of spin along the thumb. There is instead a family of causal properties in terms of which gifted experimenters describe and deploy electrons in order to investigate something else, for example weak neutral currents and neutral bosons. We know an enormous amount about the behaviour of electrons. It is equally important to know what does not matter to electrons. Thus we know that bending a polarized electron beam in magnetic coils does not affect polarization in any significant way. We have hunches, too strong to ignore although too trivial to test independently: for example dust might dance under changes of direction of polarization. Those hunches are based on a hard-won sense of the kinds of things electrons are. (It does not matter at all to this hunch whether electrons are clouds or waves or particles.)

WHEN HYPOTHETICAL ENTITIES BECOME REAL

Note the complete contrast between electrons and neutral bosons. I am told that nobody can yet manipulate a bunch of neutral bosons, if there are any. Even weak neutral currents are only just emerging from the mists of hypothesis. By 1980 a sufficient range of convincing experiments had made them the object of investigation. When might they lose their hypothetical status and become commonplace reality like electrons? When we use them to investigate something else.

I mentioned the desire to make a better gun than PEGGY II. Why? Because we now "know" that parity is violated in weak neutral interactions. Perhaps by an even more grotesque statistical analysis than that involved in the parity experiment, we can isolate just the weak interactions. That is, we have a lot of interactions, including say electromagnetic ones. We can censor these in various ways, but we can also statistically pick out a class of weak interactions as precisely those where parity is not conserved. This would possibly give us a road to quite deep investigations of matter and anti-matter. To do the statistics one needs even more electrons per pulse than PEGGY II could hope to generate. If such a project were to succeed, we should be beginning to use weak neutral currents as a manipulable tool for looking at something else. The next step towards a realism about such currents would have been made.

CHANGING TIMES

Although realisms and anti-realisms are part of the philosophy of science well back into Greek prehistory, our present versions mostly descend from debates about atomism at the end of the nineteenth century. Anti-realism about atoms was partly a matter of physics: the energeticists thought energy was at the bottom of everything, not tiny bits of matter. It also was connected with the positivism of Comte, Mach, Pearson and even J. S. Mill. Mill's younger associate

Alexander Bain states the point in a characteristic way in his textbook, *Logic, Deductive and Inductive.* It was all right for him to write in 1870 that:

> Some hypotheses consist of assumptions as to the minute structure and operation of bodies. From the nature of the case these assumptions can never be proved by direct means. Their merit is their suitability to express phenomena. They are Representative Fictions.

"All assertions as to the ultimate structure of the particles of matter," continues Bain, "are and ever must be hypothetical. . . ." The kinetic theory of heat, he says, "serves an important intellectual function." But we cannot hold it to be a true description of the world. It is a Representative Fiction.

Bain was surely right a century ago. Assumptions about the minute structure of matter could not be proved then. The only proof could be indirect, namely that hypotheses seemed to provide some explanation and helped make good predictions. Such inferences need never produce conviction in the philosopher inclined to instrumentalism or some other brand of idealism.

Indeed the situation is quite similar to seventeenth-century epistemology. At the time knowledge was thought of as correct representation. But then one could never get outside the representations to be sure that they corresponded to the world. Every test of a representation is just another representation. "Nothing is so much like an idea as an idea," as Bishop Berkeley had it. To attempt to argue for scientific realism at the level of theory, testing, explanation, predictive success, convergence of theories, and so forth is to be locked into a world of representations. No wonder that scientific anti-realism is so permanently in the race. It is a variant on the "spectator theory of knowledge."

Scientists, as opposed to philosophers, did in general become realists about atoms by 1910. Despite the changing climate, some anti-realist variety of instrumentalism or fictionalism remained a strong philosophical alternative in 1910 and in 1930. That is what the history of philosophy teaches us. The lesson is: think about practice, not theory. Anti-realism about atoms was very sensible when Bain wrote a century ago. Anti-realism about *any* submicroscopic entities was a sound doctrine in those days. Things are different now. The "direct" proof of electrons and the like is our ability to manipulate them using well-understood low-level causal properties. I do not of course claim that reality is constituted by human manipulability. Millikan's ability to determine the charge of the electron did something of great importance for the idea of electrons: more, I think, than the Lorentz theory of the electron. Determining the charge of something makes one believe in it far more than postulating it to explain something else. Millikan gets the charge on the electron: better still. Uhlenbeck and Goudsmit in 1925 assign angular momentum to electrons, brilliantly solving a lot of problems. Electrons have spin, ever after. The clincher is when we can put a spin on the electrons, polarize them and get them thereby to scatter in slightly different proportions.

There are surely innumerable entities and processes that humans will never know about. Perhaps there are many that in principle we can never know about. Reality is bigger than us. The best kind of evidence for the reality of a postulated or inferred entity is that we can begin to measure it or otherwise understand its causal powers. The best evidence, in turn, that we have this kind of understanding is that we can set out, from scratch, to build machines that will work fairly reliably, taking advantage of this or that causal nexus. Hence, engineering, not theorizing, is the best proof of scientific realism about entities. My attack on scientific antirealism is analogous to Marx's onslaught on the idealism of his day. Both say that the point is not to understand the world but to change it. Perhaps there are some entities which in theory we can know about only through theory (black holes). Then our evidence is like that furnished by Lorentz. Perhaps there are entities which we shall only measure and never use. The experimental argument for realism does not say that only experimenter's objects exist.

I must now confess a certain scepticism, about, say, black holes. I suspect there might be another representation of the universe, equally consistent with phenomena, in which black holes are precluded. I inherit from Leibniz a certain distaste for occult powers. Recall how he inveighed against Newtonian gravity as occult. It took two centuries to show he was right. Newton's aether was also excellently occult. It taught us lots. Maxwell did his electromagnetic waves in aether and Hertz confirmed the aether by demonstrating the existence of radio waves. Michelson figured out a way to interact with the aether. He thought his experiment confirmed Stokes's aether drag theory, but in the end it was one of many things that made aether give up the ghost. The sceptic like myself has a slender induction. Long-lived theoretical entities, which don't end up being manipulated, commonly turn out to have been wonderful mistakes.[3]

NOTES

[1] "I put forward three sentiments, namely interest in an indefinite community, recognition of the possibility of this interest being made supreme, and hope in the unlimited continuance of intellectual activity, as indispensable requirements of logic . . . these three sentiments seem to be pretty much the same as the famous trio of Charity, Faith and Hope. . . ." C. Hartshorne and P. Weiss (eds.), *The Collected Papers of C. S. Peirce,* Volume 2, Section 665.

[2] The popular account given below relies on generous conversations with some of the experimenters, and also on the in-house report, "Parity violation in polarized electron scattering," by Bill Kirk, *SLAC Beam Line* no. 8 October, 1978.

[3] In the discussion above, weak neutral bosons are used as an example of purely hypothetical entities. In January 1983 CERN announced observing the first such particle W in proton–antiproton decay at 540 GeV.

S T U D Y   Q U E S T I O N S   F O R   T O P I C   V

1. Chemists have a well-developed explanation for the formation of ice from liquid water. Recall that every water molecule contains two hydrogen atoms and one oxygen atom. The hydrogen atom of one molecule is attracted by unobservable electrostatic forces to the oxygen atom of another molecule. These forces of attraction are essential for explaining the chemical formation of ice from liquid water.

   Based on van Fraassen's antirealism, (a) is the formation of ice from liquid water physically real?; and (b) is the force of electrostatic attraction between the water molecules real? Explain and defend your answers.

2. Based on Stace's antirealism, (a) is the formation of ice from liquid water physically real? Use the explanation of ice from question 1 to defend your answer. Also, (b) are the forces of electrostatic attraction between water molecules physically real, according to Stace's antirealism? Again defend your answer.

3. According to van Fraassen, why is the distinction between observable entities and unobservable entities so important in science?

4. Churchland raises objections to van Fraassen's distinction between observable objects and unobservable objects. Which *one* of the following claims best represents Churchland's own view on the possibility of distinguishing observable from unobservable entities? Explain: (a) We can never provide a reasonable demarcation between observable and unobservable entities; (b) in the context of evaluating a scientific theory, we can separate observable from unobservable entities, but there is no philosophical importance placed on such a separation; and (c) in the context of evaluating a scientific theory, we can separate observable from unobservable entities, and such a distinction is central to our preference for observable entities over unobservable entities.

5. The atomic composition of water has been detected in experiments by the use of modern instruments known as X-ray diffraction devices. When such an instrument is used, a certain amount of energy, called X-rays, impinges on the material under examination, leading to observable results. According to Hacking's conception of instrumentation, does the use of this modern instrument provide scientists with a pure "picture" of atomic properties without any theoretical and experimental interference? Answer "yes" or "no," and defend your answer by appeal to Hacking's article.

6. What exactly are the similarities and differences between the following two claims, based on Giere's conception of scientific realism: (a) within the context of a physical law of nature the term "gravitational force" refers to the real force of gravity; (b) within the context of a theoretical model from physics, the concept of gravitational force replicates the real force of gravity.

7. Based on Giere's conception of scientific realism, does it make sense to say that our best scientific models provide a perfect copy of every real property of nature? Why or why not?

8. What exactly does McMullin mean by the fertility of a scientific theory, and why is fertility so important for evaluating a theory according to him?

BIBLIOGRAPHY

Aronson, J. *A Realist Philosophy of Science.* London: Macmillan, 1984.
Burtt, E. A. *The Metaphysical Foundations of Modern Science.* London: Routledge and Kegan Paul, 1949.
Cartwright, N. *How the Laws of Physics Lie.* Oxford: Clarendon, 1983.
Cassirer, E. *Substance and Function and Einstein's Theory of Relativity.* Chicago: Open Court, 1923.

Colodny, R., ed. *Paradigms and Paradoxes.* Pittsburgh: U Pittsburgh P, 1972.

Devitt, M. *Realism and Truth.* Oxford: Basil Blackwell, 1984.

Dummett, M. *Truth and Other Enigmas.* Cambridge: Harvard UP, 1978.

Fine, A. *The Shaky Game: Einstein, Realism, and the Quantum Theory.* Chicago: U Chicago P, 1986.

Hanson, N. R. *Patterns of Discovery.* Cambridge: Cambridge UP, 1958.

Harré, R. *Varieties of Realism: A Rationale for the Natural Sciences.* Oxford: Basil Blackwell, 1986.

Harré, R. and E. Madden. *Causal Powers.* Oxford: Basil Blackwell, 1977.

Leplin, J., ed. *Scientific Realism.* Berkeley: U California P, 1984.

Maxwell, G. "The Ontological Status of Theoretical Entities." *Minnesota Studies in the Philosophy of Science,* vol. III. Ed. H. Feigl and G. Maxwell. Minneapolis: U Minnesota P, 1962, pp. 3–27.

Putnam, H. "Why There Isn't a Ready-made World." *Realism and Reason.* Cambridge: Cambridge UP, 1983, pp. 205–28.

Van Fraassen, B. "Empiricism and the Philosophy of Science." *Images of Science: Essays on Realism and Empiricism with a Reply from Bas C. van Fraassen.* Ed. P. M. Churchland and C. W. Hooker. Chicago: U Chicago P, 1985, pp. 245–308.

CREDITS AND ACKNOWLEDGMENTS

READING 1 David Hume, "Sceptical Doubts Concerning the Operations of the Understanding," from *Enquiries Concerning Human Understanding and Concerning the Principles of Morals,* L.A. Selby-Bigge, ed., 3rd edition, Oxford: Clarendon Press, 1975, pp. 25-39. Reprinted by permission of Oxford University Press.

READING 2 Rudolf Carnap, "The Confirmation of Laws" from *Philosophical Foundations of Physics: An Introduction to the Philosophy of Science.* Copyright ©1966 by Basic Books, Inc., © 1994 by Hanna Carnap Thost. All rights reserved under Pan American and International Copyright Conventions. Reprinted by permission of Mrs. Thost.

READING 3 Karl R. Popper, "Science: Conjectures and Refutations," from *Conjectures and Refutations: The Growth of Scientific Knowledge.* New York: Harper & Row, pp. 33-59. Reprinted by permission of Mr. A.R. Mew and Mrs. M. Mew.

READING 4 Imre Lakatos, "History of Science and Its Rational Reconstructions," in R. Buck and R.S. Cohen, eds., *PSA 1970: In Memory of Rudolf Carnap.* Boston Studies in the Philosophy of Science: Volume VIII. Dordrecht-Holland: D. Reidel Publishing Company, pp. 91-104, 122-136. Reprinted with kind permission from Kluwer Academic Publishers.

READING 5 Norwood Russell Hanson, "Observation," from *Patterns of Discovery.* New York: Cambridge University Press, pp. 4-24. Reprinted with permission of Cambridge University Press.

READING 6 Hilary Putnam, "What Theories Are Not," from *Mathematics, Matter and Method: Philosophical Papers, Volume I,* 2nd edition. Cambridge: Cambridge University Press, 1975, pp. 215-220. Reprinted with the permission of Cambridge University Press. Article originally published in *Logic, Methodology, and Philosophy of Science,* edited by Ernest Nagel, Patrick Suppes, and Alfred Tarski. Reprinted with the permission of Stanford University Press. © 1962 by the Board of Trustees of the Leland Stanford Junior University.

READING 7 Frederick Suppe, "What's Wrong with the Received View on the Structure of Scientific Theories?" from *The Semantic Conception of Theories and Scientific Realism.* Urbana, Illinois: University of Illinois Press, 1989, pp. 39-41, 62-77. Copyright 1989 by the Board of Trustees of the University of Illinois. Used with the permission of the author and the University of Illinois Press.

READING 8 Carl G. Hempel, "Laws and Their Role in Scientific Explanation," from *Philosophy of Natural Science.* Englewood Cliffs, New Jersey: Prentice-Hall, Inc. © 1966, pp. 47-69. Reprinted by permission of Prentice-Hall, Inc., Upper Saddle River, NJ.

READING 9 Michael Scriven, "Explanations, Predictions, and Laws," in H. Feigl and G. Maxwell, eds., *Minnesota Studies in the Philosophy of Science, Volume 3: Scientific Explanation, Space and Time.* Minneapolis: University of Minnesota Press, © 1962, pp. 170-196. Reprinted by permission of University of Minnesota Press.

READING 10 Nancy Cartwright, "The Truth Doesn't Explain Much," from *How the Laws of Physics Lie.* Oxford: Oxford University Press, 1983, pp. 44-53. Reprinted by permission of Oxford University Press.

READING 11 Philip Kitcher, "Explanatory Unification," from *Philosophy of Science 48* (1981), pp. 507-531. Used by permission of the author.

READING 12 Wesley Salmon, "Why Ask, 'Why?'?: An Inquiry Concerning Scientific Explanation." Proceedings and Addresses of the American Philosophical Association, Vol. 51, No. 6 (August 1978), pp. 683-705. Copyright © 1978 Wesley Salmon. Reprinted by permission.

READING 13 Rom Harré, "Explanation," from *The Philosophies of Science,* Second Edition, Oxford: Oxford University Press, 1972, Chapter 6, pp. 168-183. Reprinted by permission of Oxford University Press.

READING 14 Mary Hesse, "Material Analogy," from *Models and Analogies in Science.* Notre Dame, Indiana: University of Notre Dame Press, 1966, pp. 57-81, 86-87, 93-100. Copyright © 1966 by the University of Notre Dame Press. Reprinted by permission.

READING 15 Thomas Kuhn, from *The Structure of Scientific Revolutions,* Second Edition. Chicago: University of Chicago Press, 1970, pp. 1-9, 23-34, 92-110. Copyright 1970 by the University of Chicago Press. Reprinted with permission.

READING 16   Thomas Kuhn, "Objectivity, Value Judgment, and Theory Choice," from *The Essential Tension: Selected Studies in Scientific Tradition and Change*. Chicago: University of Chicago Press, 1977, pp. 320–339. Copyright 1977 by the University of Chicago Press. Reprinted with permission.

READING 17   Larry Laudan, "Dissecting the Holist Picture of Scientific Change," from *Science and Values: An Essay on the Aims of Science and their Role in Scientific Debate*. Berkeley, California: University of California Press, 1984, pp. 67–102. Copyright © 1984 The Regents of the University of California. Reprinted by permission.

READING 18   Karl Popper, "The Rationality of Scientific Revolutions," in Rom Harré, ed., *Problems of Scientific Revolution: Progress and Obstacles to Progress in the Sciences*. Oxford: Oxford University Press, 1975, pp. 73–79, 82–101. Reprinted by permission of Mr. A.R. Mew and Mrs. M. Mew.

READING 19   Barry Barnes and David Bloor, "Relativism, Rationalism and the Sociology of Knowledge," in M. Hollis and S. Lukes, eds., *Rationality and Relativism*. Cambridge, Massachusetts: MIT Press, 1982, pp. 21–47.

READING 20   Bruno Latour, selections from "Opening Pandora's Black Box" and "Laboratories" in *Science in Action: How to Follow Scientists and Engineers Through Society*. Cambridge, Massachusetts: Harvard University Press, © 1987, pp. 1–17, 97–100. Reprinted by permission of the publisher.

READING 21   Carl G. Hempel, "Scientific Rationality: Analytic vs. Pragmatic Perspectives," reproduced from *Rationality To-Day* edited by Theodore F. Geraets, Copyright University of Ottawa Press, 1979, pp. 292–304.

READING 22   Nelson Goodman, "Words, Works, Worlds," (Chapter I) from *Ways of Worldmaking*. Indianapolis, Indiana: Hackett Publishing Company, © 1978, pp. 1–22.

READING 23   W.T. Stace, "Science and the Physical World," from *Man Against Darkness*. Copyright © 1967 by University of Pittsburgh Press. Reprinted by permission of the University of Pittsburgh Press.

READING 24   Bas C. van Fraassen, "Arguments Concerning Scientific Realism" in *The Scientific Image*. Oxford: Clarendon Press, 1980, pp. 6–19. Reprinted by permission of Oxford University Press.

READING 25   Paul M. Churchland, "The Ontological Status of Observables: In Praise of the Superempirical Virtues," in P.M. Churchland and C.A. Hooker, eds., *Images of Science*. Chicago: University of Chicago Press, 1985, pp. 35–47. Copyright 1985 by the University of Chicago Press. Reprinted with permission.

READING 26   Ronald N. Giere, "Constructive Realism," from *Explaining Science: A Cognitive Approach*. Chicago: University of Chicago Press, pp. 92–110. Copyright by the University of Chicago Press. Reprinted with permission.

READING 27   Ernan McMullin, "A Case for Scientific Realism," in J. Leplin, editor, *Scientific Realism*. Berkeley, California: University of California Press, 1984, pp. 8–40. Copyright © 1984 The Regents of the University of California. Reprinted by permission.

READING 28   Ian Hacking, "Experimentation and Scientific Realism," from *Representing and Intervening*. Cambridge: Cambridge University Press, 1983, pp. 262–275. Reprinted with the permission of Cambridge University Press.